Guides to Library of Congress

SUBJECT HEADINGS *and* CLASSIFICATION *on*

PEACE AND INTERNATIONAL CONFLICT RESOLUTION

from the

UNITED STATES INSTITUTE OF PEACE

Washington, D.C.

The United States Institute of Peace
1550 M Street, N.W.
Washington, D.C. 20005

The views expressed in this book are those of the editors alone. They do not necessarily reflect views of the United States Institute of Peace.

Library of Congress Cataloging in Publication Data

Guides to Library of Congress subject headings and classification on peace and international conflict resolution.
p. cm.
ISBN 1-878379-05-4
1. Subject headings—Peace. 2. Classification—Book—Peace. 3. Peace—Abstracting and indexing. 4. Subject headings—International relations. 5. Classification—Books—International relations. 6. International relations—Abstracting and indexing. 7. Subject headings, Library of Congress. 8. Classification, Library of Congress. I. United States Institute of Peace.
Z695.1.P38G84 1990
025.4'9—dc20 90-4203
CIP

This volume was edited under contract by Judith A. Kessinger.

Printed in the United States of America

First printing 1990
$30.00 single copy

Contents

Preface

The United States Institute of Peace is pleased to publish the first *Guides to Library of Congress Subject Headings and Classification on Peace and International Conflict Resolution*. Many publishers, catalogers, and others responsible for the mechanics of information retrieval have approached the peace and security field with an overly narrow view that has tended to restrict ease of access to much of the relevant information and materials. This book represents an initial effort to address these problems by facilitating access to a broad range of cataloged materials for users interested in peace and international conflict resolution and for the librarians who catalog and assist others in using these materials.

The special significant of this publication lies in its timeliness and its breadth. Our era is one of dramatic and hopeful change in many parts of the world, symbolized by the movement toward democracy in Eastern and Central Europe; sadly, however, it is also marked by continuing and even increasingly bloody conflicts, in other regions of the world.

The scope of the *Guides* may surprise some readers, especially in the inclusion of substantial military and related information. It is our view that, just as nonviolent resistance is part of the lexicon of peace so is deterrence one valid approach to conflict avoidance or management. Therefore the somewhat overlapping fields of conflict management, conflict resolution, peacemaking, peacekeeping, and peacebuilding should be as intellectually all-encompassing as possible to be most useful for researchers and scholars.

We would like to thank Judith A. Kessinger, who recently completed 20 years of service at the Library of Congress and has served as the editor of this manual. Mrs. Kessinger's careful and diligent effort has resulted in a publication which we believe to be unique in our broad subject area.

Special thanks are also due to Mary K. D. Pietris, Chief of the Library of Congress Office for Subject Cataloging Policy, and her staff, for their guidance during the preparation of this publication.

Ambassador Samuel W. Lewis
President
United States Institute of Peace

Introduction

Peace and securities courses are developing at a rapid rate in colleges and universities across the United States. Special libraries and special collections are also evolving. In response to this rapid growth of interest in our subject area, the Jeannette Rankin Library Program of the United States Institute of Peace has undertaken this project. If your library already has a collection of materials that have been cataloged using Library of Congress subject headings and classification, the use of this guide should not conflict with your existing catalog.

This volume is based on the twelfth edition of *Library of Congress Subject Headings* (LCSH 12) and on the changes to these headings through October 11, 1989 and on the Library of Congress classification schedules through 1988. It presents subject headings and classification numbers of special importance to persons interested in peace, war, international conflict resolution, and related topics, and provides assistance in using these headings to locate material on these subjects. This volume is not a substitute for LCSH 12, which should be consulted for a complete list of Library of Congress subject headings on all topics.

The Institute worked with the existing Library of Congress system because it is the most widely used in the library world and has been developed and maintained by a large staff of experts, in contrast to depending on a single author. Librarians new to the literature of peace and security studies will already be familiar with the terminology and structure of the Library of Congress system and thus should find it easier to implement immediately. In addition, if a library's collections include other topics, a more diverse terminology is easily available by consulting the full volumes of LCSH.

This is a first effort to cover an enormously diverse and complex field. Therefore, the United States Institute wants to hear from librarians and researchers as to how this might be best revised and updated for a future edition. We are particularly interested to hear from the users of this manual on any or all of the following questions:

1. Does the Introduction provide enough assistance on using the headings in the guide and in understanding the Library of Congress system of constructing headings?
2. Are the free-floating subdivisions provided in the Introduction useful? If so, are they appropriately placed? Should they be moved to an appendix?
3. Are the Library of Congress terms provided too broad in their coverage? Or too narrow?
4. Are there specific headings that you would recommend removing?
5. Have headings been omitted that should be added?
6. Is the arrangement of the material into sections acceptable?
7. Would a similar guide to the Dewey Classification System be useful? Or an annotation of the current guide with Dewey numbers?
8. Do you have any other comments, either general or specific, about the *Guides*?

Please send your response to:

Jeanne Bohlen, Director
Jeannette Rankin Library Program
United States Institute of Peace
1550 M Street NW, Suite 700
Washington, DC 20005

Guide to Library of Congress Subject Headings
on
Peace and International Conflict Resolution

Introduction

Arrangement of the guide

The Guide to Library of Congress Subject Headings on Peace and International Conflict Resolution is divided into three sections. Part One consists of topics. Part Two contains place names. Part Three lists wars and other armed conflicts.

How to use this guide

Library of Congress subject headings cover many topics and are quite specific. In trying to determine what subject heading or headings you should use to locate material, search for the most specific subject you can find. For example, **International relations** is a very broad term covering relations among nations. If you are interested in materials on a particular aspect of international relations, look in this guide to see whether the heading is present. If you cannot find the subject for which you are searching, look at **International relations** or another broad heading such as **Peace, War, International law,** or **World politics** and follow the reference structure explained below. Some headings consist of a topic, subdivided further by the name of a place, e.g., **Human rights—Latin America**. Part One contains headings of this type. Other headings emphasize place, with topics expressed in subdivisions. Headings of this type are located in Part Two. For example, Part Two will give you the heading **United States** with the subdivision **Foreign relations** as well as additional chronological subdivisions covering all periods in the history of American foreign relations. To find headings for individual wars and other armed conflicts, consult Part Three.

Subject headings

The subject headings in this guide are presented in a form similar to that used in *Library of Congress Subject Headings*. Each heading is in boldface type. It may be followed by the code (May Subd Geog), a class number, and a scope note. References associated with the heading, if any, are listed below, followed by subdivisions of the subject heading.

Geographic subdivisions

Headings followed by the code (May Subd Geog) may be subdivided by place. Generally, if the place is a country or a region larger than a country, the name is used immediately after the heading or subdivision. If the place is a region, state, province, city, etc., within a country, the name of the country precedes the name of the locality.

Example: **Refugees—France—Paris**

The major exceptions to this rule are the United States, Canada, Great Britain, and the Soviet Union, where the states, provinces, etc., serve as the gathering device.

Example: **Communication—England—London**

not

Communication—Great Britain—London

Class numbers

Some headings are followed by Library of Congress class numbers. Generally class numbers are included only when there is a close correspondence between the heading and the number. Library of Congress cataloging practice is to assign a class number that matches the first, and most important, subject heading assigned to the work being cataloged.

Scope notes

Scope notes, which appear below the headings to which they apply, are provided to define headings, to indicate the manner in which a heading is to be used, or to show how a heading differs from related topics.

References

USE references are made from an unauthorized term to an authorized one. Under the heading referred to, the code UF (Used for) precedes the terms not used. The codes USE and UF are reciprocal.

Example: Military and civilian power
USE Civil-military relations

Civil-military relations
UF Military and civilian power

Subject headings are linked to other related subject headings through cross references expressed as Broader Terms (BT) and Narrower Terms (NT).

Example: **Peace**
BT International relations

International relations
NT Peace

Because this guide is divided into three parts, a heading given as a broader or narrower term may be found in a different part of the guide from the heading with which it is associated.

Example: **European federation**
BT Europe—Politics and government
(This heading appears in Part One : Topics)

Europe—Politics and government
NT European federation
(This heading appears in Part Two : Places)

Users of this guide should search the lists for the heading or headings in which they are interested and follow the reference structure under these headings to lead them to broader or narrower concepts that may also be of interest to them.

Subdivisions

Library of Congress subject headings are used with subdivisions to indicate subtopics, places, time periods, or the form of the material. Subdivisions that apply only to specific headings are printed under the headings. Other subdivisions, called free-floating, may be used under any appropriate heading. *The Subject Cataloging Manual: Subject Headings* contains many special lists of free-floating subdivisions for use under various types of headings. Selections from four of these lists are provided below for use with the headings in this guide. *The Subject Cataloging Manual: Subject Headings* should be consulted for complete information on all free-floating subdivisions.

Free-floating subdivisions of general application

—Anecdotes
Use under names of countries, cities, etc., names of individual persons and corporate bodies, uniform titles of sacred works, and under topical headings.

—Archival resources (May Subd Geog)
Use under names of countries, cities, etc., and under topical headings for brief descriptions of the types of documents and historical records about a particular place or topic available in an institution or institutions.

—Archives
Use under names of individual persons, corporate bodies, educational institutions, and families, and under types of corporate bodies and educational institutions, classes of persons, and ethnic groups for collections of documents or historical records, including notes, correspondence, minutes, photographs, legal papers, etc.

—Audio-visual aids
Use under topical headings for catalogs of audiovisual materials.

—Audiotape catalogs
Use under names of countries, cities, etc., names of individual persons and corporate bodies, and under topical headings for lists or catalogs of audiotapes.

—Biblical teaching
Use under religious or secular topics for works on the theological and/or ethical teachings of the Bible, or its individual parts, on that topic.

—Bibliography
Use under any type of subject heading.

—Bibliography—Catalogs
Use under any type of subject heading.

—Bibliography—Microform catalogs
Use under subjects for catalogs that list works stored in microform editions.
See also **—Microform catalogs**

—Bibliography—Union lists
Use under subjects for catalogs of materials on those subjects held by two or more libraries.
See also **—Union lists**

—Biography
Use under names of countries, cities, etc., names of individual literary authors and corporate bodies, uniform titles of sacred works, and under classes of persons, ethnic groups, and historic events.

—Capture, [date]
Use under individual castles, forts, etc.

—Caricatures and cartoons
Use under names of individual persons, families, and corporate bodies, and under classes of persons, ethnic groups, individual wars, and topical headings for collections or discussions of caricatures or pictorial humor about those subjects.

—Case studies
Use under names of countries, cities, etc., and individual corporate bodies, and under topical headings.

—Censorship
Use under wars and topical headings, especially forms of communication.

—Chronology
Use under names of individual persons, uniform titles of sacred works, and topical headings that are inherently historical.
See also **—History—Chronology**

—Citizen participation

Use under topical headings for works on the participation of citizens in carrying out an activity.

—Communication systems

Use under names of individual corporate bodies and under types of industries, institutions, installations, and disciplines.

—Computer-assisted instruction

Use under topical headings for works on an automated method of instruction in which a student interacts directly with instructional materials stored in a computer.

—Congresses

Use under any type of subject heading.

—Controversial literature

Use under religious and philosophical topics for works that argue against or express opposition to a doctrine, belief, practice, school of thought, etc.

—Cross-cultural studies

Use under topical headings for works which report the results of cross-cultural studies on those topics or discuss the methods and techniques of conducting such studies.

—Data processing

Use under names of individual corporate bodies and under topical headings.

—Decision making

Use under topical headings for works on the process of arriving at decisions for action, including attempts to formulate a general theory based on mathematical analysis and psychological experiment.

—Defense measures

Use under types of industries, utilities, installations, etc., for measures undertaken for their protection during times of conflict.

—Dictionaries

Use under uniform titles of sacred works and under topical headings.

—Directories

Use under names of countries, cities, etc., individual corporate bodies, classes of persons, ethnic groups, Christian denominations, types of organizations, and topical headings for individual directories containing names, addresses, and other identifying data.

—Discipline

Use under names of individual corporate bodies and under types of corporate bodies, classes of persons, individual religions, and Christian denominations for the enforcement of rules affecting conduct or action.

—Documentation

Use under topical headings for works on the processes by which documents on those topics are made available.

—Drama

Use under names of countries, cities, etc., names of individual persons other than literary authors, names of individual corporate bodies, and under classes of persons, ethnic groups, individual wars, and topical headings for collections of plays or individual plays on those subjects.

—Early works to 1800

Use under names of countries, cities, etc., and appropriate topical headings to designate individual works written or issued before 1800.

—Economic aspects (May Subd Geog)

Use under topical headings.

See also **—Economic conditions** under names of countries, cities, etc., and under classes of persons and ethnic groups for works discussing the economic history or economic conditions in general of a place, class of persons, or ethnic group.

—Equipment and supplies

Use under names of individual corporate bodies and under disciplines, types of industries, processes, services, laboratories, institutions, and individual wars.

—Evaluation

Use under names of individual corporate bodies and under types of institutions, products, services, equipment, activities, projects, and programs for works on methods of assessing or appraising those subjects or for works on both the methods and results of assessing them.

—Fiction

Use under names of countries, cities, etc., names of individual persons other than literary authors, names of individual corporate bodies, and under classes of persons, ethnic groups, individual wars, and topical headings for collections of stories or novels on those topics. Also use under names of individual persons other than literary authors and historic events for individual works of biographical or historical fiction.

—Film catalogs

Use under any type of subject heading.

—Finance

Use under names of individual nongovernmental corporate bodies and under types of industries, services, technical operations, etc., for works on the raising and expenditure of funds. See also **—Appropriations and expenditures** under names of countries, cities, etc., and individual government agencies.

—Folklore

Use under names of countries, cities, etc., and under classes of persons, ethnic groups, and topical headings for works discussing those topics as themes in folklore and for collections of folklore texts on those subjects.

—Forecasting

Use under names of countries, cities, etc., and under topical headings.

—Foreign influences

Use under headings for civilizations of places, or particular aspects of those civilizations, including philosophies, intellectual life, etc.

—Government policy

Use under classes of persons, ethnic groups, and topical headings not inherently governmental.

See also headings of the type **[topic] and state** and **[topic] policy.**

—Handbooks, manuals, etc.

Use under names of countries, cities, etc., and individual corporate bodies, and under topical headings.

—Historiography

Use under names of countries, cities, etc., and individual corporate bodies, uniform titles of sacred works, and under classes of persons, ethnic groups, and topical headings.

—History

Use under names of countries, cities, etc., and individual corporate bodies, uniform titles of sacred works, and under classes of persons, ethnic groups, and topical headings.

—History—16th century

Use under names of individual corporate bodies and topical headings.

—History—17th century

Use under names of individual corporate bodies and topical headings.

—History—18th century

Use under names of individual corporate bodies and topical headings.

—History—19th century

Use under names of individual corporate bodies and topical headings.

—History—20th century

Use under names of individual corporate bodies and topical headings.

—History—Chronology

Use under names of countries, cities, etc., and individual corporate bodies, and under ethnic groups, and topical headings not inherently historical.

See also **—Chronology**

—History—Philosophy

Use under names of countries, cities, etc., and under topical headings.

—History—Sources

Use under names of countries, cities, etc., and individual corporate bodies, and under classes of persons, ethnic groups, and topical headings not inherently historical for collections or discussions of contemporary writings such as legal documents, letters, diaries, family papers, etc., assembled at a later time to serve as source materials for use by students, scholars, etc., in their research on the subject.

See also **—Sources**

—Humor

Use under names of countries, cities, etc., names of individual persons and corporate bodies, uniform titles of sacred works, and under topical headings.

—Indexes

Use under names of countries, cities, etc., individual works (author-title or title entries), and under topical headings.

—Influence

Use under names of individual persons and corporate bodies, uniform titles of sacred works, types of organizations, religions, and individual wars for works discussing their influence.

—Information services (May Subd Geog)

Use under names of countries, cities, etc., names of individual persons, corporate bodies, and military services, and under topical headings.

—Inspection

Use under names of individual military services and under types of merchandise, products, equipment, engineering structures, and buildings.

—Juvenile literature

Use under any type of subject heading.

—Library resources (May Subd Geog)

Use under names of countries, cities, etc., names of individual persons and corporate bodies, and under classes of persons, ethnic groups, and topical headings for works describing the resources and special collections available on those subjects.

—Literary collections

Use under names of countries, cities, etc., individual persons other than literary authors, and individual corporate bodies, and under classes of persons, ethnic groups, individual wars, and topical headings for collections including several literary forms.

—Maintenance and repair

Use under types of objects, including machinery, vehicles, structures, etc., requiring maintenance and repair.

—Management

Use under names of individual corporate bodies, including government agencies, and under types of industries, industrial plants and processes, special activities, etc.

—Manuscripts

Use under names of individual literary authors, individual works entered under title, uniform titles of sacred works, and under groups of authors, literatures, and topical headings.

—Manuscripts—Catalogs

—Manuscripts—Indexes

—Manuscripts—Microform catalogs

—Maps

Use under names of countries, cities, etc., and individual corporate bodies, and under topical headings for individual maps or collections of maps.

—Maps—Bibliography

Use under names of countries, cities, etc., and individual corporate bodies, and under topical headings.

—Methodology

Use under disciplines for works on both the theory and practice of procedures to be followed.

—Microform catalogs

Use under names of individual institutions and collections for catalogs that list works stored in those institutions or collections in microform editions.

See also **—Bibliography—Microform catalogs**

—Moral and ethical aspects

Use under non-religious or non-ethical topics for works that discuss moral and/or ethical questions regarding the topic.

—Museums

Use under names of individual corporate bodies, and under ethnic groups, individual wars, and topical headings for which phrase headings for the type of museum have not been established.

—Outlines, syllabi, etc.

Use under topical headings for brief statements of the principal elements of a subject to be studied, usually arranged by headings and subheadings.

—Papal documents

Use under topical headings for collections of documents and other papal pronouncements on the topic.

—Periodicals

Use under any type of subject heading.

—Periodicals—Bibliography

Use under subjects for lists of serials or periodicals on a subject.

—Periodicals—Bibliography—Catalogs

Use under subjects for lists of serials or periodicals held by one organization or library, assembled as a private collection, or issued by an individual publisher.

—Periodicals—Bibliography—Union lists

Use under subjects for catalogs of serials or periodicals on those subjects held by two or more libraries.

—Periodicals—Indexes

—Philosophy

Use under names of individual persons other than philosophers and under topical headings.

—Pictorial works

Use under names of ancient (extinct) cities, individual persons, families and named entities, such as individual parks, structures, etc., and under classes of persons, ethnic groups, individual wars, and topical headings.

—Planning

Use under types of activities, facilities, industries, services, etc.

—Poetry

Use under names of countries, cities, etc., names of individual persons other than literary authors, names of individual corporate bodies, and under classes of persons, ethnic groups, individual wars, and topical headings for collections of poetry and individual poems on those subjects.

—Political activity

Use under names of individual corporate bodies and military services, and under classes of persons, individual Christian denominations, and types of corporate bodies for works on the political participation of those persons or organizations.

—Posters

Use under names of individual persons and corporate bodies, classes of persons, ethnic groups, individual wars, and topical headings for collections and/or discussions of posters about those subjects.

—Privileges and immunities

Use under names of individual international agencies and legislative bodies and under types of organizations and educational institutions.

—Prophecies

Use under names of individual persons, uniform titles of sacred works, and under classes of persons and individual wars.

—Psychological aspects

Use under topical headings other than religious topics for works on the influence of conditions, activities, objects, etc., on the mental condition or personality of individuals.

—Psychology

Use under uniform titles of sacred works, religions, and religious topics for the psychological aspects of those works or topics. Also use under classes of persons and ethnic groups for the mental processes or characteristics of those persons.

—Public opinion

Use under names of individual persons and corporate bodies, and under classes of persons, ethnic groups, individual wars, and topical headings for works on public opinion on those persons or topics.

—Quotations, maxims, etc.

Use under names of countries, cities, etc., and under topical headings.

—Registers

Use under names of countries, cities, etc., and individual corporate bodies, and under classes of persons, ethnic groups, individual wars, types of objects, etc., for lists of names without addresses or other identifying data.

—Religion

Use under names of countries, cities, etc., names of individual persons and corporate bodies, and under ethnic groups and types of institutions.

—Research (May Subd Geog)

Use under names of countries, cities, etc., and under classes of persons, ethnic groups, and topical headings.

—Research grants (May Subd Geog)

Use under names of individual corporate bodies and under topical headings.

—Safety measures

Use under names of individual military services and under topical headings.

—Sex differences

Use under topical headings.

—Siege, [date]

Use under individual castles, forts, etc.

See also **—History—Siege, [date]** under names of countries, cities, etc.

—Sieges

Use under individual castles, forts, etc.

—Simulation methods

Use under topical headings.

—Social aspects (May Subd Geog)

Use under topical headings for works that discuss the effect of the item, activity, discipline, etc., and modern society on each other.

See also **—Social conditions** under names of countries, cities, etc., for works on the social history of the place.

—Societies, etc.

Use under names of individual persons, corporate bodies, classes of persons, ethnic groups, and topical headings for works discussing two or more societies or institutions related to those subjects.

—Sociological aspects

Use under types of institutions for works discussing the impact of the inherent nature of the institution on group interaction within the institution and vice versa.

—Software

Use under topical headings for actual software items, i.e. machine-readable editions.

—Songs and music

Use under names of individual persons and corporate bodies, and under ethnic groups and topical headings.

—Sources

Use under individual works (author-title or title entries), historical topics, and headings for systems of law for collections of writings compiled for scholars. Also use under names of individual persons for works discussing the individual's sources of ideas or inspiration.

See also **—History—Sources**.

—Statistical methods

Use under topical headings for discussions of the methods of solving problems in those fields through the use of statistics.

—Statistics

Use under names of countries, cities, etc., names of individual corporate bodies, classes of persons, ethnic groups, and topical headings for works consisting of or discussing statistics about those subjects.

—Study and teaching (May Subd Geog)

Use under names of countries, cities, etc., individual persons, and corporate bodies, and under classes of persons, ethnic groups, and topical headings for works on methods of study and teaching on those subjects.

—Study and teaching—Audio-visual aids

Use under names of countries, cities, etc., individual persons, and corporate bodies, and under classes of persons, ethnic groups, and topical headings for works on the use of audiovisual aids in the learning and teaching of those subjects.

—Study and teaching —Simulation methods

Use under topical headings.

—Study and teaching (Continuing education) (May Subd Geog)

—Study and teaching (Elementary) (May Subd Geog)

—Study and teaching (Graduate) (May Subd Geog)

—Study and teaching (Higher) (May Subd Geog)

—Study and teaching (Preschool) (May Subd Geog)

—Study and teaching (Primary) (May Subd Geog)

—Study and teaching (Secondary) (May Subd Geog)

—Tables

Use under topical headings.

—Textbooks

Use under topical headings for works about textbooks on those topics.

—Transportation

Use under names of individual military services, and under classes of persons, types of objects, merchandise, and individual wars for works on transportation of or applied to these topics.

—Union lists

Use under types of printed or nonbook materials for catalogs of those materials held by two or more libraries.

See also **—Bibliography—Union lists**

—Video tape catalogs

Use under any type of subject heading.

—Vocational guidance (May Subd Geog)

Use under names of individual corporate bodies and military services and under occupations, fields of endeavor, and types of industries for works describing careers in those organizations or fields and/or offering advice on how to prepare for, enter, and succeed in those careers.

Free-floating subdivisions for use under headings for military services

Types of headings designated by the category: Headings for names of individual military services, including military organizations at the state or province level such as national guards. Also included are subject headings formed using the free-floating subdivisions **—Armed Forces** and **—National Guard** under names of regions and countries, and the free-floating subdivision **—Militia** under names of places larger than cities, and headings established using **—Armed Forces** under names of international agencies having armed forces.

Examples: **Great Britain. Army; Italy. Marina; Germany. Kriegsmarine; Japan. Rikugun; Texas. National Guard; Ohio—Militia; United Nations—Armed Forces; Warsaw Treaty Organization—Armed Forces.**

The category does not include names of subordinate organizational units lower than a branch of the armed forces, such as divisions, regiments, fleets, squadrons, etc.

Period subdivisions: The subdivisions **—History** and **—Recruiting, enlistment, etc.** may be further subdivided on a free-floating basis by subdivisions for wars or armed conflicts in which the military service took part. The subdivisions may be formed based on headings for wars established either directly under their names or as subdivisions under place names.

Special provisions: Several of the subdivisions listed below may be used only under military services for which an equivalent corporate body subheading does not exist or cannot be established. If the concept exists as a corporate body, assign the name heading instead of the topical subdivision. For example, the subdivision **—Artillery** may be used under **United States. Army** because the artillery no longer constitutes a separate corporate entity in the organization of the United States Army.

—Abbreviations
—Abstracts
—Accounting
—Aerial gunners
—Aerographers
—Afro-American troops
—Afro-Americans
—Aides
—Air controlmen
—Air police (1)
—Airborne troops
—Airborne troops—Communication systems
—Aircrew survival equipmentmen
—Airfield management specialists
—Airmen
—Airmen—Recreation
—Ambulances
—Anecdotes
—Appointments and retirements
—Apprentices
—Appropriations and expenditures
—Archives
—Armored troops
—Artificers' handbooks
—Artillery
—Artillery—Drill and tactics
—Aviation
—Aviation—Ground support (2)
—Aviation—Job descriptions
—Aviation—Safety measures
—Aviation (ASW) technicians
—Aviation boatswain's mates
—Aviation electricians
—Aviation electronics technicians
—Aviation fire control technicians
—Aviation guided missilemen
—Aviation machinists
—Aviation maintenance administrationmen
—Aviation mechanics
—Aviation ordnance men
—Aviation storekeepers

—Aviation structural mechanics
—Aviation structural mechanics (Safety equipment)
—Aviation supplies and stores
—Aviation support equipment technicians
—Bandmasters
—Barracks and quarters
—Barracks and quarters—Furniture
—Barracks and quarters—Heating and ventilation
—Barracks and quarters—Lighting
—Biography
—Biography—Dictionaries
—Biography—Portraits
—Boat officers
—Boats
—Boatswains
—Boatswain's mates
—Boiler technicians
—Builders
—Caricatures and cartoons
—Cavalry (3)
—Cavalry—Drill and tactics (3)
—Chaplains (4)
—Chaplain's assistants
—Civic action
—Civil functions
—Civilian employees
—Clerical work
—Collier service
—Colonial forces (5) (May Subd Geog)
—Combat sustainability
—Commando troops
—Commissariat (6)
—Communication systems
—Construction electricians
—Construction mechanics
—Cost control
—Cruise, [date]
—Cryptologic technicians
—Cryptologic technicians, Administrative
—Damage controlmen
—Data processing
—Data processing technicians
—Data systems technicians
—Demobilization
—Dental care (May Subd Geog)
—Dental technicians
—Diaries
—Disbursing clerks
—Documents
—Draftsmen
—Drill and tactics
—Drill manuals
—Electric installations
—Electric installations—Safety measures

—Electrician's mates
—Electronic installations
—Electronic installations—Maintenance and repair
—Electronic technicians
—Energy consumption
—Engineering aids
—Enginemen
—Equipment
—Equipment—Maintenance and repair
—Equipment—Quality control
—Equipment—Testing
—Equipment operators
—Examinations
—Facilities
—Facilities—Law and legislation
—Facilities—Maintenance and repair
—Fiction
—Field service
—Finance
—Finance offices
—Fire control technicians (Ballistic missile fire control)
—Fire control technicians (Missile)
—Fire controlmen
—Firearms
—Firearms—Markings
—Firemen
—Firing regulations
—Flags
—Flight officers
—Flight surgeons
—Food service specialists
—Foreign countries
—Foreign service (May Subd Geog)
—Forms
—Fuel
—Gas turbine system technicians (Mechanical)
—Gays
—General staff officers
—Ground support (7)
—Guard duty
—Guided missile personnel
—Guided missile personnel—Training of (May Subd Geog)
—Guided missile personnel—Training of—Aids and devices
—Gunners
—Gunner's mate technicians
—Gunner's mates
—Gunner's mates (Missiles)
—Handbooks, manuals, etc.
—Handbooks, manuals, etc.—Indexes
—Headquarters
—Hispanic Americans
—Historiography
—History
—History—Revolution, 1775–1783, [War of 1812, etc.] (8)

—History—Chronology
—History, 16th century
—History, 17th century
—History, 18th century
—History, 19th century
—History, 20th century
—Honorific unit titles
—Hospital ships
—Humor
—Ice breaking operations
—Indian troops
—Indians
—Information services (May Subd Geog)
—Insignia
—Inspection
—Instrumentmen
—Intelligence specialists
—Interior communications electricians
—Inventory control
—Job descriptions
—Journalists
—Juvenile films
—Juvenile literature
—Lawyers
—Leaves and furloughs
—Legalmen
—Lists of vessels
—Lithographers
—Machine-gun drill and tactics
—Machinist's mates
—Management
—Maneuvers
—Mascots
—Masters-at-arms
—Medals, badges, decorations, etc.
—Medical care (May Subd Geog)
—Medical care—Law and legislation
—Medical examinations (May Subd Geog)
—Medical personnel
—Medical personnel—Malpractice
—Medical supplies
—Medical technologists
—Memorial certificates
—Messes
—Metalsmiths
—Military capital (9)
—Military construction operations
—Military construction operations—Cold weather conditions
—Military construction operations—Law and legislation
—Military life
—Military life—Caricatures and cartoons
—Military police (10)
—Military police—Foreign auxiliaries
—Mine companies

—Minorities
—Mobilization
—Motorcycle troops
—Non-commissioned officers
—Non-commissioned officers' handbooks
—Nuclear propulsion plant operators
—Nurses
—Occupational specialties
—Officer efficiency reports
—Officers
—Officers—Autographs
—Officers—Biography
—Officers—Classification
—Officers—Correspondence
—Officers—Diaries
—Officers' clubs
—Officers' handbooks
—Officers on detached service
—Officials and employees (11)
—Operational readiness
—Operations officers
—Operations specialists
—Order-books
—Ordnance and ordnance stores
—Ordnance and ordnance stores—Influence of environment
—Ordnance and ordnance stores—Inspection
—Ordnance and ordnance stores—Materials
—Ordnance and ordnance stores—Quality control
—Ordnance and ordnance stores—Security measures
—Ordnance facilities
—Organization
—Organization—Charts, diagrams, etc.
—Painting of vessels
—Parachute troops
—Patternmakers
—Pay, allowances, etc.
—Pay, allowances, etc.—Law and legislation
—Personnel management
—Personnel management—Law and legislation
—Personnel records
—Petty officers
—Petty officers' handbooks
—Photographers
—Physical training
—Pictorial works
—Poetry
—Political activity
—Postal clerks
—Postal service
—Prisons (12)
—Prisons and prison ships (13)
—Procurement
—Procurement—Automation
—Promotions

—Provisioning (14)
—Public relations
—Radarmen
—Radio installations
—Radiomen
—Records and correspondence
—Recruiting, enlistment, etc.
—Recruiting, enlistment, etc.—Revolution, 1775–1783, [War of 1898, etc.]
—Recruiting, enlistment, etc.—Law and legislation
—Registers
—Registers of dead
—Regulations
—Religious life
—Remount service
—Reorganization
—Reserve fleets
—Reserves
—Reserves—Pay, allowances, etc.
—Reserves—Personnel records
—Reserves—Promotions
—Rum ration
—Safety measures
—Sanitary affairs
—Sea life
—Seamen's handbooks
—Search and rescue operations
—Security measures
—Service clubs
—Service craft
—Shore patrol (16)
—Signaling
—Signalmen
—Ski troops
—Small-boat service
—Social services (17)
—Societies, etc.
—Songs and music
—Sports
—Staff corps
—Staffs
—Statistics
—Stewards
—Storekeepers
—Submarine forces
—Supplies and stores
—Supplies and stores—Classification
—Supplies and stores—Law and legislation
—Supplies and stores—Quality control
—Supplies and stores—Standards (May Subd Geog)
—Surgeons
—Tactical aviation (May Subd Geog)
—Target practice
—Test shooting
—Torpedo companies

—Tradevmen
—Transport of sick and wounded
—Transport service
—Transportation
—Transportation supplies and stores
—Trials of vessels
—Uniforms
—Unit cohesion
—Utilitiesmen
—Vocational guidance (May Subd Geog)
—Wage fixing
—Warrant officers
—Watch duty
—Weapons systems
—Weapons systems—Costs
—Weapons systems—Maintenance and repair
—Weapons systems—Maintenance and repair—Data processing
—Weapons systems—Reliability
—Weapons systems—Testing
—Women
—Women's reserves
—Yeomen

(1) Use only under air forces.

(2) Do not use under air forces.

(3) Do not use under **United States. Army**; use **United States. Army. Cavalry** and **United States. Army. Cavalry—Drill and tactics** instead, as explained above.

(4) Do not use under **[place]—Armed Forces**; use **Chaplains, Military—[place]**.

(5) Use only under the military services of countries having colonial forces.

(6) Do not use under navies.

(7) Use only under air forces.

(8) The subdivision **—History—Revolution, 1775–1783** is not valid under **United States. Army**. Use **United States. Continental Army—History** instead.

(9) Do not use under **[place]—Armed Forces**; use **Military capital—[place]**.

(10) Do not use under air forces or navies.

(11) Use only under **[place]—Armed Forces** and under names of government agencies responsible for the operation of individual military services, e.g. **United States. Dept. of the Army—Officials and employees**.

(12) Do not use under navies.

(13) Use only under navies.

(14) Use only under navies.

(15) The subdivision **—Recruiting, enlistment, etc.—Revolution, 1775–1783** is not valid under **United States. Army**. Use **United States. Continental Army—Recruiting, enlistment, etc.** instead.

(16) Use only under navies.

(17) Do not use under **[place]—Armed Forces**; use **Military social work—[place]**.

Free-floating subdivisions used under names of places

Types of headings included: The subdivisions listed below may be used, within the limitations of the footnotes, as free-floating subdivisions under headings for geographic place names including continents, regions, islands, countries, states, provinces, and equivalent jurisdictions, counties, headings for metropolitan areas, suburban areas, and regions based on names of cities. They may be used, except as footnoted, under names of cities and city sections.

—Air defenses
—Air defenses, Civil
—Air defenses, Military
—Annexation to ... (1)
—Appropriations and expenditures
—Archival resources (May Subd Geog)
—Armed Forces (2) (May Subd Geog)
—Bibliography
—Biography
—Boundaries (May Subd Geog)
—Church history
—Church history—16th century
—Church history—17th century
—Church history—18th century
—Church history—19th century
—Church history—20th century
—Civil defense
—Civil defense—Law and legislation
—Civilization
—Civilization—16th century (1)
—Civilization—17th century (1)
—Civilization—18th century (1)
—Civilization—19th century (1)
—Civilization—20th century (1)
—Civilization—Foreign influences
—Civilization—Philosophy
—Claims
—Claims vs. ...
—Coast defenses (1)
—Colonial influence
—Colonies (2)
—Colonization
—Commerce (May Subd Geog)
—Commercial policy (2)
—Commercial treaties (2)
—Congresses
—Defenses (2)
—Defenses—Law and legislation (2)
—Dependency on ... (2)
—Dependence on foreign countries (2)
—Diplomatic and consular service (2) (May Subd Geog)
—Diplomatic and consular service—Buildings (2)
—Diplomatic and consular service—Privileges and immunities (2)
—Diplomatic and consular service—Selection and appointment (2)
—Diplomatic and consular service—Travel restrictions (2)
—Economic conditions
—Economic integration (3)
—Economic policy
—Emigration and immigration
—Emigration and immigration—Economic aspects
—Emigration and immigration—Government policy

—Emigration and immigration—Social aspects
—Ethnic relations
—Exiles (1)
—Forecasting
—Foreign economic relations (May Subd Geog)
—Foreign public opinion (2)
—Foreign public opinion, British, [French, Italian, etc.] (2)
—Foreign relations (2) (May Subd Geog)
—Foreign relations—Executive agreements (2)
—Foreign relations—Law and legislation (2)
—Foreign relations—Philosophy (2)
—Foreign relations—Treaties (2)
—Foreign relations administration (2)
—Frontier troubles (1)
—Handbooks, manuals, etc.
—Historical geography
—Historical geography—Maps
—Historiography
—History
—History—Autonomy and independence movements (1)
—History—Blockade, [date]
—History—Bombardment, [date]
—History—Chronology
—History—Errors, inventions, etc.
—History—Partition, [date]
—History—Philosophy
—History—Prophecies
—History—Siege, [date]
—History—Sources
—History, Local
—History, Military
—History, Military—Religious aspects
—History, Naval (3)
—International status
—Juvenile literature
—Kings and rulers
—Library resources (May Subd Geog)
—Maps
—Military policy (2)
—Military policy—Religious aspects (2)
—Military relations (May Subd Geog)
—Military relations—Foreign countries
—Militia (1)
—National Guard (2)
—National security (2)
—National security—Finance (2)
—National security—Finance—Law and legislation (2)
—National security—Law and legislation (2)
—Naval militia (1)
—Neutrality
—Nonalignment (2)
—Politics and government
—Politics and government—Caricatures and cartoons
—Politics and government—Humor

—Politics and government—Philosophy
—Race relations
—Relations (May Subd Geog)
—Relations—Foreign countries
—Religion
—Religion—16th century
—Religion—17th century
—Religion—18th century
—Religion—19th century
—Religion—20th century
—Social conditions
—Strategic aspects
—Study and teaching (May Subd Geog)
—Study and teaching (Continuing education) (May Subd Geog)
—Study and teaching (Elementary) (May Subd Geog)
—Study and teaching (Graduate) (May Subd Geog)
—Study and teaching (Higher) (May Subd Geog)
—Study and teaching (Preschool) (May Subd Geog)
—Study and teaching (Primary) (May Subd Geog)
—Study and teaching (Secondary) (May Subd Geog)
—Territorial expansion (2)
—Territories and possessions (2)
—Travel regulations (1)

(1) Do not use under cities.

(2) Use only under countries or under regions larger than countries.

(3) Use only under regions larger than countries.

Free-floating subdivisions used under headings for individual wars

Types of headings: These subdivisions may be used under headings for individual wars entered directly under their names or as subdivisions under place names. The category includes armed conflicts called by other names, such as coups, revolutions, insurrections, uprisings, civil wars, etc. It does not include individual battles of wars, nor unarmed disturbances, such as riots, demonstrations, protests, strikes, etc.
Special provisions:

1. Subdivisions on this list with the notation (May Subd Geog) are further subdivided by place only when used after a war established directly under its own name, e.g. **World War, 1939–1945**. For a civil war or internal armed conflict, the subdivisions on this list are not further subdivided by place.

2. The subdivisions **—Participation, Foreign and Participation, [nationality]** are not used under the headings **World War, 1914–1918** or **World War, 1939–1945**. For the participation of a particular country in one of the world wars, see **[name of war]—[country]**.

—Aerial operations
—Aerial operations, American, [British, etc.]
—Afro-Americans
—Almanacs
—Amphibious operations
—Anecdotes
—Anniversaries, etc.
—Anti-aircraft artillery operations
—Antiquities

—Armistices
—Art and the war, [revolution, etc.] (1)
—Artillery operations
—Artillery operations, American, [British, French, etc.]
—Atrocities
—Autographs
—Balloons (May Subd Geog)
—Baptists, [Catholic Church, etc.]
—Basques
—Battlefields (May Subd Geog)
—Battlefields—Guide-books
—Biography
—Biography—Dictionaries
—Biological warfare
—Blacks (May Subd Geog)
—Blockades
—Bomb reconnaissance
—Buddhism, [Islam, etc.]
—Camouflage
—Campaigns (May Subd Geog)
—Campaigns—Eastern (2)
—Campaigns—Western (2)
—Caricatures and cartoons
—Cartography
—Casualties, (Statistics, etc.)
—Causes
—Cavalry operations
—Censorship (May Subd Geog)
—Centennial celebrations, etc.
—Chaplains (May Subd Geog)
—Chemical warfare
—Children (May Subd Geog)
—Chronology
—Civilian relief (May Subd Geog)
—Claims
—Collaborationists (May Subd Geog)
—Collectibles (May Subd Geog)
—Commando operations (May Subd Geog)
—Communications
—Concentration camps (May Subd Geog)
—Confiscations and contributions (May Subd Geog)
—Congresses
—Conscientious objectors (May Subd Geog)
—Conscript labor (May Subd Geog)
—Cossacks
—Counterfeit money
—Cryptography
—Deportations from [region or country]
—Desertions (May Subd Geog)
—Destruction and pillage (May Subd Geog)
—Diplomatic history (3)
—Dogs
—Draft resisters (May Subd Geog)
—Drama

—Economic aspects (May Subd Geog)
—Education and the war, [revolution, etc.] (1)
—Electronic intelligence (May Subd Geog)
—Engineering and construction
—Equipment and supplies
—Evacuation of civilians (May Subd Geog)
—Exhibitions
—Fiction
—Finance (May Subd Geog)
—Flags
—Food supply (May Subd Geog)
—Forced repatriation
—Foreign public opinion (4)
—Foreign public opinion, Austrian, [British, etc.] (4)
—Fuel supplies
—German Americans
—Giftbooks
—Government in exile
—Graffiti
—Gypsies (May Subd Geog)
—Health aspects (May Subd Geog)
—Historiography
—Horses (May Subd Geog)
—Hospitals (May Subd Geog)
—Humor
—Indians
—Influence
—Japanese Americans
—Jews (May Subd Geog)
—Jews—Rescue (May Subd Geog)
—Journalism, Military (May Subd Geog)
—Journalists
—Jungle warfare
—Language (New words, slang, etc.)
—Law and legislation (May Subd Geog)
—Libraries
—Literary collections
—Literature and the war, [revolution, etc.] (1)
—Logistics (May Subd Geog)
—Manpower (May Subd Geog)
—Maps
—Medals
—Medical care (May Subd Geog)
—Military currency
—Military intelligence (May Subd Geog)
—Missing in action (May Subd Geog)
—Monuments (May Subd Geog)
—Moral and ethical aspects
—Motion pictures and the war, [revolution, etc.] (1)
—Museums (May Subd Geog)
—Music and the war, [revolution, etc.]
—Name
—Naval operations
—Naval operations—Submarine

—Naval operations, American, [British, etc.]
—Occupied territories
—Pamphlets
—Participation, Afro-American, [Indian, etc.]
—Participation, Female
—Participation, Foreign
—Participation, German, [Irish, Swiss, etc.]
—Participation, Immigrant
—Participation, Jewish
—Participation, Juvenile
—Peace
—Personal narratives
—Personal narratives, American, [French, etc.]
—Personal narratives, Confederate
—Personal narratives, Jewish
—Photography
—Pictorial works
—Pigeons
—Poetry
—Portraits
—Postal service
—Posters
—Prisoners and prisons
—Prisoners and prisons, British, [German, etc.]
—Prizes, etc.
—Propaganda
—Prophecies
—Protest movements (May Subd Geog)
—Protestant churches
—Psychological aspects
—Public opinion
—Radar
—Reconnaissance operations
—Reconnaissance operations, American, [German, etc.]
—Refugees
—Regimental histories (May Subd Geog)
—Registers
—Registers of dead (May Subd Geog)
—Religious aspects
—Reparations
—Riverine operations
—Riverine operations, American, [British, etc.]
—Science
—Scouts and scouting
—Search and rescue operations (May Subd Geog)
—Secret service (May Subd Geog)
—Sermons
—Social aspects (May Subd Geog)
—Societies, etc.
—Songs and music
—Sounds
—Study and teaching (May Subd Geog)
—Tank warfare
—Technology

—Territorial questions (May Subd Geog)
—Theater and the war, [revolution, etc.] (1)
—Transportation
—Treaties
—Trench warfare
—Trophies
—Tunnel warfare
—Underground literature (May Subd Geog)
—Underground movements (May Subd Geog)
—Underground printing plants (May Subd Geog)
—Unknown military personnel
—Unknown military personnel, American, [British, etc.]
—Veterans (May Subd Geog)
—Veterinary service (May Subd Geog)
—War work (May Subd Geog)
—War work—American Legion
—War work—Boy Scouts
—War work—Catholic Church, [Methodist Church, etc.]
—War work—Churches
—War work—Elks
—War work—Girl Scouts
—War work—Red Cross
—War work—Salvation Army
—War work—Schools
—War work—Young Men's Christian Associations
—War work—Young Women's Christian Associations
—Women (May Subd Geog)

(1) Complete the subdivision by repeating the generic term for the type of engagement contained in the heading, e.g. **Spain—History—Civil War, 1936–1939—Art and the war; United States —History—Revolution, 1775–1783—Literature and the revolution.**

(2) Use only under the headings: **World War, 1914–1918; World War, 1939–1945.**

(3) Use only under wars established directly under the name of the war. For other wars, use **[country]—Foreign relations—[period].**

(4) Do not use under the headings: **World War, 1914–1918; World War, 1935–1945.**

Part One : Topics and Events

This section contains subject headings for topics and events. Some examples are: **Asylum, Right of; Balance of power; Boundary disputes; Communism and nonviolence; Détente; Counterinsurgency; German reunification question (1949-); Historic peace churches; International economic relations; Iran-Contra Affair, 1985- ; Jewish-Arab relations; Neutrality; Nuclear arms control**.

A few headings for corporate bodies, with their subdivisions, are also included. Examples are: **League of Nations; United Nations; United States. Army**. Most corporate bodies, including societies, government agencies, international agencies, and individual military services, are not included nor does the list contain names of persons or individual treaties. These headings can be found in the Library of Congress publication *Name Authorities Cumulative Microfiche Edition.*

The subdivisions of general application listed in the Introduction may be used with these headings, if appropriate. The military services subdivisions may be used under names of individual military services, e.g., **United States. Army; United States. Navy**.

A-bomb
USE Atomic bomb

ABM (Antiballistic missiles)
USE Antimissile missiles

Absolutism
USE Despotism

Abuse of power
USE Despotism

Access to the sea (International law)
BT Transit by land (International law)

Achille Lauro Hijacking Incident, 1985
UF Hijacking of the Achille Lauro, 1985
BT Hijacking of ships—Italy

Acquisition of territory (May Subd Geog)
[JX4088-JX4098]
UF Territory, Acquisition of
BT Territory, National
NT Annexation (International law)
Occupancy (International law)
—Cases

Act of state
UF State, Act of
BT International law
Sovereignty
—Cases

Activism, Student
USE Student movements

Admirals (May Subd Geog)
BT Naval biography

Adriatic question

Adversary in the Bible
USE Enemy in the Bible

Advisors, Political
USE Political consultants

Aerial bombing
USE Bombing, Aerial

Aerial bombs
USE Bombs

Aerial observation
USE Aeronautics, Military—Observations

Aerial reconnaissance
[UG760-UG765]
Here are entered works limited to the aerial examination of enemy territory concerning installations, movements, resources, strength, etc.
UF Reconnaissance, Aerial
BT Military reconnaissance
NT Reconnaissance aircraft

Aerial rockets
USE Rockets (Aeronautics)
Rockets (Ordnance)

Aerial strategy
USE Air warfare

Aerial warfare
USE Air warfare

Aeronautics, Military (May Subd Geog)
[UG630-UG635]
UF Military aeronautics
Military aviation
BT Armaments
Military art and science
SA subdivision Aviation under names of individual armies; subdivision Aerial operations under individual wars; and names of individual air forces
NT Air bases
Air pilots, Military
Air power
Air warfare
Airplanes, Military
Anti-submarine warfare
Naval aviation
—Law and legislation (May Subd Geog)
NT Air warfare (International law)
—Observations
Here are entered works on military aerial observations in general, including aerial reconnaissance and surveillance, monitoring of friendly ground forces, observation of friendly artillery fire, etc.
UF Aerial observation

Aerospace law
USE Space law

African cooperation
BT International cooperation

African relations
USE Pan-Africanism

Africa specialists
USE Africanists

Africanists (May Subd Geog)
[DT19.5-DT19.6]
UF Africa specialists
BT Area specialists

Afro-Asian politics
[DS33.3]
UF Asian-African politics
BT World politics

Agents provocateurs (May Subd Geog)
BT Spies

Aggression (International law)
BT Arbitration, International
Crimes against peace
International law
Mediation, International
War (International law)

Aggressiveness (Psychology) (May Subd Geog)
[BF575.A3]
NT Violence

Agreements, International
USE Treaties

Air bases (May Subd Geog)
UF Military air bases
Naval air bases
BT Aeronautics, Military
Military bases

Air bases, American, [British, Russian, etc.] (May Subd Geog)

Air defenses
Here are entered general works on preventing air attack or minimizing its military and civil effects.
UF Defenses, Air
BT Civil defense
SA subdivision Air defenses under names of countries, cities, etc.
NT Antiairborne warfare
Gases, Asphyxiating and poisonous—War use

Air defenses, Civil
Here are entered works on the protection of civilians from air attack.
BT Civil defense
SA subdivision Air defenses, Civil under names of countries, cities, etc.

Air defenses, Military
[UG625; UG630-UG635]
Here are entered works on preventing and minimizing the military effects of air attack.
BT Air warfare
SA subdivision Air defenses, Military under names of countries, cities, etc.
NT Antiaircraft missiles
Antimissile missiles
Ballistic missile defenses
Surface-to-air missiles

Air forces (May Subd Geog)
BT Air power
Armed Forces
SA names of individual air forces

Air pilots, Military (May Subd Geog)
[UG626-UG626.2]
UF Military air pilots
BT Aeronautics, Military
NT Fighter pilots

Air interdiction
[UG700-UG705]
UF Interdiction, Air
BT Air warfare
Strategy
Tactics

Air piracy
USE Hijacking of aircraft

Air power
BT Aeronautics, Military
NT Air forces

Air space (International law)
USE Airspace (International law)

Air-to-air rockets (May Subd Geog)
UF Aircraft rockets
BT Rockets (Ordnance)

Air-to-surface missiles
UF Missiles, Air-to-surface
BT Guided missiles

Air warfare
[UG630]
UF Aerial strategy
Aerial warfare
BT Aeronautics, Military
War
SA subdivision Aerial operations under individual wars
NT Air defenses, Military
Air interdiction
Airplanes, Military
Antiairborne warfare
Bombing, Aerial
Chemical warfare

Air warfare (International law)
BT Aeronautics, Military—Law and legislation
War (International law)

Air weapons
BT Munitions

Airborne troops
SA subdivision Airborne troops under names of individual armies
NT Antiairborne warfare
Parachute troops

Aircraft, Reconnaissance
USE Reconnaissance aircraft

Aircraft rockets
USE Air-to-air rockets

Airplanes, Military (May Subd Geog)
[UG1240-UG1245]
UF Military airplanes
BT Aeronautics, Military
Air warfare
SA subdivision Aviation supplies and stores under individual armies, navies, etc.
NT Bombers
Fighter planes
Reconnaissance aircraft

Airspace (International law)
UF Air space (International law)
Freedom of the air
BT International law
Sovereignty
Space law

Alien property (May Subd Geog)
UF Foreign property
BT Aliens
International law

Aliens (May Subd Geog)
[JX4255-JX4270]
Here are entered works on persons who are not citizens of the country in which they reside.
NT Alien property
Calvo doctrine and clause
Diplomatic protection
Drago doctrine
Repatriation
Self-determination, National

Aliens, Illegal (May Subd Geog)
UF Illegal aliens
BT Emigration and immigration law

All-volunteer forces
USE Military service, Voluntary

Allegiance (May Subd Geog)
[JC328; JX4203-JX4270]
UF Political loyalty
BT Loyalty
NT Self-determination, National

Alliances
[JX4005]
UF Treaties of alliance
BT International relations
Treaties

Allied operations (Military science)
USE Combined operations (Military science)

Alsace-Lorraine question
[DC639-DC642]

Alternative defense
USE Civilian-based defense

Ambassadors (May Subd Geog)
[JX1625-JX1894]
UF Embassies
BT Diplomatic and consular service
Diplomats
International relations
NT Diplomatic privileges and immunities
Nuncios, Papal

American military bases
USE Military bases, American

Amish (May Subd Geog)
The subdivisions printed under Catholic Church may be used under this heading.
BT Mennonites
—Doctrines

Amphibious warfare
Here are entered works on the joint operation of air, land, and sea forces to establish troops on shore, as developed in World War II. General works on the landing of waterborne or airborne troops on hostile territory, including the tactics of transporting, landing and establishing such troops and their supplies, and combat during the landing phase are entered under Landing operations.
UF Joint operations (Military science)
SA subdivision Amphibious operations under individual wars

Anarchism (May Subd Geog)
[HX821-HX970.7]
UF Anarchy
BT Government, Resistance to

Anarchists (May Subd Geog)

Anarchy
USE Anarchism

Ancient civilization
USE Civilization, Ancient

Ancient history
USE History, Ancient

Angary, Right of
UF Requisitions (of neutral vessels and cargoes)
Right of angary
BT International law
War, Maritime (International law)

Anglo-Iranian Oil Dispute, 1951-1954

Annexation (International law)
BT Acquisition of territory
International law
Territory, National
SA subdivision Annexation to [country] under names of territories annexed

Anchluss movement, 1918-1938

Anthropo-geography (May Subd Geog)
UF Human geography
NT Geography, Political
Human territoriality
Regionalism

Anthropology, Theological
USE Man (Theology)

Anti-Americanism (May Subd Geog)
UF Antiamericanism
BT United States—Foreign public opinion

Anti-apartheid movements (May Subd Geog)
BT Civil rights movements

Anti-Catholicism (May Subd Geog)
[BX1766]
BT Prejudices—United States
—United States
NT Nativism

Anti-colonialism
USE Anti-imperialist movements
Colonies

Anti-communist movements (May Subd Geog)
BT Communism
NT Propaganda, Anti-communist

Anti-fascist movements (May Subd Geog)
BT Fascism
NT Anti-Nazi movement

Anti-imperialist movements (May Subd

Geog)
Here are entered works discussing collectively organizations and movements, whose stated purpose is to work against what they regard as imperialism, i.e. the policy or practice of a country extending power over other states or areas of the world, often by annexing territory.
UF Anti-colonialism
Antiimperialist movements
BT Social movements

Anti-Japanese movements, Korean
USE Korean resistance movements, 1905-1945

Anti-Nazi movement (May Subd Geog)
UF German resistance movement
BT Anti-fascist movements
National socialism

Anti-nuclear movement
USE Antinuclear movement

Anti-submarine warfare
UF ASW
BT Aeronautics, Military
NT Mines, Submarine

Anti-war movements
USE Peace movements

Anti-war poetry
This heading may be used with the following qualifiers: Bengali; English, e.g. Anti-war poetry, English.

Antiairborne warfare
UF Warfare, Antiairborne
BT Air defenses
Air warfare
Airborne troops
Tactics

Antiaircraft missiles
UF Missiles, Antiaircraft
BT Air defenses, Military
Guided missiles
NT Antimissile missiles
Surface-to-air missiles

Antiamericanism
USE Anti-Americanism

Antiballistic missiles
USE Antimissile missiles

Antiimperialist movements
USE Anti-imperialist movements

Antimilitarism
USE Militarism

Antimissile missiles
UF ABM (Antiballistic missiles)
Antiballistic missiles
BT Air defenses, Military
Antiaircraft missiles
Guided missiles

Antinuclear movement (May Subd Geog)
UF Anti-nuclear movement
Nuclear freeze movement
Protest movement, Antinuclear
BT Social movements

Antipathies
USE Prejudices

Antisemitism (May Subd Geog)
[DS145]
BT Prejudices
Race relations
NT Jews—Persecutions

Antisemitism and Christianity
USE Christianity and antisemitism

Antisemitism and socialism
USE Socialism and antisemitism

Antitank warfare
USE Tank warfare

Antiwar movements
USE Peace movements

Apartheid (May Subd Geog)
Here are entered works on the political, economic, and social policies of the government of South Africa designed to keep racial groups in South Africa and Namibia separated.
UF Separate development (Race relations)

Arab civilization
USE Civilization, Arab

Arab refugees
USE Refugees, Arab

Arabic speaking countries
USE Arab countries

Arabic studies
USE Arab countries—Study and teaching
Civilization, Arab—Study and teaching

Arabic studies specialists
USE Arabists

Arabism
[DS38]
NT Panarabism
Panislamism

Arabists (May Subd Geog)
[DS37.5]
UF Arabic studies specialists

Arabs and Islam
[BP190.5.A67]
Here are entered works on the role of Islam in the history of the Arabs, as well as works on the role of the Arabs in the history of Islam, the specifically Arab features of Islam, and the doctrine of the Arabs as the chosen people of Islam, whether these topics are treated individually or collectively.
UF Islam and Arabs

Arbitration, International
[JX1901-JX1991]
UF International arbitration
BT International cooperation
International law
International relations
Negotiation
Pacific settlement of international disputes
Peace
Peaceful change (International relations)
Treaties
War (International law)
NT Aggression (International law)
Commissions of inquiry, International
Diplomatic negotiations in international disputes
International courts

Area research
USE Area studies

Area specialists (May Subd Geog)
[D16.25]
BT Area studies
NT Africanists
Developing country specialists
International relations specialists
Sovietologists

Area studies (May Subd Geog)
[D16.25]
Here are entered general works on area studies, and with local subdivision, works on area studies carried out in specific places. Works on area studies about a particular region, country, etc., are entered under the name of the region, country, etc., with the subdivision Research or the subdivision Study and teaching.
UF Area research
SA subdivision Research or Study and teaching under names of countries, cities, etc.
NT Area specialists

Armaments
Here are entered general works on military strength, including military personnel, munitions, natural resources and industrial war potential. Works on the implements of war and the industries producing them are entered under the heading Munitions. Works on the armament of a particular country are entered under the name of the country with the subdivision Defenses.
BT Military art and science
NT Armed Forces
Armies
Arms control
Disarmament
Industrial mobilization
Munitions
Navies

Armed conflict termination
USE War—Termination

Armed Forces
UF Military, The
BT Armaments
Military art and science
SA specific branches of the Armed Forces under names ofcountries; and subdivision Armed Forces under names of countries, regions, international organizations, etc.
NT Air forces
Armies
Combatants and noncombatants (International law)
Marines
Military service, Voluntary
National service
Navies
Paramilitary forces
Sociology, Military
Soldiers
Strategic forces
—Appropriations and expenditures
UF Defense budgets
SA subdivision Appropriations and expenditures under names of individual defense agencies, and subdivision Armed Forces—Appropriations and expenditures under names of countries.
—Civic action
Here are entered works on the non-military use of armed forces for social and economic development.
UF Military civic action
SA subdivision Civic action under names of individual military services
—Equipment
—Foreign countries
SA subdivision Armed Forces—Foreign countries under names of countries
NT Military occupation
—Mobilization
[UA910]
UF Military mobilization
SA subdivisions Demobilization and Mobilization under names of individual military services
—Officers
—Political activity
BT Civil-military relations
Political participation
—Prayer-books and devotions
Subdivided by language
—Procurement
[UC260]
UF Defense procurement
Procurement, Military
SA subdivision Procurement under names of individual military services
NT Arms control impact statements
Military capital
—Recruiting, enlistment, etc.
USE Recruiting and enlistment
—Regulations
Here are entered works on the rules of conduct of the armed forces for their personnel's behavior, conduct, demeanor, etc.
SA subdivision Armed Forces—Regulations under names of countries, etc., and subdivision Regulations under names of individual military services
—Reserves
UF Military reserves
Reserves, Military
SA subdivision Armed Forces—Reserves under names of countries; and subdivision Reserves under names of individual military services
—Supplies and stores
—Vocational guidance
UF Military service as a profession
SA subdivision Vocational guidance under names of individual military services

Armed Forces and mass media (May Subd Geog)
UF Mass media and Armed Forces

Armed Forces and women
USE Women and the military

Armed Forces newspapers
USE Journalism, Military

Armed Neutrality, 1780 and 1800
USE Neutrality, Armed

Armenian question
[DS194-DS195]

Armies (May Subd Geog)
UF Army
BT Armaments
Armed Forces
Military art and science
SA names of individual armies
NT Artillery
Disarmament
Infantry
Mercenary troops
Militarism
Recruiting and enlistment
Sociology, Military
Standing army
—Equipment
[UC460-UC465]
—Maneuvers
USE Military maneuvers
—Non-commissioned officers
SA subdivision Non-commissioned officers under names of individual armies
—Officers
[UB410-UB415]
SA subdivision Officers under names of individual armies
—Organization
SA subdivision Organization under names of individual armies
—Staffs
[UB220-UB225]
UF Military staffs
SA subdivision Staffs under names of individual armies

Armies, Colonial
UF Colonial armies
SA subdivision Colonial forces under names of individual armies

Armies, Cost of
[UA17]
UF Cost of armies
BT War, Cost of
NT Military capital

Armistices
[JX5173]
UF Ceasefire
Truces
BT Peace
War (International law)
SA subdivision Armistices under individual wars
NT Flags of truce

Arms and armor (May Subd Geog)
[HD9743; U799-U825]
UF Weapons
BT Military art and science
NT Nonlethal weapons
Ordnance

Arms control
[JX1974]
Here are entered works on plans, arrangements, or processes resting upon explicit or implicit international agreement which govern the numbers, types, or performance characteristics of weapons systems and/or the numerical strength, organization, equipment, deployment, or employment of the armed forces of the parties involved. Works on the reduction, either unilaterally or internationally, in the personnel and/or equipment of armed forces are entered under Disarmament.
BT Armaments
Security, International
War
NT Arms control impact statements
Nuclear arms control
—Verification
[UA12.5]
UF Verification of arms control

Arms control impact statements (May Subd Geog)
Here are entered works on the preparation and use of arms control impact statements. Actual impact statements, as well as works on impact statements relating to specific projects, activities, policies, etc., are entered here and also under the project, activity, etc.
UF Impact statements, Arms control
BT Armed Forces—Procurement
Arms control
Weapons systems

Arms proliferation
USE Arms race

Arms race (May Subd Geog)
Here are entered works on the competitive build-up and improvement of the military power of two or more nations or blocs, particularly as regards weapons.
UF Arms proliferation
Proliferation of arms
BT Armaments
—Religious aspects
—Buddhism, [Christianity, etc.]

Arms sales
USE Military assistance
Munitions

Army
USE Armies

Army-McCarthy controversy, 1954
USE McCarthy-Army controversy, 1954

Army of Great Britain
USE Great Britain. Army

Army of the United States
USE United States. Army

Army posts
USE Military bases

Army schools
USE Military education

Arrangements, Mutual
USE Deals

Art and nationalism
USE Nationalism and art

Art and nuclear warfare (May Subd Geog)
UF Nuclear warfare
BT Art and war

Art and revolutions (May Subd Geog)
UF Revolutions and art
BT Arts and revolutions
SA subdivision Art and the revolution under individual revolutions

Art and war
Here are entered works on the relation between art and war, including the functions of art in wartime and the mobilization and specialized services of artists in the war effort.
UF War and art
SA subdivisions Art and the war; Art and the revolution, etc., under individual wars
NT Art treasures in war
War memorials

Art treasures in war (May Subd Geog)
BT Art and war
Cultural property, Protection of (International law)

Artillery (May Subd Geog)
BT Armies
SA subdivision Artillery under names of individual armies; also subdivision Artillery operations under individual wars; and names of individual artilleries

Arts and revolutions (May Subd Geog)
UF Revolutions and the arts
NT Art and revolutions

Asian-African politics
USE Afro-Asian politics

Asian cooperation
BT International cooperation
NT South Asian cooperation

Assassination (May Subd Geog)
[HV6278]
UF Political murder
Political violence
BT Political crimes and offenses
SA subdivisions Assassination; Assassination attempt, [date]; and Assassination attempts under names of individual persons
—Investigation (May Subd Geog)
[HV8079.A74]
—Religious aspects
—Buddhism, [Christianity, etc.]

Assassins (May Subd Geog)
UF Death squads

Astronautics, Military (May Subd Geog)
Here are entered works on the military applications of space sciences. Works on interplanetary warfare, attacks on earth from outer space, or warfare among the nations of earth in outer space, are entered under Space warfare.
UF Military astronautics
NT Space surveillance
Space warfare
Space weapons

Asylum, Right of
[HV8652-HV8654; JX4275-JX4399]
UF Right of asylum
Sanctuary (Law)
BT Church and state
International law
Neutrality
—Cases
NT Colombian-Peruvian asylum case
—Religious aspects
—Buddhism, [Christianity, etc.]
—United States
NT Sanctuary movement

Ataturkism
USE Kemalism

Atomic bomb (May Subd Geog)
UF A-bomb
BT Bombs
Nuclear weapons
NT Radioactive fallout
—Blast effect
—Physiological effect
—Safety measures
BT Civil defense
War damage, Industrial

Atomic bomb (International law)
USE Nuclear weapons (International law)

Atomic bomb victims (May Subd Geog)
Here are entered works on the victims of atomic bomb warfare. Works on the victims of nuclear weapons tests are entered under Nuclear weapons testing victims.
UF Victims of atomic bombings
BT War victims

Atomic warfare
USE Nuclear warfare

Atomic warfare and literature
USE Nuclear warfare and literature

Atomic warfare in motion pictures
USE Nuclear warfare in motion pictures

Atomic weapons
USE Nuclear weapons

Atomic weapons, Tactical
USE Tactical nuclear weapons

Atomic weapons and disarmament
USE Nuclear disarmament

Atomic weapons information
USE Nuclear weapons information

Atrocities (May Subd Geog)
SA subdivision Atrocities under individual wars
NT Massacres
Persecution

Atrocities, Political
USE Political atrocities

Attitude (Psychology) (May Subd Geog)
[BF327]
NT Attitude change
Dogmatism
Prejudices

Attitude change
UF Change of attitude
BT Attitude (Psychology)

Authoritarianism (May Subd Geog)
BT Political science
NT Despotism
Fascism
National socialism
Totalitarianism

Authority
[BD209; BF637.A87; HM271]
BT Political science
NT Divine right of kings
Power (Philosophy)

Autonomy
UF Independence
Self-government
BT International law
Political science

Sovereignty

B-2 Bomber
UF Stealth bomber
BT Supersonic bombers

Bacteriological warfare
USE Biological warfare

Balance of power
[D217; JX1318]
UF Power, Balance of
Power politics
BT International relations
Great powers

Balance of trade (May Subd Geog)
[HF1014]
UF Trade balance
Trade deficits
BT International trade

Balkan question
USE Eastern question (Balkan)

Ballistic missile defenses (May Subd Geog)
Here are entered works on systems designed to detect, identify, track, and destroy incoming enemy strategic ballistic missiles before they detonate on target.
UF Defenses, Ballistic missile
BT Air defenses, Military
Ballistic missiles
—United States
NT Strategic Defense Initiative

Ballistic missiles (May Subd Geog)
Here are entered works on high-altitude, high-speed atomic missiles which are self-propelled and guided in the first stage of flight only, after which the trajectory becomes natural and uncontrolled. Works on powered and guided missiles are entered under Rockets (Ordnance) and Guided missiles.
UF Missiles, Ballistic
BT Guided missiles
Rockets (Aeronautics)
SA names of specific missiles
NT Ballistic missile defenses
Fleet ballistic missile weapons systems
Intercontinental ballistic missiles
Intermediate-range ballistic missiles

Banned persons (South Africa)
Here are entered works on people who, under the provisions of the South African Internal Security Act, are unable to travel or speak with anyone without written permission from the authorities.
UF Persons under banning orders (South Africa)
BT Political prisoners—South Africa

Bargaining
USE Negotiation

Bargains
USE Deals

Bases, Military
USE Military bases

Battle groups, Naval
USE Naval battle groups

Battle termination
USE Disengagement (Military science)

Battlefield photographers
USE War photographers

Battlefields (May Subd Geog)
BT Battles
SA subdivision Battlefields under individual wars

Battle-songs
USE War-songs

Battles (May Subd Geog)
[D25]
UF Fighting
BT Military art and science
Military history
Sieges
War
SA subdivision Campaigns under individual wars
NT Battlefields
Imaginary wars and battles

Battles, Naval
USE Naval battles

Battles in art

Battles in literature
BT War in literature

Battleships (May Subd Geog)
BT Warships

Bays (International law)
[JX4137]

Behavior, Human
USE Human behavior

Behavior, Self-protective
USE Self-protective behavior

Beirut Hostage Crisis, Beirut, Lebanon, 1985
USE TWA Flight 847 Hijacking Incident, 1985

Belize question
UF British Honduras question
Guatemala-British Honduras dispute

Belligerency
[JX4571-JX5187]
BT War (International law)
NT Combatants and noncombatants (International law)

Belligerent occupation
USE Military occupation

Bering Sea controversy
UF Fur-seal arbitration

Berlin crisis
USE Berlin question (1945-)

Berlin question (1945-)
UF Berlin crisis
BT German reunification question (1949-)
NT Berlin wall (1961-)

Berlin wall (1961-)
BT Berlin question (1945-)

Bias (Psychology)
USE Prejudices

Bible
—Enemy
USE Enemy in the Bible
—Ethics
USE Ethics in the Bible
—Military history
USE Military history in the Bible
—Palestine
USE Palestine in the Bible
—Politics
USE Politics in the Bible
—Theology
[BS543]
Here are entered works on the theology of the Bible, considered apart from the later theology of the church.
BT Theology, Doctrinal
SA subdivision Biblical teaching under subjects
—Violence
USE Violence in the Bible

Bikini Nuclear Tests, 1946
USE Operation Crossroads, 1946

Biological warfare (May Subd Geog)
[UG447.8]
UF Bacteriological warfare
Germ warfare
BT War
SA subdivision Biological warfare under individual wars

Biological warfare (International law)
BT War (International law)

Biological weapons
[UG447.8]
UF Weapons, Biological
BT Munitions

Biopolitics
UF Political behavior
BT Human behavior
Political science
Sociobiology

Black nationalism (May Subd Geog)
UF Nationalism, Black
Separatism, Black

Blockade
[JX5225]
UF Blockade running
BT Sanctions (International law)
War

SA subdivisions History—Blockade, [date] under names of countries, cities, etc., and Blockades under individual wars
NT Continuous voyages (International law)
Contraband of war
Search, Right of

Blockade, Pacific
[JX4494]
UF Pacific blockade
BT Embargo
War, Maritime (International law)

Blockade running
USE Blockade

Bolshevism
USE Communism

Bomb damage to industry
USE War damage, Industrial

Bomb reconnaissance
Here are entered works on the location, identification, and application of safety measures as protection against unexploded bombs which have been set to detonate.
BT Bombs
Civil defense
SA subdivision Bomb reconnaissance under individual wars

Bombardment (May Subd Geog)
[JX5117]
Here are entered works on sustained military attacks on cities, military positions, etc., with bombs, shells, rockets or other explosive missiles.
UF Aerial attacks on cities
BT War, Maritime (International law)
War (International law)
SA subdivision History—Bombardment, [date] under names of countries, cities, etc.; and subdivision Aerial operations under individual wars
NT Bombing, Aerial

Bombers (May Subd Geog)
BT Airplanes, Military
Bombardment
Strategic forces
SA headings for individual bombers
NT Bombing, Aerial
Supersonic bombers

Bombing, Aerial (May Subd Geog)
Here are entered works on military bombardments by means of bombs dropped from the air.
UF Aerial bombing
BT Air warfare
Bombardment
Bombers
Bombs
SA subdivision History—Bombardment, [date] under names of countries, cities, etc.; and subdivision Aerial operations under individual wars

Bombings (May Subd Geog)
Here are entered works on the use of explosive devices for the purposes of political terrorism, protest, etc.
UF Terrorist bombings
BT Political crimes and offenses
Terrorism

Bombs
Here are entered general works on bombs and works on bombs launched from aircraft.
UF Aerial bombs
NT Atomic bombs
Bomb reconnaissance
Bombing, Aerial
Hydrogen bomb
Neutron bomb

Bonapartism (May Subd Geog)
[JC359]
Here are entered works on attachment to and advocacy of the policies of Napoleon Bonaparte, involving belief in a concentration of power in the executive, an imperial form of state, a centralized administration, an imperialistic foreign policy, and the embodiment of the power of the state in the personality of the leader.
BT Imperialism

Booty (International law)
[JX5295-JX5313]
UF Captured property
BT Confiscations
Enemy property
Military occupation
Prizes
War (International law)

Border disputes
USE Boundary disputes

Border patrols (May Subd Geog)
UF Boundary patrols
Surveillance by border patrols
NT Coastal surveillance

Borders (Geography)
USE Boundaries

Boundaries
[JC323; JX4111-JX4145]
Here are entered works on boundaries in general. Works on boundaries of specific regions, countries, etc., are entered under the name of the place with the subdivision Boundaries. Works on the boundaries between two countries, etc., are entered under the name of each country with the subdivision Boundaries—[other country].
UF Borders (Geography)
Boundary lines
Frontiers
Geographical boundaries
International boundaries
Political boundaries
BT Geography, Political
International law
International relations
Territorial waters
Territory, National
SA subdivision Boundaries under names of countries, states, etc.; and subdivision Territorial questions under individual wars
NT Ethnic barriers

Boundary disputes
Here are entered works on boundary disputes in general. Works on boundary disputes in specific regions, countries, etc., are entered under the name of the place with the subdivision Boundaries. Works on boundary disputes between two countries, etc., are entered under the name of each country with the subdivision Boundaries—[other country].
UF Border disputes
Disputes, Boundary
Territorial boundary disputes
SA subdivision Boundaries under names of regions, countries, etc.; and subdivision Territorial questions under individual wars

Boundary lines
USE Boundaries

Boundary patrols
USE Border patrols

Brainwashing (May Subd Geog)
UF Forced indoctrination
BT Psychological warfare

British Honduras question
USE Belize question

Broadcasting, International
USE International broadcasting

Buddhism (May Subd Geog)
—Doctrines
NT Man (Buddhism)

Buddhism and communism
USE Communism and Buddhism

Buddhism and politics
[BQ4570.S7]
UF Politics and Buddhism
BT Buddhism and state

Buddhism and state (May Subd Geog)
UF State and Buddhism
BT Religion and state
NT Buddhism and politics

Buddhist ethics
UF Ethics, Buddhist

Buffer states (May Subd Geog)
UF States, Buffer
BT Geopolitics

Bushwhackers
USE Guerrillas

Business and politics (May Subd Geog)
UF Politics and business
BT Politics, Practical

Business enterprises, International
USE International business enterprises

CBD (Civilian-based defense)
USE Civilian-based defense

CBR warfare
USE Biological warfare
Chemical warfare
Nuclear warfare

Calvo doctrine and clause
[JX5485.C2]
BT Aliens
Claims
Diplomatic protection

Campaign consultants
USE Political consultants

Campaign management (May Subd Geog)
BT Elections
Politics, Practical

Capitulations, Military
UF Military capitulations
Surrender
BT Military law
Sieges
War (International law)

Capture at sea
[JX5228]
Here are entered works on enemy property taken at sea. Works on the treatment of enemy property taken on land are entered under Enemy property.
UF Captured property
Property captured at sea
BT Seizure of vessels and cargoes
NT Ransom

Captured property
USE Booty (International law)
Capture at sea
Enemy property

Cargoes, Seizure of
USE Seizure of vessels and cargoes

Casualties, Mass
USE Mass casualties

Catholic Church (May Subd Geog)
The subdivisions used under Catholic Church may also be used under headings for other Christian denominations.
UF Roman Catholic Church
—Clergy
—Diplomatic service
[BX1908; JX1801-JX1802]
NT Nuncios, Papal
—Doctrines
—History
NT Counter-Reformation
—Influence
—Missions (May Subd Geog)
—Political activity
—Relations (diplomatic) (May Subd Geog)
Here are entered works on the dealings and affairs between the Catholic Church and political jurisdictions.
—Treaties
NT Concordats

Catholic Church and socialism
USE Socialism and Catholic Church

Catholic Church and world politics
[BX1793]
UF World politics and Catholic Church
BT Christianity and international affairs
—Papal documents

Catholic Church and Zionism
BT Zionism and the Catholic Church

CBD (Civilian-based defense)
USE Civilian-based defense

Ceasefire
USE Armistices

Central Asian question
USE Eastern question (Central Asia)

Change of attitude
USE Attitude change

Chauvinism and jingoism
UF Jingoism
BT Nationalism
Patriotism
Political ethics
NT Civil religion

Chemical warfare (May Subd Geog)
[UG447-UG447.65]
UF CBR warfare
BT War
SA subdivision Chemical warfare under individual wars
—Safety measures

Chemical warfare (International law)
BT War (International law)

Chemical-weapon-free zones (May Subd Geog)
BT Disarmament

Chemical weapons
[UG447.65]
UF Weapons, Chemical
BT Munitions

Children and war (May Subd Geog)
[BF723.W3]
UF War and children
SA subdivision Children under individual wars

Children of Holocaust survivors (May Subd Geog)
BT Holocaust, Jewish (1939-1945)
Holocaust survivors

Chinese reunification question, 1949-
UF Reunification of China question, 1949-

Christian denominations
USE Christian sects

Christian ethics (May Subd Geog)
[BJ1190-BJ1278]
UF Ethics, Christian
Moral theology
BT Religious ethics
NT Social ethics
Ten commandments

Christian sects (May Subd Geog)
UF Christian denominations
Sects, Christian
SA names of individual sects
NT Amish
Catholic Church
Church of the Brethren
Mennonites
Society of Friends

Christian Zionism (May Subd Geog)
Here are entered works dealing with Christian support for the establishment and preservation of a Jewish state in Palestine.
BT Zionism

Christianity (May Subd Geog)
Here are entered works on the Christian religion including its origin, beliefs, practices and influence treated collectively. Works on the institutional history of the church are entered under Church history.
—Early church, ca. 30-600
—Middle Ages, 600-1500
—Modern period, 1500-
—16th century
—17th century
—18th century
—19th century
—20th century

Christianity and antisemitism
UF Antisemitism and Christianity

Christianity and international affairs
[BR115.I7]
UF Church and international affairs
International affairs and Christianity
BT Church and the world
Religion and international affairs
World politics
NT Catholic Church and world politics
Society of Friends and world politics

Christianity and justice (May Subd Geog)
[BR115.J8]
UF Justice and Christianity

Christianity and other religions
For works limited to relations with one religion, an additional subject entry is made under the name of the religion with

the subdivision Relations—Christianity, e.g. Buddhism—Relations—Christianity.

—Buddhism

—Confucianism

—Hinduism

—Islam

—Judaism

—Shinto

—Sikhism

—Taoism

—Zoroastrianism

Christianity and politics
[BR115.P7]
UF Politics and Christianity
BT Church and state
Church and the world

Christianity and socialism
USE Socialism and Christianity

Christianity and the world
USE Church and the world

Christians (May Subd Geog)
—Persecutions
USE Persecution

Church and international affairs
USE Christianity and international affairs

Church and international organization
UF International organization and church

Church and state (May Subd Geog)
[BV629-BV631; JC510-JC514]
UF State and church
BT State, The
NT Asylum, Right of
Christianity and politics

—Baptists, [Catholic Church, etc.]

—Germany
—History
—1933-1945
BT Germany—Politics and government—1933-1945
Nationalsozialistische Deutsche Arbeiter-Partei
NT German-Christian movement

—Soviet Union
—History
—1917-

Church and the world
[BR115.W6]
Here are entered works on the position and responsibilities of the Christian Church in a secular society.
UF Christianity and the world
World and the church
NT Christianity and international affairs
Christianity and politics

Church history
Here are entered works on the institutional history of the church. Works on the Christian religion including its origin, beliefs, practices and influence treated collectively are entered under Christianity.
SA subdivision Church history under names of countries, cities, etc.

—Primitive and early church, ca. 30-600

—3rd century

—4th century

—6th century

—Middle Ages, 600-1500

—11th century

—12th century

—Modern period, 1500-

—Reformation, 1517-1648
USE Reformation

—17th century

—18th century

—19th century

—20th century

—1945-

Church of the Brethren (May Subd Geog)
The subdivisions printed under Catholic Church may be used under this heading.

Citizen participation
USE Political participation

Citizenship (May Subd Geog)
[JF800-JF823; JK1751-JK1788]
UF Nationality (Citizenship)
BT Political science
NT Self-determination, National

Citizenship (International law)
BT International law

Civics
This heading may be used with the following qualifiers: Austrian; Barbadian; Bolivian; Brazilian; British; Bulgarian; Cameroon; Canadian; Chinese; Dutch; Ecuadorian; French; Greek; Hungarian; Indonesian; Italian; Japanese; Korean; Malaysian; Pakistani; Peruvian; Philippine; Russian; Salvadoran; Senegalese; Vietnamese; Zairian, e.g. Civics, Austrian.
UF Civics, American
BT Political science
Social ethics

Civics, America
USE Civics

Civil defense
[UA926-UA928.5]
UF Defense, Civil
Emergency preparedness
SA subdivision Civil defense under names of countries, cities, etc.; and subdivision Evacuation of civilians under individual wars
BT War damage, Industrial
NT Air defenses
Air defenses, Civil
Bomb reconnaissance
Chemical warfare—Safety measures
Evacuation of civilians
Mass casualties

—Law and legislation
SA subdivision Civil defense—Law and legislation under names of countries, cities, etc.

Civil defense (International law)
BT International law

Civil disobedience
USE Government, Resistance to

Civil liberties
USE Civil rights

Civil-military relations (May Subd Geog)
UF Military and civilian power
Military-civil relations
BT Executive power
Sociology, Military
NT Armed Forces—Political activity
Civil supremacy over the military

Civil religion (May Subd Geog)
Here are entered works describing a collection of shared national beliefs, symbols, and rituals that are borrowed from religion but free of association with any single religious sect and which function as a source of meaning and social solidarity.
UF Religion, Civil
BT Chauvinism and jingoism
Nationalism—Religious aspects
Religion and state

Civil rights (May Subd Geog)
[JC571-JC628]
Here are entered works on citizens' rights as established by law and protected by constitution. Works on the rights of persons regardless of their legal, socioeconomic or cultural status and as recognized by the international community are entered under Human rights.
UF Civil liberties
BT Human rights
SA subdivision Civil rights under classes of persons and names of ethnic groups
NT Equality before the law
Freedom of movement
Freedom of speech
Political rights

—Religious aspects
[BL65.C58]
—Baptists, [Catholic Church, etc.]
—Buddhism, [Christianity, etc.]
BT Liberation theology

Civil rights (International law)
USE Human rights

Civil rights (Islamic law)

Civil rights (Jewish law)

Civil rights and socialism (May Subd Geog)
UF Communism and civil rights
Socialism and civil rights

Civil rights movements (May Subd Geog)
UF Liberation movements (Civil rights)
Protest movements (Civil rights)
BT Social movements
NT Anti-apartheid movements

Civil supremacy over the military (May Subd Geog)
UF Civilian control of the military
Supremacy of the civil authority
BT Civil-military relations

Civil war
[JX4541]
UF Rebellions
BT Government, Resistance to
International law
Revolutions
War
NT Insurgency

Civilian-based defense
[UA10.7]
Here are entered works on a nonviolent, non-military national defense strategy designed to repulse invasions and prevent internal takeovers by preparing the people and institutions of society to be noncooperative and defiant to government by aggressors.
UF Alternative defense
CBD (Civilian-based defense)
Nonviolent defense
BT National security

Civilian control of the military
USE Civil supremacy over the military

Civilization
[CB]
SA subdivision Civilization under names of countries, cities, etc.
NT Comparative civilization
Migrations of nations
Progress
—Philosophy
NT Philosophical anthropology
Regression (Civilization)

Civilization, Ancient
[CB311]
UF Ancient civilization

Civilization, Arab
[DS215]
Here are entered works on all periods of the civilization of the Arab countries as a whole, or on the pre-Islamic and modern periods only.
UF Arab civilization
Arab countries—Civilization
—20th century
—Study and teaching (May Subd Geog)
UF Arabic studies

Civilization, Comparative
USE Comparative civilization

Civilization, Islamic
Here are entered works on the medieval civilization of the Middle East, North Africa and Arab Spain collectively. Works on the civilization of the Islamic countries of all periods, or the pre-Islamic and modern periods only, are entered under Islamic countries—Civilization. Modern works of a predominantly religious nature calling for a civilization based on the teachings of Islam are entered under Islam—20th century.
UF Islamic civilization
—Study and teaching (May Subd Geog)
UF Islamic studies

Civilization, Medieval
[CB351-CB355]
UF Medieval civilization

Civilization, Modern
[CB357-CB425]
UF Modern civilization
—17th century
—18th century
—19th century
—20th century
—1950-

Civilization, Occidental
[CB245]
UF Occidental civilization
Western civilization
—Oriental influences
USE East and West

Civilization, Oriental
[CB253]
UF Oriental civilization
—Occidental influences
USE East and West

Civilization and war
USE War and civilization

Clandestine literature
USE Underground literature

Classified defense information
USE Defense information, Classified

Claims
[HJ8903-HJ8963; JX238]
UF International claims
War claims
BT Finance, Public
International law
War
SA subdivision Claims under individual wars and under names of countries, cities, etc.; also under names of claimants subdivision Claims vs. [name of country or party against which claims are brought]
NT Calvo doctrine and clause
Drago doctrine
Exhaustion of local remedies (International law)
Military occupation damages
Restitution and indemnification claims (1933-)

Coastal surveillance (May Subd Geog)
[VG50-VG55]
For works on coastal surveillance performed by specific organizations, an additional subject entry is made under the name of the organization.
UF Surveillance, Coastal
BT Border patrols

Coexistence
USE subdivision Foreign relations under names of countries
International relations
Peace
World politics—1945-

Collaborationists
USE subdivision Collaborationists under individual wars
Treason

Cohesiveness (Military science)
USE Unit cohesion (Military science)

Cold War
Here are entered works on the post World War II rivalry between western capitalist nations led by the United States and eastern communist nations led by the Soviet Union.
BT World politics—1945-

Collective security
USE Security, International

Collectivism (May Subd Geog)
NT Communism
Fascism
Socialism

College students (May Subd Geog)
—Political activity
BT Politics, Practical

Colombian-Peruvian asylum case
UF Peruvian-Colombian asylum case
BT Asylum, Right of—Cases
Extradition—Cases

Colombo plan
USE Economic assistance—Asia, Southeastern
Technical assistance—Asia, Southeastern

Colonial armies
USE Armies, Colonial

Colonialism
USE Colonies
Imperialism
World politics

Colonies
[JV]
Here are entered general works on colonies and colonialism, subdivided

further by Africa, America, Asia, or Oceania, if appropriate. Works discussing collectively the colonies ruled by a country or other jurisdiction are entered under the name of the country or jurisdiction subdivided by Colonies. Headings of the type [country]—Colonies may be further subdivided by the regions and topics that appear as subdivisions under Great Britain—Colonies. Works on the colonial period of individual regions or countries are entered under the name of the region or country with appropriate subdivision.

Works on the influence of former colonial policies and structures on the existing institutions of former colonies are entered under the current name of the region or country with subdivision Colonial influence.

Topical subjects subdivided by place may also be subdivided further by Colonies.

UF Anti-colonialism

—Administration
[JV412-JV485]
SA subdivision Colonies—Administration under names of countries
NT Military government of dependencies

Colonies (International law)
[JX4027]
BT International law

Colonization
[HD171-HD179; HD301-HD1130]
BT Imperialism
SA subdivision Colonization under names of countries, etc.
—Religious aspects

Combat
UF Fighting
Military combat
NT Battles
Combat sustainability (Military science)
Disengagement (Military science)

Combat, Submarine boat
USE Submarine boat combat

Combat patrols
UF Patrols, Combat
BT Military art and science
Military reconnaissance

Combat photography
USE War photography

Combat sustainability (Military science)
Here are entered works on the capability of military equipment and personnel to maintain the necessary level and duration of combat activity.
BT Combat
Military art and science
SA subdivision Combat sustainability under names of individual military services

Combatants and noncombatants (International law)
UF Noncombatants (International law)
BT Armed Forces
Belligerency
Military law
War (International law)
NT Guerrillas (International law)
Levies en masse

Combined operations (Military science)
[U260]
Here are entered works on operations conducted by forces of two or more allied nations acting together for the accomplishment of a single mission. Works on joint operations conducted by elements of more than one service of the same nation are entered under Unified operations (Military science)
UF Allied operations (Military science)
BT Military art and science
Strategy
Tactics

Comity of nations
[JX4081]
UF Courtesy of nations
International courtesy
Nations, Comity of
BT International law
International relations

Command of troops
[UB210]
Here are entered works on the exercise of military leadership and power of decision by a commander over his subordinates by virtue of authority, rank, and responsibility.
UF Troops, Command of
BT Military art and science
SA subdivision Military leadership under names of individual persons

Commando troops
[U262]
UF Rangers (Military science)
Troops, Commando
BT Counterinsurgency
Guerrilla warfare
Infantry
SA subdivision Commando troops under names of individual military services and subdivision Commando operations under individual wars
NT Special forces (Military science)

Commissions of inquiry, International
[JX1971]
UF International commissions of inquiry
BT Arbitration, International
International relations
Peaceful change (International relations)

Commercial policy
[HF1410-HF1411]
UF Foreign trade policy
BT International economic relations
SA subdivision Commercial policy under names of countries
NT Commercial treaties

Common good
UF Good, Common
BT Political science

Communalism (May Subd Geog)
Here are entered works on a system or principle of community organization in which rival groups, religious, ethnic, etc., are devoted to their own interests rather than to those of the whole society.
BT Ethnic relations
Ethnocentrism

Communication (May Subd Geog)
Here are entered works on human communication, including both the primary techniques of language, pictures, etc., and the secondary techniques, such as the press and radio.
UF Mass communication
BT Sociology
NT Communication, International
Persuasion (Psychology)
Written communication
—Government policy
USE Communication policy
—International cooperation
UF International flow of news
Mass media—International cooperation
—Methodology
—Psychological aspects
—Religious aspects
—Baptists, [Catholic Church, etc.]
—Buddhism, [Christianity, etc.]
—Research
—Sex differences
—Social aspects (May Subd Geog)
—Study and teaching (May Subd Geog)

Communication, International
Here are entered works discussing systems of global mass communication
UF International communication
BT Communication

Communication and culture (May Subd Geog)
UF Culture and communication

Communication in politics (May Subd Geog)
UF Political communication
BT Political science
NT Mass media—Political aspects
Propaganda
Public relations and politics

Communication policy (May Subd Geog)
UF Communication—Government policy
State and communication

Communications, Military
[UA940-UA945]
UF Military communications
Naval communications

SA subdivision Communication systems under names of individual military services; and subdivision Communications under individual wars
NT Military telecommunication
Transportation, Military

Communism (May Subd Geog)
[HX1-HX780.9]
Here are entered works on revolutionary ideologies or movements inspired by Marx and advocating the abolition of private property, dictatorship of the proletariat, and gradual disappearance of the state. Present day communist movements are characterized by collective ownership of the means of production and totalitarian, single party governments.
UF Bolshevism
Communist movements
Maoism
Marxism
BT Collectivism
Totalitarianism
NT Anti-communist movements
Communist state
Communist strategy
Communists
Dictatorship of the proletariat
Marxian economics
Permanent revolution theory
—1945-
—United States
—1917-

Communism and Buddhism
UF Buddhism and communism

Communism and Christianity (May Subd Geog)
UF Christianity and communism
—Catholic Church
[BX1396.4]

Communism and civil rights
USE Civil rights and socialism

Communism and individualism (May Subd Geog)
[HX550.I45]
UF Individualism and communism

Communism and international law
USE International law and socialism

Communism and international relations
[HX550.I5]
UF International relations and communism
NT Communist countries—Foreign relations

Communism and Islam
USE Islam and communism

Communism and Judaism
UF Judaism and communism

Communism and liberty (May Subd Geog)
[HX550.L52]
UF Liberty and communism

Communism and mass media (May Subd Geog)
[HX550.M35]
UF Mass media and communism

Communism and nationalism
USE Nationalism and communism

Communism and nonviolence
[HX550.N66]
UF Nonviolence and communism

Communism and nuclear warfare (May Subd Geog)
[HX545]
UF Nuclear warfare and communism

Communism and religion
[HX536]
UF Religion and communism

Communism and society
UF Marxian sociology
Society and communism

Communism and youth
USE Socialism and youth

Communism and Zionism
UF Zionism and communism

Communist ethics
[BJ1390]
UF Ethics, Communist
BT Ethics
Social ethics
Totalitarian ethics

Communist leadership (May Subd Geog)
[HX518.L4]
BT Leadership

Communist state
[JC474]
UF State, Communist
BT Communism
Socialism
State, The

Communist strategy
UF Strategy, Communist
BT Communism
World politics—1945-

Communist movements
USE Communism

Communists (May Subd Geog)
BT Communism

Comparative civilization
UF Civilization, Comparative
BT Civilization

Comparative government
UF Government, Comparative
BT Political science
SA subdivision Politics and government under names of countries, cities, etc.

Comparison of cultures
USE Cross-cultural studies

Competition, International
UF International competition
World economics
BT International relations
International trade
NT Commercial treaties

Competitive behavior
USE Competition (Psychology)

Competition (Psychology)
UF Competitive behavior

Compromise (Ethics)
[BJ1430-BJ1438]
BT Ethics

Compulsory military service
USE Draft

Computer war games (May Subd Geog)
[U310]
UF Video war games
BT War games

Concentration camps (May Subd Geog)
UF Detention camps
Internment camps
BT Political crimes and offenses
Prisoners of war
SA subdivision Concentration camps under individual wars

Concert of Europe
UF European concert
BT Europe—Politics and government—1815-1871
Great powers
International organization

Conciliation, International
USE Mediation, International

Concordats
[BX1401-BX1691; BX1790]
BT Catholic Church—Relations (diplomatic)—Treaties
Church and state
International law
International relations
Treaties

Condominium (International law)
[JX4068.C7]
BT International law
Sovereignty

Conferencia de Guayaquil, Guayaquil, Ecuador, 1822
USE Guayaquil Interview, Guayaquil, Ecuador, 1822

Confiscations (May Subd Geog)
BT War (International law)
SA subdivision Confiscations and contributions under individual wars
NT Booty (International law)
Enemy property

Requisitions, Military

Conflict control
USE Conflict management

Conflict management (May Subd Geog)
Here are entered works which discuss the process of reducing, resolving or suppressing conflict in social and organizational settings, producing constructive rather than destructive results.
UF Conflict control
Conflict resolution
Dispute settlement
Management of conflict
BT Negotiation
NT Mediation
—Religious aspects
—Buddhism, [Christianity, etc.]

Conflict resolution
USE Conflict management

Conflict resolution, International
USE Pacific settlement of international disputes

Conflicts, Ethnic

Conflicts, Low-intensity (Military science)
USE Low-intensity conflicts (Military science)

Confucian ethics
UF Ethics, Confucian

Confucianism (May Subd Geog)
—Doctrines

Confucianism and state (May Subd Geog)
UF State and Confucianism
BT Religion and state

Confucianism and world politics
UF World politics and Confucianism

Conquest, Right of
UF Right of conquest
BT International law

Conscientious objection (May Subd Geog)
Here are entered works on refusal on moral or religious grounds to bear arms in military conflicts or to serve in the armed forces.
BT Military ethics
War—Moral and ethical aspects
NT Selective conscientious objection

Conscientious objectors (May Subd Geog)
[UB341-UB342]
UF Objectors, Conscientious
BT Pacifists
SA subdivision Conscientious objectors under individual wars
NT National service
Women conscientious objectors

Conscript labor
USE Forced labor

Conscription, Military
USE Draft

Consensus (Social sciences)
NT Democracy
Legitimacy of government
Political stability

Commercial treaties
[HF1721-HF1733]
UF Trade agreements (Commerce)
BT Commercial policy
Competition, International
SA subdivision Commercial treaties under names of countries

Conservatism (May Subd Geog)
UF Neo-conservatism
BT Political science
Sociology
NT Conservative literature
—Religious aspects
—Buddhism, [Christianity, etc.]

Conservatism in the press (May Subd Geog)

Conservative literature (May Subd Geog)
Here are entered works on publications associated with political conservatism.
UF Literature, Conservative
BT Conservatism

Conspiracies (May Subd Geog)
BT Political crimes and offenses
Subversive activities
Treason

Consular jurisdiction
[JX1698]
UF Jurisdiction, Consular
BT Consular law
Consuls
Diplomatic and consular service
Exterritoriality
NT Diplomatic privileges and immunities

Consular law
[JX1625-JX1894]
Here are entered works on the legal status of foreign consuls and the legal aspects of consular service in general. Works on the law governing the consular service of an individual country are entered under the name of that country with the subdivision Diplomatic and consular service.
UF Law, Consular
BT Consuls
Diplomatic and consular service
International law
NT Consular jurisdiction

Consular reports (May Subd Geog)
UF Reports, Consular
BT Diplomatic and consular service

Consuls (May Subd Geog)
[JX1694-JX1698]
BT Diplomatic and consular service
Diplomats
International law
International relations
SA subdivision Diplomatic and consular service under names of countries
NT Consular jurisdiction
Consular law

Continuous voyages (International law)
[JX5234]
UF Voyages, Continuous (International law)
BT Blockade
Neutral trade with belligerents
Prize law
War, Maritime (International law)
NT Rule of 1756 (International law)

Contraband of war
[JX5231-JX5232]
UF Requisitions (of neutral vessels and cargoes)
Ships, Requisition of
BT Blockade
Jurisdiction over ships at sea
Neutrality
Prize law
Search, Right of
Seizure of vessels and cargoes
War, Maritime (International law)

Contragate, 1985
USE Iran-Contra Affair, 1985-

Contras
USE Counterrevolutionists

Conventional warfare
USE Warfare, Conventional

Conventions (Treaties)
USE Treaties

Conventions, Pan-American
USE Pan-American treaties and conventions

Convoys, Naval
USE Naval convoys

Cooperation (Psychology)
USE Cooperativeness

Cooperation, Intellectual
USE Intellectual cooperation

Cooperation, International
USE International cooperation

Cooperativeness
UF Cooperation (Psychology)

Corfu Channel case
BT Government liability (International law)

Corruption (in politics) (May Subd Geog)
UF Political corruption
Political scandals
BT Political crimes and offenses
Political ethics
NT Elections—Corrupt practices
—United States

NT Iran-Contra Affair, 1985-
Watergate Affair, 1972-1974

Cosmopolitanism
USE Internationalism

Cost of armies
USE Armies, Cost of

Cost of navies
USE Navies, Cost of

Cost of war
USE War, Cost of

Counter-Reformation (May Subd Geog)
BT Catholic Church—History

Counter-revolutionaries
USE Counterrevolutionists

Counterespionage
USE Intelligence service

Counterguerrilla warfare
USE Counterinsurgency

Counterintelligence
USE Intelligence service

Counterinsurgency (May Subd Geog)
[U241]
UF Counterguerrilla warfare
BT Guerrilla warfare
Insurgency
NT Commando troops
Special forces (Military science)

Counterrevolutionists (May Subd Geog)
UF Contras
Counter-revolutionaries

Counterrevolutions (May Subd Geog)
[JC492]
BT Revolutions

Coups d'état (May Subd Geog)
[JC494]
Here and with local subdivision are entered general and comprehensive works discussing coups d'état collectively. Works on individual coups d'état are entered under the name of the country with appropriate historical subdivision.
BT Government, Resistance to
History
Political science
Revolutions

Courtesy of nations
USE Comity of nations

Courts, International
USE International courts

Credibility
USE Truthfulness and falsehood

Crime and war
USE War and crime

Crimes against foreign heads of state
USE Offenses against foreign heads of state

Crimes against humanity
BT International offenses
NT Deportation
Forced labor
Genocide
War crimes

Crimes against peace
UF Incitement to war
Peace, Crimes against
War, Incitement to
War propaganda
BT Peace
War (International law)
NT Aggression (International law)

Crisis management (May Subd Geog)
NT Nuclear crisis control

Crisis management in government (May Subd Geog)
UF Government crisis management

Crisis stability (Nuclear warfare)
USE Nuclear crisis stability

Cross-cultural studies (May Subd Geog)
UF Comparison of cultures
Intercultural studies
Transcultural studies
SA subdivision Cross-cultural studies under topics

Cruise missiles
[UG1312.C7]
UF Missiles, Cruise
BT Guided missiles

Crusades
[D151-D173]
BT Middle Ages—History
NT Templars
—First, 1096-1099
—Second, 1147-1149
—Third, 1189-1192
—Later, 13th, 14th, and 15th centuries
—Fourth, 1202-1204
—Fifth, 1218-1221
—Sixth, 1228-1229
—Seventh, 1248-1250
—Eighth, 1270

Cuban Missile Crisis, Oct. 1962
UF Missile Crisis, Cuba and the United States, 1962

Cuban question
[F1783-F1786]
—To 1895
—1895-1898

Cultural exchange programs
USE Exchange of persons programs
Intellectual cooperation

Cultural relations
UF Cultural exchange programs
Intercultural relations
BT Intellectual cooperation
International relations
SA subdivision Relations under names of countries, cities, etc.
NT Exchange of persons programs

Cultural pluralism
USE Pluralism (Social sciences)

Cultural property, Protection of (International law)
BT War (International law)

Culture and communication
USE Communication and culture

Culture and guilt
USE Guilt and culture

Culture and international relations
USE International relations and culture

Culture conflict (May Subd Geog)
UF Conflict of cultures
BT Race relations
NT East and West
North and South

Current events
Here are entered works on the study and teaching of current events. Accounts, discussions, etc., of the events themselves are entered under headings for the time period covered.

De facto doctrine
UF De facto government
BT Executive power
Military occupation
Revolutions

De facto doctrine (International law)
USE Recognition (International law)
De facto doctrine
Military occupation

De facto government
USE De facto doctrine
Recognition (International law)

Deals (May Subd Geog)
Here are entered works on bargains or arrangements for mutual advantage.
UF Arrangements, Mutual
Bargains
Mutual arrangements
BT Negotiation

Death squads
USE Assassins

Deceit
USE Deception

Deception
UF Deceit
Subterfuge
BT Truthfulness and falsehood

NT Disinformation

Deception (Military science)
BT Military art and science

Decision-making (May Subd Geog)
UF Making decisions
SA subdivision Decision making under topics
BT Policy sciences

Decision-making (Ethics)
[BJ1419]
UF Ethics of decision-making
BT Ethics

Declaration of war
USE War, Declaration of

Decline of civilization
USE Regression (Civilization)

Decolonization (May Subd Geog)
BT Colonies
Imperialism
Sovereignty

Defectors (May Subd Geog)
UF Turncoats
BT Refugees, Political

Defense, Civilian-based
USE Civilian-based defense

Defense budgets
USE Armed Forces—Appropriations and expenditures

Defense contracts (May Subd Geog)
UF Military contracts
SA subdivision Procurement under names of individual military services

Defense economics
USE Disarmament—Economic aspects
War—Economic aspects

Defense industries (May Subd Geog)
Here are entered works on industries producing war weapons, supportive equipment, and supportive services.
NT Military-industrial complex

Defense information, Classified (May Subd Geog)
UF Classified defense information
Military secrets
Secret defense information
BT Espionage
Military policy
Official secrets
NT Nuclear weapons information

Defense procurement
USE Armed Forces—Procurement

Defense research
USE Military research

Defenses
USE Industrial mobilization

Defenses, Air
USE Air defenses

Defenses, Ballistic missile
USE Ballistic missile defenses

Defensive (Military strategy)
[U162]
BT Strategy
SA subdivision Defenses under names of countries, etc.

Democracy
[JC421-JC458]
BT Consensus (Social sciences)
Political science
—Religious aspects
—Buddhism, [Christianity, etc.]

Denazification
[D802.G3]
BT Germany—Politics and government—1945-
Nationalsozialistische Deutsche Arbeiter-Partei
Reconstruction (1939-1951)—Germany

Denial of justice (May Subd Geog)
[JX4263.D45]
UF Justice, Denial of
BT Diplomatic protection
International law
NT Exhaustion of local remedies (International law)

Denuclearized zones
USE Nuclear-weapon-free zones

Dependent nations
USE Dependency

Dependency
Here are entered general, theoretical works which discuss the subordination of the economic, social, cultural or political development of regions or countries to other regions or countries.
UF Dependent nations
BT Colonies
Imperialism
SA subdivision Dependency on foreign countries or Dependency on [place] under names of countries, etc.

Deployment (Strategy)
BT Strategy

Deportation (May Subd Geog)
[JX4261]
UF Expulsion
BT Crimes against humanity
Emigration and immigration law
SA subdivision Deportations from [region or country] under individual wars; and subdivision Emigration and immigration under names of countries
NT Asylum, Right of
Self-determination, National

Desaparecidos
USE Disappeared persons

Desert warfare
[U167.5]
BT War

Despotism
[JC375-JC392]
UF Absolutism
Abuse of power
Tyranny
BT Authoritarianism
Political science

Destalinization
USE Political rehabilitation—Soviet Union

Detection of nuclear weapons tests
USE Nuclear weapons—Testing—Detection

Detection of underground nuclear explosions
USE Underground nuclear explosions—Detection

Détente
[JX1393.D46]
BT International relations
World politics

Detention camps
USE Concentration camps

Deterrence (Strategy)
[U162.6]
BT Military policy
Psychology, Military
Strategy
NT No first use (Nuclear strategy)
Strategic forces
—Religious aspects
—Buddhism, [Christianity, etc.]

Developing countries in mass media (May Subd Geog)
BT Mass media

Developing countries in motion pictures

Developing countries in the press (May Subd Geog)

Developing country specialists (May Subd Geog)
BT Area specialists

Dialectical materialism
[B809.8]
UF Materialism, Dialectical
BT Philosophy, Marxist
Socialism

Diaspora
USE Israel and the Diaspora

Diaspora of the Jews
USE Jews—Diaspora

Dictators (May Subd Geog)
[JC495]

BT Heads of state
Kings and rulers

Dictatorship of the proletariat
BT Communism
Totalitarianism

Diplomacy
[JX1621-JX1894]
BT History
International relations
SA subdivision Foreign relations under names of countries, etc.; and subdivision Diplomatic history under individual wars
NT Diplomatic documents
Diplomatic negotiations in international disputes
Diplomatic protests
Diplomats
Notification (International relations)
Prior consultation (International law)
Protection of interests (International relations)
Summit meetings
Treaties
Ultimatums
—Language
[JX1677]
BT Languages—Political aspects

Diplomatic and consular service (May Subd Geog)
[JX1621-JX1894]
Here are entered works on diplomatic and consular officials of various countries stationed abroad in several countries. Works on diplomatic and consular officials of various countries stationed in a specific country are entered under Diplomatic and consular service—[place]. Works on diplomatic and consular officials of a specific country are entered under [place]—Diplomatic and consular service. Works on diplomatic and consular officials of a specific country stationed in a specific country are entered under [place]—Diplomatic and consular service—[place].
UF Consular service
Embassies
Foreign service
BT Government missions
SA subdivisions Diplomatic and consular service and Armed Forces—Foreign service under names of countries, etc.
NT Ambassadors
Catholic Church—Diplomatic service
Consular jurisdiction
Consular law
Consular reports
Consuls
Diplomatic couriers
Diplomatic privileges and immunities
Diplomatic protection
Embassy buildings
Exterritoriality
Foreign agents
Foreign offices
Military attachés

Diplomatic correspondence
USE Diplomatic documents

Diplomatic couriers (May Subd Geog)
BT Diplomatic and consular service

Diplomatic documents
Here are entered works on the nature and handling of diplomatic correspondence in general and under the aspect of international law. Collections of diplomatic papers are entered under the subject to which they refer.
UF Diplomatic correspondence
Diplomatic papers
Documents, Diplomatic
BT Diplomacy
Diplomatic and consular service
International law
International relations

Diplomatic negotiations in international disputes
[JX4473]
UF Negotiations in international disputes
BT Arbitration, International
Diplomacy
International relations
Pacific settlement of international disputes

Diplomatic papers
USE Diplomatic documents

Diplomatic privileges and immunities
[JX1671-JX1672]
BT Ambassadors
Consular jurisdiction
Diplomatic and consular service
Exterritoriality
Immunities of foreign states
Privileges and immunities
SA subdivision Privileges and immunities under names of individual international organizations and under names of countries with subdivision Diplomatic and consular service
NT International agencies—Privileges and immunities

Diplomatic protection
[JX4263.P7-JX4263.P8]
Here are entered works on assistance provided by diplomatic representatives to their nationals to secure their legal rights in the host country.
UF Protection of citizens abroad
BT Aliens
Diplomatic and consular service
International law
International relations
NT Calvo doctrine and clause
Denial of justice
Diplomatic protests
Exhaustion of local remedies (International law)
Intervention (International law)

Diplomatic protests
UF Protests, Diplomatic
BT Diplomacy
Diplomatic protection
International law

Diplomats (May Subd Geog)
BT Diplomacy
International law
International relations
Statesmen
NT Ambassadors
Consuls
Military attachés
Nuncios, Papal
Travel restrictions, Diplomatic
Women diplomats

Direct action
NT Government, Resistance to
Passive resistance
Terrorism

Directed-energy weapons
[UG486.5]
UF Weapons, Directed-energy
BT Ordnance
Weapons systems
—Law and legislation (May Subd Geog)
BT War (International law)

Disappeared persons (May Subd Geog)
[HV6322-HV6322.3]
Here are entered works on persons who have disappeared and are presumed to have been illegally imprisoned or killed for political reasons.
UF Desaparecidos

Disarmament
[JX1974]
Here are entered works on the reduction, either unilaterally or internationally, in the personnel and/or equipment of armed forces. Works on plans, arrangements, or processes resting upon explicit or implicit international agreement which govern the number, types, or performance characteristics of weapons systems and/or the numerical strength, organization, equipment, deployment or employment of the armed forces of the parties involved are entered under Arms control.
UF Limitation of armament
BT Armaments
Armies
International relations
Military art and science
Navies
War
NT Chemical-weapon-free zones
Nuclear disarmament
—Economic aspects (May Subd Geog)
[HC79.D4]
UF Defense economics
—Inspection
[UA12.5]
UF Inspection of disarmament
—Religious aspects
—Baptists, [Catholic Church, etc.]
—Buddhism, [Christianity, etc.]

Disarmament, Nuclear
USE Nuclear disarmament

Disaster casualties
USE Mass casualties

Discipline, Military
USE Military discipline

Discipline, Naval
USE Naval discipline

Disclosing official secrets
USE Official secrets

Discussion
BT Leadership
NT Negotiation

Disengagement (Military science)
UF Battle termination
BT Combat

Disinformation (May Subd Geog)
Here are entered works on false, misleading, or trivial information deliberately planted by an intelligence organization to confuse another nation's intelligence operations.
BT Deception

Dismemberment of nations
BT International law
Sovereignty

Dispersion of the Jews
USE Jews—Diaspora

Displaced persons
USE Refugees, Political

Dispute settlement
USE Conflict management

Disputes, Boundary
USE Boundary disputes

Divided states
USE Partition, Territorial

Divine right of kings
[JC389]
UF Kings, Divine right of
BT Authority
Kings and rulers
Monarchy
Political science

Documents, Diplomatic
USE Diplomatic documents

Dogmatism
[BF698.35.D64]
BT Attitude (Psychology)

Downing of Korean Air Lines Flight 007, 1983
USE Korean Air Lines Incident, 1983

Draft (May Subd Geog)
[UB340-UB355]
Here are entered works on conscription for service in a country's armed forces.
UF Compulsory military service
Conscription, Military
Military conscription
Military service, Compulsory
Selective service
BT National service
Recruiting and enlistment
SA subdivision Recruiting, enlistment, etc., under individual military services
—**Law and legislation** (May Subd Geog)
BT Military law

Draft dodgers
USE Draft resisters

Draft registration (May Subd Geog)
UF Military draft registration
Registration, Draft
Selective service registration

Draft resisters (May Subd Geog)
[UB341-UB342]
UF Draft dodgers
Resisters, Draft
SA subdivision Draft resisters under individual wars

Drago doctrine
[JX1393.D8]
BT Aliens
Claims
International law
Intervention (International law)
Monroe doctrine

Dragon Project
BT Nuclear energy—Research—International cooperation

Drang nach Osten
[DD119.2]
BT Imperialism
Pangermanism

Dropshot Plan
BT Imaginary wars and battles
Nuclear warfare
Strategy
World politics—1945-
World War III

Drug enforcement
USE Narcotics, Control of

Drug dealers
USE Narcotics dealers

Drug traffic (May Subd Geog)
UF Narcotic traffic
Smuggling of drugs
Trafficking in drugs
—Prevention
USE Narcotics, Control of

Duress (International law)
BT International law

Druzes (May Subd Geog)
BT Islamic sects

East and West
[CB251]
Here are entered works on both acculturation and cultural conflict between Oriental and Occidental civilizations.
UF Orient and Occident
Civilization, Occidental—Oriental influences
Civilization, Oriental—Occidental influences
BT Culture conflict

Eastern question
[D371-D375; D461-D469]
BT Europe—Politics and government—1789-1900

Eastern question (Balkan)
[D461-D469; JX1319]
UF Balkan question

Eastern question (Central Asia)
[D378]
UF Central Asian question

Eastern question (Far East)
[DS515-DS519;JX1321]
UF Far Eastern question
Open door policy (Far East)

Economic assistance (May Subd Geog)
Here are entered works on international economic aid given in the form of technical assistance, loans, gifts, or relief grants.
This heading may be used with national and regional qualifiers, e.g. Economic assistance, American—Latin America. The following qualifiers have been authorized for use: American; Arab countries; Australian; Austrian; Belgian; British; Canadian; Chinese; Communist; Cuban; Danish; Dutch; East European; Finnish; French; Hungarian; Irish; Italian; Japanese; Kuwaiti; New Zealand; Norwegian; Portuguese; Saudi Arabian; Soviet; Swedish; Swiss; United Arab Emirates; Venezuelan; West German.
UF Foreign aid program
Foreign assistance
NT Lend-lease operations (1941-1945)
Technical assistance
—**Asia, Southern**
UF Colombo plan
—**Individualism**

Economic development
Here are entered general works on the theory and policy of economic development. Works restricted to a particular area are entered under the name of the area with subdivisions Economic conditions, Economic policy, or Industries.
NT Developing countries

Economic relations, Foreign
USE International economic relations

Economic sanctions (May Subd Geog)
This heading is subdivided locally by the name of the country against which the

economic sanctions are applied. It may be used with qualifiers to indicate the region or country applying the sanctions, e.g. Economic sanctions, American—Cuba. The following qualifiers have been authorized for use: American; Arab countries; Bahraini; Canadian; Dutch; European; French; Swedish.
UF Sanctions, Economic
BT Sanctions (International law)
NT Embargo

Economics of war
USE War—Economic aspects
War, Cost of

Education, International
USE International education

Education, Military
USE Military education

Education, Naval
USE Naval education

Education and nationalism
USE Nationalism and education

Education and war
USE War and education

Educational exchanges (May Subd Geog)
Here are entered works dealing with international exchanges of educational personnel (students, educators, research scholars, specialists, etc.) supplies, and materials.
UF Exchanges, Educational
International educational exchanges
BT Intellectual cooperation
NT Students, Interchange of
Teachers, Interchange of
—Law and legislation (May Subd Geog)

Effect of wars on housing
USE Housing—Effect of wars on

Eisenhower doctrine
BT Middle East—Foreign relations—United States
United States—Foreign relations—Middle East

Election monitoring (May Subd Geog)
UF Monitoring, Election
Poll watching
BT Elections

Elections (May Subd Geog)
[JF1001-JF1191; JK1951-JK2246]
UF Electoral politics
BT Political science
Politics, Practical
SA subdivisions Elections and Elections, [date] under names of individual legislative bodies
NT Campaign management
Election monitoring
Presidents—Election
—Corrupt practices
BT Corruption (in politics)
Political crimes and offenses

Electoral politics
USE Elections

Electronic intelligence
Here are entered works on the collections and processing for subsequent intelligence purposes, of foreign noncommunication electromagnetic radiations.
UF Electronic spying
Intelligence, Electronic
BT Intelligence service
Military intelligence
SA subdivision Electronic intelligence under individual wars

Electronic spying
USE Electronic intelligence
Electronics in espionage

Electronics in espionage
UF Electronic spying
BT Espionage—Equipment and supplies

Embargo
[JX4491]
BT Economic sanctions
International law
Sanctions (International law)
War, Maritime (International law)
NT Blockade, Pacific
Reprisals

Embassies
USE Ambassadors
Diplomatic and consular service
Embassy buildings

Embassy buildings (May Subd Geog)
UF Embassies
—Takeovers
UF Embassy sieges
Takeover of embassies
BT Political crimes and offenses
Sieges
Terrorism

Embassy sieges
USE Embassy buildings—Takeovers

Emergency legislation
USE War and emergency legislation

Emergency powers
USE Executive power
War and emergency powers

Emigrants
USE Immigrants

Emigration and immigration
[JV6001-JV9500]
Here are entered works dealing with migration from one country to another, or from one section of a country to another or to a section of another country.
UF Immigration
International migration
SA subdivision Emigration and immigration under names of countries, cities, etc., for works that discuss the process of migrating across international boundaries from a particular place, and/or migrating across international boundaries to a particular place
NT Population transfers
Repatriation
Return migration
—Government policy
SA subdivision Emigration and immigration—Government policy under names of regions, countries, etc.
—Religious aspects
BT Refugees, Religious
—Baptists, [Catholic Church, etc.]
—Buddhism, [Christianity, etc.]

Emigration and immigration law (May Subd Geog)
UF Immigration law
NT Aliens, Illegal
Deportation
Freedom of movement
Repatriation

Emperor worship
[BL465]
BT Kings and rulers—Religious aspects

Emperor worship, Japanese
[BL2211.E46]
UF Japanese emperor worship

Emperor worship, Roman
[DG124]
UF Roman emperor worship

Emperors
[D107]
UF Rulers
BT Heads of state
Kings and rulers
Monarchy
SA subdivision Kings and rulers under names of countries
NT Roman emperors

Ends and means
[BJ84.E5]
UF Means and ends
BT Ethics
Philosophy

Enemy in the Bible
UF Adversary in the Bible
Bible—Enemy

Enemy property
Here are entered works on the treatment of enemy property taken on land. Works on enemy property taken at sea are entered under Capture at sea.
UF Captured property
BT Confiscations
SA subdivision Confiscations and contributions under individual wars

NT Booty (International law)
Military occupation damages

Enhanced radiation weapons
USE Neutron weapons

Enlistment
USE Recruiting and enlistment

Envelopment (Military science)
[U167.5.E57]
BT Military art and science
Tactics

Environmental protection (May Subd Geog)
—International cooperation

Environmental radioactivity
USE Radioactive pollution

Equality (May Subd Geog)
UF Inequality
BT Political science
Sociology
NT Individualism
—Religious aspects
[BL65.E68]
—Buddhism, [Christianity, etc.]

Equality before the law (May Subd Geog)
BT Civil rights
Justice

Equality of states
[JX4003]
BT International law
Sovereignty

Escalation (Military science)
BT Military art and science
War

Espionage (May Subd Geog)
This heading may be qualified to indicate the region or country carrying out the espionage, e.g. Espionage, American—Soviet Union. The following qualifiers have been authorized for use with this heading: American; British; Bulgarian; Communist; German; Israeli; Italian; Japanese; North Korean; Pakistani; Polish; Russian; South Korean; Spanish; West German.
UF Spying
BT Intelligence service
Secret service
Sovereignty, Violation of
Subversive activities
SA subdivision Secret service under individual wars
NT Defense information, Classified
Spies
Trials (Espionage)
—Equipment and supplies
NT Electronics in espionage

Espionage, Space
USE Space surveillance

Estrada doctrine
USE Recognition (International law)

Ethics (May Subd Geog)
[BJ1-BJ1725]
UF Moral philosophy
Morality
BT Philosophy
NT Communist ethics
Decision-making (Ethics)
Ends and means
Fascist ethics
Good and evil
Justice
Military ethics
Moral education
Moral rearmament
Peace
Political ethics
Power (Philosophy)
Religious ethics
Right and wrong
Social ethics
Totalitarian ethics

Ethics, Buddhist
USE Buddhist ethics

Ethics, Christian
USE Christian ethics

Ethics, Communist
USE Communist ethics

Ethics, Confucian
USE Confucian ethics

Ethics, Hindu
USE Hindu ethics

Ethics, Jewish
UF Jewish ethics
NT Good and evil (Judaism)

Ethics, Military
USE Military ethics

Ethics, Political
USE Political ethics

Ethics, Religious
USE Religious ethics

Ethics, Sikh
USE Sikh ethics

Ethics, Social
USE Social ethics

Ethics, Socialist
USE Socialist ethics

Ethics, Taoist
USE Taoist ethics

Ethics, Totalitarian
USE Totalitarian ethics

Ethics in the Bible
[BS680.E84]
UF Bible—Ethics

Ethnic barriers
BT Boundaries

Ethnic conflict
USE Ethnic relations

Ethnic minorities
USE Minorities

Ethnic relations
UF Conflict, Ethnic
Ethnic conflict
Interethnic relations
Relations among ethnic groups
BT Sociology
SA subdivision Ethnic relations under names of regions, countries, cities, etc.
NT Communalism
Culture conflict
Pluralism (Social sciences)

Ethnocentrism (May Subd Geog)
BT Nationalism
Prejudices
BT Communalism
Racism

European communities
Here are entered works on the European communities discussed collectively. Works on an individual community, such as the European Economic Community, and works on a common institution or service of the European communities are entered under the appropriate name heading.
BT European federation

European cooperation
Here are entered works on cooperation among European countries in several fields of activity.
BT International cooperation
NT Scandinavian cooperation

European Economic Community (May Subd Geog)
Here are entered works on the European Economic Community as an international body. This heading may be subdivided geographically to indicate relationships with specific regions or countries.

European federation
[D1060]
Here are entered works on efforts to achieve the political unity of European countries.
UF Federation of Europe
BT Europe—Politics and government
Federal government
Regionalism (International organization)
NT European communities

Evacuation of civilians (May Subd Geog)
UF Civilians, Evacuation of
BT Civil defense
SA subdivision Evacuation of civilians under individual wars

Evil
USE Good and evil

Evil, Non-resistance to
[BR115.W2; HM278]
UF Non-resistance to evil
NT Government, Resistance to

Ex-prisoners of war (May Subd Geog)
UF Returned prisoners of war
BT Prisoners of war

Exchange of nuclear weapons information
USE Nuclear weapons information

Exchange of persons programs
This heading may be used with the following regional or national qualifiers: American; Australian; Chinese; German; Hungarian; Japanese; Latin American; Russian; Scandinavian; Soviet; Ukrainian.
UF Cultural exchange programs
International exchange of persons programs
BT Cultural relations
Intellectual cooperation
SA subdivision Relations under names of countries, cities, etc.
NT Students, Interchange of
Teachers, Interchange of

Exchange of population
USE Population transfers

Executive agreements
BT Executive power
International law
International relations
Treaties
SA subdivision Foreign relations—Executive agreements under names of countries

Executive power (May Subd Geog)
UF Emergency powers
Power, Executive
BT Political science
NT Civil-military relations
Civil supremacy over the military
De facto doctrine
Treaty-making power
War and emergency powers

Exhaustion of local remedies (International law)
UF Local remedy rule
BT Claims
Denial of justice
Diplomatic protection
Government liability (International law)
International law

Exiles
[JX4261]
Here are entered works on persons banished from their home or country by vested authority as a punitive measure.
SA subdivision Exile, [date] under names of persons other than literary authors and subdivision Exiles under names of countries, etc.
NT Expatriation
Governments in exile

Expatriation (May Subd Geog)
[JX4226]
BT Aliens
Exiles
International law

Extermination, Jewish
USE Holocaust, Jewish (1939-1945)

Exterritoriality
[JX1671-JX1672; JX4175]
UF Extraterritoriality
Jurisdiction, Exterritorial
BT Diplomatic and consular service
Immunities of foreign states
International law
Privileges and immunities
NT Consular jurisdiction
Diplomatic privileges and immunities

Extradition (May Subd Geog)
[JX4275-JX4399]
BT International law
—Cases
NT Colombian-Peruvian asylum case

Extraterritoriality
USE Exterritoriality

Fallout, Radioactive
USE Radioactive fallout

Far Eastern question
USE Eastern question (Far East)

Fascism (May Subd Geog)
UF Neo-fascism
BT Authoritarianism
Collectivism
NT Anti-fascist movements
Fascists
Propaganda, Fascist
—Argentina
NT Peronism
—Germany
Here are entered works on post-World War II fascist and neo-Nazi movements. Works on fascism in Germany during the Nazi regime are entered under National socialism.
UF Neo-Nazism
BT National socialism

Fascist ethics
UF Ethics, Fascist
BT Ethics
Social ethics
Totalitarian ethics

Fascists (May Subd Geog)
BT Fascism

Fedayeen
BT Palestinian Arabs

Federal government (May Subd Geog)
[JC355]
Here are entered works on the division of powers between the central government and state or provincial and local governments in federal systems.
BT Political science
Republics
SA subdivision Politics and government under names of individual federal states
NT European federation
Imperial federation
Latin American federation

Federation, Imperial
USE Imperial federation

Federation, International
USE International organization

Federation of Europe
USE European federation

Federation of Latin America
USE Latin American federation

Fighter pilots (May Subd Geog)
[UG626-UG626.2]
UF Pilots, Fighter
BT Air pilots, Military

Fighter plane combat (May Subd Geog)
BT Air warfare

Fighter planes (May Subd Geog)
[UG1242.F5]
BT Airplanes, Military
NT LCSH contains headings for individual types of fighter planes that have not been included in this guide

Fighting
USE Battles
Combat
Military art and science
Naval art and science
War

Finance, International
USE International finance

Finance, Military
USE War, Cost of

Finance, Public (May Subd Geog)
UF Public finance
SA subdivision Appropriations and expenditures under names of countries, cities, government agencies, institutions, etc.
NT Claims
War, Cost of
War finance
—United States
—To 1789
—1789-1800
—1801-1861
—1861-1875
—1875-1900
—1901-1933
—1933-

Finance, War
USE War, Finance

Firearms (May Subd Geog)
Here are entered works on weapons from which a bullet, ball, or shell is hurled by the action of explosives.
UF Weapons
BT Arms and armor
SA subdivision Firearms under individual military services
NT Ordnance

First strike (Nuclear strategy)
Here are entered works on preemptive strategic nuclear attacks designed to destroy an enemy's strategic forces before they can be used against one's own strategic forces.
BT Preemptive attack (Military science)
Targeting (Nuclear strategy)

Flags of truce
UF Truce, Flags of
BT Armistices
Protective signs (International law)
War (International law)

Fleet ballistic missile weapons systems
[V990-V995]
BT Ballistic missiles
Strategic forces
Weapons systems

Folklore and nationalism (May Subd Geog)
UF Nationalism and folklore

Forced indoctrination
USE Brainwashing

Forced labor (May Subd Geog)
UF Conscript labor
Labor, Forced
SA subdivision Conscript labor under individual wars
BT Crimes against humanity

Forced labor (International law)
BT International law

Forces, Paramilitary
USE Paramilitary forces

Forecasting
[CB158]
UF Futurology
Prediction
SA subdivision Forecasting under names of countries, cities, etc., and under subjects
NT International relations—Forecasting

Foreign agents (May Subd Geog)
[JX1896]
UF Agents, Foreign
Foreign propagandists
Propagandists, Foreign
BT Diplomatic and consular service
Propaganda

Foreign aid program
USE Economic assistance
Military assistance
Technical assistance

Foreign assistance
USE Economic assistance
Military assistance
Technical assistance

Foreign economic relations
USE International economic relations

Foreign military bases
USE Military bases, Foreign

Foreign military sales
USE Military assistance
Munitions

Foreign news (May Subd Geog)
Here are entered works on journalistic practices in reporting news about foreign events. When the heading is subdivided by place, the subdivision refers to the locality where the news is released.
UF International flow of news
News, Foreign
World news
—Censorship

Foreign offices
BT Diplomatic and consular service
International law
International relations
SA names of individual foreign offices

Foreign opinion
USE subdivision Foreign public opinion under names of countries, etc., and under individual wars

Foreign property
USE Alien property

Foreign relations
USE subdivision Foreign relations under names of countries International relations

Foreign relations administration
USE subdivision Foreign relations administration under names of countries

Foreign relations specialists
USE International relations specialists

Foreign trade
USE International trade

Foreign trade policy
USE Commercial policy

Foreign visitors
USE Visitors, Foreign

Fortification (May Subd Geog)
[UG400-UG409]
UF Forts
BT Military art and science
SA subdivision Defenses under names of countries and names of individual forts

Forts
USE Fortification

France. Armée
Subdivisions for use under individual military services are listed in the Introduction.
UF Army of France

Francoism
BT Spain—Politics and government—1939-1975
Spain—Politics and government—1975-

Francs-tireurs
USE Guerrillas

Free cities
USE Internationalized territories

Free speech
USE Freedom of speech

Freedom
USE Liberty

Freedom (Islam)
[BP190.5]
BT Islam—Doctrines

Freedom (Jewish theology)
BT Judaism—Doctrines

Freedom (Theology)
BT Theology, Doctrinal
NT Liberation theology

Freedom of information (May Subd Geog)
UF Information, Freedom of
Intellectual freedom
Right to know
BT Civil rights
NT Government and the press
Government information

Freedom of information (International law)
BT International law

Freedom of movement (May Subd Geog)
UF Movement, Freedom of
BT Civil rights
Emigration and immigration law
Liberty

Freedom of movement (International law)
BT International law

Freedom of religion (May Subd Geog)
Here are entered works on the right or privilege of acting according to one's own view of religion without undue restraints or within reasonably formulated and legally specified limits.
BT Civil rights

Freedom of religion (International law)
BT International law

Freedom of speech (May Subd Geog)
UF Free speech
Intellectual freedom
Speech, Freedom of
BT Civil rights
NT Sedition

Freedom of the air
USE Airspace (International law)

Freedom of the seas
[D580; JX4423-JX4425; JX5203-JX5268]
UF Seas, Freedom of
BT International law
Sea-power
War, Maritime (International law)
NT Jurisdiction over ships at sea

Frontiers
USE Boundaries

Fur-seal arbitration
USE Bering Sea controversy

Futurology
USE Forecasting

Garrison towns
USE Military towns

Gas warfare
USE Gases, Asphyxiating and poisonous—War use

Gases, Asphyxiating and poisonous (May Subd Geog)
UF Poison gas
—War use
[UG447]
UF Gas warfare
BT Air defenses
Military art and science
War (International law)

General will
[JC328.2]
UF Will, General
BT Authority

Generals (May Subd Geog)
[U51-U54]
NT Women generals

Genocide (May Subd Geog)
BT Crimes against humanity
International offenses
Race relations
Racism
Terrorism
NT Holocaust, Jewish (1939-1945)
Trials (Genocide)

Geographical boundaries
USE Boundaries

Geography, Historical
Here are entered works which take a historical approach to the geography of countries, regions, etc., at a particular time in the past. Works limited to an individual country, region, etc., are entered under the name of the place with the subdivision Historical geography.
UF Historical geography
BT History

Geography, Political
[JC319]
Here are entered works on the branch of geography that deals with human governments, the boundaries and subdivisions of political units, and the situations of cities.
NT Political geography
BT Anthropo-geography
NT Boundaries
Geopolitics
Territory, National

Geopolitics (May Subd Geog)
[JC319-JC323]
BT Geography, Political
International relations
Political science
NT Buffer states

Germ warfare
USE Biological warfare

German-Christian movement
[BR856]
BT Church and state—Germany—History—1933-1945
Germany—Church history—1933-1945
National socialism

German resistance movement
USE Anti-Nazi movement

German reunification question (1949-)
UF Reunification of Germany, Proposed (1949-)
NT Berlin question (1945-)
Rapacki plan

Glasnost
Here are entered works on the official policy of openness in Soviet society initiated in 1985 and resulting in public and candid discussion of political, economic, and cultural issues.

Glassboro Conference, 1967

Good and evil
[BJ1400-BJ1408.5]
UF Evil
BT Ethics
Philosophy
NT Guilt

Good and evil (Hinduism)
[BJ1400-BJ1408]
BT Hindu ethics

Good and evil (Islam)
[BJ1400-BJ1405]
BT Islamic ethics
—Koranic teaching
[BP134.G65]

Good and evil (Judaism)
BT Ethics, Jewish
NT Holocaust (Jewish theology)

Good faith (International law)
BT International law

Good offices
USE Mediation, International

Government
USE Political science

Government, Comparative
USE Comparative government

Government, Resistance to (May Subd Geog)
[JC328.3]
UF Civil disobedience
Resistance to government
BT Direct action
Evil, Non-resistance to
Political crimes and offenses
Political ethics
Political science
SA subdivision Protest movements under individual wars
NT Anarchism
Civil war
Coups d'état
—Religious aspects
BT Religion and state
—Buddhism, [Christianity, etc.]

Government and the press (May Subd Geog)
UF Press and government
State and the press
BT Freedom of information
Government information
NT Official secrets

Government crisis management
USE Crisis management in government

Government information (May Subd Geog)
UF Government secrecy
Information, Government
BT Freedom of information
NT Government and the press
Official secrets

Government liability (International law)
UF International claims
BT International law
Sovereignty
NT Exhaustion of local remedies (International law)
Immunities of foreign states
—Cases
NT Corfu Channel case

Government missions (May Subd Geog)
UF Missions, Government
BT International relations
NT Diplomatic and consular service
Economic assistance
Military missions
Technical assistance

Government missions, American (May Subd Geog)

Government secrecy
USE Government information
Official secrets

Governments, Legitimacy of
USE Legitimacy of governments

Governments in exile
UF Refugee governments
BT Exiles
International law
International relations
Refugees, Political
Sovereignty
State, The
SA subdivision Governments in exile under individual wars

Great Britain. Army
Subdivisions for use under individual military services are listed in the Introduction.
UF Army of Great Britain

Great powers
UF Powers, Great
Superpowers
BT Balance of power
International law
International relations
States, Size of
World politics
NT Concert of Europe

Ground-to-air missiles
USE Surface-to-air missiles

Guaranty, Treaties of
[JX4171.G8]
UF Treaties of guaranty
BT International relations
Neutrality
Sovereignty
Treaties

Guatemala-British Honduras dispute
USE Belize question

Guayaquil Interview, Guayaquil, Ecuador, 1822
[F2235.36]
UF Conferencia de Guayaquil, Guayaquil, Ecuador, 1822

Guernica (Painting)
USE Picasso, Pablo, 1881-1973. Guernica

Guerrilla warfare
[U240]
UF Unconventional warfare
BT Insurgency
War
NT Counterinsurgency

Guerrillas (May Subd Geog)
[D25.5]
Here are entered general and historical works. Works on the military aspects of guerrilla warfare are entered under Guerrilla warfare. International legal aspects of guerrilla warfare are entered under Guerrillas (International law).
UF Bushwhackers
Franc-tireurs
Maquis
Partisans
BT National liberation movements
SA subdivision Underground movements under individual wars
NT Women guerrillas

Guerrillas (International law)
[JX5123]
BT Combatants and noncombatants (International law)
War (International law)
War crimes

Guided missiles
UF Missiles, Guided
BT Rockets (Ordnance)
NT Air-to-surface missiles
Antiaircraft missiles
Antimissile missiles
Ballistic missiles
Cruise missiles
MX (Weapons system)
Surface-to-air missiles
Trident (Weapons systems)

Guilt
[BF575.G8; BJ1471.5]
BT Ethics
Good and evil

Guilt and culture (May Subd Geog)
UF Culture and guilt

H-bomb
USE Hydrogen bomb

Heads of state (May Subd Geog)
[JF251]
BT Executive power
Statesmen
NT Dictators
Emperors
Kings and rulers
Offenses against foreign heads of state
Presidents
Prime ministers
Women heads of state

Hijacking of aircraft (May Subd Geog)
Subdivided by national registry of aircraft
UF Air piracy
—France
NT Entebbe Airport Raid, 1976
—United States
NT TWA Flight 847 Hijacking Incident, 1985

Hijacking of ships (May Subd Geog)
—Italy
NT Achille Lauro Hijacking Incident, 1985

Hijacking of TWA Flight 847, 1985
USE TWA Flight 847 Hijacking Incident, 1985

Hijacking of the Achille Lauro, 1985
USE Achille Lauro Hijacking Incident, 1985

Hindu ethics
[BJ121-BJ123]
UF Ethics, Hindu
NT Good and evil (Hinduism)

Hinduism (May Subd Geog)
—Doctrines
NT Man (Hinduism)

Hinduism and politics (May Subd Geog)
[BL1215.P65]
UF Politics and Hinduism
BT Hinduism and state

Hinduism and socialism
USE Socialism and Hinduism

Hinduism and state
UF State and Hinduism
BT Religion and state
NT Hinduism and politics

Hispanidad
USE Pan-Hispanism

Hispanoamericanism
USE Pan-Hispanism

Historic peace churches (May Subd Geog)
Here are entered works discussing collectively the Mennonites, Society of Friends, and the Church of the Brethren, known since 1935 as historic peace churches, which have peace as their central doctrine.
UF Peace churches, Historic
BT Protestant churches

Historical geography
USE Geography, Historical

Historical materialism
Here are entered works on the Marxian theory of human history.
BT Dialectical materialism
History—Philosophy

History
[D, E, F]
SA subdivision History under specific subjects and under names of countries, states, cities, etc.
NT Coups d'état
Diplomacy
Geography, Historical
Migrations of nations
Military history
Naval history
Political science
World history
—Philosophy
[D16.7-D16.9]
UF Philosophy of history
SA subdivision History—Philosophy under names of countries, etc.
NT Historical materialism

History, Ancient
[D51-D90]
UF Ancient history

History, Medieval
USE Middle Ages—History

History, Military
USE Military history

History, Modern
[D204-D725]
UF Modern history
—16th century
—17th century
—18th century
—19th century
—20th century
—1945-

History, Naval
USE Naval history

History, Political
USE World politics

History and personality
USE Personality and history

Holocaust, Jewish (1939-1945) (May Subd Geog)
Here are entered works on the genocide of European Jews during World War II.
UF Extermination, Jewish (1939-1945)
Jewish holocaust (1939-1945)
BT Genocide
Jews—Persecutions
NT Children of Holocaust survivors
Holocaust (Christian theology)
Holocaust survivors
Righteous Gentiles in the Holocaust
—Causes
—Errors, inventions, etc.
—Personal narratives
Here are entered works consisting of personal accounts of the Jewish Holocaust.
—Reparations
BT Restitution and indemnification claims (1933-)

Holocaust (Christian theology)
[BT93]
BT Holocaust, Jewish (1939-1945)

Holocaust (Jewish theology)
BT Good and evil (Judaism)

Holocaust memorials (May Subd Geog)
BT War memorials

Holocaust survivors (May Subd Geog)
Here are entered works on Jews who survived the Jewish Holocaust of 1939-1945, with emphasis on their lives since 1945.
UF Survivors, Holocaust
BT Holocaust, Jewish (1939-1945)
NT Children of Holocaust survivors

Holy war (Islam)
USE Jihad

Home rule (Ireland)
BT Ireland—Politics and government

Home rule (Scotland)
[DA765]
BT Scotland—Politics and government

Home rule (Wales)
BT Wales—Politics and government

Hospitalers (May Subd Geog)
[BX2825]
BT Military religious orders

Hostage Crisis, Beirut, Lebanon, 1985
USE TWA Flight 847 Hijacking Incident, 1985

Hostage negotiations (May Subd Geog)
BT Hostages
Negotiation

Hostages
[JX5143]
BT Terrorism
War (International law)
NT Hostage negotiations
—Iran
NT Iran Hostage Crisis, 1979-1981
—United States
NT Iran Hostage Crisis, 1979-1981

Hostilities
USE War
War, Declaration of
War, Maritime (International law)
War (International law)

Housing
—Effect of wars on
[HD7287.5]
UF Effect of wars on housing
BT War damage to buildings

Human behavior
Here are entered general works on the observable patterns of human actions and reactions.
UF Behavior, Human
BT Biopolitics
Self-protective behavior

Human geography
USE Anthropo-geography

Human rights (May Subd Geog)
[JC571-JC628]
Here are entered works on the rights of persons regardless of their legal, socioeconomic or cultural status and as recognized by the international community. Works on citizens' rights as established by law and protected by constitution are entered under Civil rights.
UF Civil rights (International law)
Rights, Human
Rights of man
NT Civil rights
—Religious aspects
—Baptists, [Catholic Church, etc.]
—Buddhism, [Christianity, etc.]

Human territoriality
UF Territoriality, Human
BT Anthropo-geography

Hydrogen bomb
UF H-bomb
BT Bombs
Nuclear weapons
NT Radioactive fallout

ICBM
USE Intercontinental ballistic missiles

Ideal states
USE Utopias

Ideology
[B823.3]
BT Philosophy
Political science

Illegal aliens
USE Aliens, Illegal

Illegal literature
USE Underground literature

Imaginary revolutions
UF Revolutions, Imaginary
BT Imaginary wars and battles
Revolutions

Imaginary wars and battles
[D445; JX1964; U313; V253]
UF Imaginary battles
Wars and battles, Imaginary
BT Battles
Military art and science
Naval art and science
War
NT Dropshot Plan
Imaginary revolutions

Immigrants (May Subd Geog)
Here are entered works on foreign-born persons who enter a country intending to become permanent residents or citizens. This heading may be locally subdivided by names of places where immigrants settle. For works discussing emigrants from a particular place, an additional heading is assigned to designate the nationality of origin of the emigrant group and the place to which they have immigrated.
UF Emigrants
NT Women immigrants

Immigration
USE Emigration and immigration

Immigration law
USE Emigration and immigration law

Immunities and privileges
USE Privileges and immunities

Immunities of foreign states (May Subd

Geog)
UF Sovereign immunity (International law)
BT Jurisdiction (International law)
Privileges and immunities
Sovereignty
NT Diplomatic privileges and immunities
Exterritoriality

Imperial federation
[DA18; JN276]
UF Federation, Imperial
BT Great Britain—Colonies
Imperialism

Imperialism
UF Colonialism
Neocolonialism
BT Political science
SA subdivision Foreign relations under names of countries
NT Bonapartism
Colonies
Colonization
Decolonization
Dependency
Drang nach Osten
Imperial federation

Incitement to war
USE Crimes against peace

Indemnification claims (1933-)
USE Restitution and indemnification claims (1933-)

Indemnity
[JX5326]
BT International law
NT Reparations
Requisitions, Military

Independence
USE Autonomy

Indigenous peoples (May Subd Geog)
[HV3176-HV3177; JV305-JV317]
Here are entered works on the position in society and relations with governing authorities of the aboriginal inhabitants of colonial areas or modern states where the aboriginal peoples are not in control of the government.
Topical subdivisions may not be used with this heading.
UF Native races

Individualism (May Subd Geog)
[B824; HM136; JC571]
BT Equality
Political science
Sociology
—Religious aspects
—Buddhism, [Christianity, etc.]

Individualism and Communism
USE Communism and individualism

Industrial mobilization (May Subd Geog)
[UA18]
UF Defenses
Mobilization, Industrial
BT Armaments
Military art and science
War—Economic aspects
NT Military supplies
Munitions
—Law and legislation

Industry and war
USE War—Economic aspects

Inequality
USE Equality

Infantry
[UD]
BT Armies
SA names of individual infantries
NT Commando troops

Infiltration (Military science)
BT Military art and science

Information, Freedom of
USE Freedom of information

Injustice
USE Justice

Inspection of disarmament
USE Disarmament—Inspection

Insurgency (May Subd Geog)
[JC328.5]
UF Rebellions
BT Civil wars
Political crimes and offenses
Revolutions
NT Counterinsurgency
Guerrilla warfare
Peasant uprisings
Subversive activities
Terrorism

Insurrections
USE Revolutions

Intellectual cooperation
[AS4; JC362]
UF Cooperation, Intellectual
Cultural exchange programs
BT International cooperation
SA subdivision Relations under names of countries, etc.
NT Cultural relations
Educational exchanges
Exchange of persons programs
Internationalism

Intellectual freedom
USE Freedom of information
Freedom of speech

Intelligence, Electronic
USE Electronic intelligence

Intelligence officers (May Subd Geog)
BT Intelligence service

Intelligence service (May Subd Geog)
UF Counterespionage
Counterintelligence
NT Electronic intelligence
Espionage
Intelligence officers
Military intelligence
—Law and legislation (May Subd Geog)

Inter-American conferences
UF Pan American conferences
BT Pan-Americanism
SA individual conferences and congresses

Inter-American conventions
USE Pan-American treaties and conventions

Inter-American cooperation
USE Pan-Americanism

Inter-American treaties
USE Pan-American treaties and conventions

Intercontinental ballistic missiles
[UG1312.I2]
UF ICBM
BT Ballistic missiles
Strategic forces
NT MX (Weapons system)
—Mobile basing

Intercontinental bombers
USE Supersonic bombers

Intercultural studies
USE Cross-cultural studies

Interdependence of nations
USE International cooperation
International economic relations
International organization
International relations

Interdiction, Air
USE Air interdiction

Interests, Protection of (International relations)
USE Protection of interests (International relations)

Interethnic relations
USE Ethnic relations

Intermediate-range ballistic missiles
UF IRBM
BT Ballistic missiles

Internal security (May Subd Geog)
UF Security, Internal

International affairs and Christianity
USE Christianity and international affairs

International affairs and religion
USE Religion and international affairs

International affairs and technology
USE Technology and international affairs

International agencies (May Subd Geog)
Here are entered works on public international organizations and agencies of international government. Individual organizations are entered under the name heading for the organization.
UF International associations
International organizations
Non-governmental organizations
United Nations—Specialized agencies
BT International cooperation
—**Privileges and immunities**
UF International officials and employees—Privileges and immunities
BT Diplomatic privileges and immunities
Privileges and immunities
SA subdivision Privileges and immunities under names of individual international organizations

International agreements
USE International obligations

International agreements
USE Treaties

International arbitration
USE Arbitration, International

International associations
USE International agencies

International boundaries
USE Boundaries

International broadcasting (May Subd Geog)
UF Broadcasting, International

International business enterprises (May Subd Geog)
UF Business enterprises, International
International corporations
Multinational corporations
Transnational corporations
—**Law and legislation** (May Subd Geog)

International civil service
USE International officials and employees

International claims
USE Government liability (International law)

International commissions of inquiry
USE Commissions of inquiry, International

International communication
USE Communication, International

International competition
USE Competition, International

International conciliation
USE Mediation, International

International corporations
USE International business enterprises

International conflict resolution
USE Pacific settlement of international disputes

International cooperation
[JC362]
Here are entered general works on international cooperative activities with or without the participation of government.
UF Cooperation, International
Interdependence of nations
World order
BT International law
International relations
SA subdivision International cooperation under subjects which do not lend themselves to the phrase form of heading
NT African cooperation
Arbitration, International
Asian cooperation
Economic assistance
European cooperation
Intellectual cooperation
International agencies
International education
International police
Internationalism
Pacific Area cooperation
Pan-Americanism
Scandinavian cooperation
South Asian cooperation
Technical assistance

International courtesy
USE Comity of nations

International courts
UF Courts, International
BT Arbitration, International
International law
International relations
Pacific settlement of international disputes
Peaceful change (International relations)

International economic integration
UF Economic integration, International
BT International economic relations
SA subdivision Economic integration under continents and regions for works discussing the integration of the economics of a group of countries and names of international organizations established to integrate the economies of various countries.

International education (May Subd Geog)
Here are entered works on education for international understanding, world citizenship, etc.
UF Education, International
BT International cooperation
Peace
NT Students, Interchange of

International economic relations
[HF1351-HF1359]
Here are entered works on economic relations among nations. Works on the foreign economic relations of countries, cities, etc., are entered under headings of the type [place]—Foreign economic relations, further subdivided by place, if appropriate. If so subdivided, a second heading is assigned with the place names in reverse position.
UF Economic relations, Foreign
Foreign economic relations
Interdependence of nations
BT International relations
SA subdivision Foreign economic relations under names of countries
NT Economic assistance
International economic integration
International trade
Technical assistance
—**Religious aspects**
—**Buddhism, [Christianity, etc.]**

International exchange of persons programs
USE Exchange of persons programs

International exchange of students
USE Students, Interchange of

International federation
USE International organization

International finance
UF Finance, International
BT International economic relations

International flow of news
USE Communication—International cooperation
Foreign news

International lakes (May Subd Geog)
UF Lakes, Right of navigation on
BT International law

International law (May Subd Geog)
[JX2001-JX5810]
UF Law, International
BT International relations
SA subdivision Law and legislation under topics of international concern; and subdivision International status under names of countries, cities, etc.
NT Act of state
Aggression (International law)
Airspace (International law)
Alien property
Angary, Right of
Annexation (International law)
Arbitration, International
Asylum, Right of
Autonomy
Boundaries
Citizenship (International law)
Civil defense (International law)
Civil war
Claims
Colonies (International law)
Comity of nations
Concordats
Condominium (International law)
Conquest, Right of
Consular law
Consuls
Denial of justice

Diplomatic documents
Diplomatic protection
Diplomatic protests
Diplomats
Dismemberment of nations
Drago doctrine
Duress (International law)
Embargo
Equality of states
Exclaves
Executive agreements
Exhaustion of local remedies (International law)
Expatriation
Exterritoriality
Extradition
Forced labor (International law)
Foreign offices
Freedom of information (International law)
Freedom of movement (International law)
Freedom of religion (International law)
Freedom of the seas
Good faith (International law)
Government liability (International law)
Governments in exile
Great powers
Indemnity
International cooperation
International courts
International lakes
International obligations
International offenses
Intervention (International law)
Jurisdiction (International law)
Jurisdiction over ships at sea
Missing persons (International law)
Neutrality
Notification (International law)
Nuclear ships (International law)
Pacta sunt servanda (International law)
Political crimes and offenses
Postliminy
Prior consultation (International law)
Protective signs (International law)
Protectorates
Public policy (International law)
Recognition (International law)
Refugees, Political—Legal status, laws, etc.
Repatriation
Sanctions (International law)
Self-defense (International law)
Servitudes (International law)
Sovereignty
State succession
Territorial waters
Territory, National
Third parties (International law)
Torture (International law)
Transit by land
Treaties
Ultimatums
Unilateral acts (International law)
Uti possidetis (International law)
War, Maritime (International law)
War (International law)
Warships—Visits to foreign ports

—Interpretation and construction

—Philosophy

—Sources
NT Treaties

International law (Islamic law)

International law and socialism
UF Communism and international law
Socialism and international law

International mediation
USE Mediation, International

International migration
USE Emigration and immigration

International news
USE Foreign news

International obligations
[JX4171.03]
Here are entered works on obligations between states.
UF International agreements
BT International law

International offenses
[JX5415-JX5445]
Here are entered works on criminal violations of international law.
UF International criminal law
BT International law
NT Aggression (International law)
Crimes against humanity
Crimes against peace
Genocide
Sovereignty, Violation of
Terrorism
War crimes

International officials and employees
[JX1995]
UF International civil service
BT International agencies
International organization
SA subdivision Officials and employees under names of international agencies
—Privileges and immunities
USE International agencies—Privileges and immunities

International organization
Here are entered works on theories and efforts leading toward world-wide or regional political organization of nations.
UF Federation, International
Interdependence of nations
International federation
World federation
World government
World order
BT International relations
Peace
Political science
SA names of individual organizations
NT Concert of Europe
International officials and employees
International police
International trusteeships
Latin American federation
Mandates
Reconstruction (1914-1939)
Reconstruction (1939-1951)
Regionalism (International organization)

International organization and the church
USE Church and international organization

International organizations
USE International agencies

International police
[JX1981.P7]
UF Peacekeeping forces
Police, International
BT International cooperation
International organization
International relations
Sanctions (International law)
Security, International

International politics
USE World politics

International propaganda
USE Propaganda, International

International relations
Here are entered theoretical works on the relations among the nations of the world. Works on general political history and historical accounts of relations among nations are entered under World politics. Works on the foreign relations of an individual country are entered under the name of the country with the subdivision Foreign relations.
UF Coexistence
Foreign relations
Interdependence of nations
Peaceful coexistence
World order
SA subdivision Foreign relations and Foreign relations administration under names of countries; and names of international alliances, congresses, treaties, etc.
NT Alliances
Ambassadors
Arbitration, International
Balance of power
Catholic Church—Relations (diplomatic)
Comity of nations
Commissions of inquiry, International
Competition, International
Concordats
Consuls
Cultural relations
Détente
Diplomacy
Diplomatic documents
Diplomatic negotiations in international disputes
Diplomatic protection
Diplomats
Disarmament
Executive agreements
Foreign offices
Geopolitics
Government missions
Governments in exile
Great powers
Guaranty, Treaties of
International cooperation
International courts
International economic relations

International law
International organization
International police
Jihad
Mediation, International
Middle powers
Monroe doctrine
Nationalism
Neutrality, Armed
Nonalignment
Notification (International relations)
Nuclear crisis control
Pacific settlement of international disputes
Pan-Pacific relations
Peace
Peaceful change (International relations)
Plebiscite
Prior consultation (International law)
Propaganda, International
Reconstruction (1914-1939)
Reconstruction (1939-1951)
Security, International
Treaties
Ultimatums
War
Warships—Visits to foreign ports

—Forecasting
BT Forecasting

—Psychological aspects
BT Political psychology

International relations and communism
USE Communism and international relations

International relations and culture (May Subd Geog)
UF Culture and international relations

International relations literature (May Subd Geog)
UF Literature, International relations

International relations specialists (May Subd Geog)
UF Foreign relations specialists
NT United States foreign relations specialists
Women international relations specialists
BT Area specialists
Policy scientists

International relief (May Subd Geog)
UF Relief, International
SA subdivision Civilian relief under individual wars

International rivers (May Subd Geog)
[JX4150]
UF Rivers, Right of navigation on

International security
USE Security, International

International territories
USE Internationalized territories

International trade
[HF1371-HF1379]
Here are entered works on trade among nations. Works on foreign trade of specific countries, cities, etc., are entered under headings of the type [place]—Commerce, further subdivided by place, if appropriate. If so subdivided, a second heading is assigned with the place names in reverse positions.
UF Foreign trade
BT International economic relations
NT Competition, International

International trusteeships (May Subd Geog)
[JX4021-JX4023]
UF Nonselfgoverning territories
Trust territories
Trusteeships, International
United Nations—International trusteeships
BT International organization
Internationalized territories
Protectorates

International visitors
USE Visitors, Foreign

Internationalism
[JC361]
Here are entered works on the doctrine that the focus of political activity should be the universal human condition rather than the narrow interests of a particular nation.
UF Cosmopolitanism
BT Intellectual cooperation
International cooperation
NT Internationalists

Internationalism in literature

Internationalists (May Subd Geog)
BT Internationalism

Internationalized territories
[JX4068.I6]
UF Free cities
International territories
Territories, International
BT Sovereignty
NT International trusteeships
Mandates

Internment camps
USE Concentration camps

Internment of warships
USE Warships, Internment of

Interplanetary warfare
USE Space warfare

Intervention (International law)
[JX4481]
UF Military intervention
BT Diplomatic protection
International law
War (International law)
NT Drago doctrine
Jurisdiction (International law)
Monroe doctrine

Intolerance
USE Toleration

Iran-Contra Affair, 1985-
[E876]
UF Contragate, 1985-
Irangate, 1985-
BT Corruption (in politics)—United States
Military assistance, American—Iran
Military assistance, American—Nicaragua

Iran Hostage Crisis, 1979-1981
BT Hostages—Iran
Hostages—United States

Iran specialists
USE Iranologists

Irangate, 1985-
USE Iran-Contra Affair, 1985-

Iranologists
[DS271.6-DS271.7]
UF Iran specialists

IRBM
USE Intermediate-range ballistic missiles

Irish question
[DA947-DA965]

Irish unification question
UF Unification of Ireland

Islam (May Subd Geog)
Here are entered works on the religion of which Muhammad is the prophet. Works on the community of believers in this religion are entered under Muslims. Works on the group of countries in which the majority of the people are Muslims or in which Islam is the established religion are entered under Islamic countries.
UF Mohammedanism
NT Islamic fundamentalism
Koran

—1800-

—20th century
[BP163]

—Doctrines
[BP165.5-BP166.94]
UF Islamic theology
Muslim theology
NT Freedom (Islam)
Man (Islam)

—Relations

—Judaism
Here are entered works on relations between the religions of Islam and Judaism. When this heading is assigned duplicate entry is made under Judaism—Relations—Islam. Works on the conflicts between the Arab countries and Israel are entered under Israel-Arab conflicts. Works that discuss collectively the relations between Arabs and Jews, including religious, ethnic, and ideological relations, are entered under Jewish-Arab relations, subdivided further by dates, if appropriate.

—Study and teaching (May Subd Geog)
UF Islamic studies

Islam and Arabs
USE Arabs and Islam

Islam and communism
USE Communism and Islam

Islam and justice
[BP173.43]
UF Justice and Islam
BT Religion and justice

Islam and politics (May Subd Geog)
[BP173.7]
UF Politics and Islam
BT Islam and state

Islam and socialism
USE Socialism and Islam

Islam and state (May Subd Geog)
[BP173.6]
UF State and Islam
BT Religion and state
NT Islam and politics
Jihad
—Koranic teaching
BT Koran—Political science

Islam and world politics
[BP173.5]
UF World politics and Islam

Islamic civilization
USE Civilization, Islamic

Islamic ethics
[BJ1291]
UF Ethics, Islamic
Muslim ethics
NT Good and evil (Islam)
Koran—Ethics
Truthfulness and falsehood (Islam)

Islamic fundamentalism (May Subd Geog)
UF Fundamentalism, Islamic
BT Islam

Islamic holy war
USE Jihad

Islamic sects (May Subd Geog)
[BP191-BP223]
NT Druzes
Shīʻah
Sunnites

Islamic studies
USE Civilization, Islamic—Study and teaching
Islam—Study and teaching
Islamic countries—Study and teaching

Isolationism
USE Neutrality

Israel and the Diaspora
UF Diaspora
BT Jews—Diaspora
Zionism

Israeli Missile Boats Incident, Cherbourg, France, 1969
UF Missile Boats Incident, Cherbourg, France, 1969

Japanese emperor worship
USE Emperor worship, Japanese

Jewish-Arab relations
Here are entered works that discuss collectively the relations between Arabs and Jews, including religious, ethic, and ideological relations, subdivided further by dates, if appropriate.
UF Palestine problem
—To 1917
—1917-
—1917-1949
—1949-
—1949-1967
—1967-1973
—1973-
BT Palestinian Arabs
NT Gaza Strip—History—Palestinian Uprising, 1987-
West Bank—History—Palestinian Uprising, 1987-

Jewish ethics
USE Ethics, Jewish

Jewish holocaust (1939-1945)
USE Holocaust, Jewish (1939-1945)

Jewish refugees
USE Refugees, Jewish

Jewish theology
USE Judaism—Doctrines

Jews (May Subd Geog)
BT Judaism
SA subdivision Jews under individual wars
—Diaspora
Here are entered works dealing with the dispersion of the Jewish people beyond the confines of Palestine, together with a description of life, attitude, and outlook in their new surroundings.
UF Diaspora of the Jews
Dispersion of the Jews
BT Minorities
NT Israel and the Diaspora
—Persecutions
BT Antisemitism
Political atrocities
NT Holocaust, Jewish (1939-1945)
Refugees, Jewish
—Religion
USE Judaism
—Soviet Union
NT Refuseniks

Jihad
[BP182]
UF Holy war (Islam)
Islamic holy war
Muslim holy war
BT International relations
Islam and state
War
War—Religious aspects—Islam

Jingoism
USE Chauvinism and jingoism

Joint operations (Military science)
USE Amphibious warfare
Landing operations
Unified operations (Military science)

Journalism, Military (May Subd Geog)
UF Armed Forces newspapers
Military journalism
BT War correspondents
SA subdivision Journalism, Military under individual wars

Judaism (May Subd Geog)
UF Jews—Religion
NT Religious Zionism
—Doctrines
[BM600-BM603]
UF Jewish theology
NT Freedom (Jewish theology)
Man (Jewish theology)
—Relations
—Buddhism, [Christianity, Islam, etc.]
—Islam
Here are entered works on relations between the religions of Judaism and Islam. When this heading is assigned, duplicate entry is made under Islam—Relations—Judaism.

Judaism and communism
USE Communism and Judaism

Judaism and politics
[BM645.P64]
UF Politics and Judaism
BT Judaism and state

Judaism and socialism
USE Socialism and Judaism

Judaism and state
[BM538.S7]
UF State and Judaism
BT Religion and state
NT Judaism and politics
Zionism

Judaism and Zionism
USE Zionism and Judaism

Jungle warfare
[U167.5.J8]
BT War
SA subdivision Jungle warfare under individual wars

Jurisdiction (International law)
UF International jurisdiction
BT International law
Intervention (International law)
Sovereignty
NT Immunities of foreign states

Jurisdiction, Exterritorial
USE Exterritoriality

Jurisdiction, Territorial
UF Territorial jurisdiction
BT Territory, National
NT Leased territories
Territorial waters

Jurisdiction over aircraft (May Subd Geog)
BT Airspace (International law)

Jurisdiction over ships at sea
BT Freedom of the seas
International law
War, Maritime (International law)
NT Contraband of war
Search, Right of

Just war doctrine
BT War—Moral and ethical aspects
War—Religious aspects
War (Philosophy)

Justice
[JC578]
UF Injustice
BT Ethics
NT Equality before the law
—Biblical teaching

Justice (Jewish theology)
BT Religion and justice

Justice (Philosophy)
[B105.J 87]
BT Philosophy

Justice (Virtue)
[BV4647.J8]

Justice and Christianity
USE Christianity and justice

Justice and Islam
USE Islam and justice

Justice and politics (May Subd Geog)
UF Politics and justice

Justice and religion
USE Religion and justice

KAL Flight 007 Incident, 1983
USE Korean Air Lines Incident, 1983

Kemalism
[DR590]
Here are entered works on the political, economic, and social principles advocated by Kemal Ataturk designed to create a modern republican secular Turkish state.
UF Ataturkism

Kidnapping (May Subd Geog)
[HV6595-HV6604]
SA subdivision Kidnapping, [date] under names of individual persons
NT Ransom

Killing (Ten Commandments)
USE Ten Commandments—Murder

Kings, Divine right of
USE Divine right of kings

Kings and rulers
[D107; D352.1; D399.7; D412.7; JC374-JC408; JF253]
UF Kings and rulers, Modern
Monarchs
Rulers
BT Heads of state
Political science
SA subdivisions Kings and rulers and Queens under names of geographic areas and ethnic groups
NT Dictators
Divine right of kings
Emperors
Presidents
—Religious aspects
BT Divine right of kings
SA subdivision Kings and rulers—Religious aspects under names of regions, countries, and ethnic groups
NT Emperor worship
—Succession
BT Monarchy

Kings and rulers, Ancient

Kings and rulers, Medieval

Kings and rulers, Modern
USE Kings and rulers

Knighthood, Orders of
USE Orders of knighthood and chivalry

Knights Templars (Monastic and military order)
USE Templars

Koran
[BP100-BP130]
BT Islam
—Ethics
[BP134.E84]
BT Islamic ethics
—Political science
UF Political science and Koran
NT Islam and state—Koranic teaching

Korean Air Lines Incident, 1983
UF Downing of Korean Air Lines Flight 007, 1983
KAL Flight 007 Incident, 1983
Shooting Down of Korean Air Lines Flight 007, 1983
BT World politics, 1975-1985

Korean resistance movements, 1905-1945
UF Anti-Japanese movements, Korean

Korean reunification question (1945-)
UF Reunification of Korea (1945-)

Kremlinologists
USE Sovietologists

Labor, Forced
USE Forced labor

Lakes, Right of navigation on
USE International lakes

Landing operations
Here are entered general works on the landing of waterborne or airborne troops on hostile territory, including the tactics of transporting, landing and establishing such troops and their supplies. Works on the joint operation of air, land, and sea forces to establish troops on shore, as developed in World War II, are entered under Amphibious warfare.
UF Joint operations (Military science)
BT Transportation, Military
Unified operations (Military science)

Languages
—Political aspects
Here are entered general works on the political aspects of languages. Works on the political aspects of the languages ofa particular place are entered under [place]—Languages—Political aspects.
BT Nationalism
SA subdivision Languages—Political aspects under names of countries, cities, etc.
NT Diplomacy—Language
Treaties—Language

Latin American federation
UF Federation of Latin America
Latin American integration
BT International organization
Pan-Americanism
Pan-Hispanism

Latin American integration
USE Latin American federation

Latin American specialists
USE Latin Americanists

Latin Americanists (May Subd Geog)
UF Latin America specialists

Law, Consular
USE Consular law

Law, Martial
USE Martial law

Law, Naval
USE Naval law

Law and politics
UF Politics and law
BT Power (Social sciences)
State, The

Leadership
[HM141; UB210]
BT Psychology, Military
Sociology
NT Discussion
Political leadership

League of Nations (May Subd Geog)
[JX1975]
BT International cooperation
Peace
—Buildings
—Caricatures and cartoons
—Exhibitions
—Finance
—Membership
—Officials and employees
—Postal service
—Privileges and immunities
—Publicity
—Sanctions

Leagues of armed neutrality
USE Neutrality, Armed

Leased territories
[JX4099]
UF Territories, Leased
BT Jurisdiction, Territorial
Protectorates
Territory, National

Left (Political science)
USE Right and left (Political science)

Legislative power (May Subd Geog)
[JF441-JF483]]
UF Power, Legislative
SA subdivision Power and duties under names of individual legislative bodies
NT Civil supremacy over the military
Treaty-making power
War and emergency powers

Legitimacy of governments (May Subd Geog)
UF Governments, Legitimacy of
BT Consensus (Social sciences)
Revolutions
Sovereignty
State, The

Leninism
USE Communism

Lend-lease operations (1941-1945)
[D753.2]
BT Economic assistance

Leticia Dispute, 1932-1934
BT Colombia—Foreign relations—Peru
Peru—Foreign relations—Colombia

Levies en masse
BT Combatants and noncombatants (International law)
War (International law)

Lex talionis
UF Retaliation (Law)
BT Revenge

Lex talionis (Islamic law)

Liberalism
[HM276]
BT Liberty
Political science

Liberation movements (Civil rights)
USE Civil rights movements

Liberation movements, National
USE National liberation movements

Liberation theology
[BT83.57]
BT Freedom (Theology)
Theology, Doctrinal
NT Civil rights—Religious aspects—Christianity

Liberty
[HM271; JC585-JC599]
UF Freedom
BT Democracy
Political science
NT Freedom of movement
Liberalism

Liberty and communism
USE Communism and liberty

Liberty and socialism
USE Socialism and liberty

Library of Congress World War II Recorded History Collection
USE World War II Recorded History Collection

Limitation of arms
USE Disarmament

Limited war
[UA11.5]
BT Military policy
Strategy
War
NT Low-intensity conflicts (Military science)

Literature, Conservative
USE Conservative literature

Literature, International relations
USE International relations literature

Literature, Policy science
USE Policy science literature

Literature, Political science
USE Political science literature

Literature and nationalism
USE Nationalism and literature

Literature and revolutions
UF Revolutions and literature
NT Revolutionary literature

Literature and war
USE War and literature

Local remedy rule
USE Exhaustion of local remedies (International law)

Logistics
[U168]
BT Military art and science
SA subdivision Logistics under individual wars; and subdivision Procurement under names of individual military services
NT Combat sustainability (Military science)
Military supplies

Logistics, Naval
[V179]
UF Naval logistics
BT Naval art and science
Naval tactics

Low-intensity conflicts (Military science) (May Subd Geog)
Here are entered works on non-nuclear operations ranging from terrorism and small wars to revolutions and counterrevolutions, which require limited military, paramilitary, or mixed political-economic-military responses that are short of national mobilization and that often occur in conjunction with host regimes and third countries.
UF Conflicts, Low-intensity (Military science)
Protracted conflicts (Military science)
Small wars
Wars, Small
BT Limited war

Loyalty
[BJ1533.L8]
NT Patriotism

Lying
USE Truthfulness and falsehood

Macedonian question
[D651.M3; DR701.M4]

Machiavellianism (Psychology)
BT Ethics

Man
—Animal nature
BT Philosophical anthropology
NT Sociobiology

Man (Buddhism)
BT Buddhism—Doctrines

Man (Christian theology)
[BT700-BT701.2]
Here are entered works on the Christian theology of humankind.
BT Theology, Doctrinal

Man (Hinduism)
BT Hinduism—Doctrines

Man (Islam)
[BP166.7]
BT Islam—Doctrines
—Koranic teaching

Man (Jewish theology)
BT Judaism—Doctrines

Man (Shinto)
BT Shinto—Doctrines

Man (Sikhism)
BT Sikhism—Doctrines

Man (Theology)
[BL256; BS661]
Here are entered works on the theology of humankind from the perspective of two or more of the world's religions.
UF Anthropology, Theological
Theological anthropology

Management of conflict
USE Conflict management

Mandates (May Subd Geog)
[D650.T4-D651; JX1975.49; JX4021-JX4023]
UF League of Nations—Mandatory system
BT International organization
Internationalized territories

Maneuver warfare
Here are entered works on warfare concentrating on defeating the enemy by rapidly maneuvering so as to disrupt his cohesion and ability to react, rather than by physically destroying his forces.
UF Warfare, Maneuver
BT Military maneuvers
Tactics
Warfare, Conventional

Maneuvers, Military
USE Military maneuvers

Manifest destiny (United States)
USE Messianism, Political—United States

Maoism
USE Communism

Maquis
USE Guerrillas

Mariel Boatlift, 1980
UF Boatlift, Mariel, 1980
Cuban Boatlift, 1980

Marines (May Subd Geog)
BT Armed Forces

Maritime war
USE War, Maritime (International law)

Martial law
UF Law, Martial
BT War
War (International law)
NT State of siege

Marxian economics
BT Communism
Socialism

Marxian philosophy
USE Philosophy, Marxist

Marxian sociology
USE Communism and society

Marxism
USE Communism
Socialism

Marxist philosophy
USE Philosophy, Marxist

Mass casualties
UF Casualties, Mass
Disaster casualties
BT Civil defense

Mass communication
USE Communication
Mass media

Mass media (May Subd Geog)
Here are entered works on the modern means of mass communication.
UF Mass communication
NT Developing countries in mass media
—International cooperation
USE Communication—International cooperation
—Political aspects (May Subd Geog)
BT Communication in politics

Mass media and Armed Forces
USE Armed Forces and mass media

Mass media and communism
USE Communism and mass media

Mass media and Zionism (May Subd Geog)
UF Zionism and mass media

Massacres (May Subd Geog)
BT Atrocities

Materialism, Dialectical
USE Dialectical materialism

Mayaguez Crisis, May 1975
[E865]
BT United States—Foreign relations—1974-1977

McCarthy-Army controversy, 1954
[UB23]
UF Army-McCarthy controversy, 1954
BT United States—National security

Means and ends
USE Ends and means

Mediation, International
[JX4475]
UF Conciliation, International
Good offices
International conciliation
International mediation
BT International relations
Pacific settlement of international disputes
Peace
Peaceful change (International relations)
War (International law)
NT Aggression (International law)

Mediatized states
BT Sovereignty

Medieval civilization
USE Civilization, Medieval

Medieval history
USE Middle Ages—History

Mennonites (May Subd Geog)
[BX8101-BX8143]
Here are entered works on Mennonite denominations treated collectively, works for which the individual Mennonite denomination cannot be identified, and works on Mennonites as a class of persons.
The subdivisions printed under Catholic Church may be used under this heading.
BT Christian sects
NT Amish
Old Colony Mennonites
Old Order Mennonites
—Doctrines

Mercenary troops (May Subd Geog)
UF Troops, Mercenary
BT Armies
Soldiers

Messianism, Political (May Subd Geog)
UF Political messianism
BT Nationalism
NT Sebastianism
—United States
UF Manifest destiny (United States)

MIA's
USE Missing in action

Middle Ages
[CB351-CB355]
—History
UF Medieval history
NT Crusades

Middle Eastern studies
USE Middle East—Study and teaching

Middle powers
Here are entered works on states which are weaker than the great powers in the world but significantly stronger than the minor powers and small states with which they normally interact.
UF Powers, Middle
BT International relations
States, Size of
World politics

Migration, Return
USE Return migration

Migrations of nations
[D135-D149]
Here are entered works on mass migrations of peoples.
UF Nations, Migrations of

Militarism (May Subd Geog)
[UX1937-JX1964; U21; UA10]
UF Antimilitarism
BT Armies

Military policy
Sociology, Military
War

NT War, Cost of

—Religious aspects

—Buddhism, [Christianity, etc.]

Military, The
USE Armed Forces

Military aeronautics
USE Aeronautics, Military

Military aid
USE Military assistance

Military air bases
USE Air bases

Military air pilots
USE Air pilots, Military

Military airplanes
USE Airplanes, Military

Military and civilian power
USE Civil-military relations

Military art and science (May Subd Geog)
UF Fighting
SA subdivision Military aspects under types of industries; also subdivision Warfare under ethnic groups; and headings beginning with the word Military.
NT Aeronautics, Military
Armaments
Armed Forces
Armies
Battles
Combat patrols
Combat sustainability (Military science)
Combined operations (Military science)
Command of troops
Deception (Military science)
Disarmament
Envelopment (Military science)
Escalation (Military science)
Fortification
Gases, Asphyxiating and poisonous—War use
Imaginary wars and battles
Industrial mobilization
Infiltration (Military science)
Logistics
Morale
Operational readiness (Military science)
Ordnance
Paramilitary forces
Preemptive attack (Military science)
Requisitions, Military
Sieges
Special forces (Military science)
Special operations (Military science)
Spies
Tactics
Terrain study (Military science)
Transportation, Military
Unified operations (Military science)
Unit cohesion (Military science)
Veterans
War games
Warfare, Primitive

—History
[U27-U43]
BT Military history
Naval history

—Study and teaching
USE Military education

—Terminology
[U26]
UF Military terms

Military assistance
This heading may be used with the following qualifiers to designate the country or region providing the assistance: American; Australian; British; Chinese; Communist; European; French; Israeli; Portuguese; Russian; South Korean; West German. When the heading is used with a qualifier, it may be subdivided by place to indicate the country receiving the assistance.
UF Arms sales
Foreign aid program
Foreign assistance
Military aid
Sale of military equipment

Military assistance, American (May Subd Geog)
BT Mutual security program, 1951-
NT Offshore procurement program, 1951-
Security Assistance Program

—Iran
NT Iran-Contra Affair, 1985-

—Nicaragua
NT Iran-Contra Affair, 1985-

Military astronautics
USE Astronautics, Military

Military atrocities
USE subdivision Atrocities under individual wars

Military attachés (May Subd Geog)
UF Attachés
BT Diplomatic and consular service
Diplomats

Military aviation
USE Aeronautics, Military

Military bases (May Subd Geog)
UF Army posts
Bases, Military
Posts, Military
Stations, Military
NT Air bases
Navy-yards and naval stations

Military bases, American (May Subd Geog)
UF American military bases

Military bases, Soviet (May Subd Geog)
UF Soviet military bases

Military bases, Foreign
[UA15.5]
UF Foreign military bases

Military biography
[U51-U55]
BT Military history
SA subdivision Biography under names of armies

Military capital (May Subd Geog)
[UA17]
Here are entered works on the aggregate value of the durable physical assets of the defense establishment, including the military equipment, facilities, spare parts, and ordnance that provide military capability over an extended period of time.
UF Military assets
BT Armed Forces—Procurement
Armies, Cost of
SA subdivision Military capital under names of individual armies, navies, etc.

Military capitulations
USE Capitulations, Military

Military civic action
USE Armed Forces—Civic action

Military-civil relations
USE Civil-military relations

Military combat
USE Combat

Military communications
USE Communications, Military

Military contracts
USE Defense contracts

Military discipline
[UB790-UB795]
Here are entered works on the maintenance of discipline, military disciplinary power, and offenses subject to disciplinary action.
UF Discipline, Military
NT Naval discipline

Military draft registration
USE Draft registration

Military education (May Subd Geog)
[U400-U714]
UF Army schools
Education, Military
Military art and science—Study and teaching
Military schools
Military training
NT Military missions
Military training camps

Military ethics
[U22]
UF Ethics, Military
BT Ethics
Morale
NT Conscientious objection

Military geography (May Subd Geog)
[UA985-UA997]

UF Geography, Military
SA subdivision Strategic aspects under names of regions, countries, etc.

Military government (May Subd Geog)
NT Military government of dependencies

Military government of dependencies
[JV423]
BT Colonies—Administration
Martial law
Military government
Political science
NT Military occupation

Military history
[D25]
UF History, Military
Wars
BT History
SA subdivision History, Military under names of countries, cities, etc; names of particular wars, battles, etc.; and subdivision History under names of individual armies.
NT Battles
Military art and science—History
Military biography
Military policy
Naval art and science—History
Sieges

Military history, Ancient
NT Military history in the Bible

Military history, Medieval

Military history, Modern
—16th century
—17th century
—18th century
—19th century
—20th century

Military history in the Bible
UF Bible—Military history
Wars in the Bible

Military-industrial complex (May Subd Geog)
Here are entered works on the community of interests created between armed services officials and manufacturers of weapons and defense matériel.
BT Defense industries

Military intelligence
BT Intelligence service
SA subdivision Military intelligence under individual wars
NT Electronic intelligence
Military surveillance
Propaganda analysis
U-2 Incident, 1960
—Equipment and supplies
—Finance
—Law and legislation (May Subd Geog)

Military journalism
USE Journalism, Military

Military law (May Subd Geog)
Here are entered works on the government and regulation of the armed services as a separate system of jurisprudence
NT Capitulations, Military
Combatants and noncombatants (International law)

Military maneuvers (May Subd Geog)
[U250-U255; UD460-UD465]
UF Armies—Maneuvers
Maneuvers, Military
BT Tactics
SA subdivision Maneuvers under names of individual armies
NT Maneuver warfare
War games

Military mines
USE Mines, Military

Military missions
[UA16]
UF Missions, Military
Missions, Naval
Naval missions
BT Government missions
International relations
Military education

Military mobilization
USE Armed Forces—Mobilization

Military necessity
[JX5135.M5]
UF Necessity, Military
BT War (International law)

Military occupation
[JX4093; JX5003]
UF Belligerent occupation
De facto doctrine (International law)
Occupation, Military
Occupied territory
BT Armed Forces—Foreign countries
Military government of dependencies
War (International law)
SA subdivisions History and Politics and government under names of territories occupied; and subdivision Occupied territories under individual wars
NT Booty (International law)
De facto doctrine
Military occupation damages

Military occupation damages (May Subd Geog)
UF Occupation damages, Military
BT Claims
Enemy property
Military occupation
Requisitions, Military
War damage compensation

Military oceanography (May Subd Geog)
[V396-V396.5]
UF Oceanography, Military
BT Naval art and science

Military photography
USE Photography, Military

Military planning (May Subd Geog)
UF Planning, Military
BT Military policy

Military policy
[UA1]
UF Defense policy
BT Military history
Sociology, Military
War
SA subdivision Military policy under names of countries
NT Deterrence (Strategy)
Limited war
Militarism
Military planning
Warfare, Conventional

Military psychology
USE Psychology, Military

Military reconnaissance
[U220]
UF Reconnaissance, Military
BT Military surveillance
SA subdivision Reconnaissance operations under individual wars
NT Aerial reconnaissance
Combat patrols
Naval reconnaissance
Photographic reconnaissance systems
Terrain study (Military science)
U-2 Incident, 1960

Military relations
USE subdivision Military relations under countries, etc.

Military religious orders (May Subd Geog)
[CR4701-CR4785]
BT Orders of knighthood and chivalry
NT Hospitalers
Templars
Teutonic Knights

Military research (May Subd Geog)
[U390-U395]
UF Defense research
Research, Military

Military sales
USE Military assistance
Munitions

Military schools
USE Military education

Military secrets
USE Defense information, Classified

Military service, Compulsory
USE Draft

Military service, Voluntary (May Subd Geog)
[UB320-UB325]

UF All-volunteer forces
Volunteer army
BT Armed Forces
National service
Recruiting and enlistment
SA subdivision Recruiting, enlistment, etc., under names of individual military services
—**Law and legislation** (May Subd Geog)

Military service as a profession
USE Armed Forces—Vocational guidance

Military social work (May Subd Geog)
[UH750-UH769]
UF Social service, Military
SA subdivision Social services under names of individual military services

Military sociology
USE Sociology, Military

Military space surveillance
USE Space surveillance

Military spending
USE subdivision Appropriations and expenditures under names of individual defense agencies and subdivision Armed Forces—Appropriations and expenditures under names of countries

Military staffs
USE Armies—Staffs

Military strategy
USE Strategy

Military supplies
[UC260-UC267]
UF Army supplies
Supplies, Military
BT Industrial mobilization
Logistics
SA subdivisions Equipment and Supplies and stores under names of individual military services; and subdivision Equipment and supplies under individual wars

Military surveillance (May Subd Geog)
[UG475]
UF Surveillance, Military
BT Military intelligence
NT Military reconnaissance
Space surveillance

Military telecommunication
[UG590]
UF Telecommunication, Military
BT Communications, Military

Military terms
USE Military art and science—Terminology

Military towns (May Subd Geog)
Here are entered works on cities and towns on which the military has had a pervasive influence.
UF Garrison towns
Towns, Military

Military training
USE Military education

Military training camps (May Subd Geog)
[U290-U295]
UF Training camps, Military
BT Military education

Military vehicles
USE Vehicles, Military

Mine planting
USE Mines, Military

Mines, Military
[U490]
UF Military mines
Mine planting

Mines, Submarine (May Subd Geog)
[UG490-UG497]
UF Submarine mines
BT Anti-submarine warfare
Mines, Submarine

Minorities (May Subd Geog)
[D-F; JC311]
Here are entered general works on racial, religious, ethnic, or other minority groups.
UF Ethnic minorities
NT Jews—Diaspora
Nationalities, Principle of
Population transfers
SA subdivisions Ethnic relations and Race relations under individual countries, cities, etc.
—**Political activity**

Missile Boats Incident, Cherbourg, France, 1961
USE Israeli Missile Boats Incident, Cherbourg, France, 1969

Missile Crisis, Cuba and the United States, 1962
USE Cuban Missile Crisis, Oct. 1962

Missiles, Antiaircraft
USE Antiaircraft missiles

Missiles, Ballistic
USE Ballistic missiles

Missiles, Cruise
USE Cruise missiles

Missiles, Guided
USE Guided missiles

Missiles, Surface-to-surface
USE Surface-to-surface missiles

Missing in action
UF MIA's
BT Prisoners of war
Soldiers
SA subdivision Missing in action under individual wars

Missing persons (International law)
BT International law

Missions, Government
USE Government missions

Missions, Military
USE Military missions

Missions, Naval
USE Military missions

Mobilization, Industrial
USE Industrial mobilization

Modern civilization
USE Civilization, Modern

Modern history
USE History, Modern

Mohammedanism
USE Islam

Mohammedans
USE Muslims

Monarchs
USE Kings and rulers

Monarchy
[JC374-JC408]
BT Executive power
NT Divine right of kings
Kings and rulers—Succession
Sovereignty

Monitoring, Election
USE Election monitoring

Monroe doctrine
[JX1425]
BT International relations
Intervention (International law)
Pan-Americanism
NT Drago doctrine

Moral development (May Subd Geog)
[BF723.M54]
UF Ethical development
BT Moral education

Moral education
UF Character education
Ethical education
BT Ethics

Moral rearmament
[BJ10.M6]
BT Ethics

Moral theology
USE Christian ethics

Morale
[U22]
BT Military art and science
Sociology, Military
NT Military ethics
War—Psychological aspects

Moslems
USE Muslims

Motion pictures in propaganda (May Subd Geog)
BT Propaganda

Mountain warfare
[UD460-UD465]
BT War

Multiculturalism
USE Pluralism (Social sciences)

Multinational corporations
USE International business enterprises

Munitions (May Subd Geog)
[HD9743; JX5390; UF530-UF537]
Here are entered general works on the implements of war and the industries producing them. Works on military strength including military personnel, munitions, natural resources and industrial war potential are entered under Armaments.
UF Arms sales
Foreign military sales
Military sales
Sale of military equipment
Weapons industry
BT Armaments
Industrial mobilization
War—Economic aspects
SA subdivision Equipment and supplies under individual wars
NT Air weapons
Biological weapons
Chemical weapons
Military-industrial complex
Space weapons
Weapons systems
—Law and legislation (May Subd Geog)
BT Neutrality
War, Maritime (International law)
War (International law)
—Religious aspects
—Buddhism, [Christianity, etc.]

Murder (Ten commandments)
USE Ten commandments—Murder

Music and war
UF War and music
SA subdivision Music and the war, Music and the revolution, etc., and Songs and music under individual wars

Muslim countries
USE Islamic countries

Muslim holy war
USE Jihad

Muslims (May Subd Geog)
UF Mohammedans
Moslems
BT Islam
—India
—Politics and government
NT Pakistan movement

Mutual arrangements
USE Deals

Mutual defense assistance program
USE Mutual security program, 1951-

Mutual security program, 1951-
[UA12]
UF Mutual defense assistance program
BT Security, International
NT Military assistance, American
Offshore procurement program, 1951-

MX (Weapons systems)
BT Guided missiles
Intercontinental ballistic missiles

Narcotic traffic
USE Drug traffic

Narcotics, Control of (May Subd Geog)
UF Drug enforcement
Drug traffic—Prevention

Narcotics dealers (May Subd Geog)
UF Drug dealers

National characteristics
This heading may be used with the following regional and national qualifiers: African; Albanian; American; Antillean; Arab; Argentine; Australian; Basque; Belgian; Brazilian, Breton; British, Bulgarian; Canadian; Catalan; Chilean; Costa Rican; Cuban; East German; East Indian; Egyptian; English; Eritrean; European; Finnish; French; Gallegan; German; Greek; Hungarian; Indonesian; Irish; Israeli; Italian; Japanese; Korean; Latin American; Malagasy; Mexican; New Zealand; Nigerian; Panamanian; Paraguayan; Philippine; Prussian; Puerto Rican; Romanian; Russian; Salvadoran; Scandinavian; Scottish; Serbian; Sicilian; Singapore; Spanish; Sudanese; Swedish; Swiss; Thai; Ukrainian; Venezuelan; Vietnamese; Welsh; West German.
UF National psychology
Psychology, National
BT Nationalism

National characteristics in literature

National consciousness
USE Nationalism

National defenses
USE subdivision Defenses under names of countries, etc.

National liberation movements (May Subd Geog)
Here are entered works dealing with minority or other groups in armed rebellion against a colonial government, or against a national government charged with corruption or foreign domination. In general this heading is applicable only to the post World War II period.
UF Liberation movements, National
BT Nationalism
Revolutions
NT Guerrillas

National psychology
USE National characteristics

National security
SA subdivision National security under names of countries
NT Civilian-based defense
—Law and legislation
SA subdivision National security—Law and legislation under names of countries
—Religious aspects
—Baptists, [Catholic Church, etc.]
—Buddhism, [Christianity, etc.]

National self-determination
USE Self-determination, National

National service (May Subd Geog)
UF Alternative military service
Service, National
BT Armed Forces
Conscientious objectors
Recruiting and enlistment
NT Draft
Military service, Voluntary
Technical assistance
—Law and legislation (May Subd Geog)

National socialism
[DD253]
Here are entered works on fascism in Germany during the Nazi regime. Works on post-World War II fascist and neo-Nazi movements are entered under Fascism—Germany.
UF Nazism
BT Authoritarianism
NT Anti-Nazi movement
Fascism—Germany
German-Christian movement
—Religious aspects

National socialists (May Subd Geog)
UF Nazis

National state
UF Nation-state
BT Nationalism
State, The
NT Nationalities, Principle of

National territory
USE Territory, National

Nationalism
[JC311-JC323]
UF National consciousness
BT International relations
Patriotism
Political science
NT Chauvinism and jingoism
Ethnocentrism
Folklore and nationalism
Languages—Political aspects
Messianism, Political
National characteristics

National liberation movements
National state
Nationalities, Principle of
Regionalism
Self-determination, National

—**Religious aspects**
UF Nationalism and religion
NT Civil religion
—**Baptists, [Catholic Church, etc.]**
—**Buddhism, [Christianity, etc.]**

—**France**
NT Occitan movement

Nationalism and art (May Subd Geog)
UF Art and nationalism

Nationalism and communism (May Subd Geog)
UF Communism and nationalism

Nationalism and education (May Subd Geog)
UF Education and nationalism
Nationalism in education

Nationalism and folklore
USE Folklore and nationalism

Nationalism and literature (May Subd Geog)
UF Literature and nationalism
NT Nationalism in literature

Nationalism and religion
USE Nationalism—Religious aspects

Nationalism and socialism (May Subd Geog)
UF Socialism and nationalism

Nationalism in education
USE Nationalism and education

Nationalism in literature
BT Nationalism and literature

Nationalism in music
UF Nationalism and music

Nationalism in the press (May Subd Geog)

Nationalists (May Subd Geog)

Nationalities, Principle of
UF Nationality, Principle of
Principle of nationalities
BT Minorities
National state
Nationalism
Self-determination, National

Nationality, Principle of
USE Nationalities, Principle of

Nationalsozialistische Deutsche Arbeiter-Partei
NT Church and state — Germany—History—1933-1945 Denazification

Nations, Comity
USE Comity of nations

Nations, Migrations of
USE Migrations of nations

Nations, Small
USE States, Small

Native races
USE Indigenous peoples

Nativism
Here are entered works on the policy of favoring the native inhabitants of a country over immigrants and, particularly in American history, of favoring native Protestants over Catholic immigrants.
BT Anti-Catholicism—United States

Naval air bases
USE Air bases

Naval art and science
UF Fighting
Naval warfare
War, Maritime
BT War
SA headings beginning with the word Naval
NT Imaginary wars and battles
Logistics, Naval
Naval battle groups
Naval strategy
Navy-yards and naval stations
NT Ordnance, Naval
Privateering
Riverine operations
Sea control
Sea-power
Submarine warfare
War games, Naval
Warships
Warships—Scuttling of

—**History**
[V25-V55]
BT Naval history

—Study and teaching
USE Naval education

Naval aviation
[VG90-VG95]
UF Aviation, Naval
BT Aeronautics, Naval
SA subdivision Aviation under names of navies; and subdivision Aerial operations under individual wars

Naval bases
USE Navy-yards and naval stations

Naval battles (May Subd Geog)
[D27]
UF Battles, Naval
Naval warfare
War, Maritime
BT Sea control
Sea-power
SA subdivision History, Naval under names of countries, etc.; subdivision Naval operations under individual wars

Naval battle groups (May Subd Geog)
UF Battle groups, Naval
BT Naval art and science

Naval biography (May Subd Geog)
Here are entered works on persons engaged in any area of naval and maritime activity. For biographical works on individual classes of persons engaged in such activities, see the subdivision Biography under classes of persons. For biographies of members of navies, see subdivision Biography under names of individual navies.
NT Admirals
Seamen

Naval communications
USE Communications, Military

Naval convoys (May Subd Geog)
[V182]
UF Convoys, Naval
BT Naval tactics

Naval convoys (International law)
[JX5268]
UF Convoys, Naval (International law)
BT War, Maritime (International law)

Naval discipline (May Subd Geog)
UF Discipline, Naval
BT Military discipline

Naval education (May Subd Geog)
[V400-V695]
UF Education, Naval
Naval art and science—Study and teaching
Naval schools

Naval history
UF History, Naval
Wars
BT History
SA subdivision History, Naval under names of countries and subdivision History under names of individual navies.
NT Naval art and science—History
Privateering
Warships, Scuttling of

Naval history, Ancient
[D95]

Naval history, Modern
—**20th century**
[D436]

Naval law (May Subd Geog)
[VB350-VB785]
UF Law, Naval
BT International law
NT Prize law
Warships—Law and legislation

Naval logistics
USE Logistics, Naval

Naval maneuvers
[V245]
UF Maneuvers, Naval
BT Tactics
SA subdivision Maneuvers under names of

individual navies
NT War games, Naval

Naval missions
USE Military missions

Naval ordnance
USE Ordnance, Naval

Naval policy
USE Sea-power

Naval reconnaissance
[V190]
UF Reconnaissance, Naval
BT Military reconnaissance

Naval research (May Subd Geog)
UF Research, Naval

Naval schools
USE Naval education

Naval ships
USE Warships

Naval shipyards
USE Navy-yards and naval stations

Naval strategy
BT Naval art and science
Sea-power
Sea control

Naval tactics
[V167-V178]
UF Naval warfare
War, Maritime
BT Tactics
NT Logistics, Naval
Naval convoys
Sea control
War games, Naval

Naval visits to foreign ports
USE Warships—Visits to foreign ports

Naval war games
USE War games, Naval

Naval warfare
USE Naval art and science
Naval battles
Naval tactics
War, Maritime (International law)

Navies (May Subd Geog)
[VA37-VA42]
BT Armaments
Armed Forces
SA names of individual navies
NT Disarmament
Submarine forces

Navies, Cost of
[VA20-VA25]
UF Cost of navies
BT War, Cost of

Navy-yards and naval stations (May Subd Geog)
[V220-V240; VA67-VA70]
UF Naval bases
Naval shipyards
Stations, Navy-yards and naval
BT Military bases
Naval art and science

Navy-yards and naval stations, American (May Subd Geog)

Nazis
USE National socialists

Nazism
USE National socialism

Necessity, Military
USE Military necessity

Negotiation
[BF637.N4]
UF Bargaining
BT Discussion
NT Arbitration, International
Conflict management
Deals
Hostage negotiations
Treaties

Negotiations in international disputes
USE Diplomatic negotiations in international disputes

Neo-fascism
USE Fascism

Neo-conservatism
USE Conservatism

Neocolonialism
USE Colonies
Imperialism

Neutral trade with belligerents
BT Neutrality
War, Maritime (International law)
War (International law)

Neutralism
USE Neutrality
Nonalignment

Neutrality
[JX5355-JX5397]
Here are entered works on the status of states resulting from their adoption of impartiality toward belligerent states, and on the consequent rights and duties created between the neutral states and the belligerents under international law. Works on the foreign policy of states who do not identify themselves with the major power blocs but retain the option of becoming aligned when necessary are entered under Nonalignment.
UF Isolationism
Neutralism
BT International law
Privateering
Security, International
States, Small
SA subdivision Neutrality under names of countries, etc.
NT Asylum, Right of
Guaranty, Treaties of
Munitions
Neutral trade with belligerents
Passage of troops
Transit by land
Unneutral service

Neutrality, Armed
UF Armed Neutrality, 1780-1800
Leagues of armed neutrality
BT International relations
War (International law)

Neutron bomb
[UG1282.N48]
BT Bombs
Neutron weapons

Neutron weapons
UF Enhanced radiation weapons
Weapons, Neutron
BT Nuclear weapons
NT Neutron bomb

New Left (May Subd Geog)
Here are entered works on the radical leftist movement, active especially during the 1960's and 1970's, composed of diverse groups and political tendencies but united in its demand for major changes in the socio-economic-political system.
UF Left, New
BT Radicalism
Social movements

New states
USE States, New

News, Foreign
USE Foreign news

NGOs (International agencies)
USE Non-governmental organizations

No first use (Nuclear strategy)
[U264]
Here are entered works on the principle that a military power, in the event of war, would not be the first to resort to the tactical or strategic use of nuclear weapons.
BT Deterrence (Strategy)

Non-governmental organizations (May Subd Geog)
Here are entered works dealing with international organizations created and financed independent of governments and having a non-profit function in the developing countries.
UF NGOs (International agencies)
Private and voluntary organizations (International agencies)
BT International agencies

Non-resistance to evil
USE Evil, Non-resistance to

Non-violence
USE Nonviolence

Nonaligned nations
USE Nonalignment

Nonalignment
[JX1393.N54]
Here are entered works on the foreign policy of states who do not identify themselves with the major power blocs but retain the option of becoming aligned when necessary. Works on the status of states resulting from their adoption of impartiality toward belligerent states, and on the consequent rights and duties created between the neutral states and the belligerents under international law are entered under Neutrality.
UF Neutralism
Nonaligned nations
BT International relations
SA subdivision Nonalignment under names of countries, etc.

Noncombatants (International law)
USE Combatants and noncombatants (International law)

Non-lethal weapons
USE Nonlethal weapons

Nonlethal weapons (May Subd Geog)
UF Non-lethal weapons
BT Arms and armor

Nonnuclear warfare
USE Warfare, Conventional

Nonproliferation, Nuclear
USE Nuclear nonproliferation

Nonrecognition of governments
USE Recognition (International law)

Nonselfgoverning territories
USE International trusteeships

Nonviolence
UF Non-violence
NT Passive resistance
—Biblical teaching
—Religious aspects
—Baptists, [Catholic Church, etc.]
—Buddhism, [Christianity, etc.]

Nonviolence and communism
USE Communism and nonviolence

Nonviolent defense
USE Civilian-based defense

Nonviolent noncooperation
USE Passive resistance

Normandy Invasion, 1944 (Planning)
USE Operation Overlord

North and South
[CB261]
Here are entered works on both acculturation and culture conflict between civilizations of colder and warmer areas.
UF South and North
BT Culture conflict

North Atlantic Treaty Organization (May Subd Geog)
—Armed Forces (May Subd Geog)

Notification (International relations)
BT Diplomacy
International law
International relations

Nuclear arms control (May Subd Geog)
[JX1974.7-JX1974.76]
UF Nuclear weapons control
BT Arms control
Nuclear nonproliferation
Nuclear weapons
—Verification
[UA12.5]
UF Verification of nuclear arms control

Nuclear crisis control (May Subd Geog)
[JX1974.8]
UF Control of nuclear crises
Crisis control, Nuclear
BT Crisis management
International relations
NT Nuclear warfare

Nuclear crisis stability
[U263]
UF Crisis stability (Nuclear warfare)
Stability, Nuclear crisis
BT Nuclear warfare

Nuclear disarmament (May Subd Geog)
[JX1974.7-JX1974.76]
UF Atomic weapons and disarmament
Disarmament, Nuclear
BT Disarmament
NT Nuclear-weapon-free zones
Unilateral nuclear disarmament

Nuclear energy (May Subd Geog)
UF Atomic energy
Nuclear power
—Government policy (May Subd Geog)
—Law and legislation (May Subd Geog)
—Religious aspects
—Baptists, [Catholic Church, etc.]
—Buddhism, [Christianity, etc.]
—Research (May Subd Geog)
—International cooperation
NT Dragon Project

Nuclear explosions
NT Underground nuclear explosions

Nuclear-free zones
USE Nuclear-weapon-free zones

Nuclear freeze movement
USE Antinuclear movement

Nuclear nonproliferation
Here are entered works on international control over the transfer and use of nuclear equipment, material, and technology, aimed at preventing the spread of nuclear explosive capability.
UF Nonproliferation, Nuclear
BT Technology transfer

Nuclear pollution
USE Radioactive pollution

Nuclear-powered warships
USE Nuclear warships

Nuclear ships (International law)
BT International law

Nuclear strategy
USE Nuclear warfare

Nuclear submarines (May Subd Geog)
[V857.5]
UF Nuclear-powered submarines
BT Nuclear warships
Submarine boats
NT Trident (Weapons systems)

Nuclear targeting
USE Targeting (Nuclear strategy)

Nuclear terrorism (May Subd Geog)
Here are entered works on terrorism targeted at nuclear sites or involving threats to use nuclear weapons.
UF Terrorism, Nuclear
BT Terrorism

Nuclear threshold (Strategy)
Here are entered works on the level of violence or threat beneath which military operations can be conducted without causing nuclear war.
UF Threshold, Nuclear (Strategy)
BT Nuclear warfare
Warfare, Conventional

Nuclear underground explosions
USE Underground nuclear explosions

Nuclear warfare
[U263]
UF Atomic warfare
CBR warfare
Nuclear strategy
Nuclear war
BT War
NT Dropshot Plan
Nuclear crisis stability
Nuclear threshold (Strategy)
Targeting (Nuclear strategy)
—Environmental aspects (May Subd Geog)
NT Nuclear winter
—Religious aspects
—Baptists, [Catholic Church, etc.]
—Buddhism, [Christianity, etc.]
—Targeting
USE Targeting (Nuclear strategy)
—Termination
[U263]
UF Termination of nuclear warfare

Nuclear warfare (International law)

Nuclear warfare and art
 USE Art and nuclear warfare

Nuclear warfare and communism
 USE Communism and nuclear warfare

Nuclear warfare and literature (May Subd Geog)
 UF Atomic warfare and literature
 BT War and literature

Nuclear warfare in motion pictures
 UF Atomic warfare in motion pictures

Nuclear warships (May Subd Geog)
 UF Nuclear-powered warships
  Warships, Nuclear
 BT Warships
 NT Nuclear submarines

Nuclear-weapon-free zones (May Subd Geog)
 [JX1974.735-JX1974.74]
 UF Denuclearized zones
  Nuclear-free zones
 BT Nuclear disarmament
 —Europe
  NT Rapacki plan

Nuclear weapons (May Subd Geog)
 [U264]
 UF Atomic weapons
  Weapons, Nuclear
 BT Ordnance
 NT Atomic bomb
  Hydrogen bomb
  Neutron weapons
  Tactical nuclear weapons
 —Inventory control
 —Safety measures
 —Testing
  NT Operation Crossroads, 1946
  —Detection

Nuclear weapons, Tactical
 USE Tactical nuclear weapons

Nuclear weapons (International law)
 UF Atomic bomb (International law)
  Nuclear warfare (International law)
 BT War (International law)

Nuclear weapons control
 USE Nuclear arms control

Nuclear weapons disarmament
 USE Nuclear disarmament

Nuclear weapons industry (May Subd Geog)
 [HD9744.N83-HD9744.N834]

Nuclear weapons information (May Subd Geog)
 This heading may be used with the following nationality qualifiers: American; French
 UF Atomic weapons information
  Exchange of nuclear weapons information
 BT Defense information, Classified
 —Law and legislation (May Subd Geog)

Nuclear weapons plants (May Subd Geog)

Nuclear winter (May Subd Geog)
 UF Winter, Nuclear
 BT Nuclear warfare—Environmental aspects

Nuncios, Papal (May Subd Geog)
 [BX1908]
 UF Papal nuncios
 BT Ambassadors
  Catholic Church—Diplomatic service
  Diplomats

Objectors, Conscientious
 USE Conscientious objectors

Occidental civilization
 USE Civilization, Occidental

Occitan movement
 [DC607.9]
 BT Regionalism—France
  Nationalism—France

Occupation, Military
 USE Military occupation

Occupancy (International law)
 BT Acquisition of territory
  International law

Occupied territory
 USE Military occupation

Oceanography, Military
 USE Military oceanography

Offenses against foreign heads of state (May Subd Geog)
 UF Crimes against foreign heads of state
 BT Heads of state

Offensive (Military strategy)
 [U162]
 BT Military policy
  Strategy

Official secrets (May Subd Geog)
 UF Disclosing official secrets
  Government secrecy
  Secrecy in government
  Secrets, Official
  Secrets of state
 BT Government and the press
  Government information
 NT Defense information, Classified

Offshore procurement program, 1951-
 BT Military assistance, American
  Munitions
  Mutual security program, 1951-

Old Colony Mennonites
 [BX8129.O4]
 BT Mennonites

Old Order Mennonites (May Subd Geog)
 [BX8129.O43]
 BT Mennonites

Oligarchy (May Subd Geog)
 [JC419]
 BT Political science

Open city (International law)
 UF City, Open (International law)
 BT War—Protection of civilians
  War (International law)

Open door policy (Far East)
 USE Eastern question (Far East)

Operation Crossroads, 1946
 UF Bikini Nuclear Tests, 1946
 BT Nuclear weapons—Testing

Operation Overlord
 Here are entered works on the military planning and diplomatic negotiations for the Normandy invasion.
 UF Normandy Invasion, 1944 (Planning)

Operational readiness (Military science)
 Here are entered works on the capability and readiness of military equipment and personnel to perform the mission or functions for which they were organized or designed.
 UF Preparedness (Military science)
 BT Military art and science
 SA subdivision Operational readiness under names of individual military services

Opinion, Public
 USE Public opinion

Opposition (Political science)
 UF Political opposition
 BT Political science

Orders of knighthood and chivalry (May Subd Geog)
 [CR4501-CR6305]
 UF Knighthood, Orders of
 BT Military religious orders

Ordnance
 [UF520-UF630]
 BT Armaments
  Arms and armor
  Firearms
  Military art and science
 SA subdivision Ordnance and ordnance stores under names of individual military services
 NT Nuclear weapons
  Weapons systems

Ordnance, Naval
 UF Naval ordnance
 BT Naval art and science

Organization of American States

Organization of American States. General Assembly
 —Resolutions

Orient and Occident
  USE East and West

Oriental civilization
  USE Civilization, Oriental

Orientalists (May Subd Geog)

Origin of the state
  USE State, The—Origin

Pacific Area cooperation
  BT International cooperation

Pacific blockade
  USE Blockade, Pacific

Pacific relations
  USE Pan-Pacific relations

Pacific settlement of international disputes
  UF Conflict resolution, International
    International conflict resolution
    International disputes, Pacific settlement of
    Peaceful settlement of international disputes
  BT International relations
  NT Arbitration, International
    Diplomatic negotiations in international disputes
    International courts
    Mediation, International

Pacifism
  Here are entered works on the renunciation on moral grounds of offensive or defensive military action. Works on social movements advocating peace are entered under Peace movements.
  BT Peace
    Sociology, Military
  NT Pacifists
  —Biblical teaching
  —Religious aspects
    —Baptists, [Catholic Church, etc.]
    —Buddhism, [Christianity, etc.]

Pacifism in literature

Pacifists (May Subd Geog)
  [JX1962]
  BT Pacifism
    Peace
  NT Conscientious objectors

Pacta sunt servanda (International law)
  [JX4171.P3]
  BT International law
    International obligations
    Treaties

Pakistan movement
  BT Muslims—India—Politics and government

Palestine in Christianity

Palestine in Islam

Palestine in Judaism

Palestine in the Bible
  UF Bible—Palestine

Palestine problem
  USE Jewish-Arab relations

Palestinian Arabs (May Subd Geog)
  UF Palestinians
  NT Fedayeen
    Jewish-Arab relations

Palestinians
  USE Palestinian Arabs

Pan-Africanism
  UF African relations
  BT Regionalism (International organization)

Pan American conferences
  USE Inter-American conferences

Pan-American treaties and conventions
  UF Conventions, Pan-American
    Inter-American conventions
    Inter-American treaties
    Treaties, Pan-American
  BT Pan-Americanism
    Treaties

Pan-Americanism
  Here are entered works on the solidarity, actual or potential, of the Americas, including works on cooperation in all fields of activity.
  UF Inter-American cooperation
  BT America—Politics and government
    International cooperation
    Regionalism (International organization)
  NT Inter-American conferences
    Latin American federation
    Monroe doctrine
    Pan-American treaties and conventions

Pan-Arabism
  USE Panarabism

Pan-Germanism
  USE Pangermanism

Pan-Hispanism
  UF Hispanidad
    Hispanoamericanism
  NT Latin American federation

Pan-Islamism
  USE Panislamism

Pan-Latinism
  USE Panlatinism

Pan-Pacific relations
  [DU29]
  UF Pacific relations
  BT International relations

Pan-Slavism
  USE Panslavism

Pan-Turianism
  [DS17]
  UF Pan-Turkism
    Turkism

Pan-Turkism
  USE Pan-Turianism

Panarabism
  [DS38]
  UF Pan-Arabism
  BT Arabism
    Panislamism

Pangermanism
  [DD119]
  UF Pan-Germanism
  NT Drang nach Osten

Panislamism
  UF Pan-Islamism
  BT Arabism
  NT Panarabism

Panlatinism
  [D448]
  UF Pan-Latinism

Panslavism
  [D377; D449]
  UF Pan-Slavism

Parachute troops
  [UG630-UG635]
  UF Paratroops
  BT Aeronautics, Military
    Airborne troops
  SA subdivision Parachute troops under names of armies and subdivision Armed Forces—Parachute troops under names of countries

Paramilitary forces (May Subd Geog)
  UF Forces, Paramilitary
  BT Armed Forces
    Military art and science

Paratroops
  USE Parachute troops

Parliamentary government
  USE Representative government and representation

Participation, Political
  USE Political participation

Partisans
  USE Guerrillas

Partition, Territorial
  UF Divided states
    Partitioned states
    States, Divided
    States, Partitioned
    Territorial partition
  SA subdivision Partition with dates under history of individual countries, etc.

Partitioned states
USE Partition, Territorial

Partner cities
USE Sister cities

Passage of troops
[JX5397.P3]
BT Neutrality
Transit by land (International law)
War (International law)

Passive resistance (May Subd Geog)
UF Nonviolent noncooperation
Satyagraha
BT Direct action
Nonviolence

Patriotic societies (May Subd Geog)

Patriotism (May Subd Geog)
[JC329; JK1758-JK1759]
BT Loyalty
NT Chauvinism and jingoism
Nationalism

Patrols, Combat
USE Combat patrols

Peace
[JX1901-JX1991]
UF Coexistence
Peaceful coexistence
BT Ethics
International relations
SA subdivision Peace under individual wars
NT Arbitration, International
Armistices
Crimes against peace
International education
International organization
League of Nations
Mediation, International
Pacifism
Pacifists
Peace treaties
Peaceful change (International relations)
Sociology, Military
—Biblical teaching
—Religious aspects
UF Peace (Theology)
Religion and peace
—Baptists, [Catholic Church]
—Buddhism, [Christianity, etc.]
—Research
UF Peace science
—Study and teaching (May Subd Geog)
UF Peace studies

Peace, Crimes against
USE Crimes against peace

Peace, Prayers for
USE Prayers for peace

Peace (Philosophy)
BT Philosophy

Peace (Theology)
USE Peace—Religious aspects

Peace and teenagers
USE Teenagers and peace

Peace and women
USE Women and peace

Peace and youth
USE Youth and peace

Peace Day
[JX1936.5]

Peace in art

Peace in literature

Peace making
USE Reconciliation

Peace movements (May Subd Geog)
Here are entered works on social movements advocating peace. Works on the renunciation on moral grounds of offensive or defensive military action are entered under Pacifism.
UF Anti-war movements
Antiwar movements
Protest movements, War
War protest movements
BT Social movements
SA subdivision Protest movements under individual wars

Peace rug (Canvas embroidery)
USE United Nations peace rug (Canvas embroidery)

Peace science
USE Peace—Research

Peace studies
USE Peace—Study and teaching

Peace treaties
[JX5181]
UF Treaties of peace
BT Peace
Treaties

Peaceful change (International relations)
BT International relations
Peace
World politics
NT Arbitration, International
Commissions of inquiry, International
International courts
Mediation, International
Security, International
Treaties—Revision

Peaceful coexistence
USE subdivision Foreign relations under names of countries
International relations
Peace
World politics—1945-

Peaceful settlement of international disputes
USE Pacific settlement of international disputes

Peacekeeping forces
USE International police
United Nations—Armed Forces

Peacemaking
USE Reconciliation

Peasant uprisings (May Subd Geog)
UF Uprisings, Peasant
BT Insurgency
Revolutions
SA headings for specific uprisings

Penalties (International law)
USE Sanctions (International law)

People's democracies
Here are entered works on a form of government in communist-dominated countries that is considered a transitional stage to a fully communist regime.
BT Political science
Socialism

Perestroika
Here are entered works on the restructuring of Soviet society initiated by General Secretary Mikhail Gorbachev. When this heading is assigned, additional headings are assigned as appropriate, e.g. Soviet Union—Politics and government—1985-

Permanent revolution theory
[HX550.K48]
Here are entered works on the theory by which proletarian socialist revolution begins in a relatively underdeveloped country and spreads to more developed countries, proceeding permanently until socialism is achieved throughout the world.
BT Communism
Revolutions
Revolutions and socialism
Socialism

Peronism
[F2849-F2849.2]
BT Fascism—Argentina

Perry's Expedition to Japan, 1852-1854
USE United States Naval Expedition to Japan, 1852-1854

Persecution (May Subd Geog)
UF Christians—Persecution
Religious persecution
BT Atrocities
NT Jews—Persecutions
Massacres
Political persecution
Refugees, Religious

Personality and history
[D16.9]
UF History and personality

Personality and politics
[BF698.9.P6]
UF Politics and personality

Persons under banning orders (South Africa)
USE Banned persons (South Africa)

Persuasion (Psychology)
BT Communication

Philosemitism (May Subd Geog)
Here are entered works dealing with pro-Jewish attitudes of non-Jews.

Philosophical anthropology
[BD450]
UF Anthropology, Philosophical
Man (Philosophy)
BT Civilization—Philosophy

Philosophy
SA subdivision Philosophy under topical headings
NT Ends and means
Good and evil
Ideology
Justice (Philosophy)
Peace (Philosophy)
Power (Philosophy)
War (Philosophy)

Philosophy, Marxist (May Subd Geog)
[B809.8]
UF Marxian philosophy
Marxist philosophy
NT Dialectical materialism

Philosophy of history
USE History—Philosophy

Photographers, War
USE War photographers

Photographic reconnaissance systems
UF Reconnaissance, Photographic
BT Aerial reconnaissance
Military reconnaissance

Photography, Military (May Subd Geog)
Here are entered works on the military applications of photography such as mapping, reconnaissance, training, etc. Works on photography in war for the purposes of historical documentation are entered under War photography.
UF Military photography

Photography, War
USE War photography

Picasso, Pablo, 1881-1973. Guernica
UF Guernica (Painting)

Pillage (May Subd Geog)
BT War crimes
SA subdivision Destruction and pillage under individual wars

Pilots, Fighter
USE Fighter pilots

Planning, Military
USE Military planning

Plebiscite (May Subd Geog)
[JC55.P7; JX4054]
BT International relations
Political science

Pluralism (Social sciences) (May Subd Geog)
UF Cultural pluralism
Multiculturalism
BT Ethnic relations
Race relations

Point four program
USE Technical assistance, American

Poison gas
USE Gases, Asphyxiating and poisonous

Polarization (Social sciences)
BT Political science
Sociology

Policy science literature
UF Literature, Policy science

Policy sciences
UF Public policy management
SA subdivision Government policy under subjects; and headings of the type [topic] and state and [topic] policy
NT Decision-making
Political planning

Policy scientists (May Subd Geog)
UF Public policy experts
NT International relations specialists

Polish question
[DK4182]
Here are entered works on the attempts to restore the kingdom of Poland, and the influence of the partition of Poland on the general politics of Europe.

Political alienation (May Subd Geog)
BT Political psychology

Political atrocities (May Subd Geog)
UF Atrocities, Political
SA subdivision Atrocities under individual wars
NT Jews—Persecutions

Political behavior
USE Biopolitics
Political participation
Political psychology
Political sociology
Politics, Practical

Political boundaries
USE Boundaries

Political communication
USE Communication in politics

Political consultants (May Subd Geog)
UF Advisors, Political
Campaign consultants
BT Politics, Practical

Political corruption
USE Corruption (in politics)

Political crimes and offenses (May Subd Geog)
[HV6254-HV6321]
UF Crimes, Political
Political offenses
BT International law
Political ethics
Political science
NT Assassination
Bombings
Concentration camps
Conspiracies
Corruption (in politics)
Elections—Corrupt practices
Embassy buildings—Takeovers
Government, Resistance to
Insurgency
Sedition
Sovereignty, Violation of
Terrorism
Treason
Trials (Political crimes and offenses)

Political crimes and offenses (Islamic law) (May Subd Geog)

Political ethics (May Subd Geog)
UF Ethics, Political
Political science—Moral and ethical aspects
BT Ethics
Political science
NT Chauvinism and jingoism
Government, Resistance to
Political crimes and offenses

Political history
USE World politics

Political indicators (May Subd Geog)
BT Political statistics

Political leadership (May Subd Geog)
Here are entered works on the exercise of leadership in political activities.
BT Leadership

Political messianism
USE Messianism, Political

Political instability
USE Political stability

Political loyalty
USE Allegiance

Political murder
USE Assassination

Political opposition
USE Opposition (Political science)

Political participation (May Subd Geog)
UF Citizen participation
Participation, Political
Political behavior
BT Political rights
SA subdivision Political activity under names of individual corporate bodies, types of corporate bodies, Christian denominations, and classes of persons.
NT Armed Forces—Political activity

Catholic Church—Political activity
Minorities—Political activity

Political parties (May Subd Geog)
[JF2011-JF2111]
BT Political science
SA names of individual parties; and subdivision Politics and government under names of countries, cities, etc.
NT Right and left (Political science)

Political persecution (May Subd Geog)
[JC585-JC599]
UF Political repression
BT Persecution

Political planning (May Subd Geog)
UF Public policy
BT Policy sciences
Politics, Practical

Political prisoners (May Subd Geog)
UF Prisoners, Political
Prisoners of conscience
NT Women political prisoners
—South Africa
USE Banned persons (South Africa)

Political psychology
UF Political behavior
Psychology, Political
BT Political science
NT International relations—Psychological aspects
Political alienation
Propaganda
Public opinion

Political purges (May Subd Geog)
UF Purges, Political

Political refugees
USE Refugees, Political

Political rehabilitation (May Subd Geog)
Here are entered works on the restoration of political rights to victims of totalitarian regimes through amnesty, party reinstatement, or public recognition during their lifetime or posthumously.
UF Rehabilitation, Political—Soviet Union
Destalinization

Political representation
USE Representative government and representation

Political repression
USE Political persecution

Political rights (May Subd Geog)
Here are entered works on rights of citizens to participate, directly or indirectly, in the establishment or administration of government.
BT Civil rights
NT Political participation

Political satire
This heading may be used with the following qualifiers: American; Arabic; Austrian; Catalan; English; French; German; Gujarati; Italian; Romanian; Spanish, e.g. Political satire, American.
UF Satire, Political
SA subdivisions Politics and government—Humor and Politics and government—Caricatures and cartoons under names of countries, cities, etc.

Political scandals
USE Corruption (in politics)

Political science (May Subd Geog)
Here and with local subdivision are entered works on the discipline of political science. Works on the political processes of individual regions, countries, cities, etc., are entered under the name of the place subdivided by Politics and government.
UF Government
Political theory
Politics
BT History
NT Authoritarianism
Authority
Autonomy
Biopolitics
Citizenship
Civics
Common good
Communication in politics
Comparative government
Conservatism
Coups d'état
Democracy
Despotism
Divine right of kings
Elections
Equality
Executive power
Geopolitics
Government, Resistance to
Ideology
Imperialism
Individualism
International organization
Kings and rulers
Liberalism
Liberty
Military government of dependencies
Nationalism
Oligarchy
Opposition (Political science)
People's democracies
Polarization (Social sciences)
Political crimes and offenses
Political ethics
Political parties
Political psychology
Political sociology
Political statistics
Politics, Practical
Power (Social sciences)
Protectorates
Public opinion
Radicalism
Representative government and representation
Republics
Revolutions
Right and left (Political science)
Separation of powers
Socialism
Sovereignty
States, Size of
States, Small
Subsidiarity
Territory, National
Utopias
World politics
—Bibliography
—History
[JA81-JA84]
Here are entered works on the history of political science as a discipline. Works on political history, conditions and institutions are entered under World politics and under names of regions, countries, cities, etc., subdivided by Politics and government.
UF State, The—History of theories
—Moral and ethical aspects
USE Political ethics
—Philosophy
USE Political philosophy
—Study and teaching (May Subd Geog)

Political science and the Koran
USE Koran—Political science

Political science in the Bible
USE Politics in the Bible

Political science literature
UF Literature, Political science

Political scientists (May Subd Geog)

Political sociology
UF Political behavior
BT Political science
Sociology

Political stability (May Subd Geog)
UF Political instability
Stability, Political
BT Consensus (Social sciences)

Political statistics
BT Political science
SA subdivision Politics and government—Statistics under names of countries, cities, etc.

Political theory
USE Political science

Political violence
USE Assassination
Bombings
Government, Resistance to
Revolutions
Sabotage
Terrorism
Violence

Politicians (May Subd Geog)
BT Statesmen

Politics
USE Political science
Politics, Practical

Politics, Practical (May Subd Geog)
Here are entered works on practical political methods in political party work, electioneering, etc.
UF Political behavior
Politics
Practical politics
BT Political science
SA subdivision Politics and government under names of countries, states, etc., and headings beginning with the word Political
NT Business and politics
Campaign management
College students—Political activity
Elections
Political consultants
Political planning
Public relations and politics
Students—Political activity
Television in politics
Youth—Political activity

Politics and Buddhism
USE Buddhism and politics

Politics and Christianity
USE Christianity and politics

Politics and Hinduism
USE Hinduism and politics

Politics and Islam
USE Islam and politics

Politics and Judaism
USE Judaism and politics

Politics and law
USE Law and politics

Politics and personality
USE Personality and politics

Politics and public relations
USE Public relations and politics

Politics and the press
USE Press and politics

Politics and war
UF War and politics
BT Power (Social sciences)

Politics in the Bible
[BS680.P45]
UF Bible—Politics
Political science in the Bible

Poll watching
USE Election monitoring

Pollution across boundaries
USE Transboundary pollution

Population transfers
Here are entered works on the mass transfer of ethnic groups from one country to another.
UF Exchange of population
Transfer of population
BT Emigration and immigration
Minorities
—Germans, [Slovaks, Turks, etc.]

Post-attack rehabilitation of industry
USE War damage, Industrial

Postliminy
[JX5187]
BT International law
War, Maritime (International law)
War (International law)
NT Restitution and indemnification claims (1933-)

Posts, Military
USE Military bases

Power (Christian theology)
BT Theology, Doctrinal

Power (Philosophy)
[BD438]
BT Authority
Ethics
Philosophy

Power (Social sciences)
BT Political science
Sociology
NT Politics and war

Power, Balance of
USE Balance of power

Power, Executive
USE Executive power

Power, Legislative
USE Legislative power

Power politics
USE Balance of power

Powers, Great
USE Great powers

Powers, Middle
USE Middle powers

Powers, Protecting
USE Protecting powers

Powers, Separation of
USE Separation of powers

POW's
USE Prisoners of war

Prayers for peace
[BV283.P4]
UF Peace, Prayers for

Prediction
USE Forecasting

Preemptive attack (Military science)
BT Military art and science
Strategy
NT First strike (Nuclear strategy)

Prejudices (May Subd Geog)
[BF575.P9]
UF Antipathies
Bias (Psychology)
BT Attitude (Psychology)
NT Anti-Catholicism
Antisemitism
Ethnocentrism
Racism

Preparedness (Military science)
USE Operational readiness (Military science)

Presidential succession
USE Presidents—Succession

Presidents (May Subd Geog)
[JF255]
BT Heads of state
Kings and rulers
—Election
[JF285]
BT Elections
—Succession
UF Presidential succession

Press and government
USE Government and the press

Press and politics (May Subd Geog)
UF Politics and the press

Press and propaganda (May Subd Geog)
UF Propaganda and press

Prime ministers (May Subd Geog)
BT Executive power
Heads of state
NT Women prime ministers

Primitive warfare
USE Warfare, Primitive

Principle of nationalities
USE Nationalities, Principle of

Prior consultation (International law)
UF Consultation, Prior (International law)
BT Diplomacy
International law
International relations

Prisoners, Political
USE Political prisoners

Prisoners of conscience
USE Political prisoners

Prisoners of war (May Subd Geog)
[JX5141]
When subdivided by place, the name of the place may designate either the current location of prisoners of war, or the place of origin. For prisoners of war of a particular nationality held in another country two headings are assigned: 1. Prisoners of war—[country of nationality]. 2. Prisoners of war—[place where held].
UF POW's
War prisoners
BT War (International law)
War victims

SA subdivision Prisoners and prisons under individual wars
NT Concentration camps
Ex-prisoners of war
Missing in action
—Family relationships
—Psychology
BT Psychology, Military

Private and voluntary organizations (International agencies)
USE Non-governmental organizations

Privateering (May Subd Geog)
[JX5231]
BT Naval art and science
Naval history
War, Maritime (International law)
NT Neutrality
Reprisals
Search, Right of

Privileges and immunities (May Subd Geog)
UF Immunities and privileges
NT Diplomatic privileges and immunities
Exterritoriality
International agencies—Privileges and immunities

Protestantism and Zionism
UF Zionism and Protestantism

Prize-courts (May Subd Geog)
[JX5263]
BT Prize law
War, Maritime (International law)

Prize law (May Subd Geog)
[JX5245-JX5266]
UF Requisitions (of neutral vessels and cargoes)
Ships, Requisition of
BT Prizes
War, Maritime (International law)
NT Continuous voyages (International law)
Contraband of war
Prize-courts

Prize money (May Subd Geog)
[VB280-VB285]
BT Naval law
Prizes

Prizes (May Subd Geog)
[JX5245-JX5266]
SA subdivision Prizes, etc. under individual wars
NT Booty (International law)
Prize law
Prize money

Procurement, Military
USE Armed Forces—Procurement

Profiteering (May Subd Geog)
BT War—Economic aspects
War, Cost of
SA subdivision Economic aspects under individual wars

Progress
[HM101]
UF Social progress
BT Civilization
—Religious aspects
—Buddhism, [Christianity, etc.]

Proliferation of arms
USE Arms race

Propaganda
This heading may be used with the following qualifiers and subdivided further by place: American; Anti-American; Anti-Bulgarian; Anti-communist; Anti-German; Anti-Israeli; Anti-Japanese; Anti-Polish; Anti-Russian; Anti-Soviet; Arab; Argentine; Australian; British; Capitalist; Chinese; Communist; Confederate; East German; European; Fascist; French; Israeli; Italian; Japanese; Portuguese; Roman; Russian; South African; Soviet; Ukrainian; West German; Zimbabwean; Zionist, e.g. Propaganda, Fascist—Europe
[HM263]
BT Communication in politics
Political psychology
SA subdivision Propaganda under individual wars
NT Foreign agents
Government publicity
Motion pictures in propaganda
NT Propaganda, International
Propaganda analysis
Radio in propaganda
Rumor
Television in propaganda
Theater in propaganda

Propaganda, International
UF International propaganda
BT International relations
Propaganda
World politics

Propaganda analysis
BT Military intelligence
Propaganda

Propaganda and press
USE Press and propaganda

Propaganda in radio
USE Radio in propaganda

Propaganda in television
USE Television in propaganda

Propaganda in the theater
USE Theater in propaganda

Property captured at sea
USE Capture at sea

Protecting powers (May Subd Geog)
Here are entered works on neutral or third parties that consent to protect the nationals of an absent state in the event of a war or conflict.
UF Powers, Protecting

Protection of interests (International relations)
Here are entered works on the representation of the interests of an absent state by a neutral or third party in the event of a break in diplomatic relations.
UF Interests, Protection of (International relations)
BT Diplomacy

Protective signs (International law)
[JX5147]
BT International law
NT Flags of truce

Protectorates
[JX4021-JX4023]
BT Colonies
International law
Political science
NT International trusteeships
Servitudes (International law)

Protest movements (Civil rights)
USE Civil rights movements

Protest movements, War
USE Peace movements

Protestantism and Zionism
UF Zionism and Protestantism

Protests, Diplomatic
USE Diplomatic protests

Protracted conflicts (Military science)
USE Low-intensity conflicts (Military science)

Psychological warfare
[UB275-UB277]
Here are entered general works dealing with methods used to undermine the morale of the civilian population and the military forces of an enemy country.
UF War of nerves
BT War
SA subdivision Psychological aspects under individual wars

Psychology, Military
[U22.3]
UF Military psychology
BT Sociology, Military
NT Deterrence (Strategy)
Leadership
Prisoners of war—Psychology
Psychology, Naval

Psychology, National
USE National characteristics

Psychology, Naval
UF Naval psychology
BT Psychology, Military

Psychology, Political
USE Political psychology

Public finance
USE Finance, Public

Public opinion (May Subd Geog)
[HM261]
UF Opinion, Public
BT Political psychology
Political science
SA subdivision Public opinion under names of individual persons, corporate bodies, and topical subjects; also subdivision Attitudes under classes of persons and ethnic groups; also subdivision Public opinion or Foreign public opinion under individual wars; and subdivision Foreign public opinion under names of countries, etc.
NT Rumor

Public policy
USE Political planning

Public policy (International law)
BT International law

Public policy (Islamic law) (May Subd Geog)

Public policy experts
USE Policy scientists

Public policy management
USE Policy sciences

Public relations and politics
UF Politics and public relations
BT Communication in politics
Politics, Practical

Purges, Political
USE Political purges

Quakerism
USE Society of Friends

Quakers (May Subd Geog)
—Biography
UF Society of Friends—Biography

Race relations
BT Sociology
SA subdivision Race relations under names of regions, countries, etc.
NT Antisemitism
Culture conflict
Genocide
Pluralism (Social sciences)
—Religious aspects
For works limited to a place, an additional subject heading is assigned for the name of the place with the subdivision Race relations.
—Baptists, [Catholic Church, etc.]
—Buddhism, [Christianity, etc.]

Racism (May Subd Geog)
Here are entered works on racism as an attitude as well as works on both attitude and overt discriminatory behavior directed against racial or ethnic groups.
UF Race prejudice
BT Ethnocentrism
Prejudices
NT Antisemitism
Genocide
—Religious aspects
—Buddhism, [Christianity, etc.]

Radicalism (May Subd Geog)
UF Counter culture
BT Political science
NT New Left

Radio in propaganda
UF Propaganda in radio
BT Propaganda

Radioactive fallout (May Subd Geog)
UF Fallout, Radioactive
BT Atomic bomb
Hydrogen bomb
Radioactive pollution

Radioactive pollution (May Subd Geog)
UF Environmental radioactivity
Nuclear pollution
Radioactivity, Environmental

Radioactivity, Environmental
USE Radioactive pollution

Rangers (Military science)
USE Commando troops

Ransom (May Subd Geog)
BT Kidnapping

Rapacki plan
BT Europe—Politics and government—1945-
German reunification question (1949-)
Nuclear-weapon-free zones—Europe
World politics—1955-1965

Ratification of treaties
USE Treaties—Ratification

Reason of state
BT State, The
War and emergency powers

Rebellions
USE Civil war
Insurgency
Revolutions

Rebus sic stantibus clause (International law)
BT Treaties—Termination

Recognition (International law)
[JX4044; JX9574]
UF De facto government
Estrada doctrine
Nonrecognition of governments
BT International law
War (International law)

Reconciliation
UF Peace making
Peacemaking
—Religious aspects
—Baptists, [Catholic Church, etc.]
—Buddhism, [Christianity, etc.]

Reconnaissance, Aerial
USE Aerial reconnaissance

Reconnaissance, Military
USE Military reconnaissance

Reconnaissance, Naval
USE Naval reconnaissance

Reconnaissance, Photographic
USE Photographic reconnaissance

Reconnaissance aircraft (May Subd Geog)
[UG1242.R4]
UF Aircraft, Reconnaissance
BT Aerial reconnaissance
Airplanes, Military

Reconnaissance operations
USE subdivision Reconnaissance operations under individual wars

Reconstruction (1914-1939) (May Subd Geog)
BT International organization
International relations

Reconstruction (1939-1951) (May Subd Geog)
BT International organization
International relations
—Religious aspects
—Germany
NT Denazification

Recruiting and enlistment
[UB320-UB345; VB260-VB275]
UF Armed Forces—Recruiting, enlistment, etc.
Enlistment
BT Armies
SA subdivision Recruiting, enlistment, etc., under individual military services
NT Draft
Military service, Voluntary
National service

Reformation (May Subd Geog)
UF Church history—Reformation, 1517-1648
NT Peasants' War, 1524-1525
—Causes

Refugee governments
USE Governments in exile

Refugees (May Subd Geog)
Here are entered works that discuss collectively persons who have fled from their homes or countries to live elsewhere because of wars, natural disasters, political instability, religious persecution, etc.
NT Refugees, Political
Women refugees
—Government policy (May Subd Geog)
—Legal status, laws, etc. (May Subd Geog)

Refugees, Arab
UF Arab refugees

BT Refugees

Refugees, Jewish (May Subd Geog)
UF Jewish refugees
BT Refugees, Political
NT Holocaust survivors

Refugees, Political (May Subd Geog)
Here are entered works on persons who have fled their native land because of political persecution or instability.
UF Displaced persons
Political refugees
BT Refugees
SA subdivision Refugees under individual wars
NT Defectors
Governments in exile
Refugees, Arab.
Refugees, Jewish
—Legal status, laws, etc. (May Subd Geog)

Refugees, Religious (May Subd Geog)
UF Religious refugees
BT Persecution
NT Emigration and immigration—Religious aspects

Refuseniks (May Subd Geog)
Here are entered works on Soviet citizens, especially Jews, whose applications for permits to emigrate from the Soviet Union have not been granted.
BT Jews—Soviet Union

Region of war
BT War (International law)
NT Theater of war

Regionalism (May Subd Geog)
BT Nationalism
—France
NT Occitan movement

Regionalism (International organization)
[JX1979]
BT International organization
NT European federation
Pan-Africanism
Pan-Americanism

Registration, Draft
USE Draft registration

Regression (Civilization)
UF Decline of civilization
BT Civilization—Philosophy

Rehabilitation, Political
USE Political rehabilitation

Relations among ethnic groups
USE Ethnic relations

Religion, Civil
USE Civil religion

Religion and communism
USE Communism and religion

Religion and international affairs
UF International affairs and religion
BT International relations
NT Christianity and international affairs

Religion and justice
[BL65.J87]
BT Justice and religion
NT Christianity and justice
Islam and justice
Justice (Jewish theology)

Religion and peace
USE Peace—Religious aspects

Religion and politics (May Subd Geog)
[BL65.P7]
UF Politics and religion

Religion and socialism
USE Socialism and religion

Religion and state (May Subd Geog)
UF State and religion
SA headings for individual religions and state
NT Civil religion
Government, Resistance to—Religious aspects Temporal power of religious rulers

Religions (Proposed, universal, etc.)
[BL390]
Here are entered works advocating or proposing a universal or world religion.
UF Universal religion

Religious ethics
[BJ1188]
UF Ethics, Religious
BT Ethics
SA headings for ethics of individual religions, e.g. Christian ethics

Religious tolerance (May Subd Geog)
[BR1610]
Here are entered general works on religious tolerance. Works on an individual religion's or denomination's position on the issue of religious tolerance are entered under this heading subdivided by the name of the religion or denomination.
BT Toleration
—Baptists, [Catholic Church, etc.]
—Buddhism, [Christianity, etc.]

Religious Zionism (May Subd Geog)
[DS150.R3-DS150.R39]
BT Judaism
Zionism

Reparations
Here are entered works on payment made by one country to another for damage during war.
BT Indemnity
SA subdivision Reparations under individual wars

Repatriation (May Subd Geog)
[JX4231]
Here are entered works which discuss the legal or administrative aspects of returning to a country of origin.
BT Emigration and immigration law
International law
SA subdivisions Forced repatriation and Refugees under individual wars
NT Aliens

Reports, Consular
USE Consular reports

Reprisals
[JX4486]
UF Countermeasures (International law)
BT Embargo
Privateering
War, Maritime (International law)
NT Retorsion

Representative government and representation (May Subd Geog)
[JF1051-JF1075]
UF Parliamentary government
Political representation
Self-government
BT Political science

Republics
BT Political science
NT Federal government

Requisitions, Military (May Subd Geog)
[JX5321; UC15]
UF Military requisitions
BT Indemnity
Martial law
Military art and science
War—Economic aspects
War (International law)
SA subdivision Confiscations and contributions under individual wars
NT Military occupation damages

Requisitions (of neutral vessels and cargoes)
USE Angary, Right of
Contraband of war
Prize law
War, Maritime (International law)

Research, Military
USE Military research

Research, Naval
USE Naval research

Reservations to treaties
USE Treaties—Reservations

Resisters, Draft
USE Draft resisters

Restitution and indemnification claims (1933-) (May Subd Geog)
Here are entered works on the restoration to the original owners or their successors of property confiscated or involuntarily transferred under the Nazi regime in

Germany, the Fascist regime in Italy, or during the second World War, in countries under German domination, and on the indemnification for the loss of property and other injuries suffered due to persecution.
UF Indemnification claims (1933-)
BT Claims
NT Holocaust, Jewish (1939-1945)—Reparations
Postliminy

Retaliation (Law)
USE Lex talionis

Retorsion
UF Retortion
BT Reprisals

Retortion
USE Retorsion

Return migration (May Subd Geog)
Here are entered works which discuss the social or demographic aspects of emigrants' return to their country of origin.
UF Migration, Return
BT Emigration and immigration

Returned prisoners of war
USE Ex-prisoners of war

Reunification of China question, 1949-
USE Chinese reunification question, 1949-

Reunification of Germany, Proposed (1949-)
USE German reunification question (1949-)

Reunification of Korea (1945-)
USE Korean reunification question (1945-)

Reunification of Vietnam (1954-1976)
USE Vietnamese reunification question (1954-1976)

Revenge
[BF637.R48; BV4627.R4]
UF Vengeance
NT Lex talionis

Revision of treaties
USE Treaties—Revision

Revolutionaries
USE Revolutionists

Revolutionary ballads and songs (May Subd Geog)
BT Revolutionary poetry
War-songs

Revolutionary literature (May Subd Geog)
This heading may be used with the following qualifiers: African (Portuguese); Cuban; English; French; German; Greek (Modern); Indonesian; Italian; Latin American; Philippine; Philippine (English); Polish; Portuguese; Salvadoran; Spanish; Vietnamese; Yugoslav.
BT Literature and revolutions

Revolutionary poetry
This heading may be used with the following qualifiers and subdivided further by place: African (Portuguese); Algerian (French); American; Brazilian; Bulgarian; Canadian; Chinese; Colombian; Croatian; Dominica; English; French; Georgian; Ghanian (English); Grenadian (English); Guinean (French); Guyanese; Hindi; Hungarian; Italian; Japanese; Latin American; Macedonian; Mexican; Nicaraguan; Nigerian (English); Norwegian, Persian; Polish; Puerto Rican; Romanian; Russian; Serbian; Slovenian; Somali; South African (English); Spanish American; Telegu; West Indian (English); Yugoslav; Zimbabwean (English).
NT Revolutionary ballads and songs

Revolutionary women
USE Women revolutionists

Revolutionists (May Subd Geog)
UF Revolutionaries
NT Women revolutionists

Revolutionists in literature

Revolutionists' wives (May Subd Geog)

Revolutions (May Subd Geog)
[HM281-HM283; JC491]
UF Insurrections
Political violence
Rebellions
BT Political science
War
SA subdivision History—Revolution, [date] under names of countries, etc.
NT Civil war
Counterrevolutions
Coups d'état
De facto doctrine
Imaginary revolutions
Insurgency
Legitimacy of governments
National liberation movements
Peasant uprisings
Permanent revolution theory
State of siege
—Philosophy
—Religious aspects
—Buddhism, [Christianity, etc.]

Revolutions, Imaginary
USE Imaginary revolutions

Revolutions and art
USE Art and revolutions

Revolutions and literature
USE Literature and revolutions

Revolutions and socialism (May Subd Geog)
[HX550.R48]
UF Socialism and revolutions
NT Permanent revolution theory

Revolutions and the arts
USE Arts and revolutions

Revolutions in motion pictures

Resistance to government
USE Government, Resistance to

Right (Political science)
USE Right and left (Political science)

Right and left (Political science)
UF Left (Political science)
Right (Political science)
BT Political science

Right and wrong
[BJ1410-BJ1418]
BT Ethics

Right of angary
USE Angary, Right of

Right of asylum
USE Asylum, Right of

Right of search
USE Search, Right of

Right to know
USE Freedom of information

Righteous Gentiles in the Holocaust (May Subd Geog)
UF Righteous of the nations (Judaism)
BT Holocaust, Jewish (1939-1945)

Rights, Human
USE Human rights

Rights of man
USE Human rights

River warfare
USE Riverine operations

Riverine operations (May Subd Geog)
Here are entered works on operations conducted by military forces organized to cope with and exploit the unique characteristics of a riverine area, to locate and destroy hostile forces, and/or to achieve or maintain control of the riverine area.
UF River warfare
Warfare, Riverine
BT Naval art and science
SA subdivision Riverine operations under individual wars

Rivers, Right of navigation of
USE International rivers

Rockets (Aeronautics)
UF Aerial rockets
NT Ballistic missiles

Rockets (Ordnance)
[UF767]
UF Aerial rockets
NT Guided missiles
Surface-to-surface missiles

Air-to-air rockets

Roman Catholic Church
USE Catholic Church

Roman emperor worship
USE Emperor worship, Roman

Roman emperors
BT Emperors

Royal visits
USE Visits of state

Rule of 1756 (International law)
BT Continuous voyages (International law)
Unneutral service

Rulers
USE Emperors
Kings and rulers

Rumor
BT Propaganda
Public opinion

SDI (Ballistic missile defense system)
USE Strategic Defense Initiative

Sabotage (May Subd Geog)
UF Political violence
BT Subversive activities
Terrorism

Sale of military equipment
USE Military assistance
Munitions

SAM
USE Surface-to-air missiles

Safe-conducts
[JX5151]
BT War (International law)

Sailors
USE Seamen

Samizdat
USE Underground literature—Soviet Union

Sanctions, Economic
USE Economic sanctions

Sanctions (International law)
[JX1246; JX1975.6]
UF Penalties (International law)
BT International law
War (International law)
SA subdivision Sanctions under names of international organizations of nations
NT Blockade
Economic sanctions
Embargo
International police

Sanctuary (Law)
USE Asylum, Right of

Sanctuary movement (May Subd Geog)
Here are entered works on American religious congregations that publicly give shelter to illegal aliens or refugees from Central America.
UF Movement, Sanctuary
BT Asylum, Right of—United States

Satyagraha
USE Passive resistance

Scandinavian cooperation
BT European cooperation
International cooperation

Scandinavianism
[DL57]

Schleswig-Holstein question

Schlieffen Plan
BT Strategy

Scuttling of warships
USE Warships, Scuttling of

Sea control
Here are entered works on the strategic and tactical employment of land or sea-based forces of a country at the time its maritime interests are threatened, so as to gain or exploit control of the sea or deny its use to the enemy.
UF Control of the sea
BT Naval art and science
Naval strategy
Naval tactics
Sea-power
Strategy
Tactics
NT Naval battles
Submarine warfare

Sea-power (May Subd Geog)
Here are entered works on long term questions of naval strength, including weapons, installations, national resources, etc., allowing a country to maintain control of the sea and the air space above.
UF Naval policy
SA subdivision History, Naval under names of countries; and names of individual navies
NT Freedom of the seas
Naval battles
Naval strategy
Sea control
Warships

Seamen (May Subd Geog)
UF Sailors
BT Naval biography

Search, Right of
[JX5268]
UF Right of search
BT Blockade
Neutrality
Privateering
War, Maritime (International law)
NT Contraband of war

Seas, Freedom of the
USE Freedom of the seas

Sebastianism
[DP165]
BT Messianism, Political

Secrecy in government
USE Official secrets

Secret defense information
USE Defense information, Classified

Secret service (May Subd Geog)
[HV7961]
SA subdivision Secret service under individual wars
NT Espionage

Secrets, Official
USE Official secrets

Secrets of state
USE Official secrets

Sects, Christian
USE Christian sects

Security, Internal
USE Internal security

Security, International
[JX1901-JX1995]
UF Collective security
International security
BT International relations
Peaceful change (International relations)
NT Arms control
International police
Mutual security program, 1951-
Neutrality
Security Assistance Program

Security Assistance Program
[UA12]
BT Military assistance, American
Security, International

Security offenses
USE Subversive activities

Sedition (May Subd Geog)
BT Political crimes and offenses
Subversive activities
NT Trials (Sedition)
BT Freedom of speech
Subversive activities

Seizure of vessels and cargoes
UF Cargoes, Seizure of
Vessels, Seizure of
BT Jurisdiction over ships at sea
NT Angary, Right of
Capture at sea
Contraband of war
Search, Right of
Unneutral service
War, Maritime (International law)

Selective conscientious objection (May Subd

Geog)
Here are entered works on refusal to participate in a particular military conflict considered immoral without also refusing to participate in other military operations.
BT Conscientious objection

Selective service
USE Draft

Selective service registration
USE Draft registration

Self-defense (International law)
[JX4071-JX4077]
BT International law
War (International law)

Self-defense (Islamic law) (May Subd Geog)

Self-determination, National
[JX4054]
UF National self-determination
BT Allegiance
Citizenship
Nationalism

Self-government
USE Autonomy
Democracy
Representative government and representation

Self-protective behavior (May Subd Geog)
[BF697.5.S45]
UF Behavior, Self-protective
BT Human behavior

Separate development (Race relations)
USE Apartheid

Separation of powers (May Subd Geog)
Here are entered works on the division of powers between the executive, legislative, and judicial branches of government.
UF Powers, Separation of
BT Executive power
Legislative power
Political science

Servitudes (International law)
[JX4068.S5]
BT International law
Protectorates
Sovereignty

Shi'ah (May Subd Geog)
[BP192-BP194.9]
BT Islamic sects
—Doctrines

Shiites (May Subd Geog)
[BP193]

Shinto (May Subd Geog)
—Doctrines
NT Man (Shinto)

Shinto and state
[BL2223.S8]
UF State and Shinto
BT Religion and state

Ships, Requisition of
USE Angary, Right of
Contraband of war
Prize law
War, Maritime (International law)

Shooting Down of Korean Air Lines Flight 007, 1983
USE Korean Air Lines Incident, 1983

Siege, State of
USE State of siege

Sieges (May Subd Geog)
[JX5117]
Here are entered historical works on sieges.
BT Military art and science
Military history
War
SA subdivision History—Siege, [date] under names of countries, cities, etc., and subdivisions Siege, [date] or Sieges under names of castles, forts, etc.
NT Battles
Bombardment
Capitulations, Military
Embassy buildings—Takeovers

Sikh ethics
[BJ1290.5]
UF Ethics, Sikh

Sikhism (May Subd Geog)
—Doctrines
NT Man (Sikhism)

Sister cities
Here are entered general works on the concept of sister cities. Works on individual sister cities are entered under the names of the individual cities with appropriate topical subdivision, with an additional entry under the heading Sister cities.
UF Partner cities

Size of states
USE States, Size of

Slavophilism
[DK38]

Small nations
USE States, Small

Small states
USE States, Small

Small wars
USE Low-intensity conflicts (Military science)

Smuggling of drugs
USE Drug traffic

Social ethics
[HM216]
UF Ethics, Social
BT Ethics
NT Communist ethics
Fascist ethics
Political ethics
Socialist ethics

Social movements (May Subd Geog)
NT Anti-imperialist movements
Antinuclear movement
Civil rights movement
New Left
Peace movements
White supremacy movements

Social progress
USE Progress

Social service, Military
USE Military social work

Social stability (May Subd Geog)
UF Stability, Social
BT Sociology

Socialism (May Subd Geog)
Here are entered works on a variety of social and political doctrines or movements which advocate collective ownership of the means of production, a more equitable distribution of wealth, and democratic processes for achieving these ends, and which, in Marxist theory, represent the transitional stage between capitalism and communism.
[HX1-HX550]
UF Marxism
Socialist movements
BT Collectivism
Democracy
NT Communist state
Dialectical materialism
Marxian economics
People's democracies
Permanent revolution theory

Socialism and antisemitism
UF Antisemitism and socialism

Socialism and Catholic Church (May Subd Geog)
[BX1396.3]
UF Catholic Church and socialism
BT Socialism and Christianity

Socialism and Christianity (May Subd Geog)
UF Christianity and socialism
NT Socialism and Catholic Church

Socialism and civil rights
USE Civil rights and socialism

Socialism and Hinduism
UF Hinduism and socialism

Socialism and Islam
[HX550.I8]
UF Islam and socialism

Socialism and international law
USE International law and socialism

Socialism and Judaism
[HX550.J4]
UF Judaism and socialism

Socialism and liberty (May Subd Geog)
[HX550.L52]
UF Liberty and socialism

Socialism and nationalism
USE Nationalism and socialism

Socialism and religion (May Subd Geog)
UF Religion and socialism

Socialism and society
[HX542]
UF Society and socialism

Socialism and youth (May Subd Geog)
UF Communism and youth
Youth and socialism

Socialism and war
USE War and socialism

Socialist ethics
[BJ1388]
UF Ethics, Socialist
BT Ethics
Social ethics

Socialist movements
USE Socialism

Socialists (May Subd Geog)
[HX23]

Society and communism
USE Communism and society

Society and socialism
USE Socialism and society

Society and war
USE War and society

Society of Friends (May Subd Geog)
The subdivisions printed under Catholic Church may be used under this heading.
UF Quakerism
BT Christian sects
—Biography
USE Quakers—Biography
—Doctrines

Society of Friends and world politics
[BX7748.I65]
UF World politics and the Society of Friends
BT Christianity and international affairs

Sociobiology
BT Man—Animal nature

Sociology (May Subd Geog)
Here and with local subdivision are entered works on the discipline of sociology. Works on the social conditions of particular regions, countries, cities, etc., are entered under the name of the place subdivided by Social conditions.
NT Communication
Conservatism
Equality
Ethnic relations
Individualism
Leadership
Polarization (Social sciences)
Political sociology
Power (Social sciences)
Race relations
Social ethics
Social stability
Subsidiarity

Sociology, Military (May Subd Geog)
UF Military sociology
BT Armed Forces
Armies
Peace
War
NT Civil-military relations
Militarism
Military policy
Morale
Pacifism
Psychology, Military

Soldiers (May Subd Geog)
[U1-U145; U750-U773]
BT Armed Forces
SA subdivision Military life under names of individual armies
NT Generals
Mercenary troops
Military biography
Missing in action
Women soldiers

Soldiers' songs
USE War-songs

South and north
USE North and south

South Asian cooperation
BT Asian cooperation
International cooperation

Sovereignty
[JX4041-JX4068]
BT International law
Monarchy
Political science
NT Act of state
Airspace (International law)
Autonomy
Condominium (International law)
Decolonization
Dismemberment of nations
Equality of states
Exclaves
Government liability (International law)
Guaranty, Treaties of
Immunities of foreign states
Internationalized territories
Jurisdiction (International law)
Legitimacy of governments
Mediatized states
Servitudes (International law)
State, The
—Cases

Sovereign immunity (International law)
USE Immunities of foreign states

Sovereignty, Violation of (May Subd Geog)
UF Violation of sovereignty
BT International offenses
Political crimes and offenses
NT Espionage
Subversive activities
Treason

Soviet military bases
USE Military bases, Soviet

Soviet Union specialists
USE Sovietologists

Sovietologists (May Subd Geog)
UF Kremlinologists
Soviet Union specialists
BT Area specialists

Space espionage
USE Space surveillance

Space law
UF Aerospace law
NT Airspace (International law)

Space surveillance
[UG1500-UG1530]
Here are entered works on the conducting of military surveillance from space.
UF Espionage, Space
Military space surveillance
Space espionage
Surveillance, Space
BT Astronautics, Military
Military surveillance

Space warfare
[UG1530]
Here are entered works on interplanetary warfare, attacks on earth from outer space, and warfare among the nations of earth in outer space.
UF Interplanetary warfare
Warfare, Space

Space weapons
UF Star Wars weapons
Weapons, Space
BT Munitions
Space warfare
Weapons systems

Space weapons (International law)

Special forces (Military science) (May Subd Geog)
UF Special operations forces (Military science)
BT Commando troops
Counterinsurgency
Guerrilla warfare
Military art and science
Special operations (Military science)

Special operations (Military science)
UF Unconventional warfare

BT Military art and science
NT Special forces (Military science)

Special operations forces (Military science)
USE Special forces (Military science)

Speech, Freedom of
USE Freedom of speech

Spheres of influence
[JV355; JX4021-JX4023]

Spies (May Subd Geog)
[JX5121; UB270; VB250]
UF Spying
BT Espionage
Military art and science
SA subdivisions Secret service and Under-ground movements under individual wars
BT Subversive activities
War (International law)
NT Agents provocateurs
Women spies

Spying
USE Espionage
Spies

Stability, Nuclear crisis
USE Nuclear crisis stability

Stability, Political
USE Political stability

Stability, Social
USE Social stability

Standing army
[U104]
BT Armies
SA names of individual standing armies

Star Wars weapons
USE Space weapons

Star Wars (Ballistic missile defense system)
USE Strategic Defense Initiative

State, Act of
USE Act of state

State, Communist
USE Communist state

State, The
[JC]
BT Sovereignty
NT Church and state
Governments in exile
Law and politics
Legitimacy of governments
—History of theories
USE Political science—History
—Origin
UF Origin of the state

State and church
USE Church and state

State and communication
USE Communication policy

State and Confucianism
USE Confucianism and state

State and Hinduism
USE Hinduism and state

State and Islam
USE Islam and state

State and Judaism
USE Judaism and state

State and religion
USE Religion and state

State and Shinto
USE Shinto and state

State and the press
USE Government and the press

State and Zoroastrianism
USE Zoroastrianism and state

State of siege (May Subd Geog)
UF Siege, State of
BT Martial law
Revolutions
War
War and emergency powers

State succession
[JX4053]
UF States, Creation of
Succession of states
BT International law

State visits
USE Visits of state

States, Buffer
USE Buffer states

States, Creation of
USE State succession

States, Divided
USE Partition, Territorial

States, Ideal
USE Utopias

States, New
UF New states
Young states
—Diplomatic and consular service
[JX1625-JX1699]
—Foreign relations
—Politics and government

States, Partitioned
USE Partition, Territorial

States, Size of
UF Size of states
BT Political science
NT Great powers
Middle powers
States, Small

States, Small
[JC365]
UF Nations, Small
Small nations
Small states
BT Political science
States, Size of
NT Neutrality

Statesmen (May Subd Geog)
NT Diplomats
Heads of state
Politicians

Stations, Military
USE Military bases

Stations, Navy-yards and naval
USE Navy-yards and naval stations

Stealth bomber
USE B-2 Bomber

Straits question
BT Eastern question (Balkan)

Strategic Defense Initiative
[UG740-UG745]
UF SDI (Ballistic missile defense system)
Star Wars (Ballistic missile defense system)
BT Ballistic missile defenses—United States

Strategic forces (May Subd Geog)
BT Armed Forces
Deterrence (Strategy)
Strategy
NT Bombers
Fleet ballistic missile weapons systems
Intercontinental ballistic missiles

Strategy
[U161-U163]
UF Military strategy
BT War
SA subdivision Strategic aspects under names of regions, countries, etc.
NT Air interdiction
Combined operations (Military science)
Defensive (Military strategy)
Deployment (Strategy)
Deterrence (Strategy)
Dropshot Plan
Limited war
Offensive (Military strategy)
Preemptive attack (Military science)
Schlieffen Plan
Sea control
Strategic forces
Tactics
Unified operations (Military science)
Warfare, Conventional

Strategy, Communist
USE Communist strategy

Student movements (May Subd Geog)
UF Activism, Student
NT Students—Political activity

Students (May Subd Geog)
—Political activity
BT Politics, Practical
Student movements

Students, Interchange of (May Subd Geog)
UF International exchange of students
BT Educational exchanges
Exchange of persons programs
International education
—Law and legislation (May Subd Geog)

Students and war
UF War and students
BT Sociology, Military

Submarine boat combat
[V214.5]
UF Combat, Submarine boat
BT Anti-submarine warfare
Submarine warfare

Submarine boats (May Subd Geog)
[V857-V859; VM365-VM367]
UF Submarines
BT Warships
NT Nuclear submarines

Submarine forces
[V857-V859]
BT Navies
Submarine warfare
SA subdivision Submarine forces under names of individual navies

Submarine mines
USE Mines, Submarine

Submarine warfare
[V210-V214.5]
UF Warfare, Submarine
BT Naval art and science
Sea control
War
War, Maritime (International law)
SA subdivision Naval operations under individual wars
NT Submarine forces

Submarines
USE Submarine boats

Subsidiarity
BT Political science
Sociology

Subterfuge
USE Deception

Subversive activities (May Subd Geog)
UF Security offenses
Unconventional warfare
BT Insurgency
Sovereignty, Violation of
NT Espionage
Sabotage
Sedition
Spies
Terrorism
Treason

Succession of states
USE State succession

Summit diplomacy
USE Summit meetings

Summit meetings (May Subd Geog)
Here are entered works on meetings of heads of government of great powers held to conduct diplomatic negotiations and ease international tensions. This heading may be subdivided locally by the name of the place where a particular summit meeting is held.
UF Summit diplomacy
BT Diplomacy
Visits of state

Sunnis
USE Sunnites

Sunnites
[BP175.S8]
UF Sunnis
BT Islamic sects

Superpowers
USE Great powers

Supersonic bombers
[UG1242.B6]
UF Intercontinental bombers
BT Bombers
NT B-2 Bomber

Supremacy of the civil authority
USE Civil supremacy over the military

Surface-to-air missiles
[UF625]
UF Ground-to-air missiles
SAM
BT Air defenses, Military
Antiaircraft missiles
Guided missiles

Surface-to-surface missiles (May Subd Geog)
UF Missiles, Surface-to-surface
BT Rockets (Ordnance)

Surrender
USE Capitulations, Military

Surveillance, Coastal
USE Coastal surveillance

Surveillance, Military
USE Military surveillance

Surveillance, Space
USE Space surveillance

Surveillance by border patrols
USE Border patrols

Tactical nuclear weapons (May Subd Geog)
UF Atomic weapons, Tactical
Nuclear weapons, Tactical
BT Nuclear weapons

Tactics
[U164-U167]
UF Military tactics
BT Military art and science
Strategy
War
SA subdivision Drill and tactics under names of individual military services
NT Air interdiction
Antiairborne warfare
Combined operations
Disengagement (Military science)
Envelopment (Military science)
Maneuver warfare
Military maneuvers
Naval maneuvers
Naval tactics
Sea control
Tunnel warfare
Unified operations (Military science)
War games

Takeover of embassies
USE Embassy buildings—Takeovers

Tank warfare
UF Antitank warfare
BT War
SA subdivision Tank warfare under individual wars

Tanks (Military science) (May Subd Geog)
BT Vehicles, Military

Taoism (May Subd Geog)
—Doctrines

Taoist ethics
[BJ1290.8]
UF Ethics, Taoist

Targeting (Nuclear strategy)
UF Nuclear targeting
Nuclear warfare—Targeting
BT Nuclear warfare
First strike (Nuclear strategy)

Technical assistance (May Subd Geog)
This heading may be used with the following qualifiers and subdivided further by place to indicate the region or country offering the assistance and the place receiving it: American; Australian; Austrian; Belgian; Brazilian; British; Canadian; Chinese; Communist; Cuban; Danish; Dutch; Egyptian; Finnish; French; German; Hungarian; Israeli; Italian; Japanese; Latin American; New Zealand; Norwegian; Scandinavian; Soviet; Spanish; Swiss; Venezuelan; West German.
UF Foreign aid program
Foreign assistance
BT Economic assistance
Government missions
International cooperation
International economic relations
National service

Technical assistance, American (May Subd Geog)

UF Point four program Technical assistance, American—Europe

—Europe
USE Technical assistance, American

—Asia, Southeastern
NT Colombo plan

Technology and international affairs
UF International affairs and technology
NT Technology transfer

Technology transfer (May Subd Geog)
This heading may be subdivided by the region or country receiving the technology. Where applicable, an additional heading may be used with subdivision for the region or country transferring the technology.
UF Transfer of technology
BT Technology and international affairs
NT Nuclear nonproliferation

Teenagers and peace (May Subd Geog)
UF Peace and teenagers

Telecommunication, Military
USE Military telecommunication

Television in politics (May Subd Geog)
UF Television broadcasting—Political aspects
BT Politics, Practical

Television in propaganda
UF Propaganda in television
BT Propaganda

Templars (May Subd Geog)
[CR4735-CR4755]
UF Knights Templars (Monastic and military order)
BT Crusades
Military religious orders

Ten commandments
[BS1281-BS1285.5; BV4655-BV4710]
UF Commandments, Ten

—Murder
[BV4664]
UF Killing (Ten commandments)
Murder (Ten commandments)

Tenentismo
[F2537]
BT Brazil—Politics and government—1889-1930

Termination of nuclear warfare
USE Nuclear warfare—Termination

Termination of treaties
USE Treaties—Termination

Termination of war
USE War—Termination

Terrain study (Military science) (May Subd Geog)
BT Military art and science
Military reconnaissance

Territorial boundary disputes
USE Boundary disputes

Territorial expansion
USE subdivision Territorial expansion under regions and countries

Territorial partition
USE Partition, Territorial

Territorial waters (May Subd Geog)
[JX4122-JX4141]
UF Three-mile limit
BT International law
Jurisdiction, Territorial
Territory, National
NT Boundaries

Territoriality, Human
USE Human territoriality

Territories, International
USE Internationalized territories

Territories, Leased
USE Leased territories

Territories and possessions
USE subdivision Territories and possessions under names of regions and countries

Territory, Acquisition of
USE Acquisition of territory

Territory, National (May Subd Geog)
[JX4085-JX4150]
UF National territory
BT Geography, Political
International law
Political science
SA subdivision Territorial questions under individual wars
NT Acquisition of territory
Annexation (International law)
Boundaries
Jurisdiction, Territorial
Leased territories
Territorial waters

Terrorism (May Subd Geog)
[JX1981.T45; JX5420]
UF Political violence
BT Direct action
Insurgency
International offenses
Political crimes and offenses
Subversive activities
NT Bombings
Embassy buildings—Takeovers
Genocide
Hostages
Nuclear terrorism
Sabotage
Terrorists
Trials (Terrorism)

—Religious aspects
—Baptists, [Catholic Church, etc.]
—Buddhism, [Christianity, etc.]

Terrorism, Nuclear
USE Nuclear terrorism

Terrorism in art

Terrorism in mass media (May Subd Geog)

Terrorism in television (May Subd Geog)

Terrorism victims
USE Victims of terrorism

Terrorist bombings
USE Bombings

Terrorists (May Subd Geog)
BT Terrorism
NT Women terrorists

Teutonic Knights
[CR4759-CR4775; DK4600.P77]
BT Military religious orders

—Relations (diplomatic) (May Subd Geog)
—Treaties

Theater in propaganda
UF Propaganda in the theater
BT Propaganda

Theater of war
BT Region of war
War (International law)

Theological anthropology
USE Man (Theology)

Theology, Doctrinal (May Subd Geog)
[BT65-BT84]
Here are entered works on the doctrines of Christianity treated collectively.
UF Christian doctrine
SA subdivision Doctrines under individual Christian denominations
NT Bible—Theology
Freedom (Theology)
Liberation theology
Man (Christian theology)
Power (Christian theology)

Third parties (International law)
BT International law

Toleration
UF Intolerance
NT Religious tolerance

Tomb of the Unknowns (Va.)
BT War memorials—Virginia

Torture (May Subd Geog)

Torture (International law)
BT International law

Torture victims (May Subd Geog)
UF Victims of torture

Totalitarian ethics
[BJ1392]
UF Ethics, Totalitarian
BT Ethics

Totalitarianism
NT Communist ethics
Fascist ethics

Totalitarianism
[JC481]
Here are entered works discussing (in theory and in its various manifestations) a highly centralized government under the control of a political group permitting no rival loyalties or parties.
NT Authoritarianism
NT Communism
Dictatorship of the proletariat
Totalitarian ethics

Towns, Military
USE Military towns

Trade agreements (Commerce)
USE Commercial treaties

Trade balance
USE Balance of trade

Trade deficits
USE Balance of trade

Trading with the enemy
[JX5270-JX5271]
BT War (International law)

Trafficking in drugs
USE Drug traffic

Training camps, Military
USE Military training camps

Trans World Airlines Flight 847 Hijacking Incident, 1985
USE TWA Flight 847 Hijacking Incident, 1985

Transboundary pollution (May Subd Geog)
UF Pollution across boundaries
Transnational pollution

Transcultural studies
USE Cross-cultural studies

Transfer of population
USE Population transfers

Transfer of technology
USE Technology transfer

Transit by land (International law)
BT International law
Neutrality
War (International law)
NT Access to the sea (International law)
Passage of troops

Transnational corporations
USE International business enterprises

Transnational pollution
USE Transboundary pollution

Transportation, Military (May Subd Geog)
[UC270-UC360; VC550-VC580]
UF Military transportation
BT Communications, Military
Military art and science
SA subdivisions Transport of sick and wounded; Transport service and Transportation under names of individual military services

Treason (May Subd Geog)
UF Collaborationists
BT Political crimes and offenses
Sovereignty, Violation of
Subversive activities
SA subdivision Collaborationists under individual wars
NT Conspiracies
Trials (Treason)

Treaties
[JX120-JX191; JX195-JX1989; JX4161-JX4171]
UF Agreements, International
Conventions (Treaties)
International agreements
BT Diplomacy
International law
International relations
Negotiation
NT Alliances
Arbitration, International
Concordats
Executive agreements
Guaranty, Treaties of
Pacta sunt servanda (International law)
Pan-American treaties and conventions
Peace treaties
Treaty-making power
Unequal treaties
Uti possidetis (International law)

—Accession

—Collections

—Interpretation and construction
[JX4171.I6]

—Language
BT Languages—Political aspects

—Provisional application

—Ratification
[JX4171.R3]
UF Ratification of treaties

—Reservations
UF Reservations to treaties

—Revision
[JX4171.R45]
UF Revision of treaties
Treaty revision
BT Peaceful change (International relations)

—Termination
[JX4171.T5]
UF Termination of treaties
NT Rebus sic stantibus clause (International law)

Treaties, Pan-American
USE Pan-American treaties and conventions

Treaties of alliance
USE Alliances

Treaties of guaranty
USE Guaranty, Treaties of

Treaties of peace
USE Peace treaties

Treaty-making power (May Subd Geog)
BT Executive power
Legislative power
Treaties

Treaty revision
USE Treaties—Revision

Trials (Espionage) (May Subd Geog)
BT Espionage

Trials (Genocide) (May Subd Geog)
BT Genocide

Trials (Political crimes and offenses) (May Subd Geog)
BT Political crimes and offenses

Trials (Sedition) (May Subd Geog)
BT Sedition

Trials (Terrorism)
BT Terrorism

Trials (Treason) (May Subd Geog)
BT Treason

Trident (Weapons systems)
[V993]
BT Fleet ballistic missile weapons systems
Guided missiles
Nuclear submarines

Troops, Command of
USE Command of troops

Troops, Commando
USE Commando troops

Troops, Mercenary
USE Mercenary troops

Truce, Flags of
USE Flags of truce

Truces
USE Armistices

Trust territories
USE International trusteeships

Trusteeships, International
USE International trusteeships

Truthfulness and falsehood
[BJ1420-BJ1428]
UF Credibility
Lying
Untruthfulness
NT Deception

Truthfulness and falsehood (Islam)
BT Islamic ethics

Tunnel warfare (May Subd Geog)
UF Warfare, Tunnel
BT Tactics

SA subdivision Tunnel warfare under individual wars

Turkism
USE Pan-Turanianism

Turncoats
USE Defectors

TWA Flight 847 Hijacking Incident, 1985
UF Beirut Hostage Crisis, Beirut, Lebanon, 1985
Hijacking of TWA Flight 847, 1985
Hostage Crisis, Beirut, Lebanon, 1985
Trans World Airlines Flight 847 Hijacking Incident, 1985
BT Hijacking of aircraft—United States

Tyranny
USE Despotism

U-2 Incident, 1960
BT Military intelligence
Military reconnaissance

Ultimatums
BT Diplomacy
International law
International relations

Unconventional warfare
USE Guerrilla warfare
Subversive activities

Underground literature (May Subd Geog)
Here are entered works about publications issued clandestinely and contrary to government regulation.
UF Clandestine literature
Illegal literature
SA subdivision Underground literature under individual wars
—Soviet Union
UF Samizdat

Underground nuclear explosions (May Subd Geog)
UF Nuclear underground explosions
BT Nuclear weapons—Testing
—Detection
UF Detection of underground nuclear explosions

Unequal treaties
[JX4171.U5]
BT Treaties

Unification of Ireland
USE Irish unification question

Unified operations (Military science)
[U260]
Here are entered works on joint operations conducted by elements of more than one service of the same nation. Works on operations conducted by forces of two or more allied nations acting together for the accomplishment of a single mission are entered under Combined operations (Military science).
UF Joint operations (Military science)
BT Military art and science
Strategy
Tactics
NT Amphibious warfare

Unilateral acts (International law)
BT International law

Unilateral nuclear disarmament (May Subd Geog)
[JX1974.7]
BT Nuclear disarmament

Unit cohesion (Military science)
Here are entered works on the ability of military unit members to work well together and demonstrate loyalty to each other and their unit.
UF Cohesiveness (Military science)
BT Military art and science
SA subdivision Unit cohesion under names of individual military services

United Nations (May Subd Geog)
[JX1977-JX1977.8]
—Anecdotes
—Anniversaries
—Armed Forces (May Subd Geog)
UF Peacekeeping forces
—Buildings
—Caricatures and cartoons
—Commissions
—Discography
—Economic assistance
—Emblem and flag
—Environmental policy
—Film catalogs
—Finance
—Headquarters
—Humor
—Information services (May Subd Geog)
—International trusteeships
USE International trusteeships
—Juvenile literature
—Language policy
—Membership
—Non-governmental advisory organizations
—Observers
USE United Nations and non-member nations
—Officials and employees (May Subd Geog)
—Pictorial works
—Population assistance
—Postage-stamps
—Privileges and immunities
—Publicity
—Resolutions
—Sanctions
—Songs and music
—Specialized agencies
USE International agencies
—Statistical services
—Technical assistance
BT Technical assistance
—Treaty-making power
—Veto
USE United Nations—Voting
—Voting
UF United Nations—Veto

United Nations. General Assembly
—Proceedings
Here are entered works on the debates, business meetings, resolutions, documents, etc., of the U.N. General Assembly, treated collectively.

United Nations. Security Council
—Proceedings
Here are entered works on the debates, business meetings, resolutions, documents, etc., of the U.N. Security Council, treated collectively.
—Resolutions

United Nations.

Trusteeship Council
—Proceedings
Here are entered works on the debates, business meetings, resolutions, documents, etc., of the U.N. Trusteeship Council, treated collectively.

United Nations and learned institutions, societies, etc.

United Nations associations

United Nations and non-member nations
[JX1977.25]
UF United Nations—Observers

United Nations peace rug (Canvas embroidery)
UF Peace rug (Canvas embroidery)

United States. Air Force
For a list of subdivisions used under individual air forces, see the Introduction to this guide.

United States. Army
For a list of subdivisions used under individual armies, see the Introduction to this guide.

United States. Army Air Forces

United States. Dept. of Defense

United States. Marine Corps

United States. Navy
For a list of subdivisions used under individual navies, see the Introduction to this guide.

United States foreign relations specialists (May Subd Geog)
BT International relations specialists

United States Naval Expedition to Japan, 1852-1854
[DS809]

UF Perry's Expedition to Japan, 1852-1854

Universal religion
USE Religions (Proposed, universal, etc.)

Unneutral service
BT Neutrality
War, Maritime (International law)
NT Rule of 1756 (International law)

Untruthfulness
USE Truthfulness and falsehood

Uprisings, Peasant
USE Peasant uprisings

Uti possidetis (International law)
BT Boundaries
International law
Treaties
War (International law)

Utopias
[HX806-HX811]
UF Ideal states
States, Ideal
BT Political science

Vehicles, Military (May Subd Geog)
UF Military vehicles
BT Transportation, Military
NT Tanks (Military science)

Vengeance
USE Revenge

Verification of arms control
USE Arms control—Verification

Verification of nuclear arms control
USE Nuclear arms control—Verification

Vessels, Seizure of
USE Seizure of vessels and cargoes

Veterans (May Subd Geog)
BT Military art and science
SA subdivision Veterans under individual wars
NT Veterans, Disabled
Women veterans

Veterans, Disabled (May Subd Geog)
UF Disabled veterans
BT Veterans
War victims

Victims of terrorism (May Subd Geog)
UF Terrorism victims

Victims of atomic bombings
USE Atomic bomb victims

Victims of torture
USE Torture victims

Victims of war
USE War victims

Video war games
USE Computer war games

Vietnam Moratorium, October 15, 1969

Vietnam Veterans Memorial (Washington, D.C.)
BT War memorials—Washington (D.C.)

Vietnamese reunification question (1954-1976)
[DS556.9]
UF Reunification of Vietnam (1954-1976)

Violation of sovereignty
USE Sovereignty, Violation of

Violence (May Subd Geog)
UF Political violence
BT Aggressiveness (Psychology)
—Religious aspects
—Baptists, [Catholic Church, etc.]
—Buddhism, [Christianity, etc.]

Violence in literature

Violence in mass media
—Law and legislation (May Subd Geog)

Violence in motion pictures

Violence in television (May Subd Geog)
—Law and legislation (May Subd Geog)

Violence in the Bible
UF Bible—Violence

Visitors, Foreign (May Subd Geog)
UF Foreign visitors
International visitors
SA subdivision Relations under names of countries, etc.
NT Visits of state

Visits of state (May Subd Geog)
This heading is subdivided locally by the name of the place visited.
UF Royal visits
State visits
BT Visitors, Foreign
NT Summit meetings

Volunteer army
USE Military service, Voluntary

Voyages, Continuous (International law)
USE Continuous voyages (International law)

Walloon Movement
BT Belgium—Politics and government

War
UF Fighting
Wars
BT International relations
SA headings for individual wars, revolutions, etc.
NT Air warfare
Arms control
Battles
Biological warfare
Blockade
Chemical warfare
Civil war
Claims
Desert warfare
Disarmament
Escalation (Military science)
Guerrilla warfare
Imaginary wars and battles
Jihad
Jungle warfare
Limited war
Martial law
Militarism
Military policy
Mountain warfare
Naval art and science
Nuclear warfare
Psychological warfare
Revolutions
Sieges
Sociology, Military
State of siege
Strategy
Submarine warfare
Tactics
Tank warfare
Warfare, Conventional
Winter warfare
Women in war
—Biblical teaching
—Casualties (Statistics, etc.)
[D25.5; UH215]
UF War casualties
SA subdivision Casualties (Statistics, etc.) under individual wars
BT War victims
—Economic aspects (May Subd Geog)
[HB195]
Here are entered works dealing with the economic causes of war, and with the effect of war and preparation for war on industrial and commercial activity.
UF Defense economics
Economics of war
Industry and war
War and industry
SA subdivision Economic aspects under individual wars
NT Profiteering
War damage, Industrial
War damage to buildings
War finance
—Environmental aspects (May Subd Geog)
—Fiction
USE War stories
—Medical aspects
UF Medicine and war
SA subdivision Medical care under individual wars
—Moral and ethical aspects
SA subdivision Moral and ethical aspects under individual wars
NT Conscientious objection
Just war doctrine
—Mythology
—Poetry
USE War poetry
—Posters
USE War posters
—Protection of civilians

[JX5144]
Here are entered works on the rights, under international law, of civilians in the hands of belligerent powers, and on measures to protect such rights.
BT War (International law)
NT Open city (International law)

—Psychological aspects
BT Morale
SA subdivision Psychological aspects under individual wars
NT Psychological warfare

—Quotations, maxims, etc.
UF War proverbs

—Religious aspects
UF War and religion
SA subdivision Religious aspects under individual wars
NT Just war doctrine
—Baptists, [Catholic Church, etc.]
—Buddhism, [Christianity, etc.]
—Islam
NT Jihad
—Koranic teaching

—Social aspects
USE War and society

—Termination
UF Armed conflict termination
Termination of war

War (Greek law)

War (International law)
[JX4505-JX5326]
UF Hostilities
BT International law
NT Aggression (International law)
Air warfare (International law)
Arbitration, International
Armistices
Belligerency
Biological warfare (International law)
Bombardment
Booty (International law)
Capitulations, Military
Chemical warfare (International law)
Combatants and noncombatants (International law)
Confiscations
Crimes against peace
Cultural property, Protection of (International law)
Directed-energy weapons—Law and legislation
Flags of truce
Gases, Asphyxiating and poisonous—War use
Guerrillas (International law)
Hostages
Intervention (International law)
Levies en masse
Martial law
Mediation, International
Military law
Military necessity
Military occupation
Munitions—Law and legislation
Neutral trade with belligerents
Neutrality, Armed
Nuclear weapons (International law)
Open city (International law)
Passage of troops
Postliminy
Prisoners of war
Recognition (International law)
Region of war
Requisitions, Military
Safe-conducts
Sanctions (International law)
Self-defense (International law)
Space weapons (International law)
Spies
Theater of war
Trading with the enemy
Transit by land (International law)
Uti possidetis (International law)
War—Protection of civilians
War, Declaration of
War, Maritime (International law)
War crimes

War (Islamic law)

War (Jewish law)

War (Roman law)

War, Causes of
USE subdivision Causes under individual wars

War, Cost of
UF Cost of war
Economics of war
Finance, Military
BT Militarism
NT Armies, Cost of
Navies, Cost of
Profiteering
War finance

War, Declaration of (May Subd Geog)
[JF256; JX4552-JX4564]
UF Declaration of war
Hostilities
BT War (International law)

War, Incitement to
USE Crimes against peace

War, Maritime
USE Naval art and science
Naval battles
Naval tactics

War, Maritime (International law)
[JX5203-JX5268]
UF Hostilities
Maritime war
Naval warfare
Requisitions (of neutral vessels and cargoes)
BT International law
War (International law)
NT Angary, Right of
Blockade, Pacific
Bombardment
Continuous voyages (International law)
Contraband of war
Embargo
Freedom of the seas
Jurisdiction over ships at sea
Munitions—Law and legislation
Naval convoys (International law)
Neutral trade with belligerents
Postliminy
Privateering
Prize-courts
Prize law
Reprisals
Search, Right of
Submarine warfare
Unneutral service
Warships, Internment of

War (Philosophy)
BT Philosophy
NT Just war doctrine

War and children
USE Children and war

War and civilization
[CB481]
UF Civilization and war

War and crime (May Subd Geog)
UF Crime and war

War and education
UF Education and war
SA subdivisions Education and the war; Education and the revolution, etc., under individual wars

War and emergency legislation (May Subd Geog)
UF Emergency legislation
War legislation
SA subdivision Law and legislation under individual wars
NT War and emergency powers

War and emergency powers (May Subd Geog)
[JF256; JK339; JK560]
UF Emergency powers
War powers
BT Executive power
Legislative power
War and emergency legislation
NT Reason of state
State of siege

War and literature (May Subd Geog)
UF Literature and war
SA subdivisions Literature and the war; Literature and the revolution, etc., under individual wars
NT Nuclear warfare and literature

War and music
USE Music and war

War and politics
USE Politics and war

War and religion
USE War—Religious aspects

War and socialism (May Subd Geog)
[HX545]
UF Socialism and war

War and society
UF Society and war
War—Social aspects
BT Sociology
War
SA subdivision Social aspects under individual wars

War and students
USE Students and war

War and women
USE Women and war

War correspondents (May Subd Geog)
SA subdivision Journalists under individual wars
NT Journalism, Military

War crime trials (May Subd Geog)
[JX5433-JX5445]
UF Trials (War crimes)
BT War crimes

War crimes
[D625-D626]
BT Crimes against humanity
International offenses
War (International law)
SA subdivisions Atrocities and Destruction and pillage under individual wars
NT Guerrillas (International law)
Pillage
War crime trials

War criminals (May Subd Geog)

War damage, Industrial (May Subd Geog)
[UA929.5-UA929.9]
UF Bomb damage to industry
Post-attack rehabilitation of industry
BT War—Economic aspects
NT Atomic bomb—Safety measures
Civil defense

War damage compensation (May Subd Geog)
Here are entered works on indemnification of property owners by the government, through insurance or by other means, for damage suffered because of enemy attack or counter-measures against it.
NT Military occupation damages

War damage to buildings (May Subd Geog)
UF Bomb damage to buildings
BT War—Economic aspects
NT Housing—Effect of wars on

War films (May Subd Geog)
SA subdivisions Motion pictures and the war; Motion pictures and the revolution, etc., under individual wars

War finance
[HJ135]
Here are entered general works on the financing of war. War finance of individual countries is entered under Finance, Public subdivided by country.
UF Finance, War
BT Finance, Public
War—Economic aspects
War, Cost of
SA subdivision Finance under individual wars

War games
[U310]
UF Wargames
BT Military art and science
Military maneuvers
Tactics
NT Computer war games

War games, Naval
UF Naval war games
BT Naval art and science
Naval maneuvers
Naval tactics

War in art

War in literature
NT Battles in literature

War legislation
USE War and emergency legislation

War maps
USE subdivision Historical geography—Maps under names of countries and subdivision Maps under individual wars

War memorials (May Subd Geog)
BT Art and war
SA subdivision Monuments under individual wars
NT Holocaust memorials
—Virginia
NT Tomb of the Unknowns (Va.)
—Washington (D.C.)
NT Vietnam Veterans Memorial (Washington, D.C.)

War photographers (May Subd Geog)
UF Battlefield photographers
Photographers, War

War photography (May Subd Geog)
Here are entered works on photography in war for the purposes of historical documentation. Works on the military applications of photography, such as mapping, reconnaissance, training, etc., are entered under Photography, Military.
UF Combat photography
Photography, War
SA subdivision Photography under individual wars

War poetry
This heading may be used with the following qualifiers and subdivided further by place: American; Arabic; Australian; Canadian; Chinese; English; French; French-Canadian; German; Israeli; Latvian; Macedonian; Nicaraguan; Oriental; Polish; Provencal; Russian; Sinhalese; Slavic, Slovenian; Spanish; Tamil.
UF War—Poetry

War posters (May Subd Geog)
This heading may be used with the following qualifiers and subdivided further by place: American; Italian; Russian; Spanish.
UF War—Posters
SA subdivision Posters under individual wars

War propaganda
USE Crimes against peace
subdivision Propaganda under individual wars

War protest movements
USE Peace movements

War proverbs
USE War—Quotations, maxims, etc.

War relief
Here are entered works on official or private assistance to civilians during war time.
SA subdivision Civilian relief under individual wars

War resistance movements
USE subdivision Underground movements under individual wars

War-songs (May Subd Geog)
UF Battle-songs
Soldiers' songs
SA subdivision Songs and music under names of individual military services, individual wars, veteran organizations, etc.
NT Revolutionary ballads and songs

War stories
This heading may be used with the following qualifiers: American; Chinese; Cuban; English; German; Greek (Modern); Israeli; Japanese; Korean; New Zealand; Russian; Ukrainian.
UF War—Fiction
SA subdivision Fiction under individual wars

War victims (May Subd Geog)
UF Victims of war
NT Atomic bomb victims
Prisoners of war
Veterans, Disabled
War—Casualties (Statistics, etc.)
—Legal status, laws, etc. (May Subd Geog)

War widows (May Subd Geog)
[UB400-UB405]
UF Widows, War

War work
USE subdivision War work under individual wars

Warfare, Antiairborne
USE Antiairborne warfare

Warfare, Conventional
UF Conventional warfare
Nonnuclear warfare
BT Military policy
Strategy
War
NT Maneuver warfare
Nuclear threshold (Strategy)

Warfare, Maneuver
USE Maneuver warfare

Warfare, Primitive (May Subd Geog)
UF Primitive warfare
BT Military art and science

Warfare, Riverine
USE Riverine operations

Warfare, Space
USE Space warfare

Warfare, Submarine
USE Submarine warfare

Warfare, Tunnel
USE Tunnel warfare

Wargames
USE War games

Wars
USE headings for individual wars, battles, etc.
Military history
Naval history
War

Wars, Small
USE Low-intensity conflicts (Military science)

Wars in the Bible
USE Military history in the Bible

Warsaw Treaty Organization
—Armed Forces

Warships (May Subd Geog)
[V750-V980]
UF Naval ships
BT Naval art and science
Sea-power
SA name headings of individual ships
NT Battleships
—Law and legislation (May Subd Geog)
BT Naval law
—Visits to foreign ports
UF Naval visits to foreign ports
BT International law
International relations

Warships, Internment of
UF Internment of warships
BT Neutrality
War, Maritime (International law)

Warships, Nuclear
USE Nuclear warships

Weapons, Neutron
USE Neutron weapons

Warships, Scuttling of
UF Scuttling of warships
BT Naval art and science
Naval history

Watergate Affair, 1972-1974
[E860]
BT Corruption (in politics)—United States

Weapons
USE Arms and armor
Firearms

Weapons, Biological
USE Biological weapons

Weapons, Chemical
USE Chemical weapons

Weapons, Nuclear
USE Nuclear weapons

Weapons, Space
USE Space weapons

Weapons industry
USE Munitions

Weapons systems
BT Munitions
Ordnance
SA subdivision Weapons systems under the Armed Forces of individual countries and their branches
NT Arms control impact statements
Fleet ballistic missile weapons systems
Space weapons
—Maintenance and repair
—Production control

Western civilization
USE Civilization, Occidental

White Australia policy
Here are entered works on the restrictive Australian immigration policy designed to limit entry and settlement of non-Europeans in Australia.

White supremacy movements (May Subd Geog)
Here are entered works on social movements advocating the supremacy of the Caucasian race over other races.
BT Social movements

Widows, War
USE War widows

Will, General
USE General will

Winter, Nuclear
USE Nuclear winter

Winter warfare
[U167.5.W5]
BT War

Women—Political activity
USE Women in politics

Women and peace
[JX1965]
UF Peace and women

Women and the Armed Forces
USE Women and the military

Women and the military (May Subd Geog)
[U21.75]
UF Armed Forces and women
Women and the Armed Forces
BT Armed Forces

Women and war (May Subd Geog)
UF War and women
SA subdivision Women under individual wars

Women conscientious objectors (May Subd Geog)
[UB341-UB342]
BT Conscientious objectors

Women diplomats (May Subd Geog)
BT Diplomats

Women generals (May Subd Geog)
BT Generals

Women guerrillas (May Subd Geog)
BT Guerrillas

Women heads of state (May Subd Geog)
BT Heads of state
Women in politics

Women immigrants (May Subd Geog)
BT Immigrants

Women in combat (May Subd Geog)
BT Combat
Women soldiers

Women in politics
UF Women—Political activity
BT Politicians
NT Women heads of state
Women prime ministers
Women revolutionists

Women in war (May Subd Geog)
BT War
SA subdivision Women under individual wars

Women international relations specialists (May Subd Geog)
BT International relations specialists

Women political prisoners (May Subd Geog)
BT Political prisoners

Women prime ministers (May Subd Geog)
BT Prime ministers
Women in politics

Women revolutionists (May Subd Geog)
UF Revolutionary women
BT Revolutionists

Women in politics

Women soldiers (May Subd Geog)
BT Soldiers
SA subdivision Armed Forces—Women under names of countries and subdivision Participation, Female under individual wars

Women spies (May Subd Geog)
[UB270]
BT Spies

Women refugees (May Subd Geog)
BT Refugees

Women terrorists (May Subd Geog)
[HV6431-HV6433]
BT Terrorists

Women veterans (May Subd Geog)
BT Veterans

World and the church
USE Church and the world

World economics
USE Competition, International

World federation
USE International organization

World government
USE International organization

World history
BT History

World news
USE Foreign news

World order
USE International cooperation
International organization
International relations

World politics
Here are entered works on general political history and historical accounts of relations among the nations of the world. Theoretical works are entered under International relations. Works on the foreign relations of an individual country are entered under the name of the country with the subdivision Foreign relations. Works on the foreign relations between two countries are entered under headings of the type [place]—Foreign relations—[place] with an additional heading for the places in reverse order, e.g. 1. United States—Foreign relations—Soviet Union. 2. Soviet Union—Foreign relations—United States.
UF Colonialism
History, Political
International politics
Political history
BT Political science
SA subdivisions Foreign relations and Politics and government under names of countries
NT Afro-Asian politics
Christianity and international affairs
Détente
Great powers
Middle powers
Peaceful change (International relations)
Propaganda, International
World War III
—To 1900
—19th century
—1900-1918
—1900-1945
—20th century
—1919-1932
—1933-1945
—1945-
UF Coexistence
Peaceful coexistence
NT Cold War
Communist strategy
Dropshot Plan
—1945-1955
—1955-1965
NT Rapacki plan
—1965-1975
—1975-1985
NT Korean Air Lines Incident, 1983
—1985-1995

World politics and Confucianism
USE Confucianism and world politics

World politics and the Catholic Church
USE Catholic Church and world politics

World politics and the Society of Friends
USE Society of Friends and world politics

World War II Recorded History Collection
UF Library of Congress World War II Recorded History Collection

Written communication (May Subd Geog)
Here are entered works on written language as a form of communication or discourse.
BT Communication

Young Ireland movement
Here are entered works on an Irish nationalist movement of the 1840's that advocated the study of Irish history and the revival of Irish language as a means of developing Irish nationalism and achieving independence.

Young nations
USE States, New

Youth
—Political activity
BT Politics, Practical

Youth and peace (May Subd Geog)
[JX1965.5]
UF Peace and youth

Youth and socialism
USE Socialism and youth

Zionism (May Subd Geog)
BT Judaism and state
NT Christian Zionism
Israel and the Diaspora
Religious Zionism

Zionism and the Catholic Church
USE Catholic Church and Zionism

Zionism and communism
USE Communism and Zionism

Zionism and Judaism
UF Judaism and Zionism

Zionism and mass media
USE Mass media and Zionism

Zionism and Protestantism
USE Protestantism and Zionism

Zionists (May Subd Geog)

Zoroastrianism and state
[BL1590.S73]
UF State and Zoroastrianism
BT Religion and state

Part Two : Place Names

This section contains subject headings for place names, with an emphasis on the major regions and countries of the world. Other names of jurisdictions may be found in the Library of Congress name authorities list. The Library of Congress policy is to use the current name of a jurisdiction that has undergone name changes, unless the boundaries of the place have changed substantially. For example, materials about Ceylon may be found by looking under the current name for the country, Sri Lanka. If you are interested in locating materials about the political history, foreign relations, military history, or naval history of an individual region or country, you will find the appropriate subject headings in this section. The free-floating subdivisions under places listed in the Introduction may also be used under these headings.

Afghanistan
—Politics and government
—1973-

Africa
—Foreign relations (May Subd Geog)
—1945-1960
—1960-
—Politics and government
—1945-
—1945-1960
—1960-

Africa, Central
Here are entered works on the region of Africa that includes what are now the Central African Republic, Gabon, Zaire, and the Congo (Brazzaville).
UF Central Africa
—Politics and government
—1884-1960

Africa, East
Here are entered works dealing collectively with Kenya, Uganda, and Tanzania.
UF East Africa

Africa, Eastern
Here are entered works on the area extending from Sudan and Ethiopia to Mozambique.
UF Eastern Africa
—Politics and government
—To 1886
—1886-1918
—1918-1960
—1960-

Africa, French-speaking Equatorial
Here are entered works dealing collectively with Central African Republic, Chad, Congo (Brazzaville), and Gabon.
UF French-speaking Equatorial Africa
—Foreign relations (May Subd Geog)
—1884-1960
—1960-
—Politics and government
—1884-1960
—1960-

Africa, French-speaking West
Here are entered works dealing collectively with Benin, Burkina Faso, Guinea, Ivory Coast, Mali, Mauritania, Niger, Senegal, and Togo.
UF French-speaking West Africa
—Foreign relations (May Subd Geog)
—1884-1960
—1960-
—Politics and government
—1884-1960
—1960-

Africa, North
Here are entered works dealing collectively with Morocco, Algeria, Tunisia, and Libya.
UF Barbary States
North Africa

Africa, Northeast
Here are entered works dealing collectively with Sudan, Ethiopia, Somalia, and Djibouti.
UF Horn of Africa
Northeast Africa
—Foreign relations (May Subd Geog)
—1974-
—Politics and government
—1900-1974
—1974-

Africa, Northwest
Here are entered works on the area extending eastward from Morocco, Spanish Sahara, and Mauritania to include Libya and Chad.
UF Northwest Africa

Africa, Portuguese-speaking
Here are entered works dealing collectively with the countries of Angola, Cape Verde, Guinea-Bissau, Mozambique, and Sao Tome and Principe.
UF Portuguese-speaking Africa

Africa, Southern
Here are entered works on the area south of Zaire and Tanzania. Works on the Republic of South Africa are entered under South Africa.
UF Southern Africa
—Foreign relations (May Subd Geog)
—1975-
—Politics and government
—1975-

Africa, Sub-Saharan
UF Sub-Saharan Africa
—Foreign relations (May Subd Geog)
—1960-
—Politics and government
—1884-1960
—1960-

Africa, West
UF West Africa
—Politics and government
—To 1884
—1884-1960
—1960-

America
—Foreign relations (May Subd Geog)
—20th century
—Politics and government
—20th century

Angola
—Foreign relations (May Subd Geog)
—To 1975
—1975-
—Politics and government
—1855-1961
—1961-1975
—1975-

Albania
—Foreign relations (May Subd Geog)
—1944-
—Politics and government
—1912-1944
—1944-

American-Mexican Border Region
USE Mexican-American Border Region

Antarctic regions

Antilles, French
USE West Indies, French

Arab countries
Here are entered works treating collectively the Arabic speaking countries of Asia and Africa, or of Asia only. Works on the region consisting of Asia west of Pakistan, northeastern Africa, and occasionally Greece and Pakistan are entered under Middle East.
UF Arabic speaking states
BT Islamic countries
Middle East
—Civilization
USE Civilization, Arab
—Politics and government
—1945-
—Study and teaching (May Subd Geog)
UF Arabic studies

Arabia
USE Arabian Peninsula

Arabian Peninsula
Here are entered works on the countries of the peninsula of Southwest Asia, comprising Bahrain, Kuwait, Oman, Qatar, Saudi Arabia, United Arab Emirates, Yemen (Yemen Arab Republic), and Yemen (Yemen People's Republic).
UF Arabia

Arctic regions

Argentina
—Foreign relations (May Subd Geog)
—1817-1860
—1860-1910
—1910-1943
—1943-1955
—1955-1983
—1983-
—Politics and government
—To 1810
—1776-1810
—1810-
—1810-1817
—1817-1860
—1860-1910
—1910-
—1910-1943
—1943-
—1943-1955
—1955-
—1955-1983
—1983-

Armenia
Here are entered works on the historic kingdom and region of Armenia as a whole to 1920. Works on the parts of Armenia incorporated into other countries after 1920 are entered under the name of the individual region or republic.

Asia
—Politics and government
—1945-

Asia, Central
Here are entered works on the inland part of Asia, extending from the Caspian Sea in the west to, and including, northwestern China and Mongolia in the east, and from southern Siberia in the north to, and including, northern Iran and Afghanistan in the south.
UF Central Asia

Asia, East
USE East Asia

Asia, South
USE South Asia

Asia, Southeastern
Here are entered works dealing collectively with the mainland and insular regions of Asia lying south of China and east of India, including Burma, Thailand, Laos, Cambodia, Vietnam, Malaysia, Singapore, Brunei, Indonesia, and the Philippines.
UF Southeast Asia
Southeastern Asia
—Politics and government
—1945-

Asia Minor
USE Turkey

Atlantic Islands
USE Islands of the Atlantic

Atlantic Ocean

Australasia

Australia
—Foreign relations (May Subd Geog)
—1900-1945
—1945-
—Politics and government
—To 1900
—1901-1945
—1945-

Austria
UF Austro-Hungarian Monarchy
—Foreign relations (May Subd Geog)
—1519-1740
—18th century
—1740-1780
—1780-1790
—1789-1900
—1792-1835
—1815-1848
—1848-1867
—1867-1918
—20th century
—1918-1938
—1945-1955
—1955-
—Politics and government
—14th century
—16th century
—17th century
—18th century
—1740-1780
—1740-1789
—1740-1848
—1780-1790
—1789-1900
—1815-1848
—1848-1918
—1867-1918
—20th century
—1918-
—1918-1938
—1938-1945
—1945-

Austro-Hungarian Monarchy
USE Austria

Bahamas
—Politics and government
—1973-

Balkan Peninsula
UF Balkan States
—Foreign relations (May Subd Geog)
—20th century
—Politics and government
—19th century
—20th century

Balkan States
USE Balkan Peninsula

Baltic States

Bangladesh
—Politics and government
—1971-

Barbary States
USE Africa, North

Basutoland
USE Lesotho

Bavaria (Germany)
—Politics and government
—1777-1918
—1918-1945
—1945-

Bechuanaland
USE Botswana

Belgian Congo
USE Zaire

Belgium
—Foreign relations (May Subd Geog)
—1914-1951
—1951-
—Politics and government
NT Walloon Movement
—1814-1830
—1830-1914
—1914-
—1914-1951
—1951-

Benelux countries
Here are entered works dealing collectively with Belgium, the Netherlands, and Luxemburg.
UF Low countries

Benin
UF Dahomey
—Foreign relations (May Subd Geog)
—1960-
—Politics and government
—To 1960
—1960-

Berlin (Germany)
This heading is used for East Berlin, West Berlin, or both treated together. As a geographic subdivision, this heading is used directly.
—History—Blockade, 1948-1949
—Politics and government
—1945-

Biafra
USE Nigeria, Eastern

Bohemia (Czechoslovakia)
—Politics and government
—1848-1918

Bolivia
—Politics and government
—1825-1879
—1879-1938
—20th century
—1938-1952
—1952-1982
—1982-

Borderlands, Mexican-American
USE Mexican-American Border Region

Botswana
UF Bechuanaland
—Foreign relations (May Subd Geog)
—1966-
—Politics and government
—To 1966
—1966-

Brazil
—Foreign relations (May Subd Geog)
—1822-1889
—1889-1930
—20th century
—1930-1954
—1954-1964
—1964-1985
—1985-
—Politics and government
—1763-1821
—1822-
—1822-1889
—1889-
—1889-1930
NT Tenentismo

—20th century
—1930-1954
—1954-1964
—1964-1985
—1985-

British Isles
Here are entered works on the non-jurisdictional island group comprising the islands of Great Britain, Ireland, and smaller adjacent islands.

British West Indies
USE West Indies, British

Bulgaria
—Foreign relations (May Subd Geog)
—1878-1944
—1944-
—Politics and government
—1878-1944
—1944-

Burma
—Foreign relations (May Subd Geog)
—1948-
—Politics and government
—1824-1948
—1948-

Byzantine Empire
[DF501-DF649]
—Foreign relations (May Subd Geog)
—527-1081
—1081-1453
—Politics and government
—To 527
—527-1081
—1081-1453

Cambodia
UF Kampuchea
—Politics and government
—To 800
—800-1444
—1975-

Cameroon
Here are entered works about the United Republic of Cameroon, as well as works on the same territory when known by other names such as Cameroons or the German protectorate Kamerun.
—Politics and government
—To 1960
—1960-
—1960-1982
—1982-

Canada
—Foreign relations (May Subd Geog)
—1914-1945
—1945-
—Politics and government
—To 1763
—1763-1791
—1763-1867
—1775-1783
—1791-1841
—19th century
—1837-1838
—1841-1867
—1867-
—1867-1914
—20th century
—1914-
—1914-1945
—1945-
—1945-1980
—1980-

Caribbean Area
Here are entered works on the region that lies between continental North and South America and consists of the archipelago of the West Indies, the Caribbean Sea and the adjacent mainland regions, including Southern Mexico, the countries of Central America, Colombia, and Venezuela.
—Foreign relations (May Subd Geog)
—1945-
—Politics and government
—1945-

Catalonia (Spain)
—Politics and government
—19th century
—20th century

Central Africa
USE Africa, Central

Central African Republic
—Politics and government
—1966-1979
—1979-

Central America
—Foreign relations (May Subd Geog)
—1979-
—Politics and government
—To 1821
—1821-1951
—1951-
—1951-1979
—1979-

Central Asia
USE Asia, Central

Central Europe
Here are entered works on the area included in the basins of the Danube, Elbe, and Rhine rivers.
UF Europe, Central

Ceylon
USE Sri Lanka

Chad
—Politics and government
—1960-

Chile
—Foreign relations (May Subd Geog)
—1920-1970
—1970-
—Politics and government
—1565-1810
—1810-
—1810-1824
—1824-1920
—War with Peru, 1879-1882
—Revolution, 1891
—1920-1970
—1970-1973
—1973-

China
—Foreign relations (May Subd Geog)
—To 1644
—1644-1912
—20th century
—1912-1949
—1949-
—1949-1976
—1976-
—History, Military
—1949-
—History, Naval
—To 1644
—1644-1912
—1912-1949
—1949-
—Politics and government
—To 221 B.C.
—221 B.C.-220 A.D.
—221 B.C.-960 A.D.
—220-589
—581-907
—907-979
—960-1279
—960-1644
—1260-1368
—1368-1644
—1644-1912
—18th century
—19th century
—20th century
—1912-1928
—1912-1949
—1928-1937
—1937-1945
—1945-1949
—1949-
—1949-1976
—1976-

Colombia
—Foreign relations
—1974-
—Peru
NT Leticia Dispute, 1932-1934
—Politics and government
—To 1810
—19th century
—1810-
—1819-1831
—1832-1886
—1858-1861
—1861-1863
—1863-1885
—1886-1903
—20th century
—1903-1930
—1930-1946
—1946-
—1946-1974
—1974-

Common market countries
USE European Economic Community countries

Commonwealth of Nations
Here are entered works on Great Britain and the self-governing dominions.

Communist countries
[D847]
UF Iron curtain lands
Soviet bloc
—Foreign relations (May Subd Geog)
BT Communism and international relations

Congo (Democratic Republic)
USE Zaire

Congo Free State
USE Zaire

Costa Rica
—Politics and government
—To 1821
—1821-1948
—1948-1986
—1986-

Countries, French-speaking
USE French-speaking countries

Cuba
—Foreign relations (May Subd Geog)
—1959-
—Politics and government
—1810-1899
—1868-1878
—1878-1895
—1895-
—1895-1898
—1899-1902
—1902-1906
—1906-1909
—1909-1933
—1933-1959
—1959-
—Revolution, 1959

Cyprus
—Politics and government
—1960-

Czechoslovakia
—Foreign relations
—1945-

Denmark
—Foreign relations (May Subd Geog)
—1241-1397
—1448-1660
—1660-1814
—1766-1808
—19th century
—1814-1849
—1849-1866
—1866-1900
—1900-
—1912-1947
—1940-1945
—1947-1972
—1972-
—Politics and government
—1241-1397
—1448-1660
—1660-1814
—1766-1808
—19th century
—1814-1849
—1849-1866
—1866-1900
—1900-
—1912-1947
—1947-
—1947-1972
—1972-

Developing countries
Here are entered comprehensive works on those countries having relatively low per capita incomes in comparison with North American and Western European countries.
This heading may be subdivided by those topical subdivisions used under names of regions, countries, etc., and may be used as a geographic subdivision under those topics authorized for local subdivision.
UF Emerging nations
Third World
Underdeveloped areas
BT Economic development

DMZ (Korea)
USE Korean Demilitarized Zone (Korea)

Danzig-Westpreussen (Germany)
USE Prussia, West (Poland)

Dominican Republic
—Politics and government
—1844-1930
—1930-1961
—1961-

Dutch East Indies
USE Indonesia

East
USE Orient

East Africa
USE Africa, East

East Asia
Here are entered works dealing collectively with China, Japan, Korea, Taiwan, Hong Kong, and Macao.
UF Asia, East
Far East

East Germany
USE Germany (East)

East Prussia (Germany)
USE Prussia, East (Poland and R.S.F.S.R.)

Eastern Africa
USE Africa, Eastern

Eastern Europe
USE Europe, Eastern

Ecuador
—Politics and government
—To 1809
—1809-1830
—1830-
—1830-1895
—1895-1944
—1944-1984
—1984-

Egypt
—Foreign relations (May Subd Geog)
—19th century
—20th century
—1952-
—1970-1981
—1981-
—Politics and government
—To 332 B.C.
—332-30 B.C.
—30 B.C.-640 A.D.
—640-1882
—1882-1952
—1919-1952
—1952-
—1970-
—1970-1981
—1981-

El Salvador
—Foreign relations (May Subd Geog)
—1979-
—Politics and government
—To 1838
—1838-1944
—20th century
—1944-1979
—1979-

Emerging nations
USE Developing countries

England
—Foreign relations (May Subd Geog)
Here and with local subdivision are entered works on foreign relations between England and other parts of Great Britain prior to Union. Works on foreign relations between England and other countries are entered under Great Britain —Foreign relations. Works on relations between England and a specific country are entered under Great Britain—Foreign relations—[country] with an additional heading for [country]—Foreign relations—[Great Britain].
—History
USE Great Britain—History
—Politics and government
USE Great Britain—Politics and government

Equatorial Guinea
UF Spanish Guinea
—Politics and government
—1968-
—1968-1979
—1979-

Eritrea (Ethiopia)
—Politics and government

—1890-1941
—1941-1952
—1952-1962
—1962-

Estonia
—Politics and government
—1918-1940
—1944-

Ethiopia
—Foreign relations (May Subd Geog)
—To 1889
—1889-1974
—1974-
—Politics and government
—1889-1974
—1974-

Europe
UF Western Europe
—Foreign relations
—1815-1871
—1871-1918
—1918-1945
—1945-
—Politics and government
NT European federation
—476-1492
—1492-1517
—1492-1648
—1517-1648
—17th century
—1648-1715
—1648-1789
—18th century
—1789-1815
—1789-1900
NT Eastern question
—1815-1848
—1815-1871
NT Concert of Europe
—1848-1871
—1871-1918
—20th century
—1918-1945
—1945-
NT Rapacki plan

Europe, Central
USE Central Europe

Europe, Eastern
Here are entered works on the area east of the Oder and Neisse rivers extending south to the Adriatic.
UF Eastern Europe
—Foreign relations
—1945-
—Politics and government
—19th century
—1918-1945
—1945-

Europe, French-speaking
UF French-speaking Europe

Europe, German-speaking
UF German-speaking Europe

Europe, Northern
UF Northern Europe

Europe, Southern
UF Southern Europe

European Economic Community countries
Here are entered works dealing collectively with the member countries of the European Economic community as a geographic region. As a place name this heading may be used under topical subjects or may receive topical subdivisions.
UF Common market countries

Far East
USE East Asia

Finland
—Foreign relations (May Subd Geog)
—1917-1945
—1945-
—Politics and government
—1809-1917
—20th century
—1917-1945
—1945-

Flanders
Here are entered works on the Flemish region in its greatest geographical extension, from the French department of Nord north of Dunkirk, through the Dutch-speaking area of Belgium, including all the former lands of the county of Flanders, to the Dutch province of Zeeland south of the West Scheldt.
As a geographic subdivision this heading is used directly.

France
—Foreign relations (May Subd Geog)
—To 987
—16th century
—1589-1610
—1589-1789
—1610-1643
—1643-1715
—1715-1774
—1774-1793
—1789-1815
—1792-1815
—19th century
—1814-1830
—1815-1848
—1815-1870
—1830-1848
—1848-1870
—1852-1870
—1870-1940
—1914-1940
—1940-1945
—1945-
—1945-1958
—1958-1969
—1969-1981
—1981-
—History, Military
—1328-1589
—17th century
—1610-1643
—1643-1715
—18th century
—1715-1789
—1774-1793
—1789-1815
—19th century
—20th century
—History, Naval
—18th century
—19th century
—Politics and government
—To 987
—987-1328
—1226-1270
—1285-1314
—1316-1322
—1328-1589
—1422-1461
—1461-1483
—16th century
—1515-1547
—1560-1574
—1562-1598
—1589-1610
—1589-1789
—17th century
—1610-1643
—1643-1715
—18th century
—1715-1774
—1774-1793
—1789-
—Revolution, 1789-1799
—1789-1815
—1789-1900
—1799-1815
—19th century
—1814
—1814-1830
—1830-1848
—1848-1852
—1848-1870
—1852-1870
—1870-1940
—20th century
—1914-1940
—1940-1945
—1945-
—1945-1958
—1958-
—1969-1974
—1974-1981
—1981-

Francophone countries
USE French-speaking countries

French Guiana
—Politics and government
—To 1814
—1814-1947
—1947-

French Guinea
USE Guinea

French-speaking countries
UF Countries, French-speaking
Francophone countries

French-speaking Equatorial Africa
USE Africa, French-speaking Equatorial

French-speaking Europe
USE Europe, French-speaking

French-speaking West Africa
USE Africa, French-speaking West

French Sudan
USE Mali

French West Indies
USE West Indies, French

Gabon
—Politics and government
—1960-

Gambia
—Politics and government
—1965-

Gaza Strip
As a geographic subdivision, this heading is used directly.

German Democratic Republic
USE Germany (East)

German Federal Republic
USE Germany (West)

German-speaking Europe
USE Europe, German-speaking

Germany
Here are entered works on Germany for the pre-1949 period, the Territories under Allied Occupation, and East Germany and West Germany collectively for the post-1949 period.
—Foreign relations (May Subd Geog)
—To 1517
—1517-1648
—1648-1740
—1789-1900
—1848-1870
—1871-
—1871-1888
—1871-1918
—1888-1918
—20th century
—1918-
—1918-1933
—1933-1945
—1945-
—Politics and government
—To 1517
—843-1273
—1138-1254
—1138-1273
—1273-1517
—1298-1308
—1517-1648
—1648-1789
—18th century
—1740-1786
—1740-1806
—1789-1900
—19th century
—1806-1815
—1806-1848
—1815-1866
—1848-1849
—1848-1870
—1866-1871
—1871-
—1871-1888
—1871-1918
—1871-1933
—1888-1918
—20th century
—1918-1933
UF Weimar Republic, 1918-1933
—1933-1945
UF Third Reich, 1933-1945
NT Church and state—Germany—History—1933-1945
—1945-
NT Germany (East)—History—Uprising, (1953) (June)

Germany (East)
Here are entered works on the Democratic Republic, established in 1949, and works on the eastern part of the former jurisdiction, Germany.
UF East Germany
German Democratic Republic

Germany (West)
Here are entered works on the Federal Republic established in 1949, and works on the western part of the former jurisdiction, Germany.
UF German Federal Republic
West Germany
—Politics and government—1982-

Ghana
—Foreign relations
—1957-
—Politics and government
—To 1957
—1957-1979
—1979-

Gibraltar
As a geographic subdivision, this heading is used directly.

Golan Heights
As a geographic subdivision, this heading is used directly.

Great Britain
Here are entered works on the United Kingdom of Great Britain and Northern Ireland as well as works on the island of Great Britain.
—Colonies
The subdivisions listed below may be used under any heading of the type [country]—Colonies.
NT Imperial federation
—Administration
—Boundaries (May Subd Geog)
—Defenses
—Emigration and immigration
—History
—Race relations
—Africa
—America
—Asia
—Oceania
—Foreign relations (May Subd Geog)
—1066-1485
—1154-1399
—1422-1461
—1485-1603
—16th century
—1509-1547
—1558-1603
—1603-1625
—1603-1688
—1625-1649
—1649-1660
—1660-1688
—1660-1714
—1689-1702
—1689-1714
—18th century
—1702-1714
—1714-1727
—1714-1837
—1727-1760
—1760-1789
—1760-1820
—1789-1820
—1800-1837
—19th century
—1820-1830
—1837-1901
—20th century
—1901-1910
—1901-1936
—1910-1936
—1936-1945
—1945-
—History, Military
—Roman period, 55 B.C.-449 A.D.
—Anglo-Saxon period, 449-1066
—Medieval period, 1066-1485
—Tudors, 1485-1603
—Stuarts, 1603-1714
—18th century
—1789-1820
—19th century
—20th century
—History, Naval
—Tudors, 1485-1603
—Stuarts, 1603-1714
—18th century
—19th century
—20th century
—Politics and government
UF England—Politics and government
—To 1485
—449-1066
—1066-1154
—1066-1485
—1154-1189
—1154-1399
—1216-1272
—1272-1307
—1307-1327
—1327-1377
—1377-1399
—1399-1485
—1461-1483
—1485-
—1485-1509
—1485-1603

—1509-1547
—1547-1553
—1553-1558
—1558-1603
—1603-1625
—1603-1649
—1603-1714
—1625-1649
—1642-1649
—1642-1660
—1649-1660
—1660-1688
—1660-1714
—Revolution of 1688
—1689-1702
—18th century
—1702-1714
—1714-1727
—1714-1760
—1714-1820
—1714-1837
—1727-1760
—1760-1789
—1760-1820
—1789-1820
—1800-1837
—19th century
—1820-1837
—1837-1901
—20th century
—1901-1910
—1901-1936
—1936-
—1936-1945
—1945-
—1945-1964
—1964-1979
—1979-

Greece
—Foreign relations (May Subd Geog)
—To 146 B.C.
—1821-
—1821-1862
—1863-1917
—20th century
—1917-1935
—1935-1967
—1967-1974
—1974-
—Politics and government
—To 146 B.C.
—146 B.C.-323 A.D.
—1453-1821
—19th century
—1821-
—1821-1832
—1832-1862
—1863-1913
—20th century
—1913-1917
—1917-1935
—1935-1967
—1967-1974
—1974-

Greenland
As a geographic subdivision this heading is used directly.

Grenada
—Politics and government
—To 1974
—1974-

Guatemala
—Foreign relations (May Subd Geog)
—1945-
—Politics and government
—To 1821
—1821-
—1821-1945
—1945-1985
—1985-

Guiana
Here are entered works on the region between the Orinoco, Negro, and Amazon Rivers and the Atlantic Ocean, including Surinam, Guyana, French Guiana, southeastern Venezuela and northern Brazil.

Guinea
UF French Guinea
—Foreign relations (May Subd Geog)
—1958-
—Politics and government
—To 1958
—1958-1984
—1984-

Guinea-Bissau
UF Portuguese Guinea
—Politics and government
—To 1974
—1974-

Guyana
—Politics and government
—To 1803
—1803-1966
—1966-

Haiti
—Foreign relations (May Subd Geog)
—1804-1844
—Politics and government
—To 1791
—1791-1804
—1804-
—1804-1844
—1844-1934
—20th century
—1934-1977
—1971-1986
—1986-

Holy Land
USE Palestine

Holy Roman Empire

Homelands (South Africa)
UF Bantustans (South Africa)

Honduras
—Politics and government
—To 1838
—1838-1933
—1933-1982
—1982-

Horn of Africa
USE Africa, Northeast

Hungary
—Foreign relations (May Subd Geog)
—1849-1867
—1918-1945
—1945-
—Politics and government
—1683-1848
—19th century
—1849-1867
—1849-1918
—1867-1918
—20th century
—1918-1945
—1945-

Iceland
—Politics and government
—18th century
—19th century
—20th century

India
—Foreign relations (May Subd Geog)
—To 1765
—1765-1857
—1857-1919
—1919-1947
—1947-1984
—1984-
—Politics and government
—To 997
—997-1765
—1765-1947
—19th century
—1857-1919
—20th century
—1919-1947
—1947-
—1975-1977
—1977-

Indian Ocean Islands
USE Islands of the Indian Ocean

Indian Ocean Region

Indian sub-continent
USE South Asia

Indo-Pacific Region
Here are entered works on the combined regions of the Indian and Pacific Oceans, including the islands of the Indian Ocean, South India, Sri Lanka, the Malay Peninsula, Indonesia, the Philippines, and the Southwest Pacific islands.

Indochina
Here are entered works on the area comprising Laos, Cambodia, and Vietnam.

Indonesia
UF Dutch East Indies
—Politics and government
—1478-1798
—1798-1942
—20th century

—1942-1949
—1950-1966
—1966-

Iran
UF Persia
—**Foreign relations** (May Subd Geog)
—**To 640**
—**1941-1979**
—**1979-**
—**Politics and government**
—**20th century**
—**1925-1979**
—**1941-1979**
—**1979-**

Ireland
Here are entered works on the Republic of Ireland and on the island of the British Isles called Ireland.
—**Foreign relations** (May Subd Geog)
—**1922-**
—**Politics and government**
NT Home rule (Ireland)
—**To 1172**
—**1172-1603**
—**16th century**
—**17th century**
—**18th century**
—**1760-1820**
—**1800-1837**
—**19th century**
—**1837-1901**
—**20th century**
—**1901-1910**
—**1910-1921**
—**1922-**
—**1922-1949**
—**1949-**

Iron curtain lands
USE Communist countries

Islamic countries
[DS36-DS40]
UF Muslim countries
NT Arab countries
—**Civilization**
Here are entered works on the civilization of the Islamic countries in general, or during the pre-Islamic and modern periods only, as well as non-Islamic culture during the medieval period. Works on the Islamic civilization of the medieval period in the Islamic countries, or the Middle East, North Africa, and Arab Spain collectively are entered under Civilization, Islamic.
—**Study and teaching** (May Subd Geog)
UF Islamic studies

Islamic Empire
Here are entered works dealing with the Middle East alone, or the Middle East, North Africa, and Islamic Spain as a whole, during the period 622-1517.

Islands of the Atlantic
UF Atlantic Islands

Islands of the Indian Ocean
UF Indian Ocean Islands

Islands of the Pacific
UF Pacific Ocean Islands

Italy
—**Foreign relations** (May Subd Geog)
—**476-1268**
—**1268-1492**
—**1492-1559**
—**1559-1789**
—**1815-1870**
—**1849-1870**
—**1870-1915**
—**20th century**
—**1914-1945**
—**1922-1945**
—**1945-1976**
—**1976-**
—**Politics and government**
—**476-1268**
—**1268-1559**
—**1559-1789**
—**18th century**
—**1789-1815**
—**1789-1900**
—**19th century**
—**1815-1870**
—**1870-**
—**1870-1915**
—**20th century**
—**1914-1945**
—**1915-1922**
—**1922-1945**
—**1943-1947**
—**1945-**
—**1945-1976**
—**1976-**

Ivory Coast
—**Politics and government**
—**To 1960**
—**1960-**

Jamaica
—**Politics and government**
—**To 1962**
—**1962-**

Japan
—**Foreign relations** (May Subd Geog)
—**To 1600**
—**To 1868**
—**1600-1868**
—**1868-**
—**1868-1912**
—**20th century**
—**1912-1945**
—**1945-**
—**History, Military**
—**To 1868**
—**1868-**
—**1868-1945**
—**1945-**
—**History, Naval**
—**To 1868**
—**1868-**
—**Politics and government**
—**To 794**
—**To 1868**
—**794-1185**
—**794-1600**
—**1185-1333**
—**1185-1600**
—**1333-1600**
—**1336-1573**
—**1600-1868**
—**1868-**
—**1868-1912**
—**20th century**
—**1912-1926**
—**1912-1945**
—**1926-1945**
—**1926-1989**
—**1945-**
—**1989-**

Jerusalem
As a geographic subdivision, this heading is used directly.

Jordan

Kampuchea
USE Cambodia

Kenya
—**Politics and government**
—**To 1963**
—**1963-1978**
—**1978-**

Korea
Here are entered works on Korea as a whole for the pre-1948 period.
—**Foreign relations** (May Subd Geog)
—**1864-1910**
—**1945-**
—**Politics and government**
—**1392-1910**
—**1864-1910**
—**1910-**
—**1910-1945**
—**1945-1948**

Korea (North)
Here are entered works on the Democratic People's Republic of Korea, established in 1948.
UF North Korea

Korea (South)
Here are entered works on the Republic of Korea, established in 1948.
UF South Korea
—**Politics and government**
—**1948-1960**
—**1960-**

Korean Demilitarized Zone (Korea)
UF DMZ (Korea)
Neutral Buffer Zone, Korean (Korea)

Laos
—**Politics and government**
—**1975-**

Latin America
—**Foreign relations** (May Subd Geog)
—**1948-**
—**Politics and government**
NT Latin American federation
—**To 1830**

—**19th century**
—**1806-1830**
—**1830-1948**
—**20th century**
—**1948-**
—**1980-**

Lebanon
—**Politics and government**
—**1946-**
—**1946-1975**
—**1975-**

Leeward Islands (West Indies)
As a geographic subdivision, this heading is used directly.

Lesotho
UF Basutoland
—**Politics and government**
—**To 1966**
—**1966-**

Liberia
—**Politics and government**
—**To 1944**
—**1944-1971**
—**1971-1980**
—**1980-**

Libya
—**Foreign relations** (May Subd Geog)
—**1969-**
—**Politics and government**
—**1912-1951**
—**1969-**

Lithuania
—**Politics and government**
—**1918-1945**
—**1945-**

Low countries
USE Benelux countries

Madagascar
UF Malagasy Republic
—**Politics and government**
—**1947-1960**
—**1960-**

Malagasy Republic
USE Madagascar

Malawi
UF Nyasaland
—**Foreign relations** (May Subd Geog)
—**1964-**
—**Politics and government**
—**1964-**

Malay Archipelago
Here are entered works dealing collectively with the island region consisting of Indonesia, Philippines, Borneo, and New Guinea.

Malaya
Here are entered works on the Federation of Malaya prior to its merger into Malaysia in 1963, as well as the present mainland states of the country of Malaysia.
As a geographic subdivision, this heading is used indirectly through Malaysia.

Malaysia
Here are entered works on the country formed by the merger in 1963 of the Federation of Malaya, Sabah (formerly called North Borneo), and Sarawak.

Mali
UF French Sudan

Martinique
As a geographic subdivision, this heading is used directly.

Mauritania
—**Politics and government**
—**1960-**

Mauritius
—**Politics and government**
—**To 1968**
—**1968-**

Mediterranean Region
—**Foreign relations** (May Subd Geog)
—**1945-**
—**Politics and government**
—**1945-**

Mediterranean Region, Western
USE Western Mediterranean

Mexican-American Border Region
UF American-Mexican Border Region
Borderlands, Mexican-American

Mexico
—**Foreign relations** (May Subd Geog)
—**1821-1861**
—**1861-1867**
—**1867-1910**
—**1910-**
—**1910-1946**
—**1946-**
—**1946-1970**
—**1970-**
—**Frontier troubles**
—**To 1910**
—**1910-**
—**Politics and government**
—**To 1519**
—**1540-1810**
—**19th century**
—**1810-**
—**1810-1821**
—**1821-1861**
—**1861-1867**
—**1867-1910**
—**20th century**
—**1910-1946**
—**1946-1970**
—**1970-**

Middle East
Here are entered works on the region consisting of Asia west of Pakistan, northeastern Africa, and occasionally Greece and Pakistan. Works treating collectively the Arabic-speaking countries of Asia and Africa, or of Asia only, are entered under Arab countries.
UF Near East
—**Foreign relations**
—**United States**
NT Eisenhower doctrine
—**Politics and government**
—**1914-1945**
—**1945-**
—**Study and teaching** (May Subd Geog)
UF Middle Eastern studies

Mogul Empire

Morocco

Mozambique
—**Politics and government**
—**To 1975**
—**1975-**

Namibia
UF Southwest Africa
—**Politics and government**
—**1884-1915**
—**1946-**

Near East
USE Middle East

Nepal

Netherlands
UF Holland
—**Foreign relations** (May Subd Geog)
—**1556-1648**
—**1648-1714**
—**1648-1795**
—**1714-1795**
—**1778-1783**
—**1815-**
—**1830-1898**
—**1898-1948**
—**1948-**
—**Politics and government**
—**1477-1556**
—**1556-1648**
—**1648-1714**
—**1648-1795**
—**1714-1795**
—**1795-1815**
—**1830-**
—**1830-1898**
—**1898-1948**
—**1940-1945**
—**1945-**

Netherlands Antilles

Neutral Buffer Zone, Korean (Korea)
USE Korean Demilitarized Zone (Korea)

New Spain
Here are entered works on the viceroyalty of New Spain (1535-1821), the Spanish colonial territory comprising at its greatest extent, Mexico, the Caribbean Islands, Central America north of Panama, the coast of Venezuela, Florida, the present southwestern U.S., and the Philippines.

New Zealand
—Foreign relations (May Subd Geog)
—1945-
—Politics and government
—1972-

Nicaragua
—Foreign relations (May Subd Geog)
—1979-
—Politics and government
—To 1838
—1838-1909
—20th century
—1909-1937
—1937—1979
—1979-

Niger

Nigeria
—Foreign relations (May Subd Geog)
—1960-
—Politics and government
—To 1960
—1960-
—1960-1975
—1975-1979
—1979-1983
—1984-

Nigeria, Eastern
UF Biafra

North Africa
USE Africa, North

North America

North Atlantic Region

North Korean
USE Korea (North)

Northeast Africa
USE Africa, Northeast

Northern Europe
USE Europe, Northern

Northern Ireland
—Politics and government
—1969-

Northern Rhodesia
USE Zambia

Northwest Africa
USE Africa, Northwest

Norway
—Foreign relations (May Subd Geog)
—1808-1814
—1814-1905
—1905-
—1905-1945
—1945-
—Politics and government
—1030-1397
—1397-1660
—1397-1814
—1766-1808
—1814-1905
—1905-
—1940-1945
—1945-

Oceania
Here are entered comprehensive works on the islands of the Pacific Ocean belonging to the island groups of Melanesia, Micronesia, and Polynesia.
UF South Pacific Region

Oder-Neisse Line (Germany and Poland)

Orient
Here are entered works on the region that extends from the Mediterranean and Red Seas to the Pacific Ocean, encompassing the Middle East, South Asia, East Asia, Southeast Asia, etc., but excluding Siberia.
UF East

Ottoman Empire
USE Turkey—History—Ottoman Empire, 1288-1918

Pacific Area
UF Pacific Ocean Region

Pacific Ocean

Pacific Ocean Islands
USE Islands of the Pacific

Pacific Ocean Region
USE Pacific Area

Pais Vasco (Spain)
—Politics and government
—20th century

Pakistan
UF West Pakistan
—Politics and government
—1971-

Palestine
Here are entered works on the region on the eastern coast of the Mediterranean Sea that in ancient times was called the Land of Canaan, later the Kingdoms of Israel and Judah, and in modern times comprises the entire state of Israel, as well as the various disputed territories.
UF Holy Land
—History—Partition, 1947
—Politics and government
—1929-1948
—1948-

Panama
—Politics and government
—1821-1903
—1903-1946
—1946-

Panama Canal (Panama)

Papal States
—Politics and government
—1815-1870

Papua New Guinea
—Politics and government
—To 1975
—1975-

Paraguay
—Politics and government
—To 1811
—1811-1870
—1870-1938
—20th century
—1938-1954
—1954-1989
—1989-

Pays Basque (France)
UF Basque (France)

Persia
USE Iran

Persian Gulf

Persian Gulf Region
Here are entered works on the countries bordering the Persian Gulf, comprising Saudi Arabia, Iraq, Iran, and the Persian Gulf States.

Persian Gulf States
Here are entered works on the eastern Arabian countries of Bahrain, Kuwait, Qatar, Oman, and the United Arab Emirates.

Peru
—Foreign relations (May Subd Geog)
—1968-
—Colombia
NT Leticia Dispute, 1932-1934
—Politics and government
—To 1548
—1548-1820
—1820-1829
—1829-
—1829-1919
—1919-
—1919-1968
—1968-1980
—1980-

Philippines
—Foreign relations (May Subd Geog)
—1946-
—1946-1973
—1973-
—Politics and government
—1896-1898
—1898-1935
—1935-1946
—1946-
—1946-1973
—1973-

Poland
—Foreign relations (May Subd Geog)
—To 1572
—1572-1763
—1763-1796
—1918-1945
—History, Military
—1795-1918
—1918-

—Politics and government
—To 1572
—1572-1763
—1763-1796
—1796-1918
—1918-1945
—1945-
—1945-1980
—1980-

Polar regions
Here are entered works dealing with both the Antarctic and Arctic regions.

Portugal
—Foreign relations (May Subd Geog)
—17th century
—18th century
—19th century
—1910-1933
—1933-1974
—1974-
—Politics and government
—1580-
—1580-1640
—1640-1656
—1656-1683
—1706-1750
—1750-1777
—1777-1816
—1789-1900
—1816-1826
—1826-1853
—1828-1834
—1834-1853
—1853-1861
—1861-1889
—1889-1908
—1900-1910
—20th century
—1910-1926
—1910-1974
—1926-1933
—1933-1974
—1974-

Portuguese Guinea
USE Guinea-Bissau

Portuguese-speaking Africa
USE Africa, Portuguese-speaking

Prussia (Germany)
—Foreign relations (May Subd Geog)
—1688-1713
—18th century
—1740-1786
—1740-1815
—1786-1797
—1786-1806
—1806-1815
—1815-1870
—1848-1849
—17th century
—1640-1740
—1740-1786
—1740-1815
—1786-1797
—1789-1900
—1797-1840
—1806-1848
—1815-1870
—1840-1861
—1848-1849
—1848-1866
—1870-1947
—1918-1933
—1933-1945

Prussia, East (Poland and R.S.F.S.R.)
UF East Prussia (Germany)

Prussia, West (Poland)
UF Danzig-Westpreussen (Germany)
West Prussia (Germany)

Regained Territories (Poland)
USE Western and Northern Territories (Poland)

Rhodesia, Northern
USE Zambia

Rhodesia, Southern
USE Zimbabwe

Roman Empire
USE Rome

Romania
—Foreign relations
—To 1711
—1821-1914
—1914-1944
—1944-
—Politics and government
—To 1711
—1711-1821
—19th century
—1821-1866
—1866-1914
—20th century
—1914-1944
—1944-

Rome
UF Roman Empire
—Foreign relations (May Subd Geog)
—510-30 B.C.
—265-30 B.C.
—30 B.C.-284 A.D.
—30 B.C.-476 A.D.
—284-476
—306-363
—History, Military
—30 B.C.-476 A.D.
—510-30 B.C.
—265-30 B.C.
—30 B.C.-68 A.D.
—30 B.C.-284 A.D.
—30 B.C.-476 A.D.
—117-138
—284-476

Russia
USE Soviet Union

Sahara

Sahel
Here are entered works on the region of West Africa which exends from northern Senegal and southern Mauritania generally easterly to South Central Chad.

Scandinavia
Here are entered works on the region composed of Denmark, Norway, and Sweden, and sometimes expanded to include Finland and Iceland.
—Politics and government
—1945-

Scotland
—Politics and government
NT Home rule (Scotland)
—1371-1707
—16th century
—17th century
—1625-1649
—1649-1660
—1660-1688
—1689-1745
—18th century
—19th century
—20th century

Senegal
—Politics and government
—To 1960
—1960-

Serbia
—Politics and government
—1804-
—1804-1918
—1918-1945
—1945-

Seychelles
As a geographic subdivision, this heading is used directly.
—Politics and government
—To 1976
—1976-

Siam
USE Thailand

Sierra Leone
—Politics and government
—To 1808
—1808-1896
—1896-1961
—1961-

Silesia, Upper (Poland and Czechoslovakia)
—History
—Partition, 1919-1922

Somali
—Foreign relations (May Subd Geog)
—1960-
—Politics and government
—1960-

South Africa
Here are entered works on the Republic of South Africa. Works on the area south of the countries of Zaire and Tanzania are entered under Africa, Southern.
—Foreign relations (May Subd Geog)
—1948-1961
—1961-1978
—1978-
—History, Military

—1961-
—Politics and government
—To 1836
—1836-1909
—20th century
—1909-1948
—1948-1961
—1961-1978
—1978-

South America
—Politics and government
—1806-1830
—1830-
—20th century

South Asia
Here are entered works on the subcontinent of India, which in addition to India includes Afghanistan, Pakistan, Bangladesh, Nepal, and Bhutan on the mainland, and Sri Lanka and the Maldives in the Indian Ocean.
UF Asia, South Indian sub-continent

South Korea
USE Korea (South)

South Pacific Region
USE Oceania

Southeast Asia
USE Asia, Southeastern

Southeastern Asia
USE Asia, Southeastern

Southern Cone of South America
Here are entered works on the part of South America that includes Chile, Argentina, Uruguay, and southeastern Brazil.

Southern Europe
USE Europe, Southern

Southern Rhodesia
USE Zimbabwe

Soviet bloc
USE Communist countries

Soviet Union
UF Russia
—**Foreign relations** (May Subd Geog)
—To 1689
—1689-1725
—1689-1800
—1762-1796
—19th century
—1801-1825
—1825-1855
—1855-1881
—1881-1894
—1894-1917
—1917-
—1917-1945
—1945-
—1953-1975
—1975-1985
—1985-
—History, Military
—To 1801
—1801-1917
—1917-
—Politics and government
—To 1533
—1533-1613
—1613-1689
—1689-1800
—19th century
—1801-1825
—1825-1855
—1855-1881
—1881-1894
—1894-1917
—20th century
—1904-1914
—1917-
—1917-1936
—1936-1953
—1945-
—1953-1985
—1985-

Spain
—**Foreign relations** (May Subd Geog)
—1479-1516
—1516-1556
—1516-1700
—1556-1598
—1621-1665
—18th century
—19th century
—1808-1814
—1814-1886
—1886-1931
—20th century
—1931-1939
—1939-1975
—1975-
—History, Naval
—16th century
—17th century
—18th century
—Politics and government
—To 1479
—1479-1516
—1516-1556
—1516-1700
—1556-1598
—1598-1621
—17th century
—1621-1665
—1665-1700
—1700-1746
—18th century
—1759-1788
—1788-1808
—19th century
—1808-1814
—1813-1833
—1814-1868
—1833-1868
—1868-1875
—1875-1885
—1886-1931
—20th century
—1923-1930
—1931-1939
—1939-1945
—1939-1975
—1975-

Spanish Guinea
USE Equatorial Guinea

Sri Lanka
UF Ceylon
—Politics and government
—1978-

Sub-Saharan Africa
USE Africa, Sub-Saharan

Sudan
—Politics and government
—1956-

Sudan (Region)
Here are entered works on a region of north central Africa south of the Sahara and Libyan deserts and north of the rainy tropics, extending across the African continent from the west coast to the mountains of Ethiopia.

Sudetenland (Czechoslovakia)

Suez Canal (Egypt)

Surinam
—Politics and government
—To 1814
—1814-1950
—1950-

Swaziland
—Politics and government
—To 1968
—1968-

Sweden
—**Foreign relations** (May Subd Geog)
—1523-1654
—1523-1718
—1660-1697
—1697-1718
—1718-1814
—1792-1809
—1809-1818
—1814-1905
—1844-1857
—1905-1950
—1950-
—Politics and government
—1397-1523
—1523-1560
—1523-1564
—1599-1611
—1604-1611
—1632-1654
—1660-1697
—1697-1718
—1718-1772
—1718-1814
—1771-1792
—1789-1900
—1792-1809
—1809-1818
—1814-1905
—1818-1844
—1872-1907
—1905-
—1905-1950
—1950-1973
—1973-

Switzerland
—Foreign relations (May Subd Geog)
—1945-
—Politics and government
—1032-1499
—1499-1648
—1648-1789
—1789-1815
—1815-
—1848-
—20th century
—1945-

Taiwan
—Foreign relations (May Subd Geog)
—1945-
—History, Military
—1945-
—Politics and government
—To 1895
—1895-1945
—1945
—1945-1975
—1975-1988
—1988-

Tanganyika
Here are entered works limited in subject coverage to the historical, political, or cultural aspects of Tanganyika for the period before the merger of 1964. Works on other subjects relating to Tanganyika for any pre-merger period are entered under Tanzania.

Tanzania
Here are entered works on the jurisdiction of Tanzania formed in 1964 by the merger of Tanganyika and Zanzibar for all periods and subjects.
—Politics and government
—1964-

Thailand
UF Siam
—Foreign relations (May Subd Geog)
—To 1782
—Politics and government
—To 1782

Third Reich, 1933-1945
USE Germany—Politics and government—1933-1945

Third World
USE Developing countries

Tibet (China)
—Politics and government
—1951-

Togo
—Politics and government
—1922-1960
—1960-

Trinidad and Tobago

Turkey
UF Asia Minor
—Foreign relations (May Subd Geog)
—1918-1960
—1960-
—History—Ottoman Empire, 1288-1918
UF Ottoman Empire
—Politics and government
—19th century
—1829-1878
—1878-1909
—1909-
—1909-1918
—1918-1960
—1960-1980
—1980-

Uganda
—Politics and government
—1890-1962
—1962-1971
—1971-1979
—1979-

Ukraine
—Politics and government
—1917-
—1945-

Underdeveloped areas
USE Developing countries

United States
—Civilization
—To 1783
—1783-1865
—19th century
—1865-1918
—20th century
—1918-1945
—1945-
—1970-
—Foreign public opinion
NT Anti-Americanism
—Foreign relations (May Subd Geog)
—To 1865
—Colonial period, ca. 1600-1775
—Revolution, 1775-1783
—1783-1815
—1783-1865
—1789-1797
—Constitutional period, 1789-1809
—1797-1801
—1801-1809
—1801-1815
—1809-1812
—1809-1817
—War of 1812
—1815-1861
—1817-1825
—1825-1829
—1829-1837
—1841-1845
—1845-1849
—1849-1853
—1853-1857
—1857-1861
—1861-1865
—1865-
—1865-1898
—1865-1921
—1869-1877
—1881-1885
—1897-1901
—War of 1898
—20th century
—1901-1909
—1909-1913
—1913-1921
—1921-1923
—1923-1929
—1929-1933
—1933-1945
—1945-
—1945-1953
—1953-1961
—1961-1963
—1963-1969
—1969-1974
—1974-1977
NT Mayaguez Crisis, May 1975
—1977-1981
—1981-1989
—1989-
—Middle East
NT Eisenhower doctrine
—History, Military
—To 1900
—20th century
—Religious aspects
—History, Naval
—To 1900
—20th century
—National security
NT McCarthy-Army controversy, 1954
—Politics and government
—Colonial period, ca. 1600-1775
—French and Indian War, 1755-1763
—Revolution, 1775-1783
—1783-1789
—1783-1809
—1783-1865
—1789-1797
—Constitutional period, 1789-1809
—1789-1815
—1797-1801
—War with France, 1798-1800
—19th century
—1801-1809
—1801-1815
—1809-1817
—War of 1812
—1815-1861
—1817-1825
—1825-1829
—1829-1837
—1837-1841
—1841-1845
—War with Mexico, 1845-1848
—1845-1849
—1845-1861
—1849-1853
—1849-1861
—1849-1877
—1853-1857
—1857-1861
—Civil War, 1861-1865
—1865-1869
—1865-1877
—1865-1883
—1865-1900
—1865-1933
—1869-1877
—1877-1881

—1881-1885
—1885-1889
—1889-1893
—1893-1897
—1897-1901
—War of 1898
—20th century
—1901-1909
—1901-1953
—1909-1913
—1913-1921
—1919-1933
—1921-1923
—1923-1929
—1929-1933
—1933-1945
—1933-1953
—1945-
—1945-1953
—1953-1961
—1961-1963
—1963-1969
—1969-1974
—1974-1977
—1977-
—1977-1981
—1981-1989
—1989-

Uruguay
—Foreign relations (May Subd Geog)
—1904-1973
—Politics and government
—To 1810
—1810-
—1810-1830
—1830-1875
—1875-1904
—1904-1973
—1973-

Venezuela
—Foreign relations (May Subd Geog)
—1830-1935
—1958-
—Politics and government
—To 1810
—1810-1830
—1830-
—1830-1935
—20th century
—1908-1935
—1935-
—1935-1958
—1958-

Vietnam
—Politics and government
—1858-1945
—20th century
—1945-1975
—1975-

Wales
—Politics and government
NT Home rule (Wales)
—20th century

Weimar Republic, 1918-1933
USE Germany—Politics and government—1918-1933

West Africa
USE Africa, West

West Bank
As a geographic subdivision, this heading is used directly.

West Germany
USE Germany (West)

West Indies
Here are entered works on the extended archipelago that separates the Caribbean Sea from the rest of the Atlantic Ocean, and consists of the Bahamas and the Greater and Lesser Antilles.

West Indies, British
UF British West Indies

West Indies, French
UF Antilles, French
French West Indies

West Pakistan
USE Pakistan

West Prussia (Germany)
USE Prussia, West (Poland)

Western and Northern Territories (Poland)
Here are entered works which discuss the former German areas of Poland that lie east of the Oder-Neisse Line.
UF Regained Territories (Poland)

Western Europe
USE Europe

Western Mediterranean
UF Mediterranean Region, Western

Western Sahara
UF Spanish Sahara
—Politics and government
—1884-1975
—1975-

Yugoslavia
—Foreign relations (May Subd Geog)
—1918-1945
—1945-
—Politics and government
—1918-1945
—1945-

Zaire
UF Belgian Congo
Congo (Democratic Republic)
Congo Free State
—Foreign relations (May Subd Geog)
—1960-
—Politics and government
—1885-1908
—1908-1960
—1960-

Zambia
UF Northern Rhodesia
Rhodesia, Northern
—Foreign relations (May Subd Geog)
—1964-
—Politics and government
—To 1964
—1964-

Zanzibar
Here are entered works on the island of Zanzibar for all periods and subjects. Works on the jurisdiction of Tanzania formed in 1964 by the merger of Tanganyika and Zanzibar are entered under Tanzania.
As a geographic subdivision, this heading is used indirectly through Tanzania.
—Politics and government
—To 1964
—1964-

Zimbabwe
UF Rhodesia, Southern
Southern Rhodesia
—Foreign relations (May Subd Geog)
—1890-1965
—1965-1980
—1980-
—History, Military
—1965-1980
—Politics and government
—1890-1965
—1965-1979
—1979-1980
—1980-

Part Three : Wars and Other Conflicts

This section contains most of the Library of Congress subject headings for wars and other armed conflicts. Some conflicts with indigenous peoples and local uprisings of little national or international significance have been omitted. Individual battles have not been included. Free-floating subdivisions under individual wars, provided in the Introduction, may be used, as appropriate, with any of these headings.

Acarnanian Revolt, Greece, 1836
USE Greece—History—Acarnanian Revolt, 1836

Achinese War, Indonesia, 1873-1904
USE Indonesia—History—Achinese War, 1873-1904

Afghan Wars
UF India—History—Afghan Wars, 1838-1919

Afghanistan
—History
[DS355-DS371.2]
—Soviet Occupation, 1979-1989
[DS371.2]
UF Soviet Invasion of Afghanistan, 1979-1989

Albania
—History
[DR927-DR977.25]
—Turkish Wars, 15th century
—Uprising, 1912
—Peasant Uprising, 1914-1915
—June Revolution, 1924

Albanian-Venetian War, 1447-1448
[DR960.5]

Alexandrine War, 48-47 B.C.
[DT92.7]

Algeria
—History
[DT283.7-DT296]
—Revolution, 1954-1962
UF French-Algerian War, 1954-1962

American Civil War
USE United States—History—Civil War, 1861-1865

American Invasion of Grenada, 1983
USE Grenada—History—American invasion, 1983

American Revolution
USE United States—History—Revolution, 1775-1783

Anglo-Boer War, 1899-1902
USE South African War, 1899-1902

Anglo-Dutch War, 1652-1654
[DJ193]
UF Great Britain—History—Anglo Dutch War, 1652-1654
Netherlands—History—Anglo Dutch War, 1652-1654

Anglo-Dutch War, 1664-1667
[DJ180-DJ182]
UF Great Britain—History—Anglo Dutch War, 1664-1667
Netherlands—History—Anglo Dutch War, 1664-1667

Anglo-Dutch War, 1780-1784
[DJ205-DJ206]
UF Great Britain—History—Anglo Dutch War, 1780-1784
Netherlands—History—Anglo Dutch War, 1780-1784

Anglo-French Intervention in Egypt, 1956
USE Egypt—History—Intervention, 1956

Anglo-French War, 1294-1298

Anglo-French War, 1512-1513
[DA337; DC108]

Anglo-French War, 1666-1667
[D274.5-D274.6]

Anglo-French War, 1755-1763
[DA500-DA510; DC133; DD409-DD412.8]

Anglo-French War, 1778-1783
[DA510; DC136]

Anglo-French War, 1793-1802
[DC220-DC222]

Anglo-Spanish War, 1718-1720
[DA498-DA499; DP194]

Anglo-Spanish War, 1739-1748
UF Jenkins' Ear, War of

Anglo-Spanish War, 1762-1763
[DA505-DA512; DP199]

Anglo-Spanish War, 1779-1783
[DA505-DA512; DP199]

Angola
—History
[DT1314-DT1436]
—Revolution, 1961-1975
—Civil War, 1975-
—South African Invasion, 1975-1976
UF South African Invasion of Angola, 1975-1976
—South African Incursions, 1978-
UF South African Incursions into Angola, 1978-

Arab countries
—History
[DS37-DS39.2]
—Arab Revolt, 1916-1918

Argentina
—History
[F2827-F2849.22]
—English Invasions, 1806-1807
—War of Independence, 1810-1817
—Revolution, 1833
—Revolution, 1890
—Revolution, 1930
—Revolution, 1955
—Coup d'état, 1966

Argentine-Brazilian War, 1825-1828
[F2725]
UF Brazilian-Argentine War, 1825-1828

Armada, 1588
[DA360]
UF Spanish Armada

Austria
—History
[DB35-DB99.2]
—Revolution, 1848-1849

Austrian Succession, War of, 1740-1748
[D291-D294; DB72
UF War of the Austrian Succession, 1740-1748

Austro-Italian War, 1866
[DG558]
UF Italy—History—Austro-Italian War, 1866

Austro-Prussian War, 1866
[DD436-DD440]
UF Prussia (Germany)—History—Austro-Prussian War, 1866
Seven Weeks' War

Austro-Sardinian War, 1848-1849
[DG553]

Austro-Turkish War, 1661-1664
[DB62]
UF Turkey—History—War with Austria, 1661-1664

Austro-Turkish War, 1683-1699
[DB62]
UF Turkey—History—War with Austria,
1683-1699

Austro-Turkish War, 1716-1718
[DR545]

Austro-Turkish War, 1737-1739
[DR548]

Austro-Turkish War, 1788-1790
[DR555.7]

Balkan Peninsula
—History
[DR32-DR48.5]
—War of 1912-1913

Baltic States
—History
[DK502.7]
—Revolution, 1917-1921

Bangladesh
—History
[DS394.5-DS395.7]
—Revolution, 1971
UF Pakistan—History—Civil War, 1971

Barbarian Invasions of Rome
USE Rome—History—Germanic Invasions, 3d-6th centuries

Barons' War, 1263-1267
USE Great Britain—History—Barons' War, 1263-1267

Basuto War, 1865-1866
USE Sotho-Free State War, 1865-1866

Bavaria (Germany)
—History
[DD801.B35-B43]
—Revolution, 1848-1849
—Revolution, 1918-1919

Bavarian Succession, War of, 1778-1779
[DD801.B376]
UF War of the Bavarian Succession, 1778-1779

Bay of Pigs invasion
USE Cuba—History—Invasion, 1961

Belgium
—History
[DJ503-DJ692]
—Revolution, 1789-1790
—Invasion of 1792
—Peasants' War, 1798
—Revolution, 1830-1839
—Revolution, 1848-1849

Biafran Conflict, 1967-1970
USE Nigeria—History—Civil War, 1967-1970

Boer War, 1899-1902
USE South African War, 1899-1902

Bohemia (Czechoslovakia)
—History
—Hussite Wars, 1419-1436
[DB2105-DB2111]
UF Hussite Wars, Bohemia, Czechoslovakia, 1419-1436

Bolivia
—History
[F3320.3-F3327]
—Wars of Independence, 1809-1825
—War with Chile, 1879-1884
USE War of the Pacific, 1879-1884
—Coup d'état, 1943
—Revolution, 1946
—Revolution, 1952
—Revolution, 1964
—Coup d'état, 1979
—Coup d'état, 1980

Boxer Rebellion, China, 1899-1901
USE China—History—Boxer Rebellion, 1899-1901

Brazil
—History
[F2520.3-2538.5]
—Quebra-Quilos' Revolt, 1874
—Dutch Conquest, 1624-1654
—War of the Emboabas, 1707-1709
—Revolution, 1822
—Revolution, 1842
—Naval Revolt, 1893-1894
UF Federalist Revolution, Brazil, 1893-1894
—Conselheiro Insurrection, 1897
—Naval Revolt, 1910
UF Chibata Revolt, 1910
—Contestado Insurrection, 1912-1916
—Revolution, 1924-1925
—Revolution, 1930
—Uprising, 1935
—Revolution, 1938
—Revolution, 1964

Brazilian-Argentine War, 1825-1828
USE Argentine-Brazilian War, 1825-1828

Bulgaria
—History
[DR65-DR93.34]
—Uprising, 1040
—Uprising, 1185
—Peasant Uprising, 1850
—Uprising, 1876
—Vladaya Uprising, 1918
—Uprising, 1923 (June)
—Uprising, 1923 (September)
—September Uprising, 1944

Bulgarian-Serbian War, 1885
USE Serbo-Bulgarian War, 1885

Bundschuh Insurrections, 1493-1517
[DD174.4]
UF Peasants' War, 1493-1517

Burmese War, 1824-1826

Burmese War, 1852

Burmese War, 1885 (May Subd Geog)
[DS479.7]

Cambodia
—History
[DS554.5-DS554.842]
—Civil War, 1970-1975

Calmar War, 1611-1613
USE Kalmar War, 1611-1613

Cambodian-Vietnamese Conflict, 1977-
[DS554.84-DS554.842]
UF Vietnamese-Cambodian Conflict, 1977-

Cameroon
—History
[DT572-DT578.4]
—Coup d'état, 1964

Canada
—History
[F1022-F1034.3]
—Rebellion, 1837-1838
—Fenian invasions, 1866-1870

Castro, War of, 1642-1644
UF War of Castro, 1642-1644

Catalonia (Spain)
—History
[DP302.C619-C68]
—Revolution, 1640
—Revolution, 1934

Central African Republic
—History
[DT546.365-DT546.384]
—Coup d'état, 1979

Chaco War, 1932-1935
[F2688.5]

Chad
—History
[DT546.457-DT546.483]
—Civil War, 1965-

Chibata Revolt, 1910
USE Brazil—History—Naval Revolt, 1910

Chile
—History
[F3073-F3101]
—War of Independence, 1810-1824
—Insurrection, 1851
—Insurrection, 1859
—War with Spain, 1865-1866
—War with Bolivia and Peru, 1879-1884
USE War of the Pacific, 1879-1884
—Revolution, 1891
—Naval Revolt, 1931
—Coup d'état, 1973

Chimurenga War, 1966-1980
USE Zimbabwe—History—Chimurenga War, 1966-1980

China
—History
[DS733-DS779.29]
—Opium War, 1840-1842
—Taiping Rebellion, 1850-1864
—Nien Rebellion, 1853-1868
—Foreign intervention, 1857-1861
—Boxer Rebellion, 1899-1901
UF Boxer Rebellion, China, 1899-1901
—Revolution, 1911-1912
—Revolution, 1913
—Revolution, 1915-1916
—Tsinan Incident, 1928
—Sian Incident, 1936
—Southern Anhui Incident, 1941
—Civil War, 1945-1949
—Cultural Revolution, 1966-1969

Chinese-French War, 1884-1885
[DS549]
UF Franco-Chinese War, 1884-1885
Sino-French War, 1884-1885

Chinese-Japanese War, 1894-1895
[DS765-DS767]
UF Japanese-Chinese War, 1894-1895
Sino-Japanese War, 1894-1895

Chinese...
SA headings for wars beginning with the word Sino

Chremonidean War
USE Greece—History—Chremonidean War, 267-262 B.C.

Colombia
—History
[F2251-F2277]

—War of Independence, 1810-1822
—Civil War, 1860-1862
—Revolution, 1899-1903
—Coup d'état, 1953

Communist Insurrection, Malayan, 1948-1960
USE Malaya—History—Malayan Emergency, 1948-1960

Contestado Insurrection, 1912-1916
USE Brazil—History—Contestado Insurrection, 1912-1916

Crimean War, 1853-1856
[DK214-DK215.95]
BT Russo-Turkish Wars, 1676-1878

Cristero Rebellion, 1926-1929

Cuba
—History
[F1772-F1788.22]
—Insurrection, 1849-1851
—Insurrection, 1868-1878
—Revolution, 1879-1880
UF Little War, Cuba, 1879-1880
—Revolution, 1895-1898
—Revolution, 1933
—Moncada Barracks Attack, 1953
UF Moncada Barracks Attack, Cuba, 1953
—Revolution, 1959
UF Cuban Revolution, 1959
—Invasion, 1961
UF Bay of Pigs invasion
Cuban invasion, 1961

Cuban invasion, 1961
USE Cuba—History—Invasion, 1961

Cuban Revolution, 1959
USE Cuba—History—Revolution, 1959

Cyprian War, 1570-1571
[DR515-DR516]

Cyprus
—History
[DS54.5-DS54.9]
—Cyprus Crisis, 1963
—Cyprus Crisis, 1974-

Czechoslovakia
—History
[DB2044-DB2232]
—Coup d'état, 1948
—Intervention, 1968-
UF Soviet invasion of Czechoslovakia, 1968-

Dacian War, 1st, 101-102
[DG59.D3]

Dacian War, 2nd, 105-106
[DG59.D3]

Dano-Swedish War, 1643-1645
[DL190]

Dano-Swedish War, 1657-1660
[DL192]

Dano-Swedish War, 1675-1679
USE Scanian War, 1675-1679

Denmark
—History
[DL144-DL263.3]
—The Count's War, 1534-1536
—Coup d'état, 1536
—Northern Seven Years' War, 1563-1570
USE Northern Seven Years' War, 1563-1570
—Coup d'état, 1660
—Coup d'état, 1784
—War of 1807-1814

Devolution, War of, 1667-1668
[D275-D276]
UF Franco-Spanish War, 1667-1668
War of Devolution, 1667-1668

Dominican Republic
—History
[F1937-F1938.58]
—American occupation, 1916-1924
—Invasion, 1959
—Coup d'état, 1963
—Revolution, 1965
—Revolution, 1973
—Uprising, 1984

Dutch-Swedish War, 1658-1659
USE Swedish-Dutch War, 1658-1659

Easter Rebellion, 1916
USE Ireland—History—Sinn Fein Rebellion, 1916

Ecuador
—History
[F3723-F3738.4]
—Wars of Independence, 1809-1830
—Revolution, 1895
—Coup d'état, 1925

Ecuador-Peru Conflict, 1941
[F3737]
UF Peru-Ecuador Conflict, 1941

Ecuador-Peru Conflict, 1981
[F3738]
UF Peru-Ecuador Conflict, 1981

Egypt
—History
[DT74-DT107.87]
—Invasion of Saint Louis, 1249
—Insurrection, 1919
—Revolution, 1952
—Intervention, 1956
UF Anglo-French Intervention in Egypt, 1956
Israel-Arab War, 1956

El Salvador
—History
[F1485.5-F1488.42]
—Revolution, 1944
—Revolution of 1948

El Salvador-Honduras Conflict, 1969
[F1488]
UF Honduras-El Salvador Conflict, 1969

Entebbe Airport Raid, 1976
[DS119.7]
UF Operation Jonathan, 1976
Rescue of hijack victims at Entebbe Airport, 1976

Eritrea (Ethiopia)
—History
[DT394-DT397]
—Revolution, 1962-

Estonia
—History
[DK503.37-DK503.77]
—Revolution of 1905
—Revolution, 1917-1918
—War of Independence, 1918-1920
—Communist Coup, 1924

Ethiopia
—History
[DT380.5-DT387.954]
—Rebellion, 1928-1930
—Coup d'état, 1960
—Revolution, 1974

Ethiopian-Italian War, 1895-1896
USE Italo-Ethiopian War, 1895-1896

Ethiopian-Italian War, 1935-1936
USE Italo-Ethiopian War, 1935-1936

Ethiopian-Somali Conflict, 1977-1979
USE Somali-Ethiopian Conflict, 1977-1979

Ethiopian-Somali Conflict, 1979-
USE Somali-Ethiopian Conflict, 1979-

European War ...
USE World War ...

Falkland Islands War, 1982
[F3031.5]

Federalist Revolution, Brazil, 1893-1894
USE Brazil—History—Naval Revolt, 1893-1894

Finland
—History
[DL1024-DL1135.5]
—Revolution, 1917-1918

First Coalition, War of the, 1792-1797
[DC220-222]
UF War of the First Coalition, 1792-1797
BT Napoleonic Wars, 1800-1814

First World War
USE World War, 1914-1918

France
—History-
[DC35-DC423]
—Cabochien Uprising, 1413
—Wars of the Huguenots, 1562-1598
UF Huguenot Wars
—Revolution, 1789

—**Revolution, 1789-1790**
—**Revolution, 1789-1791**
—**Revolution, 1789-1792**
—**Revolution, 1789-1793**
—**Revolution, 1789-1794**
—**Revolution, 1789-1795**
—**Revolution, 1789-1796**
—**Revolution, 1789-1797**
—**Revolution, 1789-1799**
—**Revolution, 1790**
—**Revolution, 1790-1792**
—**Revolution, 1790-1793**
—**Revolution, 1790-1794**
—**Revolution, 1791**
—**Revolution, 1791-1792**
—**Revolution, 1791-1793**
—**Revolution, 1791-1794**
—**Revolution, 1791-1795**
—**Revolution, 1791-1796**
—**Revolution, 1791-1797**
—**Revolution, 1792**
—**Revolution, 1792-1793**
—**Revolution, 1792-1794**
—**Revolution, 1792-1795**
—**Revolution, 1792-1796**
—**Revolution, 1792-1797**
—**Revolution, 1792-1799**
—**Revolution, 1793**
—**Revolution, 1793-1794**
—**Revolution, 1793-1795**
—**Revolution, 1793-1796**
—**Revolution, 1793-1797**
—**Revolution, 1793-1798**
—**Revolution, 1793-1799**
—**Revolution, 1794**
—**Revolution, 1794-1795**
—**Revolution, 1794-1796**
—**Revolution, 1794-1797**
—**Revolution, 1795**
—**Revolution, 1795-1796**
—**Revolution, 1795-1797**
—**Revolution, 1795-1799**
—**Revolution, 1796**
—**Revolution, 1796-1797**
—**Revolution, 1796-1799**
—**Revolution, 1797**
—**Revolution, 1797-1798**
—**Revolution, 1797-1799**
—**Revolution, 1797-1802**
—**Revolution, 1798**
—**Revolution, 1799**
—**Invasion of 1814**
—**July Revolution, 1830**
—**February Revolution, 1848**
—**Coup d'état, 1851**

Franco-Chinese War, 1884-1885
USE Chinese-French War, 1884-1885

Franco-German War, 1870-1871
[DC281-DC326]
UF Franco-Prussian War, 1870-1871

Franco-Prussian War, 1870-1871
USE Franco-German War, 1870-1871

Franco-Spanish War, 1635-1659
[DC124.45]
UF Spanish-French War, 1635-1659

Franco-Spanish War, 1667-1668
USE Devolution, War of, 1667-1668

French-Algerian War, 1954-1961
USE Algeria—History—Revolution, 1954-1962

Gambia
—**History**
[DT509.5-DT509.83]
—**Coup d'état, 1981**

Gaul
—**History**
[DC62]
—**Gallic Wars, 58-51 B.C.**

Gaza Strip
—**History**
[DS110.G3]
—**Palestinian Uprising, 1987-**
UF Intifada, West Bank and Gaza Strip, 1987-
Palestinian Uprising, West Bank and Gaza Strip, 1987-
BT Jewish-Arab relations—1973-

Germany (East)
—**History**
[DD281.5-DD289]
—**Uprising, 1953 (June)**
BT Germany—Politics and government—1945-

Ghana
—**History**
[DT510.5-DT512.34]
—**Coup d'état, 1966**
—**Coup d'état, 1972**
—**Coup d'état, 1979**
—**Coup d'état, 1981**

Gladiators, War of the, 73-71 B.C.
USE Rome—History—Servile Wars, 135-71 B.C.

Golden Temple Assault, Amritsar, India, 1984
USE India—History—Golden Temple (Amritsar) Assault, 1984

Gothic War, Italy, 535-555
USE Italy—History—Gothic War, 535-555

Grand Alliance, War of the, 1689-1697
[D279-D280]
UF War of the Grand Alliance, 1689-1697
Nine Years' War, 1689-1697

Great Britain
—**History**
[DA20-DA592]
—**Barons' War, 1263-1267**
UF Barons' War, 1263-1267
—**Wars of the Roses, 1455-1485**
UF Wars of the Roses, 1455-1485
—**Western Rebellion, 1549**
—**Rebellion of 1569**
—**Civil War, 1642-1649**
—Anglo Dutch War, 1652-1654
USE Anglo-Dutch War, 1652-1654
—Anglo Dutch War, 1664-1667
USE Anglo-Dutch War, 1664-1667
—**Revolution of 1688**
—Anglo Dutch War, 1780-1784
USE Anglo-Dutch War, 1780-1784

Greco-Turkish War, 1897
[DF827; DR575]
UF Turco-Greek War, 1897

Greco-Turkish War, 1921-1922
[DF845.5-DF845.58]
UF Turco-Greek War, 1921-1922

Greece
—**History**
[DF207-DF854.32]
—**Dorian invasions, ca. 1125-1025 B.C.**
—**Messenian Wars, 735-460 B.C.**
UF Messenian Wars
—**Persian Wars, 500-449 B.C.**
—**Ionian Revolt, 499-494 B.C.**
—**Peloponnesian War, 431-404 B.C.**
UF Peloponnesian War, 431-404 B.C.
—**Corinthian War, 395-386 B.C.**
—**Third Sacred War, 355-346 B.C.**
UF Sacred War, Greece, 355-346 B.C.
Third Sacred War, Greece, 355-346 B.C.
—**Galatian Invasion, 279-278 B.C.**
—**Chremonidean War, 267-262 B.C.**
UF Chremonidean War
—**War of Independence, 1821-1829**
—**Acarnanian Revolt, 1836**
UF Acarnanian Revolt, Greece, 1836
—**Revolution, 1848**
—**Arta Revolt, 1854**
—**Revolution, 1862**
—**Coup d'état, 1909**
—**Civil War, 1944-1949**
—**Coup d'état, 1967 (April 21)**
—**Coup d'état, 1967 (December 13)**
—**Coup d'état, 1973 (May 22-23)**

Grenada
—**History**
[F2056]
—**Coup d'état, 1979**
—**American invasion, 1983**
UF American invasion of Grenada, 1983

Guatemala
—**History**
[F1465.5-F1466.7]
—**Revolution, 1871**
—**October Revolution, 1944**
—**Revolution, 1954**

Guinea
—**History**
[DT543.5-DT543.827]
—**Portuguese Invasion, 1970**
—**Coup d'état, 1984**

Guinea-Bissau
—History
[DT613.5-DT613.83]
—Revolution, 1963-1974
—Coup d'état, 1980

Gulf War, 1980-1988
USE Iran-Iraq War, 1980-1988

Haiti
—History
[F1918-F1928.23]
—Revolution, 1791-1804
—Revolution, 1843

Honduras
—History
[F1505.5-F1508.33]
—Coup d'état, 1904
—Revolution, 1919

Honduras-El Salvador Conflict, 1969
USE El Salvador-Honduras Conflict, 1969

Huguenot Wars
USE France—History—Wars of the Huguenots, 1562-1598

Hundred Years' War, 1339-1453
[DC96-DC105]

Hungary
—History
[DB921-DB957]
—Uprising of 1848-1849
—Revolution, 1918-1919
—Revolution, 1956

Hussite Wars, Bohemia, Czechoslovakia, 1419-1436
USE Bohemia—History—Hussite Wars, 1419-1436

Illyrian wars
[DG246]

India
—History
[DS433-DS481]
—Mysore War, 1790-1792
UF Mysore War, 1790-1792
—Mysore War, 1799
UF Mysore War, 1799
—Afghan Wars, 1838-1919
USE Afghan Wars
—Sepoy Rebellion, 1857-1858
UF Sepoy Rebellion
—Golden Temple (Amritsar) Assault, 1984
UF Golden Temple Assault, Amritsar, India, 1984

India-Pakistan Conflict, 1947-1949 (May Subd Geog)
[DS385.9]
UF Kashmir War, 1947-1949
Pakistan-India Conflict, 1947-1949

India-Pakistan Conflict, 1965
[DS386]
UF Pakistan-India Conflict, 1965

India-Pakistan Conflict, 1971
[DS388]
UF Pakistan-India Conflict, 1971

Indian-Chinese Border Dispute, 1957-
USE Sino-Indian Border Dispute, 1957-

Indochinese War, 1946-1954 (May Subd Geog)
[DS552-DS557]

Indonesia
—History
[DS633-DS644.4]
—Java War, 1825-1830
UF Java War, Indonesia, 1825-1830
—Achinese War, 1873-1904
UF Achinese War, Indonesia, 1873-1904
—Revolution, 1945-1949
—Coup d'état, 1965

Intifada, West Bank and Gaza Strip, 1987-
USE Gaza Strip—History—Palestinian Uprising, 1987-
West Bank—History—Palestinian Uprising, 1987-

Iran
—History
[DS270-DS318]
—War with Great Britain, 1856-1857
—Revolution, 1979
UF Islamic Revolution, Iran, 1979

Iran-Iraq War, 1980-1988 (May Subd Geog)
[DS318.85]
UF Gulf War, 1980-1988

Iranian-Iraqi Conflict, 1980-1988
Iraqi-Iranian Conflict, 1980-1988
Persian Gulf War, 1980-1988

Iranian-Iraqi Conflict, 1980-1988
USE Iran-Iraq War, 1980-1988

Iraq
—History
[DS70.82-DS79.66]
—Zanj Rebellion, 868-883
UF Zanj Revolt, 868-883
—Revolt of 1920
—Revolution, 1958
—Revolution, 1963

Iraqi-Iranian Conflict, 1980-1988
USE Iran-Iraq War, 1980-1988

Ireland
—History
[DA909-DA965]
—Rebellion of 1641
—War of 1689-1691
—Rebellion of 1798
—Emmet's Rebellion, 1803
—Rising of 1848
—Sinn Fein Rebellion, 1916
UF Easter Rebellion, 1916
—Civil War, 1922-1923

Islamic Revolution, Iran, 1979
USE Iran—History—Revolution, 1979

Israel-Arab Border Conflicts, 1949- (May Subd Geog)
BT Israel-Arab conflicts

Israel-Arab conflicts (May Subd Geog)
Here are entered works on the conflicts between the Arab countries and Israel.
NT Israel-Arab Border Conflicts, 1949-
Israel-Arab War, 1948-1949
Israel-Arab War, 1967
Israel-Arab War, 1973
Lebanon—History—Israeli intervention, 1982-1984

Israel-Arab War, 1948-1949 (May Subd Geog)
[DS126.9-DS126.99]
BT Israel-Arab conflicts

Israel-Arab War, 1956
USE Egypt—History—Intervention, 1956
Sinai Campaign, 1956

Israel-Arab War, 1967 (May Subd Geog)
[DS127-DS127.9]
UF Six Day War, 1967
BT Israel-Arab conflicts

Israel-Arab War, 1973
[DS128.1-DS128.19]
UF Yom Kippur War, 1973
BT Israel-Arab conflicts

Israeli intervention in Lebanon, 1982-1984
USE Lebanon—History—Israeli intervention, 1982-1984

Italo-Ethiopian War, 1895-1896
[DT387.3]
UF Ethiopian-Italian War, 1895-1896

Italo-Ethiopian War, 1935-1936
[DT387.8]
UF Ethiopian-Italian War, 1935-1936

Italo-Turkish War, 1911-1912
USE Turco-Italian War, 1911-1912

Italy
—History
[DG201-DG583]
—Gothic War, 535-555
UF Gothic War, Italy, 535-555
—Expedition of Charles VIII, 1494-1496
—Uprising, 1831
—Revolution of 1848
—War of 1859
—War of 1860-1861
—Austro-Italian War, 1866
USE Austro-Italian War, 1866

Jacobite Rebellion, 1715
[DA814.3]

Jacobite Rebellion, 1719
[DA814.4]

Jacobite Rebellion, 1745-1746
[DA814.5]

Jamaica
—History
[F1878-F1887]
—Maroon War, 1795-1796
—Slave Insurrection, 1831
—Insurrection, 1865

Japan
—History
[DS833-DS890.3]
—Iwai Rebellion, 527-528
—Shohei Revolt, 936-941
—Tengyo Revolt, 938-940
—Earlier Nine Years' War, 1051-1062
—Later Three Years War, 1083-1087
—Hogen and Heiji Insurrections, 1156-1159
—Gempei Wars, 1180-1185
—Jokyu Revolt, 1221
—Period of civil wars, 1480-1603
—Keich Peasant Uprising, 1614-1615
—Oshio Heihachiro Rebellion, 1837
—Civil War, 1868

Japanese-Chinese Conflict, 1937-1945
USE Sino-Japanese Conflict, 1937-1945

Japanese-Chinese War, 1894-1895
USE Chinese-Japanese War, 1894-1895

Japanese-Russian Border Conflicts, 1932-1941
USE Russo-Japanese Border Conflicts, 1932-1941

Japanese-Russian War, 1904-1905
USE Russo-Japanese War, 1904-1905

Java War, Indonesia, 1825-1830
USE Indonesia—History—Java War, 1825-1830

Jenkins' Ear, War of
USE Anglo-Spanish War, 1739-1748

Jugurthine War, 111-105 B.C.
[DG255]

Kalmar War, 1611-1613
[DL710]
UF Calmar War, 1611-1613

Kashmir War, 1947-1949
USE India-Pakistan Conflict, 1947-1949

Korea
—History
[DS904.8-DS917.55]
—Mongolian invasions, 1231-1270
—Japanese invasions, 1592-1598
—Manchu invasions, 1627-1637

Korea (South)
—History
[DS917.6-DS922.42]
—Yosun Rebellion, 1948
—April Revolution, 1960
—May Revolution, 1961

Korean War, 1950-1953 (May Subd Geog)
[DS918-DS921.8]

Lamian War, 323-322 B.C.
[DF235.5]

Latin America
—History
[1409.6-F1418]
—Wars of Independence, 1806-1830

Latvia
—History
[DK504.37-DK504.79]
—Revolution of 1905

Lebanon
—History
[DS80-DS87.53]
—Intervention, 1958
—Civil War, 1975-1976
—Israeli intervention, 1982-1984
UF Israeli intervention in Lebanon, 1982-1984

Liberation, Wars of, 1813-1814
USE Wars of Liberation, 1813-1814

Liberia
—History
[DT630.8-DT636.53]
—Coup d'état, 1980

Lithuania
—History
[DK505.37-DK505.79]
—Revolution, 1830-1832
—Revolution, 1863
—Revolution of 1905

Little War, Cuba, 1879-1880
USE Cuba—History—Revolution, 1879-1880

Livonian War, 1557-1582

Macedonian War, lst, 215-205 B.C.
[DG251]
BT Punic War, 2nd, 218-201 B.C.

Macedonian War, 2d, 200-196 B.C.
[DG251]

Macedonian War, 3d, 171-168 B.C.
[DF238-DF238.9; DG251.6]

Madagascar
—History
[DT469.M282-DT469.M297]
—French invasion, 1895
—Menalamba Rebellion, 1895-1899
—Revolution, 1947

Malawi
—History
[DT3194-DT3237]
—Chilembwe Rebellion, 1915

Malaya
—History
—Malayan Emergency, 1948-1960
UF Communist Insurrection, Malayan, 1948-1960

Mali
—History
[DT551.5-DT551.82]
—Coup d'état, 1968

Manchurian Incident, 1931
USE Mukden Incident, 1931

Maratha War, 1775-1782
[DS473]

Maratha War, 1803
[DS475.3]

Maratha War, 1816-1818
[DS475.6]

Marcomannic War, 167-180

Messenian Wars
USE Greece—History—Messenian Wars, 735-460 B.C.

Mexican War, 1845-1848
USE United States—History—War with Mexico, 1845-1848

Mexico
—History
[F1223-F1236.6]
—Conquest, 1519-1540
—Wars of Independence, 1810-1821
—European intervention, 1861-1867
—Revolution, 1910-1920
—Revolution, 1923-1924

Moncada Barracks Attack, Cuba, 1953
USE Cuba—History—Moncada Barracks Attack, 1953

Monferrato War, 1613-1618

Mongol Invasion, Poland, 1241
USE Poland—History—Mongol Invasion, 1241

Montenegrin-Turkish War
USE headings beginning with the words Turco-Montenegrin War

Moroccan-Spanish War, 1859-1860
USE Spanish-Moroccan War, 1859-1860

Mozambique
—History
[DT3330-DT3398]
—War of 1894-1895
—Revolution, 1964-1975

Mukden Incident, 1931
[DS783.8]
UF Manchurian Incident, 1931

Musso, War of, 1531-1532
[DQ114]

Mysore War, 1790-1792
USE India—History—Mysore War, 1790-1792

Mysore War, 1799
USE India—History—Mysore War, 1799

Namibia
—History
[DT1564-DT1648]
—Herero Revolt, 1904-1907

Napoleonic Wars, 1800-1814
[DC226.2DC249]
NT First Coalition, War of the, 1792-1797
Peninsular War, 1807-1814
Second Coalition, War of the, 1798-1801
Walcheran Expedition, 1809
Wars of Liberation, 1813-1814
—Proposed invasion of England, 1793-1805

Nepalese War, 1814-1816

Netherlands
—History
[DJ95-DJ292]
—Wars of Independence, 1556-1648
—Anglo Dutch War, 1652-1654
USE Anglo-Dutch War, 1652-1654
—Anglo Dutch War, 1664-1667
USE Anglo-Dutch War, 1664-1667
—Anglo Dutch War, 1780-1784
USE Anglo-Dutch War, 1780-1784

Nicaragua
—History
[F1525.5-F1528.22]
—English invasion, 1780-1781
—Filibuster War, 1855-1860
—Revolution, 1909-1910
—Revolution of 1912
—Revolution, 1926-1929
—Uprising, 1978
—Revolution, 1979

Nigeria
—History
[DT515.52-DT515.84]
—Coup d'état, 1966 (January 15)
—Coup d'état, 1966 (July 29)
—Civil War, 1967-1970
UF Biafran Conflict, 1967-1970
—Coup d'état, 1983

Nine Years' War, 1689-1697
USE Grand Alliance, War of the, 1689-1697

Northern Seven Years' War, 1563-1570
[DL188.5]
UF Three Crowns' War, 1563-1570

Northern War, 1700-1721
[DL733-DL743]
UF Sweden—History—Northern War, 1700-1721

Norway
—History
[DL443-DL535]
—Scottish Expedition, 1612
—Hannibal's War, 1644-1645
—War of 1807-1814

October Revolt, Thailand, 1973
USE Thailand—History—Student Uprising, 1973

Oman
—History
—Dhofar War, 1964-1976

Onin War, 1467-1477

Operation Jonathan, 1976
USE Entebbe Airport Raid, 1976

País Vasco (Spain)
—History
[DP302.B41-55]
—Carlist Wars, 1873-1876

Pakistan
—History
[DS381-DS388.2]
—Civil War
USE Bangladesh—History—Revolution, 1971

Pakistan-India Conflict, 1947-1949
USE India-Pakistan Conflict, 1947-1949

Pakistan-India Conflict, 1965
USE India-Pakistan Conflict, 1965

Pakistan-India Conflict, 1971
USE India-Pakistan Conflict, 1971

Palestine
—History
[DS115.5-DS128]
—Arab rebellion, 1936-1939

Palestinian Uprising, West Bank and Gaza Strip, 1987-
USE Gaza Strip—History—Palestinian Uprising, 1987-
West Bank—History—Palestinian Uprising, 1987-

Panama
—History
[F1565.5-F1567]
—Revolution, 1903
—Coup d'état, 1968

Paraguay
—History
[F2679.35-F2689]
—Revolution of the Comuneros, 1721-1735
—War of Independence, 1810-1811
—Revolution, 1922-1923
—Revolution, 1936
—Revolution, 1947

Paraguayan War, 1865-1870 (May Subd Geog)
[F2687]
UF Triple Alliance, War of the, 1865-1870
War of the Triple Alliance, 1865-1870

Parthian War, 113-117
[DG294]

Peasants' Revolt, 1381
USE Tyler's Insurrection, 1381

Peasants' War, 1493-1517
USE Bundschuh Insurrection, 1493-1517

Peasants' War, 1524-1525
[DD181-DD183]

Peasants' War, 1595-1597

Peasants' War, 1626

Peloponnesian War, 431-404 B.C.
USE Greece—History—Peloponnesian War, 431-404 B.C.

Peninsular War, 1807-1814 (May Subd Geog)
[DC231-DC233]
BT Napoleonic Wars, 1800-1814
NT Spain—History—Napoleonic Conquest, 1808-1813

Persian Gulf War, 1980-1988
USE Iran-Iraq War, 1980-1988

Peru
—History
[F3430.3-F3448.4]
—Conquest, 1522-1548
—Insurrection of Tupac Amara, 1780-1781
—War of Independence, 1820-1829
—Revolution of 1872
—War with Chile, 1879-1884
USE War of the Pacific, 1879-1884
—Revolution, 1930
—Coup d'état, 1968

Peru-Ecuador Conflict, 1941
USE Ecuador-Peru Conflict, 1941

Peru-Ecuador Conflict, 1981
USE Ecuador-Peru Conflict, 1981

Philippines
—History
[DS667-DS686.2]
—Insurrection, 1896-1898
—Insurrection, 1899-1901
—Revolution, 1986

Poland
—History
[DK4123-DK4442]
—Mongol Invasion, 1241
UF Mongol Invasion, Poland, 1241
—Rebellion of Zebrzydowski, 1606-1609
—Uprising of Kostka Napierski, 1651
—Rebellion of Lubomirski, 1665-1666
—Revolution of 1794
—Revolution, 1830-1832
—Partisan Campaign, 1833
—Revolution of 1846
—Revolution of 1848
—Revolution, 1863-1864
—Revolution of 1905
—Wars of 1918-1921
—Coup d'état, 1926
—Uprising, 1956

Polish-Brandenburg War, 1656-1657
[DK4306.35]

Polish-Russian War
USE headings beginning with the words Russo-Polish War

Polish Succession, War of, 1733-1738
[DK4326.5]
UF War of the Polish Succession, 1733-1738

Polish-Swedish War, 1617-1629
USE Swedish-Polish War, 1617-1629

Polish-Swedish War, 1655-1660
USE Swedish-Polish War, 1655-1660

Polish-Teutonic Knights' War, 1409-1411
[DK4261]

Polish Turkish Wars, 1683-1699
USE Turco-Polish Wars, 1683-1699

Portugal
—History
[DP535-DP682.2]
—Revolution, 1640
—Revolution, 1820
—Uprising, 1846
—Revolution, 1910
—Revolution, 1926
—Revolution, 1974
—Coup d'état, 1975

Prussia (Germany)—History—Austro-Prussian War, 1866
USE Austro-Prussian War, 1866

Punic War, 1st, 264-241 B.C.
[DG243-DG244]

Punic War, 2d, 218-201 B.C.
[DG247-DG249]

Punic War, 3d, 149-146 B.C.
[DG252.6]

Punic wars
SA headings for individual Punic wars

Rescue of hijack victims at Entebbe Airport, 1976
USE Entebbe Airport Raid, 1976

Rhodesian War, Zimbabwe, 1966-1980
USE Zimbabwe—History—Chimurenga War, 1966-1980

Rohilla War, 1774
[DS473]

Romania
—History
[DR215-DR267.5]
—Revolution, 1821
—Revolution, 1848
—War of Independence, 1876-1878
BT Russo-Turkish War, 1877-1878
—Peasants' Uprising, 1888
—Peasants' Uprising, 1907

Rome
—History
[DG201-DG365]
—Servile Wars, 135-71 B.C.
UF Gladiators, War of the, 73-71 B.C.
—Social War, 90-88 B.C.
—Mithridatic Wars, 88-63 B.C.
—Revolt of Sertorius, 82-72 B.C.
—Civil War, 49-48 B.C.
—Civil War, 43-31 B.C.
—Civil War, 68-69
—Germanic Invasions, 3d-6th centuries
UF Barbarian invasions of Rome

Ruanda-Urundi
—History
—Civil War, 1959-1962
[DT450.43]

Russian Revolution, 1917-1921
USE Soviet Union—History—Revolution, 1917-1921

Russo-Finnish War, 1939-1940
[DL1095-DL1105]
UF Soviet-Finnish War, 1939-1940
Winter War, 1939-1940

Russo-Japanese Border Conflicts, 1932-1941
[DS784]
UF Japanese-Russian Border Conflicts, 1932-1941

Russo-Japanese War, 1904-1905
[DS516-DS517]
UF Japanese-Russian War, 1904-1905

Russo-Polish War, 1632-1634
[DK4303.4]

Russo-Polish War, 1658-1667

Russo-Polish War, 1792
[DK4336]

Russo-Polish War, 1919-1920
[DK4404-DK4409]

Russo-Swedish War, 1554-1557
[DL703]

Russo-Swedish War, 1608-1617
[DL711]

Russo-Swedish War, 1656-1658
[DL725]

Russo-Swedish War, 1741-1743
[DL755]

Russo-Swedish War, 1788-1790
[DL766]

Russo-Swedish War, 1808-1809 (May Subd Geog)
[DL790]

Russo-Turkish War, 1736-1739
[DR548]

Russo-Turkish War, 1768-1774
[DR553]

Russo-Turkish War, 1787-1792
[DR555.7]

Russo-Turkish War, 1806-1812
[DR561]

Russo-Turkish War, 1828-1829
[DR564]

Russo-Turkish War, 1877-1878 (May Subd Geog)
[DR573]

Russo-Turkish Wars, 1676-1878
NT Crimean War, 1853-1856

Sacred War, Greece, 355-346 B.C.
USE Greece—History—Third Sacred War, 355-346 B.C.

Scandinavia
—History
[DL44.8-DL:87]
—The Count's War, 1534-1536

Scanian War, 1675-1679
UF Dano-Swedish War, 1675-1679

Schleswig-Holstein War, 1848-1850
[DL217-DL223]

Schleswig-Holstein War, 1864
[DL236-DL239]

Schmalkaldic War, 1546-1547
[DD184-DD184.7]

Scotland
—History
[DA750-DA890]
—War of Independence, 1285-1371
—Wallace's Rising, 1297-1304
—Revolution of 1688

Second Coalition, War of the, 1798-1801
[DC271]
UF War of the Second Coaliltion, 1798-1801
BT Napoleonic Wars, 1800-1814

Second World War
USE World War, 1939-1945

Senegal
—History
[DT549.47-DT549.83]
—Coup d'état, 1962

Sepoy Rebellion
USE India—History—Sepoy Rebellion, 1857-1858

Serbia
—History
—Insurrection, 1788
—Insurrection, 1804-1813
—Revolt, 1883

Serbo-Bulgarian War, 1885
[DR354]
UF Bulgarian-Serbian War, 1885

Serbo-Turkish War, 1876
[DR353]

Serbo-Turkish War, 1877-1878
[DR353.5]

Seven Weeks' War
USE Austro-Prussian War, 1866

Seven Years' War, 1756-1763
[DD409-DD412.8]
UF Silesian War, 3d, 1756-1763

Seychelles
—History
[DT469.S452-DT469.S483]
—Coup d'état, 1977
—Coup d'état, 1981

Sicilian Expedition, Italy, 415-413 B.C.
[DF229.65-DF229.69]

Sicilian Expedition, Italy, 1718-1720

Sicilian Vespers, Italy, 1282
[DG867.3]

Sikh War, 1845-1846
[DS477.1]

Sikh War, 1848-1849
[DS477.63]

Silesian War, 1st, 1740-1742
[DD406-DD407]

Silesian War, 2d, 1744-1745
[DD406-DD407]

Silesian War, 3d, 1756-1763
USE Seven Years' War, 1756-1763

Silesian wars
SA headings for individual Silesian wars

Sinai Campaign, 1956
[DS110.5]
UF Israel-Arab War, 1956

Sino-French War, 1884-1885
USE Chinese-French War, 1884-1885

Sino-Indian Border Dispute, 1957-
[DS480.85]
UF Indian-Chinese Border Dispute, 1957-

Sino-Japanese Conflict, 1937-1945 (May Subd Geog)
[DS777.52-DS777.533]
UF Japanese-Chinese Conflict, 1937-1945

Sino-Japanese War, 1894-1895
USE Chinese-Japanese War, 1894-1895

Sino-Vietnamese Conflict, 1979 (May Subd Geog)
[DS559.915-DS559.916]
UF Vietnamese-Chinese Conflict, 1979

Six Day War, 1967
USE Israel-Arab War, 1967

Somali-Ethiopian Conflict, 1977-1979
[DT387.952]
UF Ethiopian-Somali Conflict, 1977-1979

Somali-Ethiopian Conflict, 1979-
[DT387.952]
UF Ethiopian-Somali Conflict, 1979-

Sotho-Free State War, 1865-1866
[DT2133]
UF Basuto War, 1865-1866

South Africa
—History
[DT1772-DT1969]
—Frontier Wars, 1811-1878
—Usutu Uprising, 1888
—Rebellion, 1914-1915

South Africa—History—Soweto Uprising, 1976
UF Soweto Uprising, South Africa, 1976

South African Incursions into Angola, 1978-
USE Angola—History—South African Incursions, 1978-

South African Invasion of Angola, 1975-1976
USE Angola—History—South African Invasion, 1975-1976

South African War, 1899-1902 (May Subd Geog)
[DT1890-DT1920]
UF Anglo-Boer War, 1899-1902
Boer War, 1899-1902

South America
—History
[F2230.3-F2237]
—Wars of Independence, 1806-1830

Soviet-Finnish War, 1939-1940
USE Russo-Finnish War, 1939-1940

Soviet Invasion of Afghanistan, 1979-1989
USE Afghanistan—History—Soviet Occupation, 1979-1989

Soviet Invasion of Czechoslovakia, 1968-
USE Czechoslovakia—History—Intervention, 1968-

Soviet Union
—History
[DK36-DK290.3]
—Rebellion of Stenka Razin, 1667-1671
—Streltsy Revolt, 1698
—Astrakhan Uprising, 1705-1706
—Bulavin Uprising, 1707-1709
—Rebellion of Pugachev, 1773-1775
—Kandiyevka Uprising, 1861
—Revolution of 1905
—February Revolution, 1917
—Revolution, 1917-1921
UF Russian Revolution, 1917-1921
—Allied intervention, 1918-1920

Soweto Uprising, South Africa, 1976
USE South Africa—History—Soweto Uprising, 1976

Spain
—History
[DP56-DP272.4]
—Napoleonic Conquest, 1808-1813
BT Peninsular War, 1807-1814
—Revolution, 1820-1823
—Carlist War, 1833-1840
—Revolution, 1854
—Carlist War, 1873-1876
—Revolution, 1931
—Civil War, 1936-1939
UF Spanish Civil War, 1936-1939
—Coup d'état, 1981

Spanish American War, 1898
USE United States—History—War of 1898

Spanish Armada
USE Armada, 1588

Spanish Civil War, 1936-1939
USE Spain—History—Civil War, 1936-1939

Spanish-French War, 1635-1659
USE Franco-Spanish War, 1635-1659

Spanish-Moroccan War, 1859-1860
[DT324]
UF Moroccan-Spanish War, 1859-1860

Spanish Succession, War of, 1701-1714
[D281-D283]
UF War of the Spanish Succession, 1701-1714

Sri Lanka
—History
[DS489.5-DS489.86]
—Rebellion, 1818
—Rebellion, 1848
—Rebellion, 1971

Sudan
—History
[DT155.3-DT157,67]
—Civil War, 1955-1972
—Coup d'état, 1985

Surinam
—History
[F2420.3-F2425]
—Coup d'état, 1980
—Coup d'état, 1982

Swabian War, 1499
[DQ106-DQ107]

Sweden
—History
[DL643-DL879]
—Northern War, 1700-1721
USE Northern War, 1700-1721
—Insurrection, 1743
—Revolution, 1772

Swedish-Dutch War, 1658-1659
[DL192]
UF Dutch-Swedish War, 1658-1659

Swedish-Polish War, 1617-1629
[DL712]
UF Polish-Swedish War, 1617-1629

Swedish-Polish War, 1655-1660
[DL725]
UF Polish-Swedish War, 1655-1660

Swedish-Russian War
USE headings beginning with the words Russo-Swedish War

Syria
—History
[DS94.9-DS98.3]
—Insurrection, 1925-1927

Taiwan
—History
—Insurrection, 1895

Tanzania-Uganda War, 1978-1979
USE Uganda-Tanzania War, 1978-1979

Thai-Indochinese Conflict, 1940-1941
[DS585]

Thailand
—History
[DS570.95-DS586]
—Pak Nam Incident, 1893
—Student Uprising, 1973
UF October Revolt, Thailand, 1973
—Coup d'état, 1976
—Coup d'état, 1985

Third Sacred War, Greece, 355-346 B.C.
USE Greece—History—Third Sacred War, 355-346 B.C.

Third World War
USE World War III

Thirteen Years' War, 1454-1466
[DK4271]

Thirty Years' War, 1618-1648
[D251-D271]

Three Crowns' War, 1563-1570
USE Northern Seven Years' War, 1563-1570

Tibet (China)
—History
[DS785]
—Uprising of 1959

Titto Meer's Revolt, India, 1831

Triple Alliance, War of the, 1865-1870
USE Paraguayan War, 1865-1870

Tunisia
—History
[DT253.4-DT264.49]
—Conquest, 1573

Turco-Egyptian Conflict, 1831-1840
[DS97.5]
UF Egyptian-Turkish Conflict, 1831-1840

Turco-Greek War, 1897
USE Greco-Turkish War, 1897

Turco-Greek War, 1921-1922
USE Greco-Turkish War, 1921-1922

Turco-Italian War, 1911-1912
[DR586]
UF Italo-Turkish War, 1911-1912

Turco-Montenegrin Wars, 1711-1714

Turco-Montenegrin War, 1858

Turco-Montenegrin War, 1876-1878
[DR1881]

Turco-Polish Wars, 1683-1699
[DK4311]
UF Polish Turkish Wars, 1683-1699

Turco-Russian War
USE headings beginning with the words Russo-Turkish War

Turco-Serbian War
USE headings beginning with the words Serbo-Turkish War

Turkey
—History
[DR436-DR601]
—Invasion of Timur, 1402
—Wars with Persia, 1576-1639
—War with Austria, 1661-1664
USE Austro-Turkish War, 1661-1664
—War with Austria, 1683-1699
USE Austro-Turkish War, 1683-1699
—Rebellion, 1703
—Revolution, 1909
—Revolution, 1918-1923
—Revolution, 1960
—Coup d'état, 1971
—Coup d'état, 1980

Tyler's Insurrection, 1381
[DA235]
UF Peasants' Revolt, 1381
Wat Tyler's Insurrection, 1381

Uganda-Tanzania War, 1978-1979
[DT433.283]
UF Tanzania-Uganda War, 1978-1979

Ukraine
—History
[DK508.444-DK508.843]
—Uprising, 1768
—Revolution of 1905
—Revolution, 1917-1921

United States
—History
[E171-E883]
—King William's War, 1689-1697
—Queen Anne's War, 1702-1713
—King George's War, 1744-1748
—French and Indian War, 1755-1763
—Revolution, 1775-1783
UF American Revolution
—Tripolitan War, 1801-1805
—War of 1812
UF War of 1812
—War with Algeria, 1815
—War with Mexico, 1845-1848
UF Mexican War, 1845-1848
—Civil War, 1861-1865
UF American Civil War
—War of 1898
UF Spanish American War, 1898

Uruguay
—History
[F2720-F2729.52]
—Great War, 1843-1852
—Revolution, 1886
—Revolution, 1897
—Revolution, 1935
—Coup d'état, 1973

Vendean War, 1793-1800
[DC218]

Venezuela
—History
[F2301-F2349]
—Insurrection of the Comuneros, 1781
—War of Independence, 1810-1823
—Federal Wars, 1858-1863
—Anglo German Blockade, 1902
—Revolution, 1902-1903
—Revolution, 1945
—Coup d'état, 1948
—Revolution, 1958

Venice (Italy)
—History
—Turkish Wars, 1453-1571
—Turkish Wars, 17th century
—Turkish Wars, 18th century

Vietnam
—History
[DS556.49-DS559.916]
—Trung Sisters' Rebellion, 39-43
—Lam Son Uprising, 1418-1428
—Insurrection, 1771-1802
—Coup d'état, 1963

Vietnamese-Cambodian Conflict, 1977-
USE Cambodian-Vietnamese Conflict, 1977-

Vietnamese Conflict, 1961-1975 (May Subd Geog)
[DS557-DS559.9]

Waldshut, War of, 1468
[DQ100]
UF War of Waldshut, 1468

War of 1812
USE United States—History—War of 1812

War of the Bavarian Succession, 1778-1779
USE Bavarian Succession, War of, 1778-1779

War of Castro, 1642-1644
USE Castro, War of, 1642-1644

War of Devolution, 1667-1668
USE Devolution, War of, 1667-1668

War of the First Coalition, 1792-1797
USE First Coalition, War of the, 1792-1797

War of the Grand Alliance, 1689-1697
USE Grand Alliance, War of the, 1689-1697

War of the Pacific, 1879-1884 (May Subd Geog)
[F3097]
UF Bolivia—History—War with Chile, 1879-1884
Chile—History—War with Bolivia and Peru, 1879-1884
Peru—History—War with Chile, 1879-1884

War of the Polish Succession, 1733-1738
USE Polish Succession, War of, 1733-1738

War of the Second Coalition, 1798-1801
USE Second Coalition, War of the, 1798-1801

War of the Spanish Succession, 1701-1714
USE Spanish Succession, War of, 1701-1714

War of the Triple Alliance, 1865-1870
USE Triple Alliance, War of the, 1865-1870

Wars of Liberation, 1813-1814
[DC236-DC238.5]
UF Liberation, Wars of, 1813-1814
BT Napoleonic Wars, 1800-1814

Wars of the Roses, 1455-1485
USE Great Britain—History—Wars of the Roses, 1455-1485

Warsaw (Poland)
—History
—Uprising of 1943
—Uprising of 1944

Wat Tyler's Insurrection, 1381
USE Tyler's Insurrection, 1381

West Bank
—History
[DS110.W47]
—Palestinian Uprising, 1987-
UF Intifada, West Bank and Gaza Strip, 1987-
Palestinian Uprising, West Bank and Gaza Strip, 1987-
BT Jewish-Arab relations—1973-

Winter War, 1939-1940
USE Russo-Finnish War, 1939-1940

World War, 1914-1918 (May Subd Geog)
[D501-D680]
UF First World War

World War, 1939-1945 (May Subd Geog)
[D731-D838]
UF Second World War

World War III
UF Third World War
BT World politics
NT Dropshot Plan

Yom Kippur War, 1973
USE Israel-Arab War, 1973

Zanj Revolt, 868-883
USE Iraq—History—Zanj Rebellion, 868-883

Zaire
—History
[DT650.2-DT663]
—Civil War, 1960-1965
—Shaba Invasion, 1977
—Shaba Uprising, 1978

Zanzibar
—History
[DT449.Z26-Z29]
—Revolution, 1964

Zimbabwe
—History
[DT2914-DT3000]
—Ndebele Insurrection, 1896-1897
—Chimurenga War, 1966-1980
UF Chimurenga War, 1966-1980
Rhodesian War, Zimbabwe, 1966-1980

Guide to Library of Congress Classification on Peace and International Conflict Resolution

Introduction

This guide contains portions of the Library of Congress classification schedules for materials on peace and international conflict resolution. Peace and security studies is an interdisciplinary field and draws on materials from philosophy, psychology, ethics, religion, history, economics, sociology, political science, international law, military science, and naval science. This guide brings together under one cover the classification schedules needed by catalogers to classify peace and security studies materials and may also be used by reference librarians, scholars, and students to locate works of interest for research and teaching in this field.

Portions of the Library of Congress classification schedules listed below are included in this guide. If you do not find the information for which you are searching here, please consult the complete Library of Congress classification schedules. Some explanatory material not found in the official editions of the LC schedules has been added to assist users of this guide. Additions and changes are made weekly to the classification schedules at the Library of Congress. This guide includes material from these schedules through 1988.

—A: General works
—B: Philosophy
—BF: Psychology
—BJ: Ethics
—BL-BX: Religion
—C: Auxiliary sciences of history
—D: History (Europe, Asia, Africa, Oceania)
—E-F: History (United States, Canada, Latin —America)
—H-HJ: Economics
—HM-HX: Sociology
—JA-JQ: Political science
—JX: International law and international relations
—U: Military science
—V: Naval science
—Z: Bibliography
—Appendix: Cutter list for regions and countries

(AS) ACADEMIES AND LEARNED SOCIETIES

2.5 International associations
4 Individual associations
e.g. UNESCO
Official documents
.U8A1-5 Serials
.U8A6-Z Monographs. By title
.U82 Committees. By name, A-Z
.U825 Reports of national delegations. By country, A-Z
.U83 Individual authors, A-Z
4.Z9 Projects for intellectual cooperation. By author, A-Z
Associations, funds, foundations, etc.
911.A2A-Z General works
.A4-Z Special, A-Z
Including Nobel prizes
Under each association, fund, etc.:
.xA1-4 Official serials
.xA5-7 Official monographs
.xA8-Z Nonofficial publications. By author, A-Z

(B) PHILOSOPHY (GENERAL)

For general philosophical treatises and introductions to philosophy, see BD

105 Special topics in philosophy, A-Z
Class here special topics not limited to an individual time period or country
.J87 Justice
.L45 Liberty. Freedom
Cf. JC585+, Political theory
.P4 Peace
.V5 Violence
.W3 War
Ancient philosophy (600 B.C.-430 A.D.)
General works
110 Latin
111 English
112 French
113 German
115 Other. By language, A-Z
e.g. .I7 Italian
Occident
Greece
By period
Third period
Individual philosophers
Plato
395 Criticism and interpretation
398 Special topics, A-Z
.E8 Ethics
Evil, see .G65
.G65 Good and evil
.J87 Justice
Politics, see JC
721 Medieval philosophy (430-1450)
722 By region or country, A-Z

738 Special topics, A-Z
.A87 Authority
.C65 Conscience
.I33 Ideology
775 Renaissance
Class works that are not primarily philosophical with their subjects in other classes, e.g. civilization, theology, etc.
776 By region or country, A-Z
780 Special topics, A-Z
.L52 Liberty
.M3 Man
Modern philosophy (1450/1600-)
General works
791 English
792 French
793 German
794 Italian
795 Spanish and Portuguese
796 Russian and other Slavic
798 Other languages, A-Z
799 Comparative philosophy
Special topics and schools of philosophy
Under each topic:
.AlA-Z Periodicals, societies, etc.
.A3-Z General works
809.8 Dialectical materialism. Marxist philosophy
.82 By region or country, A-Z
823.3 Ideology
Imperialism, see JC359
824 Individualism
Cf. BJ1474, Ethics
HM136, Sociology
.4 Liberty. Freedom
Cf. JC585+, Political theory
844 Violence

(BD) SPECULATIVE PHILOSOPHY

General philosophical works

Introductions to philosophy
Early works through 1800
10 Latin
11 English and American
12 French and Belgian
13 German
15 Other (not A-Z)

Epistemology. Theory of knowledge
General works
150-158 Early through 1800 (Table)
161-168 1801- (Table)
171 Truth. Error. Certitude
Cf. BJ1420+, Ethics
181 Origin and sources of knowledge
.5 Comprehension of knowledge
201 Limits of knowledge
209 Authority
215 Belief. Faith

220 Objectivity
Relativity of knowledge
221 General works
222 Subjectivity
232 Value. Worth

Ontology

Life
Including general works on the philosophy of life
Cf. BJ, Ethics
430 Early works through 1800
431 1801-
435 General special
436 Love
437 Struggle
438 Power
439 Self-deception
450 Philosophical anthropology

(BF) PSYCHOLOGY

Consciousness. Cognitive psychology
Cf. BD150+, Epistemology
BD430+, Ontology
309 Periodicals. Societies. Serials.
311 General works
315 The unconscious mind
318 Learning
321 Apperception. Attention
323 Special topics, A-Z
Authoritarianism, see BF698.35.A87
Conscious attitudes, see BF327
Dogmatism, see BF698.35.D64
.L5 Listening
.O2 Observation
325 Comprehension. Understanding
327 Attitude. Conscious attitudes
341 Nature and nurture
Class here only the psychological aspects of this topic
343 General special
441 Thought and thinking
442 Reasoning
443 Abstraction. Conceptualization
444 Information processing
445 Categorization
446 Comparison
447 Judgment
448 Decision making
Cf. BJ1419, Ethics
449 Problem solving
Affection. Feeling. Emotion
Emotion
Including psychological and philosophical works
531-538 General works (Table)
Popular works
550-558 Early through 1850 (Table)
561-568 1851- (Table)
575 Special forms of emotion, etc., A-Z
.A3 Aggressiveness. Violence

.A5 Anger
.A85 Assertiveness
.C8 Courage
.F5 Fighting
.F66 Friendship
.G44 Generosity
.H6 Hostility
.P9 Prejudice
.T45 Threat
.T7 Trust
Violence, see .A3
Will. Volition. Choice. Control
General works
608 Early through 1850
611-618 1851- (Table)
619 Commitment
620-628 Freedom of the will (Table)
Class here psychological works only
Cf. BJ1460+, Ethics
BV741, Religious liberty
JC571, Political theory
632 Self-control. Willpower
Cf. BJ, Ethics
632.5 Manipulation or control by others
633 Brainwashing
Applied psychology
636.A1A-Z Periodicals. Societies. Serials
.A2-Z General works
637 Special topics, A-Z
.A87 Authority
Cf. BF723.A78, Child psychology
HM271, Social psychology
.C45 Communication
.D42 Deception
.I48 Interpersonal conflict
.L4 Leadership
.N4 Negotiation
.P4 Persuasion
.R4 Reconciliation
.R57 Risk-taking
.T77 Truthfulness and falsehood
697 Differential psychology. Individuality
.5 Special aspects, A-Z
.S45 Self-preservation.
Self-protective behavior
Personality
698.A1A-Z Periodicals. Societies. Serials
.A2-Z General works
.2 Personality change
698.3 Personality types
.35 Special, A-Z
.A87 Authoritarianism
.C45 Charisma
.D64 Dogmatism
.N44 Negativism
.4 Personality assessment
Special topics, A-Z
.C63 Cognition and personality

.C8 Culture and personality. Culture conflict
.P6 Politics and personality
.S63 Social aspects of personality
Developmental psychology
712 Periodicals. Societies. Serials
713 General works
Child psychology
723 Special topics, A-Z
.A35 Aggressiveness
.A4 Anger
.A76 Attitude change
.F5 Fighting
.P75 Prejudice. Antipathy
.T8 Truthfulness and falsehood
.W3 War (Reactions to)
Adolescence. Youth
724.3 Special topics, A-Z
.A34 Aggressiveness
.A55 Anger
751 Psychology of nations
753 General special
755 By nation, A-Z
778 Psychology of values, meaning
Cf. BD232, Philosophy
789 Psychology of other special subjects, A-Z
.E94 Evil
.J8 Justice
War, see U22.3
818 Character
Cf. BJ1518+, Ethics
Popular works
821-828 Early through 1850 (Table)
831-838 1851- (Table)

(BJ) ETHICS

Periodicals. Serials
1 American and English
2 French and Belgian
3 German
4 Italian
5 Spanish and Portuguese
8 Other languages, A-Z
Societies
10 International societies and movements, A-Z
Under each movement:
.x General works
.x2 Local groups. By name, A-Z
e.g. .M6 Moral re-armament
General (Table 6)
11 American and English
19 Congresses
66 Study and teaching. Research
69 Comparative ethics
History
Cf. BJ1001+, General works
71-78 General works (Table)
84 Special topics, A-Z
.E5 Ends and means

	By period
101	Ancient
161	Greece and Rome
	Including Greek ethics (General)
171	Special topics, A-Z
231	Medieval
251	Special topics, A-Z
271	Renaissance
281	Special topics, A-Z
	Modern (1700-)
301-308	General works (Table)
	By period
311	18th century
315	19th century
319	20th century
324	Special topics, A-Z
	General works, treatises, and textbooks
991	Latin
	English
	General works
1001	Through 1700
1005	1701-1800
1006	1801-1860
1008	1861-1900
1011	1901-1960
1012	1961-
	Elementary textbooks. Outlines
1021	Early through 1800
1025	1801-
1031	General special
	French and Belgian
	General works
1051	Through 1700
1054	1701-1800
1057	1801-1860
1059	1861-1900
1063	1901-
	German
	General works
1101	Through 1700
1104	1701-1800
1107	1801-1860
1111	1861-1900
1114	1901-
	Italian
	General works
1131	Early through 1800
1132	1801-
	Russian and other Slavic
	General works
1135	Early through 1800
1136	1801-
	Spanish and Portuguese
	General works
1141	Early through 1800
1142	1801-
	Scandinavian and Icelandic
	General works

Class	Subject
1151	Early through 1800
1152	1801-
	Swiss
	General works
1161	Early through 1800
1162	1801-
1185	Other languages, A-Z
1188	Religious ethics
	Christian ethics
.5	Periodicals. Serials
.7	Societies
1189	Congresses
1199	Dictionaries. Encyclopedias
1200	Study of Christian ethics. Historiography. Methodology
	History
1201-1208	General works (Table)
	By period
1212	Early Christian
1217	Medieval
	Modern
1221	Through 1700
1224	1701-1800
1227	1801-1900
1231	1901-
	General works
	Early through 1800
1240	Latin
1241-1248	Other languages (Table)
	1801-
1249	Catholic works
1250	Orthodox Eastern works
.5	Other Eastern churches' works
1251-1258	Other languages (Table)
1261-1268	Elementary textbooks. Outlines (Table)
1275	General special
1278	Special, A-Z
	.C66 Conscience
	.G6 Golden rule
.5	Ethical philosophers, A-Z
1280	Jewish ethics
	By period
1281	Ancient. Pre-Christian
1282	Medieval
	Modern
1283	Through 1800
1284	1801-1900
1285	1901-
1286	Special topics, A-Z
	.G64 Golden rule
	.R4 Reconciliation
	.T7 Truthfulness and falsehood
1287	Ethical philosophers, A-Z
	Under each unless otherwise specified:
	.x Collected works (original language)
	.x2 Translations. By language, A-Z

.x3 Separate works, A-Z
.x4 Biography and criticism
1290 Jaina ethics
.5 Sikh ethics
.8 Taoist ethics
1291 Islamic ethics
1295 Zoroastrian ethics
1388 Socialist ethics
1390 Communist ethics (20th century)
.5 Study and teaching. Research
1392 Totalitarian ethics
Special topics
For ethics of specific disciplines, see BL-Z
Good and evil
General works
1400 Early through 1800
1801-
1401 English
1401 French
1402 German
1404 Italian
1405 Other languages, A-Z
1406 Origin of evil. Depravity of human nature
1408 Value of evil
.5 Moral judgment
Right and wrong
1410 Early through 1800
1411-1418 1801- (Table)
1419 Decision making
Cf. BF448, Psychology
Truth and falsehood. Lying
Cf. BD171, Epistemology
1420-1428 General works (Table 6)
1429 Mental reservation
.3 Self-deception
.5 Secrecy
1430-1438 Compromise. Toleration (Table)
1458.5 Authority
1459 Obedience
.5 Nonviolence
Freedom of the will
1460-1468 General works (Table)
.5 General special
1471 Conscience
.5 Guilt
1474 Altruism and egotism
.3 Humanitarianism
1490 Revenge
Individual ethics. Character. Virtue
General works
1520 Early through 1800
1521-1528 1801- (Table)
1531 General special
1533 Special virtues, A-Z
.B7 Brotherliness
.C58 Concord
.H7 Honesty
.J9 Justice

1534 Vices
1535 Special vices, A-Z
.A6 Anger
.C7 Cruelty

Table for B-BJ
Language Subdivisions

(0) Early works
Including Latin and Greek
(1) .A1-3 Polyglot
.A4-Z English and American
(2) French
(3) German
(4) Italian
(5) Spanish and Portuguese
(6) Russian and other Slavic
(7)
(8) Other, A-Z

When the class numbers ending 0-8 indicate early works, use 0 for Latin or Greek and 1-8 for other languages as shown in the table.

Where six numbers have been assigned, 6=Other, A-Z (including Russian and other Slavic).

Translations are usually classified with the original language.

(BL) RELIGIONS

55 Religion and civilization
65 Religion in relations to other subjects, A-Z
Atomic energy, see .N83
.A85 Atomic warfare
.C58 Civil rights
.H78 Human rights
.I55 International affairs
.J87 Justice
.N3 Nationalism
.N83 Nuclear energy
Nuclear warfare, see .A85
.P4 Peace
.P7 Politics
.R3 Race
.R48 Revolutions
.S8 The state
.W2 War
Religions of the world
Including historical and comparative works
75 Early through 1800
80 1801-1950
.2 1951-
History
For early works, see BL75
96 Ancient
97 Medieval
98 Modern
.5 Civil religion
390 Proposed, universal, or world religions
410 Religions in relation to one another
History and principles of religions
European

Classical religion and mythology
Greek
795 Special topics, A-Z
.W28 War
Asian
By religion
Hinduism
1200 Early through 1800
1201 1801-1946
1202 1947-
1211 Controversial works against Hinduism
Doctrines. Theology
1212.72 General works. Introductions
Special doctrines
1213.54 Man
Religious life
1214.32 Special topics, A-Z
.V56 Violence and nonviolence
1215 Relations to special subjects, A-Z
.P4 Peace
.P65 Politics
.R34 Race
.S83 State (Theoretical works)
.3 Relation of Hinduism to other religions
.5 General special
.7 Special, A-Z
Buddhism, see BQ
Christianity, see BR
Islam, see BP
Judaism, see BM
By region or country
India
2018 Sikhism
.15 Relation to other religions
Christianity, see BR
Islam, see BP
.2 Theology
.5 Special topics, A-Z
.N65 Nonviolence
.R44 Religious tolerance
Japan
2220 Shinto
.6 Controversial works against Shinto
2221 Doctrines. Theology
2222.2 Relation to other religions
Special
.23 Buddhism
Christianity, see BR
Judaism, see BM
2223 Relation to other subjects, A-Z
.S8 State

(BM) JUDAISM

Relation of Judaism to special subjects
534 Religions
535 Christianity. Jews and Christianity
Judaism and Islam, see BP173.J8
536 Other religions, A-Z

Buddhism, see BQ4610.J8
.S5 Shinto
537 Civilization
Including influence of Judaism
538 Other, A-Z
.A8 Atomic warfare
Conscientious objectors, see .P3
Nuclear warfare, see .A8
.P3 Peace and war
Socialism, see HX550.J4
.S7 State and society
Violence and nonviolence, see .P3
War and peace, see .P3
General works on the principles of Judaism
Modern works
560 1801-1950
561 1951-
565 General special
585 Controversial works against the Jews
590 Jewish works against Christianity
591 Jewish works against Islam
Dogmatic Judaism
600 Early through 1950
601 1951-
627 Man
630 Sin
645 Other topics, A-Z
.J8 Justice
.P64 Politics
.R3 Race

(BP) ISLAM, THEOSOPHY, ETC.

Islam

50 History
52 General special
.5 Muslims in non-Muslim countries
Sacred books
Koran
Works about the Koran
130 General works
.1 Criticism
.4 Commentaries, Exegesis. Interpretation
132 Theology. Teachings of the Koran
134 Special topics, A-Z
.E8 Ethics
.G65 Good and evil
.J4 Jews. Judaism
.P6 Political science
General works on Islam
160 Early through 1800
161 1801-1950
.2 1951-
163 General special
166 Theology
Including Sunnite theology
Special doctrines
.7 Man
.75 Sin

168 Apostasy from Islam

169 Works against Islam and the Koran

171 Relation of Islam to other religions

.5 Toleration

172 Relation to Christianity

.5 Special denominations, sects, etc., A-Z

173 Other, A-Z

.B9 Buddhism

.H5 Hinduism

.J8 Judaism

.S5 Sikhism

.T45 Theosophy

.25 Islamic sociology

For Islam and socialism/communism, see HX

.43 Justice

.44 Civil rights

.45 Equality

.5 Islam and world politics

.55 Islam and nationalism

.6 Islam and state

.65 Islam and religious liberty

.7 Islam and politics

174 The practice of Islam

182 Jihad (Holy War)

190.5 Other topics, A-Z

.B74 Brotherliness

.R3 Race. Race relations

.W35 War

191 Branches, sects, and modifications of Islam

Sunnites, see BP166+

Shiites

192 History

General works

193.3 Early works through 1800

.5 1801-

194 Theology. Doctrine

Special topics, see BP166+

.15 Relations to other religions

.16 Relations to Sunnites

.17 Relations to Sufism

.18 Other, A-Z

.185 Shi'ah and politics

Theosophy

573 Special topics, A-Z

.P3 Peace

.P7 Political science

(BQ) BUDDHISM

General works

4000 Early through 1800

4005 1801-1945

1946-

4011 Polyglot

4012 English

4013 Chinese

4014 French

4015 German

4016 Japanese

4018 Other languages, A-Z
4020 Textbooks. Outlines
4034 General special
4045 Controversial works against Buddhism
Doctrines
Introductions
4131 Polyglot
4132 English
4133 Chinese
4134 French
4135 German
4136 Japanese
4138 Other languages, A-Z
Formal treatises
4140 Early through 1800
4145 1801-1945
4150 1945-
4570 Special topics, A-Z
.M34 Man. Buddhist anthropology
.P4 Peace
Politics, see .S7
.R3 Race
.S7 State. Politics
.V5 Violence and nonviolence
.W3 War
4600 Relation to other religions
4605 General special
4610 Special, A-Z
Christianity, see BR
.C6 Confucianism
.H6 Hinduism
Islam, see BP
.J3 Jainism
.J8 Judaism
Shinto, see BL
.T3 Taoism
.Z6 Zoroastrianism

(BR) CHRISTIANITY (GENERAL)

115 Relation to special subjects, A-Z
.A83 Atomic energy
.A85 Atomic warfare
Democracy, see .P7
.I63 Individualism
.I7 International affairs
.J8 Justice
Cf. BV4647.J8, Justice (Virtue)
Nuclear energy, see .A83
Nuclear warfare, see .A85
Peace, see BT736.4
.P7 Politics. Democracy
.P77 Progress
Race, see BT734+
War, see BT736.2
127 Relation to other religions
128 Special, A-Z
.A16 African religions
.A2 Ancient religions

.A77 Asian religions (General)
.B8 Buddhism
.C4 Chinese religions
.C43 Confucianism
.G4 Germanic religions
.G8 Greek religions and philosophies
.H5 Hinduism
Islam, see BP172
.J35 Japanese religions
Judaism, see BM535
.R7 Roman religions and culture
.S5 Shinto
.S6 Sikhism
.Z6 Zoroastrianism

Persecution
For persecution of individual sects, see BX
1600 Early through 1800
1601 1801-1950
.2 1951-
History
By region or country
1607 Great Britain
1608 Other, A-Z
e.g. .C7 Communist countries
1609.5 Dissent
1610 Tolerance and toleration

(BS) BIBLE

General

Works about the Bible
680 Special topics, A-Z
Cf. BS1199, Topics in the Old Testament
BS2417, Topics in the teachings of Jesus
BS2545, Topics in the New Testament
.A93 Authority
.C63 Conflict management
.E84 Ethics
.G6 Good and evil
.J8 Justice
.N6 Nonviolence
.P37 Patriotism
.P4 Peace
.P45 Political science
.P5 Power
.R2 Race
.W2 War

Old Testament

Works about the Old Testament
1199 Special topics, A-Z
.E8 Ethics
Evil, see .G65
.G65 Good and evil
.J8 Justice
.N3 Nationalism
.P4 Peace
.P6 Politics
.V56 Violence

.W2 War
Special parts of the Old Testament
Historical books
Pentateuch
Deuteronomy
Decalog. Ten Commandments
Criticism, commentaries, etc.
1285 Early through 1950
1951-
.2 Criticism
.3 Commentaries
.4 Sermons. Meditations
New Testament
Works about the New Testament
2415.A4-Z The teachings of Jesus
2417 Special teachings, A-Z
.A4 Aggression
.E8 Ethics
.P2 Pacifism
.P6 Political teachings
.R3 Race relations
.V56 Violence
.W2 War
2545 Special topics, A-Z
.B7 Brotherliness
.C55 Church and state
.C57 Concord
.C58 Conscience
.E8 Ethics
.J8 Justice
.P4 Pacifism
.P5 Peace
.P6 Political science
.P66 Power
.W3 War

(BT) CHRISTIANITY (DOCTRINAL THEOLOGY)

Formal treatises
70 Early through 1800
75 1801-1950
.2 1951-
77 Popular works
Christology
Life of Christ
Special topics
Public life
Sermon on the Mount
General works
380.A33-Z Early through 1950
.2 1951-
382 The beatitudes
Creation
696 Life. Reverence for life
Man. Doctrinal anthropology
700 Early through 1800
701 1801-1950
.2 1951-
702 General special

715 Sin
720 Original sin
722 Guilt
730 Accountability. Moral responsibility
734 Man and race
.2 Race relations (General)
736 Man and state
Cf. BV629, Church and state
.15 The Christian and violence
.2 The Christian and war
Including the arms race
.4 The Christian and peace
.6 The Christian and nonviolence
738 Man and society
.15 Theology of civil rights
.25 Theology of power
.3 Theology of revolution

(BV) CHRISTIANITY (PRACTICAL THEOLOGY)

Ecclesiastical theology
Special aspects of church institutions
Church and state (General)
Church and civil government. Passive obedience
Cf. BX1790+, Catholic Church
JK, JN, Political theory
General works
629 Early through 1800
630.A3-Z 1801-1950
.2 1951-
Practical Religion. The Christian life
Moral theology
Virtues
4647 Individual virtues, A-Z
.B7 Brotherliness
.J8 Justice
.N6 Nonresistance
.P33 Patriotism
.P35 Peace
Precepts from the Bible
4655 Ten Commandments
By commandment
4680 Sixth commandment
Cf. BT736.2, The Christian and war
JX1937+, Peace literature

(BX) CHRISTIAN DENOMINATIONS

Catholic Church
Controversial works against Catholics
1763 Early through 1800
1765 1801-1950
.2 1951-
1766 Anti-Catholicism. Antipapism
Class here descriptive or historical works
Catholic Church and state (General)
Including diplomatic relations
1790 Early through 1950
1791 1951-
1793 Catholic viewpoint on political theory

Including world politics, international relations, etc.
Diplomatic relations with individual countries
These works class in BX1401+ (not included in this guide)
1795 Special topics, A-Z
.A85 Atomic warfare
.C58 Civil rights
.E44 Emigration and immigration
.N66 Nonviolence
Nuclear warfare, see .A85
.P43 Peace
.W37 War
Government and organization
1908 Legates. Nuncios
Cf. JX1801+, Diplomatic services

Friends. Society of Friends. Quakers

Collected works
7615 Several authors
7617 Individual authors
Including religious works of William Penn and George Fox
General works. Doctrines
7730 Early through 1800
7731 1800-1950
.2 1951-
Sermons. Tracts
Class sermons on special topics with the subject
7733.A1 Several authors
.A3-Z Individual authors
By author or title, A-Z
7748 Special topics, A-Z
.C5 Civil government
Conscientious objectors, see UB
.I65 International activities
.L37 Liberty
.R3 Race relations
.S2 Sacredness of human life
.S4 Self-defense
.W2 War
German Baptist Brethren. Church of the Brethren
General works. Doctrines
7821 Early through 1950
.2 1951-
Sermons. Tracts
Class sermons on special topics with the subject
7827.A1 Several authors
.A3-Z Individual authors
By author and title, A-Z
Lutheran Churches
8074 Special topics, A-Z
.P4 Peace
Mennonites
8109 Collected works
.M3-5 Menno Simons' works
Collected works
.M3 Dutch
.M31 Selections
.M32-33 English

.M34-35 French
.M36-37 German
.M4 Other languages, A-Z
Individual works
Dat fundamentum
.M5 Dutch
.M52 English
.M55 German
General works
8120 Early through 1800
8121 1801-1950
.2 1951-
Sermons. Tracts
Class sermons on special topics with the subject
8127.A1 Several authors
.A3-Z Individual authors
8128 Special topics, A-Z
.P4 Peace
8129 Individual branches of Mennonites, A-Z
For Old Mennonites, see BX8120+
e.g. .A1 Collective
.A5 Amish Mennonites
.A6 Old Order Amish Mennonite Church
.M5 Mennonite Church
Methodism
8349 Special topics, A-Z
.P43 Peace
Mormons. Church of Jesus Christ of Latter-Day Saints
8643 Special topics, A-Z
.P6 Politics. Church and state
.W3 War
Shakers
9789 Special topics, A-Z
.W2 War and peace

(CB) HISTORY OF CIVILIZATION

Class here general works only; for individual countries, see D-F
3 Periodicals. Societies. Serials
.5 Congresses
15 Historiography
Biography of historians
17 Collective
18 Individual, A-Z
19 Philosophy. Theory
20 Study and teaching
General works
Early through 1800
23 Latin
25 American and English
27 French
29 German
31 Italian
33 Spanish
35 Other, A-Z
1801-
American
51 1801-1849
53 1850-1950

57 Elementary textbooks. Juvenile works
59 1951-1973
English
61 1801-1849
63 1850-1950
67 Elementary textbooks. Juvenile works
68 1951-1973
69 American and English, 1974-
.2 Elementary textbooks. Juvenile works
French
71 1801-1849
73 1850-1950
77 Elementary textbooks. Juvenile works
78 1951-
.2 Elementary textbooks. Juvenile works
German
81 1801-1849
83 1850-1950
87 Elementary textbooks. Juvenile works
88 1951-
Italian
91 1801-1849
93 1850-1950
94 1951-
Spanish
101 1801-1849
103 1850-1950
104 1951-
113 Other languages, A-Z
151 General special
Forecasts of future developments and progress
Class here general works only. For forecasting in relation to special topics, see the subject
158 Methodology
Special forecasts. By author or title
160 Published through 1950
161 1951-
195 Civilization and race
197 General special
Special civilizations
201 Caucasian. Aryan
Europe
For works on European civilization limited to individual centuries before 1800, see CB353.7+
203 General works
204 19th century
205 20th century
206 Alpine. Celtic
213 Nordic
214 General special
216 Anglo-Saxon
224 Mediterranean. Latin
226 Spanish
231 Slavic
235 Black
241 Semitic
245 Occidental. Western
251 East and West. Oriental and Occidental

Including cultural relations and culture conflict
253 Oriental. Eastern
255 Buddhist
256 Confucian
261 North and South
Including cultural relations and culture conflict
271 Developing countries
281 Other
By period
305 Protohistory
311 Ancient
331 Early Christian
351 Medieval
353 General special
.7 7th century
.8 8th century
354 10th century
.3 11th century
.6 12th century
355 13th century
357 Modern
358 General special
359 Renaissance and Reformation
361 Renaissance
365 14th century
367 1401-1550
369 1551-1600
401 16th-17th centuries
411 18th century
415 19th century
417 General special
425 1900-1970
426 Juvenile works
427 General special
428 1971-
429 Juvenile works
430 General special
Relation to special topics
440 Astronautics and civilization
448 Economic conditions and civilization
451 Imperialism and civilization
465 Ocean and civilization
478 Technology/science and civilization
481 War and civilization

(CJ) NUMISMATICS

Medals and medallions
Medieval and modern
5793 Special subjects, A-Z
Class works on medals issued by an individual society with the society in classes A-Z
.P4 Peace

(CR) HERALDRY

Chivalry and knighthood
Orders
History and description
General works

4651 Through 1800
4653 1801-
By period
4657 Early
4659 Medieval
4661 Modern
4701 Military-religious orders
4705 General special
International orders
Order of Saint John of Jerusalem
Including Knights Hospitalers, Knights of Rhodes, and Knights of Malta
4715 Sources and documents
4717 Statutes, regulations, etc.
4715 Lists and arms of knights
4723 History
4725 General special
4731 By region or country, A-Z
Under each country:
.x General works
.x2 Local, A-Z
Order of the Temple (Knights Templars)
4735 Sources and documents
4737 Statutes, regulations, etc.
4739 Lists and arms of knights
4743 History
4749 General special
4755 By region or country, A-Z
Under each country:
.x General works
.x2 Local, A-Z
Teutonic Knights
Cf. CR4991, Austrian order
4759 Sources and documents
4765 History
For the Teutonic Knights in East Prussia, see DK4600.P77
4775 By country, German state, A-Z
By region or country
Europe
Austria
4991 Teutonic Knights

(D) HISTORY (GENERAL)

Including Europe (General). For individual countries, see the country

For subarrangement for individual biography, see tables at the end of the D schedule

13 Historiography
.5 By region or country, A-Z
Biography of historians
14 Collective
15 Individual, A-Z
16 Methodology
Special topics
.16 Psychohistory
.2 Study and teaching
.25 General special

Including area studies
By country
.3 United States
.4 Other countries, A-Z
.5 Schools, by place or name, A-Z
Philosophy of history
.7 To 1800
.8 1801-
.9 Special topics
Periodicity, historical materialism, etc.
World histories
17 Works written before 1525
18 Works written from 1525 to 1800
20 1801-
21 Textbooks. Outlines
.3 General special
.5 Historical geography
24 Historical events not restricted to one country or period
Including disasters as historic events
25 Military history (General)
Including Europe; for individual countries, see DA-DU; E-F
.A2 Dictionaries. Chronological tables
.A3-Z General works
.5 General special
.9 Pamphlets
27 Naval history (General)
Including Europe; for individual countries, see DA-DU; E-F
31 Political and diplomatic history (General)
Including Europe; for individual countries, see DA-DU; E-F
32 General special
33 Pamphlets
34 Relations between Europe and individual countries, A-Z
For relations between Europe and individual countries limited to 1945- , see D1065

Ancient history

56 Historiography
Biography of historians
.5 Collective
.52 Individual, A-Z
e.g. .H45 Herodotus
General works
To 1525, see D17
57 1525-
58 Works by classical historians
Class here translations, except into Latin, and criticism and commentaries dealing primarily with historical events of works by Diodorus, Herodotus, Polybius, etc. Original texts, Latin translations, and philological commentaries and criticism class in PA (which is not included in this guide)
59 Textbooks
62 General special
95 Naval history

Medieval and Modern History (Treated together)
Including Europe; for individual countries, see DA-DU

102 General works
103 Textbooks
104 General special

105 Political and diplomatic history
106 Biography and memoirs (Collective)
107 Kings and rulers

Medieval History

Including Europe; for individual countries <u>see</u> DA-DU

113 Sources and documents. Chronicles
116 Historiography
Biography of historians
.5 Collective
.7 Individual, A-Z
General works
117.A2 Early
Chronicles, <u>see</u> D113
.A3-Z Modern
118 Textbooks. Outlines
By period
121 Early to 10th century
123 9th-10th centuries
Later, <u>see</u> D135+
128 Military and naval history
131 Political history
135 Migrations of nations
137 Goths (General). Visigoths
138 Ostrogoths
139 Vandals
141 Huns. Attila
143 Battle of Chalons, 451
145 Lombards
147 Slavs
148 Normans
149 Other special (not A-Z)
Crusades
Sources and documents
151 Collections of chronicles
152 Individual chronicles
156 Biography
For memoirs, <u>see</u> the individual crusade
157 General works
158 Textbooks. Outlines
160 Other
First crusade, 1096-1099
161 Sources
.1 Memoirs and contemporary accounts
.2 General works
.3 Pamphlets
.5 Part taken by individual countries, A-Z
Second crusade, 1147-1149
162 Sources
.1 Memoirs and contemporary accounts
.2 General works
.3 Pamphlets
.5 Part taken by individual countries, A-Z
Third crusade, 1189-1193
163.A2 Sources
.A3 Memoirs and contemporary accounts
.A4-Z General works
.3 Pamphlets
.5 Part taken by individual countries, A-Z

Fourth crusade, 1196-1198; 1204-1219
Siege of Constantinople, 1203-1204
164.A2 Sources
.A3 Memoirs and contemporary accounts
.A4-Z General works
.3 Pamphlets
.5 Part taken by individual countries, A-Z
165 Fifth crusade, 1217-1221
Siege of Damietta, 1218-1219
166 Sixth crusade, 1228-1229
167 Seventh crusade, 1248-1250
168 Eighth crusade, 1270
169 Children's crusade, 1212
171 Later crusades. Crusades in the east
172 General special
173 Crusades in the West
Latin Kingdom of Jerusalem. Latin Orient
176 Sources and documents
177 Chronicles
Biography, memoirs, journals
180 Collective
181 Individual, A-Z
General works
Chronicles, <u>see</u> D177
182.A2 Early to 1800
.A3-Z 1801-
183 General special
Later medieval
200 11th-15th centuries
201 11th-12th centuries
11th century
.3 Sources and documents
.4 General works
12th century
.7 Sources and documents
.8 General works
202 13th-15th centuries
13th century
.3 Sources and documents
.4 General works
14th century
.7 Sources and documents
.8 General works
203 15th century

Modern history, 1453-
Including Europe; for individual countries, <u>see</u> DA-DU; E-F
206 Historiography
208 General works
209 Textbooks
210 General special
214 Military history
215 Naval history
217 Political and diplomatic history. European concert. Balance of power
1453-1648
Including 16th century
219 Periodicals
220 Sources and documents
221 Reports and communications of ambassadors, etc. By accrediting

country, A-Z
Biography and memoirs
226 Collective
.6 Military and naval
.7 Rulers, kings, queens, etc.
.8 Individual, A-Z
228 General works
229 Pamphlets
231 General special
234 Political and diplomatic history
1601-1715. 17th century
242 Sources and documents
Biography and memoirs
244 Collective
.5 Public men
.6 Military and naval
.7 Rulers, kings, queens, etc.
.8 Individual, A-Z
246 General works
247 General special
Thirty Years' War, 1618-1648
251 Sources and documents
256 Memoirs, A-Z
258 General works
259 Pamphlets
260 Other
General special
261 Causes
262 Bohemia, 1618-1623, and Palatinate
263 Denmark, 1623-1629
264 Sweden, 1630-1635
265 1635-1648
267 Special events, battles, etc., A-Z
e.g. .E3 Edict of Restitution, 1629
.L3 Leipzig, Battle of, 1631
.U6 Ulm, Truce of, 1647
269 Peace of Westphalia, 1648
270 Biography of participants, A-Z
.A2 Collective
271 Relations of individual countries, A-Z
1648-1715
273.A2A-Z Sources and documents
.A3-Z General works
Anglo-Dutch wars, see DJ180+
.5 General special
Biography and memoirs
Collective, see D244
274 Individual, A-Z
.5 Anglo-French War, 1666-1667
.6 Treaty of Breda, 1667
275 War of Devolution, 1667-1668
.5 Pamphlets
276 Special events, battles, etc., A-Z
e.g. .A3 Aix-la-Chapelle, Peace of, 1668
277 Dutch War, 1672-1678
.5 General special
278 Special events, battles, etc., A-Z
.5 Peace of Nijmegen, 1678-1679

279 War of the Grand Alliance, 1688-1697
.5 General special
280 Special events, battles, etc., A-Z
.5 Peace of Ryswick, 1697
War of Spanish Succession, 1701-1714
281.A2 Sources and documents
.A3-Z Memoirs and early works
.5 General works
282 General special
.5 Pamphlets
283 Special events, battles, etc., A-Z
.5 Treaty of Utrecht, 1713
Including the Treaty of Baden, 1714; and the Treaty of Rastatt, 1714
1715-1789. 18th century
284 Sources and documents
Biography and memoirs
285 Collective
.5 Public men
.7 Rulers, kings, queens, etc.
.8 Individual, A-Z
286 General works
287 Diplomatic history
.5 Quadruple Alliance, 1718
.7 Treaty of Hanover, 1725
.8 Treaty of Seville, 1729
288 Other special
289 1740-1789
.4 Family Pact, Fontainebleau, 1743
.5 Family Pact, Paris, 1761
290 Pamphlets
War of Austrian Succession, 1740-1748
291 Sources and documents
292 General works
.8 Pamphlets
293 Silesian campaigns. International relations
Military history, <u>see</u> DD406+
.2 Rhine and Danube, 1741-1744
.3 Special events, battles, etc., A-Z
.4 Italy, 1741-1748
.5 Special events, battles, etc., A-Z
.55 Other
.6 Netherlands, 1743-1748
.7 Special events, battles, etc., A-Z
.8 Colonial. Naval operations
.9 Special events, battles, etc., A-Z
294 Peace of Aix-la-Chapelle, 1748
1750-1789
295 Political and military history
History of the armed neutrality of 1780; Treaty of Versailles, 1783, etc.
Cf. JX5383, International law
297 Seven Years' War
General international aspects only
299 1789-
Including 18th and 19th centuries together
1789-1815
301 Periodicals. Sources and documents

304 Biography and memoirs, A-Z
308 General works
309 Other
Revolutionary and Napoleonic wars, see DC220+
19th century. 1801-1914/1920
351 Sources and documents
Biography and memoirs
352 Collective
.1 Rulers, kings, etc.
.2 Queens, princesses, etc.
.5 Public men
.8 Individual, A-Z
358 General works
.5 Popular works
359 Europe in the 19th century
Class sources, biography, etc. pertaining to Europe in D351+
.7 General special
361 Military history
362 Naval history
363 Political and diplomatic history
371 Eastern question
372 General special
373 Early history to 1800
374 19th century
375 General special
.3 Conference and Treaty of Berlin, 1878
Cf. JX1383, International relations
20th century, see D461+
376 Relations of individual countries, A-Z
Slavs and Panslavism
377 Slavs
.3 Panslavism
Especially political works
.5 By country, A-Z
378 Central Asian question
.5 By country, A-Z
East Asia, see DS515+
383 1815-1830
Including Holy Alliance and Quadruple Alliance, 1815
385 1830-1848
387 1848
1848-1859
388 Sources and documents
389 General works
1860-1870
391 Sources and documents
392 General works
393 Pamphlets
1871- . Later 19th century
394 Sources and documents
395 General works
396 Military history
397 Political and diplomatic history
Including Franco-Russian alliance. Triple Alliance, 1882
398 Other
Biography and memoirs
399 Collective
.6 Public men

.7 Rulers, kings, etc.
.8 Queens, princesses, etc.
400 Individual, A-Z
20th century
410 Periodicals. Societies
411 Sources and documents
Biography and memoirs
412 Collective
.6 Public men
.7 Rulers, kings, etc.
.8 Queens, princesses, etc.
413 Individual, A-Z
.5 Historiography
416 Pamphlets
421 General works
422 Popular works
424 Europe in the 20th century
Class periodicals, sources, etc., in D410+
431 Military history
436 Naval history
437 Air warfare
Political and diplomatic history
441 Sources and documents
443 General works
445 General special
Including imaginary wars and future world politics
446 Anglo-Saxon supremacy
447 Pangermanism (International)
Cf. DD119, German imperialism
448 Panlatinism
.5 Panceltism
449 Panslavism
450 Pamphlets
Diplomatic history
451 Sources and documents
453 General works
455 General special
457 Pamphlets
460 Little Entente, 1919-
Eastern question
Cf. D371+, Eastern question in the 19th century
461 Sources and documents
462 Conferences, etc., by date
463 General works
465 General special
468 Pamphlets
469 By country, A-Z
Central Asian question
1901-1914, see D378
471 1914-
472 By country, A-Z
East Asia, see DS515+

World War, 1914-1918
(World War I)

501 Periodicals.
502 Societies
Cf. D570.A+, American Legion, etc.
503 Museums, exhibitions, etc.

Art exhibitions class in the N schedule, which is not included in this guide
504 Congresses, conferences, etc.
505 Sources and documents
Biography
507 Collective
Individual, see individual countries, D-F
510 Dictionaries
511 Causes. Origin. Aims
512 Austria
513 Serbia
514 Russia. Panslavism
515 Germany
516 France
517 Great Britain
Including colonies in general
518 Belgium
519 Japan
520 Other countries, A-Z
521 General works
522 Pictorial works.
.22 Films, slides, etc. Catalogs
.23 Motion pictures about the war
.25 Posters
.4 Study and teaching
.42 Historiography
.5 Outlines
.6 Examinations, questions, etc.
.7 Juvenile works. Elementary textbooks
523 General special
524 Ethical and religious aspects
Including prophecy
525 Pamphlets, sermons, etc.
War poetry, see class P, which is not included in this guide
526 Satire, caricature, etc.
.2 English
.3 French
.5 German
.7 Other languages, A-Z
528 Guides to the battlefields
Special, see the battle
.5 Beginnings of the war. Mobilization
Military operations
529 Collections of official reports
General works, see D521
Special arms
.3 Infantry
.4 Cavalry
.5 Artillery
.7 Engineers
.9 Other special, A-Z
Cf. D600+, Aerial and tank operations
Cf. D570+, Individual countries
530 Western
531 German
Including memoirs by Falkenhayn, Hindenburg, and Ludenforff
Special
.5 German local history, A-Z

539 Austrian. Austro-Hungarian
.5 Special, A-Z
e.g. .C8 Czechoslovak troops
.7 Local history, A-Z
540 Hungarian
.5 Special, A-Z
541 Belgian and operations in Belgium
542 Individual campaigns, battles, etc., A-Z
e.g. .M7 Mons
.Y6 Ypres, 1st Battle of, 1914
.Y7 Ypres, 2d Battle of, 1915
.Y72 Ypres, 3d Battle of, 1917
544 Anglo-French. Allies
545 Individual campaigns, battles, etc., A-Z
e.g. .M3 Marne, Battle of the, 1914
.V25 Verdun, Battle of, 1914
.V3 Verdun, Battle of, 1916
English
546.A1-19 Societies
.A2-Z General works
Special
547 Individual by region or name, A-Z
e.g. .A1 Colonies (General)
.A8 Australia
.C2 Canada
.C6 Coldstream Guards
.8 English local history, A-Z
548 French
Special
.9 Other special, A-Z
Including colonial
549.5 Other countries, A-Z
e.g. .P8 Portugal
Including colonies
.P82 Local history, A-Z
550 Eastern. Russia (General)
551 Russo-German
Including Poland, Volhynia, etc.
552 Individual campaigns, battles, etc., A-Z
556 Russo-Austrian
557 Individual campaigns, battles, etc., A-Z
558 Siberia
559 Northern Russia
560 Balkan
561 Serbian
562 Individual campaigns, battles, etc., A-Z
563.A2 Bulgarian
.A3-Z Individual campaigns, battles, etc., A-Z
564.A2 Montenegrin
.A3-Z Individual campaigns, battles, etc., A-Z
565.A2 Romanian
.A3-Z Individual campaigns, battles, etc., A-Z
566 Turkey and the Middle East
567.A2 Turco-Russian
.A3-Z Individual campaigns, battles, etc., A-Z
568.A2 Turco-Egyptian
.A3-Z Individual campaigns, battles, etc., A-Z
.2 Egypt

.3 Dardanelles. Gallipoli
.4 Arabia
.5 Mesopotamia. Assyria
.6 Syria
.7 Palestine
.8 Iran
.9 West Turkestan and Khurasan
569.A2 Italian
.A25 Divisions, regiments, etc. By author, A-Z
.A3-Z Individual campaigns, battles, etc., A-Z
e.g. .V5 Vittorio Veneto, Battle of, 1918
.2 Greece. Macedonian campaign
.3 Individual campaigns, battles, etc., A-Z
.5 Albania
570 United States
Societies
.A1 American Legion
.A12 By state, A-W
.A13 By city, A-Z
.A14 Auxiliary
.A14A1-4 Official publications
.A14A5 Nonofficial publications
.A14A6-W By state, A-W
.A14Z9 Pamphlets
.A15 Other societies, A-Z
.A2 Serials. Official bulletins, etc.
.A4-Z General works on participation in the war
.A4 Official
.A5-Z Nonofficial
.1 General special
.15 Pamphlets
Causes, see D619
Military operations
General works, see D570.A4+
Individual battles, see D545
Naval operations
General works, see D589.U5+
.45 General special
Including Marine Corps (general)
Aerial operations
General works, see D606
.65 General special
.72 Transportation service
.73 Special, A-Z
.75 Services of supply
.8 Special topics, A-Z
.A6 Alien enemies
.C4 Civil liberty
Cf. JC591, Political theory
.C5 Commissions of foreign nations, A-Z
Conscientious objectors, see UB342.U5
.C7 Council of National Defense
.C8 Councils of defense
By state, A-W
.M5 Missions to the United States
.M6 Individual missions, A-Z
.N3 National Research Council
.P7 Political prisoners

Prisons and prisoners, see D627
.R4 Registration
Repatriation, see JX4265
.S4 Seizure of German ships
570.85 By state, A-W
e.g. .A2-21 Alabama
Under each:
(1) General
(2) Local, A-Z
.87 Outlying possessions, A-Z
e.g. .H3 Hawaii
.9 Personal narratives, A-Z
Cf. D640, Personal narratives (General)
For military biography, see E745
571 Japanese
572 Individual battles, etc., A-Z
573 Colonial
574 German
575 African
576 Individual colonies, A-Z
577 Pacific, Asian, etc.
578 Individual colonies, A-Z
580 Naval operations
581 Anglo-German. Blockade
582 By engagement, ship, A-Z
e.g. .D8 Dresden (Cruiser)
.J8 Jutland, Battle of, 1916
583 Franco-Austrian. French
584 By engagement, ship, etc., A-Z
Japanese, see D571+
585 Russian
586 Egyptian
587 Turkish
588 Italian
589 Other, A-Z
e.g. .U5-8 United States
.U5 Documents
.U6 General works
.U7 By engagement, ship, A-Z
.U8 Awarding of medals
590 Submarine operations
591 German
592 By engagement, ship, etc., A-Z
e.g. .L8 Lusitania (Steamship)
593 English
594 By engagament, ship, etc., A-Z
595 Other, A-Z
600 Aerial operations
602 English
603 French
604 German
605 Russian
606 United States
607 Other, A-Z
.3 Engineering operations
608 Tank operations
610 Diplomatic history
Cf. JX1392, International law

611 General special
Including neutrality
613 Peace efforts during the war
Cf. D642+, Peace at close of war
.5 Ford Peace Expedition
614 Separate treaties, A-Z
e.g. .A2 Collections
.B8 Bucharest, 1918
Individual countries
615 Belgium. Belgian neutrality
616 Greece
617 Italy. Italian neutrality
Cf. D520.I7, Origin of war in Italy
618 South America
For individual countries, see D621
619 United States. American neutrality
Including reasons for American participation
.3 German propaganda, espionage, etc.
.5 Individual cases, A-Z
620 German Americans and the war
621 Other countries, A-Z
Special topics
622 Catholic Church and the war
623.A2 Occupied territory
.A3-Z By country, A-Z
625 Atrocities. War crimes. Trials
626 By country, A-Z
627 Prisoners and prisons
.A1 Periodicals. Societies
.A2 General works
.A3-Z In individual countries, A-Z
Under each: .A1-19, Periodicals
628 Medical care. Hospitals. Red Cross
629 By country, A-Z
630 Biography, A-Z
e.g. .C3 Cavell, Edith
631 Press. Censorship. Publicity
632 American press
633 Other special
635 Economic aspects
636.A2 Alien enemies
.A3-Z By country, A-Z
637 Relief work. Charities. Refugees
638 By country, A-Z
639 Other special topics, A-Z
For topics applicable only to the United States, see D570.8
.A6 Amnesty
.A64 Anarchism
.A7 Anthropology. Race relations
.C4 Children. Orphans
.C5 Christian Science
.C54 Church of England
.C75 Cryptography
.D45 Democracy and the war
.D5 Deportations
.E2 Education and the war
.E3 United States
.E45 France

.F9 Friends, Society of
.I2 Idealism
.I5 Illegitimacy. War babies
.J4 Jews
Including the Jewish pogroms in Ukraine
.M37 Mennonites
.M4 Merchant marine
.M5 By country, A-Z
.M8 Mutinies
.M82 By country, A-Z
.N2 Naturalized subjects in belligerent countries
.N3 By country, A-Z
Cf. D570.8.A6; D620, United States
.P5 Population and the war
.P6 Propaganda
.P7 By country, A-Z
.P77 Protest movements
.P78 Protestant churches
.P87 Public opinion
.P88 By country, A-Z
Quakers, see .F9
.R4 Religious aspects
.S15 Salvation Army
.S2 Science and technology
Cf. UG447, Chemical warfare
.S6 Socialism
.S7 Spies. Secret service
.S8 Individual, A-Z
.S9 Supplies
.T8 Transportation
Cf. D570.72+, United States
.W7 Women

Personal narratives
Cf. D570.9, United States
640.A2A-Z Collective
.A22-Z Individual, A-Z
641 Armistice
Peace
Cf. D613+, Peace efforts during the war
642 Sources and documents
643 Treaty with Central powers
Germany. Versailles Treaty, 1919
.A2 Collected texts
.A3-4 Preliminary discussions
.A5 Texts and drafts. By date
.A51 Protocol
.A55 Reservations. By date
.A6 Official discussions. By date
.A65 Other official. By date
.A67 Peace resolution (U.S. Congress). By date
.A68 Treaty of peace, United States and Germany. By date
.A7-Z Nonofficial discussions
Other countries
Austria, 1919
.A8 Texts. By date
.A81 Other official. By date
.A83 Treaty of peace, United States and Austria. By date
.A9 Discussions

Bulgaria, 1919
.B5 Texts. By date
.B6 Discussions
Hungary
.H7 Texts and drafts (other than the United States). By date
.H75 Other official. By date
.H8 Treaties, United States and Hungary. By date
.H9 Nonofficial discussions
Turkey, 1920
.T8 Texts. By date
644 General works
645 General special
646 Pamphlets
647.A2 Peace commissions (Personnel)
.A3-Z By country, A-Z
Special topics
648 Indemnity and reparation
649 By region or country, A-Z
Other special, A-Z
.B7 Bridges of the Rhine
.D5 Disarmament (German)
Eastern question, see D645
.I6 Inter-allied Military Commission of Control in Germany
.J4 Jews
.M5 Military occupation of the Rhine
.R8 Ruhr River and Valley
.T4 Territorial questions
651 Individual regions or countries, A-Z
Including territorial questions by country
.A4 Africa
.A41 Africa, German East
.A42 Africa, German Southwest
.A4 Albania and Epirus
.A7 Armenia
.A95 Austria
.A98 Azerbaijan
.B2 Baltic States
.B25 Banat
.B3 Belgium
.B4 Bessarabia
.B8 Bulgaria
.C3 Cameroon
.C4 China
.C5 Relations of America to Shantung
.C6 Relations of Japan to Shantung
.C7 Other countries, A-Z
.C75 Circassia
.C78 Croatia
.C8 Cuba
.C9 Czechoslovakia
.D3 Dalmatia
.E3 Egypt
.E8 Estonia
France
General works
.F5Al-29 Collections
.F5A3 Comprehensive treaty texts
.F5A4-Z Other

Relations of United States to France
.F6A2 Treaty text
.F6A3 United States official publications. By date
.F6A4 French official publications. By date
.F6A6-Z Nonofficial works
.F7 Relations of other countries
.G18 Galicia
.G2 Georgia
Germany
.G3A2 Collections
Treaty text, see D643
.G3A3-Z General works
.G4 Gorz
.G5-7 Great Britain
Subdivided like France
.G8 Greece
.H7 Hungary
.I5 Istria
.I6-8 Italy
Including Fiume
Subdivided like France
.J3-5 Japan
Subdivided like France
Kamerun, see .C3
.L4 Latvia
.L45 Lebanon
.L5 Lithuania
.L8 Luxemburg
.M3 Macedonia
.M4 Mesopotamia
.M7 Montenegro
.N3 Nauru
.N5 Nicaragua
.P2 Pacific Islands (German)
.P3 Palestine
.P4 Persia. Iran
.P7 Poland
.P75 Portugal
.P8 Posen
.P89 Prussia, East
.P9 Prussia, West
.S13 Saar Valley
.S3 Samoa (Western)
.S4 Schleswig
Serbia, see .Y8
.S5 Silesia, Upper
.S53 Slovenia
.S7 Styria
.S9 Syria
.T5 Thrace
.T7 Togoland
.T8 Transylvania
.T85 Trieste
.T9 Turkey
.T95 Tyrol
.U6 Ukraine
.Y8 Yugoslavia
.Y9 Relations of other countries to Yugoslavia, A-Z

Fiume, see .I6+

Reconstruction. Postwar period

652 Sources and documents

653 General works

655 Other

Individual countries

657 United States

658 By state, A-W

659 Other countries, A-Z

663 Celebrations. Memorials. Monuments

665 Other

670 United States

671 Veterans Day (Armistice Day) services and addresses

673 States, A-W

675 Cities, A-Z

e.g. .A74 Tomb of the Unknowns

680 Other countries, A-Z

Period between World Wars, 1919-1939

720 General works

723 General special

725 Pamphlets

726 European civilization

.5 Fascism

727 Political and diplomatic history

728 Rome-Berlin axis

World War, 1939-1945
(World War II)

731 Periodicals. Serials

732 Societies

733.A1A-Z Museums, exhibitions, etc.

.A2-Z By region or country, A-Z

Under each country:

.x General works

.x2 By city, A-Z

734.A1A-Z Congresses, conferences, etc.

.A2-Z Individual

735 Sources and documents

.A1 Collection and preservation of war records

.A7 Atlantic Declaration, August 14, 1941

Biography

736 Collective

Individual, see country of the individual, D-F, other appropriate class for biography, or D811+, Personal narratives

740 Dictionaries

741 Causes. Origins. Aims

742 By country, A-Z

743 General works

.2 Pictorial works

.22 Films, slides, etc. Catalogs

.23 Motion pictures about the war

.25 Posters

.4 Study and teaching

.42 Historiography

Including criticism of books on the war

.5 Outlines

Including chronology of the war

.6 Examinations, questions, etc.

.7 Juvenile works. Elementary textbooks
.9 Pamphlets
744 General special
.4 Ethical and religious aspects
.5 By region or country, A-Z
.6 Social aspects
.7 By region or country, A-Z
War poetry, see class P, which is not included in this guide
745 Satire, caricature, etc.
.2 English
.3 French
.5 German
.7 Other languages, A-Z
747 Guides to the battlefields
Special, see the individual battle
748 Diplomatic history
749 General special. Neutrality
.5 Separate treaties during the war, A-Z
By country
750 Great Britain
751 Germany
752 France
.8 The Americas. Neutrality
753 United States. Neutrality
Cf. D742.U5, Reasons for participation
.2 Lend-lease agreements, by country, A-Z
.3 Enemy propaganda, espionage, etc.
754 Other regions or countries, A-Z
Military operations. The war effort
General works, see D743
By period
755 September 1939-December 1941
.1 September 1939-May 1940
.2 1940
.3 1941
.4 1942
.5 1943
.6 1944
.7 1945
.8 VE Day to VJ Day
By region
756 Western
.3 General special
.5 Individual campaigns, battles, A-Z
e.g. .A7 Ardennes, Battle of the, 1944-1945
757 Germany
.1 Armies
.9 Local, A-Z
759 Great Britain
760.8 Local history, A-Z
e.g. .L7 London
761 France
Special
.1 Armies
.9 Other, A-Z
.F7 France combattante. French volunteer force. Free French forces
762 Local history, A-Z

e.g. .P3 Paris
763 Other countries, A-Z
e.g. .B4 Belgium
.B42 Local history, A-Z
.D4 Denmark
.D42 Local history, A-Z
.I2 Iceland
.I8 Italy
.I82 Local history, A-Z
.L9 Luxemburg
.M3 Malta
.N4 Netherlands
.N42 Local history, A-Z
.N6 Norway
.N62 Local history, A-Z
.S5 Sicily
763.5 Arctic regions
Including Greenland
764 Eastern.
Soviet Union (General), see D764
.3 Individual campaigns, battles, A-Z
e.g. .S7 Stalingrad, Battle of, 1942-1943
.7 Local history, A-Z
765 Poland
.2 Local history, A-Z
e.g. W3 Warsaw
.3 Finland
.35 Local history, A-Z
.4 Austria
.45 Local history, A-Z
.5 Czechoslovakia
.55 Local history, A-Z
.56 Hungary
.562 Local history, A-Z
766 Balkans and the Middle East
By country
.3 Greece
.32 Local history, A-Z
.4 Romania
.42 Local history, A-Z
.6 Yugoslavia
.62 Local history, A-Z
.7 Other countries, A-Z
e.g. .A4 Albania
.C7 Crete
.S9 Syria
.8 Africa
.82 North Africa
.84 East Africa
By country
.9 Egypt
.92 Ethiopia
.93 Libya
.95 Zaire. Belgian Congo
.96 French Equatorial Africa
.97 South Africa
.99 Other countries, A-Z
767 East Asia. Battle of the Pacific

Including military and naval operations
By country
.2 Japan
.25 Local history, A-Z
e.g. .H6 Hiroshima
.N3 Nagasaki
.255 Korea
.3 China
.35 Cochin China
.352 Local history, A-Z
e.g. .S3 Saigon
.4 Philippines
.45 French Indochina
.47 Thailand
.5 Malay Peninsula
.55 Singapore
.6 India. Burma
.7 Indonesia
.8 Australia
.82 Local history, A-Z
.85 New Zealand
.852 Local history, A-Z
.9 Pacific Islands
.917 Gilbert Islands
.92 Hawaii
.94 Midway Islands
Cf. D774.M5, Battle of Midway
.95 New Guinea
.98 Solomon Islands
.99 Other islands, A-Z
768 The Americas
.15 Canada
.18 Latin America
.2 Mexico
.3 Brazil
769 United States
.A1-15 Societies
.A5-Z General works on participation
.1 General special
Reasons for American participation, see D742.U5
.15 Pamphlets
Military operations
General works, see D769.A5-Z
.2 General special
Individual battles, see D756.5; D767, etc.
.8 Special topics, A-Z
.A6 Aliens
Including evacuation and relocation of Japanese Americans
.C4 Civil liberty
Conscientious objectors, see UB342.U5
Economic aspects, see HC106.4
Espionage, see D753.3
.F6 Foreign population
.P7 Political prisoners
Prisoners and prisons, see D805.U5
.85 By state, A-W
Under each:

(1) General
(2) Local, A-Z
.87 Outlying possessions, A-Z
Hawaii, see D767.92
770 Naval operations
Including freedom of the seas and battle of the Atlantic
771 Anglo-German
772 By engagement, ship, etc., A-Z
e.g. .B5 Bismark (Battleship)
773 United States
774 By engagement, ship, etc., A-Z
e.g. .A7 Arkansas (Battleship)
.M5 Midway, Battle of, 1942
775 Anglo-Italian
.5 By engagement, ship, etc., A-Z
777 Japan
.5 By engagement, ship, etc., A-Z
779 Other countries, A-Z
780 Submarine operations
Including submarine chasers
781 Germany
782 By engagement, ship, etc., A-Z
783 United States
.5 By engagement, ship, etc., A-Z
.6 Japan
.7 By engagement, ship, etc., (not A-Z)
784 Other countries, A-Z
785 Aerial operations
U.S. Strategic Bombing Survey
.U57 General works
.U58 By industry, A-Z
.U6 European War
.U63 Pacific War
786 Great Britain
787 Germany
788 France
790 United States
792 Other countries, A-Z
793 Tank operations
794 Cavalry operations
.5 Commando operations
Special topics
798 Press. Censorship. Publicity
799 By region or country, A-Z
800 Economic aspects (General)
801.A2 Alien enemies
.A3-Z By country, A-Z
United States, see D769.8.A6
802.A2 Occupied territory
Including works on resistance and underground movements in occupied countries
.A3-Z By region or country, A-Z
Under each country:
.x General works
.x2 Local, A-Z
803 Atrocities. War crimes. Trials
804 By country (accused of commiting atrocity), A-Z
e.g. .G4 Germany

Special trials
.G42 Nuremberg Trial of Major German War Criminals, 1945-1946
.G425 Subsequent proceedings, 1946-1949, by defendant A-Z
.G43 Other trials, A-Z

.3 Jewish Holocaust
.35 Errors, inventions, etc.
Including works claiming that the Holocaust did not happen

805 Prisoners and prisons
.A1 Periodicals and societies (General)
.A2 General works
.A3-Z Individual countries, A-Z
Class works with the country in which the prisons or prisoners are located
Under each: .A1-19, Periodicals
e.g. .U5 United States
Cf. D769.8.A6, Japanese American relocation centers

806 Medical care. Hospitals. Red Cross
807 By country, A-Z
808 Relief work. Refugees
809 By country, A-Z
e.g. .U5 United States
Including American relief in other countries

810 Other special topics, A-Z
.A6 Anarchism
.A7 Art and the war
.B3 Bacterial warfare
.B66 Bomb reconnaissance
.C26 Cartography
.C4 Children. Orphans
.C5 Churches
.C53 Adventists
.C56 Baptists
.C6 Catholic Church
.C62 Christian Science
.C63 Church of the Brethren
.C64 Evangelical and Reformed Church
.C65 Friends, Society of
.C66 Lutheran Church
.C665 Mennonites
.C67 Methodist
.C674 Nihon Kirisuto Kyodan
.C6745 Orthodox Eastern Church
.C68 Presbyterian Church
Quakers, see .C65
.C69 Civil defense
For technical works, see UA926+
.C7 Communications
.C8 Confiscation
.C82 Conscientious objectors
.C88 Cryptography
.D5 Deportation
.D6 Destruction and pillage
.E2 Education and the war
.E3 United States
.E5 Other countries, A-Z
.G6 Governments in exile

.G9 Gypsies
.J4 Jews
Cf. D804.3+, Holocaust
.L64 Logistics
.L642 By country, A-Z
.M8 Muslims
.N2 Naturalized subjects in belligerent countries
.N3 By country, A-Z
Cf. D769.8.A6, United States
.P4 Photography
.P6 Propaganda
.P7 By country, A-Z
.P76 Protest movements
.P8 Public opinion
.P85 By country, A-Z
.R3 Race relations
.S2 Science and technology
.S42 Search and rescue
.S45 By region or country, A-Z
.S47 Shinto
.S6 Socialism
.S7 Spies. Secret service. Military intelligence
.S8 Individual spies, A-Z
.T8 Transportation
Including merchant marine
.W7 Women
.Y74 Youth
Personal narratives
For collective military biography, see D736; for individual biography, see country of the individual, DA-F
811.A2A-Z Collective
.A3-Z Individual
.5 Noncombatants
Including collective and individual
812 Armistice
813 By country, A-Z
Peace
814 Sources and documents
Surrender documents, by country
.1 Germany
.2 Italy
.3 Japan
.4 Council of Foreign Ministers (General)
.413 Meeting in London, September-October, 1945
.415 Meeting in Moscow, December, 1945
.42 Meeting in Paris, April, 1946
.425 Meeting in Paris, June-July, 1946
.43 Meeting in New York, November-December, 1946
.44 Meeting in Moscow, March-April, 1947
.45 Meeting in London, November-December, 1947
.46 Meeting in Paris, May-June, 1949
.47 Meeting in Berlin, January-February, 1954
Treaties with Axis powers
.55 Collections
.56 Peace conferences (General)
.565 Paris Conference, July-October, 1946
.6 Germany
.7 Italy

.8 Japan
.9 Other countries, A-Z
815 General works
816 General special
.5 Pamphlets
Special topics
818 Indemnity and reparation
819 By country, A-Z
820 Other special topics, A-Z
.D5 Disarmament
.P7 Population transfers
.P72 By nationality, A-Z
.T4 Territorial questions
By country, see D821
821 By country, A-Z
e.g. .L5 Lithuania
.T8 Transylvania
.Y8 Yugoslavia
Including Trieste
Reconstruction
824 Sources and documents
825 General works
826 Pamphlets
By country
827 United States
828 By state, A-W
829 Other, A-Z
830 Celebrations. Memorials. Monuments
By country
833 United States
835 By state, A-W
836 By city, A-Z
838 Other countries, A-Z
e.g. .G6 Great Britain
.G7 Local, A-Z

Post-War History (1945-)

839 Periodicals. Societies
.2 Congresses. Conferences
.3 Sources and documents
Biography
.5 Collective
.7 Individual, A-Z
840 General works
842 General special
e.g. Refugees
.5 1945-1965
843 Political and diplomatic history
844 Pamphlets
845 North Atlantic Treaty, 1949
847 Communist countries. Soviet bloc
.2 Warsaw pact, 1955
848 1965-
849 Political and diplomatic history
.5 Pamphlets
850 Communist countries. Soviet bloc

Developing Countries

880 Periodicals. Societies

881 Congresses
882 Sources and documents
883 General works
887 Foreign and general relations
888 Relations with individual countries, A-Z

EUROPE (GENERAL)

Individual countries, see DA-DR

History
To 1945, see D1+
1945-
1050 Periodicals. Sources and documents
.5 Congresses. Conferences
1050.8 Study and teaching
.82 By region or country, A-Z
Under each country:
.x General works
.x2 Schools. By place, A-Z
1051 General works
1053 General special
1055 Social life and customs. Civilization
1058 Political and diplomatic history
1060 European federation
Cf. JN15, Constitutional history
1065 Relations with individual countries, A-Z
For relations with individual countries prior to 1945, see D34
Biography
1070 Collective
1072 Public men
1073 Rulers, kings, etc.
1074 Queens, princesses, etc.
1075 Individual, A-Z

(DA) GREAT BRITAIN

4 Study and teaching
British Empire. Commonwealth of Nations
Class here works on Great Britain, the dominions, colonies, etc., treated together
Individual dominions and colonies, see DS-DU, F, etc.
10 Periodicals. Societies
.5 General works
16 History
18 Political history
.2 Relations with commonwealth countries.
By region or country, A-Z

ENGLAND

20 Periodicals. Societies
26 Sources and documents
History
Biography
28 Collective
.1 Kings and rulers
.2 Queens
.35 Houses, noble families, A-Z
.4 Public men
30 General works
General special

40 Political history
Class works on political parties, institutions, etc., with political science
Class works on the political history of individual periods and reigns with the period, e.g. DA566.7, 20th century
41 Medieval (General)
42 Modern (General)
45 Diplomatic history. Foreign and general relations
Class general works on the diplomatic history of a period with the period, e.g. DA589.8. For works on relations with a specific country regardless of period, see DA47+
Relations with individual countries, A-Z
Europe, see D34, D1065
47.1 France
.2 Germany
.3 Netherlands
.6 Rome
.65 Russia. Soviet Union
.7 Scandinavia
.8 Spain
United States, see E183.8.G7
.9 Other, A-Z
Military history
49 Periodicals. Societies
50 General works
52 Dictionaries
54 Biography (Collective)
58 Roman
59 Anglo-Saxon
60 Medieval
65 Modern
66 16th-17th centuries
.1 Biography and memoirs, A-Z
67 18th century
.1 Biography and memoirs, A-Z
68 19th century
.1 Biography and memoirs, A-Z
.12 1801-1825
.22 1825-1850
.A1 Collective
.32 1850-1900
69 20th century
Cf. DA566.5, Military and naval history treated together (20th century)
.3 Biography and memoirs, A-Z
70 Naval history
72 Dictionaries
74 Biography (Collective)
77 General special
80 Medieval
85 Modern
86 16th-17th centuries
.1 Biography and memoirs, A-Z
Elizabethan. 1558-1603
.21 Collective
.22 Individual, A-Z
.62 Later Stuart, 1660-1714
.8 Individual battles. By date
Subarranged by author, A-Z

87 18th century
.1 Biography and memoirs, A-Z
.5 Individual battles. By date
Subarranged by author, A-Z
.7 Other special
88 19th century
.1 Biography and memoirs, A-Z
.5 Individual battles. By date
Subarranged by author, A-Z
89 20th century
Cf. DA566.5, Military and naval history treated together (20th century)
.1 Biography and memoirs, A-Z
.5 Air force history
Cf. UG635.G7, Military aeronautics
.6 Biography and memoirs, A-Z
By period, see the period or reign
118 National characteristics. Patriotism
By period
130 Early and medieval to 1485
135 Earliest to 1066
140 Celts. Pre-Romans
145 Romans
Biography and memoirs
.2 Collective
.3 Individual, A-Z
152 Saxons
445-871
General works, see DA152
.5 Biography, A-Z
871-1066
General works, see DA152
158 Danish invasions, rule, etc. (General), 1017-1042
Medieval, 1066-1485
170 Sources and documents. Contemporary works
175 General works
177 Biography (Collective)
Normans, 1066-1154
190 Sources and documents
195 General works
.8 Battle of Stamford Bridge, 1066
196 Battle of Hastings, 1066
197 William I, 1066-1087
.5 William II, 1087-1100
198 Henry I, 1100-1135
.5 Stephen, 1135-1154
Biography of contemporaries, A-Z
.9 Collective
199 Individual, A-Z
Angevins, 1154-1216
200 Sources and documents. Contemporary works
205 General works
206 Henry II, 1154-1189
207 Richard I, 1189-1199
208 John, 1199-1216
209 Biography of contemporaries, A-Z
Plantagenets, 1216-1399
220 Sources and documents. Contemporary works

225 General works
227 Henry III, 1216-1399
.5 Barons' War, 1263-1267
228 Biography and memoirs of contemporaries, A-Z
229 Edward I, 1272-1307
230 Edward II, 1307-1327
231 Biography and memoirs of contemporaries, 1272-1327, A-Z
233 Edward III, 1327-1377
234 Edward, Prince of Wales
235 Richard II, 1377-1399
Including Tyler's Insurrection
237 Biography and memoirs of contemporaries, 1327-1399, A-Z
Lancaster-York, 1066-1485
240 Sources and documents. Contemporary works
245 General works
247 Biography and memoirs of contemporaries, A-Z
250 Wars of the Roses, 1455-1485
255 Henry IV, 1399-1413
256 Henry V, 1413-1422
257 Henry VI, 1422-1461
258 Edward IV, 1461-1483
259 Edward V, 1483
260 Richard III, 1483-1485
Including Battle of Bosworth Field, 1485
300 Modern, 1485-
304 Biography and memoirs (Collective)
305 Houses, noble families, etc.
306 Special, A-Z
307 Public men
Tudors, 1485-1603
310 Sources and documents. Contemporary works
315 General works
316 Pamphlets
Biography and memoirs
317 Collective
.1 Kings, queens, etc.
.15 Houses, noble families, etc., A-Z
.2 Public men
.8 Individual, A-Z
325 Early Tudors
330 Henry VII, 1485-1509
.8 Biography and memoirs of contemporaries, A-Z
Henry VIII, 1509-1547
331 Sources and documents. Contemporary works
332 General works on life and reign
Biography
333 Queens, A-Z
334 Public men, A-Z
337 1509-1527
338 1527-1533
339 1533-1547
340 1547-1558
345 Edward VI, 1547-1553
.1 Biography and memoirs of contemporaries, A-Z
347 Mary I, 1553-1558
.1 Biography and memoirs of contemporaries, A-Z
Elizabeth I, 1558-1603
350 Sources and documents. Contemporary works

352 Pamphlets. By date
355 General works on life and reign
356 General special
358 Biography and memoirs of contemporaries, A-Z
360 Armada
17th century. 1603-1702
370 Sources and documents. Contemporary works
375 General works
Biography and memoirs
377 Collective
.1 Rulers, kings, etc.
.2 Houses, noble families, A-Z
.3 Public men
378 Individual, A-Z
Early Stuarts, 1603-1642
385 Sources and documents. Contemporary works
390 General works
.1 Biography and memoirs, A-Z
392 Gunpowder Plot, 1605
394 Pamphlets, 1603-1624. By date
395 Charles I, 1625-1649
For biography, see DA396.A2
396 Biography and memoirs, A-Z
e.g. .A1 Collective
.A2 Charles I
397 General special
398 Pamphlets, 1625-1641. By date
Civil War and Commonwealth, 1642-1660
400 Sources and documents. Contemporary works
405 General works
406 General special
407 Biography and memoirs of contemporaries, A-Z
Civil War, 1642-1649
410 Sources and documents
412 Pamphlets, 1642-1649. By original date of publication
415 General works
Including local history
417 Battle of Marston Moor, 1644
419 Biography and memoirs, A-Z
Commonwealth, 1649-1660
420 Sources and documents. Contemporary works
422 Pamphlets, 1649-1660. By original date of publication
Subarranged by author
425 General works
426 Oliver Cromwell
428.5 Richard Cromwell
429 Biography and memoirs of contemporaries, A-Z
Later Stuarts, 1660-1714
430 Sources and documents. Contemporary works
432 Pamphlets. By date
435 General works
437 Biography and memoirs of contemporaries, A-Z
445 Charles II, 1660-1685
447 Biography and memoirs of contemporaries, A-Z
448 General special
Anglo-Dutch War, 1672-1674, see DJ193
.9 Monmouth and Monmouth's Rebellion, 1685
450 James II, 1685-1688

460 William and Mary, 1689-1702
For biography, see DA462.A2+
461 Lancaster Plot, 1689-1694
.3 Versailles Conspiracy, 1695
.5 Conspiracy of 1696
462 Biography and memoirs, A-Z
e.g. .A2 William III
.A3 Mary II
.A4-Z Other individual
463 Pamphlets. By original date
Subarranged by author
470 Late modern, 1702-
480 18th century
Including House of Hanover (Windsor)
483 Biography and memoirs, A-Z
486 Other
Anne, 1702-1714
490 Sources and documents
495 General works
496 Pamphlets. By original date
Subarranged by author, A-Z
497 Biography and memoirs of contemporaries, A-Z
498 1714-1760
For all biography of this period, see DA501
499 George I, 1714-1727
500 George II, 1727-1760
501 Biography and memoirs, A-Z
e.g. .A1 Collective
.A2 George I
.A3 George II
.A4-Z Other
503 Pamphlets. By original date
Subarranged by author, A-Z
505 George III, 1760-1820
For biography, see DA506
506 Biography and memoirs, A-Z
e.g. .A2 George III
.B9 Burke, Edmund
507 Pamphlets. By original date
Subarranged by author, A-Z
510 1760-1789
512 Biography and memoirs, A-Z
520 1789-1820
521 1811-1820
522 Biography and memoirs, A-Z
530 19th century
531 Pamphlets. By original date
Biography and memoirs
.1 Collective
.2 Public men
Individual, see DA536, DA563+
535 1801-1837
536 Biography and memoirs, 1801-1837/1850, A-Z
537 George IV, 1820-1830
For biography, see DA538
538 Biography and memoirs, A-Z
e.g. .A1 George IV
539 William IV, 1830-1837

540 Era of reform, 1832-1837
541 Biography and memoirs of contemporaries, A-Z
542 Pamphlets. By original date
550 Victorian era, 1837-1901
551 Pamphlets
Victoria
552 Journal, letters
553 Memoirs by contemporaries
554 Biography
558 Pamphlets
559 Other royal biography, A-Z
.7 1837-1850
560 1850-1901
561 Pamphlets
South African War, see DT1890+
Biography and memoirs
562 Collective
Gladstone
563 Speeches, letters, etc.
.3 Memoirs by contemporaries
.4 Biography
564 Other prime ministers, A-Z
565 Contemporaries, A-Z
566 20th century
.2 General special
.3 Pamphlets
.5 Military and naval history (Treated together)
Cf. DA69; DA89
.7 Political and diplomatic history
.9 Biography and memoirs, A-Z
e.g. .C5 Churchill, Winston
.E28 Eden, Anthony
Edward VII, 1901-1910
567 Biography
568 Biography and memoirs of contemporaries, A-Z
570 Reign
George V, 1910-1936
573 Biography
574 Biography and memoirs of contemporaries, A-Z
576 Reign
577 Period of World War I
For the war itself, see D501+
578 1920-1939
Edward VIII, 1936
583 Reign
George VI, 1937-1952
584 Biography
585 Biography and memoirs of contemporaries, A-Z
e.g. .A8 Attlee, Clement
.C5 Chamberlain, Neville
586 Reign
587 Period of World War II
588 1945-1952
.3 Pamphlets
1952-
.7 Political history
.8 Foreign and general relations
Elizabeth II, 1952-

590 Biography
591 Biography and memoirs of contemporaries, A-Z
592 Reign

WALES

History
713.5 Study and teaching
714 General works
By period
715 Early and medieval
716 Biography, A-Z
720 Modern
722 19th-20th centuries
Rebecca Riots, 1839-1844, etc.
.1 Biography and memoirs, A-Z

SCOTLAND

History
758 Biography (Collective)
.1 Public men
.2 Rulers, kings, etc.
Cf. DA758.s.S8, etc., House of Stuart
DA385+, English sovereigns
760 General works
General special
765 Political and diplomatic history
Including home rule
For works on individual periods or reigns, see the period
767 Military history
772 National characteristics
By period
775 Early and medieval to 1603
777 Early to 1057
.3 Earliest to 844
.5 Roman period
844-1057, see DA777
779 1057-1603
780 1057-1278
783 1278-1488
.2 War of Independence, 1285-1371
.25 John Baliol, 1292-1296
.3 Sir William Wallace, 1296-1305
.35 Special events
.38 1306-1371
.4 Robert I, 1306-1329
.41 Special events
.43 David II, 1329-1371
.45 Biography of contemporaries, A-Z
.5 1371-1488. Early Stuarts
.53 Robert II, 1371-1390
.57 Robert III, 1390-1406
.6 James I, 1406-1437
.7 James II, 1437-1460
.8 James III, 1460-1488
.9 Biography of contemporaries, A-Z
784 1488-1603
.3 Biography and memoirs, A-Z
.5 James IV, 1488-1513
.6 Battle of Flodden, 1513

.7 James V, 1513-1542
785 1542-1603
Mary Stuart, 1542-1603
786 General works on reign
787.A1 Biography
.A2 Pamphlets
.A6-Z Biography of contemporaries, A-Z
788 1567-1603. James VI
789 Gowrie Conspiracy, 1600
790 Biography and memoirs, A-Z
800 1603-1707/1745
802 Biography and memoirs
.A1 Collective
.A2-Z Individual
803 1603-1692
.1 Pamphlets. By original date
.15 1603-1625
.2 Biography and memoirs, A-Z
.3 1625-1660
Including 1625-1688
.6 1637-1649
.7 Biography and memoirs, A-Z
.73 1637-1643
.8 1649-1660
804 1660-1692/1715
.1 Biography and memoirs, A-Z
.6 Revolution, 1688
.7 Glencoe Massacre
805 1692-1707
807 The Union, 1707
809 18th century
810 Biography and memoirs, A-Z
811 Pamphlets
813 1707-1745. Jacobite movements
814 Biography and memoirs, A-Z
.2 1707
.3 1715
.4 1719
.5 1745-1746
Including Battle of Cullodon
815 19th century
816 Biography and memoirs, A-Z
817 Pamphlets
821 20th century
822 Biography and memoirs, A-Z
824 Pamphlets

IRELAND

900 Periodicals. Societies
History
909 Study and teaching
910 General works
913.5 General special
914 Military history
915 Biography and memoirs, A-Z
916 Biography (Collective)
.4 Public men
925 National characteristics
By period

930	To 1172
931	To 433
932	433-1172
.6	Danish wars, 795-1014
933	1172-1603
	Biography and memoirs
.25	Collective
.26	Individual, A-Z
.3	English conquest, 1154-1189
934	1189-1485
.5	Invasion by Edward Bruce, 1315
935	1485-1603. Tudors
936	Biography and memoirs, A-Z
937	1558-1603. Elizabeth
.3	Tyrone's Rebellion, 1597-1603
.5	Biography and memoirs, A-Z
938	Modern, 1603-
940	17th century
.5	Biography and memoirs, A-Z
941.3	1603-1625. James I
.5	1625-1649. Charles I
943	1641-1649. Irish Confederation
	Including Rebellion of 1641
944.4	1649-1660
.5	1660-1685
.7	1685-1688
945	1688-1691
946	1691-1700
947	18th century
.Z9	Pamphlets
948.A2	General special
	Biography and memoirs
.A5	Collective
.3	Individual, A-Z
.4	1782-1800
.5	1791-1800
.6	Biography and memoirs, A-Z
949	1798-1800
.5	The Union
950	19th century. Irish question
.2	1800-1848
	Biography and memoirs
.21	Collective
	Individual, A-Z
.22	O'Connell, Daniel
.23	Other, A-Z
.29	Pamphlets. By date
.3	1800-1829
.4	Tithe War, 1829-1838
.5	1838-1848
.7	Famine, 1845-1847
951	1848-1900
952	Biography and memoirs, A-Z
953	Pamphlets. By date
954	Fenians
955	1848-1868
957	1868-1900
958	Biography and memoirs, A-Z

959 20th century
960 1901-1922
962 1914-1921
963 1922-
964.A2 Political and diplomatic history. Foreign and general relations
.A3-Z Relations with individual countries, A-Z
965 Biography and memoirs, A-Z
990 Counties, regions, etc., A-Z
Northern Ireland. Ulster
.U45 Periodicals. Societies
.U452 Biography
.A1-19 Collective
.A2-Z Individual
.U46 History and description

(DB) AUSTRIA, HUNGARY, CZECHOSLOVAKIA

AUSTRIA. AUSTRO-HUNGARIAN EMPIRE

1 Periodicals. Societies
3 Sources and documents
History
36 Biography (Collective)
.1 Rulers, kings, etc.
.3 Houses, noble families, etc., A-Z
.4 Public men
General works
37 To 1800
38 1801-
40 Pamphlets
General special
Military history
By period, <u>see</u> the period
42 Periodicals. Societies
43 General works
44 Biography (Collective)
45 Naval history
Political and diplomatic history. Foreign and general relations
Class general works on the diplomatic history of a period with the period. For works on relations with specific countries regardless of the period, <u>see</u> DB49
46 Sources and documents
47 General works
48 20th century (General)
Including the Austrian question
49 Relations with individual countries, A-Z
United States, <u>see</u> E183.8
By period
51 Early and medieval to 1521
52 Biography (Collective)
53 976-1246
54 Biography, A-Z
Collective, <u>see</u> DB52
55 1246-1526
56 1246-1251
57 1251-1278
58 1278-1282
59 Biography, A-Z
Collective, <u>see</u> DB52
60 Wars with the Turks

61 Early invasions to 1606
62 1606-1791
63 Special events, by date
e.g. Siege of Vienna, see DR536
Siege of Buda, see DR536.5
1699 Peace of Carlowitz
64 Biography and memoirs, A-Z
65 1521-
.2 1521-1648
.3 Ferdinand I, 1521-1564
.4 Maximilian II, 1564-1576
.5 Rudolf II, 1576-1612
Biography and memoirs of contemporaries, A-Z
.53 Collective
.54 Individual, A-Z
.6 Mathias, 1612-1619
.7 1618-1648
Cf. D251+, Thirty Years' War
.75 Ferdinand II, 1619-1637
.8 Ferdinand III, 1637-1657
.9 Biography and memoirs of contemporaries (not identified with specific reign), A-Z
66 1648-1740
.5 General special
67 Leopold I, 1657-1705
.3 General special
.8 Biography and memoirs of contemporaries, A-Z
68 Joseph I, 1705-1711
69 Karl VI, 1711-1740
.3 General special
.5 Biography and memoirs of contemporaries, A-Z
.7 1740-1792
.8 General special
Maria Theresia, 1740-1780
70 General works on reign
71 Biography
72 Austrian succession
For works on the War of the Austrian Succession, see D291+
.5 Political and diplomatic history
73 Biography and memoirs of contemporaries, A-Z
.A2 Collective
.A3-Z Individual
74 Joseph II, 1780-1790
.3 Political and diplomatic history
.6 Writings of Joseph II
.7 Biography and memoirs of contemporaries, A-Z
.8 Leopold II, 1790-1792
1792-1815. Period of the French Revolution
75 Sources and documents
76 General works
77 Other
Congress of Vienna, see DC249
80 19th century
Biography and memoirs
.7 Collective
.8 Individual, A-Z
81 Franz I (II), 1792-1835

82 Ferdinand I, 1835-1848
.5 Pamphlets
83 Revolution, 1848
85 Franz Joseph I, 1848-1916
86 General special
Austro-Sardinian War, 1848-1849, see DG553
Schleswig-Holstein War, see DL236+
War with Italy, 1866, see DG558
War with Prussia, 1866, see DD436+
.7 Period of World War I
For the war itself, see D501+
Biography
87 Franz Joseph I
88 Elisabeth
89 Other members of the royal family, A-Z
90 Other, A-Z
90 20th century
92 Karl I, 1916-1918
93 General special
96 Republic, 1918-
97 Other
98 Biography and memoirs, A-Z
99 1938-1945. German annexation
.1 1945-1955. Allied occupation
.2 1955-

HUNGARY

901 Periodicals. Societies
903 Sources and documents
History
922 Biography (Collective)
.1 Rulers, kings, etc.
.3 Houses, noble families, etc., A-Z
.4 Public men
.8 Study and teaching
General works
924 To 1800
925 1801-
General special
.5 Military history
926 Political and diplomatic history. Foreign and general relations
Class general works on the diplomatic history of a period with the period. For works on relations with a specific country regardless of period, see DB926.3
.3 Relations with individual countries, A-Z
United States, see E183.8
By period
927 Early to 894
.3 Earliest
.5 Roman period
928 Migrations
.9 Introduction of Christianity
894-1301
929.A3A-Z Sources and documents
.A4-Z General works
.9 Pamphlets
930 Elective kings. 1301-1526
.2 Karoly Robert I, 1308-1342
.3 Lajos I, Nagy, 1342-1382

.5 The Hunyadi
.7 Hunyadi, Janos, 1444-1453
931 Matyas I, Corvinus, 1458-1490
.4 Vladislav V, 1490-1516
.7 Ludwik II, 1516-1526
.9 Biography and memoirs, A-Z
932 1526-1608
.2 Biography and memoirs, A-Z
.3 1608-1711
.4 Ferencz II, Rakoczy
.48 Biography and memoirs, A-Z
.5 1711-1792
.9 Biography and memoirs, A-Z
933 19th century. 1789-1900
.1 General special
.3 Biography and memoirs, A-Z
.5 1792-1825
934 1825-1848. Age of Reforms
935 War of 1848-1849
936 General special
Kossuth, Lajos
937 Biography
.5 Writings and speeches
Foreign relations
United States, see E183.8
939 By country, A-Z
940 1849-1900
941 Biography and memoirs, A-Z
943 1851-1866
945 1867-1900
947 20th century
948 General special
950 Biography and memoirs, A-Z
953 1914-1918
For the war itself, see D501+
955 1918-1945
Including Revolution of 1918-1919; period of World War II, etc.
956 1945-
957 Revolution of 1956

CZECHOSLOVAKIA

Class here (DB2000-DB2232) general works on Czechoslovakia, on Bohemia, and on the Czech Socialist Republic
For Moravia, see DB2300; for Slovakia, see DB2700
2000 Periodicals. Societies.
2004 Sources and documents
Ethnography
2041 National characteristics
History
2045 Biography (Collective)
2046 Rulers, kings, etc.
2047 Queens
2048 Houses, noble families, etc.
2049 Individual, A-Z
2050 Statesmen
2059 Study and teaching
General works
2061 Through 1800
2062 1801-1976

1918-1939
2195 Sources and documents
.7 Political history
2199 Foreign and general relations
Biography and memoirs
2200 Collective
2201 Individual, A-Z
2202 Munich four-power agreement
Cf. D727, European political history
1939-1945. German occupation
2205 Sources and documents
.7 Political history
2209 Foreign and general relations
Biography and memoirs
2210 Collective
2211 Individual, A-Z
1945-1968
2215 Sources and documents
.7 Political history
2219 Foreign and general relations
Biography and memoirs
2220 Collective
2221 Individual, A-Z
2222 Coup d'état, 1948
1968-
2225 Sources and documents
.7 Political history
2229 Foreign and general relations
Biography and memoirs
2230 Collective
2231 Individual, A-Z
2232 Soviet intervention, 1968. Prague spring

Local History of the Czech Lands

Moravia

History
General special
2370 Military history
For specific periods, see the period
2374 Political history
For specific periods, see the period
2375 Foreign and general relations
Class general works on the diplomatic history of a period with the period. For works on relations with a specific country regardless of period, see DB2376
2376 Relations with individual countries, A-Z
By period
Early to 1000
.7 Political history
2389 Foreign and general relations
1000-1800
2398 Political history
Biography and memoirs
2400 Collective
2401 Individual, A-Z
19th century
2408 Political history
Biography and memoirs

2410 Collective
2411 Individual, A-Z
20th century
2418 Political history
Biography
2420 Collective
2421 Individual, A-Z

Slovakia

2700 Periodicals. Societies. Serials
2703 Sources and documents
Ethnography
2741 National characteristics
2759 Study and teaching
History
General works
2761 Through 1800
2762 1801-1976
2763 1977-
General special
Military history
For specific periods, see the period
2769 Sources and documents
2770 General works
By period
2771 Early through 1620
2772 1620-1918
2773 1918-
Political history
For specific periods, see the period
2774 Sources and documents
2775 General works
Foreign and general relations
Class general works on the diplomatic history of a period with the period. For works on relations with a specific country regardless of period, see DB2778+
2776 Sources and documents
2777 General works
2778 Relations with individual countries, A-Z
By period
To 1800
2788.5 Military history
.7 Political history
2789 Foreign and general relations
Biography and memoirs
2790 Collective
2791 Individual, A-Z
1800-1918
.5 Military history
.7 Political history
2799 Foreign and general relations
Biography and memoirs
2800 Collective
2801 Individual, A-Z
Czechoslovak Republic, 1918-
2805 Sources and documents
.7 Political history
2809 Foreign and general relations
Biography and memoirs

2810 Collective
2811 Individual, A-Z
2813 1918-1939
1939-1945
.7 Political history
2819 Foreign and general relations
Biography and memoirs
2820 Collective
2821 Individual, A-Z
2822 Uprising, 1944
1945-1968
.7 Political history
2829 Foreign and general relations
Biography and memoirs
2830 Collective
2831 Individual, A-Z
1968-
.7 Political history
2839 Foreign and general relations
Biography and memoirs
2840 Collective
2841 Individual, A-Z

(DC) FRANCE

1 Periodicals
2 Societies
3 Sources and documents
34 Ethnography
Including national characteristics
History
36 Biography (Collective)
.4 Public men
.6 Rulers, kings, etc.
.7 Queens
.8 Houses, noble families, A-Z
.983 Study and teaching
General works
37 To 1815. Chronicles
38 1815-
41 Special aspects, A-Z
.R4 Regionalism
General special
Military history
44 Sources and documents
.5 Biography (Collective)
.8 Officers
45 General works
.5 Textbooks
.7 General special
.9 Pamphlets
By period
For the military history of special periods, reigns, etc., see the period of reign
46 Early
.5 16th century
.7 17th-18th centuries
47 19th-20th centuries
Naval history

Individual campaigns and battles are classed with special period
49 Sources and documents
.5 Biography (Collective)
50 General works
.A2 Works published before 1800
51 Early and medieval
.5 15th-16th centuries
52 17th-18th centuries
53 19th-20th centuries
Cf. DC368, 20th century
55 Political and diplomatic history. Foreign and general relations
Class general works on the political and diplomatic history of a period with the period. For works on relations with a specific country regardless of period, see DC59.8
56 Early and medieval
57 1515-1789
58 19th-20th centuries
59 Special topics
.8 Relations with individual countries, A-Z
United States, see E183.8+
By period
Early and medieval to 1515
60 Sources and documents
General works
.8 To 1800. Chronicles
61 1801-
62.A3-Z Gauls. Celts
64 Franks
65 Merovingians
Carlovingians
70.A1 Sources and documents
Chronicles
.A2 9th century
.A3 10th century
.A4-Z General works
Charlemagne, 768-814
Cf. DD133, Reign in Germany
73.A2 Sources and documents
General works on life and reign
.A3-Z Modern
.8 Pamphlets
.9 Carloman, 768-771
.95 Biography and memoirs of contemporaries, A-Z
74 Louis I le Pieux, 814-987
Cf. DD134, Germany
.5 Biography and memoirs of contemporaries, A-Z
75 Treaty of Verdun, 843
76 Charles I (II) le Chauve, 840-877
.3 General special
Biography and memoirs
.4 Collective
.42 Individual, A-Z
77 Louis II, 877-879
.3 Louis III, 879-882
.5 Carloman, 882-884
.8 Karl II (III), 884-887
Cf. DD134.6, Germany
.9 Siege of Paris, 885-886

78 Eudes, 888-898
79 Charles III, 898-922
.5 Robert I, 922-923
.7 Raoul, 923-936
80 Louis IV, 936-954
81 Lothaire, 954-986
.5 Louis V, 986-987
Capetians, 987-1328
82.A2 Sources and documents
.A3-Z General works
83 General special
Wars with the Albigenses
.2 Sources and documents
.3 General works
84 Hugues Capet, 987-996
85 Robert II, 996-1031
.6 Henri I, 1031-1060
.8 Biography and memoirs of contemporaries, A-Z
86 Dukes of Normandy
87 Philippe I, 1060-1108
.7 Biography and memoirs of contemporaries, A-Z
88 Louis VI, 1108-1137
.5 Political and diplomatic history
.7 Biography and memoirs of contemporaries, A-Z
89 Louis VII, 1137-1180
.7 Biography and memoirs of contemporaries, A-Z
90.A3-Z Philippe II Auguste, 1180-1223
.7 Biography and memoirs of contemporaries, A-Z
.8 Louis VIII, 1223-1226
91.A3-Z Louis IX, Saint, 1226-1270
.3 Treaty of Paris, 1259
.6 Biography and memoirs of contemporaries, A-Z
.7 Philippe II, 1270-1285
92 Philippe IV, 1285-1314
93 Louis X, 1314-1316
.3 Jean I, b. 1316
.4 Philippe V, 1316-1322
.7 Charles IV, 1322-1328
94 Biography and memoirs, 1270-1328, A-Z
1328-1515
95.A2 Sources and documents
.45 Military history
.5 Political and diplomatic history
.7 Biography and memoirs, A-Z
96 Hundred Years' War, 1339-1453
.A2 Contemporary and early
.5 General special
97 Biography and memoirs, A-Z
.5 14th century
98 Philippe VI, 1328-1350
.5 Special events, battles, A-Z
.7 Biography and memoirs of contemporaries, A-Z
99 Jean II, 1350-1364
.2 General special
.3 La Jacquerie, 1358
.5 Other events, battles, A-Z
.7 Biography and memoirs of contemporaries, A-Z
100 Charles V, 1364-1380

.3	General special
.5	Special events, battles, A-Z
.7	Biography and memoirs of contemporaries, A-Z
101	Charles VI, 1380-1422
.A2	Contemporary and early
.3	General special
.5	Special events, battles, A-Z
	e.g. .A2 Agincourt, Battle of, 1415
	Biography and memoirs of contemporaries
.6	Collective
.7	Individual, A-Z
.9	15th century
102	Charles VII, 1422-1461
.A2	Contemporary and early
.3	General special
.5	Special events, battles, A-Z
	Arranged chronologically by affixing to .5 the last two digits of the date
.8	Biography and memoirs of contemporaries, A-Z
	Jeanne d'Arc (Joan of Arc)
103.A1-29	Sources and documents
.A3-Z	General biography
	Campaigns, see DC103
106	Louis XI, 1461-1483
.3	General special
.9	Biography and memoirs of contemporaries, A-Z
107	Charles VIII, 1483-1498
.A2	Contemporary and early
	Italian expedition, see DG541
108	Louis XII, 1498-1515
.A2	Contemporary and early
109	Special
110	Modern, 1515-
	Including works on the modern period in general
	16th century
	Including wars in Italy, conflict with Austria, period of Renaissance and Reformation, religious wars, etc.
111.A2	Sources and documents
.A3-Z	General works
.3	General special
.5	Political and diplomatic history. Foreign and general relations
112	Biography and memoirs of contemporaries, A-Z
	Francois I, 1515-1547
113.A2	Sources and documents
.A3	Contemporary and early works
.A4-Z	General works
.3	General special
.5	Diplomatic history. Foreign and general relations
114	Henri II, 1547-1559
.3	General special
115	Francois II, 1559-1560
116	Charles IX, 1560-1574
.5	General special
.7	Diplomatic history. Foreign and general relations
117	Special events, A-Z
118	Massacre of Saint Bartholomew, 1572
119	Henri III, 1574-1589
120	Holy League, 1576-1593

	1589-1715
121	General works
.3	General special
.5	Diplomatic history. Foreign and general relations
.8	Biography and memoirs, A-Z
	Henri IV, 1589-1610
122	General works on reign
.3	General special
.5	Diplomatic history. Foreign and general relations
.8	Biography of Henri IV
.9	Biography and memoirs of contemporaries, A-Z
	Louis XIII, 1610-1643
123	General works
.3	Special topics
.5	Diplomatic history. Foreign and general relations
.8	Biography of Louis XIII
.9	Biography and memoirs of contemporaries, A-Z
	Anne d'Autriche, 1643-1661
124	General works
.3	Biography
.4	Fronde, 1649-1653
.45	War with Spain
	Louis XIV, 1643-1715
125	Sources and documents
126	General works
127	Special topics, A-Z
	e.g. .C3 Camisards, Revolt of
.3	Diplomatic history. Foreign and general relations
.6	Military history
.8	Naval history
.5	Public opinion formation. Internal propaganda
129	Biography and writings of Louis XIV
130	Biography and memoirs of contemporaries, A-Z
131	18th century
.5	Diplomatic history. Foreign and general relations
	Biography
.8	Collective
.9	Individual, A-Z
132	Regency of Philippe, duc d'Orleans, 1715-1723
	Louis XV, 1715-1774
133.4	Political history
.5	Diplomatic history. Foreign and general relations
.6	Military history
	Naval history, see DC52
	Biography
134	Louis XV
135	Contemporaries, A-Z
	Louis XVI, 1774-1789/1793
136.A2	Sources and documents
.A3-Z	General works on reign
.5	Political history
.6	Diplomatic history. Foreign and general relations
	Biography and memoirs
137	Louis XVI
.5	Biography and memoirs of contemporaries, A-Z
138	Antecedent history and causes of the Revolution

Revolutionary and Napoleonic Period, 1789-1815

139	Periodicals. Societies

141 Sources and documents
Biography and memoirs of contemporaries, A-Z
145 Collective
146 Individual, A-Z
148 General works
Including works on the Revolution alone or the Revolution and Consulate treated together
150 Pamphlets
General special
151 Military history
Cf. DC220+, Revolutionary and Napoleonic Wars
153 Naval history
155 Political history
157 Diplomatic history. Foreign relations
Special topics
158 Emigres
.17 Indemnity
.8 Other
Including aliens, foreign public opinion, etc.
By period
161 Assemblies to Directory, 1787/1789-1795
165 Constituent Assembly, June 17, 1789-September 30, 1791
171 Legislative Assembly, October 1, 1791-September 21, 1792
176 Convention, September 22, 1792-October 1795
186 Directory, October 1795-November 9, 1799
191 Consulate, 1799-1804
For works treating the Consulate and Revolution together, or the Consulate, Revolution, and Empire together, see D139+. For works treating the Consulate and Empire together, see D197+
Empire (First). Napoleon I, 1804-1815
Including works treating the Consulate and Empire together
197 Periodicals. Sources and documents
198 Biography and memoirs of contemporaries, A-Z
201 General works
202 General special
.1 Military history
Cf. DC151, 1789-1815
Cf. DC227+, Napoleonic wars
.3 Naval history
Cf. DC153, 1789-1815
.5 Political history
Cf. DC155, 1789-1815
.7 Diplomatic history
General works only. Special treaties and events are classed with period, DC220+
.8 Colonial policy
203 Biography of Napoleon
Writings of Napoleon
213.A1 Complete works. By date
.A2-Z Correspondence and decrees
By editor, A-Z
.2 Memoirs. By editor, A-Z
215.5 Criticism of writings
216 Bonaparte family (General)
Wars in the provinces
218 Vendean wars
Including later wars
.1 Collective biography

.2 Contemporary memoirs, A-Z
.3 Individual events, battles, A-Z
219 Avignon and Comtat-Venaissin
Revolutionary wars, 1792-1802
220 First and Second Coalitions, 1792-1802
.1 General special
.15 Pamphlets
.2 Campaigns of 1792
.3 Proposed invasion of England
.5 Campaign of 1793
.6 Campaign of 1794
.8 Campaign of 1796 (other than Italian)
221 Second coalition, 1799-1802
.5 General special
222 Individual events, battles, A-Z
.5 Treaty of Amiens, 1802
223 Wars in Italy
.4 First campaign, 1796-1797
.7 Second campaign, 1800
224 Individual events, battles, A-Z
225 Expedition to Egypt and Syria, 1798-1799
226 Individual events, battles, A-Z
Napoleonic Wars, 1800-1815
Cf. DC151, Military history, 1789-1815
.2 Sources and documents
.3 General works
.4 General special
.5 Personal narratives
.6 Special topics, A-Z
.P36 Participation, Foreign
.P362 By region or country, A-Z
.P74 Prisoners and prisons
227 Third Coalition, 1805. German-Austrian Campaign
.A1-2 Sources and documents
.A5-Z General works
.5 Individual events, battles, A-Z
229 Campaigns against Prussia, Poland and Russia, 1806-1807
230 Individual events, battles, A-Z
231 Campaigns against Portugal and Spain. Peninsular War, 1807-1814
Including narratives and letters by officers, etc., other than English
232 Special English material
Including Wellingtoniana and narratives and letters by English officers
233 Individual events, battles, A-Z
.5 Special topics, A-Z
.U53 Underground movements
234 German and Austrian campaign, 1809
Individual events, battles
.9 Treaty of Vienna, December 14
235 Russian campaign, 1812
.1 General special
.3 Preparations in Dresden, 1812
.5 Individual events, battles, A-Z
236 1813-1814. War of Liberation
.1 General special
.3 Campaign in Saxony, Germany, 1813
.6 Battle of Leipzig, October 16-19
.7 Other battles, events, A-Z
.75 1814

.8	Individual events, battles, A-Z
237	Paris in 1814
238	Abdication and Elba
238	Treaty of Paris, 1814
239	1815. First restoration and Hundred days
240	Individual events. By date
242	Battle of Waterloo, June 18, 1815
245	Austria and Italy in their relation to Napoleonic history
249	Congress of Vienna. Treaties of 1815
	Cf. JX1351, International law
	For Holy Alliance, see D363, D383
	History, 1815-
	By period
	19th century
250	Sources and documents
251	General works
252	General special
.5	Pamphlets
.7	Military history
	Biography and memoirs
254	19th century as a whole
.A2	Collective
.A3-Z	Individual
255	Early 19th century
.A2	Collective
.A3-Z	Individual
	Later 19th century, see DC280.5, DC342.8
256	Restoration, 1815-1830
	Including reign of Louis XVIII
257	Biography of Louis XVIII
	Charles X, 1824-1830
258	General works on reign
259	Biography
260	Biography and memoirs of contemporaries, A-Z
261	July Revolution, 1830
	July monarchy, 1830-1848
266	Reign of Louis Philippe
.5	Political and diplomatic history
	Biography
268	Louis Philippe
269	Contemporaries, A-Z
	February Revolution and Second Republic
270	Revolution, 1848
272	Second Republic, 1848-1851
273.6	Foreign affairs
274	Coup d'état, December 2, 1851
276	Second Empire, 1852-1870
277	Political and diplomatic history
.5	Military history
.8	Naval history
	Biography and memoirs
280	Napoleon III
	Contemporaries, 1830-1870
.45	Collective
.5	Individual, A-Z
	Franco-German or Franco-Prussian War, 1870-1871
281	Periodicals
282	Sources and documents

285 Personal narratives
289 General works
291 Pamphlets
292 Causes
e.g. Spanish succession
Cf. DC300, Diplomatic history
293 Military history
.05 Pamphlets
.1 French army
Including causes of defeat
296 German army
297 Prussian army
298 Naval history
299 Political history
300 Diplomatic history
Including general relations of Second Empire with Germany
Spanish succession, see DC292
Campaigns and battles
301 Army of the Rhine
305 Operations in the provinces
306 Sedan, September l, 1870
Siege of Paris (and Commune), 1870-1871
311.A2 Sources and documents
.A3-Z General works
312 General special
314 Personal narratives
316 Commune, 1871
321 Alsace-Lorraine annexation question
323 German occupation and evacuation
325 Results of the war, etc.
326 Reparation of damages
.5 Special topics, A-Z
.P82 Public opinion
330 Later 19th century
Third Republic, 1871-1940
334 Periodicals. Sources and documents
335 General works
339 Military history
340 Political and diplomatic history
341 Diplomatic history
Biography and memoirs
342 Collective
.1 Public men
.8 Individual, A-Z
344 Thiers, Adolphe, 1871-1873
346 MacMahon, Marie Edme Pl.M. de, duc de Magenta, 1873-1879
348 Grevy, Jules, 1879-1887
350 Carnot, Marie Francois S., 1887-1894
351 Casimir-Perier, Jean Paulo, 1894-1895
352 Faure, Felix, 1895-1899
354 Dreyfus case
361 20th century
367 Military history
368 Naval history
369 Political and diplomatic history
Moroccan question, see DT317
Biography and memoirs
371 Collective

373 Individual, A-Z
375 Loubet, Emile, 1899-1906
380 Fallieres, Clement Armand, 1906-1913
385 Poincare, Raymond, 1913-1920
387 Period of World War I
For the war itself, see D501+
389 1919-1940
391 Deschanel, Paul Eugene, 1920
393 Millerand, Alexandre, 1920-1924
394 Doumergue, Gaston, 1924-1931
395 Doumer, Paul, 1931-1932
396 Lebrun, Albert Francois, 1932-1940
397 1940-1946
Fourth Republic, 1947-1958
398 Periodicals. Sources and documents
400 General works
403 Military and naval history
404 Political and diplomatic history
Biography and memoirs
406 Collective
407 Individual, A-Z
e.g. .S3 Schuman, Robert
408 Auriol, Vincent, 1947-1953
409 Coty, Rene, 1954-1958
Fifth Republic, 1958-
411 Periodicals. Sources and documents
412 General works
416 Military and naval history
417 Political and diplomatic history
Biography and memoirs
418 Collective
419 Individual, A-Z
Gaulle, Charles de, 1958-1969
420 General works on life and administration
Pompidou, Georges, 1969-1974
421 General works on life and administration
Giscard d'Estaing, Valery, 1974-1981
422 General works on life and administration
Mitterand, François, 1981-
423 General works on life and administration

Local History

Alsace-Lorraine

638 History
By period
639 Early and medieval
640 1500-1789
641 1789-1871
642 1871-1945
643 1945-
Alsace
650 History
By period
.2 Early and medieval
.3 1500-1789
.4 1789-1871
.5 1871-1945
.6 1945-

Lorraine
655 History
By period
.2 Early and medieval
.3 1500-1789
.4 1789-1871
.5 1871-1945
.6 1945-

(DD) GERMANY

1 Periodicals
2 Societies
3 Sources and documents
Ethnography
76 National characteristics
History
85 Biography (Collective)
.4 Public men
.6 Rulers, emperors
.8 Houses, noble families, A-Z
.8 Study and teaching
General works
87 To 1600. Chronicles
88 1601-1800
89 1801-
General special
Military history
Individual campaigns and engagements are classed with the special period
99 Sources and documents
100 Biography (Collective)
.A2 General
.A3-Z Officers
101 General works
.5 General special
.7 Pamphlets
By period
102 Early to Reformation
.5 Medieval
.7 Early modern
103 19th century
104 20th century
106 Naval history
By period, see the period
Political and diplomatic history
Class works on the political and diplomatic history of a period with the period. For works on relations with a specific country regardless of period, see DD120
110 Sources and documents
112 General works
By period
Class here broad time periods only
113 Early
114 Medieval
Reformation period, see DD184
115 Modern
116 17th-18th centuries
117 19th-20th centuries

Special topics
118.5 Expansionist movements. Imperialism
119 Pangermanism
.2 Drang nach Osten
.5 German propaganda
.7 Anti-German propaganda
120 Relations with individual countries, A-Z
By period
121 Earliest to 481
125 Early and medieval to 1519
.5 Biography (Collective)
126 481-1273
.5 Empire and papacy
127 481-918
128 Merovingians, 481-752
130 Carlovingians, 752-911
133 Charlemagne, 768-814
Class here general works on Germany during the time of Charlemagne. For the life and reign of Charlemagne, see DC73
House of Saxony, 919-1024
136 Sources and documents
137 General works
.5 General special
.9 Biography, A-Z
House of Franconia
141.A2 Sources and documents
.A3-Z General works
.5 General special
.9 Biography, A-Z
Hohenstaufen period, 1125-1273
145 Sources and documents
146 General works
147 General special
.5 Biography, A-Z
149 Friedrich I Barbarossa, 1152-1190
Houses of Habsburg and Luxemburg, 1273-1519
156.A2 Sources and documents
.A3-Z General works
157 General special
158 Biography, A-Z
1438-1519. 15th century
171.A2 Sources and documents
.A3-Z General works
.5 Biography, A-Z
172 Albrecht II, 1438-1439
173 Friedrich III (IV), 1440-1493
.5 General special
174 Maximilian I, 1493-1519
.3 General special
.4 Bundschuh Insurrections
.6 German renaissance
175 Modern, 1519-
Including works on Germany since 1740
1519-1648. Reformation and Counterreformation period
Class here general history only. For works on the Reformation as a religious movement, including works on Martin Luther, see BR300+, which is not included in this guide

176.A2	Sources and documents
.A3-Z	General works
.8	General special
	Political history, see DD184
177	Biography and memoirs, A-Z
	Karl V, 1519-1558
178	Sources and documents
	General works on reign
.9	Works written before 1769
179	Works written 1769-
180	General special
.5	Biography of Karl V
.6	Correspondence and works
	Peasants' War, 1524-1525
181	Sources and documents
182	General works
183	General special
184	Schmalkaldic League and War, 1530-1547.
	Diet of Ratisbon, 1532
	Including earlier political history of the Reformation
.5	Treaty of Passau, 1552
.7	Sievershausen, Battle of, 1553
185	Ferdinand I, 1558-1564
186	Maximilian II, 1564-1676
187	Rudolf II, 1576-1612
.8	Matthias, 1612-1619
188	Ferdinand II, 1619-1637
	Biography only; reign, see DD189
.5	Ferdinand III, 1637-1657
	Biography only, reign, see DD189
.7	Ferdinand IV, 1653-1654
189	Period of the Thirty Years' War, 1618-1648
	For the war itself, see D251+
	1648-1740
190.A2	Sources and documents
.A3-Z	General works
.3	Biography and memoirs, A-Z
.4	1658-1705
	For biography of Leopold I, see DB67
.6	1705-1711
	For biography of Joseph I, see DB68
.8	1711-1740
	For biography of Karl VI, see DB69
	1740-1789. 18th century
191	Sources and documents
192	Biography and memoirs, A-Z
193	General works
194	Karl VII, 1742-1745
195	Franz I, 1745-1765
196	1765-1790
	For biography of Joseph II, see DB74
197	1789-1815
.5	Political and diplomatic history
198	1789-1806
.4	1790-1792
	For biography of Leopold II, see DB74.8
.7	1792-1806
	For biography of Leopold II, see DB81

199 1806-1815
Confederation of the Rhine, 1806-1813
19th century
201 Sources and documents
203 General works
204 General special
205 Biography and memoirs
.A2 Collective
.A3-Z Individual
206 1815-1848
207 1848-1849
.5 Special aspects
208 Prussia and Berlin
209 Local, A-Z
210 1850-1871
211 Biography and memoirs, A-Z
212 Period of war with Denmark, 1864
For the war itself, see DL236+
214 Period of Austro-Prussian War, 1866
For the war itself, see DD436+
216 Period of Franco-German War, 1870-1871
For the war itself, see DC281+
New Empire, 1871-1918
217 Sources and documents
Biography
.5 Collective
Individual
Bismarck
218.A1-29 Autobiography and family letters
.A3-Z Biography
.3 Writings
219 Other contemporaries, A-Z
220 General works
221 Political and diplomatic history
.5 Diplomatic history (treated separately)
223 Wilhelm I, 1871-1888
.9 Special topics (not A-Z)
Including war scare of 1875, etc.
224 Friedrich III, 1888
225 Political history, Wilhelm I and Friedrich III
228 Wilhelm II, 1888-1918
For biography, see DD229
.2 General special
.5 Political history
.6 Diplomatic history
.8 Period of World War I
For the war itself, see D501+
229 Biography of Wilhelm
231 Biography and memoirs of contemporaries, A-Z
e.g. .H5 Hindenburg, Paul von
232 20th century
.5 Sources and documents
Revolution and Republic, 1918-
233 Periodicals. Societies
237 General works
238 General special
240 Political and diplomatic history
Biography and memoirs

243 Collective
244 Public men
247 Individual, A-Z
e.g. .E2 Ebert, Friedrich
.H5 Hitler, Adolf
By period
248 Revolution, 1918
249 Ebert, 1919-1925
For biography, see DD247.E2
251 Hindenburg, 1925-1934
For biography, see DD231.H5
Hitler, 1933-1945.
Including National socialism
For biography of Hitler and other National socialist leaders, see DD247
253 Contemporary works
.A1 Periodicals. Societies
The Nazi Party (Nationalsozialistische Deutsche Arbeiter-Partei)
.25 General works
.29 Administrative offices
.46 Branches of the party
.49 Deutsches Jungvolk
.5 Hitlerjugend
.6 Schutzstaffel
.65 Waffenschutzstaffel
.7 Sturmabteilung
254 Propaganda in other countries
255 Individual countries, A-Z
256 Period of World War II
For the war itself, see D731+
.3 Resistance movements against the National Socialist regime
.4 Local, A-Z
.5 Postwar works on Hitler period
257 Period of Allied occupation, 1945-
.A1 Periodicals. Societies
General special
.25 Reunification question
.4 Political and diplomatic history
Biography and memoirs, see DD243+

WEST GERMANY

258 Periodicals. Societies
.2 Congresses
History
.6 Biography (Collective)
.7 General works
General special
.75 Political history
.8 Foreign and general relations
Class general works on the diplomatic history of a period with the period. For works on relations with a specific country regardless of the period, see DD258.85
.85 Relations with individual countries, A-Z
By period
.9 To 1949
259 Konrad Adenauer, 1949-1963
.4 Political history
.5 Foreign and general relations

	Biography and memoirs
.63	Collective
.7	Individual, A-Z
260	1963-
.4	Political history
.5	Foreign and general relations
	Biography and memoirs
.6	Collective
.65	Individual, A-Z
.7	Ludwig Erhard, 1963-1966
	Life and administration
.75	Kurt Kiesinger, 1966-1969
	Life and administration
.8	Willy Brandt, 1969-1974
	Life and administration
.85	Helmut Schmidt, 1974-1982
	Life and administration
262	Helmut Kohl, 1982-
	Life and administration

EAST GERMANY

280	Periodicals. Societies
.3	Congresses
.35	Sources and documents
	History
281.5	Biography (Collective)
282	General works
	General special
.5	Military history
283	Political history
284	Foreign and general relations
	Class general works on the diplomatic history of a period with the period. For works on relations with a specific country regardless of period, see DD284.5
.5	Relations with individual countries, A-Z
	By period
285	To 1949
286	1949-1961
.2	General special
.4	Political history
.5	Foreign and general relations
	Biography and memoirs
.6	Collective
.7	Individual, A-Z
287	1961-
.2	General special
.4	Political history
.5	Foreign and general relations
	Biography and memoirs
.6	Collective
.7	Individual, A-Z
288	1961-1971
189	1971-

PRUSSIA

301	Periodicals
302	Societies
303	Sources and documents
	History

343 Biography (Collective)
.4 Public men
.6 Rulers, kings, etc.
.8 Houses, noble families, A-Z
General works.
To 1800. Chronicles
347 1801-
General special
354 Military history
358 Naval history
361 Political and diplomatic history
For works on individual periods, see the period
363 Medieval
365 Modern
370 House of Hohenzollern
By period
Early to 1640
375 Sources and documents
377 General works
378 General special
1415-1640
380 Sources and documents
382 General works
383 General special
385 Period of the Reformation
387 Period of the Thirty Years' War
For the war itself, see D251+
389 Modern, 1640-
17th century
390 Sources and documents
391 Biography and memoirs, A-Z
392 General works
394 Friedrich Wilhelm, 1640-1688
.5 Political and diplomatic history
395 Biography and memoirs of contemporaries, A-Z
18th century
396.A1 Sources and documents
Biography and memoirs
.A2 Collective
.A3-Z Individual
397 General works
398 Friedrich I (III), 1688-1713
.8 Biography and memoirs of contemporaries, A-Z
399 Friedrich Wilhelm, I, 1713-1740
.8 Biography and memoirs of contemporaries, A-Z
Friedrich II der Grosse (Frederick the Great), 1740-1786
401 Sources and documents
402 Biography and memoirs of contemporaries, A-Z
403 General works on reign
.8 General special
Biography
404 Friedrich II
Works
Complete
405 In French. By editor or date
.1 In German. By editor or date
.12 In English. By editor or date
Political correspondence

.2 In French. By editor or date
.22 In German. By editor or date
.23 In English. By editor or date
406 Silesian wars, 1740-1745
.5 Diplomatic history
407 Special events, battles, A-Z
.5 Peace of Dresden, 1745
Austrian succession, see D291+, DB72
408 1745-1756
Seven Years' War
409 Sources and documents
410 Memoirs of contemporaries, A-Z
411 General works
.5 General special
412 Pamphlets
.6 Special events, battles, A-Z
.8 Peace of Hubertsburg, 1763
413 1763-1778
.2 1778-1786
414 Friedrich Wilhelm II, 1786-1797
.9 Biography and memoirs of contemporaries, A-Z
19th century
415 Sources and documents
416 Biography and memoirs, A-Z
417 General works
1789-1815. Period of the French Revolution
418 Sources and documents
.6 Biography and memoirs, A-Z
419 General works
Military history, see DC236
Friedrich Wilhelm III, 1797-1840
420 General works on reign
Biography and memoirs
421 Friedrich Wilhelm III
422 Contemporaries, A-Z
423 Confederation, 1816-1866
Friedrich Wilhelm IV, 1840-1861
424 General works on reign
Biography and memoirs
.8 Friedrich Wilhelm IV
.9 Contemporaries, A-Z
Wilhelm I, 1861-1888
425 General works on reign as king of Prussia
Biography, see DD223
Biography and memoirs of contemporaries, see DD219
429 General special
431 Prussia during the war with Denmark
Austro-Prussian War, 1866
436 Sources and documents
437 Memoirs, A-Z
438 General works
439 Special campaigns, battles, A-Z
440 Other
442 North German Confederation, 1866-1870
446 Period of Franco-German War, 1870-1871
For the war itself, see DC281+
448 New Empire, 1871-1918
Friedrich III, 1888, see DD224+

Wilhelm II, 1888-1918
General works on reign as king of Prussia
Biography, see DD229
Biography and memoirs of contemporaries, see DD231
452 Period between World Wars, 1918-1945
Biography and memoirs, see DD247
453 1918-1933
454 1933-1945

Local History and Description

801 States, provinces, etc.
e.g. Schleswig-Holstein
Including Schleswig-Holstein question
.S6335 History
By period
.S6336 Early and medieval
.S6337 16th-18th centuries
.S6338 19th-20th centuries

Berlin
860 General works
History and description
General works, see DD860
870 To 1600
871 1600-1788
875 1789-1815
876 1816-1870
878 1871-1914
879 1914-1921
880 1922-1945
881 1946-
Including the Berlin Wall
900 Other special

(DE) THE MEDITERRANEAN REGION

THE GRECO-ROMAN WORLD (GENERAL)

1 Periodicals
2 Societies
7 Biography (Collective)
Cf. D107
8 Historiography
Biography of historians and archaeologists
For classical authors, see PA, which is not included in this guide
9.A1A-Z Collective
.A2-Z Individual, A-Z
15 Study and teaching
Antiquities. Civilization. Culture
57 Works to 1800
59 Works, 1801-
61 Special topics, A-Z
.M5 Military antiquities
.N3 Naval antiquities
.P42 Peace
.P75 Propaganda
.P8 Public and political antiquities
.W35 War
72 Greco-Roman world in the time of Christ
80 History

83 General special
84 Military and naval history
85 Political history
For specific periods, see the period
.3 Foreign and general relations
Class general works on the diplomatic history of a period with the period. For works on relations with a specific country regardless of period, see DE85.5
.5 Relations with individual countries, A-Z
By period
86 Ancient to 476. Greco-Roman era
General special
88 Military and naval history
89 Political and diplomatic history
92 Beginnings of the Christian Era
94 Medieval to 1453
96 1453-1800
98 1801-1945
100 1945-

(DF) GREECE

ANCIENT GREECE

10 Periodicals
11 Societies
12 Sources and documents
Antiquities. Civilization. Culture
General works
75 Selections from classical authors
76 To 1800
77 1801-
78 General special
81 Public and political antiquities
89 Military and naval antiquities
90 Naval antiquities alone
History
.3 Study and teaching
General works
213 Classical authors (Translations)
Modern authors
.5 To 1800
214 1801-
217 General special
By period
To 1100 B.C.
220 Bronze Age. Aegean civilization
.3 Minoan civilization
.5 Mycenaean civilization
221.2 1125-500 B.C.
.3 Dorian invasions, ca. 1125-1025 B.C.
.5 Geometric period, ca. 900-700 B.C.
222 775-500 B.C. Age of Tyrants
.2 General special
224 Biography, A-Z
225 Persian wars, 499-479 B.C.
.2 General special
.25 Pamphlets
.3 Ionian revolt, 499-494
.33 Burning of Sardis, 498

.35 Capture of Miletus, 494
.37 Conquest of Thrace, 493-492
.4 Marathon, 490
.5 Thermopylae, 480
.53 Naval battles at Artemisium, 480
.6 Salamis, 480
.7 Plataea, 479
.75 Mycale, 479
.8 Capture of Sestus, 478
.9 Other special events, A-Z
226 Biography, A-Z
227 Athenian supremacy. Age of Pericles. 479-431 B.C.
.4 Pamphlets
.5 General special
Including First Delian League
.6 Capture of Eion, 476
.63 Battles of the Eurymedon, 468
.65 Revolt of Thasos, 465
.7 Third Messenian War, 464-456
.75 War with Aegina and Corinth, 459-456
.77 Athenian expedition to Egypt, 454
.8 Peace of Cimon/Callias, 449-448 B.C.
.83 Revolt of Euboea and Megara, 446-445
.85 Samian War, 440-439
.9 Other events, A-Z
228 Biography, A-Z
229 Peloponnesian War, 431-404 B.C.
For Thucydides use:
.T5 English text
By translator, A-Z
.T55 English selections
By translator, A-Z
.T56 Other languages
By language, A-Z and date
.T6 Biography and criticism
.1 Pamphlets
.2 General special
.3 First period, 431-421
.35 Second period, 421-413
.37 Third period, 413-404
.4 Siege and fall of Plataea, 429-427
.43 Revolt and capitulation of Mytilene, 428-427
.45 Fortification of Pylus, 425
.47 Capture of Sphacteria, 425
.5 Invasion of Boeotia, 424
.53 Invasion of Thrace, 424
.55 Truce, 423
.57 Peace of Nicias, 421
.6 Matinea, 418
.63 Conquest of Melos, 416
.65 Invasion of Sicily, 415
.67 Siege of Syracuse, 414-413
.69 Battle in the Great Harbor, 413
.7 Revolt of Athenian allies, 412
.73 Revolution of the Four Hundred, 411
.75 Cynossema, 411
.77 Cyzicus, 410
.8 Notium, 407

.83	Arginusae, 406
.85	Aegospotami, 405
.87	Siege and fall of Athens, 404
.9	Other events, A-Z
230	Biography, A-Z
	Spartan and Theban supremacies, 404-362 B.C.
.9	Sources and documents
231	General works
.2	General special
.25	Pamphlets
.3	Thirty tyrants, 404
.32	Expedition of Cyrus, 401-400
.35	War in Asia Minor against Persians, 399-394
.4	Corinthian War, 395-387
.45	Cnidus, 394
.5	Coronea, 394
.55	Peace of Antalcidas, 387
.6	War between Sparta and Thebes, 378-371
.7	Naxos, 376
.75	Tegyra, 375
.8	Leuctra, 371
.87	Mantinea, 362
.9	Other events, A-Z
232	Biography, A-Z
	Macedonian epoch, 359-336 B.C.
.5	Sources and documents
233	General works
.2	General special
.25	Pamphlets
.3	Operations in Chalcidice and Thrace, 358-357
.35	Social War, 357-355
.4	Sacred War, 356-346
.45	Fall of Olynthus, 348
.5	Subjugation of Thrace, 342-341
.55	Amphissian War, 339-338
.6	Chaeronea, 338
.7	Other events, A-Z
.8	Biography, A-Z
	Alexander the Great, 336-323 B.C.
234.A1	Sources and documents
.A3-Z	General works
.2	General special
.25	Pamphlets
.31	Amphictyonic Council, 336
.33	Campaigns in Thrace and Illyria, 335
.34	Destruction of Thebes, 335
.35	Battle of the Granicus, 334
.37	Conquest of Asia Minor, 334-333
.38	Issus, 333
.4	Siege of Tyre, 332
.34	Conquest of Egypt, 332
.5	Gaugamela, 331
.53	Capture of Babylon and Susa, 331
.55	Capture of Persepolis, 330
.57	Capture of Persepolis, 330
.6	Invasion of India, 327-325
.65	Mutiny at Opis, 324
.7	Other events, A-Z

.9 Biography of contemporaries, A-Z
Hellenistic period, 323-146 B.C.
235.A1 Sources and documents
.A2 History and criticism of sources
.A3-Z General works
.3 General special
.4 323-281
.45 General special
Biography and memoirs
.47 Collective
.48 Individual, A-Z
.5 Lamian War, 323-322
.7 Athenian Revolution, 286
236 280-220. Aetolian and Achaean leagues
.3 General special
.4 Galatian Invasion, 279-278
.5 Chremonidean War, 267-262
.7 Pamphlets
237 Biography. A-Z
238 220-146. Macedonian wars and Roman conquest
.3 General special
.7 Pamphlets
.9 Biography, A-Z
239 Roman epoch, 140 B.C.-323/476 A.D.
240 General special
241 Pamphlets

MEDIEVAL GREECE. BYZANTINE EMPIRE

501 Periodicals. Societies
503 Sources and documents
.8 Study and teaching
506 Biography (Collective)
.5 Rulers, kings, etc.
543 Military history
544 Naval history
545 Political history
546 Foreign and general relations
Class general works on the diplomatic history of a period with the period. For works on relations with a specific country regardless of period, see DF547
547 Relations with individual countries, A-Z
548 Empire and papacy
History
General works
To 1800. Chronicles
550 Byzantine
551 Other
552 1801-
553 Eastern Empire, 323/476-1057
.5 Pamphlets
555 323-527
Cf. DG315+
556 General special
557 Constantine the Great, 323-337
527-1057
General works, see DF553
571 527-720
581 720-886. Iconoclasts
591 886-1057

1057-1453
.8 Sources and documents
General works
To 1800. Chronicles
600 Byzantine
.5 Other
601 1801-
1204-1261. Latin Empire
610 Sources and documents
General works
.8 To 1800. Chronicles
611 1801-
619 Fall of Empire, 1261
1261-1453. Palaeologi
630 Sources and documents
631 General works
.A2 Byzantine
.A3-Z Other
632 General special
Biography and memoirs
.3 Collective
.32 Individual, A-Z
1453. Fall of Constantinople
Cf. DR502, Turkish accounts
To 1800
645 Byzantine
647 Other
649 1801-

MODERN GREECE

701 Periodicals. Societies
703 Sources and documents
History
750 Biography (Collective)
751 Rulers, kings
752 Houses, nobles families, A-Z
.8 Study and teaching
757 General works
Including works on ancient, medieval, and modern Greece treated together
Cf. DF213+, ancient alone; DF550+, medieval alone
765 Military history
For works on specific periods, see the period
775 Naval history
For works on specific periods, see the period
785 Political and diplomatic history
Class general works on the diplomatic history of a period with the period. For works on relations with a specific country regardless of period, see DF787
787 Relations with individual countries, A-Z
By period
801 Turkish rule, 1453-1821
.9 Biography and memoirs, A-Z
802 1821-
803 1821-1913. 19th century
.9 Biography and memoirs, A-Z
War of Independence, 1821-1829
804 Sources and documents
805 General works
806 Personal narratives and contemporary accounts

807 Political and diplomatic history
809 Naval history
810 Special events, battles, A-Z
811 Special topics, A-Z
.F65 Foreign participation
.F652 By region or country, A-Z
.I54 Influence
.P74 Prisoners and prisons
.R44 Religious aspects
.W64 Women
814 Pamphlets
Biography
815.A2 Collective
.A3-Z Individual, A-Z
817 Kapodistrias, 1827-1831
821 1831-1832
823 Otho I, 1833-1862
Biography and memoirs of contemporaries
.2 Collective
.3 Individual, A-Z
.6 Acarnanian Revolt, 1836
.65 Revolution, 1848
.68 Arta Revolt, 1854
.7 Revolution, 1862
825 George I, 1863-1913
826 Annexation of Thessaly and Epirus, 1881
827 War with Turkey, 1897
831 1897-1913
.5 Military League coup d'état, 1909
832 Biography and memoirs of contemporaries, A-Z
833 20th century
Biography and memoirs
835 Collective
836 Individual, A-Z
837 Constantine I, 1913-1917
Reign, 1920-1922, see DF845
838 Period of World War I
For the war itself, see D501+
843 Alexander, 1917-1920
845 Constantine I, 1920-1922
War with Turkey, 1921-1922
.5 Sources and documents
.52 General works
.53 Special events, battles, A-Z
Biography and memoirs
.57 Collective
.58 Individual, A-Z
847 George II, 1922-1924
Reign, 1935-1947, see DF849
848 Republic, 1924-1935
849 George II, 1935-1947
Civil War, 1944-1949
.5 Sources and documents
.52 General works
.53 Special events, battles, A-Z
Biography and memoirs
.57 Collective
.58 Individual, A-Z

850	Paul, 1947-1964
	Biography and memoirs of contemporaries
851.3	Collective
.5	Individual, A-Z
852	Constantine II, 1964-1967
	Biography and memoirs of contemporaries
.3	Collective
.5	Individual, A-Z
853	Period of military rule, 1967-1974
	Biography and memoirs
.3	Collective
.5	Individual, A-Z
854	Restoration of democracy, 1974-
	Biography and memoirs
.3	Collective
.32	Individual, A-Z

(DG) ITALY

ANCIENT ITALY. ROME TO 476

11	Periodicals
12	Societies
	Antiquities. Civilization. Culture
	General works
76	To 1800
77	1801-
81	Public and political antiquities
82	General special
	Cf. DG214+, Foreign and general relations
89	Military and naval antiquities
	History
203	Biography (Collective)
204	Houses, noble families, A-Z
.5	Study and teaching
	General works
207	Translations of classical authors
	Original texts class in PA
	Modern authors
208	To 1776
209	1776-
211	General special
	Foreign and general relations
	Class general works on the diplomatic history of a period with the period. For works on relations with countries outside the Roman Empire, regardless of period, see DG215
214	Sources and documents
.5	General works
215	Relations with individual countries, A-Z
	By period
221	Pre-Roman Italy
223	Etruscans
.5	Political and diplomatic history
231	Kings and Republic, 753-27 B.C.
.3	General special
.7	Pamphlets
233	Foundations and Kings, 753-510 B.C.
.2	General special
.25	Pamphlets
.3	Romulus, 753-716

.4	Numa Pompilius, 715-673
.5	Tullus Hostilius, 673-642
.6	Ancus Marcius, 642-617
.7	Tarquinius Priscus, 616-579
.8	Servius Tullius, 578-535
.9	Tarquinius Superbus, 535-510
235	Republic to First Punic War, 509-265 B.C.
.2	General special
.4	Special events to 343, by date
236	Biography, 509-343, A-Z
237	Subjection of Italy, 343-290
.2	General special
.4	Special events, by date
238	Biography, A-Z
239	290-265
.2	General special
.4	Special events, by date
240	Biography, A-Z
241	Conquest of the Mediterranean world, 264-133 B.C.
.2	General special
242	First and Second Punic Wars
243	First Punic War, 264-241 B.C.
.2	General special
.25	Pamphlets
.4	Special events, by date
244	Biography, 264-219 B.C., A-Z
245	240-231
246	Illyrian wars, 231-219 B.C.
247	Second Punic War, 218-201 B.C.
.1	Causes
.12	Siege of Saguntum, 219
.15	Hannibal in Gaul, 218
.2	Crossing the Alps, 218
.23	Ticinus, 218
.24	Trebia, 218
.26	Trasimenus, 217
.3	Cannae, 216
.33	Revolt of Southern Italy
.36	Winter at Capua, 216
.4	Nola, 215
.48	Tarentum, 212
.5	War in Sicily, 214-210
.55	Syracuse, 212
.59	War in Spain, 218-211
.6	Capua, 211
.7	Metaurus, 207
.8	Scipio in Carthage, 209
.82	Scipio in Spain, 206
.9	Invasion of Africa, 204-201
.94	Capture of Syphax, 203
.97	Zama, 202
.98	Peace with Carthage, 201
248	Biography, A-Z
249	Hannibal
.3	General special
.4	Special events after return to Carthage, by date
250	200-133 B.C.
.5	General special

Wars in the East

251 First and Second Macedonian wars, 215-196

.3 Syrian War, 191-190

.4 Aetolian War, 189

.5 Galatian War, 189

.6 Third Macedonian War, 171-168

.8 Achaean War, 147-146

Wars in the West

252 Gallic War, 200

.2 Ligurian War, 200

.3 Spanish War, 195-179

.4 Istrian War, 178

.5 Sardinian and Corsican War, 177-175

.6 Third Punic War, 149-146

.8 Numantine War, 143-133

.9 First Servile War, 134-132

253 Biography, A-Z

Fall of the Republic and establishment of the Empire, 133-27 B.C.

.5 Sources and documents

254 General works

.2 General special

.3 Pamphlets

.5 The Gracchi, 133-121

255 Jugurthine War, 111-105

.5 Cimbri and Teuroni, 113-101

256 Period of Marius and Sulla, 111-78 B.C.

.2 General special

.5 Marius (Gaius), life and times

.7 Sulla (Lucius Cornelius), life and times

257 Second Servile War, 103-99

.3 Social or Marsic War, 90-88

.5 First Civil War, 88-86

.6 First Mithridatic War, 88-84

.8 Second Civil War, 83-78

Including First and Second Civil Wars treated together

258 Pompey, life and times

.3 Third Mithridatic war, 74-61

.5 Spartacus and the Third War, 73-71

259 Conspiracy of Catiline, 65-62

260 Biography, A-Z

261 Julius Caesar

262 General special

.5 Pamphlets

263 First Triumvirate, 60 B.C.

264 War in Gaul, 58-56

Caesar's Commentaries in English, see DC62.C2

265 Pompey and Caesar

266 Civil War, 49-48

267 Dictator, 46. Death, 44

268 Second Triumvirate, 43-31

269 Other

Empire, 27 B.C.-476 A.D.

.5 Sources and documents

270 General works

271 General special

272 Civilization. Culture. Antiquities

273 Political antiquities

274 Biography (Collective)

	Constitutional empire, 27 B.C.-284 A.D.
275	Sources and documents
276	General works
.5	General special
	Twelve Caesars, 27 B.C.-96 A.D.
277	Classical authors in English translations
.5	Sources and documents
278	General works
.3	General special
.5	Pamphlets
279	Augustus, 27 B.C.-14 A.D.
281	Julian dynasty, 14-68
282	Tiberius, 14-37
283	Caligula, 37-41
284	Claudius I, 41-54
285	Nero, 54-68
.3	General special
286	68-96
287	Galba, 68-69
288	Otho-Vitellius, 69
289	Vespasian, 69-79
290	Titus, 79-81
291	Domitian, 81-96
	Biography
.6	Collective
.7	Individual, A-Z
292	96-180
	Biography and memoirs
.5	Collective
.7	Individual, A-Z
293	Nerva, 96-98
294	Trajan, 98-117
295	Hadrian, 117-138
296	Antoninus Pius, 138-161
287	Marcus Aurelius, 161-180
298	180-284
	Biography and memoirs
.5	Collective
.7	Individual, A-Z
299	Commodus, 180-192
300	Septimius Severus, 193-211
301	Caracalla, 211-217
302	Macrinus, 217-218
303	Elagabalus, 218-222
304	Severus Alexander, 222-235
305	235-284
306	Maximinus, 235-238
.3	Gordianus III, 238-244
.5	Philippus, 244-249
.7	Decius, 249-251
307	Gallus, 251-253
.3	Valerian, 253-260
.5	Gallieus, 260-268
.7	Claudius II, 268-270
308	Aurelian, 270-275
.3	Tacitus, 275-276
.5	Florianus, 276
.7	Probus, 276-282

309 Carus, 282-283
.3 Carinus and Numerianus, 283-284
284-476. Decline and fall
310 Sources and documents
311 General works
.5 Biography, A-Z
Prefer individual periods, DG313+
313 Diocletian, 284-305
314 Rival Augusti, 306-324
.8 Biography of contemporaries, A-Z
315 Constantine the Great, 306-337
Cf. DF557, Eastern Empire
316 337-364
.3 Constantine II, 337-340
.5 Constans, 337-350
.7 Constantius II, 353-361
317 Julian, 361-363
317.5 Jovian, 363-364
.7 Other, A-Z
319 Valentinian and last emperors, 364-476
Biography and memoirs
322 Collective
.5 Individual, A-Z
323 Valentinian I, 364-375
Valens, see DF559
325 375-392
326 Gratian, 375-383
329 Valentinian II, 375-392
330 Theodosius, 392-395
For general works on Theodosius as ruler of the East, see DF560
332 Honorius, 395-423
335 Joannes, 423-424
338 Valentinian III, 425-455
341 Petronius Maximus, 455
344 Avitus, 455-456
347 Majorianus, 457-461
350 Libius Severus, 461-465
353 Anthemius, 467-472
356 Olybrius, 472
359 Glycerius, 473
362 Julius Nepos, 474-475
365 Romulus Augustulus, 475-476

MEDIEVAL AND MODERN ITALY

401 Periodicals
402 Societies
403 Sources and documents
History
463 Biography (Collective)
.2 Rulers, kings
.4 Public men
Houses, noble families
.7 General
.8 Individual, A-Z
465.8 Study and teaching
General works
Including those beginning with Roman period
466 Written before 1801
467 Written 1801-

General special
Military history
Individual campaigns and engagements are classed with special period
480 Sources and documents
481 Biography (Collective)
.A2 General
.A3-Z Officers
482 General works
By period
483 Early and medieval
.5 1492-1792
484 19th-20th centuries
486 Naval history
491 Political and diplomatic history
Class works on broad time periods in DG492+. For specific time periods, prefer the period or reign, DG500+. Class works on relations with individual country regardless of period in DG499
492 Earliest to 768
493 768-1268
494 1268-1492
495 1492-1789
497 1789-1860
498 1861-1945
1945- , see DG577.2+
499 Relations with individual countries, A-Z
By period
Medieval, 476-1492
General works
500 To 1800. Chronicles
501 1801-
502 General special
503 476-1268
.A2 To 1800. Chronicles
.A3-Z 1801-
504 476-774
506 Gothic Kingdom, 489-553
511 Lombard Kingdom, 568-774
Biography
.25 Collective
.27 Individual, A-Z
515 Frankish emperors, 774-962
519 Biography, A-Z
520 German emperors, 962-1268
The Commune. Guelfs and Ghibellines
General works
522 To 1800. Chronicles
523 1801-
530 1268-1492
13th century
General works
531.A2 To 1800
.A3-Z 1801-
.8 Biography, A-Z
Renaissance. 14th-16th centuries
General works
532 To 1800
533 1801-
534 1300-1492

535 14th century
536 Biography, A-Z
537 15th century
.8 Biography, A-Z
538 Modern, 1492-
Including period of Spanish and Austrian supremacy
16th century. 1492-1618
539.A2 Sources and documents
General works
.A3-Z To 1800
540 1801-
.8 Biography and memoirs
.A1 Collective
.A2-Z Individual, A-Z
1492-1527. Invasions
General works
541.A2 To 1800
.A3-Z 1801-
.8 Biography and memoirs, A-Z
17th century
General works
543 To 1800
544 1801-
Biography and memoirs
.7 Collective
.8 Individual, A-Z
18th century
544.9 Sources and documents
545 General works
.5 Pamphlets
.8 Biography and memoirs, A-Z
1792-1815
546 Sources and documents
547 General works
Kingdom of Italy
548 Sources and documents
.2 Cispadane Republic, 1796
.4 Transpadane Republic, 1796
.6 Cisalpine Republic, 1797-1802
.8 Italian Republic, 1802-1805
549 Kingdom of Italy, 1804-1814
551 19th century
Including 1789-1848
Biography and memoirs
.7 Collective
.8 Individual, A-Z
1848-1871
552.A15 Periodicals. Societies
.A2 Sources and documents
.A3-Z General works
.5 Political and diplomatic history
Biography and memoirs
.7 Collective
.8 Individual, A-Z
553 1848-1849. Austro-Sardinian War
.2 1848
.3 1849
.5 Special events, battles, A-Z

French expedition, 1849, see DG798.5
554 1859-1860
.3 Pamphlets
.5 Special events, battles, A-Z
e.g. Expedition of the Thousand, 1860
555 1871-1947. United Italy (Monarchy)
556 Biography and memoirs, A-Z
557 Vittorio Emanuele II, 1861-1878
General special
.5 Political and diplomatic history
558 War with Austria, 1866
559 Siege and occupation of Rome, 1870
561 Umberto I, 1878-1900
564 Political and diplomatic history
566 Vittorio Emanuele III, 1900-1946
Works on the regency and reign of Umberto II are classed in DG572
.5 Political and diplomatic history
Including general and pre-Fascist
569 Pamphlets
570 Period of World War I
For the war itself, see D501+
571 1919-1945. Fascism
.A1 Periodicals. Societies
.A2 Sources and documents
.7 Resistance movements against Fascist regime
.75 March on Rome, 1922
572 Period of World War II
Including period of double occupation, regency and reign of Umberto II, and period of Provisional Government, 1943-1947
For the war itself, see D731
Biography and memoirs
574 Collective
575 Individual, A-Z
e.g. .A4 Umberto II
.M8 Mussolini, Benito
1948- . Republic
576 Periodicals. Sources and documents
.8 General works
577 Political history
.2 Foreign and general relations
By period
.5 1948-1976
Biography and memoirs
578 Collective
579 Individual, A-Z
581 1976-
Biography and memoirs
582 Collective
583 Individual, A-Z

PIEDMONT. SAVOY

610 Periodicals. Societies
611 Sources and documents
.3 Biography (Collective)
.5 House of Savoy
History
616 General works on Piedmont-Savoy, or Savoy alone

Early and medieval
617 General works on Piedmont-Savoy, or Savoy alone
Savoy
General works on the counts of Savoy, see DG611.5
.5 Piedmont
618 Modern
.2 15th-17th centuries
.5 Kingdom of Sardinia, 1718-1860
Biography and memoirs
.52 Collective
.522 Individual, A-Z
.53 Vittorio Amedeo I, 1675-1730
.54 Biography of contemporaries, A-Z
.66 1848-1849
Cf. DG553, Austro-Sardinian War
.7 Piedmont, 1860-
.72 1860-1945
.75 1945-

GENOA

Class here works on the republic, city, and province of Genoa
631 Periodicals. Societies
.2 Sources and documents
.7 Biography (Collective)
Houses, noble families
.8 Collective
.82 Individual, A-Z
History
General works
636 Modern (Written, 1801-)
.3 Written before 1801
637 Early and medieval
638 Modern

MILAN. LOMBARDY

651 Periodicals. Societies. Sources and documents
History
General works
656 Modern
.3 Early to 1800
657 Early and medieval
.1 To 452
.2 452-774. Huns, Goths, Lombards
.3 774-1100
.35 1101-1237
.37 Friedrich I Barbarossa, 1158-1185
.4 Lombard League, 1167-1183
.45 Battle of Legnano, 1176
.5 1237-1535
.65 1237-1311
.7 1311-1447
.75 1447-1450
.8 1450-1535
.9 Biography, A-Z
658 Modern
.1 1535-1714. Spanish period
.2 1714-1796. Austrian period
Biography
.23 Collective

.25 Individual, A-Z
.3 1796-1900
.4 1796-1815
.5 1815-1859. Lombardo-Venetian Kingdom
.6 1860-1900
.7 Biography, 1796-1900, A-Z
.8 1901-

VENICE

670 Periodicals. Societies
671 Sources and documents
.4 Biography (Collective)
.45 Rulers, doges
.6 Houses, noble families, A-Z
History
General works
676 Modern
.3 Early to 1800
.8 Military history
For specific periods, see the period
Political history
For specific periods, see the period
.88 Sources and documents
.9 General works
Foreign and general relations
Class general works on the diplomatic history of a period with the period. For works on relations with a specific country regardless of period, see DG676.97
.93 Sources and documents
.95 General works
.97 Relations with individual countries, A-Z
Early and medieval
General works
677.A2 To 1800
.A3-Z 1801-
Early to 811
General works
677.1.A2 To 1800
.A3-Z 1801-
.3 697-810
.35 811-991
.4 991-1096. Relations with Constantinople
.5 1096-1172. Crusades. Normans
.6 1172-1311. 13th century
.7 1311-1382. 14th century
Including war with Turks and War of Chioggia, 1378-1380
.85 1382-1501. 15th century
678 Modern
.2 Turkish wars, 1453-1571
16th century
.22 Sources and documents
General works
.23 To 1800
.235 1801-
.24 Biography and memoirs, A-Z
1595-1718. 17th century
General works
.3 To 1800
.31 1801-

.315 Marino Grimani, 1595-1605. Papal conflict
.32 Spanish conspiracy, 1618
1644-1718
For works on the war with Turkey over Candia, see DR534.2+
General works
.33 To 1800
.34 1801-
.4 1718-1797. Fall of the Republic
.5 1797-1900
.54 1815-1848
For works dealing with the Lombardo-Venetian Kingdom as a whole, see DG658.5
.7 Biography and memoirs, A-Z
.8 1901-

TUSCANY. FLORENCE

731 Periodicals. Societies
.2 Sources and documents
History
General works
736 Modern
.3 Early through 1800
.5 General special
Medieval
737.A15 Sources and documents
General works
.A2 To 1800
.A3-Z 1801-
.3 Modern
.4 Early modern. Medicean period
.42 Biography of Medici family
15th century
General works
.5 To 1800
.55 1801-
.58 Biography and memoirs, A-Z
738 16th century
.14 Biography and memoirs, A-Z
.22 1609-1737
.29 Biography and memoirs, A-Z
.3 1737-
.32 1737-1801. Lorraine dynasty
.33 General special
.39 Biography and memoirs, A-Z
.4 19th century
.42 Napoleonic period
.43 1801-1807. Kingdom of Etruria
.44 1808-1814. Under France
.5 1815-1900
.6 Biography and memoirs, A-Z
.7 20th century
.79 Biography and memoirs, A-Z

PAPAL STATES. HOLY SEE. VATICAN CITY

791 Periodicals. Societies
.2 Sources and documents
History
General works
796 Modern

.3 Early to 1800
.5 Military and naval history
797 Early and medieval
.1 To 756
.2 756-962
.3 962-1309
.5 "Babylonian captivity," 1309-1377
.55 Biography, A-Z
.6 1377-1499
.7 1499-1870
.8 1499-1605
.82 Cesare Borgia
.83 Lucrezia Borgia
.9 1605-1700
Biography and memoirs
.92 Collective
.93 Individual, A-Z
798 1700-1798
.2 1798-1799
.3 1799-1870
Biography and memoirs
.33 Collective
.34 Individual, A-Z
.35 1799-1848
.4 1848-1870
.5 1848-1849
.6 1859-1870
.7 1870. End of temporal power
799 Holy See, 1870-
800 Vatican City, 1929-

NAPLES. KINGDOM OF THE TWO SICILIES

840 Periodicals. Societies
841 Sources and documents
.4 Biography (Collective)
.5 Rulers, kings, queens
.55 Public men
.6 Houses, noble families, A-Z
For specific periods, see the period
History
General works
846 Modern
.3 Early to 1800
General special
Political history
For specific periods, see the period
.6 Sources and documents
.62 General works
Early and medieval
General works
847.A2 To 1800
.A3-Z 1801-
Early to 1016
.1 Sources and documents
.11 General works
.13 1016-1268
Biography and memoirs
.135 Collective
.136 Individual, A-Z

.14 1016-1194. Norman period
.15 1194-1268. Hohenstaufen period
.17 1268-1442. Anjou dynasty
848 Modern
    1442-1707. Spanish rule
.05 Sources and documents
.1 General works
.112 Biography and memoirs, A-Z
.2 1707-1735. Austrian rule
    Biography and memoirs
.23 Collective
.24 Individual, A-Z
.3 1735-1861. Bourbon dynasty
    Carlos III, 1735-1759
.32 Sources and documents
.33 General works
.35 1759-1815
.37 Biography and memoirs, A-Z
.38 Parthenopean Republic, 1799
.4 19th century
.42 1798-1815
.43 1806-1815
.46 1815-1860. Kingdom of the Two Sicilies
.48 Biography and memoirs, A-Z
.58 1860-1900
.6 Biography and memoirs, A-Z
849 20th century
    Biography and memoirs
.9 Collective
850 Individual, A-Z
851 1945-

SICILY

861 Periodicals. Societies
.2 Sources and documents
    History
    General works
866 Modern
.3 Early to 1800
    Early and medieval to 1409
    General works
867.A2 To 1800
.A3-Z 1801-
    Saracen period, 827-1016
.11 Arabic authors
    European authors
.12 To 1800
.13 1801-
    Norman period, 1016-1194
.19 Sources and documents
.2 General works
.21 General special
.22 1016-1061
.28 Sicily under the Hohenstaufen, 1194-1268
.29 General special
.299 1268-1282
.3 Sicilian Vespers, 1282
    1282-1409
.33 Sources and documents

.34 General works
868 Modern, 1409-
.2 1409-1504
.3 1504-1648
.35 1648-1806
.4 19th century
.42 1806-1815
.44 1815-1871
Expedition of the Thousand, see DG554.5.E96
.5 1871-1900
869 20th century
.2 1900-1945
.3 1945-

MALTA

987 Periodicals. Societies
.5 Sources and documents
History
.83 Biography (Collective)
990 General works
General special
.5 Military history
For individual campaigns and engagements, see the special period
.7 Naval history
For individual campaigns and engagements, see the special period
991 Political history
For specific periods, see the period
.5 Foreign and general relations
Class general works on the diplomatic history of a period with the period. For works on relations with a specific country regardless of period, see DG991.6
.6 Relations with individual countries, A-Z
United States, see E183.8+
By period
992 Early to 870
.2 870-1530
Biography and memoirs
.26 Collective
.27 Individual, A-Z
.3 Revolt against Monroy, 1427
.5 1530-1798. Rule of the Knights of Malta
Including wars against the Turks and their North African allies, suppression of the Jesuits, and the conquest by Napoleon
Biography and memoirs
.56 Collective
.57 Individual, A-Z
.6 Siege of Malta, 1565
.62 Rebellion of the Turkish Slaves, 1722
.65 Rebellion of the Priests, 1775
.7 1798-1964. British colonial rule
Biography and memoirs
.76 Collective
.77 Individual, A-Z
.8 1798-1802
993 1802-1947
.5 1947-1964
994 1964- . Independent
Biography and memoirs
.7 Collective

.8 Individual, A-Z

(DH) LOW COUNTRIES. BELGIUM

BELGIUM AND THE NETHERLANDS

1 Periodicals. Societies
3 Sources and documents
History
General works
106 To 1800. Chronicles
107 1801-
General special
113 Military history
For specific periods, see the period
121 Naval history
For specific periods, see the period
131 Political and diplomatic history
Special topics
136 The Scheldt question
137 Unification movements
By period
141 Early and medieval to 1384
146 Roman period
151 Frankish period
156 843-1127
159 1127-1285
162 1285-1384
1384-1555
General works
171 To 1800
172 1801-
175 1384-1477. House of Burgundy
177 Biography and memoirs, A-Z
179 1477-1555
180 Marie of Burgundy and Maximilian I, 1477-1482
181 Felipe I, 1483-1506
182 Karl V, 1506-1555
Wars of Independence, 1555-1648
185 Sources and documents
General works
186 To 1800
.5 1801-
Felipe (Philip) II, 1555-1581
General works
187 To 1800
.5 1801-
.9 Pamphlets, by date
188 Biography and memoirs of contemporaries, A-Z
191 Alba (Alva), 1567-1573
192 1573-1576
.5 Siege of Leyden, 1573-1574
193 Juan de Austria, 1576-1578
194 Alessandro Farnese, 1578-1581
195 Union of Utrecht, 1579
1581-1609
General works
196 To 1800
197 1801-
198 Leicester, 1585-1587

199 Special events, battles, A-Z
200 Pamphlets, by date
200 Armistice, 1609-1621
204 1621-1648
206 Special events, battles, A-Z
207 Pamphlets, 1609-1648, by date
For later history of Belgium and the Netherlands, see the individual countries

BELGIUM

401 Periodicals. Societies
403 Sources and documents
471 National characteristics
491 Ethnography
Including nationalism, the Flemings, and the Flemish movement
History
513 Biography (Collective)
514 Rulers, kings
515 Public men
516 Houses, noble families, A-Z
General works
517 To 1800. Chronicles
521 1801-
General special
540 Military history
Individual campaigns and engagements are classed with special period
541 Biography (Collective)
542 To 1555
543 1555-1815
545 To 1815-
551 Naval history
566 Political and diplomatic history
Class general works on the political and diplomatic history of a period with the period. For works on relations with a specific country regardless of period, see DH569
569 Relations with individual countries, A-Z
By period
571 Early and medieval to 1555
572 General special
574 Roman period
576 Frankish period
578 843-1100
580 1101-1400
581 Biography and memoirs, A-Z
582 1401-1506
583 Biography and memoirs, A-Z
584 1506-1555
585 1555-1794. Spanish and Austrian rule
591 1555-1598. 16th century
598 Biography and memoirs, A-Z
1598-1714
600 Sources and documents
601 General works
602 Biography and memoirs, A-Z
605 1598-1621
606 1621-1648
607 1648-1700
609 1701-1714

1714-1794. Austrian Netherlands
611 Sources and documents
612 General works
613 Biography and memoirs, A-Z
614 General special
615 1740-1780
For biography of Maria Theresia, see DB71
616 1780-1790
For biography of Joseph II, see DB74
Revolution, 1788-1790
Sources and documents
617 Brabant (and Liége)
.5 Liége
General works
618 Brabant (and Liége)
.5 Liége
619 1790-1792
For biography of Leopold II, see DB74.8
620 1790-1909
621 1794-1830
628 Biography and memoirs, A-Z
631 French rule, 1794-1813
641 1813-1830
645 1830-
Revolution of 1830
650 Sources and documents
651 General works
652 General special
656 Leopold I, 1831-1865
657 General special
659 Biography and memoirs of contemporaries, A-Z
665 Treaty of London, 1839
671 Leopold II, 1865-1909
Biography and memoirs of contemporaries, A-Z
675 Collective
676 Individual, A-Z
677 20th century
681 Albert, 1909-1934
682 Period of World War I. Flemish movement
For the war itself, see D501+
683 1920-
685 Biography and memoirs of contemporaries, A-Z
687 Leopold III, 1934-1951
689 Biography and memoirs of contemporaries, A-Z
690 Baudouin I, 1951-
692 Biography and memoirs of contemporaries, A-Z

(DJ) NETHERLANDS

1 Periodicals
3 Sources and documents
History
103 Biography (Collective)
104 Rulers, kings
105 Public men
106 Houses, noble families, A-Z
.5 Study and teaching
General works
107 To 1800. Chronicles

109 1800-
General special
124 Military history
Individual campaigns and engagements are classed with the special period
Naval history
Individual campaigns and engagements are classed with special period
130 Sources and documents
131 Biography (Collective)
Individual biography is classed with periods, DJ135+
132 General works
133 General special
135 Early to 1594
136 1594-1700
137 18th century
138 19th-20th centuries
Political and diplomatic history
140 Sources and documents
142 General works
Class political and diplomatic history of broad time periods in DJ145+. Class works on specific time periods in DJ170, DJ172, etc. For works on relations with special countries regardless of time period, see DJ149
145 Earliest to 1555
146 1555-1795
147 1795-
149 Relations with individual countries, A-Z
Reigning houses
150 House of Orange
By period
Early and medieval to 1555
General works
151 To 1800. Chronicles
152 1801-
1555-1795. United Provinces
154 Sources and documents
Cf. DH185, Wars of Independence
General works
155 To 1800
156 1801-
158 General special
170 1609-1621
1621-1652
General works
171 To 1800
172 1801-
173 Biography and memoirs, 1621-1702, A-Z
1652-1702
180 Sources and documents
General works
Including Anglo-Dutch wars, 1652-1667
181 To 1800
182 1801-
Willem III, 1672-1702
General works on reign
For biography, see DA462.A2
186 To 1800

187 1801-
Period of War with France, 1672-1678
For the war itself, see D277+
General works
190 To 1800
191 1801-
193 Anglo-Dutch War, 1672-1674
Stadtholders, 1702-1747
General works
196 To 1800
197 1801-
Biography and memoirs
199 Collective
.2 Individual, A-Z
Willem IV and Willem V, 1747-1795
General works
201 To 1800
202 1801-
204 Biography and memoirs of contemporaries, 1702-1795, A-Z
Anglo-Dutch War, 1780-1795
General works
205 To 1800
206 1801-
War with France, 1793-1795
General works
208 To 1800
209 1801-
210 Period of French Revolution and Napoleonic Empire, 1792-1815
211 Batavian Republic, 1795-1806
19th-20th centuries
215 Sources and documents
216 General works
219 Biography and memoirs, A-Z
226 Kingdom of Holland, 1806-1810
228 Union with France, 1810-1813
236 Kingdom of the Netherlands, 1813-1830
241 Willem I, 1815-1840
251 Willem II, 1840-1849
261 Willem III, 1849-1890
Biography and memoirs of contemporaries, A-Z
281 Wilhelmina, 1890-1948
283 Biography and memoirs of contemporaries
.A2 Collective
.A3-Z Individual, A-Z
285 Period of World War I
For the war itself, see D501+
286 1918-1939
287 1939-1948
288 Juliana, 1948-1980
289 Biography and memoirs of contemporaries, A-Z
290 Beatrix, 1980-
Biography and memoirs of contemporaries
291 Collective
292 Individual, A-Z

(DJK) EASTERN EUROPE (GENERAL)

1 Periodicals. Societies

3 Sources and documents
26 Ethnography
27 Slavic peoples (General)
Class here historical studies only; for ethnological studies, see GN549.S6, which is not included in this guide
Cf. D147, Slavic migrations
DR25, Slavs in the Balkan Peninsula
History
31 Biography (Collective)
35 Study and teaching. Slavic studies
General works
37 Through 1800
38 1801-
General special
Political history
41 Sources and documents
42 General works
By period, see the specific period
Foreign and general relations
43 Sources and documents
44 General works
By period, see the specific period
45 Relations with individual countries, A-Z
By period
46 Early and medieval to 1500
47 1500-1815
48 1815-1918
49 1918-1945
50 1945-

Local history of Eastern Europe
For regions located in specific countries, see the country

Black Sea region
66 History
Carpathian Mountain region
76 History
Danube River Valley
For the Danube River Valley of individual countries, see the country
.8 History
77 Pannonia

(DK) SOVIET UNION. POLAND

SOVIET UNION

1 Periodicals. Societies
3 Sources and documents
History
37 Biography (Collective)
.4 Statesmen
.6 Rulers, czars
.7 Houses, noble families
.8 Special, A-Z
38.8 Study and teaching
General works
39 To 1800. Chronicles
40 1801-
General special
Military history

For individual campaigns and engagements, see the special period
50 Periodicals. Societies
.5 Biography (Collective)
.8 Officers
51 General works
.7 General special
52 Early to 1613
.5 1613-1800
53 1801-1917
54 1917-
Naval history
For individual campaigns and engagements, see the period
55 Periodicals. Societies
.5 Biography (Collective)
.8 Officers
56 General works
.7 General special
57 Early to 1689
.5 1689-1800
58 1801-1917
59 1917-
Political history
Class here general works and works on broad periods of political history. For works on a specific period, see the period
60 Sources and documents
61 General works
62 Early to 1462
.3 1462-1613
.6 1613-1762
.9 1762-1917
1917- , see DK266+
Foreign and general relations
Class works on the diplomatic history of a period with the period. For works on relations with a specific country regardless of period, see DK67.5+
65 Sources and documents
66 General works
Europe
General works, see D34, D1065
Balkan Peninsula, see DR38.3
67.5 Individual countries, A-Z
Asia, see DS33.4.S65
68.7 Individual countries, A-Z
United States, see D183.8.S65
69.3 Other American countries, A-Z
Africa
General works, see DT38.9.S65
.4 Individual countries, A-Z
By period
Early to 1613
Rus' (Eastern slavs until their trifurcation into Byelorussians, Russians, and Ukrainians)
General works
70.A3-Z Through 1800. Chronicles
71 1801-
72 Early to 862
73 862-1054

80 1054-1237
90 1237-1462. Tartar (Mongol) Yoke
Muscovy
1462-1605
.8 Sources and documents
100 General works
101 Ivan III, 1462-1505
102 Basil III, 1505-1533
106 Ivan IV, The Terrible, 1533-1584
.5 General special
Biography and memoirs
.8 Collective
107 Individual, A-Z
108 Theodore I, 1584-1598
109 Boris Godunov, 1598-1605
111 1605-1613. Time of troubles
House of Romanov, 1613-1917
.8 Sources and documents
113 General works
1613-1689. 17th century
.2 Sources and documents
114 General works
.5 Biography and memoirs, A-Z
115 Michael, 1613-1645
Alexis, 1645-1676
116 Sources and documents
117 Biography and memoirs, A-Z
118 General works on life and reign
.5 Rebellion of Stenka Razin, 1667-1671
121 War with Poland
.5 War with Sweden
122 War with Turkey
.5 War with Persia
124 Theodore III, 1676-1682
125 Sophia, 1682-1689
126 Ivan V, 1682-1696
1689-1801. 18th century
127.A2 Sources and documents
.A3-Z General works
Biography and memoirs
.4 Collective
.5 Individual, A-Z
Peter I the Great, 1689-1725
129 Sources and documents
130 Biography and memoirs of contemporaries, A-Z
131 General works on life and reign
133 General special. Reforms
e.g. Revolt of the Streltsy, 1698
134 Military history
135 Wars with Turkey
136 Wars with Sweden
137 Wars with Persia
145 Foreign and general relations
150 1725-1762
.8 Biography and memoirs, A-Z
Catherine II, 1762-1796
168 Sources and documents
169 Biography and memoirs of contemporaries, A-Z

170 General works on life and reign
171 Reign only
.7 Military history
173 Foreign relations
180 Political history
183 Insurrection of Pugachev, 1773-1775
Paul I, 1796-1801
185 Sources and documents
186 General works on life and reign
187 War with France
19th century
188 Sources and documents
Biography and memoirs
.3 Collective
.6 Individual, A-Z
189 General works
Alexander I, 1801-1825
190 Sources and documents
Biography and memoirs of contemporaries, A-Z
.3 Collective
.6 Individual, A-Z
191 General works on life and reign
197 Foreign and general relations
201 Administrative reforms
Nicholas I, 1825-1855
209 Sources and documents
Biography and memoirs of contemporaries
.3 Collective
.6 Individual, A-Z
210 General works on life and reign
211 Reign only
212 Insurrection of December 1825 (Decembrists)
213.5 Russo-Khivan Expedition, 1839
214 Crimean War, 1853-1856
215 Diplomatic history
Including the Congress of Paris, 1856; Treaty of Paris, etc.
Special events, battles
.1 Alma, September 20, 1854
.3 Balaklava, October 25, 1854
.5 Inkerman, November 5, 1854
.7 Sevastopol, 1854-1855
.8 Other, A-Z
.9 The war in Asia
Russo-Turkish War, see DR564
Alexander II, 1855-1881
219 Sources and documents
Biography and memoirs of contemporaries, A-Z
.3 Collective
.6 Individual, A-Z
220 General works on life and reign
221 Reign
Including reforms and nihilism
223 Foreign and general relations
Alexander III, 1881-1894
234 Sources and documents
Biography and memoirs of contemporaries

235 Collective
236 Individual, A-Z
240 General works on life and reign
241 Reign only
246 20th century
Nicholas II, 1894-1917
251 Sources and documents
Biography and memoirs
253 Collective
254 Individual, A-Z
e.g. Lenin, Vladimir
Collected works. By date (.L3A2)
Translations. By language and date (.L3A121-129)
Selected works. By date (.L3A25)
Translations of selections. By language and date (.L3A252-259)
Correspondence (General) (.L4A3-39)
Correspondence (Individual) (.L4A4-49)
General biographical works (.L4A5-Z)
258 General works on life and reign
260 Reign only
262 State of the empire, 1904-1917
Including causes of the Revolutions of 1905 and 1917-1921
Russo-Japanese War, 1904-1905, see DS516+
Revolution of 1905
263.A1A-Z Periodicals. Societies
.A2 Sources and documents
Causes, origins, see DK262
.A3-Z General works
.15 Historiography
264 Special events
Personal narratives
.12 Collective
.13 Individual, A-Z
.2 Local revolutionary history. By place, A-Z
For the Revolution of 1905 in Estonia, see DK503.73; in Latvia, see DK504.73; in Lithuania, see DK505.73
.3 Prisoners and prisons. Exiles
.5 Other topics, A-Z
.I6 Influence
.I67 Intellectuals
.P8 Public opinion
.R45 Religious aspects
.7 Celebrations. Monuments
.8 Period of World War I
For the war itself, see D501+
Revolution, 1917-1921
265.A1-19 Periodicals. Societies
Sources and documents
.A2-4 Serials
.A5-55 Nonserials
.A553 Historiography
.A556 Study and teaching

	Biography, see DK254, DK268
	Causes, origins, see DK262
.A56-Z	General works
.15	Pictorial works
	Including satire and caricature
.19	February Revolution, 1917
.2	Military operations
	Individual campaigns, battles, see DK265.8
.3	Naval operations
.35	Individual engagements, ships, etc., A-Z
.4	Allied intervention, 1918-1920
.42	By region or country, A-Z
.5	Prisoners and prisons
	Personal narratives
.69	Collective
.7	Individual, A-Z
.8	Local revolutionary history. By place, A-Z
	For Ukrainian independence movement, see DK508.832
.9	Other topics, A-Z
	.A5 Anarchism
	.A6 Army (Political activity)
	.A7 Art and the revolution
	.C4 Children
	.C5 Civilian relief
	.D45 Democracy and the revolution
	.E2 Economic aspects
	.F5 Foreign participation
	.F52 By country, A-Z
	.I5 Influence
	.P6 Press
	.P74 Protest movements
	.P8 Public opinion
	.R3 Refugees
	.R4 Religious aspects
	.S4 Secret service. Spies
	.S6 Soviets (Councils)
	.T48 Theater and the revolution
	.W57 Women
.95	Celebrations. Monuments
266	Soviet regime, 1918-
.A2	Periodicals. Societies
.A3	Sources and documents
.A33	Historiography
.A4-Z	General works
.3	General special
	e.g. Espionage and sabotage
.45	Foreign and general relations
.5	1918-1924. Lenin
	For the biography of Lenin, see DK254.L3+
267	1925-1953. Stalin
.3	Pamphlets. By date
268	Biography and memoirs, A-Z
	e.g. .S8 Stalin, Joseph
269	Emigres
.5	Public opinion formation. Internal propaganda
270	Soviet propaganda in foreign countries
272	In individual countries, A-Z
.5	Anti-Soviet propaganda

.7 In individual countries, A-Z
273 Period of World War II
For the war itself, see D731+
1953-1982
274.A2A-Z Periodicals. Societies
.A3-Z General works
275 Biography and memoirs, A-Z
e.g. .K5 Khrushchev, Nikita
278 Soviet propaganda in foreign countries
279 In individual countries, A-Z
280 Anti-Soviet propaganda
281 In individual countries, A-Z
282 Foreign and general relations
1982-
285 Periodicals. Societies
.5 Sources and documents
286 General works
288 Political history
289 Foreign and general relations
Biography and memoirs
290 Collective
.3 Individual, A-Z
e.g. .G67 Gorbachev, Mikhail Sergeevich, 1931-

Local History of the Soviet Union

Baltic States
Including Estonia, Latvia, and Lithuania treated collectively
502.3 Periodicals. Societies
.7 History
Estonia
503 Periodicals. Societies
.15 Sources and documents
Ethnography
.34 National characteristics
History
.38 Biography (Collective)
.44 Statesmen
.49 Study and teaching
General works
.52 Through 1800
.53 1801-1980
.54 1981-
General special
Military history
For individual campaigns and engagements, see the special period
.6 Sources and documents
.62 General works
Naval history
For individual campaigns and engagements, see the special period
.63 Sources and documents
.64 General works
Political history
.65 Sources and documents
.66 General works
Foreign and general relations
For works on relations with a specific country regardless of period, see DK503.69

.67 Sources and documents
.68 General works
.69 Relations with individual countries, A-Z
By period
.7 Early to 1200
.71 1200-1600
.72 1600-1800
.73 1800-1918
.74 1918-1940
Biography and memoirs
.745 Collective
.746 Individual, A-Z
.75 1940-
Biography and memoirs
.76 Collective
.77 Individual, A-Z
Latvia
504 Periodicals. Societies
.15 Sources and documents
Ethnography
.34 National characteristics
History
.38 Biography (Collective)
.44 Statesmen
.49 Study and teaching
General works
.52 Through 1800
.53 1801-1980
.54 1981-
General special
Military history
For individual campaigns and engagements, see the special period
.6 Sources and documents
.62 General works
Naval history
For individual campaigns and engagements, see the special period
.63 Sources and documents
.64 General works
Political history
For specific periods, see the period
.65 Sources and documents
.66 General works
Foreign and general relations
For works on relations with a specific country regardless of period, see DK504.69
.67 Sources and documents
.68 General works
.69 Relations with individual countries, A-Z
By period
.7 Early to 1200
.71 1200-1600
.72 1600-1800
.73 1800-1918
.74 1918-1940
Biography and memoirs
.75 Collective

.76 Individual, A-Z
.77 1940-
Biography and memoirs
.78 Collective
.79 Individual, A-Z
Lithuania
505 Periodicals. Societies
.15 Sources and documents
Ethnography
.34 National characteristics
History
.38 Biography (Collective)
.44 Statesmen
.49 Study and teaching
General works
.52 Through 1800
.53 1801-1980
.54 1981-
General special
Military history
For individual campaigns and engagements, see the special period
.6 Sources and documents
.62 General works
Naval history
For individual campaigns and engagements, see the special period
.63 Sources and documents
.64 General works
Political history
For individual campaigns and engagements, see the special period
.65 Sources and documents
.66 General works
Foreign and general relations
For works on relations with a specific country regardless of period, see DK505.69
.67 Sources and documents
.68 General works
.69 Relations with individual countries, A-Z
By period
.7 Early to 1350
.71 1350-1600
.72 1600-1800
.73 1800-1918
.74 1918-1940
Biography and memoirs
.75 Collective
.76 Individual, A-Z
.77 1940-
Biography and memoirs
.78 Collective
.79 Individual, A-Z

Byelorussian S.S.R. White Russia
507.A2A-Z Periodicals. Societies
.15 Sources and documents
Ethnography
.34 National characteristics

History
.38 Biography (Collective)
.44 Statesmen
.49 Study and teaching
General works
.52 Through 1800
.53 1801-1980
.54 1981-
General special
Military history
For individual campaigns and engagements, see the special period
.6 Sources and documents
.62 General works
Political history
For specific periods, see the period
.65 Sources and documents
.66 General works
Foreign and general relations
For works on relations with a specific country regardless of time period, see DK504.69
.67 Sources and documents
.68 General works
.69 Relations with individual countries, A-Z
By period
.7 Early to 1300
.71 1300-1600
.72 1600-1900
.73 1900-1945
Biography and memoirs
.74 Collective
.75 Individual, A-Z
.76 1945-
Biography and memoirs
.77 Collective
.78 Individual, A-Z
Ukraine
508.A2A-Z Periodicals
.A3 Sources and documents
Ethnography
.423 National characteristics
History
.45 Biography (Collective)
.458 Statesmen
.48 Study and teaching
General works
.49 Through 1800
.5 1801-1985
.51 1986-
General special
.54 Military history
For specific periods, see the period
.554 Political history
For specific periods, see the period
.56 Foreign and general relations
Class works on foreign relations of a period with the period. Class works on relations with an individual country regardless of period in DK508.57

.57 Relations with individual countries, A-Z
By period
For works on early history of Rus', see DK70+
.66 Early to 1340
.67 1340-1569
.68 1569-1648. Period of Polish rule
1648-1775
.73 Sources and documents
.74 General works
Biography and memoirs
.75 Collective
.752 Individual, A-Z
.753 1647-1657
Biography and memoirs
.754 Collective
.755 Individual, A-Z
.756 1657-1709
Biography and memoirs
.757 Collective
.758 Individual, A-Z
.759 1709-1775
Including Uprising of 1768
Biography and memoirs
.76 Collective
.761 Individual, A-Z
1775-1917
.77 Sources and documents
.772 General works
Biography and memoirs
.78 Collective
.782 Individual, A-Z
1917-1945
.79 Sources and documents
.812 General works
Biography and memoirs
.82 Collective
.83 Individual, A-Z
.832 1917-1921
Class here works limited to the Ukrainian independence movement. For works on the Revolution in Ukraine, see DK265.8.U4
.833 1921-1944
Biography and memoirs
.834 Collective
.835 Individual, A-Z
.84 1945-
Biography and memoirs
.842 Collective
.843 Individual, A-Z
Moldavian S.S.R. Bessarabia
509.1 Periodicals. Societies
.15 Sources and documents
Ethnography
.34 National characteristics
History
.38 Biography (Collective)
.44 Statesmen
.5 Study and teaching

General works
.52 Through 1800
.53 1801-1980
.54 1981-
General special
Military history
For individual campaigns and engagements, see the special period
.6 Sources and documents
.62 General works
Political history
For specific periods, see the period
.65 Sources and documents
.66 General works
By period
Early to 1812, see DR238+
.7 1812-1918
.71 1918-1940
For works on the Revolution in Moldavia, see DK265.8.M48
Biography and memoirs
.72 Collective
.73 Individual, A-Z
.74 1940-
Biography and memoirs
.75 Collective
.76 Individual, A-Z
Russian S.F.S.R.
Class here only works that discuss the Russian S.F.S.R. since its formation in 1917. For works that discuss the same territory for the pre-1917 period, or the pre-1917 and post-1917 periods combined, see DK1+.
510 Periodicals. Societies
.15 Sources and documents
Ethnography
.34 National characteristics
History
.38 Biography (Collective)
.42 Statesmen
.49 Study and teaching
.52 General works
General special
Military history, see DK50+
.6 Political history
For specific periods, see the period
Foreign and general relations, see DK65+
By period
Early to 1917, see DK70+
.7 1917-1945
Biography and memoirs
.71 Collective
.72 Individual, A-Z
.73 1945-
Biography and memoirs
.74 Collective
.75 Individual, A-Z
Georgian S.S.R.
670 Periodicals. Societies
671.5 Sources and documents

Ethnography
673.4 National characteristics
History
.8 Biography (Collective)
674.4 Statesmen
.9 Study and teaching
General works
675.2 Through 1800
.3 1801-1980
.4 1981-
General special
Military history
For individual campaigns and engagements, see the special period
676 Sources and documents
.2 General works
Political history
For specific periods, see the period
.5 Sources and documents
.6 General works
Foreign and general relations
Class works on the foreign relations of a specific period with the period. For works on relations with a specific country regardless of period, see DK676.9+
.7 Sources and documents
.8 General works
.9 Relations with individual countries, A-Z
By period
677.1 Early to 330
.2 330-1220
.3 1220-1801
.4 1801-1921
For works on the Revolution in Georgia, see DK265.8.G4
Biography and memoirs
.5 Collective
.6 Individual, A-Z
.7 1921-
Biography and memoirs
.8 Collective
.9 Individual, A-Z
Armenian S.S.R.
For works on the territory of Armenian S.S.R. before 1920, and/or the historic kingdom and region of Armenia as a whole, see DS161+
680 Periodicals. Societies
681.5 Sources and documents
Ethnography
.4 National characteristics
History
.8 Biography (Collective)
684 Statesmen
.9 Study and teaching
General works
.3 1920-1980
.4 1981-
By period
Early to 1920, see DS181+
1920-
686.9 Sources and documents

687 General works
Biography and memoirs
.2 Collective
.3 Individual, A-Z
Azerbaijan S.S.R.
690 Periodicals
.5 Sources and documents
Ethnography
693.4 National characteristics
History
.8 Biography (Collective)
694.4 Statesmen
.9 Study and teaching
General works
695.2 Through 1800
.3 1801-1980
.4 1981-
General special
Military history
For individual campaigns and engagements, see the special period
696 Sources and documents
.2 General works
Political history
For specific periods, see the period
.5 Sources and documents
.6 General works
Foreign and general relations
Class works on relations of a specific period with the period. For works on relations with a specific country regardless of period, see DK696.9
.7 Sources and documents
.8 General works
.9 Relations with individual countries, A-Z
By period
697.1 Early to 1813
.2 1813-1917
.3 1917-
For works on the Revolution in Azerbaijan, see DK265.8.A9
Biography and memoirs
.4 Collective
.5 Individual, A-Z
Siberia
761 History
By period
764 Early through 1800
766 19th-20th centuries
Biography and memoirs
768.7 Collective
769 Individual, A-Z
770 Russian exiles
Soviet Central Asia. West Turkestan
845 Periodicals. Societies
847 Sources and documents
History
856 General works
By period
858 Early through 1919

859 1920-
860 Biography (Collective)
Kazakh S.S.R. Kazakhstan
901 Periodicals. Societies
902 Sources and documents
907 Ethnography. National characteristics
908.6 History
By period
.82 Through 500
.83 500-1400
.84 1400-1700
.85 1700-1850
.86 1850-1917
.861 1917-1945
Biography and memoirs
.862 Collective
.863 Individual, A-Z
.864 1945-
Biography and memoirs
.865 Collective
.866 Individual, A-Z
Kirghiz S.S.R.
911 Periodicals. Societies
912 Sources and documents
917 Ethnography. National characteristics
History
918.6 General works
By period
.82 Through 500
.83 500-1700
.84 1700-1917
.85 1917-1945
Biography and memoirs
.86 Collective
.87 Individual, A-Z
.871 1945-
Biography and memoirs
.872 Collective
.873 Individual, A-Z
Tajik S.S.R. Tadzhikistan
921 Periodicals. Societies
922 Sources and documents
927 Ethnography. National characteristics
History
928.13 Biography (Collective)
.144 Rulers, statesmen
.6 General works
By period
.82 To 500
.83 500-1850
.84 1850-1917
.85 1917-1945
Biography and memoirs
.852 Collective
.853 Individual, A-Z
.86 1945-
Biography and memoirs
.862 Collective

.863 Individual, A-Z
Turkmen S.S.R.
931 Periodicals. Societies
932 Sources and documents
937 Ethnography. National characteristics
History
938.13 Biography (Collective)
.144 Rulers, statesmen
.6 General works
By period
.82 To 500
.83 500-1800
.84 1800-1917
.85 1917-1945
Biography and memoirs
.852 Collective
.853 Individual, A-Z
.86 1945-
Biography and memoirs
.862 Collective
.863 Individual, A-Z
Uzbek S.S.R. Uzbekistan
941 Periodicals. Societies
942 Sources and documents
947 Ethnography. National characteristics
History
948.13 Biography (Collective)
.144 Rulers, statesmen
.55 Study and teaching
General works
.6 Through 1980
.62 1981-
General special
Military history
For individual campaigns and engagements, see the specific period
.7 Sources and documents
.72 General works
Political history
For specific periods, see the period
.73 Sources and documents
.75 General works
Foreign and general relations
.76 Sources and documents
.77 General works
.79 Relations with individual countries, A-Z
By period
.82 To 500
.83 500-1800
.84 1800-1917
.85 1917-1945
Biography and memoirs
.852 Collective
.853 Individual, A-Z
.86 1945-
Biography and memoirs
.862 Collective
.863 Individual, A-Z

POLAND

4010 Periodicals. Societies
4020 Sources and documents
Ethnography
4121 National characteristics. Patriotism. Messianism
History
4130 Biography (Collective)
4131 Rulers, kings
4137 Houses, noble families
4138 Individual, A-Z
.3 Study and teaching
General works
Through 1800, see DK4187, DK4190
4140 1801-
General special
4170 Military history
Class works on broad periods of military history in DK4172+.
Class works on individual battles, etc., with the specific period, e.g. DK4261
4171 General special
4172 Early to 1795
4173 1795-1918
4174 1918-
4177 Naval history
4178 General special
By period, see the specific period
Political history
.5 Sources and documents
4179 General works
.2 General special
By period, see the specific period
Foreign and general relations
.5 Sources and documents
4180 General works
4182 Polish question
4185 Relations with individual countries, A-Z
By period, see the specific period
4185 Relations with individual countries, A-Z
By period
To 1795
4186 Sources and documents
General works
4187 Through 1800
4188 1801-
.2 General special
To 1572
4189 Sources and documents
General works
4190 Through 1800
4200 1801-
4205 General special
4210 To 960
4212 960-1386
4213 960-1138
4227 1138-1305
.6 1305-1386
1386-1572
4249.7 Sources and documents

4250 General works
4252 General special
4260 Vladislaus II Jagiello, 1386-1434
4261 War with Teutonic Knights, 1409-1411
4262 Treaty of Horodlo, 1413
Biography and memoirs
4263 Collective
4264 Individual, A-Z
4265 Vladislaus III Warnenczyk, 1434-1444
4268 Interregnum, 1444-1447
4270 Casimir IV, 1447-1492
4271 Thirteen Years' War, 1454-1466
4272 Peace of Torun, 1466
Biography and memoirs
4273 Collective
4274 Individual, A-Z
4275 John I Albert, 1492-1501
4276 16th century
4277 Alexander, 1501-1506
4280 Sigismund I the Old, 1506-1548
4281 Battle of Obertin, 1531
Biography and memoirs
4283 Collective
4284 Individual, A-Z
4285 Sigismund II Augustus, 1548-1572
4286 General special
Livonian War, see DK4297
4287 Union of Lublin, 1569
Biography and memoirs
4288 Collective
4289 Individual, A-Z
1572-1763
.5 Sources and documents
4290 General works
4291 General special
4292 Interregnum, 1572-1573
4293 Henry III Valois, 1573-1574
4295 Stefan Batory, 1575-1586
4297 Livonian War, 1557-1582
Biography and memoirs
4298 Collective
4299 Individual, A-Z
4300 Sigismund III, 1587-1632
4301 General special
.4 Battle of Kirchholm, 1605
.5 Rebellion of Zebrzydowski, 1606-1609
Swedish-Polish War, 1617-1629, see DL712
.6 Battle of Cecora, 1620
.7 Battle of Chocim (Hotin), 1621
Biography and memoirs
.9 Collective
4302 Individual, A-Z
.5 17th century
4303 Wladyslaw IV Zygmunt, 1632-1648
.4 Russo-Polish War, 1632-1634
4305 John II Casimir, 1648-1668
4306 General special
.3 Uprising of Kostka Napierski, 1651

Swedish-Polish War, 1655-1660, see DL725
.35 Polish-Brandenburg War, 1656-1657
.4 Rebellion of Lubomirski, 1665-1666
Biography and memoirs
4307 Collective
.5 Individual, A-Z
4308 Michael Wisniowiecki, 1669-1673
4309.5 Battle of Chocim (Hotin), 1673
4310 John III Sobieski, 1674-1696
4311 Turco-Polish Wars, 1683-1699
Siege of Vienna, 1683, see DR536
.5 Battle of Podgaytsy, 1698
Biography and memoirs
.9 Collective
4312 Individual, A-Z
4314 Interregnum, 1696-1697
.5 18th century (General)
4315 Augustus II (Friedrich August I, Elector of Saxony), 1697-1733
For biography, see DD
4317 Political and diplomatic history
Northern War, 1700-1721, see DL733+
Biography and memoirs
4318 Collective
4319 Individual, A-Z
4320 Stanislaus I Leszczynski, 1704-1709
4325 Augustus III (Friedrich August II, Elector of Saxony), 1733-1763
For biography, see DD
4326 Political and diplomatic history
.5 War of Polish Succession, 1733-1738
4327 Treaty of Vienna, 1738
Biography and memoirs
.5 Collective
4328 Individual, A-Z
1763-1795. Partition period
.9 Sources and documents
4329 General works
.5 General special
4330 Stanislaus II Augustus, 1764-1795
4331 Barska Konfederacja, 1768-1772
4332 First partition, 1772
4333 Sejm, 1788-1792
4335 Targowicka Konfederacja, 1792-1793
4336 Russo-Polish War, 1792
4337 Second partition, 1793
Revolution of 1794
4339 Sources and documents
4340 General works
4342 General special
4343 Personal narratives
4344 Local revolutionary history. By place, A-Z
Biography and memoirs
4347 Collective
4348 Individual, A-Z
1795-1918. 19th century (General)
.5 Sources and documents

4349 General works
.3 General special
1795-1830
.9 Sources and documents
4350 General works
4351 General special
4353 Period of Napoleonic Wars, 1795-1815
For the wars themselves, see DC220+
Biography and memoirs
4354 Collective
4355 Individual, A-Z
1830-1864
4356 Sources and documents
4357 General works
4358 General special
Revolution of 1830-1832
4359 Periodicals. Societies
.5 Sources and documents
4360 General works
.5 General special
4362 Military operations (General)
.3 Personal narratives
.5 Local revolutionary history.
By place, A-Z
4363 Special topics, A-Z
.E3 Economic aspects
.F6 Foreign public opinion
.P7 Press
.R4 Refugees
.W66 Women
.2 Partisan Campaign, 1833
4364 Revolution of 1846
4365 Revolution of 1848
.5 Local revolutionary history.
By place, A-Z
Revolution of 1863-1864
4366 Periodicals. Societies
4368 Sources and documents
4370 General works
4372.3 General special
4373 Military operations (General)
4374 Personal narratives
4376 Local revolutionary history
By place, A-Z
4378 Special topics, A-Z
.C3 Catholic Church
.C65 Communications
.F6 Foreign participation
.F62 By country, A-Z
.F65 Foreign public opinion
.I5 Influence
.P7 Press
.R4 Refugees
.S4 Secret service. Spies
.S6 Social aspects
.T7 Transportation
.W6 Women
Biography and memoirs, 1830-1864

4379 Collective
.5 Individual, A-Z
1864-1918
.9 Sources and documents
4380 General works
4381 General special
4382 20th century (General)
Revolution of 1905
4383 Periodicals. Societies
4384 Sources and documents
4385 General works
4386 General special
4387 Personal narratives
4388 Local revolutionary history. By place, A-Z
4389 Special topics, A-Z
.P74 Press
4390 Period of World War I
For the war itself, see D501+
4392 Austrian occupation, 1915-1918
Biography and memoirs
4394 Collective
4395 Individual, A-Z
1918-1945
4397 Sources and documents
4400 General works
4402 Political history
.5 Foreign and general relations
.5 1918-1926
Wars of 1918-1921
Including Russo-Polish War, 1919-1920
4404 Periodicals. Societies
.5 Sources and documents
4405 General works
.7 Diplomatic history
4406 Military operations (General)
.5 Personal narratives
4407 Individual campaigns, battles By place, A-Z
4409 Special topics, A-Z
.P75 Prisoners and prisons
.T4 Territorial questions
.3 Treaty of Riga, 1921
.4 Coup d'état, 1926
.5 1926-1939
4410 1939-1945. Period of World War II
Including German occupation, 1939-1945
For the war itself, see D731+
4415 Russian occupation, 1939-1941
Biography and memoirs, 1918-1945
4419 Collective
4420 Individual, A-Z
1945- . People's Republic
4429 Sources and documents
4430 General works
Biography and memoirs
4434 Collective
4435 Individual, A-Z

4436 Political history

.5 Foreign and general relations

4438 1945-1956

4439 Uprising, 1956

4440 1956-1980

4442 1980-

Local history of Poland

4600 Provinces, counties, historical regions, A-Z

e.g. .G44 Gdansk Pomerania. Pomerelia (Table)

Including Royal Prussia, West Prussia, Polish Pomerania, and Danzig-Westpreussen

.O33 Oder-Neisse Line. Western and Northern Territories (Table)

.P77 East Prussia (Table)

Including the Teutonic Knights and Ducal Prussia

.S42 Silesia (Table)

Table

.x5 History (General)

.x62 Political history. Foreign and general relations

.x63 Relations with individual countries, A-Z

.x65 Early and medieval history to 1526

.x7 1526-1918

.x8 1918-1945

.85 1945-

Gdansk (Danzig)

4670 History (General)

4671 Early to 1793

4672 1793-1919

4673 1919-1945

Including the Free City of Danzig

4674 1945-

(DL) SCANDINAVIA

GENERAL

1 Periodicals. Societies

3 Sources and documents

History

44 Biography (Collective)

.1 Rulers, kings

.3 Houses, noble families, A-Z

.5 Public men

.95 Study and teaching

General special

52 Military history

For special events, see the period

53 Naval history

For special events, see the period

55 Political and diplomatic history

Class general works on the political and diplomatic history of a period with the period. For works on relations with a specific country regardless of period, see DL59

57 Scandinavianism

59 Relations with individual countries, A-Z

By period
61 To 1387
65 Northmen. Vikings
76 1387-1524
78 1524-1814
81 1814-1900
83 1901-1945
85 1914-1918
87 1945-

DENMARK

101 Periodicals. Societies
103 Sources and documents
133 Early and medieval (General)
Ethnography
141.5 National characteristics
History
144 Biography (Collective)
.1 Rulers
.3 Houses, noble families
.32 Individual, A-Z
.5 Public men
General works
147 To 1800. Chronicles
148 1801-
General special
154 Military history
For individual campaigns and engagements, see the special period
Naval history
Class works on broad periods of naval history in DL156.2+.
Class works on engagements, etc., with the specific period
156.A1 Sources and documents
.A2 Biography (Collective)
.A3-Z General works
.1 Pamphlets
.2 Early and medieval
.5 16th-18th centuries
Biography
.52 Collective
.53 Individual, A-Z
.7 19th-20th centuries
Biography
.72 Collective
.73 Individual, A-Z
158 Political history
For specific periods, see the period
159 Foreign and general relations
Class general works on the foreign and general relations of a period with the period. For works on relations with a specific country regardless of period, see DL159.5
.5 Relations with individual countries, A-Z
By period
Early and medieval to 1523
General works
Early, see 147
160 Modern
161 Earliest to 750
162 750-1042
Cf. DA159+, Invasion and rule of England

167 1042-1241
174 1241-1387
177 1387-1523
178 Margrethe, 1375/1387-1412
Cf. DL483, Reign in Norway
179 Union of Kalmar, 1397
Cf. DL485, Norway
DL694, Sweden
180 Erik VII, 1412-1439
181 Christoffer III, 1439-1448
.6 Biography and memoirs of contemporaries, 1387-1448, A-Z
182 Oldenburg dynasty, 1448-1481
183 Christian I, 1448-1481
.5 Hans, 1481-1513
.8 Christian II, 1513-1523
.9 Biography and memoirs of contemporaries, 1448-1523, A-Z
184 Modern, 1523-
185 1523-1670
Biography and memoirs
.7 Collective
.8 Individual, A-Z
186 Frederik I, 1523-1533
.8 Interregnum, 1533-1534
187 Christian III, 1534-1559
188 Frederik II, 1559-1588
.5 Northern Seven Years' War, 1563-1570
(Three Crowns' War)
.8 Biography and memoirs of contemporaries, A-Z
189 Christian IV, 1588-1648
Thirty Years' War, see D263
190 War with Sweden, 1643-1645
.3 General special
.5 Biography and memoirs of contemporaries, A-Z
191 Frederik III, 1648-1670
.5 General special
192 Dano-Swedish wars, 1657-1660
.3 Coup d'état, 1660
.8 Biography and memoirs of contemporaries, A-Z
1670-1808
193.A2 Sources and documents
.A3-Z Biography and memoirs of contemporaries, A-Z
194 General works
195 Christian V, 1670-1699
.3 General special
.8 Biography and memoirs of contemporaries, A-Z
196 Frederik IV, 1699-1730
.3 Denmark during Northern War, 1700-1721
.8 Biography and memoirs of contemporaries, 1699-1746, A-Z
197 Christian VI, 1730-1746
198 Frederik V, 1746-1766
.3 General special
.8 Biography and memoirs of contemporaries, A-Z
199 Christian VII, 1766-1808
.3 General special
.8 Biography and memoirs of contemporaries, A-Z
201 1808-1906
202 General special
204 Biography and memoirs, A-Z

205 Frederik VI, 1808-1839
206 War of 1807-1814
207 Other special
208 Biography and memoirs of contemporaries, A-Z
Frederik VII, 1848-1863
213 Sources and documents
214 General works on life and reign
215 General special
216 Pamphlets
217 Schleswig-Holstein War, 1848-1850
218 General special
219 Special events, battles, A-Z
223 Treaty of Berlin, 1850
228 Biography and memoirs of contemporaries, A-Z
229 Christian IX, 1863-1906
1863-1866
230 Sources and documents
231 General works
232 General special
.5 Pamphlets
234 Period of constitutional amendments, 1863
236 Schleswig-Holstein War, 1864
239 Political and diplomatic history
For general works on the Schleswig-Holstein question, see DD801.S6335+
Personal narratives
.5 Collective
.6 Individual, A-Z
241 The new constitution, 1866
246 1866-1873
248 1873-1906
249 Biography and memoirs of contemporaries, A-Z
250 20th century
251 General special
252 Biography and memoirs of contemporaries, A-Z
253 Frederik VIII, 1906-1912
254 Biography and memoirs of contemporaries, A-Z
255 Christian X, 1912-1947
256 Period of World War I
.5 1919-1947
257 Biography and memoirs of contemporaries, A-Z
258 Frederik IX, 1947-1972
260 Biography and memoirs of contemporaries, A-Z
261 Margrethe II, 1972-
Biography and memoirs of contemporaries, A-Z
263 Collective
.2 Royal family
.3 Other, A-Z

NORWAY

401 Periodicals. Societies
403 Sources and documents
441 Ethnography. National characteristics
History
444 Biography (Collective)
.1 Rulers, kings
.3 Houses, noble families
.5 Public men
General works

446 To 1800. Chronicles
448 1801-
General special
454 Military history
For specific campaigns and engagements, see the period
456 Naval history
For specific campaigns and engagements, see the period
458 Political and diplomatic history
Foreign and general relations
Class works on the political and diplomatic history of a specific period with the period. Class works on relations with a specific country regardless of period in DL459
459 Relations with individual countries, A-Z
By period
460 Early and medieval to 1387
461 Early to 872
462 872-1035
469 1035-1319
478 1319-1387
480 1387-1814
482 General special
483 Margrethe, 1387-1412
485 Union of Kalmar, 1397
495 Biography and memoirs
.A2 Collective
.A3-Z Individual
Napoleonic period
497 Sources and documents
498 General works
499 War of 1807-1814
1814. Union with Sweden
500 Sources and documents
501 General works
502 Biography and memoirs, A-Z
1814-1905. 19th century
503 Sources and documents
504 Biography and memoirs
.A2 Collective
.A3-Z Individual
506 General works
509 1814-1818. Karl XIII
Cf. DL792+, Life; reign as king of Sweden
511 1818-1844. Karl XIV Johan
Cf. DL816+, Life; reign as king of Sweden
513 Biography and memoirs of contemporaries, A-Z
515 1844-1859. Oskar I
Cf. DL836, Life; reign as king of Sweden
517 1859-1872. Karl XV
518 1872-1905. Oskar II
519 General special
521 Struggle for foreign representation and consuls, 1884
525 Dissolution of the Swedish-Norwegian union, 1905
526 Biography and memoirs of contemporaries, A-Z
527 20th century
528 General special
529 Biography and memoirs
.A1 Collective
.A2-Z Individual

530 Haakon VII, 1905-1957
531 Period of World War I
532 Period of World War II
533 1945-1957
534 Olav V, 1957-
535 Biography and memoirs of contemporaries, A-Z
.A1 Collective
.A6-Z Other

SWEDEN

601 Periodicals. Societies
603 Sources and documents
639 Ethnography. National characteristics
History
644 Biography (Collective)
.1 Rulers, kings
.3 Houses, noble families, A-Z
.5 Public men
645.9 Study and teaching
General works
646 To 1800. Chronicles
648 1801-
General special
654 Military history
For individual campaigns and engagements, see the specific period
656 Naval history
For individual campaigns and engagements, see the specific period
Political and diplomatic history. Foreign and general relations
Class works on broad periods of political and diplomatic history in DL658.2+. Class works on narrow periods of political and diplomatic history with the specific period. Class works on relations with individual countries regardless of period in DL659
658.A2 Sources and documents
.A3-Z General works
.2 Early to 1523
1523- , see DL658.A3-Z
.4 1523-1654
.5 1654-1720
.6 1720-1818
.8 1818-
659 Relations with individual countries, A-Z
By period
660 Early and medieval to 1523
661 Earliest to 750
662 750-1060
667 1060-1134
672 1134-1234
681 1234-1523
685 Valdemar, 1250-1274
687 Magnus I Ladulas, 1275-1290
688 Birger, 1290-1318
689 Magnus II Eriksson, 1319-1363
691 Albrecht von Mecklenburg, 1363-1388
692 1389-1397
694 Union of Kalmar, 1397
695 Biography and memoirs of contemporaries, A-Z
1397-1523
696 Sources and documents

697 General works
698 General special
699 1513-1523
700 Kristian II, 1520-1521
.9 Biography and memoirs of contemporaries, 1397-1523, A-Z
Modern , 1523-
701 Vasa dynasty, 1523-1654
702 Biography and memoirs, A-Z
703 Gustaf I Vasa, 1523-1560
.8 Erik XIV, 1560-1568
704 Johan III, 1568-1592
.2 General special
.5 Sigismund, 1592-1599
.6 17th century
.7 General special
.8 Karl IX, 1600/1604-1611
Gustaf II Adolf, 1611-1632
705.A2 Sources and documents
Biography and memoirs of contemporaries
.A3 Collective
.A4-Z Individual, A-Z
706 General works on life and reign
708 Political and diplomatic history
Military history
General works, see DL706
710 War with Denmark. Kalmar War, 1611-1613
711 War with Russia
712 War with Poland
Special events, battles
.5 Oliwa, Battle of, 1627
713 Period of the Thirty Years' War
For the war itself, see D251+
Kristina, 1632-1654
717 Sources and documents
Biography and memoirs of contemporaries
.5 Collective
718 Individual, A-Z
719 General works on life and reign
.2 Political and diplomatic history
.5 Peace with Denmark, 1645
721 Zweibrucken dynasty, 1654-1718
725 Karl X Gustaf, 1654-1660
.5 General special
.6 Swedish-Polish War, 1655-1660
.62 Special events, battles, A-Z
.O44 Oliwa, Peace of, 1660
.7 Russo-Swedish War, 1656-1658
Dano-Swedish War, 1657-1660, see DL192
727 Karl XI, 1660-1697
728 General special
729 Biography and memoirs of contemporaries, A-Z
Karl XII, 1697-1718
730 Sources and documents
732 General works on life and reign
.7 Biography and memoirs of contemporaries, A-Z
733 Northern War, 1700-1721
735 General special

736 Invasion of Denmark (Holstein)
737 Invasion of Poland
738 Invasion of Russia
739 Invasion of Turkey
740 Invasions of Norway
743 Special events, battles, A-Z
1718-1818
747 Sources and documents
748 General works
749 General special
750 Biography and memoirs, A-Z
753 Ulrika Eleonora, 1718-1720
755 Fredrik I, 1720-1751
757 General special
Biography and memoirs of contemporaries
758 Collective
759 Individual, A-Z
761 Adolf Fredrik, 1751-1771
766 Gustaf III, 1771-1792
Including Russo-Swedish War, 1788-1790
770 Biography and memoirs of contemporaries, A-Z
772 Napoleonic period
776 Gustaf IV Adolf, 1792-1809
782 Political and diplomatic history
785 Special events
790 Revolution and loss of Finland, 1809. Russo-Swedish War, 1808-1809
792 Karl XIII, 1809-1818
796 General special
801 Special events
Treaty of Orebro, 1812, etc.
805 Union with Norway, 1814
1818-1907. 19th century
807 Sources and documents
808 General works
809 General special
Biography and memoirs of contemporaries, A-Z
810 Collective
811 Individual, A-Z
Karl XIV Johan, 1818-1844
816 Sources and documents
Biography and memoirs of contemporaries, A-Z
818 Collective
819 Individual, A-Z
820 General works on life and reign
824 Reign only
828 Political history
829 Diplomatic history
830 Military history
833 Special events, by date
836 Oskar I, 1844-1859
841 Karl, XV, 1859-1872
Oskar II, 1872-1907
851 Sources and documents
852 General works on reign
854 Biography
Dissolution of union with Norway, see DL525
Biography and memoirs of contemporaries

858 Collective
859 Individual, A-Z
860 20th century
861 General special
Biography and memoirs of contemporaries
.A2 Collective
.A3-Z Individual
867 Gustaf V, 1907-1950
.5 Political and diplomatic history
868 Period of World War I
.5 1919-
Biography and memoirs of contemporaries
869 Collective
870 Individual, A-Z
872 Gustaf VI, Adolf, 1950-1973
Biography and memoirs of contemporaries
875 Collective
876 Individual, A-Z
877 Karl XVI Gustaf, 1973-
Biography and memoirs of contemporaries
878 Collective
879 Individual, A-Z

FINLAND

1002 Periodicals. Societies
1005 Sources and documents
Ethnography
1019 National characteristics
History
1024 Biography (Collective)
1027 Study and teaching
General special
Military history
For individual campaigns and engagements, see the special period
1036 Sources and documents
1037 General works
Naval history
For individual campaigns and engagements, see the special period
1040 Sources and documents
1042 General works
Political history
For specific periods, see the period
1043 Sources and documents
1044 General works
Foreign and general relations
Class general works on the diplomatic history of a period with the period. For works on relations with a specific country regardless of period, see DL1048
1045 Sources and documents
1046 General works
1048 Relations with individual countries, A-Z
By period
Early to 1523
1050 Sources and documents
1052 General works
.9 Danish rule, 1397-1523
Modern, 1523-
1055 Sources and documents
1056 General works

1523-1617
1058 Sources and documents
.5 General works
1617-1721
1060 Sources and documents
.5 General works
1721-1809
1063 Sources and documents
.5 General works
Biography
.7 Collective
.8 Individual, A-Z
.9 Russian Conquest, 1808-1809
Russian administration, 1809-1917
1065 Sources and documents
.3 General works
Biography
.4 Collective
.5 Individual, A-Z
.6 1809-1899
.8 1899-1917
20th century
1066 Sources and documents
.5 General works
.7 General special
Biography
1067 Collective
.5 Individual, A-Z
Revolution, 1917-1918. Civil War
1070 Sources and documents
1072 General works
Personal narratives
1073 Collective
.5 Individual, A-Z
1074 Local history. By place, A-Z
1075 Special topics, A-Z
.P75 Propaganda
1078 Treaty of Peace, 1918
1080 Treaty of Peace with Russia, 1920
1918-1939
1082 Sources and documents
1084 General works
1086 General special
Biography
1088 Collective
.5 Individual, A-Z
1939-1945
For World War II in Finland, and the Continuation War, 1941-1945, see D765.3+
1090 Sources and documents
1092 General works
Biography
1093 Collective
.5 Individual, A-Z
Russo-Finnish War, 1939-1940
1095 Periodicals. Societies
1096 Sources and documents
1097 General works

1098 Diplomatic history
1099 Military operations (General)
For individual battles, etc., see DL1103
Personal narratives
1102 Collective
.5 Individual, A-Z
1103 Local history. By place, A-Z
1945-
1122 Periodicals. Societies
1123 Sources and documents
1125 General works
1132 Political history
1133 Foreign and general relations
Biography
1135 Collective
.5 Individual, A-Z

(DP) SPAIN. PORTUGAL

SPAIN

1 Periodicals. Societies
3 Sources and documents
52 Ethnography. National characteristics
History
58 Biography (Collective)
59 Kings, rulers
60 Houses, noble families, A-Z
61 Public men
63.8 Study and teaching
General special
Military history
Individual campaigns and engagements are classed with special period
76.A2 Sources and documents
.A3 Biography and memoirs
.A5 Collective
.A6-Z General works
.5 General special
77 Early to 1492
.5 1492-1700
78 1701-1808
.5 1808- . 19th-20th centuries
Naval history
Individual campaigns and engagements are classed with special period
80 Sources and documents
.5 Biography and memoirs
.7 Officers
81 General works
.2 General special
.3 Early to 1492
.5 1492-1700
.6 1701-1808
.7 1808- . 19th-20th centuries
Political and diplomatic history.
Foreign and general relations
Class general works on the political and diplomatic history of a period with the period. For works on relations with a specific country, see DP86. For works on relations with

individual countries during the Civil War, 1936-1939, see DP258
83 Sources and documents
84 General works
.5 Early to 1516
1516- , see DP84
85.3 1516-1700
.5 1700-1814
.8 1814- . 19th-20th centuries
86 Relations with individual countries, A-Z
By period
91 Earliest to 711
General early and medieval, see DP98+
92 Pre-Roman period
94 Roman period, 218 B.C.-414 A.D.
96 Gothic period, 414-711
Moorish domination and the Reconquest, 711-1516. Arab period
97.4 Sources and documents
General works
98 To 1800. Chronicles
99 1801-
Moors in Spain
100 Sources and documents
General works
101 To 1800
102 1801-
Modern, 1479/1516-
160.9 Periodicals
161 General works
1479-1516. Fernando V and Isabel I
.5 Sources and documents
General works on reign
.8 To 1800
162 1801-
Biography
163 Isabel
.5 Fernando
164 General special
166 Biography and memoirs of contemporaries, A-Z
Habsburgs, 1516-1700
170 Sources and documents
General works
.8 To 1800
171 1801-
172 Karl I (V of Germany), 1516-1556
Cf. DD180.5. General biography of Karl V
174 General special
175 Biography and memoirs of contemporaries, A-Z
Felipe II, 1556-1598
176 Sources and documents
General works on life and reign
177 To 1776
178 1777-
179 General special
181 Biography and memoirs of contemporaries, A-Z
182 Felipe III, 1598-1621
183 General special
.9 Biography and memoirs of contemporaries, A-Z

184	Felipe IV, 1621-1665
185	General special
.9	Biography and memoirs of contemporaries, A-Z
186	Carlos II, 1665-1700
187	General special
189	Biography and memoirs of contemporaries, A-Z
192	Bourbons, 1700-1808
193	Biography and memoirs, A-Z
194	Felipe V, 1700-1746
.3	General special
196	Spanish succession
	For works on War of the Spanish Succession, see D281+
197	Biography and memoirs of contemporaries, A-Z
198	Fernando VI, 1746-1759
199	Carlos III, 1759-1788
.3	General special
.9	Biography and memoirs of contemporaries, A-Z
	1808-1886. 19th century
201	Sources and documents
202	Biography and memoirs
.A2	Collective
.A3-Z	Individual, A-Z
203	General works
	1808-1814. Napoleonic period
204	Sources and documents
205	General works
207	Joseph Bonaparte
	Biography, see DC216.5
208	Peninsular War period
	For the war itself, see D231+
212	Bourbon restoration, 1814-1868
214	Fernando VII, 1808; 1814-1833
.5	General special
215	Revolution, 1820-1823
.9	Biography and memoirs of contemporaries, A-Z
216	Isabel II, 1833-1868
217	General special
.5	Biography and memoirs of contemporaries, A-Z
	The Pretenders
218	General works on the Carlist movements
.3	Don Carlos I, 1788-1855
.5	Don Carlos II, 1818-1861
	Don Carlos III, see DP226
219	Carlist War, 1833-1840
220	Period of war with Morocco, 1859-1860
	For the war itself, see DT324
222	1868-1886
	Biography and memoirs
.3	Collective
.4	Individual, A-Z
224	Revolution, 1868-1870
226	Don Carlos III
228	Amadeo I, 1870-1873
	First Republic, 1873-1875
230	Sources and documents
231	General works
	Including Carlist War, 1873-1876
.3	General special

232 Alfonso XII, 1875-1885
.5 General special
233 20th century. 1886-
.8 Foreign and general affairs
Alfonso XIII, 1886-1931
234 Sources and documents
Biography and memoirs of contemporaries, A-Z
235 Collective
236 Individual, A-Z
238 General works on life and reign
243 General special
245 Period of war with America, 1898
For the war itself, see E714+
246 Period of World War I
247 1918-1931
Second Republic, 1931-1939
250.5 Sources and documents
254 General works
257 Political and diplomatic history.
Foreign and general relations
258 Relations with individual countries, A-Z
Biography and memoirs, A-Z
260 Collective
264 Individual, A-Z
e.g. .F7 Franco, Francisco
267 Alcala Zamora Y Torres, 1931-1936
268 Azana, 1936-1939
269 Civil War, 1936-1939
.A1-19 Periodicals
Sources and documents
.A2-4 Serials
.A5-55 Nonserials
Biography, see DP260+
Causes, origins, see DP257+
.A56 Historiography
.A57-Z General works
Political and diplomatic history, see DP257+
Military operations
General works, see DP269.A57-Z
.2 Individual campaigns, battles, A-Z
.27 Local history, A-Z
.3 Naval operations
.35 Individual engagements, ships, A-Z
.4 Aerial operations
.45 Foreign participation
.47 By nationality, A-Z
.5 Atrocities
.6 Prisoners and prisons
.8 Other topics, A-Z
.A7 Art and the war
.C4 Children
.E2 Economic aspects
.I5 Influence and results
.J68 Journalists
.L5 Literature and the war
.M6 Motion pictures about the war
.P8 Public opinion
.R3 Refugees

.R4 Religious aspects
.S4 Secret service. Spies
.W7 Women
.9 Personal narratives
1939-1975
.97 Sources and documents
270 General works
271 Biography and memoirs
.A2 Collective
.A3-Z Individual, A-Z
272 1975-
Biography and memoirs
.3 Collective
.4 Individual, A-Z
e.g. .J8 Juan Carlos I, King of Spain

Local History

302 Provinces, regions, etc., A-Z
e.g. Basque Provinces (General).
Pais Vasco
History
.B47 General works
.B49 Earliest
.B50 750-1492
.B51 1492-1789
.B52 1789-1815
.B53 19th-20th centuries
Catalonia
History
.C62 General works
.C64 Early to 711
.C65 Medieval
.C66 17th-18th centuries
.C67 1789-1815
.C68 19th-20th centuries
Gibraltar
History
.G38 General works
.G39 Early to 1704
.G4 18th-20th centuries

PORTUGAL

501 Periodicals. Societies
503 Sources and documents
533 Ethnography. National characteristics
History
536 Biography (Collective)
.1 Rulers, kings
.3 Houses, noble families, A-Z
.5 Public men
.95 Study and teaching
General works
537 To 1800. Chronicles
538 1801-
General special
547 Military history
Individual campaigns and engagements are classed with special period
Naval history

550 Biography and memoirs (Collective)
.5 Officers
551 General works
By period, see the special period
Political and diplomatic history. Foreign and general relations
Class works on broad periods of political and diplomatic history in DP556.2. Class works on special periods with the specific period. For works on relations with individual countries regardless of period, see DP557
555 Sources and documents
556 General works
.1 General special
.2 Early to 1580
.4 1580-
.6 1580-1816
.8 1816-
557 Relations with individual countries, A-Z
By period
Early and medieval to 1580
General works
558 To 1800. Chronicles
559 1801-
Earliest to 1095
General works
561 To 1800
562 1801-
House of Burgundy, 1095-1383
General works
568 To 1800
569 1801-
582 House of Aviz, 1385-1580
583 Discovery and explorations
585 Joao I, 1385-1433
588 Expedition to Ceuta, 1415
590 Biography and memoirs of contemporaries, A-Z
592 Duarte, 1433-1438
593 Expedition to Tangier, 1437
594 Biography and memoirs of contemporaries, A-Z
596 Affonso V, 1438-1481
598 Biography and memoirs of contemporaries, A-Z
600 Joao II, 1481-1495
602 Biography and memoirs of contemporaries, A-Z
604 Manoel I, 1495-1521
606 Biography and memoirs of contemporaries, A-Z
608 Joao III, 1521-1557
610 Biography and memoirs of contemporaries, A-Z
612 Sebastiao, 1557-1578
614 Expedition to Morocco, 1578
615 Sebastianism. Sebastianists
616 Biography and memoirs of contemporaries, A-Z
618 Henrique I, 1578-1580
1580-
General works
620 To 1800
621 1801-
622 Spanish dynasty
624 Felipe I (II of Spain), 1580-1598
625 Felipe II (III of Spain), 1598-1621

627	Felipe III (IV of Spain), 1621-1640
628	Revolution of 1640
629	Biography and memoirs of contemporaries, A-Z
632	1640-1816. House of Braganza
634	Joao IV, 1640-1656
	Biography and memoirs of contemporaries
.79	Collective
.8	Individual, A-Z
635	Affonso VI, 1656-1683
636	Pedro II, 1683-1706
.8	Biography and memoirs of contemporaries, A-Z
638	Joao V, 1706-1750
639	Jose I, 1750-1777
641	Marquis do Pombal, 1699-1782
.9	Biography and memoirs of contemporaries, A-Z
642	Maria I and Pedro III, 1777-1816
	Including biography of Maria I
643	1792-1816
644	Period of Peninsular War
	For the war itself, see DC231+
.9	Biography and memoirs of contemporaries, A-Z
	1816-1853/1908
645.A1	Sources and documents
	Biography and memoirs
.A2	Collective
.A3-Z	Individual
646	General works
650	Joao VI, 1816-1826.
	Including Revolution of 1820
651	Biography and memoirs of contemporaries, A-Z
653	Pedro IV (I of Brazil), 1826
654	Maria II, 1826-1828
655	Miguel I, 1828-1834
	Biography and memoirs of contemporaries
656	Collective
.2	Individual, A-Z
657	Wars of succession, 1826-1840
659	Maria II (restored), 1834-1853
660	Biography and memoirs of contemporaries, A-Z
	1853-1908
661.A1	Sources and documents
	Biography and memoirs
.A2-Z	Collective
.A3-Z	Individual
662	General works
664	Pedro V, 1853-1861
666	Luiz I, 1861-1889
667	Biography and memoirs of contemporaries, A-Z
668	Carlos I, 1889-1908
669	Biography and memoirs of contemporaries, A-Z
.A2	Collective
.A3-Z	Individual, A-Z
	20th century
670	Sources and documents
671	Biography and memoirs
.A2	Collective
.A3-Z	Individual, A-Z
672	General works

673 Manoel II, 1908-1910
674 Revolution, October 1910
675 Republic, 1910-
676 Biography and memoirs
.A2 Collective
.A3-Z Individual, A-Z
e.g. .S25 Salazar, Antonio de Oliveira
677 Period of World War I
678 Revolution, 1919
680 1919-1974
.5 Pamphlets
681 1974-
Biography and memoirs
682 Collective
.2 Individual, A-Z

(DQ) SWITZERLAND

1 Periodicals. Societies
3 Sources and documents
History
52 Biography (Collective)
.1 Rulers
.6 Public men
.95 Study and teaching
General works
53 To 1800. Chronicles
54 1801-
General special
59 Military history
Individual campaigns and engagements are classed with special period
Political and diplomatic history. Foreign and general relations
Class general works on the political and diplomatic history of a period with the period. For works on relations with a specific country regardless of period, see DQ76
68 Sources and documents
69 General special
Including Swiss neutrality
71 Pamphlets
73 Early and medieval to 1516
74 1516-1798
For general modern, see DQ69
75 19th-20th centuries
76 Relations with individual countries, A-Z
By period
78 Early and medieval to 1516
79 Earliest to 406
83 Teutonic tribes, 406-687
85 Carlovingian and German rule, 687-1291
Federation and Independence, 1291-1516
General works
88 To 1800. Chronicles
89 1801-
90 First Perpetual League, 1291
94 Battle of Morgarten, 1315
95 Renewal of Perpetual League, 1315
96 Battle of Sempach, 1386
97 Battle of Nafels, 1388

98 Battle of Arbedo, 1422
99 Battle of Sankt Jakob an der Birs, 1444
100 Wars of Mulhausen and of Waldshut, 1468
101 Wars of Burgundy, 1474-1477
106 Wars against Swabian League, 1499
109 Swiss in Italy.
Including Battle of Marignano, 1515
110 Biography and memoirs, A-Z
111 1516-1798
114 1516-1648
121 1648-1712
.8 Biography and memoirs, A-Z
122 1712-1798
123 Biography and memoirs
.A2 Collective
.A3-Z Individual
124 19th century
Biography
128 Collective
129 Individual, A-Z
131 1789/1798-1815
137 1789-1798
1798-1803. Helvetic Republic
141 Sources and documents
143 General works
145 Special events. By date
151 1803-1815
154 1815-1830
156 1830-1848
158 1845-1847. Sonderbund.
161 War of the Sonderbund, 1847
171 1848-1900
173 General special
Biography and memoirs
177 Collective
178 Individual
181 1848-1871
191 1871-1900
201 20th century
203 General special
205 1900-1945
Biography and memoirs
206 Collective
207 Individual, A-Z
208 1945-
Biography and memoirs
209 Collective
210 Individual, A-Z

(DR) BALKAN PENINSULA

GENERAL

1 Periodicals. Societies. Sources and documents
Ethnography
25 Slavic peoples in the Balkan Peninsula
History
33 Biography (Collective)
34.8 Study and teaching. Balkan studies
General works
35 To 1800

36 1801-
38.2 Political and diplomatic history
By period, see the period
.3 Balkan relations with individual countries, A-Z
By period
39 Early and medieval to 1500
41 1500-1800
43 1800-1900
45 1900-
Balkan War, 1912-1913
46.A2 Sources and documents
.A4-Z General works
General special
.2 Naval history
.3 Diplomatic history
Cf. D461+, Eastern question
Special campaigns
.4 Turkish
.5 Bulgarian
.6 Serbian
.7 Montenegrin
.8 Greek
.9 Local events, battles, A-Z
.95 Bucharest, Treaty of, 1913
.97 Personal narratives
47 1913-1919
48 1919-1945
.5 1945-

Local History

For regions limited to an individual country, see the country

Lower Danube Valley
49.26 History
.7 Rumelia
Thrace
Class here general works on Thrace and the ancient Thracians. For modern Bulgarian, Greek, and Turkish Thrace, see the individual country
50.46 Ethnography
Including general works on Thracians
.5 History
By period
.6 Early to 1362
.7 1362-1913. Turkish rule
.77 Preobrazhensko Uprising, 1902
.78 Personal narratives
.785 Local history, A-Z
1913-
.8 General works
Biography and memoirs
.83 Collective
.84 Individual, A-Z

BULGARIA

51 Periodicals. Societies
52 Sources and documents
Ethnography
64.15 National characteristics
History
66 Biography (Collective)

.95 Study and teaching
67 General works
General special
70 Military history
72 Political and diplomatic history. Foreign and general relations
Class general works on the political and diplomatic history of a period with the period. For works on relations with a specific country regardless of the period, see DR73
73 Relations with individual countries, A-Z
By period
74 Early to 1396
.25 Military history
.3 Early to 681
.5 First Bulgarian Empire, 681-1018
75 681-893
77 893-1018
79 Greek rule, 1018-1185
Biography and memoirs
.2 Collective
.25 Individual, A-Z
80 Second Bulgarian Empire, 1185-1396
Biography and memoirs
.2 Collective
.25 Individual, A-Z
Turkish rule, 1396-1878
81 Sources and documents
.5 General works
82 1396-1762
Biography and memoirs
.2 Collective
.25 Individual, A-Z
.3 Uprising of 1403
.5 Uprising of 1598
83 1762-1878. National revival
.2 Biography and memoirs, A-Z
.3 Uprising of 1849
.4 Uprising of 1850
.5 Uprising of 1857
.7 April Uprising, 1876
.74 Personal narratives
.75 Local. By place A-Z
.76 Special topics, A-Z
.P73 Press
.P75 Propaganda
.P83 Public opinion
84 Period of Russo-Turkish War, 1877-1878
For the war itself, see DR573
1878-1944
.9 Sources and documents
85 General works
.4 Foreign and general relations
.5 Biography and memoirs, A-Z
86 Alexander, 1879-1886
Serbo-Bulgarian War, see DR2027
.5 Interregnum, 1886-1887
87 Ferdinand, 1887-1918
.3 General special
.5 Pamphlets
.7 Period of Balkan War

For the war itself, see DR46
.8 Period of World War I
For the war itself, see D501+
.9 Vladaya Uprising, 1918
88 Biography and memoirs of contemporaries, A-Z
89 1918-1944. Boris III. 1918-1943
.2 Biography and memoirs of contemporaries, A-Z
.22 June Uprising, 1923
.3 September Uprising, 1923
.34 Personal narratives
.35 Local. By place, A-Z
.36 Special topics, A-Z
.I53 Influence
.P73 Press
.5 April events, 1925
.8 1939-1944. Period of World War II
For the war itself, see D731+
1944-
.9 Sources and documents
90 General works
92 Foreign and general relations
93 Biography and memoirs, A-Z
.3 September Uprising, 1944
.34 Personal narratives

ROMANIA

(Moldavia and Wallachia)
Cf. DK509.15+, Moldavian S.S.R.

201 Periodicals. Societies
203 Sources and documents
History
216 Biography (Collective)
.92 Study and teaching
217 General works
General special
219 Military history
225 Naval history
226 Political and diplomatic history. Foreign and general relations
Cf. D371+, D461+, Eastern question
Class general works on the political and diplomatic history of a period with the period. For works on relations with a specific country regardless of period, see DR229
229 Relations with individual countries, A-Z
By period
238 Early and medieval to 1601
239 Earliest and Roman period
240 Medieval period
.5 Biography and memoirs
.A2A-Z Collective
.A3-Z Individual, A-Z
241 Phanariote regime, 1601-1822
.5 Biography and memoirs
.A2A-Z Collective
.A3-Z Individual, A-Z
242 1822-1881. 19th century
244 1822-1866
246 1866-1876
248 1876-1881
249 Biography and memoirs, A-Z

250 1866/1881-1944
Carol I, 1881-1914
252 Sources and documents
253 Biography and memoirs of contemporaries, A-Z
255 General works on life and reign
256 Reign only
257 General special
258 Period of the Balkan War
For the war itself, see DR46
Ferdinand, 1914-1927
260 Sources and documents
261 General works on life and reign
262 Biography and memoirs of contemporaries, A-Z
263 Period of World War I
For the war itself, see D501+
264 1918-1944
265 Michael
266 Carol II, 1930-1940
Biography and memoirs of contemporaries, A-Z
.2 Collective
.3 Individual, A-Z
267 1944-
.5 Biography and memoirs, A-Z
e.g. .C4 Ceausescu, Nicolae

Local history

Transylvania
280 History
By period
.2 Earliest to 1526
.4 1526-1919
.7 1919-

TURKEY

For Ancient Asia Minor to 1453, see DS155+;
for Turkey in Asia after 1453, see DS47+
401 Periodicals. Societies
403 Sources and documents
History
Including Ottoman Empire, 1288-1918
438 Biography (Collective)
.1 Rulers
.3 Houses, noble families
.5 Public men
.94 Study and teaching
General works
439 To 1800
440 1801-
General special
448 Military history
Individual campaigns and engagements are classed with special period
451 Naval history
Individual campaigns and engagements are classed with special period
Political and diplomatic history
Class works on broad periods of political and diplomatic history in DR472+. Class works on specific periods with the period of general history. For works on relations with individual countries regardless of time period, see DR479

470 Sources and documents
471 General works
472 Earliest to 1566
473 1566-1757
474 1757-1812
475 1812-1876
476 1876-1918
Including Panislamism
477 1918-
479 Relations with individual countries, A-Z
By period
481 Earliest to 1281/1453
1281/1453-1918
General works
485 1800
486 1801-
492 Ertoghrul, 1281-1288
493 Osman I, 1288-1326
494 Murad I, 1359-1389
Including Battle of Kosovo, 1389
496 Bajazet I, 1389-1403
Including Battle of Nikopoli, 1396
.5 Solyman I, 1404-1410
.7 Musa, 1410-1413
497 Mohammed I, 1413-1451
498 Murad II, 1421-1451
Including battles of Varna, 1444, Kosovo, 1448, etc.
501 Mohammed II, 1451-1481
502 Fall of Constantinople, 1453
Mainly Turkish accounts; for general works see DF645+
.5 War with Venice, 1470-1474
.7 Siege of Rhodes, 1480
503 Bajazet II, 1481-1512
504 Selim I, 1512-1520
Solyman I the Magnificent, 1520-1566
505 Sources and documents
506 General works on life and reign
507 General special
Including Battle of Mohacs, 1526
508 Pamphlets
509 Biography and memoirs of contemporaries, A-Z
511 1566-1640. Period of decline
513 Selim II, 1566-1574
515 Cyprian War, 1570-1571. Holy League
.5 Pamphlets
516 Battle of Lepanto, 1571
519 Murad III, 1574-1595
521 Border wars with Hungary, 1575-1639
523 Wars with Persia, 1576-1639
525 Mohammed III, 1595-1603
526 Ahmed I, 1603-1617
527 Mustafa I, 1617-1623
528 Osman II, 1618-1622
529 Murad IV, 1623-1640
531 1640-1789
533 Ibrahim, 1640-1648
534 Mohammed IV, 1648-1687
.2 War of Candia, 1644-1669
.25 Pamphlets

.3 Siege of Candia, 1667-1669
.5 Other special events, A-Z
536 Siege of Vienna, 1683. Holy League against the Turks, 1684
.5 Siege of Buda, 1686
537 Solyman III, 1687-1691
539 Ahmed II, 1691-1695
541 Mustafa II, 1695-1703
.3 Rebellion of 1703
542 Ahmed III, 1703-1730
544 Russia, 1710-1713
545 Venice and Austria, 1715-1718. Austro-Turkish War, 1714-1718
547 Mahmud I, 1730-1754
548 War with Austria and Russia, 1736-1739. Peace of Belgrad, 1739
549 Osman III, 1754-1757
551 Mustafa III, 1757-1773
553 Russia, 1768-1774
554 Egypt, 1770-1777
555 Abdul-Hamid I, 1773-1789
.7 Austria and Russia, 1787-1792
1789-1861. 19th century
556 Sources and documents
557 General works
558 Biography and memoirs, A-Z
559 Selim III, 1789-1807
.5 1789-1804. War with the Suliotes
560 Mustafa, IV, 1807-1808
561 War with Russia, 1806-1812
562 Mahmud II, 1808-1839
564 War with Russia, 1828-1829
566 Abdul-Mejid, 1839-1861
567 Period of Crimean War
For the war itself. see DK214+
568 1861-1909
.8 Biography and memoirs, A-Z
569 Abdul-Aziz, 1861-1876
570 Murad V, 1876
571 Abdul-Hamid II, 1876-1909
572 General special
.5 Committee of Union and Progress (Young Turks), 1889-1908
573 War with Russia, 1877-1878
.3 General special
.4 Personal narratives
.5 Special events, battles, A-Z
.7 Treaty of San Stefano, 1878
575 Period of war with Greece, 1897
For the war itself, see DF827
583 Mohammed V, 1909-1918
584 General special
.5 Committee of Union and Progress (Young Turks), 1908-1918
586 Period of Turco-Italian War, 1911-1912
587 Period of Balkan War, 1912-1913
For the war itself, see DR46
588 Period of World War I
For the war itself, see D501+

1918-
589 Mohammed VI, 1918-1922
Including Turkish Revolution, 1918-1923
590 First Republic, 1923-1960. Kemalism
592 Biography and memoirs
e.g. Ataturk, Kamal, see .K4
.K4 Kemal, Mustafa
(Kamal Ataturk)
593 Second Republic, 1960-
600 Coup d'état, 1971
601 Coup d'état, 1980

Ancient Asia Minor to 1453, see DS155+
Turkey in Asia after 1453, see DS47+

ALBANIA

901 Periodicals. Societies
904 Sources and documents
Ethnography
924 National characteristics
History
928 Biography (Collective)
929 Rulers, kings
931 Houses, noble families
932 Individual, A-Z
933 Statesmen
938 Study and teaching
General works
.5 Through 1800
940 1801-1975
941 1975-
General special
947 Military history
For specific periods, see the period
948 Naval history
For specific periods, see the period
Political history
For specific periods, see the period
949 Sources and documents
950 General works
Foreign and general relations
Class general works on the diplomatic history of a period with the period. For works on relations with a specific country regardless of period, see DR953
951 Sources and documents
952 General works
953 Relations with individual countries, A-Z
By period
955 To 1501
958 1190-1389
959 1389-1501. Turkish Wars
Biography and memoirs
.2 Collective
.25 Individual, A-Z
960 Scanderbeg, 1443-1468
.3 Kotodeshi Plain, Battle of, 1444
.5 Albanian-Venetian War, 1447-1448
1501-1912. Turkish rule
961 Sources and documents
962 General works

963 1501-1878
Biography and memoirs
.2 Collective
.25 Individual, A-Z
964 Bushati family. 1757-1831
Biography and memoirs
.2 Collective
.25 Individual, A-Z
965 Ali Pasa, Tepedelinli, 1744-1822
1878-1912
.9 Sources and documents
966 General works
.18 Foreign and general relations
Biography and memoirs
.2 Collective
.25 Individual, A-Z
967 League of Prizren, 1878-1881
969 Uprisings, 1910-1912
1912-1944
970 Sources and documents
971 General works
Biography and memoirs
.2 Collective
.25 Individual, A-Z
972 1912-1918
973 1918-1925
974 Zogu I, 1925-1939
975 1939-1945. Period of World War II
For the war itself, see D731+
1944-
976 Sources and documents
977 General works
.18 Foreign and general relations
Biography and memoirs
.2 Collective
.25 Individual, A-Z

YUGOSLAVIA

For works limited to specific republics, see the individual republic
1202 Periodicals. Societies
1206 Sources and documents
History
1233 Biography (Collective)
1234 Rulers, kings
1235 Statesmen
1242 Study and teaching
General works
1244 Through 1800
1245 1801-1980
1246 1981-
General special
Military history
For specific periods, including individual campaigns and engagements, see the special period
1250 Sources and documents
1251 General works
Naval history
For specific periods, including individual campaigns and engagements, see the special period

1252 Sources and documents
1253 General works
Political history
For specific periods, see the period
1254 Sources and documents
1255 General works
Foreign and general relations
Class general works on the diplomatic history of a period with the period. For works on relations with a specific country regardless of period, see DR1258
1256 Sources and documents
1257 General works
1258 Relations with individual countries, A-Z
By period
1260 Early and medieval to 1500
1267 1500-1800
1800-1918
1273 Sources and documents
1274 General works
Biography and memoirs
1278 Collective
1279 Individual, A-Z
1280 1914-1918
For World War I, see D501+
1918-
1281 Sources and documents
1282 General works
.2 General special
1283 Biography and memoirs (Collective)
1918-1945
1288 Sources and documents
1289 General works
1291 Political history
1292 Foreign and general relations
Biography and memoirs
1293 Collective
1294 Individual, A-Z
1295 Peter I, 1918-1921
Cf. DR2040, Life and reign in Serbia
1296 Alexander I, 1921-1934
1297 Peter II, 1934-1945
1298 1941-1945
For World War II, see D731+
1945-1980. Tito regime
1299 Sources and documents
1300 General works on life and administration
1302 Political history
1303 Foreign and general relations
Biography and memoirs
1304 Collective
1305 Individual, A-Z
1307 1980-

Local History

Slovenia
1352 Periodicals. Societies
1355 Sources and documents
History
1376 Biography (Collective)

1383 Study and teaching
1385 General works
General special
1390 Military history
For specific periods, see the period
1391 Naval history
For specific periods, see the period
1392 Political history
For specific periods, see the period
1395 Foreign and general relations
Class general works on the diplomatic history of a period with the period. For works on relations with a specific country regardless of period, see DR1396
1396 Relations with individual countries, A-Z
By period
1398 Early and medieval to 1456
1406 1456-1814
Biography and memoirs
1410 Collective
.5 Individual, A-Z
1411 Peasant Uprising, 1573
1415 1809-1814. Slovenia as part of the Illyrian Provinces
1814-1918
1425 Political history
Biography and memoirs
1427 Collective
1428 Individual, A-Z
1430 Revolutionary events, 1848-1849
1431 1849-1918
1434 Period of World War I
For the war itself, see D501+
1918-1945
1438 Political history
Biography and memoirs
1440 Collective
1441 Individual, A-Z
1443 1941-1945
For World War II, see D731+
1945-
1447 Political history
Biography and memoirs
1449 Collective
1450 Individual, A-Z
Croatia
1502 Periodicals. Societies
1505 Sources and documents
History
1526 Biography (Collective)
1533 Study and teaching
1535 General works
General special
Military history
For specific periods, see the period
1541 Naval history
For specific periods, see the period
1545 Foreign and general relations
Class general works on the diplomatic history of a period with the period. For works on relations with a specific country regardless of period, see DR1546

1546 Relations with individual countries, A-Z
By period
1548 Early to 1102
1560 1102-1527
1566 1463-1526. Turkish invasions
For the Battle of Mohacs, 1526, see DR507
1568 1527-1918
1570 Political history
Biography and memoirs
1572 Collective
.5 Individual, A-Z
1573 Peasant Uprising, 1573
1576 1800-1849
Biography and memoirs
1577 Collective
1578 Individual, A-Z
.8 Revolutionary events, 1848-1849
1582 Period of World War I
For the war itself, see D501+
1918-1945
1586 Political history
Biography and memoirs
1588 Collective
1589 Individual, A-Z
1591 Period of World War II
For the war itself, see D731+
1945-
1595 Political history
Biography and memoirs
1597 Collective
1598 Individual, A-Z
Bosnia and Hercegovina
Class here works on Bosnia alone or Bosnia and Hercegovina treated together
1652 Periodicals. Societies
1655 Sources and documents
History
1676 Biography (Collective)
1683 Study and teaching
General special
1690 Military history
For specific periods, see the period
1692 Political history
For specific periods, see the period
1695 Foreign and general relations
Class general works on the diplomatic history of a period with the period. For works on relations with a specific country regardless of period, see DR1696
1696 Relations with individual countries, A-Z
By period
1698 Early to 1463
1712 1463-1878. Turkish rule
Biography and memoirs
1716 Collective
1717 Individual, A-Z
1720 Rebellion of 1875
.5 Personal narratives
1721 Local history. By place, A-Z
1723 1878-1918. Austrian administration

1725 Political history
Biography and memoirs
1727 Collective
1728 Individual, A-Z
1731 Annexation to Austria, 1908
1732 Period of World War I
For the war itself, see D501+
1734 1918-1945
1736 Political history
Biography and memoirs
1738 Collective
1739 Individual, A-Z
1741 Period of World War II
For the war itself, see D731+
1743 1945-
1745 Political history
Biography and memoirs
1747 Collective
1748 Individual, A-Z
Montenegro
1802 Periodicals. Societies
1805 Sources and documents
History
1827 Biography (Collective)
1834 Study and teaching
1835 General works
General special
1840 Military history
For specific periods, see the period
1841 Naval history
For specific periods, see the period
1842 Political history
For specific periods, see the period
1845 Foreign and general relations
Class general works on the diplomatic history of a period with the period. For works on relations with a specific country regardless of period, see DR1846
1846 Relations with individual countries, A-Z
By period
1848 Early to 1516
1856 1516-1782
1868 1782-1918
Biography and memoirs
1872 Collective
1873 Individual, A-Z
1878 Nicholas I, 1860-1918
Biography and memoirs of contemporaries
1879 Collective
.5 Individual, A-Z
1881 Turco-Montenegrin War, 1876-1878
1883 Period of the Balkan Wars and World War I
For the wars themselves, see DR46+; D501+
1885 1918-1945
1887 Political history
Biography and memoirs
1890 Collective
1891 Individual, A-Z
1893 Period of World War II
For the war itself, see D731+

1945-
1897 Political history
Biography and memoirs
1899 Collective
1900 Individual, A-Z
Serbia
1932 Periodicals. Societies
1935 Sources and documents
History
1956 Biography (Collective)
1963 Study and teaching
1965 General works
General special
1970 Military history
For specific periods, see the period
1972 Political history
For specific periods, see the period
1975 Foreign and general relations
Class general works on the diplomatic history of a period with the period. For works on relations with a specific country regardless of period, see DR1976
1976 Relations with individual countries, A-Z
By period
1978 Early to 1459
2001 1459-1804. Turkish rule
2003 Political history
Biography and memoirs
2004 Collective
.5 Individual, A-Z
.8 Great Emigration, 1690
2005 Insurrection, 1788
2007 1804-1918
2009 Political history
2010 Foreign and general relations
Biography and memoirs
2012 Collective
.5 Individual, A-Z
2014 Insurrections, 1804-1813
.7 Ivankovac, Battle of, 1805
2016 Milos Obrenovic I, 1814-1839
2018 Mihail Obrenovic III, 1839-1842
2019 Alexander Karadordevic, 1842-1858
Biography and memoirs
2020 Collective
.5 Individual, A-Z
2021 Milos I, 1858-1860
2022 Mihail III, 1860-1868
Biography and memoirs
2023 Collective
.5 Individual, A-Z
2024 Milan Obrenovic IV, 1868-1889
Biography and memoirs
2025 Collective
.5 Individual, A-Z
.8 Serbo-Turkish War, 1876
2026 Serbo-Turkish War, 1877-1878
.8 Revolt, 1883
2027 Serbo-Bulgarian War, 1885
2028 Alexander Obrenovic, 1889-1903

Biography and memoirs
2029 Collective
.5 Individual, A-Z
2030 Peter I, 1903-1918
Cf. DR1295
Biography and memoirs
2031 Collective
.5 Individual, A-Z
2032 Period of the Balkan Wars and World War I
For the wars themselves, see DR46+; D501+
2034 1918-1945
2036 Political history
Biography and memoirs
2038 Collective
.5 Individual, A-Z
2040 Period of World War II
For the war itself, see D731+
2042 1945-
2044 Political history
Biography and memoirs
2046 Collective
2047 Individual, A-Z
Local history of Serbia
Provinces, regions, etc.
Kosovo
2082 History
By period
2083 Early to 1389
2084 1389-1913. Turkish rule
2085 1913-1945
Kosovo as part of Serbia and Yugoslavia
2086 1945- . Autonomous region
Vojvodina
2097 History
By period
2098 Early to 1526
2099 1526-1918. Turkish and Austro-Hungarian rule
.7 Revolutionary events, 1848-1849
2100 1918-1945. Vojvodina as part of Yugoslavia
2101 1945- . Autonomous region
Macedonia
Class here works on medieval and modern Macedonia and the Socialist Republic of Macedonia
2152 Periodicals
2155 Sources and documents
History
2176 Biography (Collective)
2183 Study and teaching
2185 General works
General special
2190 Military history
For specific periods, see the period
2192 Political history
For specific periods, see the period
2195 Foreign and general relations
Class general works on the diplomatic history of a period with the period. For works on relations with a specific country regardless of period, see DR2196
2196 Relations with individual countries, A-Z

By period
2198 Early to 1389
2206 1389-1912. Turkish rule
Biography and memoirs
2210 Collective
.5 Individual, A-Z
2214 1878-1912. Independence movement
2215 Political history
2216 Foreign and general relations
Biography and memoirs
2217 Collective
2218 Individual, A-Z
2219 Kresna Uprising, 1878
2223 Ilinden Uprising, 1903
2225 Personal narratives
2226 Local history. By place, A-Z
2227 Special topics, A-Z
.F67 Foreign public opinion
2230 1912-1945
2232 Political history
2233 Foreign and general relations
Biography and memoirs
2234 Collective
2235 Individual, A-Z
2237 Period of the Balkan Wars and World War I
For the wars themselves, see DR46+; D501+
2240 1919-1945
2242 Period of World War II
For the war itself, see D731+
2244 1945-
2246 Political history
2247 Foreign and general relations
Biography and memoirs
2248 Collective
2249 Individual, A-Z

(DS) ASIA

GENERAL

1 Periodicals. Societies
2 Sources and documents
13 Ethnography
15 Indo-Europeans
16 Semites
19 Mongols
25 Tatars
26 Turks
27 Seljuks
History
32 Biography (Collective)
.8 Study and teaching
33 General works
.3 Political and diplomatic history
.4 Asian relations with individual countries, A-Z
By period
33.5 Ancient and medieval
.7 Early modern
34 19th century
For Central Asian question, see D378
35 20th century

For Central Asian question, see D471+
For Far Eastern question, see DS515+
For Middle East, see DS61+
.2 1945-

THE ISLAMIC WORLD (GENERAL)

35.3 Periodicals. Societies. Sources
.63 History
.64 Biography (Collective)
.68 Study and teaching
General special
.69 Political history
.7 Panislamism
.73 Foreign and general relations
Class general works on the diplomatic history of a period with the period. For works on relations with a specific country regardless of period, see DS35.74
.74 By region or country, A-Z
By period
Early to 1900, see DS35.63
.77 20th century

ARAB COUNTRIES (GENERAL)

36 Periodicals. Societies
.2 League of Arab States
.3 Sources and documents
History
37.2 Biography (Collective)
.6 Study and teaching
.A2A-Z General works
.7 General works
General special
.8 Military and naval history
By period, see the period
Political and diplomatic history, see DS62.8+
Arab nationalism, see DS63.6
Arab-Israeli wars, see DS126.9+
Jewish-Arab relations, see DS119.7
By period
38 Early to 622
.1 622-661
Caliphs, 632-1517
General works
.2 Early to 1800
.3 1800-
.4 Biography and memoirs of caliphs, etc.
.A2A-Z Collective
.A23-Z Individual, A-Z
By period
.5 661-750
.6 750-1258
.7 1258-1517
.8 Ottoman period, 1517-1918
.9 1798-
39 1914-
.2 Biography and memoirs
.A2A-Z Collective
.A3-Z Individual

MIDDLE EAST

41 Periodicals. Societies
42 Sources and documents
Local history and description
Cyprus
54.A2 Periodicals. Societies. Sources
.5 History
By period
.6 Early to 1571
Biography and memoirs
.62 Collective
.63 Individual, A-Z
.7 1571-1878. Turkish rule
.8 1878-1960. British period
Biography and memoirs
.82 Collective
.83 Individual, A-Z
.9 Republic, 1960-
History of the Middle East
For history of Islamic Empire, see DS38.1+
For history of Arab countries in general (including North Africa), see DS37.7
Biography
61.5 Collective
.52 Individual, A-Z
Class here biographies not elsewhere provided for under special countries and periods
.8 Study and teaching
Including area studies
.9 By region or country,A-Z
62 General works
By period
.2 Early to 622 A.D.
Medieval, see DS38.1+
.4 Modern
General special
.5 Military and naval history
By period, see the period
.8 Political and diplomatic history. Foreign and general relations
.85 Pamphlets. By date
By period
.9 Early through 1920
63 1921-1958
.1 1958-
.18 Central Treaty Organization. Baghdad Pact
.2 Middle East relations with individual countries, A-Z
e.g. .U5 United States
.3 Arab propaganda in foreign countries
.5 Nationalism
.6 Arab nationalism. Panarabism
Islam and nationalism, see BP173.5
Panislamism, see DS35.7
Palestine problem see DS119.7

IRAQ (ASSYRIA, BABYLONIA, MESOPOTAMIA)

67 Periodicals. Societies
68 Sources and documents
History
70.85 Biography (Collective)

.9 General works
.95 Political and diplomatic history. Foreign and general relations
Class general works on political and diplomatic history of a specific period with the period. For works on relations with a specific country regardless of period, see DS70.96
.96 Relations with individual countries, A-Z
By period
71 Ancient
72 Sumerians
.3 Akkadians
.5 Amorites
.52 Sutaeans
By period
73.1 4500-2200 B.C. Earliest rulers
.2 2400-607 B.C.
.25 2400-2100
.3 2100-1700
.35 Hammurabi, ca. 1800
.4 1731-1154
.45 Shalmaneser I, 1330-1310
.5 1160-1081
.53 Tiglath-Pileser I, 1115-1100
.58 Assurbelkala, 1100-1080
.6 1000-900
.7 910-607
.72 Assurnasirpal III, 884-860
.73 Shalmaneser II, 860-824
.74 Semiramis, ca. 800
.75 Shalmaneser III, 782-772
.76 Tiglath-Pileser III, 745-727
.78 Shalmaneser IV, 727-722
.8 Sargon II, 722-705
.83 Sennacherib, 705-681
.85 Esarhaddon, 681-668
.87 Assurbanipal, 668-626
.9 625-539 B.C. New Babylonian or Chaldean Empire
.91 Nabopolassar, 625-604
.92 Nebuchadnezzar II, 604-561
.93 Nabonidus, 555-538
.94 Invasion of Babylon by Cyrus, 539
.95 539-333 B.C.
75 333 B.C.-638 A.D.
76 Medieval period, 638-1517
.4 Abbasids, 750-1258
77 Turkish period, 1517-1918
79 1919-1958
.5 Faisal I, 1921-1922
.52 Ghazi I, 1933-1939
.53 Faisal II, 1939-1958
Biography and memoirs
.6 .A2 Collective
.6 .A3-Z Individual
.65 Republic, 1958-
.66 Biography and memoirs
.A2 Collective
.A3-Z Individual

LEBANON

80.A2 Periodicals. Societies

80.A3 Sources and documents
.5 Ethnography
.55 Individual elements, A-Z
.A75 Armenians
.D78 Druzes
.M37 Maronites
.P34 Palestinians
.S54 Shi'ah
History
.75 Biography (Collective)
.9 General works
.95 Political and diplomatic history.
Foreign and general relations
Class works on the political and diplomatic history of a specific period with the period. For works on relations with a specific country regardless of period, see DS80.96
.96 Relations with individual countries, A-Z
By period
81 Ancient. Phoenicians
82 333 B.C.-638 A.D.
83 Medieval, 638-1517
84 Turkish period, 1517-1918
85 Autonomy, 1861-1918
86 French Mandate and occupation, 1919-1945
87 Republic, 1941-
.2 Biography and memoirs
.A2 Collective
.A3-Z Individual
.5 Civil War, 1975-1976
.53 Israeli intervention, 1982-
Including the massacre of the Palestinian Arabs in Beirut
90 Philistines

SYRIA

92 Periodicals. Societies
.4 Sources and documents
History
.93 Biography (Collective)
95 General works
.5 Political and diplomatic history. Foreign and general relations
Class general works on the political and diplomatic history of a specific period with the period. For works on relations with an individual country regardless of period, see DS95.6
.6 Relations with individual countries, A-Z
By period
96 Early to 333 B.C.
.2 333 B.C.-634 A.D.
97 634-1516
.15 634-660
.2 Omayyads, 660-750
.3 750-1260
.4 Mamelukes, 1250-1516
.5 Turkish period, 1517-1918
.6 Biography and memoirs
.A2 Collective
.A3-Z Individual
98 French mandate, 1918-1945
.2 1946-
.3 Biography and memoirs

.A2 Collective
.A3-Z Individual

ISRAEL. PALESTINE. THE JEWS

101 Periodicals. Societies
102 Sources and documents
Jerusalem
History
Biography and memoirs
109.85 Collective
.86 Individual, A-Z
.9 General works
By period
.912 To 70 A.D.
.913 70 A.D. to 637
.916 637-1099, Muslim period
1099-1291, see D175+
.92 1244-1917, Muslim-Turkish period
.925 1800-1917
.93 1917-
.94 1967-
110 Regions, towns, etc., A-Z
Class here regions, towns, etc., west of the Jordan River, regardless of political jurisdiction
e.g. .G3 Gaza Strip
.W47 West Bank
.45 Gulf of Aqaba. Straits of Tiran
.5 Sinai Peninsula
Antiquities
111.2 Public and political
.6 Military
113.2 Ethnography. Tribes of Israel
For ancient period, see DS131
.6 Arabs. Palestinian Arabs
Including works on Palestinian Arabs in foreign countries collectively
For works on Palestinian Arabs in individual countries , see the country
.7 Arabs in Israel
.72 Druzes
History
For history of Jerusalem, see DS109.9
115 Biography (Collective)
Class here collective biography of Israel and collective biography of Jews of all countries
.3 Public men
.95 Study and teaching
General works
116 To 1800
117 1800-
General special
119.2 Military and naval history
By special period, see the period
.6 Political and diplomatic history. Foreign and general relations
Class general works on political and diplomatic history of a period with the period. For works on relations with a specific country regardless of period, see DS119.8
.65 Boundaries
.7 Jewish-Arab relations. Palestine problem
.8 Relations with individual countries, A-Z
United States, see E183.8+

By period
Earliest to 70 A.D., see DS116+
121 Earliest to 63 B.C.
.4 Canaanites
.5 Jews in Egypt
.55 Exodus to Death of Solomon
.6 Divided Kingdom
.65 Babylonian Exile to Maccabean period (586-168 B.C.)
.7 168-63 B.C. Maccabees
.8 Biography, A-Z
122 63 B.C.-70/395 A.D. Roman period
Including Hellenistic period
.3 Herod the Great, 37-4 B.C.
.4 Archelaus, 4 B.C.-6 A.D.
.5 Herod Antipas, 4 B.C.-39 A.D.
.6 Herod Philip, 4 B.C.-33 A.D.
.7 Herod Agrippa I, 37-44
.8 Herod Agrippa II, 53-70
.9 Roman domination, 70-395
Including Bar Kokba's Rebellion, 132-135
123 70 A.D.-
.5 70-638
124 General medieval and early modern to 1800
125 19th-20th centuries
.3 Biography and memoirs
For Zionists, see DS151
.A2 Collective
.A3-Z Individual
e.g. .B37 Ben-Gurion, David
.5 Period of World War I
Cf. D568.7, World War I
DS109.9, Jerusalem
126 1919-1948. British control
.3 Period of World War II
Cf. D810.J4
.4 1945-1948
.5 Republic, 1948-
.6 Biography and memoirs
.A2 Collective
.A3-Z Individual
.75 Israeli-Zionist propaganda in foreign countries
.9 Arab War, 1948-1949
.A1 Periodicals.
.A2-4 Sources and documents
.A5-Z General works
Including military operations
.92 Diplomatic history
.93 Individual countries, A-Z
.954 Medical care. Refugees
.96 Other topics, A-Z
.A3 Aerial operations
.M65 Motion pictures about the war
.N3 Naval operations
.O3 Occupied territories
.P8 Public opinion
Refugees, see DS126.954
.R4 Religious aspects
.T4 Territorial questions
.97 Personal narratives

.98 Armistices
.983 Peace
.985 Influence and results
.99 Local, A-Z
Sinai Campaigns, 1956, see DS110.5
Arab War, 1967
127.A1 Periodicals
.A2-4 Sources and documents
.A5-Z General works
Including military operations
.2 Diplomatic history
.3 Individual countries, A-Z
.54 Medical care. Refugees
.6 Other topics, A-Z
.A3 Aerial operations
.M65 Motion pictures about the war
.N3 Naval operations
.O3 Occupied territories
.P8 Public opinion
Refugees, see DS127.54
.R4 Religious aspects
.T4 Territorial questions
.7 Personal narratives
.8 Armistices
.83 Peace
.85 Influence and results
.9 Local, A-Z
128.1 Arab War, 1973
.A1 Periodicals
.A2-4 Sources and documents
.A5-Z General works
Including military operations
.12 Diplomatic history
.13 By country, A-Z
.154 Medical care. Refugees
.16 Other topics, A-Z
.A3 Aerial operations
.M65 Motion pictures about the war
.N3 Naval operations
.O3 Occupied territories
.P8 Public opinion
.R4 Religious aspects
.T4 Territorial questions
.17 Personal narratives
.18 Armistices
.183 Peace
.185 Influence and results
.19 Local, A-Z
Special topics
132 The Jewish state and Jews outside of Israel. Israel and the diaspora
Jews outside of Palestine
133 Periodicals
134 General works
Biography and memoirs, see DS115
135 By region or country, A-Z
Under each country (where three cutter numbers are indicated):
(1) General works
(2) Local, A-Z
(3) Biography and memoirs

.A1-19 Collective
.A2-Z Individual, A-Z
For North and South American countries, see E-F
e.g. Germany
.G3A2-4 Serials
.G3A5-Z History
.G31 Early and medieval
.G32 1601-1815
.G33 19th-20th centuries
.G332 1945-
.G34 Prussia
.G5 Biography, A-Z
.H9-93 Hungary
.R9 Russia. Soviet Union
.R92 History, 1917-
.R93 Local, A-Z
.R95 Biography and memoirs
.A1-19 Collective
.A2-Z Individual
United States, see E184.J5

140 Political and social conditions
.5 Economic conditions
141 Jewish question
145 Anti-Semitism
146 By region or country, A-Z
148 Assimilation
149.A5-Z Zionism. Restoration
Biography and memoirs
151.A2 Collective
.A3-Z Individual, A-Z

JORDAN

153.A2 Periodicals. Societies
.A3 Sources and documents
.5 Ethnography
.55 Individual elements, A-Z
.P34 Palestinian Arabs
History
.8 Biography (Collective)
154 General works
General special
.13 Military history
.15 Foreign and general relations
Class general works on foreign relations by period with the period.
For works on relations with a specific country regardless of period, see DS154.16
.16 Relations with individual countries, A-Z
By period
.2 Ancient
.22 Nabataeans
.3 Medieval
.4 Turkish period, 1517-1918
.5 1919-
.52 Biography and memoirs
.A2 Collective
.A3-Z Individual, A-Z
.53 Abdullah I, 1946-1951
.54 Talal I, 1951-1952
.55 Hussein I, 1952-

For regions, towns, etc., west of the Jordan River, see DS110

ASIA MINOR

155 General works on Asia Minor before 1453
  Including Greek city-states and colonies
156 Ancient states, regions, etc., A-Z
  e.g. .C3 Cappadocia
  .P5 Phrygia

ARMENIA

Class here works on the historic kingdom and region of Armenia as a whole. For works on the territories incorporated into other countries after 1920, see the country

161 Periodicals. Societies
162 Sources and documents
History
174 Biography (Collective)
.92 Study and teaching
175 General works
.3 Political and diplomatic history. Foreign and general relations
  Class general works on the political and diplomatic history of a specific period with the period. For works on relations with a specific country regardless of period, see DS175.4
.4 Relations with individual countries, A-Z
By period
181 Earliest to 428
186 428-1522. Sassanids, etc.
191 1522-1800. Turkish rule
193 Biography and memoirs
  .A2 Collective
  .A3-Z Individual, A-Z
194 1801-1900
.5 Biography and memoirs
  .A2 Collective
  .A3-Z Individual
195 1901-
.3 Biography and memoirs
  .A2 Collective
  .A3-Z Individual
.5 1914-1923
  Including independence and massacres by the Turks until the Treaty of Lausanne in 1923

ARABIAN PENINSULA. SAUDI ARABIA

201 Periodicals. Societies
202 Sources and documents
History
222 Biography (Collective)
.92 Study and teaching
223 General works
227 Political and diplomatic history. Foreign and general relations
  Class general works on political and diplomatic history of an individual period with the period. For works on relations with a specific country regardless of period, see DS228
228 Relations with individual countries, A-Z
By period
231 Earliest to 622
232 622-661
661-1517

General works
234 Oriental authors to 1800
European, modern Oriental, and other
235 To 1800
236 1800-
238 Biography and memoirs, A-Z
By period
.3 661-750
.5 750-1258
.7 1258-1517
239 1517-1635
241 1635-1740
242 1740-1873
243 1873-1914
244 1914-1932
Biography and memoirs
.49 Collective
.5 Individual, A-Z
.512 1932-
.52 Kingdom of Saudi Arabia, 1932-
Biography and memoirs
.525 Collective
.526 Individual, A-Z
By period
.53 1932-1953
.56 1953-1964
.6 1964-1975
.63 1975-
247 Local history and description
Regions, sultanates, emirates, A-Z
Regions
Persian Gulf States
.A135 History
By period
.A137 To 1919
.A138 1919-
Southern Arabia
.A145 History
By period
.A147 To 1919
.A148 1919-
Aden. Yemen (People's Democratic Republic)
.A25 History
By period
.A27 To 1919
.A28 1919-
Bahrain
.B25 History
By period
.B27 To 1919
.B28 1919-
Dubai
.D75 History
By period
.D77 To 1919
.D78 1919-
Kuwait
.K85 History
By period

.K87 To 1919
.K88 1919-
Trucial Oman. United Arab Emirates
.T85 History
By period
.T87 To 1919
.T88 1919-
Yemen
.Y45 History
By period
.Y47 To 1919
.Y48 1919-

IRAN. PERSIA

251 Periodicals. Societies
252 Sources and documents
History
271 Biography (Collective)
.8 Study and teaching
272 General works
General special
273.3 Military history
For specific periods, <u>see</u> the period
274 Political and diplomatic history. Foreign and general relations
Class general works on the political and diplomatic history of an individual period with the period. For works on relations with a specific country regardless of period <u>see</u> DS274.2
.2 Relations with individual countries, A-Z
By period
275 Ancient to 226 A.D.
276 Earliest through 640 B.C.
278 Median Empire, 640-558 B.C.
281 Persian Empire, 558-330 B.C.
282 Cyrus, 558-529
.5 Cambyses, 529-522
.6 Smerdis, 521
.7 Darius I, 521-485
283 Xerxes I, 485-465
284 Artaxerxes I, 465-424
.2 Xerxes II, 424
.3 Darius II, 424-405
.4 Artaxerxes II, 405-359
.5 Artaxerxes III, 358-338
.6 Arses, 338-336
.7 Darius III, 336-330
.9 330/323-246 B.C. Seleucids
285 Parthian Empire, 246 B.C.-226 A.D.
Modern, 226-
General works, <u>see</u> DS272
286 Sassanian Empire, 226-651
288 Arab and Mongol rule, 651-1500
292 Safawids and Afghans, 1500-1736
293 Afghan wars
.9 1736-1794
298 Kajar dynasty, 1794-1925
301 Agha Mohammed, 1794-1797
302 Fath Ali, 1797-1834
305 Mohammed, 1834-1848
307 Nasr-ed-Din, 1848-1896

.5 War with Great Britain, 1856-1857
311 Muzaffar-ed-Din, 1986-1907
313 1905-1911
315 Ahmed, 1909-1925
Biography and memoirs
.9 Collective
316 Individual, A-Z
Pahlavi dynasty, 1925-1979
.2 Periodicals. Societies
.23 Sources and documents
.3 General works
.5 Military history
.55 Naval history
.6 Political history
.8 Foreign and general relations
Biography and memoirs
.85 Collective
.9 Individual, A-Z
317 Reza Shah, 1925-1941
318 Mohammed Reza, 1941-1979
Islamic Republic, 1979-
.72 Periodicals. Societies
.74 Sources and documents
.8 General works
.822 Military history
.825 Political history
.83 Foreign and general relations
Biography and memoirs
.839 Collective
.84 Individual, A-Z
e.g. .K48 Khomeini, Ruhollah
.85 Iran-Iraq War
Iran Hostage Crisis, 1979-1981, see E183.8.I55
Local history and description
326 Persian Gulf (General)

SOUTHERN ASIA. INDIAN OCEAN REGION

331 Periodicals. Societies. Sources
History
.8 Study and teaching
340 General works
341 Political and diplomatic history. Foreign and general relations
.3 Relations with individual countries, A-Z
349.8 Islands of the Indian Ocean (General)

AFGHANISTAN

350 Periodicals. Societies. Sources
History
355 Biography (Collective)
356 General works
357.5 Political and diplomatic history. Foreign and general relations
Class general works on the political and diplomatic history of an individual period with the period. For works on relations with an individual country regardless of period, see DS357.6
Relations with individual countries, A-Z
By period
358 Earliest to 1747
359 1747-1826. Durani dynasty
19th-20th centuries
361 1826-1973

371.2 1973-
Including Soviet occupation

PAKISTAN

376 Periodicals. Societies. Sources
History
381 Biography (Collective)
.7 Study and teaching
382 General works
383.2 Military and naval history
.5 Political and diplomatic history. Foreign and general relations
.A2 General works
.A3-Z Relations with individual countries, A-Z
By period
Early through 1946, see DS451+
384 1947-
385 Biography and memoirs
.A2 Collective
.A3-Z Individual, A-Z
e.g. .J5 Jinnah, Mahomed Ali
.9 Conflict with India, 1947-1949
.A3 General works
386.A3-Z Conflict with India, 1965
387 Tashkend Conference
388.A3-Z Conflict with India, 1971-
.2 Simla Summit

BANGLADESH. EAST PAKISTAN

393 Periodicals. Societies
.2 Sources and documents
394.5 History
.7 Political and diplomatic history. Foreign and general relations
.73 Relations with individual countries, A-Z
By period
Early to 1946, see DS485.B46+
395 1947-1971
.5 1971-
.7 Biography and memoirs
.A2 Collective
.A3-Z Individual

INDIA

401 Periodicals. Societies
.5 Sources and documents
430 Ethnography. Sects
432 Individual elements, A-Z
.M84 Muslims
.S5 Sikhs
History
434 Biography (Collective)
.8 Study and teaching
General works
436.A1A-Z Oriental authors to 1850
.A2A-Z European authors to 1850
.A3-Z Modern authors
General special
Military history
Class works on broad periods of military history in DS442.2+.
For works on specific battles, engagements, etc., see the special period of general history

442.A2 Sources and documents
.A3-Z General works
.2 Early and medieval
.3 1526-1761
.5 1761-1900
.6 1901-
443 Naval history
Political and diplomatic history. Foreign and general relations
Class works on broad periods of political and diplomatic history in DS446+. Class works on specific periods of political and diplomatic history with the special period of general history. For works on relations with an individual country regardless of period, see DS450
444 Sources and documents
445 General works
446 Early to 1761
.3 1761-
.5 1761-1858
447 19th century
448 20th century
450 Relations with individual countries, A-Z
By period
451 Earliest to 997
Biography and memoirs
.9.A2A-Z Collective
.9.A3-Z Individual
452 997-1761. Moslem rule
457 997-1526
461 1526-1761. Mogul Empire
462 French in India, 1664-1765. 17th-18th centuries
Including French East India Company
.8 Biography and memoirs, A-Z
Portuguese in India, see DS498+
463 English rule, 1761-1947
469 General special
470 Biography and memoirs not identified with any particular administration, A-Z
Including Hindu rulers
Lord Clive, 1751-1767
471 Life and administration
472 Administration only
.8 Biography and memoirs of contemporaries, A-Z
.9 Verelst, Harry, 1767-1769
473 Warren Hastings, 1772-1785
Including Maratha War, 1775-1782
.3 General special
474 Sir John Macpherson, 1785-1786
.1 Marquis Cornwallis, 1786-1793
Cf. DS475.35, His administration, 1805
.2 Sir John Shore, 1793-1798
475 1798-1862. 19th century
.1 General special
.2 Biography and memoirs
.A2 Collective
.A3-Z Individual
.3 Marquis Wellesley, 1798-1805
Including Maratha War, 1803
.35 Marquis Cornwallis, 1805
Cf. DS474.1

.4 Sir George Barlow, 1805-1807
.5 Earl of Minto, 1807-1813
Including Mutiny of 1809
.6 Earl of Moira (Marquis of Hastings), 1813-1823
Including Maratha War, 1816-1818
.7 Earl Amherst, 1823-1828
Including Burmese War, 1824-1826
.8 Lord Bentinck, 1828-1835
.9 Lord Metcalf, 1835-1836
476 Earl of Auckland, 1836-1842
477 Earl of Ellenborough, 1842-1844
.1 Viscount Hardinge, 1844-1848
Including Sikh War, 1845-1846
Marquis of Dalhousie, 1848-1856
.5 Life and administration
.6 Administration only
.63 Sikh War, 1848-1849
.65 Burmese War, 1852
.8 Earl Canning, 1856-1862
Sepoy Rebellion
478.A1 Sources and documents
.A2-Z General works
479 1862-1914
.1 Biography and memoirs
.A2 Collective
.A3-Z Individual
480.4 1914-1919
.45 1919-1947
.5 Viscount Chelmsford, 1916-1921
Including Amritsar Massacre, 1919
.6 Marquis of Reading, 1921-1926
.7 Earl of Halifax, 1926-1931
.8 Marquis of Willingdon, 1931-1936
.82 Marquis of Linlithgow, 1936-1943
Including Quit India Movement, 1942
.83 Earl of Wavell, 1943-1947
1947-1977
For India-Pakistan Conflict, see DS386; DS388
.832 Periodicals. Societies
.84 General works
.842 Partition, 1947
.85 Chinese border dispute, 1957
.852 National Emergency, 1975-1977
.853 1977-
481 Biography and memoirs (20th century), A-Z
e.g. .G23 Gandhi, Indira
.G3 Gandhi, Mohandas
.N35 Nehru, Jawaharlal
Local history and description
485 Kingdoms, regions, states, A-Z
Bengal
For East Bengal, see DS393+
.B46 History
For the history of Bengal after 1947, see DS395+; DS485.B493
.B47 Early and medieval
.B48 1701-1850
.B49 1851-1947
Bengal, West

.B493 General works and history
Punjab
.P15 Biography (Collective)
.P2 History
.P3 Sikhs
Cf. DS432.S5

SRI LANKA

488 Periodicals. Societies
.2 Sources and documents
489.2 Ethnography
.25 Individual elements, A-Z
.T3 Tamils
.3 Biography (Collective)
.5 History
General special
.57 Political and diplomatic history. Foreign and general relations
Class general works on the political and diplomatic history of a specific period with the period. For relations with individual countries regardless of period, see DS489.59
.59 Relations with individual countries, A-Z
By period
.6 Early to 1505
.7 1505-1948
Biography and memoirs
.72 Collective
.73 Individual, A-Z
.8 1948-1978
Biography and memoirs
.82 Collective
.83 Individual, A-Z
e.g. .B28 Bandaranaike, Sirimavo R.D., 1916-
.84 1978-
Biography and memoirs
.85 Collective
.86 Individual, A-Z

NEPAL

493 Periodicals. Societies
.2 Sources and documents
.5 History
General special
.65 Military history
For specific periods, see the period
.7 Political and diplomatic history
For specific periods, see the period
.8 Relations with individual countries, A-Z
By period
495 Earliest to 1768
.3 1768-1951
.5 1951-
.58 Foreign and general relations
Biography and memoirs
.59 Collective
.592 Individual, A-Z

GOA. PORTUGUESE IN INDIA

History
498.3 Early to 1600

.7 1600-1961
.8 1962-

EAST ASIA. THE FAR EAST (GENERAL)

501 Periodicals. Societies
503 Sources and documents
Biography and memoirs
510 Collective
.5 Individual, A-Z
History
Including Far Eastern question
.7 Study and teaching
511 General works
By period
514 Early through 1500
.3 1501-1800
515 1801-1904
517 Russo-Japanese War, 1904-1905
.1 Naval history
.13 Political and diplomatic history
Special events, battles
.15 Battle of Yalu, 1904
.3 Siege of Port Arthur, 1904-1905
.4 Battle of Mukden, 1905
.5 Battle of Tsushima, 1905
.9 Other
Including personal narratives
518 1904-1945
.1 1945-
Relation of individual countries to East Asia
.15 China, 1945
For works on China and the Far Eastern question to 1945, see DS740.6+
.2 France
.3 Germany
.4 Great Britain
.42 India
.45 Japan
.47 Korea
.5 Netherlands
.6 Portugal
.7 Soviet Union
.8 United States
.9 Other countries, A-Z

SOUTHEASTERN ASIA (GENERAL)

520 Periodicals. Societies
.4 Sources and documents
History
524.2 Biography (Collective)
.7 Study and teaching
525 History
General special
.7 Political history
For specific periods, see the period
.8 Foreign and general relations
For specific periods, see the period
.9 Relations with individual countries, A-Z
By period
526.3 To 1500

.4 1500-1900
.6 1900-1945
.7 1945-
.9 Golden Triangle (Southeastern Asia)

BURMA

527 Periodicals. Societies
.2 Sources and documents
528.3 Biography (Collective)
History
.5 General works
General special
.6 Military history
For specific periods, see the period
.7 Political and diplomatic history. Foreign and general relations
Class general works on the political and diplomatic history of an individual period with the period. For works on relations with an individual country regardless of period, see DS528.8
.8 Relations with individual countries, A-Z
By period
529.2 Earliest to 1287
.3 1287-1824
.7 1824-1885
530 1885-1945
Biography and memoirs
.3 Collective
.32 Individual, A-Z
.4 1945-
Biography and memoirs
.52 Collective
.53 Individual, A-Z
e.g. .N9 Nu, U

INDOCHINA. FRENCH INDOCHINA

531 Periodicals. Societies
532 Sources and documents
Biography and memoirs
.A2 Collective
.A3-Z Individual
541 History
544 Military history
For specific periods, see the period
545 Naval history
.5 Political history
For specific periods, see the period
546 Foreign and general relations
For general works on the diplomatic history of a period, see the period. For works on relations with a specific country regardless of period, see DS546.5
.5 Relations with individual countries, A-Z
By period
547 To 1787
548 1787-1884
549 1884-1945
Including Chinese-French War, 1884-1855
550 1945-
Indochinese War, 1946-1954
553.A1A-Z Periodicals
.A2-Z Sources and documents
.1 General works. Military operations

.3 Individual campaigns, battles, A-Z
.5 Personal narratives
.6 Armistices. Peace negotiations
.7 Other topics (not A-Z)

Cambodia

554 Periodicals. Societies
.2 Sources and documents
.44 Ethnography
.45 Khmers
.47 Biography (Collective)
.5 History

General special

.57 Foreign and general relations

For general works on the diplomatic history of a period, see the period. For works on relations with a specific country regardless of period, see DS554.58

.58 Relations with individual countries, A-Z

By period

.6 Earliest to 1863
.62 Khmer Empire

Biography and memoirs

.63 Collective
.64 Individual, A-Z
.7 1863-1954

Biography and memoirs

.72 Collective
.73 Individual, A-Z
.8 1954-

Biography and memoirs

.82 Collective
.83 Individual, A-Z

e.g. .N6 Norodom Sihanouk Varmam

Sihanouk, see .N6

Cambodian-Vietnamese Conflict

.84 Sources and documents
.842 General works

Laos

555 Periodicals. Societies
.2 Sources and documents
.47 Biography (Collective)
.5 History

General special

.57 Foreign and general relations

For general works on the diplomatic history of a period, see the period. For works on relations with a specific country regardless of period, see DS555.58

.58 Relations with individual countries, A-Z

By period

.6 Earliest to 1893

Biography and memoirs

.62 Collective
.63 Individual, A-Z
.7 1893-1954

Biography and memoirs

.72 Collective
.73 Individual, A-Z
.8 1954-1975

Biography and memoirs

.82 Collective

.83 Individual, A-Z
.84 1975-
Biography and memoirs
.85 Collective
.86 Individual, A-Z
Vietnam
Including the Republic of Vietnam (South Vietnam)
556 Periodicals. Societies
.2 Sources and documents
.47 Biography (Collective)
History
.49 Study and teaching
.5 General works
General special
.54 Military history
For specific periods, see the period
.57 Foreign and general relations
For general works on the diplomatic history of a period, see the period. For works on relations with a specific country regardless of period, see DS556.58
.58 Relations with individual countries, A-Z
By period
.6 Earliest to 1225
Biography and memoirs
.62 Collective
.63 Individual, A-Z
.7 1225-1802
Biography and memoirs
.72 Collective
.73 Individual, A-Z
.8 1802-1954
Biography and memoirs
.82 Collective
.83 Individual, A-Z
.9 1954-1975
Biography and memoirs
.92 Collective
.93 Individual, A-Z
e.g. .N5 Ngo Dinh Diem
Vietnamese Conflict
557 Periodicals. Societies
.3 Congresses. Conferences
.4 Sources and documents
Biography
.5 Collective
Individual, see the individual country in DA-F
.7 General works. Military operations (General)
.72 Pictorial works. Satire, caricature
.73 Motion pictures about the conflict
.74 Study and teaching
.8 Individual campaigns, battles, A-Z
e.g. .T4 Tet Offensive, 1968
By country
Including foreign relations, participation in the conflict, etc.
558 United States
.2 General special
.4 Armies, divisions, etc.
.5 North Vietnam
.6 Other, A-Z

.7 Naval operations
.8 Aerial operations
.92 Guerrilla operations
559.2 Atrocities. War crimes
.3 Destruction and pillage
.4 Prisoners and prisons
.42 Economic aspects (General)
.44 Medical care
.46 Press. Censorship. Publicity
.5 Personal narratives
.6 Protest movements, anti-war demonstrations, public opinion
.62 By region or country, A-Z
Individual demonstrations are classed with the city in which they were held
.63 Relief work. Refugees
.64 Moral and religious aspects
.7 Peace negotiations, treaties, etc.
.72 Veterans
.8 Other topics, A-Z
.A4 Amnesty
.C5 Chemical and biological warfare
.C53 Children. Orphans
.C54 Churches
.C6 Communications
.C63 Conscientious objectors
.D4 Desertions
.D7 Draft resisters
.M44 Military intelligence
.M5 Missing in action
.P65 Propaganda
.P7 Psychological aspects
.S6 Social aspects
.W6 Women
.82 Celebrations. Memorials
By region or country
.825 United States
.83 Local, A-Z
.832 Other regions or countries, A-Z
.9 Local history, A-Z
.912 1975-
.916 Sino-Vietnamese Conflict, 1979
Democratic Republic (North Vietnam), 1945-
560 Periodicals. Societies
.2 Sources and documents
.6 History
General special
.68 Foreign and general relations
.69 Relations with individual countries, A-Z
Biography and memoirs
.7 Collective
.72 Individual, A-Z
e.g. .H6 Ho Chi Minh

THAILAND. SIAM

561 Periodicals. Societies
562 Sources and documents
570.5 Biography (Collective)
History
.98 Study and teaching

571 General works
573 Military history
For specific period, see the period
574 Naval history
For specific period, see the period
575 Political and diplomatic history
Class general works on the political and diplomatic history of an individual period with the period. For works on relations with a specific country regardless of period, see DS757.5
.5 Relations with individual countries, A-Z
By period
576 Earliest to 638
577 638-1809
Biography and memoirs
.2 Collective
.22 Individual, A-Z
.9 1782-1809
578 19th-20th centuries
Biography and memoirs
.3 Collective
.32 Individual, A-Z
For biography of an individual ruler, see the period of his reign
579 Phra Budalot La (Rama II), 1809-1824
580 Phra Nang Klao (Rama III), 1824-1851
581 Mongkut (Rama IV), 1851-1868
582 Chulalongkorn (Rama V), 1868-1910
583 Vajiravudh (Rama VI), 1910-1925
584 Prajadhipok (Rama VII), 1925-1935
585 Ananda Mahidol (Rama VIII), 1935-1946
586 Phumiphon Aduldet (Rama IX), 1946-

MALAYSIA. MALAY PENINSULA. STRAITS SETTLEMENTS

591 Periodicals. Sources and documents
595.5 Biography (Collective)
History
.9 Study and teaching
596 General works
.3 Political and diplomatic history. Foreign and general relations
For works on the political and diplomatic history of an individual period, see the period. For works on relations with an individual country regardless of period, see DS596.4
.4 Relations with individual countries, A-Z
By period
.5 Early to 1511
.6 1511-1946
Biography and memoirs
.52 Collective
.53 Individual, A-Z
597 1946-1963 (Federation)
Biography and memoirs
.14 Collective
.15 Individual, A-Z
.2 1963-
Biography and memoirs
.214 Collective
.215 Individual, A-Z
Local history and description
East Malaysia

Sabah. British North Borneo
.336 History
Sarawak
.37 History
Other settlements, regions, etc. A-Z
Singapore
.S75 History
.S762 Political history. Foreign and general relations
By period, see the period
.S763 Relations with individual countries, A-Z
By period
.S775 20th century

MALAY ARCHIPELAGO

603 History

INDONESIA. DUTCH EAST INDIES

611 Periodicals. Societies
613 Sources and documents
632.5 Biography (Collective)
History
.8 Study and teaching
634 General works
General special
636 Military history
For specific periods, see the period
637 Naval history
For specific periods, see the period
638 Political and diplomatic history. Foreign and general relations
Class general works on the political and diplomatic history of a specific period with the period. For works on relations with an individual country regardless of period, see DS640
640 Relations with individual countries,A-Z
By period
641 Earliest to 1478
.5 1478-1602. Muslim rule
642 1602-1798. Dutch East India Company
Biography and memoirs
.2 Collective
.22 Individual, A-Z
643 1798-1942. Colonial period
Biography and memoirs
.2 Collective
.22 Individual, A-Z
.5 1942-1945
644 1945-1966
.1 Biography and memoirs
.A2 Collective
.A3-Z Individual, A-Z
e.g. .S8 Sukarno, president
.32 Coup d'etat, 1965
.4 1966-
Islands
Sumatra
646.129 History
Java
.27 History
Borneo. Kalimantan, Indonesia
.3 General works
Celebes. Sulawesi

.47 History
Timor
.57 History
Molluccas. Maluku
.67 History
.69 Local, A-Z
e.g. .S69 South Moluccas

BRUNEI

650 Periodicals. Societies
.15 Sources and documents
History
.44 Biography (Collective)
.48 Study and teaching
.5 General works
General special
.54 Political history. Foreign and general relations
For specific periods, see the period.
For works on relations with a specific country regardless of period, see DS650.55
.55 Relations with individual countries, A-Z
By period
.56 Early to 1400
.6 1400-1906
.64 1906-1959
.7 1959-1984
.8 1984-

PHILIPPINES

651 Periodicals. Societies
653 Sources and documents
History
667.28 Study and teaching
General works
668.A2 Through 1800
.A3-Z 1801-
General special
671 Military history
By period, see the special period
672 Naval history
By period, see the special period
.5 Pirate wars
.8 Political history. Foreign and general relations
Class works on a specific period with the period. For works on relations with a specific country regardless of period, see DS673
673 Special, A-Z
Including relations with individual countries
e.g. .F7 Friars
.J3 Japan
By period
.8 Earliest to 1521
674 Spanish rule, 1521-1898
.5 Battle of Playa Honda, 1617
.8 English in Manila, 1762
.9 Biography and memoirs, A-Z
675 19th century
.5 Cavite Mutiny, 1872
Biography and memoirs
.78 Collective
.8 Individual, A-Z

676 1894-1901
.5 General special
.8 Biography and memoirs, A-Z
678 1894-1897
679 1897-1901
Cf. E712+, War of 1898
681 Political and diplomatic history
.7 Diplomatic history
682.A1-3 Military history
Including Insurrections of 1896-1898 and 1899-1901
.A5-Z Special events, battles, A-Z
683.3 Naval history
.7 Personal narratives
685 1901-
Class here works on the Philippines under United States rule, 1901-1935
.8 Biography and memoirs, A-Z
686 Commonwealth, 1935-1946
.2 Biography and memoirs
.A2 Collective
.A3-Z Individual, A-Z
.3 Quezon, 1935-1944
.4 Period of World War II.
.5 1946-1986
.6 Biography and memoirs
.A2 Collective
.A3-Z Individual, A-Z
e.g. .M35 Marcos, Ferdinand
.614 1986-
Biography and memoirs
.615 Collective
.616 Individual, A-Z
.62 Revolution, 1986

CHINA

701 Periodicals. Societies
703 Sources and documents
History
734 Biography (Collective)
.95 Study and teaching
.97 By region or country, A-Z
General works
735.A2 Through 1800
.A3-Z 1801-
General special
738 Military history
By period, see the specific period
739 Naval history
By period, see the specific period
740 Political and diplomatic history
Class works on special periods with the period. For works on relations with an individual country regardless of period, see DS740.5
.2 General special
.4 Foreign and general relations
.5 Relations with individual countries, A-Z
e.g. Great Britain
.G5 International relations
.G6 Local, A-Z

.e.g. .H6 Hong Kong

.6 China and the Far Eastern question
.61 Early through 1800
.62 1801-1860
.63 1861-1945
1945- , see DS518.15

By period
Early to 221 B.C.
741 Periodicals. Societies
.15 Sources and documents
General works
.3 Through 1800
.5 1801-
.72 Military history
.75 Political history
Biography and memoirs
.82 Collective
.85 Individual, A-Z
221 B.C.-960 A.D.
747.28 Periodicals. Societies
.33 Sources and documents
.37 General works
.43 Military history
.45 Political history
.46 Foreign and general relations
.48 Biography and memoirs (Collective)
960-1644
750.52 Periodicals. Societies
.56 Sources and documents
.64 General works
.74 Military history
.76 Naval history
.78 Political history
.82 Foreign and general relations
.86 Biography (Collective)
753.7 Tatar Conquest, 1643-1644
1644-1912
.82 Periodicals. Societies
.86 Sources and documents
754 General works
.15 Military history
.16 Naval history
.17 Political history
.18 Foreign and general relations
.19 Biography (Collective)
756 1796-1820
.33 White Lotus Rebellion, 1796-1804
757 Tao-Kuang, 1820-1850
.5 Opium War, 1840-1842
758 Hsien-feng, 1850-1861
759 Taiping Rebellion, 1850-1864
.5 Nien Rebellion, 1853-1868
760 Foreign intervention, 1857-1861
761 1861-1912
763.A2 Biography (Collective)
.5 Tung-chih, 1861-1875
Biography and memoirs of contemporaries, A-Z
.62 Collective
.63 Individual, A-Z

.65 Self-strengthening movement, 1861-1895
.7 Tien-tsin Massacre, 1870
764 Kuang-hsu, 1875-1908
Biography and memoirs of contemporaries, A-Z
.22 Collective
.23 Individual, A-Z
Chinese-Japanese War, 1894-1895
.4 Sources and documents
765 General works
Personal narratives
.3 Collective
.4 Individual, A-Z
768 Reform Movement, 1898
771 Boxer Rebellion, 1899-1901
773 Hsuan-tung, 1908-1912
.2 General special
Biography and memoirs of contemporaries
.22 Collective
.23 Individual, A-Z
Revolution of 1911-1912
.32 Sources and documents
.4 General works
.42 General special
Personal narratives
.5 Collective
.52 Individual, A-Z
.55 Local, A-Z
Republic, 1912-1949. 20th century
.83 Periodicals. Societies
.89 Sources and documents
.94 Historiography
774 General works
775.4 Military history
.5 Naval history
.7 Political history
.8 Foreign and general relations
776 Biography (Collective)
.4 1912-1928
.6 General special
Biography and memoirs
.8 Collective
Individual
Sun, Yat-sen
Writings
777.A2 Collected works. By date
.A25 Selected works. By date
.A3 Autobiography
.A4 Letters. By date
.A5 Speeches. By date
.A597-Z Biography and criticism
.15 Others, A-Z
.2 Revolution, 1913
.25 Revolution, 1915-1916
.36 Warlord period, 1916-1928
.46 Northern Expedition, 1926-1928
.462 Tsinan Incident, 1928
.47 1928-1937
.48 General special
Biography and memoirs

.487 Collective
.488 Individual, A-Z
e.g. Chiang, Kai-shek, 1887-1975
.5 Chinese-Japanese Conflict, 1931-1933
.51 Shanghai Invasion, 1932
.5134 Long March, 1934-1935
.514 Sian Incident, 1936
.518 1937-1945
.519 General special
Biography and memoirs
.5194 Collective
.5195 Individual, A-Z
Sino-Japanese Conflict, 1937-1945
.52 Sources and documents
.53 General works
Personal narratives
.5314 Collective
.5315 Individual, A-Z
.5316 Individual campaigns, battles, A-Z
.533 Other topics, A-Z
.A35 Aerial operations
.A86 Atrocities
.B55 Biological warfare
.C47 Children
.I53 Indemnity and reparation
.M3 Marco Polo Bridge Incident, 1937
.P76 Propaganda
.P82 Public opinion
.P825 By country, A-Z
.S65 Spies. Secret service
.U53 Underground movements
.534 Southern Anhui Incident, 1941
.535 1945-1949
Civil War, 1945-1949
.537 Sources and documents
.538 Historiography
.54 General works
.5425 Individual campaigns, battles, A-Z
Personal narratives
.543 Collective
.5435 Individual, A-Z
People's Republic, 1949-
1949-1976
Including comprehensive works on the People's Republic
.545 Periodicals. Societies
.546 Congresses
.547 Sources and documents
.549 General works
.65 Military history
.7 Naval history
.75 Political history
.8 Foreign and general relations
Biography and memoirs
778.A1A-Z Collective
.A2-Z Individual, A-Z
.7 Cultural Revolution, 1966-1969
1976-
779.15 Periodicals. Societies
.16 Congresses

.17 Sources and documents
.2 General works
.24 Military history
.25 Naval history
.26 Political history
.27 Foreign and general relations
Biography and memoirs
.28 Collective
.29 Individual, A-Z
Local history and description
Manchuria
783 History
By period
.4 Early to 1800
.7 19th-20th centuries
League of Nations Commission of Enquiry (The Lytton Commission)
.L4C6 Memoranda presented by China. By date
.L4J3 Memoranda presented by Japan. By date
.L42 Summary. Report. By date
.L42C6 China's discussion. By date
.L42J3 Japan's discussion. By date
.L43 Verdict of the League. By date
.L45 Summary and discussions by individual authors, A-Z
.8 Mukden Incident, 1931
784 1932-1945
.2 1945-
Tibet
General works. History and description
785.A5-Z Through 1950
786 1951-
Outer Mongolia. Mongolian People's Republic
798.5 History
.62 Political history. Foreign and general relations
By period, see the specific period
.63 Relations with individual countries,A-Z
By period
.65 Early
.75 20th century
Taiwan
.92 Periodicals. Societies
.94 Congresses
.945 Sources and documents
History
799.48 Study and teaching
.5 General works
.6 Biography (Collective)
General special
.615 Military history
.62 Political history
For specific periods, see the period
.625 Foreign and general relations
Class general works on the diplomatic history of a period with the period. For works on relations with a specific country regardless of period, see DS799.63
.63 Relations with individual countries, A-Z
By period
.65 Early to 1895
.654 Military history

.656 Political history
.658 Foreign and general relations
.7 1895-1945
.714 Military history
.716 Political history
.718 Foreign and general relations
.72 Biography and memoirs
.A2 Collective
.A3-Z Individual, A-Z
.8 1945-1975
Including works on Taiwan since 1945
.814 Military history
.816 Political history
.818 Foreign and general relations
.82 Biography and memoirs
.A2 Collective
.A3-Z Individual
.83 1975-
Biography and memoirs
.832 Collective
.833 Individual

JAPAN

801 Periodicals. Societies
802 Congresses
803 Sources and documents
History
834 Biography (Collective)
.1 Rulers. Imperial family
.5 Houses, noble families, A-Z
.95 Study and teaching
General special
838 Military history
For individual campaigns and engagements, see the specific period
By period
.5 Early to 1868
.7 1868-
839 Naval history
For individual campaigns and engagements, see the specific period
By period
.5 Early to 1868
.7 1868-
Political and diplomatic history
For specific periods, see the period
840 Sources and documents
841 General works
842 Early
845 Foreign and general relations
Class general works on the diplomatic history of a period with the period. For works on relations with a specific country regardless of period, see DS849
849 Relations with individual countries, A-Z
United States, see E183.8+
By period
850 Earliest to 1600
851 To 1185
857 1185-1603
859 Kamakura period, 1185-1333
864 Muromachi period, 1336-1573

868 Period of civil wars, 1480-1603
.6 Foreign and general relations
Japanese invasions of Korea, 1592-1598, see DS913.4
871 Tokugawa period, 1600-1868. Edo period
.7 Foreign and general relations
.77 1600-1709
Biography and memoirs
872.A1 Collective
.A2-Z Individual
874 1709-1853
Biography and memoirs
876 Collective
877 Individual, A-Z
881 1790-1853
.3 1853-1868
.45 Foreign and general relations
.5 Biography and memoirs, A-Z
.8 Perry expedition to Japan, 1853-1854
.83 Civil War, 1868-1689. Boshin War
.84 Individual campaigns, battles
.9 Modern, 1868-
.96 Foreign and general relations
.97 Biography (Collective)
Meiji (Mutsuhito), 1868-1912
882 General works on reign
War with China, see DS765+
Russo-Japanese War, see DS516+
.6 Foreign and general relations
Biography and memoirs
.7 Meiji (Mutsuhito)
883 Collective
884 Individual, A-Z
20th century
.5 Periodicals. Societies
885 General works
.48 Foreign and general relations
.5 Biography and memoirs
886 Taisho (Yoshihito), 1912-1926
887 Period of World War I
Showa (Hirohito), 1926-
888.2 General works on reign
.25 General special
.5 1926-1945
Cf. D731+, World War II
889 1945-
.15 General special
.16 Allied occupation, 1945-1952
.2 Propaganda in other countries
.3 Individual countries, A-Z
e.g. .U6 United States
.5 Foreign and general relations
Biography and memoirs
.7 Royal family (General)
.8 Hirohito
.9 Contemporaries, A-Z
1980-
.3 Foreign and general relations
Local history and description
Kyushu region

894.99 Prefectures, subregions, etc., A-Z
e.g. Okinawa
Covers only the Okinawa, Miyako, and Yaeyama groups of islands. For the Ryukyu archipelago, see Ryukyu Islands
.O375 History
By period
.O3765 Early to 1600
.O377 1600-1868
.378 1868-1945
.3785 1945-
895 Other regions, A-Z
e.g. Ryukyu Islands
.R95 History
By period
.R97 Early to 1879
.R975 1879-1945
.R98 1945-1972
.R985 1972-

KOREA

Class here general works on Korea and South Korea; for North Korea, see DS930+

901 Periodicals. Societies
.62 Sources and documents
Ethnography
904.52 National characteristics
History
905 Biography (Collective)
.2 Rulers, kings
.5 Houses, noble families
.52 Individual, A-Z
.55 Statesmen
.9 Study and teaching
General works
907.14 Through 1800
.16 1801-1976
.18 1977-
General special
Military history
For individual campaigns or engagements, see the special period
909 Sources and documents
.2 General works
Naval history
For individual campaigns or engagements, see the special period
.5 Sources and documents
.7 General works
Political history
For specific periods, see the period
.95 Sources and documents
910 General works
Foreign and general relations
Class works on the diplomatic history of a period with the period. For works on relations with a specific country regardless of period, see DS910.2
.16 Sources and documents
.18 General works
.2 Relations with individual countries, A-Z
United States, see E183.8+

	By period
911.2	Early to 935
.31	Military history
.35	Political history
.37	Foreign and general relations
912.2	Koryo period, 935-1392
.31	Military history
.35	Political history
.37	Foreign and general relations
.42	Mongolian invasions, 1231-1270
	I (Yi) dynasty, 1392-1910
913	Periodicals. Societies
.15	Sources and documents
.2	General works
.31	Military history
.35	Political history
.37	Foreign and general relations
	Biography and memoirs
.39	Collective
.392	Individual, A-Z
.4	Japanese invasions, 1592-1598
.62	Manchu invasions, 1627-1637
915.2	19th century. 1864-1910
.31	Military history
.35	Political history
.37	Foreign and general relations
	Biography and memoirs
.49	Collective
.5	Individual, A-Z
	20th century
.56	Periodicals. Societies
.572	Sources and documents
916	General works
.35	Political history
.37	Foreign and general relations
.5	Biography and memoirs, A-Z
	e.g. .R5 Rhee, Syngman
.54	Japanese rule, 1910-1945
.55	General special
	Biography and memoirs
.57	Collective
.58	Individual, A-Z
917	1945-
.35	Political history
.37	Foreign and general relations
	Biography and memoirs
.4	Collective
.42	Individual, A-Z
.52	Allied occupation. 1945-1948
.7	1948-1950
.8	Political history
.82	Foreign and general relations
	War and intervention, 1950-1953
	Including military operations
918.A1	Periodicals
	Sources and documents
.A2-4	Serials
.A5-55	Nonserials
.A56-Z	General works

.2 Individual campaigns, battles, A-Z
.8 Foreign participation
By country
919 United States
.2 Canada
.3 Great Britain
.4 Turkey
.5 China
.7 Other, A-Z
920.A2 Naval operations
.A3-Z Individual engagements, ships
.2.A2 Aerial operations
.2.A3-Z By country
.8 Atrocities
.9 Germ warfare charges
921 Prisoners and prisons
.25 Repatriation
.3 Relief work. Refugees
.4 Religious aspects
.5 Other topics, A-Z
.D4 Destruction and pillage
.G8 Guerrillas
.M5 Missing persons
.S7 Spies. Secret service
.S8 Individual, A-Z
.W64 Women
.6 Personal narratives, A-Z
.7 Armistice
.8 Reconstruction
1960-
922 Periodicals. Societies
.15 Sources and documents
.2 General works
.35 Political history
.37 Foreign and general relations
Biography and memoirs
.4 Collective
.42 Individual, A-Z
North Korea. Democratic People's Republic, 1948-
930 Periodicals. Societies
.6 Sources and documents
History
Biography
934 Collective
.5 Rulers
.55 Statesmen
.6 Individual, A-Z
.7 Historiography
.8 Study and teaching
935 General works
General special
.31 Military history
Political history
.4 Sources and documents
.5 General works
.55 General special
Foreign and general relations
.6 Sources and documents
.65 General works

.7 Relations with individual countries, A-Z

(DT) AFRICA

GENERAL

1 Periodicals. Societies. Sources and documents
.5 Congresses. Conferences
History
18 Biography (Collective)
.8 Study and teaching
20 General works
21 General special
.5 Military history
By period, see the specific period
By period
History and description
25 Early through 1500
26 1501-1700
27 1701-1800
28 1801-1884
29 1884-1945
30 1945-1960
.5 1960-
31 Political and diplomatic history. Partition. Colonies and possessions
By period, see the specific period
Relations with individual countries
Under each:
.0 General
.1 General special
.3 Early through 1800
.5 1801-1960
.7 1960-
32 Great Britain
33 France
34 Germany
35 Italy
36 Portugal
37 Spain
38 United States
.9 Other, A-Z
e.g. .S65 Soviet Union
39 Red Sea Coast. Red Sea Region

EGYPT

43 Periodicals. Societies. Sources
History
76 Biography (Collective)
.93 Study and teaching
77 General works
80 General special
81 Military history
By period, see the specific period
82 Political history. Foreign and general relations
Class general works on the political and diplomatic history of a period with the period. For works on relations with an individual country regardless of period, see DT82.5
.5 Relations with individual countries, A-Z
By period
83 Ancient and early to 638 A.D.
.A2 Through 1800

.A3-Z	1801-
85	3400-1580 B.C.
87	1580-1150 B.C.
88.5	Period of Jewish captivity
91	Persian rule, 525-332 B.C.
92	Alexander and Ptolemies, 332-30 B.C.
.A2	Through 1800
.A3-Z	1801-
93	Roman rule, 30 B.C.-638 A.D.
.A2	Through 1800
.A3-Z	1801-
94	Modern
95	Muslims, 638-1798
.5	638-1250
	Conquest. Omayyads. Abbasids, 638-868
96	1250-1517. Mamelukes
.3	Biography and memoirs
	.A2A-Z Collective
	.A3-Z Individual
97	1517-1798. Turkish rule
100	1798-1879. 19th century
	Biography and memoirs
	.A2A-Z Collective
	.A3-Z Individual
103	1798-1805
104	Mohammed Ali, 1805-1848
.5	Ibrahim, 1848
.7	Abbas I, 1848-1854
105	Mohammed Said, 1854-1863
106	Ismail, 1863-1879
107	1879-1952
.2	Biography and memoirs
	.A2A-Z Collective
	.A3-Z Individual
.3	Tewfik, 1879-1892
.4	Arabi Pasha, 1882
.6	Abbas II, 1892-1914
.7	Hussein Kamil, 1914-1917
.8	Fuad I, 1917-1936
.82	Faruq I, 1936-1952
	Republic, 1952-
.821	Periodicals. Societies
.823	Sources and documents
.825	General works
.8265	Military history
.827	Political history
.8275	Foreign and general relations
.828	Biography and memoirs
	.A2A-Z Collective
	.A3-Z Individual
	By period
.83	Nasser, Gamal Abdel, 1952-1970
.85	Sadat, Anwar, 1970-1981
.87	1981-
	Local history and description
	Cities, towns
154	Other, A-Z
	e.g. .S9 Suez (Isthmus and Canal)

SUDAN

154.1 Periodicals. Societies
.32 Sources and documents
History
155.4 Biography (Collective)
.42 Rulers, kings
.46 Statesmen
.55 Study and teaching
General works
.58 Through 1800
.6 1801-
General special
.64 Military history
For specific periods, see the period
.7 Political history
For specific periods, see the period
Foreign and general relations
Class general works on diplomatic history of a period with the period. For works on relations with an individual country regardless of period, see DT155.9
.78 Sources and documents
.8 General works
.9 Relations with individual countries, A-Z
By period
156 Early to 641
.3 641-1820
.4 1821-
.5 19th century
.6 1881-1899. Mahdiyah. Gordon. Kitchener
.7 1900-1955
Republic, 1956-
157 Periodicals. Societies
.2 Sources and documents
.3 General works
.43 Military history
.5 Political history
.6 Foreign and general relations
Biography and memoirs
.63 Collective
.65 Individual, A-Z
.67 Civil War, 1956-1972
Including Southern Sudan question
Local history and description
159.6 Provinces, regions, A-Z
e.g. .S73 Southern Region

NORTH AFRICA (GENERAL)

160 Periodicals. Societies
167 History
By period
168 Carthaginian period
170 Roman period, 146 B.C.-439 A.D.
171 Vandals, 439-534
172 Byzantine period
173 Arab conquest
174 16th-18th centuries
176 19th-20th centuries

NORTHWEST AFRICA (GENERAL)

179.2 Periodicals. Societies
.9 History

BARBARY STATES

Including Libya, Tunisia, Algeria and Morocco (Collectively)

181 Periodicals
183 Biography (Collective)
194 History
197 Political history. Foreign and general relations
Class general works on the political and diplomatic history of a period with the period. For works on relations with an individual country regardless of period, see DT197.5
.5 Relations with individual countries, A-Z
By period
198 Early to 647
199 647-1516
201 1516-1830
202 16th century
204 19th-20th century
Libya
211 Periodicals
History
224 General works
227 Political history. Foreign and general relations
Class general works on the political and diplomatic history of a period with the period. For works on relations with an individual country regardless of period, see DT227.5
.5 Relations with individual countries, A-Z
By period
228 Early to 642
229 642-1551
231 1551-1912
War with the United States, see E335
233 1801-1912
234 Turco-Italian War, 1911-1912
235 1912-1951
.5 1951-1969
236 1969-
Tunisia
241 Periodicals. Societies
243 Biography (Collective)
History
254 General works
257 Political history. Foreign and general relations
Class general works on the political and diplomatic history of a period with the period. For works on relations with an individual country regardless of period, see DT257.5
.5 Relations with individual countries, A-Z
By period
258 Early to 647
259 647-1516
261 1516-1830
262 16th century
263 1830-1881. 19th century
Biography and memoirs
.75 Collective
.76 Individual, A-Z
French Protectorate, 1881-1957

.9 Periodicals. Societies
.95 Sources and documents
264 General works
.26 Military and naval history
.27 Political history
.28 Foreign and general relations
Biography and memoirs
.29 Collective
.3 Individual, A-Z
Republic, 1957-
.35 Periodicals. Societies
.37 Sources and documents
.4 General works
.45 Military and naval history
.46 Political history
.47 Foreign and general relations
Biography and memoirs
.48 Collective
.49 Individual, A-Z
Algeria
271 Periodicals. Societies
History
284 General works
287 Political history. Foreign and general relations
Class general works on the political and diplomatic history of a period with the period. For works on relations with an individual country regardless of period, see DT287.5
.5 Relations with individual countries, A-Z
By period
288 Early to 647
289 647-1516
291 1516-1830
292 16th century
294 1830-1901
War with the United States, see E335
.5 1901-1945
.7 Biography and memoirs, A-Z
295 1945-1962
Including the Algerian Revolution
.3 Biography and memoirs, A-Z
.5 1962-
.55 Biography and memoirs, A-Z
Morocco
301 Periodicals. Societies
History
313.75 Biography (Collective)
314 General works
316 Military and naval history
317 Political history. Foreign and general relations
Class general works on the political and diplomatic history of a period with the period. For works on relations with an individual country regardless of period, see DT317.5
.5 Relations with individual countries, A-Z
By period
318 Early to 647
319 647-1516
321 1516-1830
322 16th century
323.5 Ismail, 1672-1727

324 1830-1955
Biography and memoirs
.9 Collective
.92 Individual, A-Z
1955-
325 Periodicals. Societies
.2 Sources and documents
.4 General works
.6 Military history
.7 Political history
.8 Foreign and general relations
Biography and memoirs
.9 Collective
.92 Individual, A-Z
330 Spanish Morocco
Including Ifni; Northern and Southern Zones
Sahara
333 History and description

CENTRAL AFRICA. SUB-SAHARAN AFRICA

348 Periodicals. Societies
349.2 Sources and documents
History
Study and teaching, see DT19.8
352.5 General works
.6 Biography and memoirs
By period
.65 Early
.7 Colonial
.8 Independent
353 Political and diplomatic history
.5 Relations with individual countries, A-Z
356 West Central Africa.
360 Niger River
East Central (Lake Region)
History
Biography and memoirs
362 Collective
363 Emin Pasha. Exploration and relief expedition
.2 Other individual, A-Z
.3 General works

EASTERN AFRICA

365 Periodicals. Societies
.13 Sources and documents
.5 History
General special
.59 Political history
For specific periods, see the period
.62 Foreign and general relations
Class general works on the diplomatic history of a period with the period. For works on relations with an individual country regardless of period, see DT365.63
.63 Relations with individual countries, A-Z
By period
.65 Early to 1884
.7 1884-1960
Biography and memoirs
Class biography under individual country except for those persons who are associated with more than one country or

who inhabited a region that does not correspond to a modern jurisdiction
.74 Collective
.75 Individual, A-Z
.8 1960-
Northeast Africa
Including Sudan, Ethiopia, Somalia and Djibouti (Collectively)
367 Periodicals. Societies
.5 History
General special
.59 Political history
For specific periods, see the period
.62 Foreign and general relations
Class general works on the diplomatic history of a period with the period. For works on relations with an individual country regardless of period, see DT367.63
.63 Relations with individual countries, A-Z
By period
.65 Early to 1900
.75 1900-1974
Biography and memoirs
Class biography under individual country except for those persons who are associated with more than one country or who inhabited a region that does not correspond to a modern jurisdiction.
.76 Collective
.77 Individual, A-Z
.8 1974-
Ethiopia. Abyssinia
371 Periodicals. Societies
History
.8 Study and teaching
381 General works
382.3 Political history. Foreign and general relations
Class general works on political and diplomatic history of a period with the period. For works on relations with an individual country, see DT382.5
.5 Relations with individual countries, A-Z
By period
383 Early through 1500
384 16th-18th centuries
386 19th-20th centuries
.3 Theodore II, 1855-1868
.7 John IV, 1872-1889
Biography and memoirs of contemporaries
.72 Collective
.73 Individual, A-Z
387 Menelik II, 1889-1913
.3 War with Italy, 1895-1896
.5 Lij Yasu, 1913-1916
.6 Waizeru Zauditu and Ras Taffari Makonnen, 1916-1928
.7 Haile Selassie I, 1928-1974
.8 Italo-Ethiopian War, 1935-1936
Documents
.A2 League of Nations
.A3-5 Italy
.A6 Ethiopia
.A7 Other countries, A-Z
.A8-Z General works. By author

.92 Biography and memoirs of contemporaries
.A2A-Z Collective
.A3-Z Individual
.95 1974-
.952 Somali-Ethiopian Conflict, 1977-
Biography and memoirs
.953 Collective
.954 Individual, A-Z
Eritrea
391 Periodicals. Societies
394 History
By period
.5 Early to 1890
395 1890-1941. Italian domination
.3 1941-1952. British administration
.5 1952-1962. Federation with Ethiopia
397 1962- . Annexation to Ethiopia
Including civil war and liberation movements
Somalia. Somaliland
Including Italian and British Somaliland
401 Periodicals. Societies
.15 Sources and documents
History
.6 Biography (Collective)
403 General works
General special
403.25 Political history
By period, see the specific period
.3 Foreign and general relations
Class general works on the diplomatic history of a period with the period. For works on relations with an individual country regardless of period, see DT403.4
.4 Relations with individual countries, A-Z
By period
.5 Early to 1889
Including Egyptian occupation and activities of the British East Africa Company
Biography and memoirs
.6 Collective
.7 Individual, A-Z
404 1885-1941. British Somaliland
Biography and memoirs
.2 Collective
.3 Individual, A-Z
405 1889-1941. Italian Somaliland
Biography and memoirs
.2 Collective
.3 Individual, A-Z
406 1941-1960. British military administration. United Nations Trusteeship
Biography and memoirs
.2 Collective
.3 Individual, A-Z
407 1960-
For Somali-Ethiopian Conflict, see DT387.952
Biography and memoirs
.2 Collective
.3 Individual, A-Z
Djibouti. French Territory of the Afars and Issas. French Somaliland

411 Periodicals. Societies
.13 Sources and documents
.5 History
General special
.62 Foreign and general relations
Class general works on the diplomatic history of a period with the period. For works on relations with an individual country regardless of period, see DT411.63
.63 Relations with individual countries, A-Z
By period
.65 Early to 1883
.75 1883-1977
Biography and memoirs
.76 Collective
.77 Individual, A-Z
.8 1977- . Independent
Biography and memoirs
.82 Collective
.83 Individual, A-Z
East Africa. British East Africa
Including Uganda, Kenya, and Tanzania (Collectively)
421 Periodicals. Societies
.2 Sources and documents
History
430 Biography (Collective)
431 General works
432 General special
By period
Early to 1960, see DT431
.5 1960-
Uganda
433.2 Periodicals. Societies
.213 Sources and documents
History
.252 Biography (Collective)
.257 General works
.26 Political history
By period, see the period
.262 Foreign and general relations
Class general works on the diplomatic history of a period with the period. For works on relations with an individual country regardless of period, see DT433.263
.263 Relations with individual countries, A-Z
By period
.265 Early to 1890
Biography and memoirs
.266 Collective
.267 Individual, A-Z
.27 1890-1962
Biography and memoirs
.272 Collective
.273 Individual, A-Z
.275 1962-1979
Biography and memoirs
.279 Collective
.28 Individual, A-Z
.282 1962-1971
.283 1971-1979. Amin regime
Including Uganda-Tanzania War, 1978-1979

.285 1979-

Biography and memoirs

.286 Collective

.287 Individual, A-Z

Kenya

.5 Periodicals. Societies

.513 Sources and documents

History

.552 Biography (Collective)

.557 General works

General special

.559 Political history

By period, see the period

.562 Foreign and general relations

Class general works on the diplomatic history of a period with the period. For works on relations with an individual country regardless of period, see DT433.563

.563 Relations with individual countries, A-Z

By period

.565 Early to 1886

Biography and memoirs

.566 Collective

.567 Individual, A-Z

.57 1886-1920

Biography and memoirs

.572 Collective

.573 Individual, A-Z

.575 1920-1963

.576 Biography and memoirs

.A2A-Z Collective

.A3-Z Individual

.577 Mau Mau movement

.58 1963-

.582 Biography and memoirs

.A2A-Z Collective

.A3-Z Individual, A-Z

.583 1963-1978

.584 1978-

Tanzania. Tanganyika. German East Africa

436 Periodicals. Societies

History

.5 Biography (Collective)

444 General works

General special

445 Political history

By period, see the period

.3 Foreign and general relations

Class general works on the diplomatic history of a period with the period. For works on relations with an individual country regardless of period, see DT445.5

.5 Relations with individual countries, A-Z

By period

447 Early and colonial

.2 Biography and memoirs

.A2A-Z Collective

.A3-Z Individual

448 Independent, 1961-1964

.2 1964- . United Republic of Tanzania

.25 Biography and memoirs

.A2A-Z Collective
.A3-Z Individual
449 Regions, etc., A-Z
e.g. Zanzibar
.Z26 History
By period
.Z27 Early to 1890
.Z28 1890-1963
.Z29 1963-
For works about Zanzibar and Tanganyika treated together, see DT448.2
Rwanda. Ruanda-Urundi
450 Periodicals. Societies
.28 History
General special
.3 Political history
By period, see the period
.32 Foreign and general relations
Class general works on the diplomatic history of a period with the period. For works on relations with an individual country regardless of period, see DT450.33
.33 Relations with individual countries, A-Z
By period
.34 Early to 1890
.37 1890-1916. German domination
.4 1916-1945. Belgian domination
.425 1945-1962. United National mandate. Belgian administration
Biography and memoirs
.426 Collective
.427 Individual, A-Z
.43 Civil War, 1959-1962
.435 1962-
Biography and memoirs
.436 Collective
.437 Individual, A-Z
Burundi
.5 Periodicals. Societies
.68 History
General special
.7 Political history
By period, see the period
.72 Foreign and general relations
Class general works on the diplomatic history of a period with the period. For works on relations with an individual country regardless of period, see DT450.73
.73 Relations with individual countries, A-Z
By period
.74 Early to 1890
.77 1890-1916. German domination
.8 1916-1945. Belgian domination
.84 1945-1962. United Nations mandate. Belgian administration
Biography and memoirs
.842 Collective
.843 Individual, A-Z
.85 1962-
Biography and memoirs
.852 Collective
.853 Individual, A-Z

WEST AFRICA

470 Periodicals. Societies
.2 Sources and documents
475 History
By period
476 Early to 1884
.2 1884-1960. Colonial period
.5 1960- . Independent
British West Africa
491 Periodicals. Societies
502 History
503 Other
Local
Gambia
509.5 History
General special
.62 Foreign and general relations
Class general works on the diplomatic history of a period with the period. For works on relations with an individual country regardless of period, see DT509.63
.63 Relations with individual countries, A-Z
By period
.65 Early to 1894
.7 1894-1965
.8 1965-
Ghana. Gold Coast
.97 Periodicals. Societies
510.5 History
.6 Biography (Collective)
.62 Political history. Foreign and general relations. Nationalism
Class general works on the political and diplomatic history of a period with the period. For works on relations with an individual country regardless of period, see DT510.63
.63 Relations with individual countries, A-Z
By period
511 Early to 1957
Republic, 1957-
512 1957-1979
Biography and memoirs
.2 Collective
.3 Individual, A-Z
.32 1979-
Biography and memoirs
.33 General works
.34 Individual, A-Z
Nigeria
515 Periodicals. Societies
.13 Sources and documents
History
.53 Biography (Collective)
.556 Study and teaching
.57 General works
General special
.585 Military history
By period, see the period
.59 Political history
By period, see the period
.62 Foreign and general relations
Class general works on the diplomatic history of a period

with the period. For works on relations with an individual country regardless of period, see DT515.63
.63 Relations with individual countries, A-Z
By period
.65 Early to 1861
.7 1861-1914
.75 1914-1960
Biography and memoirs
.76 Collective
.77 Individual, A-Z
.8 1960- . Independence
Biography and memoirs
.82 Collective
.83 Individual, A-Z
.832 1960-1966
.834 1966-1975
.836 1967-1970. Civil War
Cf. DT515.9.E3, Eastern Region
.838 1975-1979
.84 1979-
.9 Local history and description, A-Z
e.g. .E3 Eastern Region. Biafra
For the Civil War, 1967-1970, see DT515.836
Sierra Leone
516 Periodicals. Societies
.13 Sources and documents
.5 History
General special
.6 Political history
By period, see the period
.62 Foreign and general relations
Class general works on the diplomatic history of a period with the period. For works on relations with an individual country regardless of period, see DT516.63
.63 Relations with individual countries, A-Z
By period
.65 Early to 1787
.7 1787-1961
Biography and memoirs
.719 Collective
.72 Individual, A-Z
.8 1961- . Independent
Biography and memoirs
.819 Collective
.82 Individual, A-Z
French West Africa. West Sahara. Sahel
521 Periodicals. Societies
532 History
By period
.4 To 1884
.5 1884-1960
.6 1960-
Local history
Benin. Dahomey
541 Periodicals. Societies
.13 Sources and documents
.5 General works
General special

.62 Foreign and general relations
Class general works on the diplomatic history of a period with the period. For works on relations with an individual country regardless of period, see DT541.63
.63 Relations with individual countries, A-Z
By period
.65 Early to 1894
.75 1894-1960
.8 1960-
Biography and memoirs
.82 Collective
.83 Individual, A-Z
.84 1960-1972
.845 1972-
Guinea
543 Periodicals. Societies
.13 Sources and documents
.5 History
General special
.59 Political history
.62 Foreign and general relations
Class general works on the diplomatic history of a period with the period. For works on relations with an individual country regardless of period, see DT543.63
.63 Relations with individual countries, A-Z
By period
.65 Early to 1895
.75 1895-1958. French colony
Biography and memoirs
.76 Collective
.77 Individual, A-Z
.8 1958-
Biography and memoirs
.819 Collective
.82 Individual, A-Z
e.g. .T68 Toure, Ahmed Sekou
.822 1958-1984
Biography and memoirs
.823 Collective
.824 Individual, A-Z
.825 1984-
Biography and memoirs
.826 Collective
.827 Individual, A-Z
Ivory Coast
545 Periodicals. Societies
.13 Sources and documents
.57 History
General special
.59 Political history
By period, see the period
.62 Foreign and general relations
Class general works on the diplomatic history of a period with the period. For works on relations with an individual country regardless of period, see DT545.63
.63 Relations with individual countries, A-Z
By period
.7 Early to 1893
.75 1893-1960

Biography and memoirs
.76 Collective
.77 Individual, A-Z
.8 1960- . Independent
Biography and memoirs
.82 Collective
.83 Individual, A-Z
French-speaking Equatorial Africa
Gabon
546.1 Periodicals. Societies
.113 Sources and documents
.15 History
General special
.162 Foreign and general relations
Class general works on the diplomatic history of a period with the period. For works on relations with an individual country regardless of period, see DT546.163
.163 Relations with individual countries, A-Z
By period
.165 Early to 1886
.175 1886-1960
.18 1960- . Independent
Biography and memoirs
.182 Collective
.183 Individual, A-Z
Congo (Brazzaville)
.2 Periodicals. Societies
.213 Sources and documents
.25 History
General special
.262 Foreign and general relations
Class general works on the diplomatic history of a period with the period. For works on relations with an individual country regardless of period, see DT546.263
.263 Relations with individual countries, A-Z
By period
.265 Early to 1910
.275 1910-1960
.28 1960- . Independent
Biography and memoirs
.282 Collective
.283 Individual, A-Z
Central African Republic
.3 Periodicals. Societies
.313 Sources and documents
.35 History
General special
.362 Foreign and general relations
Class general works on the diplomatic history of a period with the period. For works on relations with an individual country regardless of period, see DT546.363
.363 Relations with individual countries, A-Z
By period
.365 Early to 1910
.37 1910-1960. French colony
.375 1960- . Independent
.38 1960-1979

Biography and memoirs
.382 Collective
.383 Individual, A-Z
e.g. .B64 Bokassa I
.384 1979-
Chad
.4 Periodicals. Societies
.413 Sources and documents
.457 History
General special
.46 By period, see the period
.462 Foreign and general relations
Class general works on the diplomatic history of a period with the period. For works on relations with an individual country regardless of period, see DT546.463
.463 Relations with individual countries, A-Z
By period
.47 Early to 1910
.475 1910-1960
.48 1960- . Independent
Biography and memoirs
.482 Collective
.483 Individual, A-Z
Niger
547 Periodicals. Societies
.13 Sources and documents
.5 History
General special
.62 Foreign and general relations
Class general works on the diplomatic history of a period with the period. For works on relations with an individual country regardless of period, see DT547.63
.63 Relations with individual countries, A-Z
By period
.65 Early to 1900
.75 1900-1960
.8 1960- . Independent
Biography and memoirs
.82 Collective
.83 Individual, A-Z
Senegal
549 Periodicals. Societies
.13 Sources and documents
.5 History
General special
.59 Political history
By period, see the period
.62 Foreign and general relations
Class general works on the diplomatic history of a period with the period. For works on relations with an individual country regardless of period, see DT549.63
.63 Relations with individual countries, A-Z
By period
.7 Early to 1895
.75 1895-1960
.8 1960- . Independent
Biography and memoirs
.82 Collective

.83 Individual, A-Z
Mali. Mali Federation. French Sudan
551 Periodicals. Societies
.13 Sources and documents
.5 History
General special
.6 Political history
By period, see the period
.62 Foreign and general relations
Class general works on the diplomatic history of a period with the period. For works on relations with an individual country regardless of period, see DT551.63
.63 Relations with individual countries, A-Z
By period
.65 Early to 1898
.7 1898-1959
.8 1959-
Including Mali Federation (1959-1960) and Mali Republic (1960-)
Biography and memoirs
.819 Collective
.82 Individual, A-Z
Mauritania
554 Periodicals. Societies
.13 Sources and documents
.57 History
General special
.59 Political history
By period, see the period
.62 Foreign and general relations
Class general works on the diplomatic history of a period with the period. For works on relations with an individual country regardless of period, see DT554.63
.63 Relations with individual countries, A-Z
By period
.65 Early to 1920
.75 1920-1960
.8 1960- . Independent
Including Moroccan annexation claims
Biography and memoirs
.82 Collective
.83 Individual, A-Z
Burkina Faso. Upper Volta
555 Periodicals. Societies
.13 Sources and documents
.57 History
General special
.59 Political history
By period, see the period
.62 Foreign and general relations
Class general works on the diplomatic history of a period with the period. For works on relations with an individual country regardless of period, see DT555.63
.63 Relations with individual countries, A-Z
By period
.65 Early to 1897
.75 1897-1960
.8 1960-
Biography and memoirs

.82 Collective
.83 Individual, A-Z
Cameroon. Cameroun. Kamerun
Formerly German West Africa
561 Periodicals. Societies
562 Sources and documents
572 History
General special
573.3 Foreign and general relations
Class general works on the diplomatic history of a period with the period. For works on relations with an individual country regardless of period, see DT573.5
.5 Relations with individual countries, A-Z
By period
574 Early to 1960
.5 1960-
576 1960-1982
Biography and memoirs
.5 Collective
577 Individual, A-Z
578 1982-
Biography and memoirs
.3 Collective
.4 Individual, A-Z
Togo. Togoland
582 Periodicals. Societies
.13 Sources and documents
.5 History
General special
.59 Political history
By period, see the period
.62 Foreign and general relations
Class general works on the diplomatic history of a period with the period. For works on relations with an individual country regardless of period, see DT582.63
.63 Relations with individual countries, A-Z
By period
.65 To 1884
.7 1884-1960. Partition
.75 French Togoland (1922-1960)
British Togoland (1922-1957),see DT511+
.8 1960- . Independent
Biography and memoirs
.819 Collective
.82 Individual, A-Z
Portuguese-speaking West Africa
591 Periodicals. Societies
602 History
Local history and description
Guinea-Bissau. Portuguese Guinea
613 Periodicals. Societies
.13 Sources and documents
.5 History
General special
.6 Political history
By period, see the period
.62 Foreign and general relations
Class general works on the diplomatic history of a period with the period. For works on relations with an

individual country regardless of period, see DT613.63
.63 Relations with individual countries, A-Z
By period
.65 Early to 1879
.75 1879-1974
Biography and memoirs
.752 Collective
.76 Individual, A-Z
e.g. .C3 Cabral, Amilcar
.77 1879-1963
.78 1963-1974. Revolution
.8 1974- . Independent
Biography and memoirs
.82 Collective
.83 Individual, A-Z
619 Spanish West Africa
Equatorial Guinea. Spanish Guinea
620 Periodicals. Societies
.13 Sources and documents
.5 History
General special
.6 Political history
By period, see the period
.62 Foreign and general relations
Class general works on the diplomatic history of a period with the period. For works on relations with a specific country regardless of period, see DT620.63
.63 Relations with individual countries, A-Z
By period
.65 Early to 1778
.7 1778-1968
.74 1968-
.75 1968-1979
Biography and memoirs
.76 Collective
.77 Individual, A-Z
.8 1979-
Biography and memoirs
.82 Collective
.83 Individual, A-Z
Liberia
621 Periodicals. Societies
631 History
General special
.5 Political history
By period, see the period
632 Foreign and general relations
Class general works on the diplomatic history of a period with the period. For works on relations with an individual country regardless of period, see the period
.5 Relations with individual countries, A-Z
By period
633 Early to 1847. American Colonization Society settlements
634 1847-1944
Biography and memoirs
.2 Collective
.3 Individual, A-Z
635 1944-1971
Biography and memoirs

.2 Collective
636 Individual, A-Z
e.g. .T8 Tubman, William V.S.
.2 1971-1980
Biography and memoirs
.3 Collective
.4 Individual, A-Z
e.g. .T63 Tolbert, William R.
.5 1980-
Biography and memoirs
.52 Collective
.53 Individual, A-Z
Zaire. Congo (Democratic Republic). Belgian Congo
641 Periodicals. Societies
652 History
General special
653 Political history
By period, see the period
.3 Foreign and general relations
Class general works on the diplomatic history of a period with the period. For works on relations with an individual country regardless of period, see DT653.5
.5 Relations with individual countries, A-Z
By period
654 Early. Congo Kingdom
655 Congo Free State, 1885-1908
657 Belgian Congo, 1908-1960
.2 Biography and memoirs
.A2A-Z Collective
.A3-Z Individual
.22 Civil War, 1960-1965
Including assassination of Patrice Lumumba
.25 1965-
Including Shaba Invasions of 1977-1978, and Kolwezi Massacre, 1978
663 Biography and memoirs (Collective)

SOUTHERN AFRICA

1001 Periodicals. Societies
1009 Sources and documents
1054 Ethnography
1055 National characteristics
1056 Ethnic and race relations
History
1064 Biography (Collective)
1070 Study and teaching
General works
1075 Through 1900
1077 1901-1975
1079 1976-
General special
1096 Military history
By period, see the period
Political history
By period, see the period
1098 Sources and documents
1099 General works
Foreign and general relations
Class general works on the diplomatic history of a period with

the period. For works on relations with an individual country regardless of period, see DT1105
1101 Sources and documents
1103 General works
1105 Relations with individual countries, A-Z
By period
1107 Early to 1890
1890-1975
1125 Periodicals. Societies
1126 Sources and documents
1130 General works
1135 Military history
1137 Political history
1139 Foreign and general relations
1142 Biography and memoirs (Collective)
1144 1890-1918
1145 1918-1945
1147 1945-1976
1975-
1155 Periodicals. Societies
1159 Sources and documents
1165 General works
1170 Military history
1172 Foreign and general relations
1174 Biography and memoirs (Collective)
1177 National liberation movements

ANGOLA

1251 Periodicals. Societies
1259 Sources and documents
1325 History
General special
1348 Political history
By period, see the period
1353 Foreign and general relations
Class general works on the diplomatic history of a period with the period. For works on relations with an individual country regardless of period, see DT1355
1355 Relations with individual countries, A-Z
By period
1357 Early to 1648
1373 1648-1885
1385 1885-1961
Biography and memoirs
1387 Collective
1388 Individual, A-Z
1961-1975. Revolution
1398 Periodicals. Societies
1400 Sources and documents
1402 General works
1405 Military history
1406 Individual events, battles, A-Z
1408 Foreign participation
1410 By region or country, A-Z
e.g. .C83 Cuba
Biography and memoirs
1415 Collective
1417 Individual, A-Z
1420 1975- . Independent

Biography and memoirs
1422 Collective
1424 Individual, A-Z
e.g. .S38 Savimbi, Jonas
1426 Agostinho Neto. 1975-1979
1428 Civil War, 1975-
1430 South African Invasion, 1975-1976
1432 Coup d'etat, 1977
1434 Jose Eduardo dos Santos, 1979-
1436 South African incursions, 1978-
Including Lusaka Accord

NAMIBIA. SOUTH-WEST AFRICA

1501 Periodicals. Societies
1509 Sources and documents
1554 Ethnography
1555 Ethnic and race relations
1556 Apartheid
History
1575 General works
General special
1579 Political history
By period, see the period
1583 Foreign and general relations
Class general works on the diplomatic history of a period with the period. For works on relations with an individual country regardless of period, see DT1585
1585 Relations with individual countries, A-Z
By period
1587 Early to 1884
1601 Afrikaner Trek, 1878-1879
1603 1884-1915. German South-West Africa
1625 1915-1946. South African Mandate under authority of the League of Nations
1638 1946- . United Nations Trusteeship. South African administration
Biography and memoirs
1640 Collective
1641 Individual, A-Z
1643 Cancellation of South African Mandate, 1966
1645 Armed struggle for national liberation, 1966-
Including South African raids on SWAPO installations in Angola, 1978-
1647 Turnhalle conference, 1975-
1648 Transitional government, 1985-

SOUTH AFRICA

1701 Periodicals. Societies
1709 Sources and documents
1754 Ethnography
1755 National characteristics
1756 Race relations
1757 Apartheid
1758 Blacks
1760 Homelands (General)
1762 Afro-Afrikaner relations
History
1774 Biography (Collective)
1780 Study and teaching
General works
1784 Through 1983

1787	1984-
	General special
1796	Military history
	By period, see the period
1798	Political history
	By period, see the period
1803	Foreign and general relations
	Class general works on the diplomatic history of a period with the period. For works on relations with an individual country regardless of period, see DT1805
1805	Relations with individual countries, A-Z
	By period
1807	Early to 1652
1813	1652-1795
1828	1795-1836. British possession
1837	Frontier Wars, 1811-1878
1840	British settlers, 1820
1848	1836-1910
	Biography and memoirs
1850	Collective
1851	Individual, A-Z
1853	Great Trek, 1836-1840
1889	Jameson Raid, 1895
	South African War, 1899-1902
1890	Periodicals. Societies
1892	Sources and documents
1894	Causes
1896	General works
	Military history
1900	British Army
1904	Afrikaner Army
1908	Individual events, battles, A-Z
1911	Foreign participation
1913	By region or country, A-Z
	Personal narratives
1915	Collective
1916	Individual, A-Z
1918	Special topics, A-Z
	.P75 Prisoners and prisons
	.P83 Public opinion
1920	Peace of Vereeniging, 1902
1921	1902-1910
1924	1910-1961
	Biography and memoirs
1926	Collective
1927	Individual, A-Z
	e.g. .S68 Smuts, Jan Christiaan
1928	1910-1948
1938	1948-1961. Afrikaner domination
1941	Sharpeville Massacre, 1960
1945	1961- . Republic of South Africa
	Biography and memoirs
1948	Collective
1949	Individual, A-Z
	e.g. .S58 Sisulu, Walter
1951	Hendrik Verwoerd, 1961-1966
	Life and administration
1953	National liberation and armed struggle by ANC begins, 1961-
1957	Balthazar Johannes Vorster, 1966-1978

Life and administration
1959 Soweto uprising, 1976
1963 Pieter Willem Botha, 1978-
Life and administration
1967 State of emergency, 1985-
Local history and description
Cape Province. Cape of Good Hope
2039 History
By period
Early to 1795, see DT1807+
2042 1795-1872
2046 1872-1910
2051 1910-
Orange Free State
2109 History
By period
2112 Early to 1854
For Great Trek, see DT1853
2124 1854-1910
2142 1910-
Natal
2229 History
By period
2232 Early to 1843
2250 1843-1910
2270 1910-
Transvaal. South African Republic
2329 History
By period
2332 Early to 1857
2347 1857-1880
2354 War of 1880-1881. First Anglo-Afrikaner War
2357 Personal narratives
2359 Individual events, battles, A-Z
2361 1881-1910
2375 1910-

BOTSWANA. BECHUANALAND

2421 Periodicals. Societies
2428 Sources and documents
2475 History
General special
2478 Political history
By period, see the period
By period
2483 Early to 1885
2490 1885-1966. Bechuanaland Protectorate. British Bechuanaland
Biography and memoirs
2492 Collective
2493 Individual, A-Z
2496 1966- . Independent
2500 Seretse Khama, 1966-1980
Life and administration
2502 Quett Masire, 1980-
Life and administration

LESOTHO. BASUTOLAND

2541 Periodicals. Societies
2549 Sources and documents
2615 History

General special
2618 Political history
By period, see the period
2623 Foreign and general relations
Class general works on the diplomatic history of a period with the period. For works on relations with an individual country regardless of period, see DT2625
2625 Relations with individual countries, A-Z
By period
2630 Early to 1868
2636 Wars with Orange Free State, 1865-1868
2638 1868-1966. Basutoland
2644 Cape rule, 1871-1884
2652 1966- . Independent
Biography and memoirs
2654 Collective
2655 Individual, A-Z
2657 1966-1986. Leabula Jonathan
Life and administration
2658 South African raid on Maseru, 1982
2660 1986-
Including 1986 coup d'etat

SWAZILAND

2701 Periodicals. Societies
2709 Sources and documents
2765 History
General special
2768 Political history
By period, see the period
2773 Foreign and general relations
Class general works on the diplomatic history of a period with the period. For works on relations with an individual country regardless of period, see DT2775
2775 Relations with individual countries, A-Z
By period
2777 To 1889
2788 1889-1968. British rule
2793 Transvaal rule, 1894-1902
2797 1968- . Independent
2802 1968-1982. Sobhuza II
Life and reign
2804 1982-1986
2806 1986- . Mswati III
Life and reign

BRITISH CENTRAL AFRICA. FEDERATION OF RHODESIA AND NYASALAND

Including works on Malawi, Zambia, and Zimbabwe treated together. For each country treated separately, see the country

2858 History
By period
Early to 1890, see DT2937
2860 1890-1923
Including general works on the British South Africa Company. For activities of the Company in specific countries, see the country
2862 1923-1953. British Protectorates
2864 1953-1964. Federation of Rhodesia and Nyasaland

ZIMBABWE. SOUTHERN RHODESIA

2871 Periodicals. Societies

2879 Sources and documents
2910 Ethnography
2912 Ethnic and race relations
History
2925 General works
General special
2928 Political history
By period, see the period
2933 Foreign and general relations
Class general works on the diplomatic history of a period with the period. For works on relations with an individual country regardless of period, see DT2935
2935 Relations with individual countries, A-Z
By period
2937 Early to 1890
2959 1890-1923. British South Africa Company administration
Biography and memoirs
2961 Collective
2963 Individual, A-Z
2972 1923-1953. British Crown Colony
Biography and memoirs
2974 Collective
2975 Individual, A-Z
2976 1953-1965
Biography and memoirs
2978 Collective
2979 Individual, A-Z
2981 1965-1980
Biography and memoirs
2983 Collective
2984 Individual, A-Z
e.g. .N56 Nkomo, Joshua
.S65 Smith, Ian
2986 Unilateral Declaration of Independence (UDI), 1965
2988 1972-1979. War of National Liberation. Second Chimurenga
2990 Personal narratives
2992 Individual events, battles, A-Z
2994 1979-1980
2996 1980- . Independent
Biography and memoirs
2998 Collective
2999 Individual, A-Z
3000 Mugabe, Robert, 1980-
Life and administration

ZAMBIA. NORTHERN RHODESIA

3031 Periodicals. Societies
3035 Sources and documents
3071 History
General special
3073 Political history
By period, see the period
3075 Foreign and general relations
Class general works on the diplomatic history of a period with the period. For works on relations with an individual country regardless of period, see DT3077
3077 Relations with individual countries, A-Z
By period
3079 Early to 1890

3091 1891-1924
3103 1924-1953. British Protectorate
Biography and memoirs
3105 Collective
3106 Individual, A-Z
3108 1953-1964
Cf. DT2864
Biography and memoirs
3110 Collective
3111 Individual, A-Z
e.g. .W45 Welensky, Roy
3113 1964- . Independent
3119 Kenneth Kaunda, 1964-
Life and administration

MALAWI. NYASALAND

3161 Periodicals. Societies
3167 Sources and documents
3201 History
General special
3204 Political history
By period, see the period
3206 Foreign and general relations
Class general works on the diplomatic history of a period with the period. For works on relations with an individual country, see DT3208
3208 Relations with individual countries, A-Z
By period
3211 To 1891
3216 1891-1953
3227 1953-1964
Cf. DT2864
3232 1964- . Independent
Biography and memoirs
3234 Collective
3235 Individual, A-Z
3236 Hastings Kamuzu Banda, 1964-
Life and administration

MOZAMBIQUE

3291 Periodicals. Societies
3293 Sources and documents
History
3337 General works
General special
3339 Political history
By period, see the period
3341 Foreign and general relations
Class general works on the diplomatic history of a period with the period. For works on relations with an individual country, see DT3343
3343 Relations with individual countries, A-Z
By period
3345 Early to 1505
3350 1505-1698
3361 1698-1891
3376 1891-1975
Biography and memoirs
3378 Collective
3379 Individual, A-Z

e.g. .M66 Mondlane, Eduardo
3387 National liberation struggle, 1964-1975
3389 1975- . Independent
Biography and memoirs
3391 Collective
3392 Individual, A-Z
1975-1986
3393 Samora Machel, 1975-1986
Life and administration
3394 1976- . Insurgency movement
3396 Nkomati Accord, 1984
3398 Joaquim Chissano, 1986-
Life and administration

(DU) OCEANIA. SOUTH SEAS

GENERAL

1 Periodicals. Societies
History
28.2 Study and teaching
.3 General works
29 Political history. Foreign and general relations. Control of the Pacific
By country
30 United States
32 Canada
40 Great Britain
50 France
60 Germany
65 Spain
66 Japan

AUSTRALIA

80 Periodicals. Sources and documents
History
.5 Study and teaching
110 General works
General special
112.3 Military history
By period, see the period
.4 Naval history
By period, see the period
113 Foreign and general relations
Class general works on the diplomatic history of a period with the period. For works on relations with an individual country regardless of period, see DU113.5
.5 Relations with individual countries, A-Z
By period
1788-1900
114 Sources and documents
115 General works
.2 Biography and memoirs
.A2A-Z Collective
.A3-Z Individual
116 1900-1945
.18 Foreign and general relations
.2 Biography and memoirs
.A2A-Z Collective
.A3-Z Individual
1945-
.9 Sources and documents

117 General works
.15 Military history
.17 Political history
.18 Foreign and general relations
Biography and memoirs
.19 Collective
.2 Individual, A-Z

NEW ZEALAND

400 Periodicals. Societies
History
420 General works
.12 To 1840
.16 1840-1876
.22 1876-1918
.26 1918-1945
Biography and memoirs
.27 Collective
.28 Individual, A-Z
.32 1945-
Biography and memoirs
.33 Collective
.34 Individual, A-Z
.5 Military history
421 Political history. Foreign and general relations
.5 Relations with individual countries, A-Z
422 Biography (General)

490 Melanesia (General)
500 Micronesia (General)
510 Polynesia (General)

SMALLER ISLAND GROUPS

Most of the islands are not included in this guide. For information about the history of these islands, see DU520+ in the complete LC classification schedules

739 New Guinea
Papua New Guinea
Including works on Papua and New Guinea (Territory)
740.5 History
.62 Political history. Foreign and general relations
By period, see the period
.63 Relations with individual countries, A-Z
By period
.7 Colonial
.75 20th century
.8 Independent
Irian Jaya. Irian Barat. Netherlands New Guinea
744.5 History

Tables for individual biography
Use the tables below to subarrange numbers and cutters for individual persons under each class number of the D schedule providing for biography and memoirs. Exception: for class numbers designating individual reigns, including the life of the ruler, cutter only for the author of the work without further subarrangement.
One number
.A2 Collected works. By date (1)
.A25 Selections. By date (1)
Including quotations

.A3 Autobiography, diaries. By date
.A4 Letters. By date
.A5 Speeches, essays. By date
.A6-Z Biography and criticism

Cutter number
.xA2 Collected works. By date (1)
.x25 Selections. By date (1)
.xA3 Autobiography, diaries. By date
.xA4 Letters. By date
.xA5 Speeches, essays. By date
.xA6-Z Biography and criticism

(1)Class here collected or selected works by the individual on general historical or political topics pertaining to the period during which he lived. For his collected or selected works on a special topics, see the topic.

(E) AMERICA

GENERAL

11 Periodicals. Societies
History
16.5 Study and teaching
18 General works
By period
.82 1492-1810
.83 1810-1900
.85 1901-

NORTH AMERICA

31 Periodicals. Societies
45 History
46 General special

DISCOVERY OF AMERICA AND EARLY EXPLORATIONS

101 General works
103 Pre-Columbian period
111 Christopher Columbus
Including biography
118 Voyages. Journal of Columbus
121 Post-Columbus period. To 1607
123 Spanish and Portuguese
125 Individual explorers, A-Z
127 English
129 Individual explorers, A-Z
131 French
133 Individual explorers, A-Z
135 Other, A-Z

UNITED STATES

General

151 Periodicals. Societies
169.1 Civilization. Intellectual life
Including national characteristics, ideals, Americanization
By period
1866-1945, see D169.1
.12 1945-

History

171 Periodicals
172 Societies

.9 Congresses
175 Historiography
Biography of historians
.45 Collective
.5 Individual, A-Z (Table I)
.8 Study and teaching
176 Biography (Collective)
.1 Presidents
Biography of each president is classed with his administration
.47 Staff
.49 Vice-Presidents
178 General works
.1 Textbooks
179 General special
.5 Historical geography
Including boundaries (general), the frontier, territorial expansion, regionalism, etc.
181 Military history
Including military history and biography of several battles or wars
Class works on individual wars with the war. For works on the military history of the 20th century, see E745
182 Naval history
Including naval history and biography of several battles or wars
Class works on individual wars with the war. For works on the naval history of the 20th century, see E746
183 Political history
By period, see the period
.7 Foreign and general relations
Class general works on the diplomatic history of a period with the period. For works on relations with an individual country regardless of period, see E183.8
.8 Relations with individual countries, A-Z
Works on relations between the United States and another country always class with the United States. For works on relations between the United States and a region larger than a country, see the region
.9 Other (not A-Z)
Colonial history, 1607-1775
186 Periodicals. Societies
Patriotic societies, e.g. Colonial Dames of America, class in separate numbers which are not included in this guide
187.5 Biography (Collective)
188 General works
By period
191 1607-1689
195 1689-1775
196 King William's War, 1689-1697
197 Queen Anne's War, 1702-1713
198 King George's War, 1744-1748
199 French and Indian War, 1755-1763
The Revolution, 1775-1783
210 Periodicals. Historical societies
Patriotic and hereditary societies class in separate numbers which are not included in this guide
204 Congresses
Biography
206 Collective
Especially military and naval leaders
Statesmen, see E302.5

207 Individual, A-Z (Table I)
Including lives of military and naval commanders and staff officers
208 General works
209 General special
Political history
Including causes and origins of the Revolution
210 General works (other than contemporary)
211 Contemporary works
221 Declaration of Independence
Including collective biography of the signers
230 Military history (General)
249 Diplomatic history
Including Treaty of Paris, 1783
.3 Foreign public opinion
271 Naval history
275 Personal narratives
.A2A-Z Collective
.A3-Z Individual
Revolution to the Civil War, 1775-1861
301 General works
Including general works covering the period 1765-1865
302 Collected works of American statesmen (Revolutionary group), A-Z (Table III)
e.g. .F8 Franklin, Benjamin
.J44 Jefferson, Thomas
Washington, George, see E312.7+ (not included in this guide)
.1 Political history
Biography (late eighteenth century)
.5 Collective
.6 Individual, A-Z (Table II)
e.g. .H23 Hancock, John
By period
303 1775-1789
310 1789-1809
.7 Foreign and general relations
311 Washington's administrations, 1789-1797
312 Biography of Washington. Washington as President
.7 Special
313 Foreign and general relations
314 Jay's Treaty, 1795
321 John Adams' administration, 1797-1801
322 Biography of Adams (Table II)
For his collected works, see E302+
323 Troubles with France, 1796-1800
331 Jefferson's administrations, 1801-1809
332 Biography of Jefferson. Jefferson as President (Table II)
.2 Special
.45 International diplomacy
Treaty negotiator with European powers, 1784; Minister to France, 1785-1789
333 Purchase of Louisiana, 1803
335 War with Tripoli, 1801-1805
336 Neutral trade and its restriction, 1800-1810
.5 Embargo, 1807-1809
337.5 Nineteenth century (General)
Early nineteenth century, 1801/1809-1845
.8 Collected works of American statesmen, A-Z (Table III)
e.g. .C55 Clay, Henry
.J3 Jackson, Andrew

338 General works
Including manifest destiny, territorial expansion, etc.
Biography
339 Collective
340 Individual, A-Z (Table II)
Jefferson's administrations, see E331+
341 Madison's administrations, 1809-1817
342 Biography of Madison (Table II)
For his collected works, see E302+
War of 1812
351 Periodicals. Societies
Biography
353 Collective
.1 Individual, A-Z (Table I)
354 General works
355 Military operations, 1812-1815
357 Political history
.2 Right of search and impressment
.9 Effects of the war
358 Diplomatic history
360 Naval history
.5 Secret service, Spies
.6 Individual spies, A-Z
361 Personal narratives, A-Z
365 War with Algeria, 1815
371 Monroe's administrations, 1817-1825
372 Biography of Monroe (Table II)
His collected works in E302+
374 Foreign and general relations
376 John Quincy Adams' administration, 1825-1829
377 Biography of Adams (Table II)
For his collected works, see E337.8+
Foreign and general relations, see E376
381 Jackson's administrations, 1829-1837
382 Biography of Jackson (Table II)
For his collected works, see E337.8+
384.8 Foreign and general relations
386 Van Buren's administration, 1837-1841
387 Biography of Van Buren (Table II)
For his collected works, see E337.8
391 W.H. Harrison's administration, 1841
396 Tyler's administration, 1841-1845
397 Biography of John Tyler (Table II)
For his collected works, see E337.8
War with Mexico, 1845-1848
Biography
Chiefly military and naval leaders
403 Collective
.1 Individual, A-Z (Table I)
404 General works
405 Military operations
407 Political history
Including causes of the war
408 Diplomatic history
Including Treaty of Guadalupe Hidalgo, 1848 and Mexican cessions of 1848
410 Naval history
411 Personal narratives
Cf. E410, Sailors' narratives

Middle nineteenth century, 1845/1848-1861
415.6 Collected works of American statesmen, A-Z (Table III)
e.g. .J65 Johnson, Andrew
.7 General works
Biography
.8 Collective
.9 Individual, A-Z (Table II)
416 Polk's administration, 1845-1849
417 Biography of Polk (Table II)
For his collected works, see E415.6+
421 Taylor's administration, 1849-1850
422 Biography of Z. Taylor (Table II)
For his collected works, see E415.6+
426 Fillmore's administration, 1850-1853
427 Biography of M. Fillmore (Table II)
429 Foreign and general relations
430 Pierce's administration, 1853-1857
Including diplomatic history
432 Biography of Pierce (Table II)
For his collected works, see E415.6+
436 Buchanan's administration, 1857-1861
437 Biography of James Buchanan (Table II)
For his collected works, see E337.8+
Civil War period, 1861-1865
456 Lincoln's administrations, 1861-1865
457 Biography of Abraham Lincoln. Lincoln as President (Table II)
.2 Special
458 Political history (Contemporary works)
459 Political history (Later works)
Civil War, 1861-1865
461 Periodicals
Biography
467 Collective
.1 Individual, A-Z (Table II)
468 General works
469 Diplomatic history
.8 Foreign public opinion
470 Military history (General)
591 Naval history (General)
1865-1900
660 Collected works of American statesmen, A-Z (Table III)
e.g. .R7 Roosevelt, Theodore
661 General works
.7 Foreign and general relations
Biography
Including biography of statesmen of the early twentieth century
663 Collective
664 Individual, A-Z (Table II)
666 Johnson's administration, 1865-1869
667 Biography of Andrew Johnson (Table II)
For his collected works, see E415.6+
669 Foreign and general relations
671 Grant's administrations, 1869-1877
672 Biography of Ulysses Grant (Table II)
673 Foreign and general relations
681 Hayes' administration, 1877-1881
682 Biography of Hayes (Table II)
686 Garfield's administration, 1881
691 Arthur's administration, 1881-1885

692 Biography of Chester Arthur (Table II)
For his collected works, see E660+
696 Cleveland's first administration, 1885-1889
697 Biography of Grover Cleveland (Table II)
701 Benjamin Harrison's administration, 1889-1893
702 Biography of Harrison (Table II)
706 Cleveland's second administration, 1893-1897
711 McKinley's first administration, 1897-1901
.6 Biography of William McKinley (Table II)
For his collected works, see E660+
713 Foreign and general relations
Including imperialism, territorial expansion, etc.
War of 1898 (Spanish-American War)
Biography
714.5 Collective
.6 Individual, A-Z (Table II)
715 General works
717 Military operations (General)
721 Political history
Including public opinion
723 Diplomatic history. Treaty of Paris, 1898
727 Naval history
Twentieth century
740 Periodicals. Societies
.5 Sources and documents
742.5 Collected works of American statesmen, A-Z (Table III)
For works of statesmen to 1921, see E660; for works of statesmen prominent after 1960, see E838.5
e.g. .E37 Eisenhower, Dwight David
.R6 Roosevelt, Franklin Delano
743 Political history
.5 Un-American activities
Including propaganda, espionage, subversive activities
744 Foreign and general relations
.5 Cultural relations
Including the work and publications of the Department of State's Office of Information and Educational Exchange; the U.S. Information Agency; Voice of America, etc.
745 Military history
Including military biography
746 Naval history
Including naval biography
Biography
747 Collective
748 Individual, A-Z (Table II)
e.g. .D22 Dawes, Charles Gates
.D868 Dulles, John Foster
751 McKinley's second administration, 1901
756 Theodore Roosevelt's administrations, 1901-1909
Including foreign and general relations
757 Biography of Roosevelt (Table II)
For his collected works, see E660+
761 Taft's administration, 1909-1913
Biography of Taft (Table II)
For his collected works, see E660+
766 Wilson's administrations, 1913-1921
767 Biography of Woodrow Wilson (Table II)
For his collected works, see E660+
768 Foreign and general relations

780 Period of World War I
Cf. D570; D619
784 1919-1933. Harding-Coolidge-Hoover era
785 Harding's administration, 1921-1923
786 Biography of Warren Harding (Table II)
For his collected works, see E742.5+
791 Coolidge's administrations, 1923-1929
792 Biography of Calvin Coolidge (Table II)
For his collected works, see E742.5+
801 Hoover's administration, 1929-1933
802 Biography of Herbert Hoover (Table II)
For his collected works, see E742.5+
806 F.D. Roosevelt's administrations, 1933-1945
Including the Roosevelt and Truman administrations treated together
807 Biography of F. D. Roosevelt (Table II)
813 Truman's administration, 1945-1953
814 Biography of Harry Truman (Table II)
835 Eisenhower's administrations, 1953-1961
836 Biography of Dwight Eisenhower (Table II)
Later twentieth century, 1961-
838 Periodicals. Societies
.3 Sources and documents
.5 Collected works of American statesmen, A-Z (Table III)
e.g. .K4 Kennedy, John Fitzgerald
839 General works
.5 Political history
.8 Un-American activities
Including propaganda, espionage, subversive activities, etc.
840 Foreign and general relations
.2 Cultural relations
Including the work of the U.S. Information Agency; the Voice of America, etc.
.4 Military, naval, air force history
.5 Biography, A-Z (Table I)
Biography (General)
.6 Collective
.8 Individual, A-Z (Table II)
e.g. .K4 Kennedy, Robert F.
.K58 Kissinger, Henry
841 Kennedy's administration. 1961-1963
Including Cuban missile crisis
842.A-Z8 Biography of John Kennedy (Table II)
For his collected works, see E838.5+
846 Johnson's administrations, 1963-1969
847 Biography of Lyndon Johnson (Table II)
For his collected works, see E838.5+
855 Nixon's administrations, 1969-1974
856 Biography of Richard Nixon (Table II)
For his collected works, see E838.5+
860 Watergate Affair
865 Ford's administration, 1974-1977
866 Biography of Gerald Ford (Table II)
For his collected works, see E838.5+
872 Carter's administration, 1977-
873 Biography of Jimmy Carter (Table II)
For his collected works, see E838.5+
Iran Hostage Crisis, 1979-1981, see E183.8.I55
876 Reagan's administration, 1981-1989
877 Biography of Ronald Reagan (Table II)

For his collected works, see E838.5+
Korean Airlines Incident, 1983, see E183.8.S65
881 Bush administration, 1989-
882 Biography of George Bush (Table II)

United States Tables

Table I—Individual Biography

.x	Cutter for the individual
.xA2	Collected works. By date
.xA25	Selected works. By date Including quotations
.xA3	Autobiography, diaries. By date
.xA4	Letters. By date
.xA5	Speeches, essays. By date
.xA6-Z	Biography and criticism

Table II—Individual Biography

1 no.	Cutter no.	
	.x	Cutter for the individual
.A3	.xA3	Autobiography, diaries By date
.A4	.xA4	Letters. By date
.A6-Z	.xA6-Z	Biography and criticism

Table III—Collected Works of American Statesmen

.x	Collected works. By date
.x2	Selected works. By date Including quotations
.x4	Essays. By date
.x5	Speeches. By date
.x9	Special libraries. By author, A-Z

(F) CANADA. LATIN AMERICA

1001 Periodicals. Societies
1005 Biography (Collective)
1021 Social life and customs. Civilization.
Intellectual life
Including national characteristics
History
1022 Periodicals
1025 Study and teaching
1026 General works
Including political history
General special
1027 French-Canadians. French Canadian question
1028 Military history
By period, see the period
.5 Naval history
By period, see the period
1029 Foreign and general relations
Class general works on the diplomatic history of a period with the period. For works on relations with an individual country regardless of period, see F1029.5
.5 Relations with individual countries, A-Z
By period
Including political history and biography
1030 1603-1763. New France
1031 1763-
.5 19th century
1032 1763-1867

1033 1867-
1034 1914-1945
.2 1945-
.3 Biography
.A2 Collective
.A3-Z Individual (Table)
e.g. .D5 Diefenbaker, John

MEXICO

1201 Periodicals. Societies
1205 Biography (Collective)
1210 Social life and customs. Civilization. Intellectual life
Including national characteristics
History
.5 Study and teaching
1226 General works
Including political history
General special
1227.5 Military and naval history
By period, see the period
1228 Foreign and general relations
Class general works on the diplomatic history of a period with the period. For works on relations with an individual country regardless of period, see F1228.5
.5 Relations with individual countries, A-Z
By period
Including political history and biography
.98 1492-1519
1229 1519-1824
1230 1519-1535
1231 1535-1810. New Spain
.5 1810-
1232 1810-1849
Including Wars of Independence, 1810-1821
.5 1849-1858/1861
1233 1849/1861-1867
Including European intervention and empire of Maximilian
.5 1867-1910
1234 1910-1946
Including Mexican Revolution
1235 1946-1970
.5 Biography
.A2 Collective
.A3-Z Individual (Table)
1236 1970-
Biography
.5 Collective
.6 Individual, A-Z (Table)
Regions, states, etc.
1249 Boundaries
Including Guatemala boundary

LATIN AMERICA (GENERAL)

1401 Periodicals. Societies
1402 Organization of American States
Class publications on special subjects with the subject
Documents
.A1-29 Serial
Nonserial
.A3 By the organization. By date

.A4A-Z By subordinate bodies, A-Z
.A5-Z Nonofficial publications
Including official publications by individual countries of the Organization
Pan American Union
Official publications
1403 By the organization
.3 By subordinate bodies
.5 Nonofficial publications
.9 Congresses
Pan-American conferences
1404 Early congresses
1405 International American Conference. By date
.A1-7 Official publications
.A8-Z4 Reports of delegations from participating countries. By country, A-Z
.Z5A-Z Works about the conference
.3 Inter-American Conference for the Maintenance of Peace, Buenos Aires, 1936
.5 Meeting of Consultation of Ministers of Foreign Affairs of American States. By date
.9 Other conferences, congresses, etc., A-Z
1407 Biography (Collective)
1408.3 Social life and customs. Civilization.
Intellectual life
Including national characteristics
.4 Inter-American Council for Education, Science and Culture
History
.9 Study and teaching
1410 General works
Including political history
By period
Including political history and biography
1411 Early to 1601
1412 1601-1830. Wars of Independence
1413 1830-1898
1414 20th century. 1898-
.2 1948-
1415 Foreign and general relations
Class general works on the diplomatic history of a period with the period. For works on relations with an individual country regardless of period, see F1416+
1416 Relations with individual countries, A-Z
United States, see F1418
1418 Relations with the United States

CENTRAL AMERICA

1421 Periodicals. Societies
History
1435.8 Study and teaching
1436 General works
Including political history
General special
Military and naval history
.5 By period, see the period
.7 Foreign and general relations
Class general works on the diplomatic history of a period with the period. For works on relations with an individual country regardless of period, see F1436.8

.8 Relations with individual countries, A-Z
By period
Including political history and biography
1437 1502-1821
1438 1821-1950
1439 1951-1979
Including Organization of Central American States
.5 1979-
British Honduras. Belize
1441 Periodicals. Societies
1442.7 Biography (Collective)
1443.8 Social life and customs. Civilization. Intellectual life
Including national characteristics
History
1445.8 Study and teaching
1446 General works
Including political history
General special
.4 Foreign and general relations
Class general works on the diplomatic history of a period with the period. For works on relations with an individual country regardless of period, see F1446.5
.5 Relations with individual countries, A-Z
By period
Including political history and biography
1447 1506-1884
.5 1884-1945
1448 1945-
1449 Regions, districts, etc., A-Z
e.g. .B7 Boundaries
.B7A1-9 General works
.B7G1-9 Guatemala
.B7M1-9 Mexico
.B7S1-9 Spain
Guatemala
1461 Periodicals. Societies
1462.7 Biography (Collective)
History
1465.8 Study and teaching
1466 General works
Including political history
General special
.1 Military and naval history
By period, see the period
.2 Foreign and general relations
.3 Relations with individual countries, A-Z
By period
.4 1523-1838
.45 1838-1945
.5 1945-1985
.7 1985-
1469 Regions, etc., A-Z
e.g. .B7 Boundaries
.B7A1-5 General
Belize, see F1449.B7
.B7A6-Z Honduras
Mexico, see F1249
El Salvador, see F1489.B7

El Salvador
1481 Periodicals. Societies
1482.7 Biography (Collective)
1483.8 Social life and customs. Civilization. Intellectual life
Including national characteristics
History
1485.8 Study and teaching
1486 General works
Including political history
General special
.1 Military and naval history
By period, see the period
.2 Foreign and general relations
Class general works on the diplomatic history of a period with the period. For works on relations with an individual country regardless of period, see F1486.3
.3 Relations with individual countries, A-Z
By period
Including political history and biography
1487 1524-1838
.5 1838-1944
1488 1944-1979
.3 1979-
Biography
.4 Collective
.42 Individual, A-Z (Table)
1489 Regions, etc., A-Z
e.g. .B7 Boundaries
.B7A1-9 General
.B7G1-9 Guatemala
.B7H1-9 Honduras

Honduras
1501 Periodicals. Societies
1502.7 Biography (Collective)
1503.8 Social life and customs. Civilization. Intellectual life
Including national characteristics
History
1505.8 Study and teaching
1506 General works
Including political history
General special
.2 Military and naval history
By period, see the period
.3 Foreign and general relations
Class general works on the diplomatic history of a period with the period. For works on relations with an individual country regardless of period, see F1506.4
.4 Relations with individual countries, A-Z
By period
1507 1502-1838
.5 1838-1933
1508 1933-1982
Biography
.2 Collective
.22 Individual, A-Z (Table)
.3 1982-
Biography
.32 Collective
.33 Individual, A-Z (Table)

1509 Regions, etc., A-Z
e.g. .B7 Boundaries
.B7A1-5 General
Guatemala, see F1469.B7
.B7A6-Z Nicaragua
El Salvador, see F1489.B7

Nicaragua
1521 Periodicals. Societies
1522.7 Biography (Collective)
1523.8 Social life and customs. Civilization. Intellectual life
Including national characteristics
History
1525.8 Study and teaching
1526 General works
Including political history
General special
.1 Military and naval history
By period, see the period
.2 Foreign and general relations
Class general works on the diplomatic history of a period with the period. For works on relations with an individual country regardless of period, see F1526.22
.22 Relations with individual countries, A-Z
By period
.25 1522-1838
.27 1838-1909
.3 1909-1937
1527 1937-1979
1528 1979-
Biography
.2 Collective
.22 Individual, A-Z (Table)
1529 Regions, A-Z
e.g. .B7 Boundaries
.B7A1-5 General
.B7A6-Z Costa Rica
Honduras, see F1509.B7

Costa Rica
1541 Periodicals. Societies
1542.7 Biography (Collective)
1543.8 Social life and customs. Civilization. Intellectual life
Including national characteristics
History
1545.8 Study and teaching
1546 General works
Including political history
General special
.2 Military and naval history
By period, see the period
.3 Foreign and general relations
Class general works on the diplomatic history of a period with the period. For works on relations with an individual country regardless of period, see F1546.4
.4 Relations with individual countries, A-Z
By period
1547 1502-1838
.5 1838-1948
1548 1948-1986
.2 1986-

Biography
.22 Collective
.23 Individual, A-Z (Table)
1549 Regions, etc., A-Z
e.g. .B7 Boundaries
.B7A1-29 General
Nicaragua, see F1529.B7
.B7A3-Z Panama

Panama
1561 Periodicals. Societies
1562.7 Biography (Collective)
1563.8 Social life and customs. Civilization. Intellectual life
Including national characteristics
History
1565.8 Study and teaching
1566 General works
Including political history
General special
.2 Military history
By period, see the period
.3 Foreign and general relations
Class general works on the diplomatic history of a period with the period. For works on relations with an individual country regardless of period, see F1566.4
.4 Relations with individual countries, A-Z
By period
.45 1501-1903
.5 1903-1952
1567 1952-
1569 Regions, etc., A-Z
e.g. B7 Boundaries
.B7A1-5 General
.B7A6-7 Canal Zone
.B7A8-Z Colombia
Costa Rica, see F1549.B7
.C2 Canal Zone. Panama Canal
For technical works on the construction and maintenance of the canal, see TC774+, which is not included in this guide

Caribbean area, see F2155+

WEST INDIES

1601 Periodicals. Societies
1607 Biography (Collective)
1609.5 Social life and customs. Civilization.
Intellectual life
Including national characteristics
History
1620.7 Study and teaching
1621 General works
Including political, military, and naval history
General special
Military and naval history, see F1621
.5 Foreign and general relations
1622 Relations with the United States
.5 Relations with other countries, A-Z
By period
Early to 1898, see F1621
1623 1898-

1741 Greater Antilles
Including Cuba, Haiti, Puerto Rico, Jamaica, and outlying islands treated together
Cuba
1751 Periodicals. Societies
1755 Biography (Collective)
1760 Social life and customs. Civilization. Intellectual life
Including national characteristics
History
1775 Study and teaching
1776 General works
Including political history
General special
.1 Military and naval history
.2 Foreign and general relations
Class general works on the diplomatic history of a period with the period. For works on relations with an individual country regardless of period, see F1776.3
.3 Relations with individual countries, A-Z
By period
1779 1492-1810
1781 1762-1763
Including siege of Havana and English occupation
1783 1810-1898
1784 Insurrection, 1849-1851
1785 1868-1895
1786 1898-1933
1787 1898-1933
.5 1933-1959
1788 1959- . Communist regime
Including Revolution and Bay of Pigs Invasion
Cf. E841+, Cuban missile crisis
.22 Biography
.A2 Collective
.A3-Z Individual (Table)
e.g. .C3 Castro, Fidel

Haiti
1912 Periodicals. Societies
1914 Biography (Collective)
History
1921 General works
Including political history
General special
.5 Military and naval history
By period, see the period
1922 Political and diplomatic history
Class general works on the diplomatic history of a period with the period. For works on relations with an individual country regardless of period, see F1922.5
.5 Relations with individual countries, A-Z
By period
1923 1492-1803
1924 1804-1843
1926 1843-1915
1927 1915-1950
1928 1950-1986
.2 1986-
Biography
.22 Collective

.23 Individual, A-Z (Table)
1929 Regions, etc., A-Z
e.g. .B7 Boundaries
Dominican Republic
1931 Periodicals. Societies
1933 Biography (Collective)
1935 Social life and customs. Civilization. Intellectual life
Including national characteristics
History
1937.8 Study and teaching
1938 General works
Including political history
General special
.1 Military and naval history
By period, see the period
.2 Foreign and general relations
Class general works on the diplomatic history of a period with the period. For works on relations with an individual country regardless of period, see F1938.25
.25 Relations with individual countries, A-Z
By period
.3 1492-1844
.4 1844-1930
.45 1916-1924. United States occupation
.5 1930-1961
.55 1961-
Biography
.57 Collective
.58 Individual, A-Z (Table)
1939 Regions, etc., A-Z
Boundaries, see F1929.B7
Puerto Rico
1951 Periodicals. Societies
1955 Biography (Collective)
History
1971 General works
Including political history
1972 General special
By period
1973 1493-1898. Spanish rule
1975 1898-1952. United States territory
1976 1952-
Biography
.2 Collective
.3 Individual, A-Z (Table)
2001 Lesser Antilles (Collective)
2131 British West Indies (Collective)
2133 History, 1943-
2141 Netherlands West Indies (Collective)
2151 French West Indies (Collective)
Caribbean Area
2155 Periodicals. Societies
2160 Biography (Collective)
2161 General works
2169 Social life and customs. Civilization. Intellectual life
Including national characteristics
History
2173 Study and teaching
2175 General works

2176 General special
2177 Foreign and general relations
Class general works on the diplomatic history of a period with the period. For works on relations with an individual country regardless of period, see F2178
2178 Relations with individual countries, A-Z
By period
Early through 1810, see F2161
2181 1811-
2183 1945-

SOUTH AMERICA

2201 Periodicals. Societies
2205 Biography (Collective)
Regions
2212 Andes Mountains (General)
2213 Pacific Coast
2214 Atlantic Coast
2216 Northern South America
2217 Southern South America
History
2217.6 Study and teaching
2231 General works
.5 General special
.7 Military history
By period, see the period
.8 Naval history
By period, see the period
2232 Foreign and general relations
Class general works on the diplomatic history of a period with the period. For works on relations with an individual country regardless of period, see F2232.2
.2 Relations with individual countries, A-Z
By period
2233 1498-1806
2235 1806-1830. Wars of independence
.3 Bolivar, Simon
Life and works
.36 Guayaquil meeting, 1822
.4 San Martin, Jose de
Life and correspondence
.5 Other liberators, A-Z (Table)
e.g. .R6 Rodriguez, Simon
2236 1830-
2237 1939-
Colombia
2251 Periodicals. Societies
2255 Biography (Collective)
2260 Social life and customs. Civilization. Intellectual life
Including national characteristics
History
2270.7 Study and teaching
2271 General works
Including political history
General special
.4 Military and naval history
By period, see the period
.5 Foreign and general relations
Class general works on the diplomatic history of a period

with the period. For works on relations with an individual country regardless of period, see F2271.52

.52 Relations with individual countries, A-Z

By period

2272 1499-1810

.5 1739-1742

2273 1810-

2274 1810-1822. War of Independence

2275 1822-1832

2276 1832-1886

.5 1886-1903

2277 1904-1946

2278 1946-1974

2279 1974-

Biography

.2 Collective

.22 Individual, A-Z (Table)

2281 Regions, etc., A-Z

e.g. .B7 Boundaries

.B7A1-9 General

Brazil, see F2554.C7

Costa Rica, see F1549.B7

.B7E1-9 Ecuador

Panama, see F1569.B7

.B7P1-9 Peru

Including Leticia question

Venezuela

2301 Periodicals. Societies

.5 Sources and documents

2305 Biography (Collective)

2310 Social life and customs. Civilization. Intellectual life

Including national characteristics

History

2320.7 Study and teaching

2321 General works

Including political history

General special

.1 Military and naval history

By period, see the period

.2 Foreign and general relations

Class general works on the diplomatic history of a period with the period. For works on relations with an individual country regardless of period, see F2321.3

.3 Relations with individual countries, A-Z

By period

Including political history and biography

2322 1498-1806/1810

2322.8 1806/1810-

2323 1806-1812

2324 1810-1830. War of Independence

2325 1830-1935

2326 1935-1958

2327 1958-

Biography

.5 Collective

.52 Individual, A-Z (Table)

2331 Regions, etc., A-Z

e.g. .B7 Boundaries

.B7 General

Brazil, see F2554.V4
.B72 Guyana
Colombia, see F2281.B7

Guyana. British Guiana
2361 Periodicals. Societies
History
2380.7 Study and teaching
2381 General works
Including political history
2382 General special
.3 Foreign and general relations
Class general works on the diplomatic history of a period with the period. For works on relations with an individual country regardless of period, see F2382.4
.4 Relations with individual countries, A-Z
By period
Including political history and biography
2382 1580-1803
2384 1803-1966
2385 1966-
2387 Regions, etc., A-Z
.B7 Boundaries
.B7A1-5 General
Brazil, see F2554.B8

Surinam. Dutch Guiana
2401 Periodicals. Societies
2405 Biography (Collective)
2421 History
Including political history
2422 General special
By period
Including political history and biography
2423 1604-1814
2424 1814-1950
2425 1950-
2427 Regions, etc., A-Z
.B7 Boundaries
.B7A1-5 General
Brazil, see F2554.D8
Guyana, see F2387.B7
.B7A6-Z French Guiana

French Guiana
2441 Periodicals. Societies
2445 Biography (Collective)
2461 History
Including political history
.5 General special
By period
2462 1626-1814
2463 1814-1946
2464 1947-
2467 Regions, etc., A-Z
.B7 Boundaries (General)

Brazil
2501 Periodicals. Societies
2505 Biography (Collective)
2510 Social life and customs. Civilization. Intellectual life
Including national characteristics
History

.7 Study and teaching
2521 General works
Including political history
General special
2522 Military and naval history
By period, see the period
2523 Foreign and general relations
Class general works on the diplomatic history of a period with the period. For works on relations with an individual country regardless of period, see F2523.5
.5 Relations with individual countries, A-Z
By period
Including political history and biography
2524 1500-1821
2526 1500-1548
2528 1549-1762
2529 1555-1567
2530 Spanish control, 1580-1640
2532 Dutch conquest, 1624-1654
2534 1763-1821
2535 1822-
2536 Empire, 1822-1889
2537 Republic, 1889-
Including 1889-1930, Naval revolt, 1893-1894, Conselheiro Insurrection, 1897, etc.
2538 1930-1954. Period of Vargas
.2 1954-1964
Biography
.A2 Collective
.A3-Z Individual (Table)
e.g. .G6 Goulart, Joao Belchoir Marques
.K8 Kubitschek, Juscelino
.25 1964-1985
Biography
.26 Collective
.27 Individual, A-Z (Table)
e.g. .G44 Geisel, Ernesto
.3 1985-
Biography
.4 Collective
.5 Individual, A-Z (Table)

Regions, etc., A-Z
2554 Boundaries
.A1-8 General
.A82 Argentina
.B6 Bolivia
.B8 Guyana
.C7 Colombia
.D8 Surinam
.F8 French Guiana
.P3 Paraguay
.P4 Peru
.U8 Uruguay
.V4 Venezuela
Paraguay
2661 Periodicals. Societies
2665 Biography (Collective)
2670 Social life and customs. Civilization. Intellectual life

Including national characteristics
History
2679.7 Study and teaching
2681 General works
Including political history
General special
.5 Military history
By period, see the period
2682 Foreign and general relations
Class general works on the diplomatic history of a period with the period. For works on relations with an individual country regardless of period, see F2682.5
.5 Relations with individual countries, A-Z
By period
Including political history and biography
2683 1527-1811
Including War of Independence
2684 1609-1769. Jesuit province
2686 1811-1870
2687 Paraguayan War, 1865-1870
Including individual battles
2688 1870-1938
.5 Chaco War, 1932-1935
Cf. F2691.C4, Chaco Boreal
2689 1938-
2691 Regions, etc., A-Z
e.g. .B7 Boundaries
.B7A1-5 General
.B7A6-Z Bolivia
Brazil, see F2554.P3
.C4 Chaco Boreal. Paraguayan Chaco
Uruguay
2701 Periodicals. Societies
2705 Biography (Collective)
2710 Social life and customs. Civilization. Intellectual life
Including national characteristics
History
2720.7 Study and teaching
2721 General works
Including political history
General special
.5 Military and naval history
By period, see the period
2722 Foreign and general relations
Class general works on the diplomatic history of a period with the period. For works on relations with an individual country regardless of period, see F2722.5
.5 Relations with individual countries, A-Z
By period
2723 1516-1811
2724 1811-
2725 1811-1830
Including Wars of independence and Argentine-Brazilian War
2726 1830-1904
2728 1904-1973
Including era of Batlle, 1902-1929
2729 1973-
Biography

.5 Collective
.52 Individual, A-Z (Table)
2731 Regions, etc., A-Z
e.g. .B7 Boundaries (General)
Argentina
2801 Periodicals. Societies
2805 Biography (Collective)
2810 Social life and customs. Civilization. Intellectual life
Including national characteristics
History
2830 Study and teaching
2831 General works
Including political history
General special
2832 Military and naval history
By period, see the period
2833 Foreign and general relations
Class general works on the diplomatic history of a period with the period. For works on relations with an individual country regardless of period, see F2833.5
.5 Relations with individual countries, A-Z
By period
Including political history and biography
2841 1516-1810
2843 1810-
2845 1806-1817
Including War of Independence
2846 1817-1861. Civil wars
.3 1829-1852. Period of Rosas
2847 1861-1910
2848 1910-1943
2849 1943-
Including Peron regime and biography of Juan Peron
.2 1955-
.22 Biography
.A2 Collective
.A3-Z Individual (Table)
Regions, etc.
2851 Andes Mountains
Including Chilean boundary question
2857 Boundaries
.A2 General
.B6 Bolivia
Brazil, see F2554.A82
Chaco Boreal dispute, see F2688.5
Chile, see F2851
.P2 Paraguay
.U7 Uruguay
3030 South Atlantic region
3031 Falkland Islands. Islas Malvinas
.5 Falkland Islands War, 1982
Chile
3051 Periodicals. Societies
3055 Biography (Collective)
3060 Social life and customs. Civilization. Intellectual life
Including national characteristics
History
3077 Study and teaching
3081 General works

Including political history
General special
3082 Military and naval history
By period, see the period
3083 Foreign and general relations
Class general works on the diplomatic history of a period with the period. For works on relations with an individual country regardless of period, see F3083.5
.5 Relations with individual countries, A-Z
By period
Including political history and biography
3091 1535-1810
3093 1810-
3094 1810-1824. War of Independence
3095 1824-1920
3097 War of the Pacific, 1879-1884. Tacna-Arica question
.3 Including individual battles and territorial questions growing out of the war
3098 Revolution of 1891
3099 1921-
3100 1970-
3101 Biography
.A2 Collective
.A3-Z Individual (Table)
e.g. .A4 Allende, Salvador
Regions, etc.
3139 Boundaries
.A1-4 General
Argentina, see F2851
.A5-Z Bolivia
Cf. F3097.3, Tacna-Arica question
Peru, see F3451.B73
Bolivia
3301 Periodicals. Societies
3305 Biography (Collective)
3310 Social life and customs. Civilization. Intellectual life
Including national characteristics
History
3310.7 Study and teaching
3321 General works
Including political history
General special
.1 Military history
By period, see the period
.2 Foreign and general relations
Class general works on the diplomatic history of a period with the period. For works on relations with an individual country regardless of period, see F3321.3
.3 Relations with individual countries, A-Z
By period
Including political history and biography
3322 1538-1809
3323 1809-1825. Wars of Independence
3324 1825-1884
Cf. F2876, War of the Pacific
3325 1884-1938
Cf. F2688.5, Chaco War
3326 1938-1982
3327 1982-

3341 Regions, etc., A-Z
e.g. .B7 Boundaries (General)
With individual countries, see the country
.C4 Chaco (Bolivian)
Chaco War, see F2688.5
Peru
3401 Periodicals. Societies
3405 Biography (Collective)
3410 Social life and customs. Civilization. Intellectual life
Including national characteristics
History
3430.7 Study and teaching
3431 General works
Including political history
General special
3432 Military and naval history
By period, see the period
3433 Foreign and general relations
Class general works on the diplomatic history of a period with the period. For works on relations with an individual country regardless of the period, see F3434
3434 Relations with individual countries, A-Z
By period
Including political history and biography
3442 1522-1548
3444 1548-1820
3446 1820-1829. War of Independence
.5 1829-
3447 1829-1919
Cf. F3097, War of the Pacific
3448 1919-1968
.2 1968-
Biography
.3 Collective
.4 Individual, A-Z (Table)
e.g. .V4 Velasco Alvarado, Juan
3451 Regions, etc., A-Z
.B7 Boundaries
.B7 General
.B71 Bolivia
Brazil, see F2554.P4
.B73 Chile
Cf. F3097.3, Tacna-Arica question
Colombia, see F2281.B7
.B75 Ecuador
Leticia question, see F2281.B7+
Ecuador
3701 Periodicals. Societies
3705 Biography (Collective)
3710 Social life and customs. Civilization. Intellectual life
Including national characteristics
History
3727 Study and teaching
3731 General works
Including political history
General special
.5 Military and naval history
By period, see the period
3732 Foreign and general relations

Class general works on the diplomatic history of a period with the period. For works on relations with an individual country regardless of period, see F3732.5

.5 Relations with individual countries, A-Z

By period

Including political history and biography

3733 1526-1809. Colonial period

3734 1809-1830. Wars of independence

3735 1830-

3736 1830-1895. Age of Moreno

3737 1895-1944

Including Peru-Ecuador Conflict, 1941

Cf. F2281.B7+, Leticia dispute

3738 1944-1984

Including Peru-Ecuador Conflict, 1981

.2 1984-

Biography

.3 Collective

.4 Individual, A-Z (Table)

3741 Regions, etc., A-Z

.B7 Boundaries (General)

With individual countries, see the country

Tables for individual biography

Use the tables below to subarrange numbers and cutters for individual persons under each class number of the F schedule providing for biography and memoirs. However, in cases where individual biography is classed in numbers designating individual periods two cutters are assigned, one for the name of the biographee, and one for the author.

One number

.A2	Collected works. By date (1)
.A25	Selected works. By date (1)
.A3	Autobiography, diaries.
.A4	Letters. By date
	Speeches, essays
.A49-499	Serials. By title
.A5	Monographs. By date
.A6-Z	Biography and criticism

Cutter number

.xA2	Collected works. By date (1)
.xA25	Selected works. By date (1)
.xA3	Autobiography, diaries
.xA4	Letters. By date
	Speeches, essays
.xA49-499	Serials
.xA5	Monographs. By date
.xA6-Z	Biography and criticism

(HB) ECONOMIC THEORY

195 Economics of war

Cf. HC79.D4, Economic impact of defense and disarmament

(HC) ECONOMIC HISTORY AND CONDITIONS (GENERAL)

Including economics of natural resources

10 Periodicals. Societies

21 General works

History

By period

31 Antiquity

33 Egypt
35 Orient
37 Greece
39 Rome
41 Middle Ages
42 15th century
51 Modern
.5 16th century
52 17th century
.5 18th century
53 19th century
54 20th century
56 World War, 1914-1918
Reconstruction
57.A15A-Z Periodicals. Societies
Documents
.A2 League of Nations
.A3A-Z Individual countries
Conferences
.A5 International
.A6 Other
.A62-Z General works
.3 Genoa conference, 1922
.4 Hague conference on the Soviet Union, 1922
.6 Monetary and economic conference, London, 1933
58 World War, 1939-1945
59 1945-
Developing countries
.69 Periodicals. Societies
.7 General works
.72 Special topics, A-Z
For list of topics, see HC79
Technical assistance. Economic assistance
Including aid by individual countries to several countries and aid to developing countries in general. For aid for a specific country, see the recipient country in HC95+
.8 Periodicals. Societies
60 General works
.5 United States Peace Corps
79 Special topics, A-Z
Class here general works only
For these topics in regions, countries, etc., see HC94+
.D4 Defense and disarmament, Economic impact of. Economics of war. Military-industrial complex
.E44 Economic development projects
.E5 Environmental policy
Military-industrial complex, see .D4
.O93 Outer space development
.P6 Poor. Poverty
.T4 Technological innovations. Technology transfer
.W4 Wealth
By region or country
Class here general works only
Individual industries class in HD and are not included in this guide

Tables

Use these tables for subarrangement where spans of numbers are indicated below:

10 numbers

	Documents
(1.A1-3)	Serials
(1.A4)	Administrative documents. By date
(1.A5-Z)	Periodicals. Societies
(3)	General works
(3.5)	Natural resources
	By period
(4)	Early
(5)	Later
	Local (used under countries only)
(7)	By state, etc., A-Z
(8)	By city, A-Z
(9)	Colonies
(10)	Special topics, A-Z
	For list of topics, see HC79

5 numbers

	Documents
(1.A1-3)	Serials
(1.A4)	Administrative documents. By date
(1.A5-Z)	Periodicals. Societies
(2)	General works
(2.5)	Natural resources
	By period
(2.5)	Early
(2.5)	Later
(3)	Local, A-Z (used under countries only)
(4)	Colonies
(5)	Special topics, A-Z
	For list of topics, see HC79

1 number

.A1A-Z	Periodicals. Societies
.A5-Z6	General works
.Z6A-Z	Natural resources
.Z7A-Z	Local, A-Z
.Z9A-Z	Special topics, A-Z
	For list of topics, see HC79

94	America
95	North America
	United States
101	Periodicals. Societies
103	General works
.7	Natural resources
	By period
104	Colonial
105	1776-1900
.6	1860-1869
.7	1870-1879
106	1901-1945
.2	World War, 1914-1918
.3	Reconstruction, 1919-1939
.4	World War, 1939-1945
.5	Reconstruction, 1919-1939
.6	1961-1971
.7	1971-1981
.8	1981-
111-120	Canada

121-130 Latin America
131-140 Mexico
141 Central America
142 Belize
143 Costa Rica
144 Guatemala
145 Honduras
146 Nicaragua
147 Panama
.5 Panama Canal Zone
148 El Salvador
151 West Indies. Caribbean Area. Greater Antilles
152 Bahamas
Greater Antilles (General), <u>see</u> HC151
.5 Cuba
153 Haiti
.5 Dominican Republic
154 Jamaica
.5 Puerto Rico
155.5 British West Indies
.6 Lesser Antilles
.7 Barbados
156 Leeward Islands
.5 Windward Islands
157.3 Trinidad and Tobago
.5 Netherlands Antilles
158 French West Indies
.5 Guadeloupe
.6 Martinique
161-170 South America
167 Regions, A-Z
171-180 Argentina
181-185 Bolivia
186-190 Brazil
188 Regions, states, A-Z
189 Cities, A-Z
191-195 Chile
196-200 Colombia
201-204.5 Ecuador
204.5 Special topics, A-Z
206-210 Guyana
211-215 Surinam
216-220 French Guiana
221-225 Paraguay
226-230 Peru
231-235 Uruguay
236-239.5 Venezuela
239.5 Special topics, A-Z
240 Europe
.9 Special topics, A-Z
241 European economic integration
.2 European Economic Community
For special topics, <u>see</u> HC240.9
.25 Relation to individual regions or countries, A-Z
.4 European Free Trade Association
For special topics, <u>see</u> HC240.9
243 Northern Europe. Baltic States (General)
.5 Sovet ekonomicheskoi vzaimopomoshchi. Council for Mutual Economic Aid. COMECON

For special topics, see HC244.Z9
244 Central Europe. Eastern Europe
.5 Southern Europe. Mediterranean area
246 Commonwealth of Nations
251-260 Great Britain. England
253 General works
By period
254 Middle ages
.4 1485-1600
.5 1600-1800
255 19th century
256 20th century
.2 World War, 1914-1918
.3 Reconstruction, 1919-1939
.4 World War, 1939-1945
.5 1945-1964
.6 1964-
Local
For England, see HC251+
257 By region, country, etc., A-Z
258 By city, A-Z
260.5 Ireland
261-270 Austria
Czechoslovakia
270.2 Periodicals. Societies
.24 General works
.25 Natural resources
By period
.26 To 1918
.27 1918-1945
.28 1945-
.29 By region, county, etc., A-Z
.292 By city, A-Z
.295 Special topics, A-Z
For list of topics, see HC79
271-280 France
274 To 1600
275 1600-1900
276 20th century
.2 1945-1981
.3 1981-
281-290.5 Germany
Including West Germany
286 20th century
.2 World War, 1914-1918
.3 Reconstruction, 1919-1945
.4 World War, 1939-1945
.5 1945-1965
.6 1965-1974
.7 1974-
287 States, A-Z
288 Regions, A-Z
289 Cities, A-Z
290 Colonies
.5 Special topics, A-Z
For list of topics, see HC79
.7-.795 East Germany
Divided like HC270.2-.295
291-300 Greece

	By period
294	Byzantine Empire
295	Modern Greece
300.2-.295	Hungary
	Divided like HC270.2-.295
301-310	Italy
310.5	Benelux countries. Low countries
311-320	Belgium
321-329.5	Netherlands
329.5	Special topics, A-Z
	For list of topics, see HC79
331-340	Soviet Union
	By period
334	To 1861
.5	1861-1917
335	1917-1950
.2	1917-1927
.3	1928-1950
.4	1928-1932
.5	1933-1937
.6	1938-1945
.7	1946-1950
336	1951-1958
.2	1959-1965
.23	1966-1970
.24	1971-1975
.25	1976-1985
.26	1986-
	Local
.9	By region, A-Z
337	By republic, A-Z
338	By city, A-Z
340	Special topics, A-Z
	For list of topics, see HC79
.2	Finland
.3	Poland
341-350	Scandinavia
351-360	Denmark
361-370	Norway
371-380	Sweden
381-390	Spain
391-394.5	Portugal
394.5	Special topics, A-Z
	For list of topics, see HC79
395-400	Switzerland
395	Periodicals. Societies
397	General works
	Local
398	Regions and cantons, A-Z
399	Cities, A-Z
400	Special topics, A-Z
	For list of topics, see HC79
401	Balkan States
402	Albania
403	Bulgaria
405	Romania
407	Yugoslavia
411-415	Asia
415.15	Middle East

.2	Cyprus
.23	Syria
.24	Lebanon
.25	Israel. Palestine
.26	Jordan
.3	Arabian Peninsula. Arabia. Persian Gulf States
.33	Saudi Arabia
.34	Yemen (Yemen Arab Republic)
.342	Yemen (People's Democratic Republic)
.35	Oman
.36	United Arab Emirates
.37	Qatar
.38	Bahrain
.39	Kuwait
.4	Iraq
416-420	Afghanistan
422	Burma
424	Sri Lanka. Ceylon
425	Nepal
426-430	China
	By period
427.6	Early to 1644
.7	1644-1912
.8	1912-1949
.9	1949-1976
.92	1976-
430.5	Taiwan
.6	South Asia
431-440	India
435.1	1918-1947
.2	1947-
440.5	Pakistan
.8	Bangladesh
441	Southeast Asia. Indochina
442	Cambodia
443	Laos
444	Vietnam
445	Thailand
.5	Malaysia
.8	Singapore
.85	Brunei
446-450	Indonesia
451-460	Philippines
460.5	East Asia
461-465	Japan
	By period
462.6	Early to 1867
.7	1867-1918
.8	1918-1945
.9	1945-
466-470	Korea
	Including South Korea
470.2	North Korea
.3	Hong Kong
471-480	Iran. Persia
491-495	Turkey
498	Arab countries
.9	Special topics, A-Z
	For list of topics, see HC79

499	Islamic countries
	Atlantic Ocean Islands
595.5	Falkland Islands
.55	Indian Ocean Islands (General)
601-610	Australia
661-670	New Zealand
681	Pacific area. Islands of the Pacific (General)
.3	Special topics, A-Z
	For list of topics, see HC79
	Communist countries
701	Periodicals. Societies
704	General works
710	Special topics, A-Z
	For list of topics, see HC79
721-730	Antarctic regions
731-740	Arctic regions
800	Africa
	Including Sub-Saharan Africa
805	North and Northwest Africa
810	Morocco
815	Algeria
820	Tunisia
825	Libya
830	Egypt
835	Sudan
840	Northeast Africa
845	Ethiopia
850	Somalia
855	Djibouti
860	East and Southeast Africa
865	Kenya
870	Uganda
875	Rwanda
880	Burundi
885	Tanzania. Tanganyika. Zanzibar
890	Mozambique
895	Madagascar
900	Southern Africa
905	South Africa
910	Zimbabwe. Southern Rhodesia
915	Zambia. Northern Rhodesia
920	Lesotho
925	Swaziland
930	Botswana. Bechuanaland
935	Malawi. Nyasaland
940	Namibia. Southwest Africa
945	Central Africa
950	Angola
955	Zaire. Congo Democratic Republic
960	Equatorial Guinea
970	French-speaking Equatorial Africa
975	Gabon
980	Congo (Brazzaville)
985	Central African Republic
990	Chad
995	Cameroon
1000	West Africa
1002	Sahel
1005	French-speaking West Africa

1010 Benin. Dahomey
1015 Niger
1020 Ivory Coast
1030 Guinea
1035 Mali
1040 Burkina Faso. Upper Volta
1045 Senegal
1050 Mauritania
1055 Nigeria
1060 Ghana
1065 Sierra Leone
1070 Gambia
1075 Liberia
1080 Guinea-Bissau. Portuguese Guinea
1085 Western Sahara. Spanish Sahara

(HD) ECONOMIC HISTORY AND CONDITIONS

PRODUCTION

Organization of production. Management of special enterprises
62.4 International business enterprises
.45 Transfer pricing

INDUSTRY

Corporations. Cartels. Trusts
2755.5 International business enterprises. Multi-national corporations (General)
Cf. HD62.4, Management
Works on international business enterprises located in a given country class in HD2770+ (not included in this guide)

(HE) TRANSPORTATION AND COMMUNICATIONS

Telecommunication industry
Radio and television broadcasting
Radio broadcasting
8697.4 International broadcasting
.45 By region or country, A-Z
.8 Political broadcasts
.85 By region or country, A-Z
Television broadcasting
8700.75 Political broadcasts
.76 By region or country, A-Z

(HF) COMMERCE

International economic relations (General)
For foreign economic relations by region or country, <u>see</u> HF1451+ (not included in this guide)

1351 Periodicals. Societies
1359 General works
International trade
1371 Periodicals. Societies
1379 General works
By region or country, <u>see</u> HF1451+ (not included in this guide)
Foreign commercial policy
1410 Periodicals. Societies
1411 General works
By region or country, <u>see</u> HF1451+ (not included in this guide)

1413 Developing countries
.5 Economic sanctions. Boycotts
1414 Competition
.3 Countertrade
.4 Exports
.5 Export controls
1416 Export and international marketing
By region or country
.5 United States
.6 Other regions or countries, A-Z
1417 Export processing zones
By region or country, see HF3000+ (not included in this guide)
1418 Free ports
.5 International economic integration
1419 Imports
By region or country, see HF3000+ (not included in this guide)
1421 Trade adjustment assistance
1425 Dumping (selling in foreign markets at lower prices than in the home market)
1428 International commodity control
1429 Foreign licensing agreements
1430 Nontariff trade barriers (General)
.5 Subsidies
Tariff policy (Protection and free trade)
Class here theoretical and controversial works
1701 Periodicals. Societies
1711 History
1713 General works
1715 Drawbacks
1716 United States
1717 Other regions or countries, A-Z
1721 Tariff. Reciprocity. Favored nation clause
For tariff acts and laws in general, see class K (not included in this guide)
1723 Colonial tariffs
Including policy
By region or country
1731.A6-Z United States
1732 Treaties with other countries, A-Z. By date
1733 Other regions or countries, A-Z
Under each country:
.x General works
.x2 Treaties with other countries, A-Z

(HJ) FINANCE

Foreign exchange. International finance
International finance. International monetary system.
International banking
3879 Periodicals. Societies
3881 General works
.5 Individual international financial institutions
.A37 African Development Bank
.A73 Arab Bank for Economic Development in Africa
.A74 Arab Fund for Economic and Social Development
.A75 Asian Development Bank
.C65 Council of Europe Resettlement Fund
.E87 European Investment Bank
.I44 Inter-American Development Bank
.I55 International Bank for Economic Co-operation

.I58 International Monetary Fund

.I84 Islamic Development Bank

.W57 World Bank

3882 Balance of payments

3883 By region or country, A-Z

3890 Developing countries

3891 Capital movements

.3 Compensatory financing

.5 Foreign loans. International lending

3892 International clearing

3893 International liquidity

3894 Monetary unions. Currency areas

(HM) SOCIOLOGY

24 Theory. Method. Relation to other subjects

36.5 Relation to war

101 Culture. Progress

106 Biological sociology

126 Unity. Solidarity

131 Association. Mutuality. Social groups

136 Individualism. Differentiation. Struggle

141 The great man. Leadership

146 Equality

201 Social elements, forces, laws

206 Environment

211 Economic

216 Moral

Including social justice, social ethics, etc.

221 Technological

Cf. CB478, Technology and civilization

251 Social psychology

258 Communication

261 Public opinion (General)

By topic, see the topic

263 Public relations. Propaganda

267 Tradition

271 Authority and freedom

276 Liberalism. Toleration

278 Passive resistance

Crowds. Revolutions. Violence

281 Theory

283 History

(HV) SOCIAL PATHOLOGY. SOCIAL WELFARE

Criminology

Criminology anthropology

Causes of crime

Environment

6189 War and crime

Crimes and offenses

Political crimes

Class here only theory and psychology of political crimes; for historical works, individual cases, etc., see D, JF-JX, K, etc.

6254 Offenses against the government

International. see JX

6273 National

6275 Treason. Conspiracy

6278 Assassination of rulers

By region or country

6285 United States
6295 Other regions or countries, A-Z
6301 Offenses against the administration, election bribery, etc.
Class here only theory and psychology; for descriptive works, history, cases, etc., see D, JF-JX, K, etc.
By region or country
6304 United States
6321 Other regions or countries, A-Z
Under each country:
.x General works
.x2 Special topics (not A-Z)
6419 Offenses against public safety
6431 Terrorism
By region or country
6432 United States
6433 Other regions or countries, A-Z
Offenses against the public order
6474 Riots and unlawful assemblies
By region or country
6477 United States
6485 Other regions or countries, A-Z
6493 Crimes against the person
6595 Kidnapping
By region or country
6598 United States
6604 Other regions or countries, A-Z
6762.A3A-Z Missing persons
.A4-Z By region or country, A-Z

(HX) SOCIALISM. COMMUNISM. ANARCHISM

19 Study and teaching
.2 By region or country, A-Z
21 History
23 Biography (Collective)
By period
26 Ancient
31 Medieval
36 Modern
38 French revolution
39 19th century
.5 Karl Marx
.A2 Collected works. By date
.A51-529 Separate works. By title
.A53-Z Biography and criticism
40 20th century
44 1945-
Special systems and movements
51 Christian socialism
54 Catholic socialism
General works and advanced textbooks
71 Through 1847
Karl Marx, see HX39.5
72 1848-1980
73 1981-
77 Democratic centralism
By region or country, see HX80+ (not included in this guide)
518 Special topics, A-Z
.C7 Self-criticism
.L4 Leadership

.R4 Revisionism
.S8 Strategy
545 Communism/socialism and war
550 Communism/socialism in relation to other topics, A-Z
.A7 Armies
.B8 Buddhism
.C58 Civil rights
.I45 Individualism
.I5 International relations
.I8 Islam
.J4 Jews. Judaism
.L52 Liberty
.M35 Mass media
.N3 Nationalism
.N66 Nonviolence
.R48 Revolutions
806 Utopias. The ideal state
For Utopian novels, see class P (not included in this guide)
807 Religious aspects
Anarchism
826 History
838 19th-20th centuries
833 General works and advanced textbooks
By region or country, see HX841+ (not included in this guide)

(JC) THE STATE

11 General works
51 Ancient state
61 Assyro-Babylonian Empire
66 Egypt
67 Hebrews
Greece
Contemporary treatises
71.A1A-Z Selections, etc. By editor, A-Z
.A2-Z By author, A-Z
.A4-7 Aristotle
.P2-6 Plato
.S6-62 Socrates
General works
72 Early works
73 Modern
75 Special, A-Z
.I5 International relations
.J8 Justice
.R4 Resistance to government
83 Rome
By period
88 The Republic
89 The Empire
Byzantine Empire
91 Contemporary treatises
93 General works
101 The Medieval state
Contemporary treatises
121 Latin
126 Arabic
131 The Modern state
By period
16th century

134 History
Contemporary treatises, see JC137+ (not included in this guide)
17th century
151 History
Contemporary treatises, see JC153+ (not included in this guide)
18th century
171 History
Contemporary treatises, see JC176+ (not included in this guide)
19th century
201 History
Contemporary treatises, see JC211+ (not included in this guide)
20th century
249 History
Treatises. By region or country
251 United States
253 Canada
255 Latin America
257 Great Britain
259 Netherlands
261 France
263 Germany
265 Italy
267 Soviet Union
269 Scandinavia
271 Spain and Portugal
273 Other
301 Origin of the state
311 Nationalism
Including minorities
313 Particularism
315 Political messianism
319 Geopolitics
321 Expansion. Acquisition of territory
323 Frontiers
325 Nature, entity, concept of the state
General special
327 Sovereignty
328 Allegiance. Loyalty
.2 Consensus. Consent of the governed
.3 Opposition
.5 Insurgency
.6 Violence
Cf. HM281, Social psychology
329 Patriotism (General)
.5 Political obligations
330 Power
.15 Public interest
.2 Stability
331 Juridical theory
336 Social and evolutionary theories
341 The state as a moral organism
348 Forms of the state
351 Simple state
352 City-state
353 Mixed state
355 Federal state

357 Confederation of states
359 Empire. Imperialism
361 The World state. Cosmopolitanism
362 Internationalism
Class here theoretical works only. For practical applications, see JX
363 Special
364 Size of states
365 Small states
Ideal states, see HX806+
Monarchy
374 Origins
375 History
381 General works. Despotism
385 Theory of kingship
387 Hereditary rights
389 Divine right of kings
Constitutional or limited monarchy
401 History
405 Treatises. Theory
Aristocracy
411 History
414 Treatises. Theory
419 Oligarchy
Democracy
421 History
423 Treatises (Theory)
For constitutional history and government, see JF
458 Pure democracy
474 Communist state. People's democracies
478 Corporate state
481 Totalitarianism. Fascism
Change of form of the state
Class here works on political theory only
Cf. D-F, History of events; HM 281+, Social psychology
491 Revolutions
492 Counterrevolutions
494 Coups d'état
495 Dictatorship
497 Legitimation; de facto government
501 Purpose, functions, and relations of the state
Special relations of the state
510 The state and religion (Theory)
For historical works, see BL-BX
512 Ancient
513 Medieval
514 Modern
571 The state and the individual. Civil rights.
Human rights
For political rights, see JF800+
For the legal aspects of human rights, see class K, which is not included in this guide
575 Equality of individuals, races, etc.
578 Equality before the law; justice
Rights of the individual
583 Life
585 Liberty
587 Freedom of action
591 Freedom of speech

596 Right of privacy
.2 By region or country, A-Z
605 Property
607 Right of assembly
609 Right of petition
621 Limitation and suspension of individual rights and guaranties
Martial law, see JF, JK, JX

(JF) CONSTITUTIONAL HISTORY AND ADMINISTRATION

CONSTITUTIONAL HISTORY (GENERAL)

Treatises
45 Early
General
51 English
52 French
53 German
54 Italian
55 Spanish and Portuguese
.5 Russian and other Slavic
56 Other languages, A-Z
Special treatises
60 New states. Developing countries
71 Constitutions, Making of
101 Constitutional limitations and interpretation
107 Advanced textbooks
American and English; others with treatises, JF52+
130 Study and teaching
195 Special constitutional questions, A-Z
.C5 Civil and military power
.R44 Regionalism
201 Organs and functions of government
Sovereignty, see JC327; JX4041+
225 Delegation of powers
229 Separation and distribution of powers
235 Checks and balances
251 Executive
Special
255 President
256 Military power. Declaration of war. War powers
260 Legislative power
269 Treaty-making power
331 Cabinet and ministerial government
Legislation. Law-making
411 History
412 Ancient
414 Medieval
416 Modern, 1800-
Treatises. Theory
421 Early to 1800
423 Later
441 Legislative powers
War, see JX; UB
477 Foreign relations
Political rights and guaranties
General only; for special countries, see JK-JQ
801 Citizenship (Theory)
Prefer JK-JQ; JX
811 Naturalization
Cf. JX4216

1001 Electoral systems. Voting
1051 Representation
1057 Representation of economic and social groups
1059 By country, A-Z
1061 Representation of minorities
1063 By country, A-Z
1071 Proportional representation
1075 By country, A-Z
1081 Corruption and election fraud
1083 Election contests
1085 Election contributions and expenditures

GOVERNMENT. ADMINISTRATION (GENERAL)
Special countries, see JK-JS; Colonies, see JV

1341 History
1700 Territorial administration
1800 Martial law
1820 Military government
Cf. JV423, Colonies
JX5003, International law

Political parties. Practical politics
The political activity of special groups is classed with the group
2011 History (Comparative)
2049 Philosophy; psychology
2051 Treatises
2061 Political parties and the administration
2075 Parties and legislation
Organization. Campaign methods
2112 Special topics, A-Z
.A4 Advertising
.C28 Campaign funds
.P8 Public relations
.T4 Television broadcasting

(JK) CONSTITUTIONAL HISTORY AND ADMINISTRATION UNITED STATES

1 Periodicals
Constitutional history
31 Comprehensive works
37 Textbooks
39 Philosophy, theory
51 Early. Origins
54 Colonial period
116 1776-1820
171.A1A-Z 1788-1798/1800
201 1821-1865
231 1966-1989/1908
261 1908-
304 Acquisition and alienation of territory
Special constitutional questions
305 Separation and delegation of powers
Treaty-making power, see JK570+; JX4161+
339 War powers of the government
General works; for war powers of President, see JK560
Government. Administration
411 History
468 Special topics, A-Z
.I6 Intelligence service
.S4 Secret and confidential information

501 The Executive
The President
511 History
558 Military power
560 In time of war
562 In time of peace
570 Treaty-making power. Foreign affairs
573 Special. By date
585 Relation to Congress
Congress
1001 Legislation
1021 History
1061 Constitution. Powers. Prerogatives
Senate
1158 History
1161 1901-
Constitution. Powers. Prerogatives
1166 History
1170 Treatises
Committees
1340 Individual committees, A-Z
Under each (using two successive cutter numbers):
(1) Documents
(2) Other works
House of Representatives
1316 History
1319 Recent
Constitution. Powers. Prerogatives
1326 History
1331 Treatises
Organization
1411 Officers. Speaker
Committees
1430 Special committees, A-Z
Subarranged:
(1) Documents
(2) Other
Politics, civil rights
1711 History
1714 Early
1717 Recent
1726 Treatises
Citizenship
1759 Education. Patriotism
1764 Political participation
Naturalization
1829 Treatises
1846 Suffrage
2249 Political corruption (General)
Political parties
2255 Party platforms, conventions, etc.
2256 Special. By year
History
General
2260 Early to 1860
2261 1860-
2263 Special, by date
2265 Treatises
Particular parties

Democratic
2313 Conventions. By date
2316 History
2317 Special. By date
Republican
2353 Conventions. By date
2356 History
2357 Special. By date

The Constitutional history and administration of countries other than the United States classes in JL-JQ. JL-JQ are not included in this guide.

(JV) COLONIES AND COLONIZATION. EMIGRATION AND IMMIGRATION

COLONIES AND COLONIZATION

General works, description, etc.
161 Early to 1700
165 18th century
171 1801-1870
175 1870-1900
185 20th century
Continents
221 Western hemisphere
226 North America
231 South America. Latin America
236 Eastern hemisphere
241 Asia and Oceania
246 Africa
261 Colonizing races; influence of race
Special
266 Teutonic
268 English
271 Dutch
273 German
276 Other
Latin
285 French
288 Spanish
291 Other
295 Acquisition of colonies
Cf. JV355+; JX4088+
305 Relations with indigenous peoples
Special
308 Policy, treatment
311 Subjection
314 Assimilation
317 Autonomy
321 Colonization and Christianity
341 Colonization and economics
351 Forms and classes of colonies
Special
355 Protectorates and spheres of influence
Cf. JX4021+, International law
358 Colonies of migration
361 Economic colonies
365 Colonization companies
368 Military colonies. Strategic posts
373 Penal colonies
377 Colonies of exploitation
381 Colonies of expansion

Cf. JC359, Imperialism
401 Colonies and the central government
Special
404 Colonial office. Home office
Administration and organization
412 Treatises
418 Administrative
420 Economic
Special
423 Military government
Individual colonizing nations, see JV500+ (not included in this guide)

EMIGRATION AND IMMIGRATION

General

Periodicals
6001.A1 International or polyglot
.A2-Z American
6002 English
6003 French
6004 German
6005 Italian
6006 Other
6021 History
By period
Under each:
(1) General
(2) Special
6023-6024 Ancient
6026-6027 Medieval to 1800
6029-6030 19th century
6032-6033 20th century
6035 Treatises
Special
6038 Relations to the state
6041 Pamphlets

Emigration

6061 History and general works
By period
Under each:
(1) General
(2) Special
6065-6066 Ancient
6068-6069 Medieval
6071-6072 17th century
6074-6075 18th century
6077-6078 19th century
6080-6081 20th century
6091 Treatises
Special
6094 Causes of emigration
6098 Economic
6101 Social
6104 Political
6107 Religious
6109 Other
6115 Effects of emigration
Special
6118 Economic
6121 Social

6124 Political and national
6127 Other
Emigration to special regions
6135 Western Hemisphere
6137 North America
6139 South America. Latin America
Eastern Hemisphere
6141 Europe
6143 Asia
6145 Africa
6147 Australia and New Zealand
6149 Oceania
By country, see JV6403+ (not included in this guide)

Immigration

History and general works, see JV6061
6201 Treatises
Special
6205 Immigration and population
6208 Racial effects of immigration
6225 Social effects of immigration
6255 Political effects
6258 Naturalization
Comparative and general works only
Cf. JF, JX
6268 Inspection and registration
6271 Regulation and control
6278 Restriction and exclusion
6308 Deportation
6312 Distribution of immigrants
6325 Promotion and assistance
6342 Assimilation
Special classes, races, etc.
6346 By class, A-Z
.M5 Migrant labor
.R4 Refugees
.W7 Women
6348 By race, A-Z
General works only; by country, see the country
.C6 Chinese

(JX) INTERNATIONAL LAW. FOREIGN RELATIONS. DIPLOMACY. INTERNATIONAL ARBITRATION

Periodicals
1 American and English
3 French and Belgian
5 German
7 Italian
9 Spanish, Portuguese, Latin American
18 Other
Societies
24 International
27 American
31 English
32 French
33 German
34 Italian
35 Spanish
38 Other

41	Congresses and conferences
54	Special. By name, A-Z
	Hague Conference, see JX1912+
	Collections. Documents. Cases
	General. Selections, sources, etc.
	By country, see JX221+
	Polyglot editions
63	Early
64	Recent
65	Latin
68	English
71	Dutch
74	French
77	German
81	Italian
84	Spanish
91	Other, A-Z
97	Pamphlets
	Diplomatic relations (Universal collections)
101	Latin and polyglot
103	English
105	French
107	German
109	Italian
111	Spanish
115	Other
	Treaties (General collections)
	Subarrange periods below as follows: (0) Latin and polyglot (1) English (2) French (3) German (4) Italian (5) Spanish (8) Other, A-Z Subarranged by title or editor
	Ancient, see JX2001
120-128	To 1700
130-138	1700-1789
140-148	1789-1815
150-158	1815-1860
160-168	1860-1900
170-178	1900-
191	Separate treaties of general character
	Including treaties of amity and commerce to which the United States is not a party
	Cf. United States treaties, JX235 Arbitration treaties, JX1985+ Boundary treaties, D-F Extradition treaties, JX4301+ Treaties of peace, D-F
	Subarrange each treaty by year, month, and date of signature or, if better known, by date of ratification Further subarrange as follows: (1) Original text, including editions in language of party of the first part if identical (2) Text in language of party of the second part (3) Text in language of third and fourth parties and translations into other languages. By language, A-Z

(4) Preliminaries, negotiations (Official documents)
(5) History. Pamphlets (Nonofficial)

Collections. By country
221-230 American
Divide by 10 number table below JX351-JX1195
231 United States
Foreign relations and diplomatic correspondence
Secretary of State
232 Report (including bureau documents)
233 Diplomatic correspondence
Class correspondence covering special events, negotiations, etc., in D, E, F
.A1-4 Serial (in chronological order of series)
.A5-59 Special
.A6-Z Relations with individual countries
234.A1 President's messages and other executive documents
Legislative documents
.A2-3 Senate
.A2 Collected
.A3 Special. By date
.A4-5 House
.A4 Collected
.A5 Special. By date
.A8-Z Other documents
Treaties and conventions
235 Separate treaties. By date
.9 Series
Main official series, . A3 by number
236 Collections, by date of first volume (or by period covered)
.5 Indexes
237 Digests of decisions, opinions, etc.
e.g. United States Attorney-general's opinions on international law questions
238 Cases, claims, etc., by name, A-Z
.A2A-Z Collections
239 Other cases. By date
245 States, A-W
351-1195 Other countries
Under each:
1 number
.A1-19 General collections
Foreign relations and diplomatic correspondence
Secretary of State. Minister of foreign affairs
.A2-29 Reports
.A3A-Z Diplomatic correspondence
.A1-4 Serial
.A5 Special. By date
.A6-Z Relations with individual countries
.A4-48 Legislative documents
.A5A-Z Other documents
.A1-5 Administrative
.A6 Digests of decisions, opinions, etc.
Treaties and conventions
.A58 Official serials
.A6 Collections. By imprint date of first volume
.A7 Separate treaties. By date
.A75 Indexes
Cases, claims, etc.

.A8A-Z By name, A-Z
.A85 By date
.A9-Z States (which at some time maintained independent foreign relations)

10 numbers

(1) General collections
Foreign relations and diplomatic correspondence
Secretary of State. Minister of foreign affairs
(2) Reports
(3) Diplomatic correspondence
.A1-4 Serial
.A5 Special. By date
.A6-Z Relations with individual countries
(4) Legislative documents
(5) Other documents
.A1-5 Administrative
.A6 Digests of decisions, etc.
Treaties and conventions
(5.9) Official serials
(6) Collections.By imprint date of first volume
(7) Separate treaties. By date
(7.5) Indexes
Cases, claims, etc.
(8) By name, A-Z
(9) By date
(10) States (which at one time maintained independent foreign relations)

Note 1: For countries that are to be given cutter numbers, use three successive numbers. Use the first for (1)-(5), the second for (6)-(7), and the third for (8)-(9)
e.g. Poland is treated here as a local of the Soviet Union and classed in JX760.P6

Note 2: For groups that have been given two numbers, use (1) for general and (2) for local

Note 3: Use of subdivisions (8) and (9)
(a) Place claims under defendant nation unless the United States or an American citizen is a party
(b) Prefer JX238 and (8), using JX239 and (9) only for claims that cannot otherwise be disposed of
(c) Group claims under name of plaintiff nation
(d) Under each claim subarrange using successive cutter numbers
e.g. .C5-62 Chilean claims
.C5 General
Documents of first contracting party
.C51 Collections. By date
.C52 Separate. By date
.C53 Other
Documents of second contracting party
.C54 Collections. By date
.C55 Separate. By date
.C56 Other
.C57 Commissions for arbitrating claims
.C6 Special claims. By name, A-Z
.C61 Special claims. By date
.C62 Nonofficial
Instead of using subdivisions .C5-57, material not dealing with a particular claim may be arranged in a single chronological series

351-360 Canada
355.9 Official serials
.A3-35 Treaty series, by series and number
361-370 Mexico
371-380 Central America
381-390 Belize. British Honduras
391-400 Costa Rica
401-410 Guatemala
411-420 Honduras
421-430 Nicaragua
431-440 Panama
441-450 El Salvador
West Indies
451-460 Cuba
461-470 Haiti
471-480 Dominican Republic
483 Puerto Rico
484 Virgin Islands of the United States
485-486 British West Indies
491-492 Danish West Indies
493-494 Dutch West Indies
495-496 French West Indies
501-510 South America
511-520 Argentina
521-530 Bolivia
531-540 Brazil
541-550 Chile
551-560 Colombia
561-570 Ecuador
Guiana
571 Guyana. British Guiana
574 Surinam. Dutch Guiana
577 French
581-590 Paraguay
591-600 Peru
601-610 Uruguay
611-620 Venezuela
621-630 Europe
631-640 Great Britain
671-680 Austria and Hungary
.C9-93 Czechoslovakia
681-690 France
691-700 Germany
701-710 Greece
711-720 Italy
721-730 Benelux countries. Netherlands and Belgium treated together
731-740 Belgium
741-750 Netherlands
751-760 Soviet Union
.P6-8 Poland
761-770 Scandinavia
771-780 Denmark
791-800 Norway
801-810 Sweden
811-820 Spain
821-830 Portugal
831-840 Switzerland
Turkey and the Balkan States

841-850 Turkey
850.A4-6 Albania
851-860 Bulgaria
861-870 Montenegro
871-880 Romania
881-890 Yugoslavia. Serbia
893 Luxemburg
895 Monaco
899 Other European, A-Z
e.g. .I3 Iceland
.S3 San Marino
900 Asia
901-910 Philippines
Former British possessions
911-920 India
920.5 Other special, A-Z
921-930 China
932-940 Indonesia. Dutch East Indies
Former French possessions
943 General and Indochina
945 Local, A-Z
947-948 Former German possessions
951-960 Japan
961-970 Korea
970.15 North Korea (People's Democratic Republic)
.5 Pakistan
971-980 Iran. Persia
981-990 The Soviet Union in Asia
991-1000 Thailand. Siam
1001-1010 Turkey in Asia
1015 Other, A-Z
Africa
1021-1030 Egypt
1040 British Africa and Union of South Africa
1041 Cape of Good Hope
1042 Orange Free State
1043 South African Republic
1045 Transvaal
1046 Rhodesia
1050 Other, A-Z
1059-1060 Former French possessions
1069-1070 Former German possessions
1079-1080 Former Italian possessions
1085 Zaire. Belgian Congo
1089-1090 Former Portuguese possessions
1099-1100 Former Spanish possessions
1101-1110 Ethiopia. Abyssinia
1121-1130 Liberia
1131-1140 Morocco
1145 Other, A-Z
1161-1170 Australia
1171-1179 New Zealand
1180 Pacific Islands
American
1181 Hawaii
1182 Other, A-Z
1184 British
1187-1188 French
1191-1192 German

1195 Other, A-Z
Digests of cases, see JX63+
1226 Dictionaries
1245 Theory, scope, relations
Cf. JX63+, Collections of sources
1246 General special
Including sanctions, compulsion, power to enforce treaties, etc.
Special
1248 Relation to municipal law
1249 Relation to social sciences
1250 Relation to political science
1251 Relation to sociology
1252 Relation to economics
1253 Relation to history
1255 Other
Codification of international law
1261 Collections. Congresses. Societies
Codes
1265 Official. By date
1268 Nonofficial. By editor
General works
1270 Early to 1860
1271-1280 Recent
1271 American and English
1273 French and Belgian
1275 German
1277 Italian
1279 Spanish, Portuguese, Latin American
1280 Other, A-Z
e.g. .R8 Russian
1281 Pamphlets
1283 Special topics
1291 Study and teaching
Cf. JX1904.5, International organization
1293 By country, A-Z
1295 By school, A-Z
1297 Outlines, syllabi
1299 Examination questions
Textbooks, see JX2001+

FOREIGN RELATIONS

Class here works on international questions treated as sources of or contributions to the theory of international law. Class diplomatic history, history of wars, etc., in D-F (History). In case of doubt, prefer history

1305 History of international relations and the development of international law
1308 Textbooks
1311 Pamphlets
By country, see JX1404+
By period
Ancient, see JX2001
Medieval, see JX2041
1315 Modern
Special
1318 Balance of power
1319 Balkan question
1321 Far Eastern question
By period
1325 1648-1713

Special
1328 Peace of Westphalia
1331 Spanish succession
1333 Pamphlets
1335 1713-1789
Treaty of Paris, see D297
1338 Special, by subject, A-Z
1341 Contemporary works
1345 1789-1815
Special
1346 Congress of Rastatt
1347 Treaty of Ghent
1349 Holy Alliance
1351 Congress of Vienna
1352 Other, A-Z
1353 Contemporary works
1358 1815-1861
Special
1361 Congress of Troppau, 1820
1363 Congress of Laibach, 1821
1365 Congress of Verona, 1822
Congress of Panama, 1826, see F1404
1367 Treaty of Paris, 1856
Including works on the Declaration of Paris and publications of the English Maritime League
1369 Contemporary works
1373 1861-1899
Special
Geneva Conference, 1864, see JX5136+; JX5243
1377 Saint Petersburg Convention, 1868
1379 London Conference, 1871
1381 Brussels Conference, 1875
1383 Berlin Conference, 1878
1385 Congo Conference, 1884-1885
1386 Other, A-Z
1387 Contemporary works
1391 20th century
1392 World War, 1914-1918
.5 World War, 1939-1945
1393 Other special, A-Z
.A8 Atlantic Union
.B74 British Honduras question
.C65 Conference on Security and Cooperation in Europe
.D46 Détente
.D8 Drago doctrine
.E8 Exterritoriality
.I53 Indian Ocean region
.I8 Italo-Ethiopian War, 1935-1936
.K6 Korean War, 1950-1951
.L3 Latin America
London Declaration, 1909, see JX5203
.M43 Mediterranean region
.N54 Nonalignment
.N57 North Atlantic region
North Atlantic Treaty Organization (NATO)
.N58-62 Official serials
.N63 Official monographs. By date
.N67A-Z General works
.P3 Pacific Islands

.R4 Rhine River and Valley
.R8 Russo-Japanese War
.S5 Sino-Japanese Conflict
.S63 South Atlantic Region
.S65 Spanish Civil War
Strategic Arms Limitation Talks, see JX1974.75
.W2 Warsaw Pact Organization

1395 Contemporary works
1398 Interoceanic canals
Class here diplomatic history only
Cf. JX4155, Treatises
1398 Panama Canal
Including Isthmian canals in general
Cf. HE537+, Traffic and tolls (not included in this guide)
TC774+, Construction and maintenance (not included in this guide)
.2 Early to 1876/79
.3 French companies
United States
.5 Documents
.6 Clayton-Bulwer Treaty, 1850
.7 Hay-Pauncefote Treaties, 1901-1902
Panama Canal Treaties, 1977
.72 Text of treaties. By date
.73 General works
Panama Republic, see F1566
.8 Nonofficial
1400 Nicaragua Canal
1401 Other American canal projects
1403 Suez Canal
Foreign relations, by country
1404 American
United States
1405 Collections
1406 History of international law in the United States
1407 History of foreign relations, diplomatic questions, etc.
By period
1411 Colonial to 1776
1412 1776-1800/15
1413 1800-/15-1861
1414 1861-1880
1415 1880-1900
1416 1900-1945
1417 1945-
Special topics
Boundary questions, see E
1421 Eastern policy
1423 Great Lakes
1425 Monroe Doctrine (Theory)
1426 Philippine annexation. War of 1898
Fisheries question, see JX238
1427 Other topics, A-Z
e.g. .E5 Embargo
.M5 Military influence
1428 Relations with individual countries
Cf. E183.8+, United States history
1515-1598 Other countries
Under each:
.A2 Collections

.A28A-Z History of the science
History and general
.A3A-Z To 1800
.A4-Z4 1800-
.Z5 Contemporary works. By date
.Z6A-Z Special topics, A-Z
.Z7 Relations with individual countries, A-Z
1515 Canada
.5 Latin America
1516 Mexico
1517 Central America
.5 Belize. British Honduras
British Honduras question, see F1449.B7
1518 Costa Rica
1519 Guatemala
1520 Honduras
1521 Nicaragua
1522 Panama
.5 Panama Canal
1523 El Salvador
1524 West Indies
.5 Bahamas
1525 Cuba
1526 Haiti
.5 Dominican Republic
1527 Jamaica
1528 Puerto Rico
.5 Virgin Islands of the United States
1529 Other, A-Z
1530 South America
1531 Argentina
1532 Bolivia
1533 Brazil
1534 Chile
1535 Colombia
1536 Ecuador
1537 Guiana
.1 Guyana. British Guiana
.3 Surinam. Dutch Guiana
.5 French Guiana
1538 Paraguay
1539 Peru
1540 Uruguay
1541 Venezuela
1542 Europe
European communities, see KJE5105+ (not included in this guide)
1543 Great Britain. England
1545 Scotland
1546 Ireland
1547 Austria
.3 Czechoslovakia
1548 France
.3 Monaco
1549 Germany
.Z7A2 International relations of the German states to one another
.3 Danzig
.5 Saar
1550 Greece
.5 Hungary

1551 Italy
1552 Papacy. Vatican City
.5 Latvia
1553 Belgium
1554 Netherlands
.5 Luxemburg
1555 Soviet Union
.3 Finland
.5 Poland
.8 Ukraine
.9 White Russia
1556 Scandinavia
1557 Denmark
1558 Iceland
1559 Norway
1560 Sweden
1561 Spain
1562 Portugal
1563 Switzerland
Turkey and the Balkan States
1564 Bulgaria
.5 Yugoslavia
1565 Montenegro
1566 Romania
1567 Serbia
1568 Turkey . Muslim countries (General)
1569 Asia
1570 China
1571 India
.5 Other former British possessions, A-Z
1572 Indochina
1573 French Indochina
1575 Indonesia. Dutch East Indies
1576 Philippines
1577 Japan
.5 Korea
1578 Iran. Persia
1579 Soviet Union in Asia
.5 Thailand. Siam
.7 Taiwan
1580 Turkey in Asia
1581 Other divisions of Asia, A-Z
1582 Africa
1583 Egypt
1584 Former British possessions, A-Z
e.g. .S7 South Africa
1585 Former French possessions, A-Z
1586 Former German possessions, A-Z
.5 Former Italian possessions, A-Z
.7 Congo Free State
1587 Former Portuguese possessions, A-Z
.5 Former Spanish possessions, A-Z
1588 Other divisions of Africa, A-Z
1589 Australia and New Zealand
1590 New South Wales
1591 New Zealand
1592 North Australia
1593 Queensland
1594 South Australia

1595 Tasmania
1596 Victoria
1597 Western Australia
1598 Pacific Islands, A-Z

DIPLOMACY. THE DIPLOMATIC SERVICE

Including foreign relations administration

Periodicals, see JX1+
1628 Societies
1631 Collections (General)
Special, see JX1700+
1632 Codes
1634 Study and teaching. Schools
1635 History. General works
By period
1638 Ancient
1641 Medieval to 1600
1643 Contemporary works
1648 Modern
By period
Under each:
(1) Histories
(2) Contemporary works
1651-1652 17th century
1654-1655 18th century
1658-1659 19th century
1661-1662 20th century
1664 Pamphlets
The Diplomatic Service
Subarrangement for topics with 2 numbers:
(1) Cases, documents, sources
(2) Treatises
1665-1666 Appointment
1668-1669 Credentials. Reception
1670 Unauthorized negotiations
1671-1672 Powers and privileges. Immunities
1674 Duties. Functions
1675 To the home government
1676 To the foreign government
1677 Diplomatic language, style
1678-1679 Ceremonials. Precedence
1681-1682 Dress
1683 Other topics, A-Z
.F6 Foreign interests
.G5 Gifts
.P7 Protection of foreign missions
1684 Organization. Administration
Special
1686-1687 Department of foreign affairs. The minister of state or foreign affairs
1691-1692 Ambassadors, envoys, etc.
1694 Consuls
1695-1696 Special topics, A-Z
Under each:
(1) Treatises
(2) Cases
.A4 Administration of estates
.J8 Jurisdiction
.P7 Police
.P8 Privileges and immunities

.T8 Trade and the consular service

1699 Other

1705-1894 By country

Tables

1 number table

- .A2-4 Collections
- .A5 Organization. Administration
- .A6-Z General works. By author

Cutter number table

- (1) Collections
- (2) Organization. Administration
- (3) General works. By author

2 number table

- Manuals, diplomatic lists
  - (1).A15-19 Serials
  - .A2 Nonserials. By date
- General works
  - .A3 Early to 1860. By date
  - .A5-Z 1860- . By author, A-Z
- (2) Organization.
  - Administration
  - Documents
    - .A2 Serial
      - Cf. JX200+
    - .A3 Special. By date
    - .A33 Upper House (Senate). By date
    - .A34 Lower House (Representatives). By date
    - .A37 Other. By date
  - .A4 Department of foreign affairs
  - .A5 Legations
  - By place
    - .A52 North America
    - .A53 South America
    - .A54 Europe
    - .A55 Asia
    - .A56 Other
    - .A58 By place, A-Z
  - .A585 Foreign legations
- .A59 Ambassadors. Envoys
- Consular service
  - Documents
    - .A6 Serial
    - .A65 Cases
      - .Z5 Individual. By date
    - .A7 Organization, duties
    - .A75 Special. By date
  - .A8-Z3 General works. By author, A-Z
  - .Z5 Civil service
  - .Z55 Messengers, interpreters
  - .Z6 Examinations for diplomatic and consular service
- .Z7A-Z Other works. By author, A-Z
- .Z8-Z States
- .Z9 Miscellaneous and uncataloged material

1705-1706 United States

1725 States, A-W

1729-1730 Canada

1731-1732 Mexico

1733-1734 Central America

1735-1736 Belize and Honduras
1737-1738 Costa Rica
1739 Guatemala
1741 Nicaragua
1742-1743 Panama
1743.5 Panama Canal
1744 El Salvador
1745 West Indies
1749-1750 Cuba
1751 Haiti
1752 Dominican Republic
1753 Jamaica
1755-1756 Puerto Rico
1756.5 Virgin Islands of the United States
1757 Other, A-Z
1758 South America
1759-1760 Argentina
1761-1762 Bolivia
1763-1764 Brazil
1765-1766 Chile
1767-1768 Colombia
1769-1770 Ecuador
1771 Guiana
1772 Guyana
.5 Surinam
.7 French Guiana
1773-1774 Paraguay
1775-1776 Peru
1777-1778 Uruguay
1779-1780 Venezuela
1781 Europe
1783-1784 Great Britain. England
1787-1788 Scotland
1789-1790 Ireland
1791-1792 Austria
1792.5 Czechoslovakia
1793-1794 France
1794.3 Monaco
1795-1796 Germany
1797-1798 Greece
1798.5 Hungary
1799-1800 Italy
1801-1802 Papacy. Vatican City
Cf. BX1908, Legates, nuncios
1802.7 Malta
1803-1804 Belgium
1805-1806 Netherlands
1806.5 Luxemburg
1807-1808 Soviet Union
1808.2 Estonia
.3 Finland
.5 Latvia
.6 Lithuania
.7 Poland
1809-1810 Scandinavia
1811-1812 Denmark
1813-1814 Iceland
1815-1816 Norway
1817-1818 Sweden

1819-1820 Spain
1821-1822 Portugal
1823-1824 Switzerland
1825-1826 Turkey and the Balkan States
1826.5 Albania
1827-1828 Bulgaria
1828.5 Yugoslavia
1829 Montenegro
1831-1832 Romania
1833-1834 Serbia
1835 Asia
1837-1838 China
1838.5 Taiwan
1839-1840 India
1841-1842 Indochina
1843-1844 French Indochina
1847-1848 Indonesia. Dutch East Indies
1849-1850 Philippines
1851-1852 Japan
1853-1854 Iran. Persia
1855-1856 Soviet Union in Asia
1857-1858 Turkey in Asia
1859 Other, A-Z
1861 Africa
1863-1864 Egypt
1854 Former British possessions, A-Z
1867 Former French possessions, A-Z
1869 Former German possessions, A-Z
1870 Former Italian possessions, A-Z
1871 Former Portuguese possessions, A-Z
1872 Former Spanish possessions, A-Z
1873 Other, A-Z
e.g. .L4-6 Liberia
1875-1876 Australia and New Zealand
1891 Pacific Islands
1893 Hawaii
1894 Others, A-Z
1896 Agents of foreign principals

PROCEDURE IN INTERNATIONAL DISPUTES: INTERNATIONAL ARBITRATION. WORLD PEACE, INTERNATIONAL ORGANIZATIONS, ETC.

Periodicals
1901 English and American
1902 French and Belgian
1903 Other
1904.5 Study and teaching. Research
1905 Handbooks, manuals, etc.
Societies, institutions, etc., for the promotion of peace
.5 Directories
International
1906 Carnegie Endowment for International Peace
.A1-3 Serials
.A4 Annual report
.A5 Charter
.A6 Announcements, circulars
United States public documents
.A63 Collections. By earliest date
.A65 Separate documents. By date
.A7-Z History

.Z5 Pamphlets
1907 Other, A-Z
1908 Local. By country, A-Z
1910 Congresses and conferences
International
The Hague Conferences
1912 Collections
1913 1st Conference (1899)
Official publications
.A1 Preliminary correspondence
.A13 Acts, proceedings
.A16 Rules
.A2A-Z Official publications by countries taking part, A-Z
Under each:
(1) Preliminary
(2) Acts, proceedings
(3) Other
.A3-4 2d Conference (1907)
Subarranged like JX1913.A1-A2
Works on the conferences. Nonofficial
1916 General
1918 Popular
1919 General special
Permanent Court of Arbitration
Cf. JX1971.5, Hague Permanent Court of International Justice
JX1990, International courts
1925 Documents
.A2 (1) Preliminary. By date
.A5 (2) Sessions
1928 General
Other international congresses
1930 Congresses with permanent organization.
By name, A-Z
Under each:
(1) Acts, proceedings
(2) History
1931 Other. By date
National congresses
United States
1932 Permanent. By name, A-Z
1933 Other. By date
1935 Other countries, A-Z
Under each:
(1) By name
(2) By date
1936 Exhibitions. Museums
.5 Celebrations, festivals
Including Peace Day
General works. History
Including popular peace literature, pacifism, and the moral and ethical aspects of peace
1937 Collections
1938 Comprehensive
By period
1941 Ancient
1942 Medieval
1944 Modern
1945 17th century
1946 18th century

19th century
1948 International arbitration, world peace
1949 Popular works
1950 International organization
20th century
1952 International arbitration, world peace
1953 Popular works
1954 International organization
1961 By country, A-Z
Prefer JX1938-JX1953
.A3 America
1962 Biography, A-Z
.A2 Collected
1963 Pamphlets
.Z9 Uncataloged materials
1964 Illustrative material. Fiction, etc.
e.g. Imaginary wars and works written to show the horrors of war
Illustrative and fictional works may also be classed as follows:
(1) Works on military tactics class in U
(2) Works showing weakness of national defense class in UA
(3) Works illustrating world politics class in D445
(4) Literary works class in P
1964.3 Labor and war
.4 Motion pictures and peace
.5 Press and peace movements
.7 Radio broadcasting and peace
1965 Women and peace movements
.5 Youth and peace movements
Theory, philosophy, see U21
Special topics
1968 Compromisory clause
1971 Courts of international arbitration
Cf. JX1925+, Hague Permanent Court of Arbitration
JX1990, International courts
.5 Permanent Court of International Justice
.6 International Court of Justice
1974 Disarmament. Arms control
Cf. HC65, Economic impact of defense and disarmament
UA12.5, Disarmament inspection
UA15+, Army budgets
.5 Conference on the limitation of armament, Washington, D.C., 1921-22
.A1-7 Documents
e.g. .A15 Preliminary documents
.A2 1st-3d plenary sessions
.A3 Proposal of the United States for limitation of naval armament
.A5 Address of President
.A6 Documents. By country, A-Z
.A7 Special missions. By country, A-Z
.A9-Z Works. By author or title, A-Z
.7 Nuclear weapons
.73 Nuclear nonproliferation
.735 Nuclear-weapon-free zones
.74 By region or country, A-Z
.75 Strategic Arms Limitation Talks I, 1969
Strategic Arms Limitation Talks II, 1979
.76 Strategic Arms Reduction Talks
.8 Nuclear crisis control
1975 League of Nations

.A1 Periodicals. Societies
.A2-5 Documents
Collected sets
.A2 By official number
.A25 By sales number
.A3 Official journal
.A37 Monthly summary
Texts of the covenant
.A39 English. By date
.A392 Other languages, A-Z
.A393 Amendments. By date
.A395 Proposed amendments. By date
.A397 Reports on application. By date
Assembly
Records
.A42 Committees
.A422 Index to the Records
.A423 Plenary meetings
.A425 Journal
.A43 Special reports of meetings. By date
.A433 List of delegates
.A435 Official guide
.A437 Miscellaneous documents. By date
.A438 Rules of procedure. By date
.A439 Reports of national delegates.
By country, A-Z
Council
.A44 Minutes
Report on the work of the League
.A4415 English
.A4416 French
.A45 Special reports. By date
.A455 Miscellaneous documents. By date
.A46 Reports of special representatives.
By country, A-Z
.A465 Rules of procedure. By date
Secretariat. Secretary-General
.A488 Serials
.A49 Nonserial documents. By date
.A5-Z General works
.5 League of Nations in relation to individual countries, A-Z
.A2 Collective
.6 Sanctions (economic and military)
.7 Geneva protocol
.8 High Commission for Refugees
.A1 General
.A3-Z By country, A-Z
.9 Miscellaneous works and pamphlets
1976 Genesis of the United Nations
Including general works on preliminary conferences
.3 Dumbarton Oaks Conversations, 1944
.4 San Francisco Conference, 1945
.5 Preparatory Commission of the United Nations
.8 Ratification of the United Nations Charter
By country, A-Z
1977 United Nations
.A1 Periodicals. Societies
Documents
Texts of the charter

.A15 English
.A16 Other languages, A-Z
.A22 Journal
Bulletin
.A3 English edition
.A314 French edition
.A315 Spanish edition
.A3155 Resolutions
By editor or compiler, A-Z
Secretariat. Secretary-General
Including subordinate departments, committees, library
.A316-359 Serials
Arranged alphabetically by subheading
.A36 Nonserial documents. By date
.A362A-Z Nonofficial publications. By author, A-Z
.A365 Administrative Tribunal
General handbooks, manuals, etc.
.A37 Serial. By title, A-Z
.A38 Nonserial. By date
.A39 Other documents. By date
.A4 General Assembly
Official records
.A41 English edition
.A417 French edition
.A418 Spanish edition
Journal
.A42 English edition
.A422 French edition
.A423-46 Other serials
.A47 Nonserial documents of individual sessions. By date
.A48 Reports of national delegations accredited to the General Assembly. Subarranged by country, A-Z, using two successive cutter numbers for serials and nonserials (by date)
.A49 Miscellaneous documents. By date
.A495A-Z Nonofficial publications. By author, A-Z
.A5 Security Council
.A51 Journal
.A515 Official records
.A52 Report to the General Assembly
.A54 Nonserial documents of meetings. By date
Prefer classification by subject
.A59 Miscellaneous documents. By date
.A593 Nonofficial publications. By author, A-Z
.A595 Selected documents. By compiler, A-Z
.A6-Z7 General works
.Z8 Popular and juvenile works
.18 Relations with regional organizations
.A2 General
.A3-Z By organization, A-Z
.2 Relations with individual countries, A-Z
.A1 Collective
.25 Relations with nonmember nations
Individual countries, see JX1977.2
.3 Relations with learned societies, universities
Class works on cooperation in special projects with the project
.A2 General works
.A3-Z By society, university, etc.
.8 Special topics about the United Nations, A-Z
.D6 Documentation

.F5 Finance
.H4 Headquarters
.L35 Languages. Translating
.M4 Membership
.O35 Officials and employees
.P8 Postal administration
.P85 Privileges and immunities
.S3 Sanctions
.T4 Technical assistance
.T7 Treaty-making power
.V4 Veto
.V6 Voting

1979 Regional organization. Regionalism
1981 Other topics, A-Z
.A35 Air force (International)
.B65 Boundary disputes
.N8 Nullity
.P3 Papacy
.T45 Terrorism

Arbitration treaties
1985 General collections
1987 United States
.A1-3 Collections
Treaties with several countries collectively
.A4 Documents. By date of signature (or, if better known, by date of ratification)
.A42A-Z General works
.A5-Z Separate treaties. By country, A-Z
1988 Other countries, A-Z (Collections)
1989 Other treaties to which the United States is not a party
Subarranged by year and month
1990 International courts
Cf. JX1971, Courts of international arbitration
.A2 General
.A3-Z Individual courts
Arbitration cases
1991 General collections
Subarrange:
.A2-28 Collections of cases of the Hague Permanent Court of Arbitration, chronologically
.A3-Z Other collections. By editor, A-Z
1995 International unions, conventions, congresses
Cf. JC362, JX1245+

INTERNATIONAL LAW

Treatises (History and theory)
Ancient
2001 Sources and documents
2005 General works
2008 Oriental states
2009 Special, A-Z
2011 Greece
2014 Special topics, A-Z
.R5 Rhodian laws
.T7 Treaties
2021 Rome
Special topics
2025 Jus feciale
2027 Jus gentium

2029 Jus sacrum
2035 Other, A-Z
2041 Medieval to 1500
2051 Special topics, A-Z
2060 Individual publicists, A-Z
e.g. .T4 Thomas Aquinas
Modern
2061 1500-1713
2066 Special topics
Individual publicists
Class here collected works and general theoretical works; f or works on special subjects, see the subject in JX4001+, etc.
For subarrangment, see tables at the end of JX
2070-2071 Alonso de la Vera Cruz
2072-2073 Ayala
2075-2076 Bodin
2081-2082 Brunus
2083 Brunus to Cumberland
2084-2085 Cumberland
2086 Cumberland to Gentilis
2087-2088 Gentilis
2091-2099 Grotius (1)
2103-2104 Hobbes
2107 Hobbes to Leibnitz
2109-2110 Leibnitz
2112-2113 Loccenius
2115-2116 Machiavelli
2117 Machiavelli to Molloy
2118-2119 Molloy
2125-2126 Peckius
2131-2139 Pufendorf (1)
2141-2142 Rachel
2144-2145 Santerna
2147-2148 Selden
2155-2156 Suarez
2157 Suarez to Vitoria
2158-2159 Vitoria
2161-2169 Wicquefort (1)
2181-2182 Zouch
2206 18th century
2215 Special topics
English publicists
2220 A to Bentham
2221-2222 Bentham
2223 Bentham to Fulbeck
2225-2226 Fulbeck
2227 Fulbeck to Rutherforth
2231-2232 Rutherforth
2233 Rutherforth to Z
Dutch publicists
2242 A to Bynkershoek
2243-2244 Bynkershoek
2245 Bynkershoek to Z
French publicists
2260 A to Mably
2261-2262 Mably
2266 Mably to Montesquieu
2271-2272 Montesquieu
2273 Montesquieu to Neyron

2272-2275	Neyron
2276	Neyron to Z
	German publicists
2303-2304	Achenwall
2305	Achenwall to Glafey
.E5	Eggers
2306-2307	Glafey
2308	Glafey to Gunther
2311-2312	Gunther to Heineccius
2314-2315	Heineccius (Heinecke)
2316	Heineccius to Kant
2321-2322	Kant
2323	Kant to Martens
.K7	Kohler, H
	Martens, G.F. von, see JX2814+
2326	Martens to Moser
2328-2329	Moser, F.C.
2332-2333	Moser, J.J.
2334	Moser to Ompteda
2335-2336	Ompteda
2339	Ompteda to Thomasius
.R7	Romer, C.H. von
2344-2345	Thomasius
2346	Thomasius to Wolff
.W2	Weidler
.W3	Wenck
2347-2348	Wolff, C. von
2349	Wolff to Z
.Z3	Zechin
	Italian publicists
2370	A to Azuni
2371-2372	Azuni
2373	Azuni to Lampredi
2374-2375	Lampredi
2379	Lampredi to Z
2388	Spanish and Portuguese publicists, A-Z
.M8	Muriel, Domingo (Morelli)
.O5	Olmeda y Leon
.O7	Ortega y Cotes
	Scandinavian publicists
2391	A to Hubner
	Eggers, see JX2305.E5
2393-2394	Hubner
2395	Hubner to Z
	Swiss publicists
2400	A to Burlamaqui
2401-2402	Burlamaqui
2406	Burlamaqui to Vattel
.F4	Felice, F.B.
2411-2419	Vattel (1)
2420	Vattel to Z
2435	Other. By country, A-Z
2441	19th century
2446	Special topics
	American publicists
2451	A to Davis, C.
.B6	Bowen, H.W.
2455-2456	Davis, C.K.
2458-2459	Davis, G.B.

2460	Davis, G.B. to Field
.D7	Duane
2464-2465	Field. D.D.
2467-2468	Gallaudet
2469	Gallaudet to Halleck
.G2	Gardner
.G4	Glenn
2475	Halleck
2478-2479	Kent
2480	Kent to Lawrence, W.B.
2481-2482	Lawrence, W.B.
2483	Lawrence to Snow
.L6	Lieber
.P7	Pomeroy
.S3	Schuyler
2486-2487	Snow
2489-2490	Story
2492-2493	Wharton
2495-2496	Wheaton
2498-2499	Woolsey
2500	Woolsey to Z
2502	Dutch publicists, A-Z
	English publicists
2503	A to Amos
2505-2506	Amos
2507	Amos to Creasy
2514-2515	Creasy
2523	Creasy to Hall
.G6	Griffith, W.
2524-2525	Hall, W.E.
2527-2528	Hertslet
2529	Hertslet to Holland
2531-2532	Holland
2533	Holland to Hosack
2538-2539	Hosack
2540	Hosack to Lawrence
2542-2543	Lawrence, T.J.
2545-2546	Levi
2548-2549	Lorimer
2550	Lorimer to Mackintosh
2552-2553	Mackintosh
2554	Mackintosh to Maine
2555-2556	Maine, Sir Henry
2558-2559	Manning
2564	Manning to Phillimore
.M5	Miller, William G.
2565-2566	Phillimore
2567	Phillimore to Polson
2572-2573	Polson
2574	Polson to Stowell
2578-2579	Stowell
2580	Stowell to Twiss
2582-2583	Twiss
2584	Twiss to Ward
.W3	Walker
2585-2586	Ward, Robert Plumer
2588-2589	Westlake
2590	Westlake to Wildman
2592-2593	Wildman

2594	Wildman to Z
	French and Belgian publicists
2607	A to Bonfils
2608-2609	Bonfils
2613	Bonfils to Cauchy
.B8	Bry, Georges
2614-2615	Cauchy
2616	Cauchy to Cussy
.C4	Chretien
2624-2625	Cussy
2626	Cussy to Despagnet
2641-2642	Despagnet
2643	Despagnet to Fauchille
2651-2652	Fauchille
2656	Fauchille to Feraud
2658-2659	Feraud-Giraud
2660	Feraud to Funck
2668-2669	Funck-Brentano
2671-2672	Garden, Guillaume de, comte
2673	Garden to Laveleye
.G2	Gerard de Rayneval
.G4	Gondon
2687-2688	Laveleye
2701	Laveleye to Nys
.L3	Leseur
.M3	Michel, C.L.S.
2702-2703	Nys
2704	Nys to Piedelievre
2714-2715	Piedelievre
2716	Piedelievre to Pradier
2725-2726	Pradier-Fodere
2728-2729	Proudhon
2730	Proudhon to Renault
2735-2736	Renault
2737	Renault to Rivier
2739-2740	Rivier
2742-2743	Rolin-Jacquemyns
2745-2746	Rouard de Card
2747	Rouard to Sorel
2751-2752	Sorel
2753	Sorel to Z
	German and Austrian publicists
2774	A to Bluntschli
2778-2779	Bulmerincq
2781-2782	Gagern
2783	Gagern to Gz
.G3	Gareis
2786	H to Heffter
.H3	Hartmann
2787-2788	Heffter
2789	Heffter to Holtzendorff
.H3	Heilborn
2791-2792	Holtzendorff
2793	Holtzendorff to Kaltenborn
2797-2798	Kaltenborn von Strachau
2799	Kaltenborn to Kamptz
2801-2802	Kamptz
2804-2805	Kluber
2806	Kluber to Lasson

2811-2812 Lasson, Adolf
2814-2815 Martens, G.F.von
2817-2818 Neumann
2819 Neumann to Oppenheim
2821-2822 Oppenheim, H.B.
2824 Oppenheim to Saalfeld
.P7 Politz
.Q3 Quaritsch
.R3 Resch
2826-2827 Saalfeld
2828 Saalfeld to Savigny
2831-2832 Savigny
2833 Savigny to Schmalz
2834-2835 Schmalz
2836 Schmalz to Schulze
.S4 Schmelzing
2838-2839 Schulze
2841-2842 Stoerk
2843 Stoerk to Z
.U6 Ullmann
Greek publicists
2844 A to Saripoulos
2845-2846 Saripoulos
2847 Saripoulos to Z
Italian publicists
2857 A to Carnazza
2858-2859 Carnazza-Amari
2860 Carnazza to Casanova
2862-2863 Casanova
2865-2866 Celli
2868-2869 Contuzzi
2870 Contuzzi to Del Bon
2872-2873 Del Bon
2875-2876 Esperson
2878-2879 Ferrero Gola
2881-2882 Fiore
2883 Fiore to Grasso
2887-2888 Grasso
2889 Grasso to Macri
2894-2895 Macri
2897-2898 Mamiani
2899 Mamiani to Morello
2904-2905 Morello
2910 Morello to Pertile
.O7 Olivi, Luigi
2914-2915 Pertile
2917-2918 Pierantoni
2919 Pierantoni to Sandona
2924-2925 Sandona
2926 Sandona to Schiattarella
2928-2929 Schiattarella
2930 Schiattarella to Z
Russian publicists
2940 A to Bergholm
2941-2942 Bergholm
2943 Bergholm to Martens
2951-2952 Martens, F.F.
2953 Martens to Z
Scandinavian publicists

2954	A to Matzen
2955-2956	Matzen
2957	Matzen to Tetens
2961-2962	Tetens
2963	Tetens to Z
	Spanish, Portuguese, Latin American publicists
2966	A to Alcorta
2967-2968	Alcorta
2969	Alcorta to Arenal
2975-2976	Arenal
2977	Arenal to Bello
2978-2979	Bello
2980	Bello to Calvo
.C3	Calcano
2984-2985	Calvo
2986	Calvo to Ferrater
.C7	Cruchaga Tocornal
.D5	Diez de Medina
2991-2992	Ferrater
2994-2995	Ferreira, R.
2996	Ferreira to Gestoso
3001-3002	Gestoso y Acosta
3003	Gestoso to Labra
3007-3008	Labra y Cadrana
3015	Labra to Lopez Sanchez
.L5	Lopez, Jose F.
3017-3018	Lopez Sanchez
3019	Lopez to Madiedo
3021-3022	Madiedo, Manuel M.
3027	Madiedo to Mozo
.M5	Montufar y Rivera Maestre
.M6	Moreira de Almeida
3028-3029	Mozo
3030	Mozo to Olivart
3034-3035	Olivart
3036	Olivart to Pando
3038-3039	Pando
3040	Pando to Pinheiro
.P4	Perez Gomar, Gregorio
3041-3042	Pinheiro-Ferreira
3043	Pinheiro to Riquelme
3045-3046	Riquelme
3047.R4	Rodriguez Sarachaga
3048-3049	Seijas
3050	Seijas to Torres Campos
3055-3056	Torres Campos
3058-3059	Tremosa y Nadal
3060	Tremosa to Z
3085	Other, by nationality, A-Z
	e.g. .H8 Hungarian
2091	20th century
3096	Special topics
	American publicists
3110	A to Hershey
.F6	Foulke, R.R.
.H3	Hall, A.B.
3131-3132	Hershey, Amos S.
2140	Hershey to Maxey
.H8	Hyde, C.C.

Class	Subject
3151-3152	Maxey
3160	Maxey to Scott
.R4	Root, Elihu
3178-3179	Scott, J. Brown
3180	Scott to Taylor
.S4	Singer, B.
.S7	Stockton, C.H.
3181-3182	Taylor, Hannis
3185	Taylor to Wilson
3191-3192	Wilson, George G.
3195	Wilson to Z
	English publicists
	Including Canadian
3205	A to Baker
3211-3212	Baker, Sir George S.
3215	Baker to Birkenhead
.B3	Baty, Thomas
3220-3221	Birkenhead, Frederick Edwin Smith
3225	Birkenhead to Oppenheim
.B8	Burns, C.D.
3264-3265	Oppenheim, Lassa F.L.
3275	Oppenheim to Smith
.P5	Plater, C.D.
3295	Smith to Z
	French and Belgian publicists
3310	A to Merignhac
3351-3352	Merignhac
3375	Merignhac to Z
	German and Austrian publicists
3425	A to Liszt
.C9	Cybichowski
.K7	Kohler
3445-3446	Liszt, Franz von
3491	Liszt to Z
.P6	Pohl, H.
.S5	Schucking, W.M.A.
.Z5	Zorn
3545	Italian publicists, A-Z
3651	Spanish, Portuguese, Latin American publicists, A-Z
3695	Other. By nationality, A-Z
	Treatises on special topics
	International persons
4000	The individual as subject of international law
4001	The state as subject of international law
4003	General special
	Including fundamental rights of states from the standpoint of international law
	Sovereign states
	General, see JX4041
4005	Unions of sovereign states. Alliances (From the standpoint of international law)
4008	Suzerain states
4011	Semisovereign, dependent, and vassal states
	Special
4015	Mediatized states
4021	Protected states. Protectorates. Mandates. International trusteeships
4023	By country, A-Z
4025	Vassal states

4027 Colonies and international law
4031 Neutralized states. Neutralization
Cf. JX1305+, Neutrality policy
JX5355+, Neutrality in war
4033 Special states, A-Z
4035 Regions: rivers, canals, etc. (General)
4041 Sovereignty and international law
Special
4044 Recognition of sovereignty
4053 Transfer of sovereignty
4054 International plebiscite
4055 State dismemberment. Civil war
Cf. JC491+, Political theory
4061 Dissolution of a state
4068 Other, A-Z
.C7 Condominium
.E92 Exclaves
.G6 Governments in exile
.I6 Internationalized territories. Free cities
.S5 Servitudes
.S8 State bankruptcy
4071 Means of protecting independence.
Self-preservation. Noninterference
Special
4077 Exterritorial self-defense
4079 Other special, A-Z
.N4 Necessity (Doctrine)
.P7 Propaganda
4081 International courtesy. Comity of nations
4084 International status of individual countries, regions, organizations
.A15 Aland Islands
.A34 Afghanistan
.A43 Algeria
.A45 Alsace
.A5 Antarctic regions
.A68 Arctic regions
.A7 Armenia
.A8 Austria
.A86 Aves Island
.B3 Bali Island
.B314 Baltic Sea
.B315 Baltic Straits
.B32 Bangladesh
.B38 Berlin
.B4 Bessarabia
.B55 Black Sea
.B8 Bukowina
.C34 Canary Islands
.C5 China
.C52 China (People's Republic of China, 1949-)
.C6 Commonwealth of Nations
.C63 Constance, Lake of
.C86 Cyprus
.C9 Czechoslovakia
.D64 Dodecanese
.D68 Dover, Strait of
.E9 Euphrates River
.F34 Falkland Islands

.G3 Germany
  Including West Germany
.G4 East Germany
.G5 Gibraltar
.G52 Gibraltar, Straits of
.H66 Hong Kong
.I7 Irian Barat
.I8 Israel
.J3 Japan
.J4 Jerusalem
.J67 Jordan (Territory under Israeli occupation, 1967-)
Kangwane (South Africa), see .S62
.K34 Kashmir
Kattegat (Denmark and Sweden), see .B315
.K45 Khuzistan, Iran. Arabistan
.K48 Kiel Canal (Germany)
.K55 Knights of Malta
.K67 Korea
.K673 North Korea
.K82 Kuril Islands
.K83 Kwantung Leased Territory
.M3 Malacca, Strait of
Middle East, see .N4
Namibia, see .S68
.N4 Near East. Middle East
.N45 Netherlands Antilles
.N65 North Sea
.P27 Pacific Islands Territory
.P28 Paracel Islands
  Including Spratly Islands
.P39 Persian Gulf
.P4 Persian Gulf States
.P65 Polar regions
.P9 Puerto Rico
.R5 Rhodesia, Southern
.R65 Romania
.R9 Ryukyu Islands
.S3 Saarland
.S32 Sabah
.S36 San Andres y Providencia (Colombia)
.S45 Senkaku Islands
.S5 Silesia
Skagerrak, see .B315
Sound, The (Denmark and Sweden), see .B315
.S62 South Africa
.S63 South China Sea Islands
.S65 Moluccas
.S68 Southwest Africa. Namibia
.S7 Spanish Sahara
.S88 Sudetenland
.S94 Svalbard
.T25 Taiwan
.T27 Tajikistan
.T3 Tangier (Zone)
.T45 Tibet
.T48 Tiran, Strait of
.T5 Titicaca Lake
.T67 Transkei
.T7 Trentino-Alto Adige, Italy

.U4 Ukraine
.V5 Vietnam
West Bank of the Jordan River, see .J67
.W45 White Russia
Right of domain and property
Territory
4085 General works
Special
4088 Acquisition of territory
Special
4093 By occupation and possession
4095 By discovery
4098 By cession. Annexation
By conquest, see JX4093
4099 Leased territories. Military bases
4111 Boundaries
By country, see D-F
Special
4115 Natural boundaries
4118 Mountains
4122 Rivers
4125 Lakes
4131 Coast. Territorial waters
4135 Three-mile limit
4137 Bays
4138 Gulfs and harbors
4141 Straits
4143 Continental shelf
4144 Contiguous zones, Maritime
.5 Economic zones, Maritime
4145 Artificial boundaries
4147 Adjoining territory. Nuisances
Cf. JX5405, Responsibility of the state for nuclear hazards
4148 Islands
4149 Archipelagoes
4150 International rivers and waterways (General)
4155 Interoceanic canals
Treaties and conventions. Treaty making
4161 Early works to 1800
Treatises
4165 English
4166 French
4167 German
4169 Other
4171 Special topics, A-Z
.A3 Accession
.C6 Clausula rebus sic stantibus
.D8 Duration
Favored nation clause, see HF1721
.G8 Guaranty treaties
.I6 Interpretation
.L3 Language
.O3 Obligation
.O32 Obsolescence
.P3 Pacta sunt servanda
.P4 Peace treaties
.P77 Provisional application
.R3 Ratification

.R37 Reciprocity
.R4 Reservations
.R45 Revision
.S72 State succession
.T5 Termination
.T6 Third parties
.U5 Unequal treaties
.V5 Violation
.W3 War
4172 Jurisdiction. Competence
4175 Exterritoriality
4185 Jurisdiction over property
4190 Jurisdiction over shipping
4195 Exterritorial crime
Consular courts, see JX1700+
Nationality. Allegiance. Citizenship
Cf. JC; JF801+; JX6111+
4203 History
4204 Ancient
4205 By state or nation, A-Z
4206 Medieval
4207 Modern
Laws. Legislation
4209 Collections of the laws of different countries
4211 General works
4215 Nationality
4216 Naturalization
4226 Expatriation
4231 Other special, A-Z
.C5 Children
.D5 Diplomatic and consular personnel
.M3 Marriage and nationality
.M5 Minorities
.O7 Option of nationality
.R5 Repatriation
.S8 Statelessness
4241 Domicile
4251 Passports
4253 By country, A-Z
4255 Aliens
Cf. JV6001+,Emigration and immigration
4261 Expulsion. Deportation
4262 Internationally protected persons
.5 Crimes against internationally protected persons
4263 Other special topics, A-Z
.A8 Arrest and imprisonment
Individual cases, see .P8
.A9 Assistance to aliens
.M6 Military service
.P6 Alien property
Including nationalization and valuation
.P7 Protection of nationals abroad by their home states
.P8 Individual cases, A-Z
e.g. . W4 White affair
.P82 Protection of stockholders abroad by their home states
.T8 Travelers in foreign countries
Special countries
4265 United States
.A1-A5 Documents

.A7-Z Monographs
4270 Other countries, A-Z
Under each:
(1) Documents
(2) Monographs
Right of asylum. Extradition
4275 Collections
Treatises
General only; prefer JX4301+
4280 Early to 1800
4281 English
4282 French and Belgian
4283 German
4284 Italian
4285 Spanish, Portuguese, Latin American
4286 Scandinavian
4288 Other, A-Z
4292 Special topics, A-Z
.L5 Legations
.P6 Political offenses
.P8 Provisional arrest
.R4 Refugees
.S5 Ships
By country
United States
4301 Documents
4302 Separate documents. By date
4305 General works
4311 Pamphlets
4316 Canada and other British America, A-Z
4318 West Indies other than British, A-Z
4321 Mexico
4326 Central America, A-Z
4335 South America, A-Z
Europe
4341 Great Britain
4345 Other European, A-Z
Asia
4351 Former United States possessions
Including Philippines
4353 Former British possessions
4357 Other former European possessions, A-Z
4365 Other, A-Z
Africa
4371 Former British possessions, A-Z
4377 Former possessions of other European countries, A-Z
4384 Other, A-Z
4387 Australia, A-Z
4391 New Zealand
Oceania
4394 United States possessions
Including Hawaii
4398 Other, A-Z
4399 Cases. By name, A-Z
Jurisdiction over the High Seas. Maritime law
Cf. JX4190, Jurisdiction over shipping
JX5203+, Maritime war
JX6271+, Commercial law
JX5239, JX5355+, Neutrality

4408 Collections
4410-4418 Treatises
Divide like JX4280-JX4288
4419 Pamphlets
4421 Codes
4422 By country, A-Z
Special topics
The open and closed sea
4423 Early works to 1800
4425 Recent
4426 Ocean bottom (Maritime law)
4427 Offshore structures. Artificial islands
4431 Navigation laws (General)
4434 Collisions at sea
4436 Shipwreck, salvage
4444 Piracy
Cf. D-F, History
G535+, Geography
4446 Cases, A-Z
4447 Slavers, slave trade
Right of visit and search, see JX5268
4449 Other special, A-Z
.A25 Access to the sea
.A5 Airports (Floating)
.A6 Angary
.D4 Death on the high seas
.N3 Nationality of ships
.R3 Responsibility for shipments
.S4 Seizure of vessels and cargoes
.S5 Shipmasters
.W27 Warships
International disputes and collisions
4471 Measures short of war
Special
4472 Diplomatic protests
4473 Diplomatic negotiations for peaceful settlement
4475 Mediation
Arbitration, see JX1901+
4481 Intervention
4484 Retorsion
4486 Reprisals
4489 Boycott
4491 Embargo
4494 Pacific blockade
Law of war
4505 Collections
4507 Codes
4508 History
4510-4518 Treatises
Divided like JX4280-JX4288
4521 Pamphlets
Philosophy and ethics of war, see U21
4525 Treaties, Effect of
4530 Region of war
Kinds of war
4541 Civil war
4552 Declaration and outbreak
Special
4556 Hostilities prior to declaration

4561 Declaration
4564 Necessity for declaration
4571 Belligerency
Special
4574 Recognition of belligerency
4581 Alliance, succor, etc.
4591 Belligerents and noncombatants
4595 Martial law
5001 Belligerent measures. Warfare
Special
5003 Invasion. Occupation
.5 Money. Occupation currency
5005 Permissable violence
5011 Devastation
5117 Bombardments and sieges
5121 Deceit, spies, etc.
Cf. UB270+, Military administration
5123 Guerrilla warfare
5124 Air warfare
5127 Arms and instruments of war
5131 Prohibited instruments and methods
5133 Special, A-Z
.A7 Atomic bomb
.C5 Chemical and biological warfare
.D55 Directed energy weapons
.G3 Gas, Poison
.I5 Incendiary weapons
5135 Special topics, A-Z
.F7 Fortifications
.M5 Military necessity
.R3 Railroads
Treatment of the wounded. Geneva and Hague conventions
Including works on the Geneva and Hague conventions collectively
Official publications
.A2-24 Geneva, 1864
.A2 Preparatory conferences and committees. Preliminary drafts
.A21 Preliminary correspondence
.A22 Proceedings
.A225 Resolutions. Final act
Text of convention
.A23 English, or French and English
.A235 Other languages, A-Z
.A24 Other documents. By country, A-Z
.A25-29 Hague (III), 1899
Subdivided like JX5136.A2-24
.A3-34 Geneva, 1906
Subdivided like JX5136.A2-24
.A35-39 Hague (X), 1907
Subdivided like JX5136.A2-24
.A4-44 Geneva, 1929
Subdivided like JX5136.A2-24
.A45-49 Geneva, 1949
Subdivided like JX5136.A2-24
.A5-54 Geneva, 1974-1977
Subdivided like JX5136.A2-24
.A9-Z Other works
5141 Prisoners of war

.A1 Texts of international conventions.By date
.A2-Z Other works
5143 Hostages
5144 Protection of civilians
.A1 Texts of international conventions. By date
.A2-Z Other works
5145 Intercourse of belligerents
Special
5147 Protective signs
5148 Flag of truce
5151 Safe conduct
5161 Deserters
5166 Termination of belligerency
Special
5169 Cartels
5173 Truces and armistices
5177 Capitulations
5181 Treaties of peace
Cf. JX4165+, JX4525
Conquest of territory, <u>see</u> JX4093
5187 Postliminium
Maritime war
Collections
5203 Congresses. Conferences. By date
5205 Other
5207 History
5210-5218 Treatises
Divide like JX4280-JX4288
5221 Pamphlets
Special topics
5225 Blockade
Cf. JX4491, JX4494
5228 Capture
Cf. JX4449.S4, Seizure of vessels
JX5295+, Enemy property
Contraband
5231 Theory
5232 Lists. By country, A-Z
5234 Doctrine of continuous voyage
5237 Innocent passage
5239 War vessels in neutral ports
5241 Privateers and letters of marque
5243 Treatment of the wounded and shipwrecked. Hospital ships
.A1 Texts of international conventions. By date
.A2-Z Other works
5244 Other topics, A-Z
.A7 Armed merchant ships
.C6 Converted merchant ships
.M6 Mines
.S8 Submarines
Prize law
5245 Collections
5250-5258 Treatises
Divide like JX4280-JX4288
5261 By country, A-Z
Special
5263 Prize courts
5266 Procedure
5268 Right of visit and search

Including convoy
Cf. JX4408+, JX5316
5270 Effect on commercial relations of belligerents
Including trading with the enemy
5271 Special topics, A-Z
.C5 Contracts
.L4 License to trade
.M6 Moratorium
5275 Enemy aliens
5276 By country, A-Z
Property in war
5278 Collections
5280-5288 Treatises
Divide like JX4280-JX4288
5291 Pamphlets
Special topics
5295 Enemy property
Including wartime control of alien property
Special
5298 Public property
5305 Private property
5311 Scientific collections, art treasures, libraries, churches
5313 By country, A-Z
5316 Neutral property and trade
5321 Requisitions
5326 Damages. Claims
Right of visit and search, see JX5268
Neutrality
Cf. JX4031+, Neutralized states
5355 Collections
5360-5368 Treatises
Divide like JX4280-JX4288
5371 Pamphlets
Special topics
5383 Armed neutrality (Theory)
Class historical works in D295
5388 Asylum. Internment
5390 Exportation of munitions of war
5391 Infractions of neutrality
5393 Fitting out of war vessels for belligerents
5395 Foreign enlistment. Filibustering
5397 Other, A-Z
.A4 Air warfare
.L6 Loans
.N4 Neutral trade with belligerents
.P3 Passage of troops and goods
.P7 Press
.R4 Refueling of warships
5401 International responsibility. International delinquencies
For responsibility or delinquency inherent in a subject listed elsewhere, see the subject, e.g. JX4263.P6, Alien property
5402 Responsibility of the state
Denial of justice to aliens, see JX4255+
5404 Nonpayment of contract debts and damages
Cf. JX1393.D8, Drago doctrine
JX5485, Calvo doctrine and clause
5405 Nuclear hazards and damages
5407 Mass media

5408 Acts of unsuccessful insurgent governments
5410 Acts of private persons
.2 Hostile acts against foreign states
.3 Injuries and losses to aliens caused by mob violence, riots, etc.
Riots against foreign missions, see JX1683.P7
5411 Responsibility of international agencies
League of Nations, see JX1975+
United Nations, see JX1976+
International unions, bureaus, etc., see JX1995
5415 International offenses
Class here works on criminal law aspects of violations of international law. For noncriminal international delinquencies or noncriminal and criminal combined, see JX5401
5417 Criminal responsibility of individuals
5418 Crimes against humanity. Genocide
5419 Offenses against peace. Aggression
.5 War crimes
Cf. D625+, World War, 1914-1918
D803+, World War, 1939-1945
JX4505+, Law of war
5420 Terrorism
.5 Vandalism
Class here works on the destruction of cultural or artistic works
Piracy at sea, see JX4444+
Hijacking of aircraft, see JX5775.C7
Slave trade, see JX4447
5425 International criminal jurisdiction and courts
5428 International criminal courts
5430-5460 Criminal trials
Subarrange individual trials using tables below:
Tables
Table A—1 number
(0) Preliminaries. By date
Proceedings
.2 Indexes and digests
.3 General. By editor
.4 Statements by participants. By author
.5 Evidence. By date
.6 Judgments and minority opinions. By author
.7 Post-trial. By author
.8 General works. By author
Table B—Cutter number
.xA15 Preliminaries. By date
Proceedings
.A2-29 Indexes and digests
.A3-39 General. By editor
.A4-49 Statements by participants. By author
.A5 Evidence. By date
.A6-69 Judgments and minority opinions. By author
.A7-79 Post-trial. By author
.A8-Z General works. By author
5430 General works
5433 War crime trials
World War, 1939-1945
.5 Collected trials
5434 General works
5436 Trials by international military tribunals
5437 Nuremberg Trial of German War Criminals, 1945-1946 (Table A)

5438 Tokyo War Crimes Trial, 1946-1948 (Table A)
Trials by national courts other than those of the country of the defendant
Collected trials
5439 War crime trials, Nuremberg, 1946-1949 (subsequent proceedings) (Table A)
5440 Other collected trials
5441 Particular trials. By first named defendant or best known name, A-Z (Table B)
.E3 Eichmann trial
.J8 Justice case
.M3 Manila trial, 1946
Trials by the courts of defendant's own country
Trials by the courts of a particular country, see the country
Trials by the courts of countries in the same region, see the region
Trials by courts of countries in different regions, see K545 (not included in this guide)
5445 Other wars
5460 Mock trials. By first named defendant or best known name, A-Z
5482 Remedies
.5 Exhaustion of local remedies
5483 Claims and reparation
Including restitution, recompensation and satisfaction
5485 Calvo doctrine and clause
Drago doctrine, see JX1393.D8
5486 By region or country, A-Z
Transportation
5701 Railways
Aeronautics
5760 Periodicals. Societies
5762 Congresses. Conferences
5763 International public agencies
5768 Collections
5769 Treaties
.A2 Collections
.A3-Z Separate treaties
5770 History
5771 General works
5775 Special topics, A-Z
.C7 Crimes abroard aircraft. Hijacking of aircraft
.L5 Licensing
.S3 Salvage
.T7 Traffic control
5810 Space law

Tables of subdivisions under individual publicists in JX2072-JX3695
Table 1—10 numbers
(1) Collections and selections
(3-8) Separate works (see note below)
(9) Criticism
Table 2—2 numbers
(1). A1 Collections and selections
.A3-Z Separate works (see note below)
(2) Criticism

Note: In Table 1 separate works are to be assigned separate numbers, 3-8, arranged by alphabetical order of original titles. Under each: Texts in original language, .A1 and date; Translations arranged alphabetically by language. In Table 2 arrange similarly using successive cutter numbers for translations. Authors having cutter numbers are arranged in the same order with the cutter number for the original title following the author number.

(U) MILITARY SCIENCE (GENERAL)

Periodicals and societies. By language
1 English
2 French
3 German
4 Other languages (not A-Z)
7 Congresses
Almanacs
By country
9 United States
10 Other countries, A-Z
11 Army lists. By country, A-Z
For special branches of the service, see UB-UG
13.A1A-Z Museums. Exhibitions
.A2-Z By region or country, A-Z
Under each country:
.x General works
.x2 Special. By city, A-Z
Collected works
14 Early through 1700
1701-
15 Several authors
17 Individual authors
20 Satire
War. Philosophy. Military sociology
Including philosophy of world peace
General works
21 Through 1945
.2 1946-
.5 Military sociology
.7 Mathematical models. Methodology
.75 Women and the military
22 Ethics. Morale
.3 Military psychology
24 Dictionaries. Encyclopedias
25 Dictionaries in two or more languages
26 Military symbols and abbreviations
27 History of military science
Cf. D-F, History of military events
29 Ancient
31 Oriental
33 Greek
35 Roman
37 Medieval
39 Modern
41 19th century
42 20th century
43 By region or country, A-Z
For the history of the military situation, defenses, army, etc., of individual countries, see UA21+
45 Historiography
Biography

For military personnel identified with military events in the history of a particular country, see D-F

51 Collective
By region or country
United States
52 Collective
53 Individual, A-Z
Other regions or countries
54 Collective
55 Individual, A-Z
General works
101 Early through 1788
102 1789-
104 General special
105 Popular works
106 Juvenile works
108 Textbooks. By author
110 Soldiers' handbooks
By country
113 United States
115 Other countries, A-Z
130 Officers handbooks
By country
133 United States
135 Other countries, A-Z
150 Military planning
By country
153 United States
155 Other countries, A-Z
Strategy
General works
161 Early through 1788
162 1789-
.6 Deterrence
163 Miscellaneous topics (not A-Z)
Tactics
General works
164 Early through 1810
165 1811-
166 Study and teaching. Training
167 General special
.5 Special topics, A-Z
.A35 Advanced guard
.D37 Deception
.D4 Desert warfare
.E57 Envelopment
.E58 Environmental warfare. War use of weather control
.F6 Forest fighting
.H3 Hand-to-hand fighting
.J8 Jungle warfare
.L5 Lightning war
.M3 Machine-gun warfare
.M6 Motorized units
.N5 Night fighting
.P6 Polar warfare
.R34 Raids
.S7 Street fighting
.W5 Winter warfare
168 Logistics

170 Field service
By country
173 United States
175 Other countries, A-Z
180 Encampments
By country
183 United States
185 Other countries, A-Z
190 Guard duty, outposts
By country
193 United States
195 Other countries, A-Z
200 Debarkation. Landing maneuvers
205 Stream crossing
210 Skirmishing
215 Rearguard action
220 Reconnaissance. Scouting. Patrols
225 Combat survival. Evasion techniques
230 Riot duty
240 Small wars. Guerrilla warfare
241 Counterinsurgency. Counterguerrilla warfare
250 Maneuvers (Combined arms)
By country
253 United States
255 Other countries, A-Z
260 Joint operations. Combined operations
261 Amphibious warfare
262 Commando tactics
263 Nuclear warfare
264 Nuclear weapons (General)
Class here technical and administrative works. For works on the nuclear weapons or warfare policy of a single nation, see the general military policy of that nation
.3 United States
.4 By region or state, A-Z
.5 Other regions or countries, A-Z
265 Military expeditions
280 Tactical rides. General staff journeys
By country
283 United States
285 Other countries, A-Z
290 Maneuver grounds. Camps of instruction
By country
293 United States
294.5 Individual camps. By name, A-Z
295 Other countries, A-Z
310 War games
312 Problems, map maneuvers, etc.
313 Imaginary wars and battles (General)
Cf. JX1964, Works on the horrors of war
UA, Individual countries
320 Physical training of soldiers
By country
323 United States
325 Other countries, A-Z
390 Military research
By region or country
393 United States
.5 General special

394 Special institutions. By place, A-Z
395 Other regions or countries, A-Z
Military education and training
400 History
401 Ancient
402 Medieval
403 Modern
General
404 Through 1800
405 1801-
.5 Juvenile works
By region or country
America
408 United States
.3 General special
Including training
.5 Examinations
409 States, A-W
United States Military Academy, West Point
410.L1 General works. Histories
.A1-5 Official works
.L3 Illustrated works
Biography
.M1 .A1-5 Collective
.A6-Z Individual
.P1 Descriptive works
412 National War College, Washington, D.C.
413 Army War College, Carlisle Barracks, Pa.
415 Command and General Staff College, Fort Leavenworth, Kansas
420 Coast Artillery School, Fort Monroe, Va.
425 Engineer School, Fort Belvoir, Va.
428 Other government schools. By name, A-Z
.5 Reserved Officers' Training Corps (R.O.T.C.)
.7 Army Specialized Training Program
429 Military instruction in colleges. By name, A-Z
.A1 General works
430 Private military schools. By name, A-Z
Under each:
Official
.xA1-4 Serial
.xA5-7 Nonserial
.xA8-Z Other works. By author, A-Z
435 Military instruction in public schools
439 Military training camps for boys. By name, A-Z
440 Canada
442 Special subjects, A-Z
443 Provinces, A-Z
444 Schools. By place, A-Z
Under each:
.C1 Regulations. By date
.H1 Registers. By date
.L1 History. By date
.R1 Miscellaneous topics. By date
445 Mexico
447 Special subjects, A-Z
448 States, A-Z
449 Schools. By place, A-Z
Divide like U444

450 Central America
453 Countries
454 Schools. By place, A-Z
Divide like U444
455 West Indies
457 Islands, A-Z
459 Schools, A-Z
Divide like U444
465 South America
Divide individual countries with 3 numbers like U466-U468
466 Argentina
467 General special
468 Schools. By place, A-Z
Divide like U444
469-471 Bolivia
472-474 Brazil
475-477 Chile
478-480 Colombia
481-483 Ecuador
Guianas
484 Guyana
485 Surinam
486 French Guiana
487 Schools. By place, A-Z
Divide like U444
488-490 Paraguay
491-493 Peru
494-496 Uruguay
497-499 Venezuela
505 Europe
Divide individual countries with 5 numbers like U550-U554
510 Great Britain
511 Special periods
512 Special subjects, A-Z
.A5 Artillery
.C2 Cavalry
.E3 Economics
.E5 Military engineering
.I5 Infantry
.L2 Language
.P7 Programmed instruction
.T5 Technology
513 Examinations (General)
549 Military training in universities, public schools. etc., Officers' Training Corps
.5 Ireland
550 Austria. Austria-Hungary
551 Special periods
552 Special subjects, A-Z
.5 Examinations
553 States, provinces, etc., A-Z
554 Schools. By place, A-Z
Under each:
.A1-19 Serials
.C1 Regulations. By date
.H1 Registers. By date
.L1 History. By date
.R1 Miscellaneous. By date

555-559	Belgium
560-564	Denmark
565-569	France
570-574	Germany
	Including West Germany
574.5-54	East Germany
575-579	Greece
580-584	Netherlands
585-589	Italy
590-594	Norway
595-599	Portugal
600-604	Soviet Union
605-609	Spain
610-614	Sweden
615-619	Switzerland
620-624	Turkey
625	Balkan States
626	Bulgaria
628	Romania
629	Yugoslavia
630	Other countries, A-Z
635	Asia
	Divide individual countries with 5 numbers like U550-U554
640-644	China
645-649	India
650-654	Japan
655-659	Iran
660	Other countries, A-Z
670	Africa
680-684	Egypt
	Divide like U550-U554
695	Other countries, A-Z
700-704	Australia
	Divide like U550-U554
705-509	New Zealand
	Divide like U550-U554
710-714	Islands of the Pacific
	Divide like U550-U554
715	Nonmilitary education in armies
	By region or country
716	United States
717	Other regions or countries, A-Z
750	Military life, manners and customs
	By period
755	Ancient
757	Special topics, A-Z
760	Medieval
763	Special topics, A-Z
765	Modern
766	American
767	English
768	French
769	German
770	Italian
771	Russian
772	Spanish
773	Other
	History of arms and armor

799 Periodicals. Societies
General works
800.A2A-Z Early through 1800
.A3-Z 1801-
804 Museums. Exhibitions
Subarranged like U13
By period
805 Ancient
810 Medieval
813 Special, A-Z
815 Modern
By region or country
818 United States
819 Other American countries, A-Z
820 Europe, A-Z
821 Asia, A-Z
822 Africa, A-Z
823 Australia
.5 New Zealand
Pacific Islands, see GN (not included in this guide)
825 Armor
850 Swords and daggers
852 History
Prefer periods, U853+, to individual countries
853 Ancient
854 Medieval
855 Modern
856 By region or country, A-Z
872 Lances. Spears
Arms for throwing projectiles
By period
873 Ancient and medieval
875 Catapults, ballistas
877 Bows
878 Crossbows
Modern
880 Guns (History and antiquities)
Cf. UF530+, Ordnance
883 Artillery to 1800/1840
884 Small arms
By period
885 Early to 1700/1800
886 1700/1800-1860
889 19th-20th century
897 By region or country, A-Z

(UA) ARMIES: ORGANIZATION, DISTRIBUTION MILITARY SITUATION

10 General works
.5 National security
.7 Civilian-based defense. Nonviolent alternative defense
11 Military policy
.5 Limited war
12 Mutual security programs
.5 Disarmament inspection. Arms control verification. Nuclear arms control verification
.8 Guards troops
13 General organization of militia
14 Colonial troops. Indigeneous troops

Special, see UA668, UA679, etc.
15 Armies of the world. Armies and navies of the world
16 Military missions
17 Cost of armaments, budgets, estimates, etc.
Cf. JX1974, Disarmament
VA20+, Cost of navies
.5 Manpower
.A2A-Z General works
.A3-Z By country, A-Z
18.A2A-Z Industrial mobilization for war and defense
.A3-Z By region or country, A-Z
19 Military statistics (Theory and method)
By region or country
Class general regimental histories in the appropriate numbers below; for regimental histories connected with individual battles, wars, etc., see D-F
21 America
22 North America
United States
General military situation, military policy, defenses, etc.
23.A1A-Z Periodicals. Societies
.A2-Z General works
Department of Defense
.2 Annual reports, serial documents
.3 Special reports
.6 History
.7 Joint Chiefs of Staff
United States Army
24.A1-149 Annual reports of the War Department
.A15-16 Annual reports of the Department of the Army
.A17-175 Annual reports of the Assistant Secretary of the Army
.A18-19 Annual reports of the Comptroller of the Army
.A2-29 Annual reports of the Adjutant General
.A3-39 Annual reports of the Military Secretary
.A4-49 Annual reports of the Inspector General
.A5-54 Annual reports of the general commanding the army
.A55-675 Annual reports of the Chief of Staff
.A7 Miscellaneous documents. By date
25 General works
.5 Army expenditures and budgets
26.A1-6 Distribution, posts, etc.
.A7-Z Special. By place, A-Z
27 Divisions, A-Z
Tactical units
.3 Armies. By number and author
.5 Divisions. By number and author
28 Infantry
29 Regiments. By number and author
30 Cavalry. Armor
31 Regiments. By number and author
32 Artillery
33 Batteries, etc., By number and author
34 Other special troops. By name, A-Z
.R36 Rangers
.S64 Special Forces. Green Berets
37 Lists of veterans
39 By state, A-W
United States militia, volunteers, and reserves.
National Guard

General works
42.A1-59 United States documents
.A6A-Z Periodicals. Societies
.A7-Z Other works. By author
45 Armed Forces women's reserves
By state, see UA50-UA549 (not included in this guide)
565 United States Army auxiliaries, A-Z
.W6 Women's Army Corp. WAC
600 Canada
.6 Distribution, posts. By place, A-Z
601 Provinces, A-Z
602 Organizations. By name, A-Z
.3 Latin America (General)
603-605 Mexico
Divide like UA600-UA602
606-608 Central America
Divide like UA600-UA602
609-611 West Indies. Caribbean Area
Divide like UA600-602
612 South America
Divide individual countries with 3 numbers like UA600-UA602
.5 South Atlantic Ocean
613-615 Argentina
616-618 Bolivia
619-621 Brazil
622-624 Chile
625-627 Colombia
628-630 Ecuador
631 Guyana
632 Surinam
633 French Guiana
634-636 Paraguay
637-639 Peru
640-642 Uruguay
643-645 Venezuela
646 Europe
Divide individual countries with 10 numbers like UA670-UA679
.3 North Atlantic Treaty Organization (NATO). Supreme Headquarters, Allied Powers, Europe (SHAPE). European Defense Community
.5 Participation by individual countries, A-Z
.53 Baltic Sea region
.55 Mediterranean region
.6 North Sea region
.7 Scandinavia
.8 Eastern Europe
.85 Northern Europe
Great Britain
647 General military situation, military policy, defenses, etc.
648 General documents
Including reports of War Department and Parliamentary papers
649 British Army
.3 Distribution, posts
.32 Special. By place, A-Z
650 Infantry
651 Regiments. By number and author
652 Regiments. By name, A-Z
653 Militia regiments. By number and author
.5 Militia organizations. By name, A-Z
654 Cavalry. Armor

655 Troops. By number and author
656 Troops. By name, A-Z
657 Militia
.3 Militia organizations. By number and author
.5 Militia organizations. By name, A-Z
658.A1A-Z Artillery
.A5-Z Divisions, A-Z
.5 Militia artillery
.A1A-Z General works
.A2-Z Special, A-Z
659 Other special troops. By name, A-Z
661 Militia. Yeomanry. Territorial Force. Reserves
Regiments, etc., see UA653+
668 Colonial troops. Indigenous troops
For individual regiments, see UA840+
Austria. Austria-Hungary
670 General military situation, military policy, defenses, etc.
671 General reports
672 Army
Including organization, history, etc.
Infantry
673.A1-5 Documents
.A6-Z4 General works
.Z6 Organizations. By number and author
.Z9A-Z Organizations. By name
674 Cavalry. Armor
675 Artillery
676 Other special troops, A-Z
677 Militia
678 Local, A-Z
679 Colonial troops. Indigenous troops
680-689 Belgium
690-699 Denmark
France
700 General military situation, military policy, defenses, etc.
701 General documents
702 Army
Including organization, history, etc.
.3 Distribution, posts
.32 Special. By place, A-Z
Infantry
703.A1-5 Documents
.A6A-Z General works
.A7 Infantry regiments of the line. By number and author
.C4A-Z Chasseurs a pied. Chasseurs alpins
.C5 Battalions. By number and author
.I6A-Z Infanterie legere d'Afrique
.I7 Battalions. By number and author
.I8 Irish regiments
.L5A-Z Legion etrangere
.T4A-Z Tirailleurs indigenes
.T45A-Z Tirailleurs algeriens
.T5 Regiments. By number and author
.T65A-Z Tirailleurs marocains
.T7 Regiments. By number and author
.T75A-Z Tirailleurs tunisiers
.T8 Regiments. By number and author
.Z5A-Z Zouaves
.Z6 Regiments. By number and author

.Z9A-Z Other organizations. By name, A-Z
Cavalry. Armor
704.A1-5 Documents
.A6A-Z General works
.A8 Divisions. By number and author
.C4A-Z Chasseurs a cheval
.C5 Regiments. By number and author
.C6A-Z Chasseurs d'Afrique
.C7 Regiments. By number and author
.C8A-Z Cuirasiers
.C9 Regiments. By number and author
.D7A-Z Dragons
.D8 Regiments. By number and author
.H8A-Z Hussards
.H9 Regiments. By number and author
.S7A-Z Spahis
.S8 Regiments. By number and author
.Z9 Other organizations. By name, A-Z
Artillery
705.A1-5 Documents
.A6-Z4 General works
.Z5A-Z Bataillons d'artillerie a pied
.Z6 Regiments. By number and author
706 Other special troops, A-Z
Territorial Army
707.A1-5 Documents
.A6-Z5 General works
.Z6 Regiments. By number and author
Colonies and colonial troops
For individual regiments, see UA840+
709.A1-5 Documents
.A6-Z General works
710-719 Germany
Including West Germany
719.3 East Germany
720-729 Greece
730-739 Netherlands
740-749 Italy
750-759 Norway
760-769 Portugal
770-779 Soviet Union
780-789 Spain
790-799 Sweden
800-809 Switzerland
810-819 Turkey
Balkan States
820 General military situation, military policy, defenses, etc.
822 Organization, history, description of armies
By country
824 Bulgaria
826 Romania
827 Yugoslavia
829 Other European countries, A-Z
830 Asia
832 Middle East. Persian Gulf Region
833 Southeast Asia Treaty Organization (SEATO)
.5 Association of Southeast Asian Nations (ASEAN)
China
835 General military situation, military policy, defenses, etc.

836 Reports
837 Army organization, history, etc.
838 Arms of the service, A-Z
839 States, provinces, etc., A-Z
India
840 General military situation, military policy, defenses, etc.
841 Reports
842 Army organization, history, etc.
843 Arms of the service, A-Z
844 States, provinces, etc., A-Z
Japan
845 General military situation, military policy, defenses, etc.
846 Reports
847 Army organization, history, etc.
848 Arms of the service, A-Z
849 States, provinces, etc., A-Z
853 Other Asian countries, A-Z
854 Arab countries
.8 Islamic countries
855 Africa
.5 Northeast Africa
.6 Southern Africa
.7 Sub-Saharan Africa
South Africa
856 General military situation, military policy, defenses, etc.
.3 Reports
.5 Army organization, history, etc.
.7 Arms of the services, A-Z
.9 Provinces, territories, etc., A-Z
858 Algeria
859 Cameroon
.3 Chad
860 Ethiopia
.5 Kenya
861 Mozambique
.3 Nigeria
.7 Zimbabwe. Southern Rhodesia
862.5 Spanish Sahara
.5 Sudan
863 Zaire
864 Zambia
865 Egypt
866 Liberia
867 Morocco
.5 Tunisia
868 Libya
869 Other African countries, A-Z
Australia
870 General military situation, military policy, defenses, etc.
871 Reports
872 Army organization, history, etc.
873 Arms of the service, A-Z
874 States and territories, A-Z
New Zealand
.3 General military situation, military policy, defenses, etc.
.4 Reports
.5 Army organization, history, etc.
.6 Arms of the services, A-Z
.7 Provincial districts, etc., A-Z

875 Pacific Islands
876 By island or island group, A-Z
Hawaii, see under United States
910 Mobilization
By country
913 United States
914 By state, A-W
915 Other countries, A-Z
917.A2A-Z Demobilization
.A3-Z By country, A-Z
920-925 Plans for attack and defense
Divide like UA910-UA915
Civil defense
Class here works on all or several aspects of civil defense.
For works on a special aspect or civil defense in relation to a particular war, see the topic or war
926.A1A-Z Periodicals. Societies
.A3-Z General works
.5 General special
Including psychological aspects
By region or country
927 United States
928 By region or state, A-Z
.5 By city, A-Z
929 Other regions or countries, A-Z
.5 War damage in industry. Industrial defense
Class here works on planning to avoid or minimize war damage to industry. For special aspects, see the special topic
By region or country
.6 United States
.7 By region or state, A-Z
.8 By city, A-Z
.9 Other regions or countries, A-Z
.95 By industry, A-Z
930 Strategic lines and bases
940-945 Military communications
Divide like UA910-UA915
950-955 Routes of travel. Distances
Divide like UA910-UA915
960-965 Roads. Highways
Divide like UA910-UA915
970-975 Waterways. Rivers
Divide like UA910-UA915
979 Other (not A-Z)
980 Telegraphic connections
Military geography
985 Periodicals. Societies
990 General works
By region or country
993 United States
995 Other regions or countries, A-Z
Europe, see UA990

(UB) MILITARY ADMINISTRATION

1 Periodicals. Societies
15 History
Including history of several countries
21-124 By region or country (Table 1 following UG1530)
General works

144 Through 1800
145 1801-1970
146 1971-
147 Military service as a profession
150-155 Interior administration
Divide like UB190-UB195
160-165 Records, returns, muster rolls, accounts, general correspondence
Divide like UB190-UB195
170-175 Adjutant generals' offices
Divide like UB190-UB195
180 Civilian personnel departments
190 Civil employees
By country
193 United States
195 Other countries, A-Z
200 Commanders. Generals. Marshals
210 Command of troops. Leadership
212 Command and control systems
220-225 Staffs of armies
Divide like UB190-UB195
230-235 Headquarters, aides, adjutants, etc.
Divide like UB190-UB195
240-245 Inspection. Inspectors
Divide like UB190-UB195
246 Security measures for defense information
By country
247 United States
248 Other countries, A-Z
249.A2A-Z Industrial security measures
.A3-Z By country, A-Z
250 Intelligence
Cf. UB475, Military surveillance
251 By country, A-Z
255 Electronic data processing of intelligence
256 By country, A-Z
260 Attachés
270 Espionage. Spies
Cf. JX5121, International law
271 By country, A-Z
Class here those works concerned with the country responsible for the activity. For spy cases in individual wars, see the war, D-F
Under each:
.x General works
.x2 Individual spies, A-Z
273 Sabotage
274 Equipment
275 Psychological warfare. Propaganda
Cf. HM263, Social psychology
By country
276 United States
277 Other countries, A-Z
280-285 Preparation of orders. Correspondence in the field
Divide like UB190-UB195
290 Cryptography
320 Enlistment, recruiting, placement, promotion
321 International relations
By country
United States

Documents
323.A2-3 Serials. Manuals
.A31-45 Special events
.A5 Miscellaneous. By date
.A6-Z Nonofficial works
325 Other countries, A-Z
340 Compulsory service. Conscription and exemption
341 Conscientious objectors
342 By country, A-Z
By country
343 United States
345 Other countries, A-Z
350 Universal service. Universal military training
By country
353 United States
355 Other countries, A-Z
407 Warrant officers. Noncommissioned officers
By country
408 United States
.5 Army
409 Other countries, A-Z
410 Officers
Including appointments, promotions, retirements, etc.
By country
United States
Documents
412.A1-2 Serial
.A4 Special. By date
.A5-Z Individual cases, A-Z
413 General works
414 Militia and volunteers
415 Other countries, A-Z
416 Minorities, women, etc., in armed forces
By country
417 United States
418 Individual groups, A-Z
.A47 Afro-Americans
.H57 Hispanic Americans
.W65 Women
419 Other countries, A-Z
Military law
For martial law, see JF1800
General works
461 Early through 1800
465 1801-
International law, see JX
By region or country
United States, see KF7201+ (not included in this guide)
Other countries, see UB505+ (not included in this guide)
770 Civil law relating to the military
By country
United States, see KF7680 (not included in this guide)
775 Other countries, A-Z
780 Military crimes and offenses
By country
783 United States
785 Other countries, A-Z
787 Mutiny
788 Desertion

790	Military discipline
	By country
793	United States
795	Other countries, A-Z

Works on military maintenance and transportation class in UC, which is not included in this guide

(UD) INFANTRY

Class here works in tactics, regulations, etc. For histories and reports of special organizations, see UA

1	Periodicals. Societies
7	Organization (General)
15	History
	Including history of several countries treated together
21-124	By region or country, A-Z (Table)
	General works
144	Early through 1800
145	1801-
157	Tactics. Maneuvers
	By region or country
160	United States
162	By region or state, A-Z
163	Canada
164	Militia
165	By region or province, A-Z
166-168	Mexico
	Divide like UD163-UD165
169	Central America
170	By region or country, A-Z
172	West Indies
173	By island or island group
175	South America
	Divide 3 number countries below like UD163-UD165
176-178	Argentina
179-181	Bolivia
182-184	Brazil
185-187	Chile
188-190	Colombia
191-193	Ecuador
195	Guyana
196	Surinam
197	French Guiana
200-202	Paraguay
203-205	Peru
206-208	Uruguay
209-211	Venezuela
215	Europe
	Divide 3 number countries below like UD163-UD165
219-221	Austria
222-224	Belgium
225-227	Denmark
228-230	France
231-233	Germany
	Including West Germany
233.5-53	East Germany
234-236	Great Britain
237-239	Greece

240-242 Netherlands
243-245 Italy
246-248 Norway
249-251 Portugal
252-254 Soviet Union
255-257 Spain
258-260 Sweden
261-263 Switzerland
264-266 Turkey
269 Other European countries, A-Z
270 Asia
Divide 3 number countries below like UD163-UD165
271-273 China
274-276 India
277-279 Japan
280 Other Asian countries, A-Z
285 Africa
Divide 3 number countries below like UD163-UD165
286-288 Egypt
292 Other African countries, A-Z
295-297 Australia
Divide like UD163-UD165
298 New Zealand
300 Pacific Islands
302 By island or island group, A-Z
380 Small arms
382 Small arms inspection
By region or country
383 United States
385 Other regions or countries, A-Z
390 Rifles
396 Shotguns
410 Pistols. Revolvers
By country
413 United States
414 By region or state, A-Z
415 Other regions or countries, A-Z
430 Militia. Reserves. Volunteer Rifle Corps
Cf. UA13, General militia organization
For history and reports of individual organizations, see UA
440 Field service
By country
443 United States
444 By region or state, A-Z
445 Other regions or countries, A-Z
450 Mounted infantry
By country
453 United States
454 By region or state, A-Z
455 Other regions or countries, A-Z
460 Mounted troops. Mountain warfare
By country
463 United States
464 By region or state, A-Z
465 Other regions or countries, A-Z
480 Airborne troops. Parachute troops
By country
483 United States
484 By region or state, A-Z

485 Other regions or countries, A-Z
490 Airmobile operations
By country
493 United States
494 By region or state, A-Z
495 Other regions or countries, A-Z

Works on horse cavalry, armored cavalry, and mechanized calvary class in UE, which is not included in this guide

(UF) ARTILLERY

1 Periodicals. Societies
6 Museums. Exhibitions
9 Dictionaries. Encyclopedias
10 Organization (General)
15 History (General)
Including several countries treated together
21-124 By region or country (Table)
130 Laws relating to ordnance departments
By country
United States, see KF7335 (not included in this guide)
135 Other countries, A-Z
General works
144 Early through 1800
145 1801-
157 Tactics, Maneuvers. Drill regulations
160-302 By region or country
Divide like UD160-UD302
520 Ordnance and small arms
By country
523 United States
524 By region or state, A-Z
525 Other regions or countries, A-Z
526 Research
By country
.3 United States
.5 Other countries, A-Z
527 Study and teaching
530 Manufacture
Including reports of ordnance factories
By country
533 United States
534 By region or state, A-Z
535 Other regions or countries, A-Z
537 By manufacturer
560 Ordnance material (Ordnance proper)
561 General special

(UG) MILITARY ENGINEERING. AIR FORCES

MILITARY ENGINEERING

1 Periodicals. Societies
15 History
Including history of several countries treated together
21-124 By region or country (Table)
Except for the United States, with the first number assigned to a country, use .Z6 for individual regiments
125 Regiments of the United States Army.
By number

Biography
127 Collective
By country, see UG21+
128 Individual, A-Z
130 Laws relating to engineer corps
By country
United States, see KF7335.E5 (not included in this guide)
135 Other countries, A-Z
General works
144 Early through 1800
145 1801-
147 General special
150 Manuals
By country
153 United States
155 Other countries, A-Z
157 Study and teaching
Tactics and regulations
160-302 By region or country
Divide like UD160-UD302
320 Maneuvers
By country
323 United States
325 Other countries, A-Z
350 Hydraulic engineering
360 Field engineering
Fortification
General works
400 Early through 1800
401 1801-
403 Field fortification
Trenches and trench warfare, see UG446
405 Permanent fortification
Fortification and defenses. By region or country
410 United States
411 By region or state, A-Z
412 By place, A-Z
Other regions or countries
Divide regions or countries with 3 numbers like UG410-UG412
413-415 Canada
416-418 Mexico
419-421 Central America
422-424 West Indies
425-527 South America
428-430 Europe
431-433 Asia
434-436 Africa
437-439 Australia
439.1-3 New Zealand
440-442 Pacific Islands
Attack and defense. Siege warfare
General works
443 Early through 1788
444 1789-
446 Trenches and trench warfare
.5 Tanks, armored cars, etc.
447 Chemical warfare. Gas and flame
.5 Special gases, A-Z
.M8 Mustard gas

.O74 Organophosphorus compounds
.P5 Phenylimido-phosgene
.6 Gas masks (Military use)
.65 Incendiary weapons
.8 Biological warfare
448 Coast defenses
For coast defenses by place, see UG410+
449 Camouflage
450 Military application of mechanical engineering
455 Military metrology
460 Military architecture and building
465 Military geology
.5 Military seismology
For seismic verification of arms control, see UA12.5
467 Military meteorology
468 Military hydrology
470 Military surveying, mapping, etc.
By region or country
472 United States
473 Other regions or countries, A-Z
475 Military surveillance
Cf. UA12.5, Disarmament inspection and arms control and nuclear arms control verification
UG1500+, Space surveillance
476 Military photography
478 Military aspects of automation
479 Military use of artificial intelligence
480 Military uses of electricity
482 Military uses of telemeter
485 Military uses of electronics
486 Military uses of lasers
.5 Directed-energy weapons
487 Military uses of infrared rays
488 Military uses of electrooptics and optoelectronics
489 Military use of information display systems
490 Land mines. Mine fields. Mine countermeasures
Cf. V856+, Submarine mines
Technical troops and other special corps
500 Technical troops
590 Military telegraphy and telephony
Including general telecommunication and wiring
Special aspects of this topic class in UG600+ (not included in this guide)

AIR FORCES. AIR WARFARE

622 Periodicals. Societies
625 History
For specific wars, see the war, D-G
By country, see UG633+
Biography
626 Collective
.2 Individual, A-Z
628 Dictionaries. Encyclopedias
630 General works
631 Juvenile works
632 General special
Including international cooperation, psychological aspects, etc.
By country
633 United States

634 By state, A-W
.5 Air bases and airfields. By name, A-Z
635 Other countries, A-Z
Under each:
.x General works
.x2 Air bases and airfields. By name, A-Z
637 Education and training
By country
638 United States
.3 By state, A-W
.5 Air Force Academy, Colorado Springs, Colo.
Divide like U410
Other schools. By place, A-Z
.8 Reserve Officers' Training Corps (R.O.T.C.)
639 Other countries, A-Z
Under each:
.x General works
.x2 Individual schools. By place, A-Z
640 Military aeronautical research
By country
643 United States
.5 By state, A-W
644 Individual establishments. By place, A-Z
645 Other countries, A-Z
670 Manuals. Regulations
By country
673 United States
674 By region or state, A-Z
675 Other regions or countries, A-Z
700-705 Tactics
Divide like UG670-UG675
730-735 Air defenses
Divide like UG670-UG675
740-745 Ballistic missile defenses
760-765 Aerial reconnaissance
Divide like UG670-UG675
For reconnaissance satellites, space surveillance, see UG1500+
770-775 Organization. Personnel management
Divide like UG670-UG675
790-795 Officers
Divide like UG670-UG675
820-825 Noncommissioned officers. Airmen
Divide like UG670-UG675
850-855 Reserves. Air National Guard
880-885 Recruiting, enlistment, etc.
1010-1015 Public relations. Press. War correspondents
1097 Air bases
By country, see UG633+
1100-1105 Equipment and supplies
Divide like UG670-UG675
1120-1125 Procurement and contracts
Divide like UG670-UG675
1200-1205 Operational
Divide topics with 6 numbers like UG670-UG675
1220-1205 Airships
1230-1235 Helicopters
1240-1245 Airplanes
Including instrumentation, recognition, camouflage
For manufacture and testing, see TL (not included in this guide)

1242 By type, A-Z
.A25 Antisubmarine aircraft
.A27 Army cooperation aircraft
.A28 Attack planes
Including dive bombers
.B6 Bombers
.D7 Drone aircraft
.E43 Electronic warfare aircraft
.F5 Fighter planes
.G85 Gunships
.R4 Reconnaissance airplanes
.T36 Tanker planes
.T67 Trainer planes
.T7 Transport planes
.V47 Vertically rising airplanes
1270-1275 Ordnance (General)
For manufacture, see UF530+
1280-1285 Bombs
For types of bombs of particular countries, prefer UG1282
1282 By type, A-Z
.A8 Atomic
Including hydrogen bombs
Cf. U264, Nuclear weapons
.F7 Fragmentation
.G8 Guided
.I6 Incendiary
.N48 Neutron
1310-1315 Missiles and rockets
For types of missiles and rockets of particular countries, prefer UG1312
1312 By type, A-Z
.A35 Air-to-air
.A6 Antimissile
Cf. UG740+, Ballistic missile defenses
.A8 Atomic
.B34 Ballistic
.C7 Cruise
.I2 ICBM
.M2 MIRV
1340-1345 Aircraft guns and small arms
1370-1375 Balloons and kites
1400-1405 Air force vehicles
1420-1425 Radar and electronics in military aeronautics
Divide like UG670-UG675
1430-1435 Infrared rays in military aeronautics
Divide like UG670-UG675

MILITARY ASTRONAUTICS. SPACE WARFARE. SPACE SURVEILLANCE

1500 Periodicals. Societies
1509 Dictionaries and encyclopedias
1515 History
1520 General works
By region or country
1523 United States
1525 Other regions or countries, A-Z
1530 Space warfare. Interplanetary defenses
Cf. UG740+, Ballistic missile defenses

Table for Class U: Regions and Countries

Unless otherwise specified the second number assigned to each country

may be used for subdivisions of the country, A-Z
21 America
22 North America
23 United States
24 By state, A-W
25 By city, A-Z
26-27 Canada
27.5 Latin America (General)
28-29 Mexico
30-31 Central America
32-33 West Indies
34 South America
36-37 Argentina
38-39 Bolivia
41-42 Brazil
43-44 Chile
45-46 Colombia
47-48 Ecuador
49 Guyana
.5 Surinam
50 French Guiana
51 Paraguay
52 Peru
53 Uruguay
54 Venezuela
55 Europe
57 Great Britain (General)
58 Special periods. By date
59 England and Wales
61 Scotland
63 Northern Ireland
64 Cities (or other special), A-Z
65-66 Austria
67-68 Belgium
69-70 Denmark
71-72 France
73-74 Germany
Including West Germany
74.5 East Germany
75-76 Greece
76.5 Ireland
77-78 Netherlands
79-80 Italy
81-82 Norway
83-84 Portugal
85-86 Soviet Union in Europe
86.5 Scandinavia (General)
87-88 Spain
89-90 Sweden
91-92 Switzerland
95 Other European countries, A-Z
99 Asia
101-102 China
103-104 India
105-106 Japan
107-108 Iran
109-110 Soviet Union in Asia
111-112 Turkey
113 Other Asian countries, A-Z

115 Africa
117-118 Egypt
119 Other African countries, A-Z
121-122 Australia
122.5 New Zealand
123 Pacific islands
124 By island or island group, A-Z

(V) NAVAL SCIENCE (GENERAL)

Periodicals and societies. By language of publication
1 English
2 French
3 German
4 Italian
5 Other languages (not A-Z)
9 Almanacs (Official)
11 Navy lists. By country, A-Z
Class with administrative documents in VA, if annual report of department is included
13.A1A-Z Museums. Exhibitions
.A2-Z By region or country, A-Z
Under each country:
.x General works
.x2 Special. By city, A-Z
23 Dictionaries and encyclopedias
24 Dictionaries in two or more languages
History and antiquities of naval science
Including history of navies and naval policy in general. For naval history, wars, and battles of individual countries, see D-F.
25 Philosophy
Including theory of sea power
27 General works
By period
29 Ancient history
31 Orientals
33 Egyptians
35 Phoenicians. Carthaginians
37 Greeks
39 Romans
41 Other special
43 Medieval history
45 Vikings
46 Other special
Modern history
47 17th-18th centuries
51 19th century
53 20th century
55 By region or country, A-Z
Biography
For military personnel identified with military events in the history of a particular country, see D-F
61 Collective
By country
United States
62 Collective
63 Individual, A-Z
64 Other countries, A-Z
Under each:
.x Collective

.x2 Individual, A-Z

General works

101 Early through 1800

103 1801-

105 General special

107 Popular works

109 Juvenile works

Naval strategy

General works

160 Through 1800

163 1801-

165 General special

167 Naval tactics

169 General special

175 Field service

Including landing operations, shore service, small arms instruction

177 Riverine operations

178 Boat attack

179 Naval logistics

180 Blockade duty

182 Convoys

185 Security measures

190 Reconnaissance. Scouting. Patrols

200 Coast defense

205 Nuclear warfare

210 Submarine warfare

214 Antisubmarine warfare

.5 Submarine boat combat

215 Marine camouflage

220 Naval ports, bases, reservations, docks

By country, see VA69+

245 Naval maneuvers

Combined operations, amphibious warfare, see U260+

250 Naval war games

252 Synthetic training methods and devices

253 Imaginary naval wars and battles

260 Physical training in navies

By region or country

263 United States

264 By region or state, A-Z

265 Other regions or countries, A-Z

390 Naval research

By country

393 United States

.5 By state, A-W

394 Special establishments. By place, A-Z

395 Other countries, A-Z

396 Military oceanography

By country

.3 United States

.4 Special establishments. By place, A-Z

.5 Other countries, A-Z

398 Electronic data processing in the naval sciences

399 Automation in the naval sciences

400 Naval education

401 History

By period

402 Ancient

403 Medieval

404 Modern
405 Through 1800
407 19th century
409 20th century
By region or country
Under each country, unless otherwise provided for, subarrange naval schools, colleges, etc., as follows:
Table
Principal national school
.A5-59 History, description
.A7-Z Other schools.
By name or place
Under each:
.x4-45 History, description
411 United States
United States Naval Academy, Annapolis
415.L1A-Z History and general works
.M1A-Z Biography
.P1A-Z Descriptive works. Life at Annapolis
420 United States Naval War College
425 Other government schools, A-Z
426 Naval Reserve Officers' Training Corps
427 V-12 program
430.A3A-Z Private naval schools
.A4-Z Individual. By name, A-Z
433 Naval training stations
434 By place, A-Z
435 Training ships. Naval apprentices
436 By name, A-Z
437 Coast Guard training
Including appointment of cadets; Coast Guard Academy, New London, Conn.
440 Canada
441 General special
442 Special subjects, A-Z
443 Provinces, regions, etc., A-Z
444 Schools, A-Z
445-449 Mexico
Divide like V440-V444
450 Central America
453 By country, A-Z
Under each (using two successive cutter numbers):
(1) General works
(2) Schools. By place, A-Z
455 West Indies
458 By island or island group, A-Z
Subarrange under each like V453
465 South America
Divide individual countries with 3 numbers like V466-V468
466 Argentina
467 General special
468 Schools, A-Z
472-474 Brazil
475-477 Chile
478-480 Colombia
481-483 Ecuador
484-484.3 Guyana
485-485.3 Surinam
486-486.3 French Guiana

488-490 Peru
491-493 Uruguay
494-496 Venezuela
500 Europe
Divide individual countries with 5 numbers like V550-V554
510 Great Britain
511 General special
512 Special subjects, A-Z
Royal Naval College, Dartmouth
515.L1A-Z History and general works
.M1A-Z Biography
.P1A-Z Descriptive works, views
522 Naval training stations
.5 By place, A-Z
523 Training ships
524 By name, A-Z
530 Private naval schools
550 Austria
551 General special
552 Special subjects, A-Z
553 Local, A-Z
554 Schools, A-Z
.5 Training ships. By name, A-Z
555-559 Belgium
560-564 Denmark
565-569 France
570-574 Germany
Including West Germany
574.51-54 East Germany
575-579 Greece
580-584 Netherlands
595-599 Portugal
600-604 Soviet Union
605-609 Spain
610-614 Sweden
620 Balkan States
621 Bulgaria
622 Romania
623 Other European countries, A-Z
625 Asia
630-634 China
635-639 India
640-644 Japan
645-649 Iran
650 Other Asian countries, A-Z
660 Africa
675-679 Egypt
680 Other African countries, A-Z
690-694 Australia
695.1-5 New Zealand
695 Pacific islands, A-Z
697 General education. Nonnaval education
By region or country
698 United States
699 Other regions or countries, A-Z
Naval observations in special wars, see D-F
720 Naval life, manners and customs, etc.
By period
725 Ancient

730 Medieval
733 General special
735 Modern
736 American
737 English
738 French
739 German
740 Italian
741 Russian
742 Spanish
743 Other, A-Z
750 War vessels
By period
755 Ancient
760 Medieval
763 General special
765 Modern
767 General special
Construction (General)
795 To 1815/1830
797 1815/1830-1860
799 1860-1900
800 1901-
Special types
815 Battleships
By navy
.3 United States
.5 Other countries, A-Z
820 Cruisers
By navy
.3 United States
.5 Other countries, A-Z
825 Destroyers
By navy
.3 United States
.5 Other countries, A-Z
826 Frigates
By navy
.3 United States
.5 Other countries, A-Z
827 Fireships
By navy
.3 United States
.5 Other countries, A-Z
830 Torpedo boats
By navy
833 United States
835 Other countries, A-Z
837 Torpedo boat service
840 Torpedo boat destroyers
850 Torpodoes
Including apparatus for projection
855 Special, A-Z
856 Submarine mines. Minesweeping
.5 By country, A-Z
857 Submarine boats. Submarine forces
.5 Nuclear submarines
By navy
858 United States

859 Other countries, A-Z
860 Revolving turrets. Monitors
865 Auxiliary vessels: Fleet train
870 Unarmored vessels
874 Aircraft carriers
By navy
.3 United States
.5 Other countries, A-Z
875 Special topics, A-Z
.F5 Flight decks
880 Minor craft
885 Minesweepers
890 Floating batteries
895 Other (not A-Z)
950 Armament
960 Installation
980 Other equipment
990 Fleet ballistic missile systems
By country
993 United States
995 Other countries, A-Z

(VA) NAVIES: ORGANIZATION. DISTRIBUTION

NAVAL SITUATION

10 General works
20 Naval expenditures. Cost of navies
25 Budgets
By country, see VA60+
40 Navies of the world
41 Popular works
42 Pictorial works
45 Organization of naval militia, reserves, etc.
By country, see VA80+
48 Mobilization
By country, see VA77+
Naval, organization, policy, etc. By country
United States
Naval situation, policy, etc. (General)
49 Periodicals. Societies
50 General works
United States Navy
Documents (General)
52.A1-19 Navy Department
.A2-29 Secretary of the Navy
.A6-67 Bureau of Navigation. Bureau of Naval Personnel
.A68-69 Office of Naval Material
.A7-79 Office of Naval Operations
.A8-89 Naval Consulting Board
Congressional documents, nonofficial reports, etc.
Cf. KF16+, Law of the United States
53.A1-69 Compilations
.A7 Special. By date
.A8-Z Nonofficial reports, statements, etc., to the Congress or its committees
54 Speeches
55 General works
By period
56 Early works through 1860

57 1861-1880
58 1881-1970
.4 1971-
59 Pictorial works
60 Naval expenditures and budgets
61 Lists of vessels
62 Distribution
.5 Naval districts
.7 Special. By number
63 Squadrons, fleets, etc. By name, A-Z
65 Ships. By name, A-Z
Training ships, see V436
66 Other units. By name, A-Z
67 Naval ports, bases, reservations, docks, etc.
68 By place, A-Z
69 Naval yards. Naval stations
70 By place, A-Z
Under each:
.A2-7 Documents
.A8-Z Other
73 Coaling stations
74 By place, A-Z
77 Mobilization
79 United States Naval Auxiliary Service
80 Naval militia, naval reserves, etc.
By state, see VA90+ (not included in this guide)
390 Organizations not localized. By name, A-Z
Including Coast Guard Women's Reserve (SPARS); Women's Naval Reserve (WAVES)
400 Canada
.5 Ships. By name, A-Z
401 By province, etc., A-Z
402 Naval militia
.5 Latin America
403-405 Mexico
Divide like VA400-VA402
406 Central America
407 By region or country, A-Z
409 West Indies
410 By island or island group, A-Z
415 South America
Divide individual countries with spans of numbers like VA400-VA402
416-418 Argentina
419-421 Bolivia
422-424 Brazil
425-427 Chile
428-430 Colombia
431-433 Ecuador
434 Guyana
435 Surinam
436 French Guiana
.5-7 Paraguay
437-439 Peru
440-442 Uruguay
443-445 Venezuela
450 Europe
Divide individual countries with spans of numbers like VA470-VA479
For naval affairs in NATO, see UA646.3
Great Britain

452 Periodicals. Societies
453 Documents (General)
454 General works
455 Naval expenditures
456 Lists of vessels
457 Squadrons, fleets, etc. By name, A-Z
458 Ships. By name, A-Z
459.A1A-Z Naval ports, bases, etc.
.A3-Z By place, A-Z
460.A1A-Z Navy yards. Naval stations
.A3-Z By place, A-Z
461.A1A-Z Coaling stations, wharves, docks
.A3-Z By place, A-Z
463 Mobilization
464 Naval militia and reserves
465 By organization, A-Z
By country
466 Scotland
467 Ireland
Austria
470 Periodicals. Societies
471 Expenditures, budgets, etc.
472 Documents (General)
473.A1-49 Lists of vessels
.A5-Z General works
474 Squadrons, fleets. By name, A-Z
475 Ships. By name, A-Z
476.A1A-Z Naval ports, bases, yards
.A3-Z By place, A-Z
477.A1A-Z Coaling stations, wharves, docks
.A3-Z By place, A-Z
478 Mobilization
479 Naval militia and reserves
480-489 Belgium
490-499 Denmark
500-509 France
510-519 Germany
Including West Germany
519.3-39 East Germany
520-529 Greece
530-539 Netherlands
540-549 Italy
550-559 Norway
560-569 Portugal
570-579 Soviet Union
580-589 Spain
590-599 Sweden
610 Balkan States
612 Bulgaria
615 Romania
617 Yugoslavia
619 Other countries, A-Z
620 Asia
Divide individual countries with spans of numbers like VA470-VA479
630-639 China
640-649 India
650-659 Japan
660 Iran
665 Thailand

667 Other Asian countries, A-Z
670 Africa
680 Former British Africa
690 Egypt
700 Other African countries, A-Z
710-719 Australia
720-729 New Zealand
730 Pacific islands
750 Individual islands and island groups, A-Z

(VB) NAVAL ADMINISTRATION

15 History (General)
Including history of several countries treated together
21-124 By region or country (Table)
General works
144 Through 1800
145 1801-1970
146 1971-
160 Interior administration
Including administration of fleets, stations, etc.
170 Civil department
190 Commanders, admirals, etc.
Including duties
200 Command of ships. Leadership
By country
203 United States
205 Other countries, A-Z
210 Headquarters, aides, etc.
212 Naval command and control systems
For military command and control systems, see UB212
220 Inspection, inspectors, etc.
By country
223 United States
225 Other countries, A-Z
230 Intelligence
Cf. V190, Reconnaissance
231 By country, A-Z
240 Attachés
250 Espionage. Spies
Cf. JX5121, International law
252 Psychological warfare. Propaganda
By region or country
253 United States
254 Other regions or countries, A-Z
255 Communications. Correspondence. Preparation of orders
257 Personnel management
By country
258 United States
.5 Other countries, A-Z
259 The Navy as a career. Vocational guidance
260 Enlisted personnel
Including recruiting, enlistment, promotion, discharge, etc.
By country
263 United States
264 By region or state, A-Z
265 Other countries, A-Z
270-275 Recruits
Divide like VB260-VB265
Including medical, physical, and mental examination

277 Demobilization. Civil employment
310 Officers
Including rank, grades, procurement, appointment, promotion, etc.
By country
313 United States
314 Individual cases, A-Z
315 Other countries, A-Z
320 Minorities, women, etc. in navies
By country
323 United States
324 Individual groups, A-Z
.A47 Afro-Americans
.G38 Gays
.W65 Women
325 Other countries, A-Z
350 Naval law
Special
353 International law
By region or country
United States, see KF7345 (not included in this guide)
Other regions or countries, see VB370+ (not included in this guide)
840 Naval discipline
By country
843 United States
845 Other countries, A-Z
850 Naval crimes and misdemeanors
By country
853 United States
855 Other countries, A-Z
860 Mutiny
By country
863 United States
865 Other countries, A-Z
867 By vessel, A-Z
870 Desertion
By country
873 United States
875 Other countries, A-Z

Works on naval maintenance class in VC, which is not included in this guide

(VD) NAVAL SEAMEN

Including enlisted personnel in general
For recruiting, enlistment, see VB260+
For physical training, see V260+
For education, see V400+

15 History (General)
Including history of several countries treated together
21-124 By region or country (Table)
General works
144 Early works through 1800
145 1801-1970
146 1971-
Tactics and maneuvers, see V167+, V245
150 Manuals
By country
153 United States
155 Other countries, A-Z

(VE) MARINES

15	History (General)
	Including history of several countries treated together
	By region or country
	United States Marine Corps
23.A1A-Z	Periodicals
.A13A-Z	Marine Corps League
.A14	By department, A-Z
.A2-79	Documents
.A2	Annual report
.A25	Regulations. By date
.A3-32	History
.A33	Registers
.A48	Manuals
.A5	Monographs. By date
	Recruiting documents
.A59	Serials. By title, A-Z
.A6	Monographs. By date
.A8-Z	General works
.22	Divisions. By number
.25	Regiments. By number
.3	Marine Corps Reserve
.4	Marine Corps Women's Reserve
	Biography
24	Collective
25	Individual, A-Z
26-124	Other regions or countries (Table)
	General works
144	Early works through 1800
145	1801-1970
146	1971-
150	Handbooks, manuals, etc.
	By country
153	United States
155	Other countries, A-Z
157	Tactics and maneuvers
430	Training camps
	By country
432	United States
434	By place, A-Z
435	Other countries, A-Z

(VF) NAVAL ORDNANCE

1	Periodicals. Societies
6	Museums. Exhibitions
	Subarranged like V13
15	History (General)
	Including history of several countries treated together
21-124	By region or country (Class V Table)
	General works
144	Through 1800
145	1801-
147	General special
150	Handbooks, manuals, etc.
	By country
153	United States
155	Other countries, A-Z
346	Naval weapons systems

Cf. V990+, Fleet missile weapons systems
By country
347 United States
348 Other countries, A-Z
350-355 Ordnance and arms (General)
Divide like VF150-VF155
Cf. UF520+, Military ordnance
357 Study and teaching
360 Research
By region or country
.3 United States
.5 Other regions or countries, A-Z
370-375 Manufacture
Divide like VF150-VF155
380 Ordnance facilities
By country
383 United States
384 Individual. By name, A-Z
385 Other countries, A-Z
390 Ordnance material (Ordnance proper)
By country
United States
393.A1-3 Documents
.A7-Z General works
395 Other countries, A-Z

(VG) MINOR SERVICES OF NAVIES

50 Coast guard and coast signal service
By country
53 United States
55 Other countries, A-Z
90 Naval aviation. Air warfare
By country
93 United States
Including Marine Corps aviation
94 By region or state, A-Z
.5 By station, field, A-Z
.6 Organizations. By name, A-Z
.7 Reserves
95 Other countries, A-Z
500 Public relations. Press. War correspondents
By country
503 United States
505 Other countries, A-Z

Works on navigation and merchant marine class in VK; works on naval architecture and shipbuilding class in VM. These subclasses are not included in this guide

Table for Class V : Regions and Countries

21 America
22 North America
23 United States
24 By state, A-W
25 By city, A-Z
26-27 Canada
27.5 Latin America (General)
28-29 Mexico
30-31 Central America

32-33 West Indies
34 South America
36-37 Argentina
38-39 Bolivia
41-42 Brazil
43-44 Chile
45-46 Colombia
47-48 Ecuador
49 Guyana
.5 Surinam
50 French Guiana
51 Paraguay
52 Peru
53 Uruguay
54 Venezuela
55 Europe
57 Great Britain (General)
59 England and Wales
61 Scotland
63 Northern Ireland
64 Cities (or other special), A-Z
65-66 Austria
67-68 Belgium
69-70 Denmark
71-72 France
73-74 Germany
Including West Germany
74.5 East Germany
75-76 Greece
76.5 Ireland
77-78 Netherlands
79-80 Italy
81-82 Norway
83-84 Portugal
85-86 Soviet Union in Europe
86.5 Scandinavia (General)
87-88 Spain
89-90 Sweden
91-92 Switzerland
96 Other European countries, A-Z
99 Asia
101-102 China
103-104 India
105-106 Japan
107-108 Iran
109-110 Soviet Union in Asia
111-112 Turkey
113 Other Asian countries, A-Z
115 Africa
117-118 Egypt
119 Other African countries, A-Z
121-122 Australia
122.5 New Zealand
123 Pacific islands
124 By island or island group, A-Z

(Z) BIBLIOGRAPHY

SUBJECT BIBLIOGRAPHY

History

6207 Special historical events, movements, A-Z
- .B9 Byzantine Empire
- .C5 Chivalry
- .C53 Orders. By country, A-Z
- .C55 By order, A-Z
  - .C55M3 Knights of Malta
  - .C55T3 Templars
  - .C55T35 Teutonic Knights
- .C97 Crusades
- .D5 Displaced persons. Refugees
- .E8 World War, 1914-1918
- .E81 Reconstruction
- .M8 Munich four-power agreement, 1938
- .N2 Napoleonic period in history
- .P4 Peninsular War, 1807-1814
- .R8 Russo-Japanese War, 1904-1905
- .R85 Russo-Turkish War, 1877-1878
- .T4 Thirty Years' War, 1618-1648
- World War, 1914-1918, see .E8+
- .W8 World War, 1939-1945
- .W81 Reconstruction

6461 International law and relations

6463 Periodicals. Societies

6464 Special topics, A-Z
- .A4 Aeronautics
- .A6 Aliens
- .B6 Blockade
- .C6 Citizenship
- .C75 Communication
- .C77 Contraband of war
- .D5 Diplomatic privileges and immunities
- .D6 Disarmament
- .E1 Eastern question
- .E5 Enemy property
- .E8 Extradition
- .I6 International organization
- .I7 Intervention
- .M2 Maritime law
- .M6 Minorities
- .N4 Neutrality
- .N62 Nonaligment
- .N65 North Atlantic Treaty Organization
- .P3 Paris, Declaration of
- .P63 Police, International
- .P9 Psychology of international relations
- .R3 Recognition
- .R33 Regionalism (International organization)
- .R4 Representatives, Diplomatic
- .R59 Rivers, International
- .S2 Sanctions
- .S62 Space law
- .S73 State succession
- .T8 Treaties
- .T84 Trusteeships (International)
- .W3 War (International law)
- .W33 War crimes
- .Z9 Peace, arbitration, etc.
  Including Permanent Court of International Justice at the Hague

6465 Foreign relations. By region or country, A-Z
  Class bibliographies on general relations between countries in Z1361, Z1609, etc. (not included in this guide)
6466 Catalogs
League of Nations
6471 Serial publications
6472 Official lists
6473 General bibliography
6474 Minor
6475 Special topics, A-Z
  .C8 Covenant
  .D5 Disarmament
  .E3 Economic conditions
  .H4 Health
  .I5 Intellectual cooperation
6476 Relation to individual countries, A-Z
6479.A1-Z8 Catalogs
  .Z9 Sale catalogs
6481.A3-Z United Nations
6482 Periodicals. Societies
6483 Special topics, A-Z
6484 By region or country, A-Z
  Under each country:
    .x General works
    .x2 Local, A-Z
6485 Catalogs
  .Z9 Sale catalogs
6721.A3-Z Military science
6722 Bibliography of early works
6723 Periodicals. Societies
6724 Special topics, A-Z
  .A25 Aeronautics (Military)
  .A3 Air defenses
  .A38 Air warfare
  .A4 Airborne troops
  .A6 Amphibious warfare
  .A8 Artillery
  .A9 Nuclear warfare
  .B6 Biography
  .B7 Bounties (Military)
  .C18 Camouflage (Military science)
  .C185 Camps
  .C2 Cavalry
  .C5 Chemical warfare
  .C58 Civil action
  .C6 Civil defense
  .C62 Communications
  .C63 Compulsory service
  .D43 Deception
  .E4 Education (Military)
  Education (Nonmilitary), see .N64
  .E5 Electronics
  Enlistment, see .R4
  .E75 Environmental aspects of war
  Espionage, see .I7
  .F67 Fortification
  .G2 Gas warfare
  .G7 Guerrilla warfare
  .G8 Guided missiles

.H6 History (Military)
.I5 Industrial mobilization
.I55 Infantry
.I7 Intelligence. Espionage
.J8 Jungle warfare
.L4 Leadership
.M3 Manpower
.M4 Mechanization (Military)
.M9 Munitions
.N37 National security
.N64 Nonmilitary education of soldiers
.O8 Ordnance
.P53 Planning (Military)
.P6 Psychological warfare
.P65 Psychology (Military)
.R4 Recruiting, enlistment, etc.
.R48 Research (Military)
.S6 Sociology (Military)
.S64 Space warfare
.S66 Special forces
.S8 Strategy
.T3 Tactics
.V4 Veterans
.W4 Weapons systems
6725 Local, A-Z
6726 Catalogs
.A9 Sale catalogs
6831.A3-Z Naval science
6832 Bibliography of early works
6833 Periodicals. Societies
6834 Special topics, A-Z
.A4 Aeronautics
.A7 Nuclear ships
.B37 Battleships
.B6 Biography
.H5 History
.S9 Submarine warfare
.T3 Tactics
.T35 Tankers
.T7 Torpedoes
6835 Local, A-Z
6836 Catalogs
.Z9 Sale catalogs
7161.A22-Z Political and social sciences
7164 Special topics, A-Z
.C7 Colonies
Communism, see .S67
.C9 Consular service
.C98 Coups d'etat
.D2 Democracy
.C15 Economic policy
.E17 Economic relations, International
.E2 Economics
.G45 Genocide
.I3 Immigration. Emigration
.I34 Imperialism
.I39 Individualism
.I8 Internationalism
.L38 Leadership

.L6 Liberty
Including civil rights, human rights, etc.
.M67 Monarchy
.N2 Nationalism
.P19 Passive resistance to government
.P2 Patriotism
.P3 Peace Corps
.P79 Political participation
.P8 Political parties
.R32 Refugees
.R34 Regionalism
.R4 Representation
.R54 Revolutions
.S67 Socialism. Communism
.T3 Terrorism
.U5 Developing countries
.V55 Violence
7165 By region or country, A-Z
7166 Catalogs
Theology and religion
7809 Liberation theology
Catholic Church
7838 Special topics, A-Z
.P54 Peace
7845 Sects, churches, movements, A-Z
.F8 Friends, Society of. Quakers
.M4 Mennonites
7853 War and religion

APPENDIX

List of Regions and Countries in One Alphabet

The Cutter numbers are intended as a guide for the best distribution of numbers and are not to be used as a fixed standard or to affect numbers already assigned

Abyssinia: see .E8
Afghanistan: .A3
Africa: .A35
Africa, Central: .A352
Africa, East: .A353
Africa, Eastern: .A354
Africa, North: .A355
Africa, Northeast: .A3553
Africa, Northwest: .A3554
Africa, Southern: .A356
Africa, Sub-Saharan: .A357
Africa, West: .A358
Albania: .A38
Algeria: .A4
America: .A45
Andorra: .A48
Angola: .A5
Antarctic regions: .A6
Antigua: .A63
Arab countries: .A65
Argentina: .A7
Armenia: .A75
Asia: .A78
Asia, Central: .A783
Asia, East: see .E18
Asia, Southeastern: .A785
Asia, Southwestern: see .N33
Australia: .A8
Austria: .A9
Bahamas: .B24
Bahrain: .B26
Balkan Peninsula: .B28
Bangladesh: .B3
Barbados: .B35
Belgium: .B4
Belize: .B42
Bengal: .B43
Benin: .B45
Bhutan: .B47
Bolivia: .B5
Botswana: .B55
Brazil: .B6
British Honduras: see .B42
Brunei: .B7
Bulgaria: .B9
Burkina Faso: see .U65
Burma: .B93
Burundi: .B94
Byzantine Empire: .B97
Cambodia: .K3
Cameroon: .C17
Canada: .C2
Canary Islands: .C23
Caribbean area: .C27
Cayman Islands: .C29
Central African Republic: .C33
Central America: .C35
Central Europe: .C36
Ceylon: see .S72
Chad: .C45
Chile: .C5
China: .C6
Colombia: .C7
Communist countries: .C725
Congo (Brazzaville): .C74
Costa Rica: .C8
Cuba: .C9
Cyprus: .C93
Czechoslovakia: .C95
Dahomey: see .D4
Developing countries: .D44
Djibouti: .D5
Dominican Republic: .D65
East: .E16
East Asia: .E18
Ecuador: .E2
Egypt: .E3
El Salvador: see .S2
Ethiopia: .E8
Europe: .E85
Europe, Central: see .C36
Europe, Eastern: .E852
Europe, Northern: .E853
Europe, Southern: .E854
European Economic Community countries: .E86
Falkland Islands: .F3
Fiji: .F4
Finland: .F5
France: F8
French Guiana: .F9
Gabon: .G2
Gambia: .G25
Germany: .G3
Germany (East): .G35
Germany (West): see .G3
Ghana: .G4
Great Britain: .G7
Greece: .G8
Greenland: .G83
Grenada: .G84
Guam: .G85
Guatemala: .G9
Guinea: .G92
Guinea-Bissau: .G93
Guyana: .G95
Haiti: .H2
Honduras: .H8
Hong Kong: . H85
Hungary: .H9
Iceland: .I2
India: .I4
Indochina: .I48
Indonesia: .I5
Iran: .I7
Iraq: .I72
Ireland: .I73
Islamic countries: .I74
Islamic Empire: .I742
Israel: .I75
Italy: .I8
Ivory Coast: .I9
Jamaica: .J25
Japan: .J3
Kampuchea: .K3
Kenya: .K4
Kiribati: .K5
Korea: .K6
Korea (North): .K7
Korea (South): see .K6
Kuwait: .K9
Laos: .L28
Latin America: .L29
Lebanon: .L4
Lesotho: .L5
Liberia: .L7
Libya: .L75
Macao: .M25
Macedonia: .M27
Madagascar: .M28
Malawi: .M3
Malaysia: .M4
Mali: .M42
Malta: .M43
Mauritania: .M44
Mauritius: .M45
Melanesia: .M5
Mexico: .M6
Micronesia: .M625
Middle East: see .N33
Mongolia: .M65
Morocco: .M8
Mozambique: .M85
Namibia: .N3
Near East: .N33
Nepal: .N35
Netherlands: .N4
New Guinea: .N43
New Zealand: .N45
Nicaragua: .N5
Niger: .N55
Nigeria: .N6
North America: .N7
Norway: .N8
Oceania: .O3
Oman: .O5
Pacific area: .P16
Pakistan: .P18
Palestine: .P19
Panama: .P2
Papua New Guinea: .P26
Paraguay: .P3
Peru: .P4
Philippines: .P6
Poland: .P7
Polynesia: .P75
Portugal: .P8
Puerto Rico: .P9
Romania: .R6
Rwanda: .R95
Sahel: .S15
Salvador: .S2
Saudi Arabia: .S33
Scandinavia: .S34
Senegal: .S38
Sierra Leone: .S5

Singapore: .S55
Somalia: .S58
South Africa: .S6
South America: .S63
South Asia: .S64
Soviet Union: .S65
Spain: .S7
Sri Lanka: .S72
Sudan: .S73
Surinam: .S75
Swaziland: .S78
Sweden: .S8
Switzerland: .S9
Syria: .S95
Taiwan: .T28
Tanzania: .T34
Thailand: .T5
Tibet: .T55
Togo: .T6
Trinidad and Tobago: .T7
Tunisia: .T8
Turkey: .T9
Uganda: .U33
United Arab Emirates: .U5
United States: .U6
Upper Volta: .U65
Uruguay: .U8
Vatican City: .V3
Venezuela: .V4
Vietnam: .V5
Yemen: .Y4
Yemen (People's Democratic Republic): .Y45
Yugoslavia: .Y8
Zaire: .Z28
Zambia: .Z33
Zimbabwe: .Z55

INDEX